GERMANY
WEST and EAST

FODOR'S MODERN GUIDES

are compiled, researched and edited by an international team of travel writers, field correspondents and editors. The series, which now almost covers the globe, was founded by Eugene Fodor.

OFFICES
New York & London

Area Editor:	ANDREA DUTTON
Executive Editor:	RICHARD MOORE
Editorial Contributors:	FRANCES HOWELL, SUSAN LESTER, GEORGE MIKES, DAVID TENNANT
Drawings:	BERYL SANDERS
Maps:	C.W. BACON, ROGER GORRINGE
Photographs:	PETER BAKER, DOUGLAS DICKINS, GERMAN NATIONAL TOURIST OFFICE

FODOR'S

GERMANY

West and East

1982

FODOR'S MODERN GUIDES, INC.

Distributed by
DAVID McKAY COMPANY, INC.
New York

All the following Guides are current (most of them also in
the Hodder and Stoughton British edition).

CURRENT FODOR'S COUNTRY AND AREA TITLES:

AUSTRALIA, NEW ZEALAND
  AND SOUTH PACIFIC
AUSTRIA
BELGIUM AND
  LUXEMBOURG
BERMUDA
BRAZIL
CANADA
CARIBBEAN AND BAHAMAS
CENTRAL AMERICA
EASTERN EUROPE
EGYPT
EUROPE
FRANCE
GERMANY
GREAT BRITAIN
GREECE
HOLLAND

INDIA & NEPAL
IRELAND
ISRAEL
ITALY
JAPAN AND KOREA
JORDAN AND HOLY LAND
MEXICO
NORTH AFRICA
PEOPLE'S REPUBLIC
  OF CHINA
PORTUGAL
SCANDINAVIA
SOUTH AMERICA
SOUTHEAST ASIA
SOVIET UNION
SPAIN
SWITZERLAND
TURKEY
YUGOSLAVIA

CITY GUIDES:

CHICAGO
LONDON
NEW YORK CITY
PARIS

ROME
SAN FRANCISCO
WASHINGTON, D.C.

FODOR'S BUDGET SERIES:

BUDGET BRITAIN
BUDGET CANADA
BUDGET CARIBBEAN
BUDGET EUROPE
BUDGET FRANCE
BUDGET GERMANY

BUDGET ITALY
BUDGET JAPAN
BUDGET MEXICO
BUDGET SPAIN
BUDGET TRAVEL IN AMERICA

USA GUIDES:

ALASKA
CALIFORNIA
CAPE COD
COLORADO
FAR WEST
FLORIDA
HAWAII

NEW ENGLAND
PENNSYLVANIA
SOUTH
SOUTHWEST
USA (in one volume)

SPECIAL INTEREST:

CIVIL WAR SITES

FOREWORD

Germany has the reputation for being an expensive country to visit, and, with the strength of the German mark against so many other currencies, this is not an entirely undeserved reputation. But the combination of low transatlantic air fares and the many advantageous offers that your travel agent can tell you about, should bring the problem of budgeting your trip into more manageable proportions. Certainly, Germany has a wide enough variety of possibilities to suit any and every pocketbook, and you can be sure that you will get value for money.

Along with such traditional strongholds of tourism as the Bavarian Alps, the Romantic Road, the Black Forest, the castled Rhine and Neckar rivers and medieval Franconia, Germany also possesses an incomparable chain of glittering cities where sophisticated modern living vies with historic fascination. Many of these maintain opera, ballet and drama companies which are among the most interesting in the world. Supported largely out of civic funds and often housed in beautifully designed performing-arts centers, these companies can afford to experiment on a scale not possible for their commercially-oriented brethren. We can heartily recommend a visit to a performance of one of these companies. If your lack of German worries you, then try the opera or ballet.

However, if cost is a major factor in planning your trip—and how many can say that it isn't!—then you should take the time and trouble to search out the tremendous range of offers available in order to come up with travel prospects that will not send your bank manager into hospital with a coronary. Don't deny yourself the pleasures of visiting one of the great, historic cities, or swanning down the popular Rhine, but balance out those parts of your holiday with visits to other, less frequented areas—North Germany, perhaps, or the quiet, forested stretches of East Bavaria. One of the very best ways to do this is to take advantage of the many cheap rail tickets that Germany offers to its visitors. The rail network in Germany is extensive and excellently maintained, so you can expect to reach even the most remote areas easily and at low cost. For many years we have been trying to persuade our readers to leave the beaten track and explore the regions which are often more truly typical of the atmosphere of a country than are the large cosmopolitan centers, and never was such a policy more valid than in today's expensive world. For not only do the more hidden areas preserve the spirit of place undiluted by foreign influence, but they are also usually less expensive.

Our coverage in this book extends to East Germany, the German Democratic Republic. The East German authorities welcome visitors from abroad, and have produced some attractive tours of their historic sites and lovely, baroque towns that are bargains in anyone's language. And, of course, one can combine a visit there with travel to other Eastern European countries.

*

The task of making this book would not have been possible without the help of numerous tourist officials and other friends. We could not possibly thank here all who have aided us in the completion of this guide, but we extend our special thanks to Mr. Guenther Nischwitz, the Director, German National Tourist Office, London; to Berolina Travel Ltd., London; to the East German Chamber of Commerce, London; and to the many staff members of the German National Tourist Offices throughout Germany who have provided us with so much information. We would like to thank, especially, Andrea Dutton who has assumed the burden of Area Editor for Germany and whose hard work has made this edition possible.

*

We would like to stress that our listings of hotels and restaurants are selections from the wide range of establishments available. We greatly appreciate letters from our readers, telling us of their experiences in using our choices, such contacts help us to have a "traveler's eye view" of things, which is not always the same as that of our professional editors. Naturally, we are interested, too, in any other points that our readers raise in connection with this Guide.

All prices quoted in this Guide are based on those available to us at time of writing, mid-1981. Given the volatility of European costs, it is inevitable that changes will have taken place by the time this book becomes available. We trust, therefore, that you will take prices quoted as indicators only, and will double-check to be sure of the latest figures.

*

Our addresses are:
in the U.S.A., Fodor's Modern Guides, 2 Park Ave., New York, NY 10016;
in Europe, Fodor's Modern Guides, 1-11 John Adam St., London WC2N 6AD.

We accept advertising in some books, but this does not affect the editor's recommendations. We include advertising because the revenue helps defray the high cost of our annual republishing, and the advertisements themselves provide information for our readers.

CONTENTS

FACTS
AT YOUR
FINGERTIPS

FACTS AT YOUR FINGERTIPS

Practical Information for the German Democratic Republic will be found in the East Germany chapter at the end of the book.

PLANNING YOUR TRIP

Devaluation—Inflation

Current international monetary problems make it impossible to budget accurately long in advance. All prices mentioned in this book are indicative of costs at the time of going to press (mid-1981). Keep a weather eye open for fluctuations while planning your trip—and while on it.

WHAT WILL IT COST. Germany had one of the lowest inflation rates in Western Europe in mid-1981 and it will probably be about the same in 1982. Even though prices have risen in the past years, the pinch felt by American and British tourists is mostly as a result of the devalued dollar and floating pound, which simply don't buy as much in Germany as they did in the good old days. Nevertheless, a vacation here can still be cheaper than one in either London, Scandinavia, much of France, Switzerland, Belgium, or even parts of Italy. Staying in the big cities, such as Frankfurt, Munich, Cologne, Düsseldorf, Berlin, etc., can be very expensive, but it is possible to stay in much less expensive places nearby and still explore the cities.

Below we give a table showing hotel costs at typical resorts during high season.

HOTEL ROOM
(in German marks)

		Major cities, Top resorts	Smaller towns	Small resorts, Countryside
Deluxe (L)	Single	100–175	70–100	—
	Double	140–285	98–170	—
Expensive (E)	Single	70–118	50–110	44–62
	Double	114–196	80–136	65–90
Moderate (M)	Single	45–100	30–70	24–45
	Double	60–160	44–90	40–75
Inexpensive (I)	Single	30–50	28–35	15–30
	Double	46–89	40–65	29–58

Breakfast, service charges and taxes included

Budget ideas. You can cut your budget considerably by visiting less-known cities, towns and summer and winter resorts. All along the Main and Neckar rivers you will find small towns as charming, if not as well known, but less expensive than Rothenburg and Heidelberg; Westphalia offers similar atmosphere at cheaper prices than the fabled Rhine towns and cities; wine lovers should explore the Palatinate instead of the classical Rhine-Mosel tour; in northern Germany the East Frisian islands from Emden on are less crowded than their more expensive sisters along the North Frisian coast; and ski enthusiasts would do well to investigate the advantages of the Harz and Eifel mountains, the Allgäu in Swabia, Kleinwalsertal, the Black Forest and, most particularly, Oberpfalz and Bayerischer Wald in East Bavaria. Known as the step-child of German tourism, East Bavaria offers excellent quality at truly bargain rates.

Apartment renting. In all the above areas there are new and comfortable vacation apartments and bungalows with 2–4 rooms accommodating up to 6 persons. Prices vary according to location, season and facilities offered, but run roughly from 115 marks per week for a small studio apartment for two, to 700 marks for a 2-story deluxe chalet for at least 5 people.

Fremdenzimmer. This is a word to remember when traveling on a budget. This means a room in a small guest house or private house: there's usually a notice with that word (or, more often, "Zimmer Frei"—room free) hanging in the window, but they are often listed with the local tourist office. The charge is about 7 marks for bed and continental breakfast, and a Fremdenzimmer can always be recommended in the smaller towns and villages.

Average local costs: shirt laundering, DM 1.40; pressing a dress, 2.50; machine dry cleaning, about 4.50 for a woman's dress, 7.50 for a man's suit. A shampoo and haircut for a man is 9–15 marks, for a woman about 20 marks for a shampoo and set, 7 for a manicure.

You will pay from 15 to 180 marks for a seat at the opera, 10 to 80 at a theater, 8 to 12 at the cinema, and if you take in a nightclub, anywhere from 30 to 100 marks—or more.

Other local costs: A quarter liter of open wine, 2.90 to 5 marks; a whisky, 3 marks up, depending on restaurant or bar; schnapps 1.60 to 3.50; a bottle of beer 1.90 (usual light beer, dark and special brews are more); coffee in a good café 2–4 marks.

In pub-restaurants grilled sausages *(würste)* with roll and potato salad DM3.50–4; escalope or roast meat DM8, steaks DM12, thick soup DM4. All meals include vegetables, VAT and service. Cigarettes from DM3 for 20, cigars from DM0.50 each.

A TYPICAL MODERATE DAY PER PERSON

	DM
Hotel room with bath, breakfast, service and tax charges included	40.00
Lunch, table d'hôte, excluding drinks	12.00
Dinner	20.00
Coffee, in café	2.40
Pastry	2.00
Beer, ½ liter glass	1.90
Wine, ¼ liter	3.50
Transportation:1 tram	1.50
1 taxi	10.00
Theater	40.00
Miscellaneous (say 10%)	14.00
	147.30

Inclusive terms, the wisest choice for almost all travelers, even if only used as a basis. 7-day packages are arranged by the German Reservation system of Frankfurt (ADZ) offering 246 packages in 165 resorts, costing around DM9 nightly for bed and breakfast and DM18 for full board. For shorter stays ask your travel agent or a German National Tourist office. Special all-inclusive rates are offered almost everywhere, but the many small towns along Lake Constance are a typical example: off-season, or better "edge-of-season" reductions range from a 3-day weekend in a private house room from DM30 per person to DM80 and up for a first class hotel. Weekly rates are 10–20 percent less.

Special weekend rates are a popular feature throughout Germany, and these usually include sightseeing and some form of entertainment. Munich's "Weekend Key" offers 1–3 night bed and breakfast from DM64–152 in standard hotels, DM108–344 in deluxe, excursion to an Alpine lake, low-cost rail trips and free entrance to many attractions included. Hamburg, Stuttgart, Düsseldorf, Mittenwald, Garmisch-Partenkirchen and many other cities offer similar reduced weekend rates. Feldberg and Schluchsee in the Black Forest offer 7 days' bed and breakfast in pensions from DM90 to DM150 between Easter and Whitsun.

Aachen, Charlemagne's great city, is offering two nights' bed and breakfast, with tours around the historic sites, the markets for which the city is renowned, the cathedral and the old town. Prices are from DM69. An excellent base for touring the Eifel/Ardennes region.

Even exclusive Baden-Baden offers special off-season weekly and weekend bargains, as does Konstanz on Bodensee. Seven hotels in Baden-Baden, and in the Freudenstadt area of the Black Forest, 16 hotels have formed pools, enabling guests to take meals at any of the member hotels.

In addition, a group of hoteliers in Habichtswald in the north of Hesse, the *Holiday Ring Habichtswald Nature Park,* offer particularly comfortable, low-cost holidays. One week's bed and breakfast costs from DM137 and there are guest houses in Breuna, Naumburg, Wolfhagen and Zierenberg-Oberelsungen. They promise comfortable rooms, hearty breakfasts and afternoon tea on Sundays, as well as special children's menus. Furthermore, they will provide a map of the area for hikers, a walking stick and flowers in all the rooms.

Although the Black Forest and volcanic Eifel region are classic walking country, Bavaria is stepping in with an intriguing tour which follows in the footsteps of King Ludwig II. Starting from Starnberg and its lake, near where he met his death, it finishes 65 miles away at Füssen close to the royal castle of Neuschwanstein. Some of Bavaria's best scenery is passed and visits are of course made to famous spots like the tiny rococo Wies Church. Economy is paramount and seven nights en route are spent in guest houses, the luggage goes ahead. Walking is confined to 12–15 miles daily.

Romantic Hotels and Restaurants is an organization of 53 hotels and restaurants in Germany and Austria run personally by their owners, and featuring old historic inns but with all modern comforts, rooms with bath and toilet, sometimes having a pool. Weekly rates in its affiliated hotels are from about DM150–350, bed and breakfast between DM50–70. Full details from P.O. Box 114 D-8757, Karlstein am Main, Seestr. 5.

For further details of other accommodations in Germany, see p. 22.

WHEN TO GO. The main tourist season in Germany lies approximately between the first of May and the end of October. This is when you go to take in events that happen at a time most convenient for tourists during the vacation season, like the Wagner Festival at Bayreuth or the hundreds of folk festivals. There is a secondary season for winter sports, particularly developed in the Bavarian Alps. You can benefit by lower transportation rates (transatlantic winter fares, for instance) and weekend rates at resorts by visiting Germany at this time of year, but naturally hotel prices in resorts primarily devoted to skiing and similar pleasures will then be at their peak (Dec.–Mar. inclusive).

 OFF-SEASON TRAVEL. This has become increasingly popular in recent years. Germany is a country with a lively theatrical, concert and night life, and winter is the big season for these activities. Transatlantic liner and roundtrip plane fares are cheaper. Hotels may combine with the locality to offer low-priced inclusive rates. Some restaurants offer special low-price menus in the winter months. Theaters and concert halls may offer reduced winter rates as part of an inclusive winter weekend and in association with the hotels and the resort.

If you can travel off season, you should know that the warmest parts of Germany are the shores of Lake Constance (Bodensee); the Bergstrasse, a strip of countryside on the east bank of the Rhine just below Frankfurt; and the Rhineland. Pre-Lent carnival merriment is greatest in the Rhineland, in Munich, in some Black Forest localities and in the Lake Constance region.

Average maximum daily temperatures in degrees Fahrenheit and centigrade:

Berlin	Jan.	Feb.	Mar.	Apr.	May	June	July	Aug.	Sept.	Oct.	Nov.	Dec.
F°	36	37	46	55	66	72	75	73	68	55	45	37
C°	2	3	8	13	19	22	24	23	20	13	7	3

Note: in the south of Germany, temperatures are a couple of degrees higher.

 SPECIAL EVENTS. In **January**, the outstanding event in the winter sports year takes place, the International Winter Sports Week at Garmisch-Partenkirchen. Berlin's Green Week gets under way with the traditional agricultural and garden show accompanied by social and sports events. At the beginning of **February** Nürnberg holds its famous toy fair and Berlin has its equally famous film festival later in the month. The Fasching season (carnival season) has its peak events such as Enthronement of Carnival Princes and Princesses, Fool's Congresses, masked balls and masked parades in January and February, particularly in Cologne, Munich, Mainz, Augsburg, Düsseldorf, Aachen, Bonn, Wiesbaden, Frankfurt, and in hundreds of smaller localities. The famous Frankfurt Spring Fair for consumer goods takes place in the first half of **March**, usually for five days only, and Munich's international Fashion Fair, Mode Woche, is usually in the last week of March.

On the last day of **April**, Walpurgis festivals occur throughout the Harz Mountains while Frankfurt holds its Fur Fair. Mannheim begins its traditional May Market, with a parade of flower floats; towards the end of April and on the last day of this month Marburg has a special May festival on the Market Square. The Hannover Industrial Fair begins the end of April and lasts into early May, which signals the opening of the festival season, with Wiesbaden staging its annual panorama of opera, drama, concerts and ballet, with the participation of foreign artists and companies, during the first three weeks of the month. At Pentecost, Rothenburg-on-Tauber commemorates a famous event in its history by putting on the traditional *Meister Trunk* play, followed by equally traditional shepherds' dances and the comic Hans Sachs Plays. Winter sports end the month in Aschau in the Bavarian Alps with the traditional May ski run.

June sees the year's most important sports event—Kiel Week, a great time for yachtsmen. The Augsburg season of open-air opera and operetta starts in the middle of the month and continues into September and Munich's ballet festival begins. On Corpus Christi Day there are parades at Freiburg and Berchtesgaden, and colorful religious processions take place in all the Catholic regions of Germany.

July is the festival month for children: the Biberach festival with 3,000 children in historical costumes; the Children's Festival at Dinkelsbühl; and the oldest Bavarian children's festival at Kaufbeuren. It is also the month of the Bach Week at Ansbach, which takes place in alternate years (next in 1981), the Lorelei Festival at St. Goarshausen on the Rhine, and the horse racing week at Bad Harzburg. But the big dates for this month are Germany's most famous musical drawing cards, the Wagner Festival at Bayreuth and Munich Opera Festival.

Horse race addicts have a big fixture at the end of **August,** the international contests at Baden-Baden's Iffezheim Week. The German Grand Prix world racing car championship run takes place at Hockenheim in early August. This is also the month of the Kulmbach beer festival.

Meanwhile, at Mainz, the Wine Market anticipates by a few days the wine festivals which break out all over the Rhineland early in **September** and succeed or overlap one another all the way into the first few days of November. There are too many of them to list, but of particular note are those of Bad Dürkheim, about the middle of the month, confusingly known as the Sausage Fair, and of Neustadt, which doesn't get under way until September 30. Before that, though, four other events in September deserve mention—the second of Frankfurt's big trade fairs, early in the month, and, about the middle, one of the most spectacular sights of the year, the Rhine in Flames illuminations, which bathe the river in fire from St Goar on one bank to St Goarshausen on the other, at the very point where the Lorelei used to wreck the Rhine boats before James Watt thwarted her by inventing the steam engine.

The second half of September is also noted for the inception of the Oktoberfest in Munich, which, to justify its name, does continue for a few days into **October.** Dating back to 1810 when King Ludwig I of Bavaria got married, this festival attracts as many as 6,000,000 visitors from Germany and abroad for two weeks of beer drinking, parades, fun-fair amusements, sideshows, dancing, and general merrymaking, plus a few congresses and exhibitions for the serious minded (if any). Cannstatt Folk Festival, dating back to 1818, is a similar event in Stuttgart.

Major auto races are held every month at Nürburgring, but the principal events take place in May, August and September. The Bremen Freimarkt, the oldest (since A.D. 965) folk festival in Germany, takes place the second half of October and in **November** St Martin day parades and festivals are held in, among other places, Heidelberg. Another November event is the Leonhardiritt, horseback parades honoring St Leonard, the patron saint of cattle and horses, taking place in Bad Tölz. As the regular winter entertainment season now sets in, the number of special events falls off but one more might be noted, Nürnberg's Christkindlmarkt, or Christ Child's Market, a fair which begins the second week of **December.** Some other major cities have similar Christmas markets.

Trade fairs and exhibitions. Detailed information can be obtained from the Central Committee for Exhibitions and Trade Fairs of German Industry and Commerce (AUMA), Lindenstr. 8, Cologne. Also in London from the German Chamber of Commerce and Industry, 11 Grosvenor Crescent, S.W.1; Collins & Endres, 36 Sackville St., W.1; Frankfurt and Hamburg Fairs and Congress Co., Leslie House, 238 High St., Poole, Dorset, BH15 1DY.

 WHERE TO GO. Unless you travel on a packaged tour, with a fixed itinerary and schedule which you can't modify, it's most unlikely that you will follow unchanged any detailed plans you make in advance. Nevertheless it is advantageous to rough out your trip. This gives you an opportunity to decide how much you can cover comfortably in the time at your disposal.

Highlights of Germany. The regions most visited for their general attractiveness are the Rhine valley (and don't forget its tributary, the Mosel); the Black Forest; the Palatinate (Pfalz) and Palatinate Forest (Pfälzer Wald); and the Bavarian Alps. Top excursions are the boat trip on the Rhine (similar cruise on the Neckar) and the auto or bus ride along the Romantic Road.

The most interesting cities are Frankfurt, for a busy bustling center; Bremen, Germany's second largest seaport, for its Hanseatic memories; Hamburg for its magnificent reconstructed harbor, Alster lakes, and nightlife, and the same city along with Stuttgart, Cologne, and Düsseldorf, for modern architecture; Cologne for its famous Gothic cathedral; Munich for its art galleries, its varied old architecture, and its gaiety; Nürnberg for its medieval aspect; Heidelberg, Marburg, Freiburg, Göttingen, Tübingen for their centuries-old universities, Gothic buildings, gabled and half-timbered façades, and student memories; Bamberg, Regensburg, Passau for great cathedrals, old patrician town houses and residential palaces; Coburg and Würzburg for great fortresses, the latter also for magnificent baroque and rococo palaces.

Also: Bayreuth for the theater and memories of Richard Wagner; Augsburg for its Renaissance buildings, mementos of the Fuggers and Welsers, the first bankers in the world; Lübeck for its Hanseatic tradition and architecture; Berlin as a political anomaly, and as a cosmopolitan city and cultural center with great international expositions, art shows, stage, music, and sporting events; Aachen for memories of the Holy Roman Empire and Trier for memories of the Roman Empire itself (along with Saalburg, the Roman garrison town preserved near Bad Homburg); and, of course, any number of medieval fairybook towns like the world-famous triad on the Romantic Road: Rothenburg-on-Tauber, Dinkelsbühl, and Nördlingen or, farther north, 1,000-year-old Goslar on the fringe of the Harz Mountains, and Hildesheim.

Garmisch-Partenkirchen, Berchtesgaden, Oberstdorf with the Kleines Walsertal, Reit im Winkl—all in Bavaria, except Kleines Walsertal, which is in Austria but can only be reached from Oberstdorf (in Allgäu), as well as the Harz Mountains, and the Bayerischer Wald, Fichtelgebirge and several other high-lying areas for mountain scenery, skiing, climbing, old folklore traditions; for native dress also Fränkische Schweiz and Frisian Islands; Bodensee for lovely lake towns and water sports; the wind-swept coasts, estuaries, and islands of the Baltic and North Sea for water sports, particularly sailing; the gracious Neuschwanstein is the most frequently photographed castle in Germany, while scores of other castles stand along the Rhine, Mosel, and Neckar valleys.

 HOW TO GO. When you have decided where you want to go, your next step is to consult a good travel agent. If you haven't one, the American Society of Travel Agents, 711 Fifth Avenue, New York 10022 and ASTA/West 4420 Hotel Circle Court, Suite 230, San Diego, CA 92108, or the Association of British Travel Agents, 50–57 Newman St., London W1P 4AH, will advise you. Whether you select *Maupintour, American Express, Thomas Cook, DER (Deutsches Reisebüro), Diners,* or a smaller organization is a matter of preference. They all have branch offices or correspondents in the larger European cities.

Travel abroad today, although it is steadily becoming easier and more comfortable, is also growing more complex in its details. As the choice of things to do, places to visit, ways of getting there, increases, so does the problem of *knowing* about all these questions. A reputable, experienced travel agent is a specialist in details, although his knowledge is almost inevitably less extensive than that of the National Tourist Office.

If you wish your agent to book you on a package tour, reserve your transportation and even your first overnight hotel accommodation, his services should cost you nothing. Most carriers and tour operators grant him a fixed commission for saving them the expense of having to open individual offices in every town and city.

If, on the other hand, you wish him to plan for you an individual itinerary and make all arrangements down to hotel reservations and transfers to and from rail and air terminals, you are drawing upon his knowledge of travel and he will make a service charge on top of the total cost of your planned itinerary. This charge may amount to 10 or 15 percent, but it will more than likely *save* you money on balance.

The German National Tourist Office *(Deutsche Zentrale für Tourismus)* can furnish you with booklets covering every aspect of travel in Germany. Its head office is at Beethovenstr. 69, Frankfurt-am-Main; cable address, Fremdenverkehr Frankfurtmain. The German National Tourist Offices abroad include:

In the United States:

New York: Rockefeller Center, 630 Fifth Avenue, Suite 2406, New York, NY 10020.

Chicago: 104 South Michigan Avenue, Chicago, Ill. 60603.

Los Angeles: Broadway Plaza, Suite 1714, 700 South Flower St., Los Angeles, California 90071.

In Canada:

Montreal: 2 Fundy, P.O. Box 417, Pl. Bonaventure, Montreal 114, P.Q., Canada H5A 1B8.

In Britain:

London: 61 Conduit Street, W.1.

DER (German Travel Service) in London is at 16 Orchard Street, London, W1H OAY.

 MEET THE GERMANS. Travelers with special interests can extend their hobbies while touring Germany, through the "Open House" program. Among many factories and workshops that welcome visitors are: *Volkswagen* at Wolfsburg near Braunschweig; *Mercedes-Benz;* the optical works of *Carl Zeiss* at Okerkochen; camera fans can visit *Zeiss Ikon* in Stuttgart; chinamaking can be seen at *Rosenthal's* workshops in Selb, Bavaria; in the Black Forest is the *Staiger* clock factory; several great wineries can be visited at Rüdesheim in Rheingau and at Trier in the Mosel-Saar-Ruwer wine district.

Contacts with individual Germans or groups can be made through the American Houses (Amerika Haus) in various cities.

 STUDENTS. German language courses for foreigners are offered by the major universities all year round, but there are special 3–4 week summer courses at the Universities of Cologne, Frankfurt, Hamburg, Munich and Stuttgart, as well as in the medieval town of Rothenburg on the Romantic Road. Other summer courses include painting again in Rothenburg, and in Dinkelsbühl and Seebruck on Chiemsee, and photography in the scenic village of Mittenwald in the Bavarian Alps. For information on language courses, write to the university of your choice or to the German Academic Exchange Services (DAAD), 11–15, Arlington Street, London, SW1, which publishes details on various courses annually during February–March. There is also IAESTE (Int. Assn. for the Exchange of Students for Technical Experience) c/o Imperial College, 178 Queens Gate, London, SW7. Various bodies have details on other courses, including language study and these are listed in the booklet *Happy Days*

in Germany issued by the German National Tourist Offices. They include the Goethe Institute, 3 Lenbachplatz, Munich.

In the U.S., for student and youth travel the basic sources of information are: the *Institute of International Education,* 809 UN Plaza, N.Y. 10017; the *Council on International Educational Exchange,* 205 East 42 St., N.Y. 10017; and *U.S. Student Travel Service,* 801 Second Ave., N.Y. 10017.

Student package tours which include short courses at European universities are organized by several American tour operators, including *University Travel,* 44 Brattle St., Cambridge, Mass. 02138; *U.S. Student Travel Service Inc.,* 801 Second Ave., New York 10017; *Academic Travel Abroad,* 280 Madison Avenue, New York, N.Y. 10016; *The American Institute for Foreign Study,* 102 Greenwich Avenue, Greenwich, Connecticut 06830; and *The New York University World Campus Program,* 2 University Place, New York, N.Y. 10003.

 CUTTING THE COST. Recently, encouraged particularly by the extension of the Youth Hostel system, foreign tourists, especially youngsters, have been participating in increasing numbers in the cheapest and ruggedest form of traveling, always popular among Germans.

Germany has over 600 **Youth Hostels,** many in romantic old castles that have been modernized, providing some 65,000 beds. Although the hotels are primarily for hikers or cyclists under 20, persons above that age are admitted when accommodations are available, except in Bavaria where the age ceiling is 27. A Youth Hostel card (16 marks) valid for one year, entitles you to reduced nightly rates (about 2 marks for youths, 4.30 for adults).

The German Youth Hostels are probably the most efficient, up-to-date and numerous of any country in the world. For information, write to *American Y.H. Inc.,* National Campus, Delaplane, Virginia 22025; *Canadian Y.H. Assn.,* 333 River Rd., Vanier City, Ottawa, Ont.; in England, *Y.H. Assn.,* 14 Southampton Street, London, W.C.2.

For **campers,** the Federal Republic has about 2,000 campsites and the German Tourist Bureau publishes a list of those considered "well" to "excellently" equipped, together with a map, index, addresses, phone numbers, and evaluations. The official camping guide of the *DCC* (German Camping Club, D 8000 Munich 40, Mandlstrasse 28) lists 1,600 camping sites and costs DM12.80. The **German Automobile Club** also publishes a detailed guide. Average charges for use of camping sites are: adults DM2–3.50 per person per night; children DM1–2; parking DM3–5. *European Campgrounds and Trailer Parks,* published by Rand McNally Co., 10 East 53 Street, New York, N.Y. 10022, is a 300-page guide to over 3,000 selected sites in all of Europe, including the eastern countries and Turkey, 29 countries in all, with maps, access instructions, and complete listings of equipment and facilities.

Other useful addresses in England are: *Camping Club of Great Britain and Ireland,* 11 Lower Grosvenor Place, London S.W.1; *The Cyclists Touring Club,* 69 Meadrow, Godalming, Surrey.

WALKING TOURS. Although the Germans have always favored walking—or hiking—holidays, these are only now beginning to catch on as far as non-German visitors are concerned, probably because people want to combine fitness and activity with their leisure time. In the past, the Black Forest and the volcanic Eifel region have been regarded as classic walking country, but now German regional tourist offices are becoming increasingly aware of the appeal to hikers of traveling light and offer varied arrangements for hikers' luggage to be sent on ahead. This service is combined with planned hiking routes and inexpensive accommodations (bed and breakfast) in inns and pensions. For example, in the Westerwald, the region east of the Rhine, you can spend seven nights en route at comfortable guesthouses; your luggage is sent ahead each morning and walking is confined to leisurely stretches of 12 to 15 miles per day. The price—including bed, breakfast and evening meal, vouchers for swimming pools and entrance to the wild-life parks of the area—is from DM311. Similar arrangements are offered in the Sauerland area of Hunau, the Black Forest, Swabian Forest, the Nature Parks of Hesse and Franconia and many other holiday resorts. It is important to make a reservation at the appropriate regional tourist office; when writing, ask for details of *Wandern ohne Gepäck* (Hiking without Luggage).

There are also some seven-day tours in the Bavarian Forest and in Lower Saxony. These are designed for motorists, with overnight stops in farmhouses.

WHAT TO TAKE. Travel light. Air travelers from North America and Canada to Germany are now subject to the "piece" luggage system: First class: two checked bags not exceeding a total dimension of 62" (158cm) each, plus 1 piece of hand luggage, maximum 39" (100cm) are carried free. Economy class: two checked bags of which neither exceeds 62" (158cm) and the two together do not exceed a total of 106" (269cm) plus 1 carry-on bag 39". Infants, at 10% of the fare, also now get a luggage allowance, excess luggage will cost $40–$50. This simplifies going through customs and lets you take fast autorail trains with room for hand baggage only.

What to Wear. The climate of Germany is much like that of the Northwest or northern New England, and somewhat more rigorous in winter than that of England. You can pack about the same clothes you would wear in either region at the same time of year. If you are going into the Alps, however, remember that the evenings are cool in high altitudes even during the summer. Take a good warm sweater and a pair of sturdy walking shoes. Finally, Germans tend to formality, although rules on how to dress are generally far more relaxed now than they were, but an evening at the theater or a dinner party is still a time for dressing up to the occasion.

Travelers checks are the best way to safeguard travel funds. They are sold by various banks and companies in terms of American and Canadian dollars and pounds sterling. There are a number of brands; *American Express, Bank of America* and *Citibank* are the leading U.S. brands. Best known and easily exchanged British travelers checks are those issued by *Thos. Cook & Son* and the banks: *Barclays, Lloyds, Midland* and *National-Westminster.*

It is now possible for British travelers to cash checks abroad for up to £50 each transaction, on production of a Barclaycard or one of many bank check cards participating in the scheme in over 30 countries, including Germany; it is also cheaper than exchanging travelers checks, though the bank cards can only be negotiated through a European bank.

 TRAVEL DOCUMENTS. Apply several months in advance of your expected departure date. **U.S. residents** must apply in person to the U.S. Passport Agency's office in Boston, Chicago, Detroit, Honolulu, Houston, Los Angeles, Miami, New Orleans, New York, Philadelphia, San Francisco, Seattle, Stamford Connecticut), or Washington D.C., or to their local County Courthouse. In some areas selected post offices can handle passport applications. If you still have your passport issued within the past 8 years, you may use this to apply by mail. Otherwise, take with you your birth certificate (or certified copy), or other proof of citizenship, two identical photographs 2 in. square full face, black/white or color, on nonglossy paper and taken within the past 6 months, proof of identity such as a driver's license, previous passport, any governmental I.D. card and $14 ($10 if applying by mail) with prior passport. Social security cards and credit cards are NOT acceptable. If you expect to travel extensively request a 48- or 96-page passport. There is no extra charge. Passports are valid 5 yrs. If your passport gets lost or stolen, immediately notify either the nearest American Consul or the Passport Office, Department of State, Washington, D.C. 20524.

If a **resident alien** you need a Treasury Sailing Permit, Form 1040C; if a non-resident alien file Form 1040NR, certifying that Federal taxes have been paid; you must present a blue or green alien card, passport, travel tickets, most recently filed Form 1040, W2 forms for most recent full year, current payroll stubs or letter. Check this is all! To return to the U.S.A. resident aliens with green cards must file Form I–131 45 days prior to departure if abroad more than 1 year. Apply for it at least six weeks before departure in person at the nearest office of the Immigration and Naturalization Service, or by mail to the Immigration and Naturalization Service, Washington, D.C.

British subjects: Apply on forms obtainable from your travel agency or main post office. The application should be sent to the Passport Office for your area (as indicated on the guidance form) or taken personally to your travel agent. Apply at least 5 weeks before the passport is required. The regional Passport Offices are located in London, Liverpool, Peterborough, Glasgow, and Newport (Mon.). The application must be countersigned by your bank manager or by a solicitor, barrister, doctor, clergyman or Justice of the Peace who knows you personally. You will need two full-face photos. The fee is £11.

British Visitor's Passport. This simplified form of passport has advantages for the once-in-a-while tourist to Germany and most other European countries.

Valid for one year and not renewable, it costs £5.50. Application must be made in person at your local post office and two passport photographs are required, together with proof of identity such as birth certificate, current pension card, or medical card. *Note:* This is not valid for East Berlin and Eastern Germany.

Visas. Nationals of the U.S.A., U.K., Commonwealth, and Eire, among others, do not need visas to enter West Germany.

 HEALTH CERTIFICATES. Not required for entry to Germany. The United States, Canada and Britain do not require a certificate of vaccination prior to re-entry. If visiting Mediterranean regions as well as Germany, it is wise to have anti-typhoid, cholera and polio jabs.

PETS. There are currently extremely rigid controls on the importation of pets into Britain, caused by the rapid spread of rabies on the Continent. All pets brought into Germany must have proof of rabies vaccination. If you are likely to be taking animals from the Continent to Britain, make very sure you have checked on the quarantine and other regulations.

GETTING TO GERMANY

From North America

 **BY AIR.** It took a whole decade for West Germany to re-establish a national airline out of the ruins of World War II and when it finally emerged in the mid-50s, bearing its pre-war name, few would have believed that it would soon become one of the giants of the skies. *Lufthansa* began operations with a modest internal service and 44-passenger planes, but she joined the jet age with everyone else, adding routes every season until they touched all six inhabited continents. At the same time, Lufthansa established a reputation for punctuality and service that is still the envy of many carriers. As the older Boeing 707 jets in her livery are gradually phased out, Lufthansa is building up a wide-body fleet of Boeing 747 Jumbo Jets, DC-10s, and Airbuses while some short-haul European and domestic routes are operated with Boeing 727s and 737s.

Lufthansa flies 747s and DC-10s from New York, Boston, Philadelphia, Chicago, Miami, San Francisco, Los Angeles, Montreal and Toronto to Frankfurt and from New York to Hamburg, Cologne/Bonn and Munich. Other services to Frankfurt are from New York by *Pan Am, TWA, Air-India* and *Pakistan International;* from Atlanta on *Delta;* from Boston on *Braniff;* from Dallas on Braniff; from Houston on Pan Am; from Miami on Pan Am; from Philadelphia on TWA; from San Juan on *Avianca;* from Vancouver, Calgary and Edmonton on *Air Canada.*

AIR FARES. In effect there are now three classes of air travel: first, economy and charter. On regularly scheduled airlines, charter-group passengers receive economy class service, but they may be paying much less for it than their neighbors who are traveling as individuals. On purely charter-flight lines the amenities may be more sparing, and the flight times longer. Nowadays scheduled carriers are allowed into the charter field and the rules for charter-group membership have been so relaxed that a wide variety of possibilities is now open. Your travel agent can advise you on the most economical rates and times to travel, on reduced 14- to 60-day excursions as well as group fares. Unless you aim to visit many European cities *en route* to your destination (in which case see Bonus Stopovers below) you will save considerably by choosing one of the various types of excursion or package-tour flights. In summer, for example, flights on Advance Purchase (APEX), which must be arranged and paid for 21 days prior to travel are available New York-Frankfurt for about $526. All airlines offer even greater savings in the off-peak periods of spring, fall and winter.

The whole field of charter flights and other cut-rate fares is covered in a thorough and up-to-date fashion in a specialized publication, *How to Fly for Less, A Consumer's Guide to Low-Cost Air Charters and Other Travel Bargains,* by Jeno Jurgen, published by Travel Information Bureau, 44 County Line Road, Farmingdale, NY 11735.

Budget-minded travelers may be tempted to take advantage of the very low standby and budget fares from a dozen American cities to Germany on scheduled or chartered flights. You select the week of travel but the airline assigns the actual date and flight during that week. Advance booking is now possible for these flights if one day's quota is sold out.

Lufthansa (in agreement with the car-hire companies) offer special "Fly and Drive" packages as well as a wide variety of other attractive schemes—"City-by-City" packages allowing for a choice in over 30 cities; "Room Service" hotel plan, with special rates; Chalet and Apartment holidays with car; a personal chauffeur/guide service; in fact a complete range of interesting and money saving possibilities. For further details contact Lufthansa.

Bonus Stopovers to Germany. If you go on one of the many charter or package plans now available, you save money but are locked into the itinerary of that particular flight or group. If you travel on a regular, fully priced ticket, you can take advantage of various stopovers along the way. Thus, between New York and Frankfurt you choose different routes each with various stopovers, all at no extra charge. Essentially, when you buy a ticket for Frankfurt you have bought 4,261 miles of transportation in each direction. You may lay them out as you see fit. For example, leaving New York you can travel first to Shannon (Eire), and then into Dublin. This allows you a stopover in Ireland at no extra fare. The itinerary then continues via Liverpool, Manchester and Birmingham to London. If you wish a Scottish stopover, you fly nonstop to Glasgow.

On the London/Frankfurt segment of the trip you may stop first in Paris, then continue via Geneva to Zürich, Stuttgart and Frankfurt. Basel can be substituted for Geneva. Other possibilities from London are: Brussels–Cologne–Frankfurt; Brussels–Paris–Frankfurt; Amsterdam–Hamburg–Hannover–Frankfurt; Amsterdam–Brussels–Düsseldorf or Cologne–Frankfurt.

You can, of course, enter Europe via many gateways. For instance, you can fly direct to Amsterdam or for that matter Geneva, Brussels, Zürich or Paris.

A northern routing takes you via Glasgow and Copenhagen, then Hamburg, Bremen, Düsseldorf or Cologne, Frankfurt.

It is also possible to visit Switzerland while traveling between two German cities. This routing could include New York to London, Amsterdam, Düsseldorf or Cologne, Zürich, Stuttgart and Frankfurt.

What about circle trip possibilities on a New York/Frankfurt ticket? Leaving New York you can fly to Shannon, Dublin, Liverpool, Manchester, Birmingham, London, Paris, Geneva, Zürich and Stuttgart before arrival in Frankfurt. Homeward bound you can visit Düsseldorf or Cologne, Bremen, Hamburg, Copenhagen and Glasgow. The fare is the same as the roundtrip. Your travel agent can help you add up the mileages and evaluate the choices.

 BY SEA. Regularly-scheduled transatlantic sailings have largely disappeared as tourists travel the quick air route, while shipping lines discover the cruise program more profitable. However, it is still possible to cross the Atlantic by sea, if you can choose your time. And once in Europe, there are innumerable and frequent short cruise possibilities in all areas, some operating out of Cuxhaven and Hamburg. Consult your travel agent.

Shipping Lines. The Cunard Line, with the superbly-equipped *Queen Elizabeth 2*, 67,107 tons, is the only one running fairly regular transatlantic services from New York to Southampton, nightly stopover, Cherbourg. Write to Cunard Line, Ltd., 555 Fifth Ave., New York, N.Y. 10017, or 1 Berkeley Street, London W1.

The *March Shipping Passenger Services* has several summer sailings between Montreal, Le Havre, London (Tilbury), Bremerhaven and Leningrad with the *Alexandr Pushkin*. The *Mikhail Lermontov* goes transatlantic from New York to the same European ports. Both vessels are 20,000 tons. Write March Shipping Passenger Services, One World Trade Center, Suite 5257, New York, N.Y. 10048 for the Baltic Shipping Co. and Polish Ocean Lines (Gdynia America Line, Inc.) which link Montreal, London, Rotterdam and Gdynia (Poland). London agents for Polish Ocean Lines are Stelp and Leighton, 238 City Road, EC1, and for Baltic Shipping Co., CTC Lines, 1–3 Lower Regent Street, SW1Y 4NN.

Many of the major cruise lines call at German ports.

Fares vary according to the shipping line, route, and season. In addition to the fare and tipping (which may add on $30 to $100), you are almost certain to spend at least an equivalent amount on incidentals during your time on board. Port taxes at disembarkation point may add $14 or more to your costs. Note: No tipping allowed and no medical expenses charged with Baltic Shipping.

If you have a flexible schedule, consider the advantages of a passenger-carrying freighter. Leisure, informality, comfort, usually no more than 12 passengers—these ships are often booked far in advance.

Waiting-list time on the North Atlantic run is now about one year. To help you choose from the 70 or so lines available, consult *Ford's Freighter Travel Guide,* PO Box 505, 22151 Clarendon St., Woodland Hills, Calif. 91365; *Pearl's Freighter Tips,* 175 Great Neck Rd., Great Neck, N.Y. 11201; *Air Marine Travel Service,* 501 Madison Ave., New York, N.Y. 10022; *Freighter Travel Club,* Box 12693, Salem, Oregon 97309; or *Traveltips Freighter Association,* Box 933, Farmingdale, N.Y. 11737.

From Great Britain

BY AIR. Few countries in the world that are not neighbors have better and more comprehensive air links with each other than Britain and Germany, and they are growing all the time. The majority of flights depart from London's Heathrow Airport. The flying time to Frankfurt is one hour and 20 minutes and both *British Airways* and *Lufthansa* have several flights every day, the former by Trident and wide-body TriStar, the latter by Airbus and Boeing 727. You can also fly from Heathrow to Frankfurt on the more infrequent services of *Malaysian Airlines System, Sunday Airways, Air-India, TWA, Pakistan International* and *Kuwait Airways.*

British Airways also operate daily flights from London's Gatwick Airport to Frankfurt. This route is also served by *Philippine Airlines* and *Air Lanka.* British Airways flies from Birmingham to Frankfurt, while both British Airways and Lufthansa fly from Manchester. The East Midlands Airport in Derbyshire is linked by DC-9 *British Midland Airways* jet to Frankfurt daily. *Air UK* flies from Southend to Dusseldorf.

Lufthansa and British Airways both have daily flights from London (Heathrow) to Munich, Hamburg, Nuremberg, Stuttgart, Cologne/Bonn, Dusseldorf, Bremen and Hannover, while British Airways and Pam Am have direct flights from Heathrow to West Berlin.

Sample return fares from London are: Frankfurt: First class (F) £230; Economy class (Y) £150; Weekend Excursion fare £75. Conditions: Travel must take place on Saturday or Sunday with maximum stay of four weeks. Charter flight £70.

Munich: (F) £275; (Y) £185; Weekend Excursion fare £90. Conditions: same as for Frankfurt; One Month Excursion £130. Conditions: Minimum stay six days, maximum stay one month. Charter flight £80. (For details of charter flights consult the national Sunday press and the London entertainment magazine, *Time Out*). Similar fares exist to other German cities.

BY TRAIN. There are two main routes from London. The one from Victoria Station to Dover, with the short sea crossing to Ostend, continues with through coaches to destinations in south and north Germany. In summer the most convenient day trains on these routes are the *Ostend–Vienna Express* and the *Nord Express.* Both leave about 10:30. From Ostend, both leave within minutes of each other, but the former reaches Cologne at 21:25 (22:25 in summer), the latter at 22:20 (23:20 in summer). Thence, the Vienna Express travels up the Rhine valley, while the Nord goes via Düsseldorf (23:00) to Hamburg and Berlin.

The second route is from Liverpool St. Station to Harwich-Hook of Holland, with day and night services. By day, you leave about 10:15, and reach Cologne by 23:00 (24:00 in summer), Bonn 30 mins. later. The more convenient night service leaves at 20:00 and arrives at The Hook in ample time to catch several trains including the Rheingold (connecting at Utrecht), which reaches Düsseldorf at 10:20 (11:20 in summer), Cologne at 10:50 (11:50 in summer), and continues up the Rhine valley. Connections at Duisburg for Frankfurt (14:30) and Munich (about 18:00). Another good train from the Hook of Holland is the Rhein Express which leaves at about 7:30 (8:30 in summer) and travels via Rotterdam, Cologne, Bonn, Mainz, Darmstadt, Heidelberg, Stuttgart, Ulm and Augsburg to Munich arriving at about 18:30 (19:30 in summer). Rail travel anywhere in Britain, plus the sea crossing to Germany, and a week, say, in the Lower Moselle with bed and breakfast at a country guesthouse costs from £80 (2 weeks from £110). A 10-day Rail Rover with unlimited travel for £10 can go with this or not.

BY BUS. *Europabus* operates through services from Victoria Coach Station, London, to Augsburg, Cologne, Frankfurt, Munich, etc., with easy travel and connections to many parts of Germany. Sample fares (at time of writing) are: London—Munich £75 return; London—Cologne £51 return; London—Garmisch-Partenkirchen £112 return.

BY CAR. The cross-channel routes for Germany are Dover–Dunkirk and Dover or Folkestone–Ostend by *Sealink;* Ramsgate-Dunkirk by *Sally Viking* line; Sheerness to Flushing by *Olau-Line;* Dover and Felixstowe to Zeebrugge by *Townsend Thoresen,* or Harwich-Hook of Holland by Sealink. All make frequent crossings taking 3½ to 8 hrs. Longer, less frequent services sail Hull-Rotterdam/Zeebrugge by *North Sea Ferries,* nightly 14 hrs, while Prins Ferries alone sails direct to Germany, Harwich–Hamburg/Bremerhaven, 20 and 16 hrs. respectively.

Several of the companies offer mini cruises to Germany; *Prins Ferries* particularly, between Harwich and Hamburg and Bremerhaven, onward to Berlin. Sealink offers packages in the areas of Upper and Eastern Bavaria, the Black Forest and Rhine/Moselle at reduced rates.

Fares for 14-ft. car and 2 passengers are from £40 on the short crossings, way. For complete tariffs, inquire of the Continental Car Ferry Centre, 52 Grosvenor Gardens, London SW1, AA, RAC, or AAA offices.

Fly-Drive. Lufthansa and Hertz have inclusive flights from London to Bremen, Düsseldorf, Cologne, Frankfurt, Hannover, Hamburg, Munich, Nürnberg and Stuttgart with car hire at these places included.

By Hovercraft. If time afloat is all important, *Seaspeed* has several daily services from Dover to Boulogne and Calais, and *Hoverlloyd* from Ramsgate (Pegwell Bay) to Calais. The craft take 250 passengers and 30 cars, crossing time about 40 minutes. *Sealink* have a jetfoil service between Dover and Ostend. The journey time is 100 minutes and there are 6 "flights" daily. The fare is the same as for the ferries, but plus a £5 supplement. No cars are carried.

Car-Sleeper Express. The Ostend–Munich service, which saved hours of tedious driving, is currently suspended, but enquire of DER in London (15 Orchard St., W1); Paris—Munich overnight is irksome and expensive, Cologne–Munich by day cheaper and easier.

From the Continent

 BY AIR. *Lufthansa* flies not only from the major cities of Western and Eastern Europe to Frankfurt but also has many routes to Hamburg, Munich, Cologne, Düsseldorf and Stuttgart as well. All European flag carriers fly to Germany; many to more than one city. Where there is no direct service, connections can easily be made at the highly efficient Rhein Main Airport near Frankfurt. Lufthansa is not permitted to fly into West Berlin while it is still administered militarily by the Americans, British, and French. *Air France* maintains the only non-stop air service between anywhere on the Continent (in this case, Paris) and West Berlin's Tegel Airport.

 BY TRAIN. Best of the many topnotch trains that join Germany with other Continental cities are the TEE (Trans Europ Express) services, a series of daytime, all-first-class electric trains. Seats must be reserved in advance, and there is also a surcharge. Full meals or refreshments are served on these trains.

Top among these is the *Rheingold,* which runs through the Rhine valley, along a very scenic route; it has a bar buffet car, a full diner, secretarial services and other amenities. It leaves Amsterdam in the early morning and Hook passengers join at Utrecht. It then goes up the valley and on to Basel, reaching there about 15:30.

Other TEE trains run from Vienna to Hannover (9½ hrs.); Brussels to Frankfort, (5 hrs.); Paris to Hamburg (9 hrs.); Amsterdam to Nürnberg (10 hrs.); Amsterdam to Munich (9½ hrs.); The Hague to Munich (12 hrs.); Milan to Bremen (11½ hrs.); Milan to Munich (7 hrs.); Zürich to Hamburg (9½ hrs.);

the Copenhagen–Hamburg–Stuttgart (13 hrs.) line is now an Intercity train, with 2 classes.

BY SEA. Between Helsinki (Finland) and Travemünde is a service with the ferry Finnjet operated by Finnlines, which can also connect with Prins Ferries' service between Hamburg and the UK (Harwich).

 BY CAR. *ADAC* (German Automobile Club), with head office in Munich, Baumgartnerstr. 53 and branch offices in all important towns of Germany, puts out an excellent map of Germany with the road conditions marked, as well as the most scenic stretches of the roads; the most interesting localities are marked in yellow and a brief description of their chief sights appears in the margin.

Motorists from Denmark can use the bridge spanning the Fehmarn Sund, after using the ferry route from Roedby in Denmark to Puttgarden in Germany. New stretches of motorway run from Skovby near Schleswig up to Flensburg, effectively linking Denmark with motorways down to the boot of Italy. Several ferryboat routes (ships loading cars are used on some of them) connect various Scandinavian ports, including Helsinki and Hango in Finland and Slite on the Swedish island of Gotland, with Travemünde near Lübeck. Townsend–Thoresen are British agents for the Gedser–Travemünde car-ferry service.

Car-Sleeper Express Trains. Motorists can save time but not money putting their car aboard one of these overnight special trains equipped with couchettes and sleepers. Many of them operate all year, but some only in summer and only on certain days of the week.

For the 81/82 season the German Railways *(Bundesbahn)* are making increased efforts to improve the services offered thus relieving the overloaded autobahns from some of their summer season transit traffic. At present cars can be loaded at 23 stations in Germany from where trains link with 19 destinations abroad. In addition car-sleepers connect main centers with Germany, of which some of the main routes are: *Christophorus Express* to Düsseldorf-Cologne-Munich; *Auto-Traum-Express* to Hamburg/Bremen-Hannover-Karlsruhe-Lörrach (near Basel), as well as daily services operated by the German Travel Service's (DER) with trains to and from Lindau, Lörrach, Munich, Sonthofen and the island of Sylt.

Three times a week during the summer season car-sleepers leave Düsseldorf on the journey to Narbonne in S.W. France, via the Rhine Valley and Frankfurt, connecting for Spain and Portugal. During the school holidays (June-August) additional connections run from Munich and Kassel. Increased services between Hamburg and Villach (on the Austrian border with Yugoslavia) offer direct links with the Yugoslavian coastal resorts.

It is of course wise to book your car-sleeper in advance, but the Bundesbahn's computerized reservation system nearly always finds a vacancy on another sleeper one or at maximum two days later.

Fares are calculated on a unit price for car and driver, every additional passenger extra. Sleeping-car or couchette are priced separately.

ARRIVING IN GERMANY

CUSTOMS. You may bring into Germany free of duty all objects intended for your personal use during your stay, including typewriters, cameras with plates or films, bicycles, rowboats, collapsible boats, sports equipment of all kinds, etc. Foodstuffs, confectionery, coffee, and drinks are limited to the amount expected to be consumed on the trip to your German destination. Travelers from European countries may bring in 200 cigarettes or 100 cigarillos or 50 cigars or 250 grams tobacco; travelers from non-European countries twice that amount; those coming from Common Market countries (including Britain) may bring in 300 cigarettes, or 150 cigarillos or 75 cigars or 400 grams of tobacco. You may bring in customs free the following alcoholic beverages: 2 liters of wine and either 1 liter of liquor or 2 liters of fortified wines (such as aperitifs) or 2 liters of sparkling wines (champagne and similar). Travelers from Common Market countries may bring in 3 liters of wine and 1½ liters of liquor.

Unless you reside in Germany, you may take out an unlimited amount of purchases duty free, provided they are not intended for commercial purposes. Simplified customs procedures have been inaugurated at all German airports; as with most Western countries, you have the choice of a quick exit through the Nothing-to-Declare channel, or you can go through the normal Customs check, if you are carrying declarable goods.

MONEY. You may bring into or take out of Germany any amount of German and foreign currency, without declaration or any other formality. You can change money at any bank, travel bureau, or railway station, or you can make purchases and pay bills in your own currency, in which case it's best to check on the exchange rate being used. The German monetary unit is the mark (DM), which is divided into 100 pfennigs. Coins are issued in the denominations of 1, 2, 5, 10 and 50 pfennigs and 1, 2, and 5 marks, and there are 5, 10, 20, 50, and 100-mark bills.

At time of writing, mid-1981, the exchange rate for the Deutschmark was about: US$1 = 2.35DM, and £1 = DM4.80. However, we advise you to check carefully on the exchange while you are planning your trip and then, while traveling, keep an eagle eye on what is happening to the mark, dollar or pound. It's a simple precaution, but it can pay handsome dividends, both in peace of mind and hard cash.

STAYING IN GERMANY

HOTELS. Residential tourist establishments comprise *hotels, Gasthöfe* or *Gasthäuser,* which are inns, that is, primarily restaurants, but with some rooms for transients, and *Fremdenheime* or pensions. When a hotel is listed as *garni* it means that it does not have a restaurant, but breakfast is available and is served either in the guest rooms or in a special breakfast room. In any given locality, the hotels are usually the most expensive, the Gasthöfe next, the pensions the cheapest. There are few localities where you can't find a single room without bath in a clean, modest pension for 12 marks minimum.

Service charges and taxes are automatically included in the room rates, as well as in the prices for meals and drinks. Continental breakfast is frequently included in the rate (always inquire), other breakfast features are always extra.

A computer hotel-reservation system is operated by ADZ, 6 Frankfurt, Untermainanlage 6, which can book a room in any hotel in Germany and also package holidays.

For brochures listing hotels in holiday regions offering special facilities for the disabled, write to *Hilfe für Behinderte e.V.*, D4 Düsseldorf, Kirchfeldstr. 149.

Romantic Hotels. There is a fascinating chain of country inns called *Romantic Hotels and Restaurants* dotted throughout both Germany and Austria. They are highly atmospheric and, while not all deluxe, brimming with charm and comfort. For details, contact Romantic Hotels and Restaurants P.O.Box 114, D-8757, Karlstein am Main. Another hotel association, called *Silence Hotels*, emphasizes quiet, green locations; write to Landgasthof, Hirsch D–7061 Ebnisee/Württemberg.

CASTLE HOTELS. Of particularly good value and interest in Germany are the castle hotels. These are old castles, often still privately owned. The simpler ones sometimes lack comfort, but the atmosphere and furnishings are authentic. Some of them are luxurious establishments, with valuable antique furnishings, private tennis courts, hunting preserves, and fishing waters. Because they are located in the country away from major centers, they have a special appeal for motorists. Various special tours, including a number of overnight stays in different castles, are available.

Prices range from DM25–DM160; average is about DM55. Inclusive tours of several castle hotels are possible; some have special features like art treasures and culinary specialities.

You can obtain a brochure *Castle Hotels in Germany* from the German National Tourist Office, from Lufthansa Airline offices, or write to the *Vereinigung der Burg und Schlosshotels,* Burghotel Trendelburg, c/o Baron von Stockhausen, D.3526 Trendelburg, West Germany.

MOTELS AND AUTOBAHN HOTELS. Autobahn Hotels (Rasthäuser) usually represent a combination of a restaurant, café, service station, and offer a number of hotel rooms. Sometimes they are similar to motels, sometimes not. You are not allowed to make a U-turn on the autobahns, so be on the lookout to select a hotel located on your lane of the autobahn; special underpasses, however, are frequently sited. There are no charges for children under 12; baby beds also available.

A folder *Autobahn Service* showing the entire motorway system and all facilities available en route, is available in English from filling stations and road houses, or from the frontier crossing points.

APARTMENTS. Bungalows or apartments usually accommodating from a minimum of two to a maximum of eight persons, including children, can be rented. The rates are relatively inexpensive (with reductions for longer stays) but the expense for gas, electricity and sometimes water is usually extra (based on meter reading). For very short stays you usually have to pay a small amount extra for the use of linen (you may also bring your own). For further information write to the provincial tourist associations mentioned in the regional chapters.

Prins Ferries operate 9 day (7 night) holidays with your car from Britain using bungalows and apartments with self-catering mostly in scenic areas of north Germany, and within easy reach of Hamburg or Bremerhaven.

 RESTAURANTS. Considerable savings can be made if you eat as the Germans do: take the table d'hôte or *Tageskarte* (daily special) lunch (offered *only* at noon), which consists of soup, main course and may or may not include a simple dessert (in the south probably not; in the north probably yes). This will cost anywhere from 6 marks in an inexpensive restaurant to 10–15 marks in a moderate establishment. If your digestion and habits require coffee and/or dessert, go to a café; the coffee served in most German restaurants (except expensive or foreign ones) is not very good. Germans eat light in the evening: potato salad and sausages, or an omelette and perhaps cheese afterwards (4–10 marks, depending on the restaurant). Some, but not all, expensive restaurants also offer table d'hôte lunches. If you eat à la carte, there is virtually no difference between lunch and dinner prices.

We grade the restaurants in our Practical Information sections at the end of each chapter as *Expensive* (E), *Moderate* (M) and *Inexpensive* (I). Naturally, the variation of prices within each category will be marked from region to region and from town to town. The approximate range is—(E) 20–40DM and up; (M) 9–20; (I) 6–10. We stress that this is only an approximation. You could, for example, pay well over these rates, in, say, Frankfurt, and under them in a small country town.

Except for a few very expensive ones, restaurants display their menu outside next to the entrance, including at lunchtime the day's special, and, of course, the prices, so you can shop around until you find the place which suits you.

Service charges are included in all restaurant prices. Menus and wine lists automatically quote prices *inclusive* of taxes and service charges.

 CONVENIENT CONVENIENCES. These are not too frequent on the street, to be found at all railroad stations, larger border crossings, in all large department stores, restaurants and entertainment spots. Apart from the international symbols for location, the letters D (for Damen, ladies) and H (for

Herren, men) are used, and in many simpler places, the 00 sign with an arrow pointing the way.

In hotels and restaurants there is usually no charge, so 20–30 pfennigs placed in the saucer of the washroom attendant will do. In other places the charge is 30 pfennigs or often 50 for the use of soap and towel; usually there is an attendant, but if not there is a lock mechanism on the door which swallows 10 pfennig pieces, so be sure to have small change.

TIPPING. In Germany, the service charges on hotel bills suffice, except for bellhops and porters (1 mark per bag or service), doormen (1 mark for calling a cab). Whether you tip the hotel concierge depends on whether he has given you any special service. Except in the case of special service in expensive hotels, chambermaids are not tipped in Germany. All service charges (10%) are included in restaurant bills, but it is customary to add the loose change or about 5% as a tip; in expensive restaurants a bit more. Because of increases in taxi fares, taxi drivers no longer expect a tip; you can add the loose change or up to 5% in case of special favor. The days of the station porter (except perhaps in some resorts and smaller towns) are over; there are instead push carts in all main railroad stations free of charge - at airports these carts cost 1 mark. In Germany you do not tip theater ushers or barmen. Hairdressers get 1.50 to 2 marks, ladies' room attendants 50 pfennigs.

MEDICAL SERVICES. The IAMAT (International Assoc. for Medical Assistance to Travellers) offers you a list of approved English-speaking doctors who have had postgraduate training in the U.S., Canada or Gt. Britain. Membership is free; the scheme is world-wide with many European countries participating. For information apply in the U.S. to Suite 5620, 350 Fifth Ave., New York 10001; in Canada, 123 Edward St., Toronto M5G 1E2. In Europe: Gotthardstrasse 17, 6300 Zug, Switzerland. A similar service with a small initial membership charge is offered by *Intermedic*, 777 Third Ave., New York, N.Y. 10017; however, there is an initial membership charge, and the subsequent fee schedule is higher than IAMAT's.

Among numerous medical insurances available to travelers from the U.K., *Europ Assistance* offers help 24 hours a day, seven days a week, including holidays, by means of a telephone service staffed by highly trained multilingual personnel. Facilities include air and road ambulances and a continent-wide network of medical advisers. Europ Assistance, 252 High Street, Croydon, Surrey CRO 1NF. has two schemes, one for independent and inclusive-tour travelers, the other for motorists. Basic price is £5.75 per person plus an additional £7.50 for winter sports; £16.60 for cars, £5.60 for caravans. This service is available only to residents of Great Britain.

Germany and Britain, as members of the EEC, have a reciprocal medical service. Obtain the explanatory leaflet (SA28) from your local Department of Health and Social Security. The Allgemeine Ortskrankenkasse in most towns supplies lists of doctors and also certificates entitling you to free treatment, if you reside in Britain.

CLOSING TIMES. The general public holidays are: 1 January, New Year's Day; Easter (Good Friday through Easter Monday); 1 May, Labor Day; Ascension Day; Whit Monday; 17 June, Day of Unity; mid-Nov. Prayer and Repentance day; 25–26 Dec., Christmas. In addition, there are several regional public and religious holidays.

In general, shops are open from 8:30 or 9 to 6 or 6:30 and close Sat. afternoons except on the first Sat. in each month. Hairdressers close Mons. Banks are open on weekdays from 8:30–1 p.m. and from 2 to 4 p.m., Thursdays until 5:30, closed on Saturday.

MAIL, TELEPHONE, TELEGRAMS. As in most European countries, the post office operates the telephone and telegraph service. Local phone calls from pay stations cost 20 pfennigs. Cheap rates on long distance calls are in effect between 6 p.m. and 8 a.m. For foreign calls, inquire at a post office or from your hotel concierge, but calls from a hotel will cost considerably more. Over half of the telephones in Germany, with the exception of parts of Bavaria, have been converted to a new system of an 8-minute time limit on calls. This means that private calls now cost 23 pfennigs for 8 minutes, and pay stations are being adjusted accordingly. Although the longer you talk the more you pay now, in many areas the local-call zone has been greatly extended so that you can make calls over long distances at local rates. The 8-minute time limit is in effect between 6 a.m. and 6 p.m. and during the night and at weekends the time is extended to 12 minutes. Cheap rates are available on international calls to European countries bordering on W. Germany between 6 p.m. and 8 a.m. The whole of W. Germany will have been converted to this system by 1982.

File telegrams at post offices or give them to your concierge. The rate inside of Germany is 72 pfennigs a word. Mail rates are: letters up to 20 grams to all destinations except Andorra, Belgium, France, Holland, Italy, Lichtenstein, Luxembourg, Monaco, San Marino, Switzerland and Vatican City, to which inland rates apply, DM1.20, postcards, DM0.70. Letters to Britain cost DM1.00. Inland, DM0.80 for letters, DM0.70 for postcards. Airletter forms, DM1.10 to all countries. There are no extra charges for air mail delivery within Europe. Cables to New York are DM1.44 per word; to London, DM0.48 per word. At the time of going to press, all mail rates will be increased as of 1 March 1982 by 10–15 pfennigs.

TIME in West Germany is one hour ahead of Britain, six hours ahead of U.S. E.S.T., so plan your phoning accordingly. Furthermore, attention should be given to the times of changeover from winter time to summer time in Germany (as of 6 April 1980 West Germany adopted East European summer time, lasting through until end of September) because this takes place a few weeks *after* Great

Britain puts its clocks forward in spring, and *before* the U.S. changeover to daylight saving time. In both cases the interim period can affect flight and rail timetables, West Germany having the same time as Great Britain until the 24 hours of changeover and being a total of 7 hours ahead of the U.S. until the latter adopts summer time. The same applies to the reversion to C.E.T. and E.S.T.

 BUSINESS PEOPLE. If you have had experience of business in the USA it will serve well in West Germany whose business personnel are used to Americans and even speak good English. Business appointments are likely to occur earlier or later in the day than in the USA or Britain; no language problems, no lack of secretarial help. Formalities are not as formal as you might imagine but cool first name terms. Reckon on DM290 to dine 4 people in a smart city restaurant, for 2 apertifs each, a 3-course meal, 2 bottles of wine, coffee, tax and service costs. Executives allow DM250 daily for living, of which about half goes on accommodation and meals.

 ELECTRIC CURRENT. In about 90 percent of locations the voltage is 220, AC current, 50 cycles. Better check before plugging in, however. Transformers to step down too high voltages can be bought in special shops everywhere, along with adapters for German sockets and plugs, which differ from the American and British varieties. New railroad sleepers have special sockets for American razors. But best take along a battery-operated razor.

LAUNDROMATS. Prolific, especially in urban areas but on side streets rather than boulevards.

 PHOTOGRAPHY. German customs regulations permit you to bring in your own cameras, plates and film without payment of duty, but as some of the world's best cameras are manufactured in this country, if you have in mind buying a new one, you might well do it here. German film is naturally good also, and there is no shortage of it. A roll of black and white film with 36 exposures will cost about 5 marks; color film, with 36 exposures and development included, about 18. If you find yourself on the border between East and West Germany, better leave your camera behind. It is unwise anywhere in the world to attempt to photograph military establishments or operations.

Important note. Those once-in-a-lifetime holiday films are vulnerable to the X-ray security machines on airports. At some, such as London's Heathrow, extra-powerful equipment is used; on most the machines are of the "low-dose" type. Both can cause films to be "fogged", and the more often the film passes through such machines, the more the fog can build up.

Warning notices are displayed sometimes, and passengers are advised to remove film—or cameras with film in them—for a hand check. But many airport authorities will not allow hand inspection and insist that all luggage pass through the detection devices.

There are two steps you should follow. First, ask for a hand inspection whenever you can. Second, buy one or more *Filmshield* lead-laminated bags, which are manufactured by the American SIMA Products Group. These will protect films from low-dosage X-rays, but should not be relied on against the more powerful machines. The bags are also available in Britain.

 SPAS. There are 250 health resorts with mineral springs in the German Spa Association. Beginning at Wiesbaden, one of the biggest, there is a notable row of them running across Hesse, not far from Frankfurt. There is quite a group in Westphalia, another concentration between the Rhine and the western frontier, from Aachen to Bad Dürkheim, and a further concentration in the southwestern corner of Germany, in Baden, with Baden-Baden as the most famous and the most chic. There are open-air thermal swimming pools at Badenweiler, Bad Hönningen on Rhine. Niederbreisig on Rhine, Schlangenbad (Taunus) and Wilbad in the Black Forest; indoor thermal swimming pools at Aachen and Badenweiler; open-air mineral swimming pools at Honnef, Stuttgart-Berg and Stuttgart-Cannstatt; an open-air brine swimming pool at Bad Rappenau; and an indoor sea water swimming pool at Norderney (constant temperature of water: 72° F). Bad Reichenhall and Bad Wiessee are very fashionable spas in Bavaria as well as Bodenmais in the Bayerischer Wald and Bad Kissingen in Franconia. Another important string of spas goes from Weserbergland (Bad Pyrmont) to Harz (Bad Harzburg).

For a complete list of spas, the nature of their springs and the ailments they alleviate, ask the German National Tourist Office. Average cost for 3 weeks' treatment is DM700–DM2100; for 4 weeks DM1300–DM3200. This includes board and lodging, doctor's fees, treatment up to a certain level, and spa tax.

 CASINOS. Here the favorite games of roulette and baccarat, played according to the international rules, exist at a number of the German spas. They are licensed, and gambling is legal. Baden-Baden, in the Black Forest, is perhaps the best known. Bad Neuenahr, in the Rhineland, boasts the largest gambling rooms, and Bad Homburg, near Frankfurt, was the place that exported roulette to Monte Carlo. Other popular casinos are located at Hittfeld by Hamburg, Hamburg itself, Travemünde on the Baltic; Westerland, on the North Sea island of Sylt; Bad Dürkheim in the Palatinate; Wiesbaden, half an hour from Frankfurt; Lindau and Constance, on Lake Constance; Garmisch-Partenkirchen, Bad Reichenhall and Bad Wiessee in the Bavarian Alps, Bad Kissingen in North Bavaria, Bad Pyrmont in Lower Saxony, Berlin, Bad Harzburg in the Harz mountains, Bad Zwischenahn in Lower Saxony, Hannover and Aachen. Minimum stakes at all games DM2–DM10.

SPORTS. Germany has always been a great country for athletics and almost every German town of any size has a stadium and athletic field, where you may see football (soccer) matches and track meets. Some of the big cities have tremendous arenas, holding up to 100,000 spectators. Watch local papers or the weekly calendars put out in many towns, for boxing, wrestling and similar events. Six-day bicycle races are popular, and are regular features especially in Munich (one of the biggest), Dortmund, Frankfurt, Hannover, Münster and Berlin. Stadiums or athletic fields often have swimming pools, where water sports events are held. Many become skating rinks in winter, where ice hockey is scheduled.

Apart from particular addresses given below, information on all sports activities may be had from any German National Tourist Office, and from local information centers.

 GOLF. There are about 130 golf courses in Germany. Daily tickets average 12 to 20 marks; on weekends and holidays 15 to 30 marks; weekly tickets between 60 and 150 marks. Clubs usually allow foreign non-members to play on their links; apply to any local golf club (see regional chapters), or for full information, write to the German Golf Assn., Rheinblickstr. 24, 6202 Wiesbaden Biebrich.

 FISHING. Trout fishing is the most popular form of this sport in Germany, where the river rainbow, lake and salmon trout are found. You can also fish for pike, carp, salmon, eel, Danube salmon, shad, perch-pike, perch, bream, barbel, chub and rudd, among others. You need a fishing permit from the local government (district, city), which will cost 10–20 marks and is valid for one year, and a local angling permit issued by the owners or lessees of the fishing waters at fees, usually low, which vary according to the length of time requested and the quality of the fishing waters.

Hotels with fishing facilities usually allow their guests to fish free of charge but you have to deliver the catch to the hotel.

Full information from *Verband der Deutschen Sportfischer*, 605 Offenbach, Bahnhofstr. 37.

GLIDING. There are about 1,000 branches of the Deutscher Aeroclub, and 14-day courses cost between DM450 and DM500. Address: Frankfurt 71, Lyoner Str. 16.

Hang gliding (Drachenfliegen) is an increasingly popular, if rather daring, sport in mountainous regions of Southern Germany where air currents and terrain are suitable (see p. 233). The name, if nothing else, should tempt the adventurous into the air—who could resist dragonflying! Information about courses and suitable areas from Drachenflug Aichach, Postfach 1112, 889 Aichach, Oberbayern.

WINTER SPORTS. Southern Bavaria is the big winter sports region, with Garmisch-Partenkirchen, where the Olympic Stadium is located, the best known center, and the Oberstdorf ski jump in Allgäu is the world's largest. There are also winter sports resorts in the Black Forest, the Harz region, the Bavarian Forest, Rhön Mountains, Fichtelgebirge, Sauerland and the Swabian mountains. From the middle of December to the end of March is the normal **skiing** season, but at the higher altitudes such as Zugspitze (near Garmisch), you can usually ski from as early as the end of November to as late as the middle of May. There's no need to bring skis with you—you can rent them or buy them here at lower prices.

For **cross-country** (or *Langlauf*) skiing, which is becoming increasingly popular (the equipment is considerably cheaper and there is no waiting at ski-lifts) as opposed to downhill (or *Alpin*) skiing there are stretches of prepared tracks (or *Loipen*) to be found in the valleys and foothills of most winter-sports centers as well as in the suburbs of larger towns in Southern Bavaria. The season is naturally rather shorter.

Ski-bobbing is on the increase here. There are runs and schools teaching the sport at Bayrischzell, Berchtesgaden, Garmisch-Partenkirchen, Füssen, and Oberstdorf in the Alps, as well as at Altglashütten, Bernau, and Feldberg in the Black Forest. Ice rinks, many open all year, are prolific.

Ski instruction costs from DM70 weekly, DM20 daily, skibob courses from DM48 weekly. Hire of skis and sticks costs from DM3 daily, DM12 weekly, ski boots DM2.50 and 10 respectively.

 CAMPING, HIKING, CYCLING, MOUNTAINEERING. Hiking and mountaineering groups are affiliated with the *Association of German Mountain and Touring Clubs,* Hospitalstr. 21b, Stuttgart, which can supply any needed information. The *Deutsche Alpenverein* (DAV), Alpenvereinshaus, Praterinsel 5, Munich 22, admits foreign members. Membership allows 50 percent reduction or more for use of their huts.

The *German Camping Club,* Mandelsstr. 28, Munich 23, publishes a guide of the camping sites in Germany at DM12.80 for non-members, free for members, and the German National Tourist Office issues a folder, *Camping in Germany.* There are also about 500 winter camping sites and their number is increasing.

Every weekend in high season VHF services of several regional broadcasting authorities give out details of available pitches on camp sites. Timings can be seen on motorways and are also listed in the Autobahn Service brochure.

Cyclists can get all the information they need from the Association of German Cyclists, *Bund Deutscher Radfahrer* (BDR), Karl Glöcknerstr. 2, Giessen/Lahn; or in Britain from the *Cyclists' Touring Club,* 69 Meadrow, Godalming, Surrey. You can bring your bicycle in with you without formality or payment of duty. At more than 250 railroad stations you can hire a cycle for DM8 a day (DM4 if you have a rail ticket), and even return it to another station.

BOATING AND CANOEING. Boating has always been a popular sport in Germany, whose rivers and canals afford a wide choice of trips through interesting scenery, whether you prefer placid waters or like to shoot rapids. Motorboats and motordriven canoes can only be brought into Germany under triptyques or *carnets de passage.* They can be obtained through touring clubs and other organizations affiliated with the Alliance Internationale de Tourisme (AIT) or the Fédération Internationale de l'Automobile (FIA). Other boats and folding canoes require no documents and can be imported without duty.

For information regarding canoeing and rowing respectively, address the *Deutsche Kanuverband,* Berta-Allee 8, Duisburg or the *Deutsche Ruderverband* Aegidiendamm 2, Hannover.

 YACHTING. The big event in Germany for yachtsmen is the annual regatta week at Kiel, usually at the end of June. Many other international regattas attract foreign yachtsmen. For full information on them, write to the German Sailing Association, Adolfstr. 26, Hamburg 50. Crews of seagoing yachts carrying normal ship's papers do not require passports or visas to enter Germany.

Lake sailing is taught in over 30 sailing schools, particularly on Chiemsee and Steinhuder Meer, largest lake in North Germany. Write: *Verband Deutscher Segelschulen,* 44 Münster, Graelstr. 45. Depending on length of course (1–3 weeks) and accommodation, courses cost from DM100–900. Self-drive yachts (cabin cruisers) may be chartered on the Moselle at about DM50 per person. Details from Yacht-Seereisen H. O. Schirrmacher, Königsallee 22, Düsseldorf.

WINDSURFING. This exhilarating, and skilful, watersport which combines sailing and surfing, has escalated in popularity on the lakes of Southern Germany so much so that it is now quite often restricted on some bathing beaches because of the increasing danger of collision between windsurfers and swimmers. From May to September it is in fact prohibited on the lakes of the Munich suburbs. Great care should be taken at all times to observe the restricted areas. Equipment can be hired at most of the large resorts on the Bavarian lakes, but it is advisable for the novice to invest in lessons in order to get full enjoyment from this sport. Courses cost around DM 25 per hour, or in blocks of 7 hours, including simulator practice and the possibility of taking the proficiency test of the Association of German Windsurfing Schools *(Verband der Deutschen Windsurfing Schulen AG).* For further information on hire of equipment and instruction centers contact the VDWS at Fasserstr. 30, 8120 Weilheim, Oberbayern (tel. (0881)–5267).

HORSERACING. Flat, jumping and trotting races and driving tournaments are held in many German cities, among the most important being the International Riding, Jumping and Driving Tournaments at Aachen in late June or early July, and the week of racing at Baden-Baden's Iffezheim track during the same month. The most important races are held at Aachen, Baden-Baden, Berlin, Bremen, Dortmund, Düsseldorf, Frankfurt, Gelsenkirchen, Hamburg (German Derby), Hannover, Cologne, Krefeld, Mönchengladbach, Mülheim, Munich, Recklinghausen, Verden on the Aller and Wiesbaden. There is totalisator betting.

RIDING. Available almost throughout Germany. Charges are from DM10 per hour, from DM15 for instruction.

MOTOR AND MOTORCYCLE RACING. Germany has a number of internationally known tracks for motor races, among which the best known are the twisting mountain track, the Nürburgring in the Eifel district; the Avus track in Berlin; on the steep Schauinsland mountain course near Freiburg; the Solitude track near Stuttgart; the Eilenriede course in Hannover; the Noris Ring at Nürnberg; the Hockenheimring near Heidelberg; and the hilly motorcycle race course at Schotten, not far from Frankfurt. The principal events of the year in this category are the international Eilenriede motorcycle race at Hannover in April; the Rhine Cup motor race on the famous Hockenheim Ring track in Baden, near Mannheim, in May; the international Feldberg motorcycle race in the Taunus mountains near Frankfurt in June; important motorcycle events in July take place alternately on the most important tracks, the international hillclimbing "Round Schotten" race at the place of the same name, and the world championship Solitude Castle race near Stuttgart.

Probably the Number One event of its kind is the German Grand Prix world championship event for Formula 1 racing cars at Hockenheim early in August. The 1,000-kilometer race for the same categories takes place in May. The important Freiburg-Schauinsland Mountain Record hill climb for racing and sports cars on the edge of the Black Forest is also held in August; in the same month, two important motorcycle events of the year, the international Noris Ring races of Nürnberg and the international Municipal Park race at Hamburg; and the international 24-hour race at the Nürburgring in June.

TRAVELING IN GERMANY

BY TRAIN. Germany has one of the best and most modern railroad services in Europe, with many new, fast trains. Best are the TEE (Trans Europ Express) trains and the Inter-City network. The latter has two classes, TEE has first class only, with a surcharge and obligatory seat reservations.

Top among the TEE trains are the *Rheingold, Diament* and *Gambrinus*. All three number among the fastest trains in Germany and are equipped with first-class amenities, including radio telephones. The *Rheingold* runs from Holland through the Rhine Valley to Basel, *Diament* traverses Germany from North to South, leaving Hamburg's main station (Hauptbahnhof) at 9.00 (10.00 summer) then running via Hannover, Würzburg, Nürnberg and Augsburg, to arrive in Munich shortly after 15.00 (16.00 summer). *Gambrinus* also runs from North to South, but after leaving Hamburg at 10.25 (11.25 summer) it branches east via Dortmund, Düsseldorf, Cologne and Stuttgart to reach Munich at 20.30 (21.30 summer) in the evening.

In other trains there are 2 classes and although there are usually enough seats, places may be reserved in advance, advisable at peak periods.

Inter-City trains connect 47 large towns at hourly intervals with interchange facilities at the same platform in five principal stations—Hannover, Cologne, Mannheim, Dortmund, and Würzburg and serve a total of seven European cities outside Germany. There is also a similar system of D-City trains with second-class accommodation as well as first-class. These services, called 'DC', run on eight supplementary and connecting lines to offer good connections between 73 major towns, and good interchange facilities. About 80 DC trains operate daily, all with buffet car services. Long distance overnight trains in Germany have both couchettes and full sleeping cars serving first and second class. About forty-five new sleeping cars have showers, the only European railway to offer this facility to travelers.

Car rentals can be arranged on TEE and Inter-City trains, and the car will be waiting for you at the station.

Telegrams may be sent from trains just by giving them to the conductor, or received on trains or in station waiting rooms, where persons to whom they are addressed will be paged. There is a self-dialling telephone service on almost all TEE and Inter-City fast trains. Any number in Germany (or abroad) can be called from soundproof booths and passengers can also receive calls. Multilingual secretaries are available on many express trains.

The Holiday Express. A brand-new style of holiday express is in operation from Hannover to Bavaria and thence on to Vienna, the Italian Riviera, Yugoslavia, France and Spain. The *TUI-Ferien-Express* (Touristik Union International Holiday Express) has been financed by the German travel agencies' organisation, Touristik Union International, in collaboration with five large travel agents and the German *Bundesbahn*. The super-luxurious red-orange-beige-brown sleepers offer a completely new-style of rail travel particularly aimed at package-tour holidaymakers. Sleeping-compartments for not more than four people, plus child, at a time, are fully airconditioned, equipped with lockers for valuables and breakfast and supper are served by stewards in air-travel style to each compartment at no extra charge. In addition each train has a TUI-Recreation Car where passengers can sit at a comfortable bar with a kiosk for snacks, browse through newspapers and magazines in the reading room, make telephone calls, buy souvenirs or listen to music and watch films related to the train's destination. For details contact one of the following German travel agencies: *Touropa, Scharnow, Hummel, Dr. Tigges* or *Twen Tours*.

A **Eurailpass** is a convenient, all-inclusive ticket that can save you money on over 100,000 miles of railroads and railroad-operated buses, ferries, river and lake steamers, hydrofoils, with some Mediterranean crossings in 16 countries of Western Europe (including Germany). It provides the holder with unlimited travel at rates of: 15 days $242, 21 days $300, 1 month $368, 2 months $495, 3 months $570; a Eurail-Youthpass valid 21 days, $320. Children under 12 go half-fare, under 4 go free. The prices cover 1st class passage, reservation fees, and TEE surcharges. Available to U.S., Canadian, Japanese and S. American residents *only,* the pass must be bought from an authorized agent before leaving for Europe. Apply through your travel agent, or to: French Railroads, Eurailpass Div., 610 Fifth Ave., New York 10020; German Railroad, 630 Fifth Ave., N.Y. 10020 and D.E.R. Travel Service, 1290 Bay St., Toronto M5R 2C3.

Inside or outside of Germany, roundtrip tickets are sold at discounts varying from 10 percent to 50 percent, depending on distance, season, period of time and traveler's age. There is a wide variety of ticket combinations at reduced rates, including a "Tourist Card", a "Mini-Group Ticket" (at least 2 adults and 1 child), and a "Senior Citizen Ticket" (50% on roundtrip tickets). An Inter-Rail ticket, for young people up to the age of 26, offers unlimited travel through 20 European countries on all rail routes, and 50% discount travel inside the Federal Republic. The price for a monthly season ticket is DM395. Reservations advisable well in advance from the Deutsches Bundesbahn ticket offices. Apply to any German National Tourist Office. Currently travelers may purchase 9- or 16-day tourist cards, using any train with 1st class tourist cards, including TEE and Inter-City trains, with no surcharge. The card also includes using the Europabus services; reduced fares apply when using the KD Rhine steamers, and when traveling by train through East Germany to West Berlin. In the high season, groups of 6–14 people get 35% off TEE and Inter-City services; 65% off for 45 or more. A Junior Rail Pass, valid 1 year, costing DM98 enables people from 12 to 23 years to buy rail tickets at half price.

Luggage service: German Railroads have a luggage service which provides the transportation of your luggage from your home (or hotel) to your destination address within Germany; you call the luggage section (Gepäckabfertigung) at your railroad station; this service is presently available in about 350 places in Germany, including about 25 tourist centers in Upper Bavaria and Black Forest which do not have railroad links and where this service is provided by the German Federal Post's bus service. NB. Stuttgart, Munich, Hamburg and Frankfurt have available one ticket for one price which covers all journeys on public transport within a given period within that city.

BY AIR. Large modern airports are located in Frankfurt, Hamburg, Munich, Hannover, Bremen, Stuttgart, Cologne/Bonn, Dusseldorf, Nurnberg and West Berlin. Except for Berlin, all of these are connected with each other by a frequent schedule maintained by Lufthansa using Boeing 727, 737 and Airbus jets. West Berlin is connected with the main German cities by *British*

Airways, Pan Am and *Air France.*

There is no meal service on internal flights but *Lufthansa* has box lunches or snacks, depending on the time of day, available for all passengers in the departure lounge, free of charge. If not consumed on board, these make good picnics later in the day. This may seem mundane to the foreign visitor, but it is much more efficient on short flights.

Sample one-way fares (all economy): Frankfurt-Munich DM185; Frankfurt-Hamburg DM215; Frankfurt-Berlin DM145; Munich-Hamburg DM310. Discount return fares are available from most German cities to Berlin. With the exception of Bremen, where municipal buses stop at the airport, there are coach or rail services into the city centres at a cost ranging from DM1.20 to DM5.

Saarbrucken, Kiel, Kassel, Westerland, Wyk, Helgoland and Sylt are linked to the main cities by the two domestic airlines, *General Air* and *DLT Luftverkehrsgesellschaft,* though many flights operate in summer only. They also fly a regional service between Helgoland and Wangerooge and St Peter-Ording. Air taxi services are available throughout Germany.

Aerial sightseeing trips can be made from Munich over the nearby Alps in 4-seater Cessnas at reasonable rates. Apply to *Bayerischer Flugdienst Transair* at Munich Airport. Similar trips can be made from the airports of Stuttgart, Dusseldorf, Hamburg, Bremen and Hannover.

 BY BOAT. There are several fast services daily between Düsseldorf, Cologne and Mainz, passing many romantic castles, old towns and the famous rocky wall of Lorelei. German cruising ships also operate on the Upper Rhine as far as Basel, on the Main between Frankfurt and Mainz, and on the Mosel, Weser and Neckar rivers. With the opening of the Europe Canal, which joins the Main and the Danube, passenger boats now cruise the Main and Canal from Lohr, Würzburg, Bamberg and Nürnberg. The Danube Shipping Co.'s *Germania, Bavaria* and *Johanna* also operate on the Inn and the Ilz, and from Deggendorf to Vilshofen and Passau. There are also services on lakes Ammersee, Chiemsee and Königsee and on the Kiel Fjord.

The *German Federal Railway* with the *Fränkische Personenschiffahrt* of Würzburg offers through rail and boat trips between Nürnberg and Aschaffenburg (30 miles from Frankfurt). The same company has regular services from Erlangen, Fürth (near Nürnberg), Forchheim, Bamberg, Würzburg, Wertheim and Gemünden. Luxury German hotel-boats are in service along the entire length of the Rhine between Basel on the German-Swiss border and Rotterdam; they run a nine-day summer tour between Rotterdam and Basel (five days up, four downstream). Departures every two-three days in both directions during season. They also carry cars.

There is a hydrofoil service between Cologne and Koblenz and a short, lower-priced cruise between Amsterdam and Frankfurt. There are also Swiss, Dutch and British companies operating on the Rhine and Mosel, some quoting inclusive costs from London. Fuller details from the German National Tourist Office. Travelers holding single or return tickets to stations south of Cologne may transfer to the steamships of the regular day services of the *KDR* (Cologne–Düsseldorf Steamship Co.) between Cologne, Mainz, Wiesbaden and Frankfurt, provided the tickets are valid for the rail section corresponding to the part traveled by steamer. A transfer ticket *(Ergänzungskarte)* may be obtained at the landing stages on the Rhine. Full information from the *KD German Rhine Line,* 170 Hamilton Ave., White Plains, N.Y. 10601, or 323 Geary St., San Francisco, Calif. 94102. In Britain: *G.A. Clubb Rhine Cruise Agency,* 35 Dover St., London W1X 3RA.

Cruise-drive Rhine holidays, based on Frankfurt, with 7 days' car hire and unlimited mileage before or after cruising, and 7 nights' accommodation in Crest Hotels are worth considering.

In summer there is a daily service between Hamburg and the island of Helgoland and between Cuxhaven and Helgoland. Daily (except Monday) services between Bremerhaven (with train connection to and from Bremen) and Helgoland have been extended through mid-October. A special fast service (2½ hours) operates between Wilhelmshaven and Helgoland. There are daily connections between Helgoland and Hornum on the island of Sylt and with Büsum on the Schleswig-Holstein coast. Several other lines connect East Frisian and North Frisian Islands with the mainland and Helgoland. Ferry services between Travemünde, near Lübeck on the Baltic, and the Danish island of Bornholm operate at least five round trips weekly with accommodation for cars.

For unlimited trips on Lake Constance, it is possible to buy a seven-day ticket at a reasonable price. These are for use on all scheduled boats of the German, Austrian and Swiss Federal Railways.

 BY BUS. Germany is well covered by bus services, most of them using coaches of the latest design, with adjustable seats, sliding and glass roofs for maximum visibility, loudspeakers, radio—even with bars, buffets and stewardesses in some. For DM7 you can buy a timetable giving the schedules of all buses operated by the Federal Railways or the post office. The latter operates a number of special long distance services in summer, while all year round its buses penetrate into some of the remote mountain regions where there are no railroads. Also available are pocket timetables at about DM2. These can also be ordered through B.A.S. (Overseas Publications) Ltd., 48–50 Sheen Lane, London S.W.14, who will advise on payment.

One of the best services is provided by the *Romantic Road Bus* between Würzburg (with connections to and from Frankfurt and Wiesbaden) and Füssen (with connections to and from Munich, Augsburg, and Garmisch-Partenkirchen at Echelsbacher Brüke); this is an all-reserved-seats bus with a stewardess and one daily service in each direction, leaving in the morning and arriving in the evening. For seat reservations write to *Bahnbusverkehrsstelle Augsburg Bahnhof.*

On urban bus services, fares vary from 80 pfennigs to DM1.50. Often *carnets* (ticket booklets) can be purchased at a saving and in a few cities *rover* tickets are available.

BY CAR. Germany encourages motor tourists to take advantage of her autobahns and fine roads by making entrance formalities as simple as possible. Only the following documents are required: international car registration (not needed for cars registered in Britain, Belgium, Holland, Denmark, France, Italy, Luxembourg, Austria, Norway, Switzerland, Sweden, and Portugal); international drivers' license (not needed if the license is issued in the country from which no international car registration is needed or if the foreign license is made out in German or accompanied by a certified German translation); the latter can be provided by the ADAC, AvD *(Automobil-Club von Deutschland)* or DTC *(Deutsche Touring Club);* state identity plate. The green international insurance card is not required (though advisable); proof of liability insurance is.

You will find Germany an ideal country for motor touring because it has excellent roads and good garage service, while the number of interesting small localities makes travel through Germany more rewarding for the motorist, who can stop at will and vary his route as he wishes, then for the train traveler. ADAC *(Allgemeiner Deutscher Automobil-Club)* representatives meet incoming ships at Hamburg and Bremen and the ferry at Puttgarten (Fehmärn Island) to assist foreign motorists. Motorists coming overland will find offices set up to aid them at the frontiers.

For help in these and other matters, the three German automobile clubs mentioned above can be of great service. All of them are ready to aid foreign motorists. Their central addresses are: ADAC, Baumgartnerstr. 53, Munich 70, tel: 76–761; AvD, Lyonerstr. 16, Frankfurt/Niederrad, tel: 66061; DTC, Amalienburgstr. 23, Munich 60, tel: 11–10–48. ADAC and AvD operate road assistance services on the entire net of the German autobahns, which are constantly patrolled by their assistance cars; emergency phones for this purpose are located at spots only 7½ miles distant from each other. Ask expressly for Road Service Assistance in English (Strassenwachthilfe) when phoning. Help over breakdowns is given freely but materials must be paid for.

ADAC also maintains four helicopters to spot trouble on the autobahns and, if need be, act as ambulances. The first of these alone has been credited with saving over 100 lives, so they are known as the "Yellow Angels." Emergency calls for foreign tourists are taken by Radio Hessen—dial 0611/1551, and Bavarian Radio's motorists' service on "Bayern 3," tel. 089–59001.

"Auto pilots," mostly young students who are also good drivers, can be picked up on the main roads entering some large cities. For a modest fee they will guide or drive you through street traffic to your hotel or take you on a tour of the sights.

The German National Tourist Office or their representatives abroad can supply you with a booklet, *Happy Days in Germany,* which lists a number of recommended routes for seeing the country.

The speed limit in built-up areas is 50 kilometers per hour (31 mph). Since the fuel crisis all roads hitherto unrestricted are limited to 100 kmh (62 mph) while on motorways there is presently no limit, but a "recommended" 130 kmh (about 80 mph) limit, which means that if you are involved in an accident at a higher speed, this fact will weigh against you. Wearing of seat belts is now compulsory.

Fuel. Gasoline (petrol) costs had, by mid-1981, steadied somewhat in Germany at around DM-1.24 per litre, a lower price than in many other European countries. West German fuel contains less lead than is customary on the continent, and it has been found that some elderly cars object to this, but it makes no difference at all to the performance of newer models. It is perfectly OK to buy cut-price petrol of the correct octane rating, i.e. Super. German filling stations are highly competitive.

Car Hire. All the larger West German towns offer a drive-yourself car hire service. Depending on the type of car and rental firm you will pay between DM44 and DM117 daily plus charges of DM0.29 and DM1 per kilometer. Some firms offer weekly rates including unlimited mileage at about DM400 (VW Polo) to DM1400 (Mercedes 280A). VAT at 12% is extra. Four-weekly rates are lower. Many airlines operate in conjunction with Hertz Europe an inclusive Fly-Drive scheme on what they call a Combination Ticket, which is to say that your air fare and car hire are costed and paid for together: the cars await flights at the airport, and can be turned in where convenient. Cars can also be rented at railroad stations and while aboard the TEE and Inter-City trains. *Auto Sixt,* a prominent car rental and purchase firm throughout Germany is represented in the U.S.A. by Auto Europe, 21 E. 40th St., N.Y. 10016.

Taxis. Available almost everywhere by hailing or telephoning. Initial charges from DM3.00 plus DM1 to DM1.50 per km; DM0.50 extra for each piece of luggage. Waiting costs about DM12.00 per hour. Meters are compulsory.

Autobahns. The autobahn (A1) from Lübeck on the Baltic to Basel (Switzerland) runs via Hamburg, Hannover (A7), Kassel, Frankfurt, Karlsruhe and Freiburg. Bremen is connected into this chain by two links: the A27 northbound to Bremerhaven, from where a new stretch of motorway is nearing completion to link up with Cuxhaven on the North Sea, and southbound to Walsrode near Hannover. Westbound from Bremen the A1 autobahn continues via Osnabrück, Münster, Dortmund, Leverkusen to Cologne. The stretch Cologne-Trier is still under construction and is expected to be completed by the mid-eighties providing a direct motorway link to the French border at Saarbrücken thus avoiding having first to travel eastwards to join the north-south autobahn at Mannheim.

The long autobahn from the Dutch border at Arnhem (A3) runs to Nürnberg (where it joins the Berlin-Munich motorway) via Duisburg, Düsseldorf, Cologne, Frankfurt and Würzburg. The continuation of this autobahn will eventually (mid-eighties) link with Passau and the Austrian border.

From these two main arteries (A1, A3), nearly all the major cities and towns are connected by autobahn, and the autobahns with each other.

Major autobahns connect Karlsruhe with Stuttgart, Bodensee, Munich and Salzburg (Austria); Duisburg with Dortmund, Aachen with Cologne, Hannover, Braunschweig and the East German border near Helmstedt (from where it proceeds to Berlin); Heilbronn with Nürnberg, providing a direct autobahn connection between Suttgart and Berlin. Major links connect Sinsheim and

Mannheim, Freiburg and Mühlhausen (French border), and Oberhausen (Dutch border—Frankfurt autobahn) with Dortmund and the Cologne-Hannover autobahn.

Among the numerous shorter links are Dortmund-Kassel section, Kassel-Giessen; Karlsruhe-Munich; Munich-Deggendorf (to the Austrian border at Passau) and Rosenheim-Kuftsein (Austrian border) in Bavaria; Bendorf-Koblenz, connecting the Frankfurt-Cologne autobahn with the Rhine valley; Würzburg-Bad Hersfeld; Würzburg-Heilbronn, making the direct Hamburg-Hannover-Stuttgart route fully operational and easing the Frankfurt flyover and the Frankfurt-Karlsruhe-Stuttgart route.

The Darmstadt-Heidelberg link alleviates the old parallel Frankfurt-Mannheim autobahn. Europe's first 2-storied tunnel is on the autobahn near Wuppertal, and the 2-mile Elbe Tunnel underpasses Hamburg on the Europastrasse 3. Northbound motorists from Hamburg towards Denmark now have the E3-A7 all the way. The approach to the coastal resorts on Lübeck Bay is eased with the opening of the section between Bad Schwartau, near Lübeck, and Neustadt–Süd; it also speeds travelers from Hamburg going to Puttgarden ferry for Denmark.

Europa-routes. All *Autobahns* in the Federal Republic are distinguished from the main roads by the preceding letter "A" followed by the motorway number. Other main roads, *Bundesstrassen,* are preceded by "B". In addition, there is a network of major European highways criss-crossing West Germany, incorporating the Autobahns but preceded by "E" for Europaroute. Do not get confused if a particular stretch of Autobahn appears with an "E" number. For example, the Autobahn A9—Hof-Munich—is also Europaroute E6.

Conversion chart. If you want to convert from miles (m) into kilometers (km), read from the center column to the right; if from kilometers into miles, from the center column to the left. Example—5 miles = 8 kilometers, 5 kilometers = 3 miles.

m		km	m		km
0.6	1	1.6	37.2	60	96.5
1.2	2	3.2	43.4	70	112.2
1.8	3	4.8	49.7	80	128.7
2.4	4	6.3	55.9	90	144.8
3.1	5	8.0	62.1	100	160.9
3.7	6	9.6	124.2	200	321.8
4.3	7	11.2	186.4	300	482.8
4.9	8	12.8	248.5	400	643.7
5.5	9	14.4	310.6	500	804.6
6.2	10	16.0	372.8	600	965.6
12.4	20	32.1	434.9	700	1,126.5
18.6	30	48.2	497.1	800	1,287.4
24.8	40	64.3	559.2	900	1,448.4
31.0	50	80.4	621.3	1,000	1,609.3

LEAVING GERMANY

 CUSTOMS ON RETURNING HOME. If you propose to take on your vacation any *foreign-made* articles, such as cameras, binoculars, expensive time-pieces and the like, it is wise to put with your travel documents the receipt from the retailer or some other evidence that the item was bought in your home country. If you bought the article on a previous trip abroad and have already paid duty on it, carry with you the receipt for this. Otherwise, on returning home, you may be charged duty (for the British, V.A.T. as well).

U.S. Customs. At this writing, Americans who are out of the United States at least 48 hours and have claimed no exemption during the previous 30 days are entitled to bring in duty-free up to $300 worth of bona fide gifts or items for their own personal use. For the next $600 worth of goods beyond the first $300, inspectors will assess a flat 10% duty, rather than hitting you with different percentages for various types of goods. For the next $600 worth of goods above the duty-free $600, there will be a flat duty of 5%. The value of each item is determined by the retail value of the goods in the country where acquired (so save your receipts). Every member of a family is entitled to this same exemption, regardless of age, and their exemptions can be pooled. Infants and children get the same exemptions as adults.

Do not bring home foreign meats, fruits, plants, soil, or other agricultural items when you return to the United States. To do so will delay you at the port of entry. It is illegal to bring in foreign agricultural items without permission, because they can spread destructive plant or animal pests and diseases. For more information, read the pamphlet "Customs Hints", or write to: "Quarantines", U.S. Dept. of Agriculture, Federal Center Bdg., Hyattsville, Maryland 20782 for leaflet No. 1083, "Travelers tips on bringing food, plant and animal products into the United States."

Purchases intended for your duty-free quota must accompany your personal baggage.

Not more than 100 cigars, 200 cigarettes, may be included in your duty free exemption, nor more than a liter (33.8 fl. oz.) of wine or liquor (none at all if your passport indicates you are from a "dry" state or are under 21 years old). Only one bottle of perfume that is trademarked in the US may be brought in, plus a reasonable quantity of other brands.

Antiques are defined as articles over 100 years old and are duty-free. You may be asked to supply proof of age.

Small gifts may be mailed to friends, but not more than one package to one address and none to your own home. Notation on package should be "Unsolicited Gift, Nature of Gift, value under $25." Tobacco, liquor and perfume are not permitted.

If your purchases exceed your exemption, list the items that are subject to the highest rates of duty under your exemption and pay duty on the items with the lowest rates. Any articles you fail to declare cannot later be claimed under your exemption. To facilitate the actual customs examination it's convenient to pack all your purchases in one suitcase.

American rates of customs duty may change, therefore it is best to check the regulations with the American Embassy before or during your visit. The Embassy in Bonn has a special attaché for Customs matters in case you have any questions or problems.

British Customs. There are few concessions, and the remarks under "Returning Home" are particularly applicable. British subjects, except those under the age of 17 years, may import duty-free from any country the following: 200 cigarettes or 100 cigarillos or 50 cigars or 250 grams of tobacco; 1 liter of spirits or 2 liters of wine in excess of 38.8% proof, and 2 liters of still table wine. Also 50 grams of perfume, ¼ liter of toilet water and £28 worth of other normally dutiable goods.

Returning from Germany (or any other EEC country), you may, *instead* of the above exemptions, bring in the following, provided you can prove they were not bought in a duty-free shop: 300 cigarettes or 150 cigarillos or 75 cigars or 400 grams of tobacco; 1½ liters of strong spirits or 3 liters of other spirits or fortified wines plus 3 liters of still table wine; 75 grams of perfume and three-eighths liter of toilet water and £120 worth of other normally dutiable goods.

Canada. In addition to personal effects, and over and above the regular exemption of $150 per year, the following articles may be brought into Canada duty-free: a maximum of 50 cigars, 200 cigarettes, 2 pounds of tobacco and 40 ounces of liquor, provided these are declared in writing to customs on arrival. Canadian Customs regulations are strictly enforced; you are recommended to check what your allowances are and to make sure you have kept receipts for whatever you may have bought abroad. Small gifts can be mailed and should be marked "Unsolicited Gift, Nature of Gift, value under $25 in Canadian Funds". For all details, ask for the Canada Customs brochure "I Declare".

 DUTY FREE is not what it once was. You may not be paying tax on your bottle of whiskey or perfume, but you are certainly contributing to somebody's profits. Duty free shops are big business these days and mark ups are often around 100 to 200%. So don't be seduced by the idea that because it's duty free it's a bargain. Very often prices are not much different from your local discount store and in the case of perfume or jewelry they can be even higher.

As a general rule of thumb, duty free stores on the ground offer better value than buying in the air. Also, if you buy duty free goods on a plane, remember that the range is likely to be limited and that if you are paying in a different currency to that of the airline, their rate of exchange often bears only a passing resemblance to the official one.

THE
GERMAN
SCENE

THE GERMANS

A Satirical Glance

by
GEORGE MIKES

The trouble with the Germans is that their greatest virtues are ridiculed, scoffed at and criticized, while their failings and vices are extolled. They are often reprimanded, for instance, for taking serious things seriously. (I admit that the English would never do such a thing and I do like them much better for it.) The Germans seem to reject the idea that everything on earth is a capital joke. That is a pity; it causes them much trouble. Maybe we should accept such an attitude as a fact.

The English, again, are reputed for admitting their own faults, while the Germans always consider themselves as being right in everything. This seems to be a basic difference, but it isn't. We are all prone to

45

admit faults we do not regard as faults; in other words, we never admit any *real* faults. So we all do what the Germans do, but we do it—I think I must say that—with more charm and humor, so it looks much better.

The Germans are more methodical in all their ways than the Americans and incomparably more methodical than the English. This, too, is often held against them. I think it was Stephen Leacock, the great Canadian humorist, who remarked that in Germany, even the birds sit in a neat row on the boughs of trees and sing in choir and harmony under a conductor-bird. At the bottom of all this there is, in the soul of all German people, and of all German birds, a great—and hopeless—desire for order. I do not think—in spite of their reputation to the contrary—that Americans or English are less fond of order than the Germans. But they like a different kind of order. The German order must *look* like order.

How to be a German

Suppose you want to become a German. First of all you have to decide what sort of German you want to become. A Prussian, a Bavarian, a Saxon—or what? Oh yes, you will still find a few elderly Bavarians who will sigh: "Oh, for the good old days, when it was still permitted to shoot at the Prussians." Or some still remember the old saying: "North of the Danube is abroad; north of the Main is hostile territory." And you will find some old Berliners who will say: "The Bavarians are the outcome of God's miscarried attempt to turn Austrians into Prussians." In Bavaria everybody counts for a "Prussian" who is not Bavarian and consequently half of Munich today is "Prussian", that is Swabian, Saxon, Pomeranian, Balt, etc. Prussia, on the other hand, has disappeared completely, and it survives only in Bavarian prejudices. You still hear murmurs in Düsseldorf about the Bavarians having plundered some of their riches; but the younger generation is very different. It is true, I heard one young woman remark about a young man: "For a Bavarian, he speaks quite good German," but this was said in his presence and meant as an affectionate leg-pull, more English in style than anything else; the truth is that the young do not care a damn. Racial prejudice is dead in young Germany—so dead that even a man from Cologne is (almost) accepted in Bonn.

The second point to remember if you want to become a German is that you do not need to be a Teutonic god. You do not need to be six feet tall, broad-shouldered, fair, blue-eyed and divine in any particular way. If your laugh chimes melodiously like churchbells sunk in the Rhine, that is all right; but if it happens to be an uproarious belly-laugh, do not worry. If you are brave and vengeful like Siegfried, good for you; but if you are meek and humble, that will do as well. If you are lean and muscular, like warriors of the Nibelungenlied, that must be good for your health; but if your girth borders on the miraculous and you have a treble chin as well as a treble neck, you are still eligible.

Whatever you do, be polite and formal, like a foreign ambassador performing his official duty. If you are addressing someone 238 times in the course of an evening, give him his full title 238 times. And if you go on meeting him for 50 years, give him his full title for 50 years. In Frankfurt I visited the house (bombed and rebuilt) where Goethe was born, and the guide always referred to Goethe's father as *Herr Rat* (Mr. Councillor). Not once did he allow himself more familiarity with a man who had been dead for about 200 years.

Be decent, well meaning and clean. Always be well dressed, whether you are a millionaire or a beggar. Frenchmen spend most of their money on food and drink and do not care how they are dressed; the Germans would go about hungry, but they are always presentably dressed. In Germany few people would give money to a poorly clad beggar. There are very few beggars in Germany but the point is that those few are exquisitely clad.

Always explain the obvious and explain it with a dogmatic air; but be highly cultured and well educated at the same time. Quote Greek authors in the original, be interested in everything and amass a huge volume of factual information. Be paternal to everybody and teach everybody his own business. Do this benevolently and full of good intentions.

The Danger of Thinking

Now I should like to speak of the German vices, which I prefer to call the Three Dangers.

The first is the Danger of Thinking. Supercilious writers and silly commentators like to remark that the trouble with people is the fact that they refuse to think. They are quite wrong. The trouble with people is that they *do* think. This trouble amounts to serious danger when people not only think, but think logically. Thinking in most cases is only a poor substitute for common sense.

The Germans do think and consequently they feel they must reduce everything to principles. Everything must be either white or black, red or blue, one thing or the other. This is a good rule, but life and things do not follow it. Everything must be analyzed, understood and pigeon-holed.

The great trouble with logical thinking is that it does not exist. No philosopher—or person—has ever arrived at any conclusion by sheer logic. The conclusion—or at least a strong inclination for a certain kind of solution—always came first. Logic was applied afterwards. Logic is always the ally of prejudice; "muddling through" is the pillar of a perhaps clumsy, but clear-cut and workable, solution.

The Danger of Working

We all used to think that the Germans' mania for hard work was one of their strongest impulses—even stronger than their mania for traveling. But on this count I am able to report a most pleasant surprise. We don't need to worry. This legend ought to disappear fast. The Germans —I am delighted to report—are almost as lazy as their neighbors. Today they work less than any other European nation and get higher wages, while the quality of their products has not risen. Employers go in fear of their employees; no waiter, for example, is ever told off, however impertinent he may choose to be. In fact, truculent clients are often asked to keep away from restaurants as they may annoy the waiters: the owner knows he may get as many clients as he wants but waiters are few and far between. Customers are kept waiting in stores while assistants finish their little chats. Strikes, too, are becoming more and more frequent. Hard work is on the decline. Work is not an important subject of conversation, it lags behind sports, jokes, politics and cars. In 1952 a room—completely in ruins—was let to me one morning and by the next day it had been rebuilt and redecorated, complete with lace cushions and Biedermayer porcelain-angels playing their harps on my bedside table. Nothing like this could happen now. Today the German working week is one of the shortest in Europe and the Swabians—the hardest workers in the lot—work even less than the rest. Theirs is a religiously mixed region and they keep *all* holidays: Catholic, Calvinist, Lutheran, etc. You often see a group of workers: six lazy Italians work hard while two industrious Germans watch them.

I do not paint this picture in order to deride the Germans but, on the contrary, to build them up. If, after the war, they felt an irresistible urge to rebuild their devastated country, and take great pride in the magnificent result, that is perfectly understandable. But after some years this urge has faded. A permanent mania for hard work would be a frightening thing; the desire to shirk is human. Work for work's sake is a repulsive and sinister inclination; to get the maximum reward for the minimum of work is a worthy, meritorious and natural desire which we condemn in others but which we all share. The Germans hate work just as much as other decent people do. They are really quite human. They *do* belong to Europe.

Prosperity and Travel-mania

It is enough to walk along the main shopping street of any large town to be able to breathe in the riches of Germany. Travel agents abound, intriguing advertisements invite you to package tours to faraway places: spend Easter in Bali, go shopping in Hong Kong, go around the world in 24 days. The advertisements try to shame you into it: you don't mean to say you haven't seen the Indian Ocean yet? Tut, tut, tut . . . Estate agents offer you properties in the Bahamas, in Morocco and Sicily, villas on the Turkish coast of Asia Minor or yachts to rent in the Caribbean. Or just take one of the great mail-order house's catalogs: 623 pages in glorious color. You can choose between several thousands of suits, coats (from mini to maxi) for men, women and children. You drop a postcard and they deliver to your home a color TV set, tropical fish, tropical birds (flamingoes, pelicans or cockatoos), medieval musical instruments or deep-diving kits, inflatable swimming pools, speed-boats, yachts, racing cars or an observatory, complete with the finest telescope.

The telescope and the villas are more significant than most people think. The Americans are, on the whole, inward-looking people; they keep watching themselves; the Germans are outward looking, they watch—perhaps too anxiously, perhaps with too large telescopes—others. After two world wars, the Germans have sincerely and finally given up all ideas of conquering Europe. Hardly have they done so, than they succeeded in conquering it without even trying. Half of Europe—at least half of Europe in the sun—belongs to them. Where tanks failed, the check-book prevailed; where valueless bombers flopped, revalued marks succeeded. And it was a *Blitzkrieg,* too: it took not much more than a decade to accomplish all this. The conquest, however, did not make the Germans too popular: no conquest does.

The Danger of German Humor

The German lack of a sense of humor has its share of responsibility in causing two world wars. This is not a sweeping statement, but a sober assessment of historical truth.

A good sense of humor, whatever its psychological origin, is the ability to see life in a rosier light. It may make one happier, but this is one's private affair. The only general importance of a sense of humor is the fact that it goes with a sense of proportion. It either produces a sense of proportion or is produced by it. If we have a sense of humor, we cannot consider our affairs terribly and overwhelmingly important. Of course, we all know that we are wonderful creatures, but our self-

admiration is at least tempered by the knowledge that we have minor
faults. Yes, we are noble, unselfish, dignified (but never pompous!),
good-hearted, brilliantly intelligent and extremely capable in almost
everything; but we are ready to admit that we do not know the railway
timetable by heart. An average German would never admit this. I heard
long, heated and acrimonious arguments about whether, on a certain
journey, one had to change at Heidelberg or not. Both sides used
weighty and convincing arguments (except the timetable itself) and the
losers, in the end, felt genuinely angry and resentful.

Dictatorship and the lack of a sense of humor go hand in hand,
because the admiration of a dictator or of an infallible dogma presup-
poses a lack of a sense of proportion. People say that a totalitarian
system could not gain a foothold in Britain or the United States because
these countries have long democratic traditions. This is a mistake. A
totalitarian system can be enforced by bayonets; traditions have very
little to do with it. But a dictator would have great difficulty in Britain
or in the United States because people would laugh at him. Hitler and
Stalin made gods of themselves in Germany and Russia, they would
have made fools of themselves in Britain or America; No, the British
would say, no one man can possibly be the greatest hero, statesman,
and scientist of all ages; and if he is, he cannot be a male beauty and
the best dancer as well. And he certainly cannot have the best hand-
writing on top of it!

The Duty of Laughter

Not that the Germans do not laugh a great deal. But observe their
pleasures and their merriment. The *Bräu* (the *Bierhalle,* or beer hall)
often looks like a temple, with its massive Gothic arches. There sit the
Germans, not simply eating yards of sausages and drinking gallons of
beer but making sacrifices to Bacchus and to the God of Good Appetite. The mood is solemn. A man must occasionally enjoy himself and
they are performing a duty now.

Along the walls are little statues on tiny shelves, all of which represent saints in the temple—Bacchanalian saints, but saints all the same.
The waitresses of the *Bräu* are dressed in gay yellow and green (they
not infrequently have enormous bosoms) and their friendly smile expresses approval of your eating and drinking a lot. But, primarily, they
do not serve you; they serve higher and livelier masters, the pagan gods
and the saints on the wall. The Germans eat and drink industriously
and conscientiously under the Gothic arches, in the shadow of grinning
statues, and go home with a gratifying feeling that their duty has been
done.

And, of course, they laugh, too. But the question is not so much at *what*, as *when?* It rather depends on the calendar. Every German understands that the time of the *Oktoberfest* and the time of *Fasching* (carnival time) are times of gaiety. They know for months beforehand that (let us say) on the third of October they will be hilariously happy. They go out to the festival and have a jolly good time because they have made a note to do so in their diary months before.

And then they let themselves really go. They shriek and shout. They sit next to each other, singing songs, rocking rhythmically, drinking beer from almost incredibly huge jugs and roasting entire oxen in one piece. The joke is that someone is fat and ugly and dances comically, with a fatuous smile on his face. The joke is that he falls on his behind. The joke is that the musicians are also enormously fat, that they wear tiny bowler hats on the top of their big round heads and play so loudly that no one can hear his own voice. Strangers dance with one another, strangers kiss one another and smack one another on certain parts of the body where they find, as a rule, plenty of surface for smacking. During the carnival parade the shop windows of Cologne have to be boarded up, otherwise they would be smashed. Not through wickedness; not with malice; only as a joke. Of course, there are many truly witty and enchanting people in Germany, just as anywhere else, but however large their number may be, they do not seem to be characteristic of the community. The beer festivals and carnival parades are characteristic.

Manners

What sort of manners should you adopt? Some old habits die hard, of course, particularly in the older people. A taxi driver could not find the house I wanted although I had given him the proper address: 21 Kreuzstrasse. Then he discovered that I meant a big newspaper's building. "Yes, that's what I want," I agreed. "Perhaps I should have told you. I'm sorry." He was most magnanimous: "Don't mention it. We all make mistakes. It would not be human if we didn't." In other words he was quite ready to forgive me *his* mistakes: it was entirely my fault that he had failed to find the house having been given the correct address, but he bore no malice against me. This type of thing still exists, but is getting rarer and rarer.

The famous German heel-clicking is out—it died a natural and unlamented death with the Nazis. Wherever you go, phrases like "*bitte schön*", "*danke schön*", "please permit me", "thank you", are bandied about. A shade too formal and stiff, you feel. Titles and ranks are also respected: they are firm guides, they establish a proper hierarchy. *Professor* is still something big in Germany, *Doktor-doktors* abound and *Frau Oberinspektors* swarm around. A President had three doctorates and all, I am told, displayed on his personal writing-paper.

Manners have improved beyond recognition but they often crack under strain. A Hungarian friend whom I met in Munich told me somewhat ruefully:

"Having lived in London for ten years before coming to Munich, I used my best London manners, trying to get a taxi on a rainy day. People pushed me aside, trampled upon me and on one occasion actually dragged me out of the taxi by force. I lost seven cabs that way. Then I said to myself: 'Hell, after all, I'm not coming from London. I come, really, from Budapest.' The next taxi was mine."

A British librarian working in Cologne had this to say: "I meet many of my clients at the bus stop every morning. They bow, they shake hands, they say how pleased they are to see me. They could not be nicer and more humble. When the bus arrives, they knock me in the belly, push me aside, board the bus and leave me gasping on the pavement."

Militarism?

"The trouble is," an American officer once told me, "that the Germans are not militaristic enough." The German army is, undoubtedly, the most easy-going in the world. Recruits can wear long hair and hippy-type beards; they do not salute their officers except their immediate superiors. Most sergeants dread the charge of being rude to recruits, and recruits—members of a citizen army—may belong to a trade union. As George Vine, an English journalist working in Bonn, remarked in his book, speaking of that famous old baton and the soldier's knapsack: "the old German soldier could become a field-marshal, the new one may become the secretary of the Trades Union Congress."

Neither are the Germans patriotic enough: they were too mild and self-effacing vis-à-vis the Gaullists and the big phrase, the bombast, the nationalistic thunder has been, for some time, more conspicuous west of the Rhine than east of it. For more than two decades, no German ventured to utter the suggestion that re-unification was a dream and East Germany might as well be recognized—or at least tolerated, accepted as a second (or, with Austria, third) German state. But Willy Brandt, during his leadership, looked at East Germany with fresh eyes and he became the little boy who discovered that the emperor was not quite so naked, and if not particularly well dressed, at least he existed.

On Sausages and Other Food

My first meal in Germany (on my last visit) was a shock. I am one of the greatest sausage-connoisseurs in the world and I believe sausages are one of the most glorious creations of human civilization. It is true that it was not the Germans but the Romans who gave humanity the sausage, but the Southern Germanic races have raised it to new heights. My disappointment was immense when in restaurants in Stuttgart and Munich I found *papaya* and *mango* and *Nasi Goreng* on the menus but no frankfurters. I am not a man of strict and uncompromising principles, but just as I would refuse to eat *bratwurst* in Jakarta, I turn away with disdain from *Nasi Goreng* in Stuttgart.

"Shish-kebab seems to be the new national dish of Germany," a German friend told me. "No self-respecting German town can exist today without at least half a dozen *Balkan Grills*. There are so many Yugoslav, Greek, Turkish, Chinese and other restaurants in Germany that you can more easily get an excellent *souvlaki* or *cevapacici* than a tolerable *Weisswürstel* (white sausage) in Munich, capital of Bavaria."

I should like to finish this short discourse with praise for the German *Würstlerei*. And this is also praise for German honesty. A *Würstlerei* is a place where you can get sausages and beer, and nothing else. My particular *Würstlerei* consisted of one tiny room, with a few chairs and some boards running along the walls, so that you could place your plate and glass on them. The walls were covered with nudes and other beauties, propagating various makes of beer. I was admiring the beauties when my eye caught a small notice which read: "Toilette in the Café Speizmann, next door, in the basement."

I was deeply impressed by this. It was the last degree of honesty, I thought, to draw all the customers' attention to the fact that there was no *toilette* on the premises. It was even more honest to point out that even the nearest *toilette,* in the Café Speizmann, was in the basement. But that little notice meant even more than that. It was the shining example of cooperation and unselfishness. Why not let the Café Speizmann have a share in the business? A fair distribution of the benefit of a blooming business, I reflected. That is what the Germans rightly call *leben und leben lassen:* to live and let live.

Johann
Sebastian
Bach
1685-1750

CREATIVE GERMANY

From Medieval to Modern

As the previous chapter has shown, it is possible to make gentle fun of the national characteristics of the Germans. Orderly, disciplined, hardworking, serious about the world and themselves they certainly are. But that is only part of the story. Below the surface the waters of the German spirit run deep, and that depth is revealed by the artistic contributions that Germany has made to the sum of the world's creative life. For centuries the Germans have explored the workings of the human spirit, not being content merely to embroider the superficial vagaries of human behavior, they have searched for the profounder levels of consciousness and the deeper strata that lie below.

Partly this searching is due to a medieval, almost haunted, element in the German spirit. For all its modernity, even today Germany is not so very far removed from the world of Grimm and Hoffman, from the belief that behind life there lurks a supernatural world, a world where human beings shade away into creatures that share human characteristics, but transcend them. Partly it is due to a relentless logicality which seeks for a reason for things that the rest of the world might take for granted, a desire to explain, to explore, to bring to the surface and expose the root causes of human behavior. It is no accident that, later in this chapter, Freud and Jung find their place among Germany's writers. Partly, too, it is due to an innate ability to tackle vast themes and encompass vast projects with a daring and skill which, outside Germany, might be considered a sign of imbalance. All these are double-edged swords. Allied to genius they can create immortal art, in the wrong hands they can create unparalleled disaster.

Before exploring German creativity in a little more detail, it must be remembered that "German" in this sense is not confined to the present boundaries of the Federal Republic. Historically, it has always been difficult to define the territory that constitutes Germany. Its borders have expanded and contracted over the centuries, advancing and retreating in response to the tides of conquest or political expediency. At one time or another the German peoples have held sway over most of central Europe, and even today the German-speaking boundaries encompass not only sundered Germany itself, but also Austria and part of Switzerland. So, to avoid confusion, it would be better to think of "Creative Germany" as covering the creativity of the German-speaking people.

Music

In no artistic field is the magnitude of the German creative achievement more clearly demonstrated than in music. If "music is the language in which soul communicates with soul" then the long procession of German composers who have been brilliant linguists is impressive. Ask anyone for a list of the ten greatest composers and inevitably a majority will be German—Bach, Haydn, Handel, Mozart, Beethoven, Schubert, Wagner, Brahms, Mahler, Strauss, any or all of them will figure. They all, in their own ways, explored the springs of the human spirit, creating a musical language that has formed the very basis for Western music.

The first flowering of German music was due very largely to the work of one prodigious family, the Bachs. They played a vital role in the development of German music for 200 years, culminating in the achievements of Johann Sebastian Bach (1685–1750). In the town of Erfurt, which swarmed with Bachs, musicians were not called musicians, they were called Bachs. Taking influences from all the earlier European schools that were accessible to him in his Thurigian backwater, Bach fused them into a completely new form. He worked through the elements that formed the staple of his career as church organist and "chapel master"—the choir, the organ, the small orchestra—and created from them a vast output of music that totally transcended anything that such a background might reasonably have been expected to produce. In 1708 he moved into the circles of ducal patronage, which, though it extended the means available to him, did not essentially change the nature of his creative output. With Bach we find yet another facet of the German spirit—a deep-seated Protestantism. Bach's most colossal achievements were his church works, the *Passion according to St. Matthew* and the *Mass in B Minor,* and these contain, recognizably, the suffering and hope of the human spirit in the face of mystical forces beyond its comprehension. After his death, Bach's works suffered an eclipse until, in the middle of the nineteenth century, they were once more made popular, partly through the efforts of another great German composer, Mendelssohn. From that time they have been recognized as a vital contribution by one of the world's great seekers after truth.

Another composer whose works suffered in popularity after his death is Handel (1685–1759). Unlike Bach, Handel left Germany and spent the bulk of his life abroad, mainly in England. Again unlike Bach, Handel was a man of the world, of the theater and court, creating operas (46 of them) and endless music for all occasions. Although *Messiah* was the work which kept his memory alive for generations, the breadth and scope of his work is only now being recognized by the public at large. Many of his operas are being revived and one or two, especially *Giulio Cesare,* have entered the regular repertory of the world's opera houses. Although Handel became proud to be an Englishman, his strengths as a composer were archetypally German, especially in the way that he was able to synthesize the influences of his native land, of Italy where he spent some time as a young man, and of British music, and create an opus which, for its breadth of expression and depth of feeling, is rivalled by very few other composers. Also, through the medium of the style of his time, which did not lend itself to deep emotional expression, he was able to create a wealth of music, for orchestra, the voice and solo instruments, that speaks with a voice of human compassion.

Among those who changed the face of European music the "Austrian," Joseph Haydn (1732–1809), must rank with the first. He originated forms of composition, the string quartet, the sonata, chamber music generally, which formed a solid basis for much that was to follow. His official position as composer and conductor to the court of Prince Esterhazy notwithstanding, he remained a simple and pious man, crystallising and defining musical trends which we now can recognize as "Classical". His long life spanned the age from Bach and Handel to Mozart, another, and the greatest, of the "Austrian" composers.

Mozart (1756–91), in his tragically short life, raised Classical music to its most perfect and scintillating form. He had the kind of genius which would be rare for any nation, and even in the list of Germany's great names is supreme. His lightness of touch and facility of expression seem almost superhuman. It is said that he could hear his music so completely in his head that he could transcribe it to paper with hardly a correction. Mozart's talent formed a perfect counterpart to the Baroque in German art, full of sunlight and controlled exuberance, skillfully handling the dramatic elements and able to suggest the darkness that lies below the surface of life without being overwhelmed by it.

The inspired procession continued with Beethoven (1770–1827), whose music, though rooted in the age of Mozart, is now understood as the first major statement of the Romantic spirit. It is here, in the nineteenth century, that Germany found one of the purest expressions of its essential nature. Romanticism sprang not only from the rich heritage of Germany's past, but also from the very woods and mountains that once sheltered the tribes whose territories grew over the years into the ducal states on which modern Germany is modelled. The Romantic age drew its lifeblood from myth and legend, from the dark forests and silent lakes, from the Germanic probing of the sadness and joy of the human spirit. Within the limitations of the music of his age, whose boundaries he significantly advanced, Beethoven joined Goethe and Schiller in this searching quest.

He also drew inspiration from his suffering and privations. At the end of his life when, living in poverty after years of magnificent but unprofitable achievement, after a series of illnesses and quite deaf, he produced some of his most stirring work. He died, taking his tenth symphony with him, because his brother was too mean to find the price of enough coal to keep the composer's room warm. In its essence, Beethoven's life and death breathed Romanticism.

In their own ways the careers of Schumann, Schubert and Mendelssohn, who followed Beethoven, all represent various aspects of the German Romantic spirit, but it was with Wagner (1813–83) that that spirit reached its apotheosis. Wagner stands at the heart of German music, indeed, in a very real sense he *is* the heart of German music. In Wagner's work much of the past, the contributions of Bach, Beethoven and Weber among others, comes to fruition. His work, too, had an ineradicable influence on many of the composers who succeeded him. He appeared at a critical point in history where the past could be gathered together, summed up and turned into great art, and from where the future could expand. Not that he founded any kind of a school. Like Michelangelo, his art was such that, though it could be imitated, it could not be built upon. The Bayreuth version of the *Ring des Nibelungen* which has been preserved on film for the first time, (1980), has shown that Wagner's masterpiece can be translated in contemporary terms, but, essentially, all his output was securely based in the myths and legends of Germany, seen through the eyes of an artist capable of envisaging the endless war between good and evil, and translating that struggle into theatrical art—even the forces needed to perform his operas are, themselves, titanic.

A visit to Bayreuth to see the Festival, will provide a glimpse into the soul of creative Germany. Though the operas of Wagner are still performed there under the direction of his family, the last few decades have turned the ritual reproduction of his work from merely museum pieces into vibrant modern stage experiences. The theater is still that which was carefully constructed under Wagner's direction—with the backing of that most bizarre of all phantasists, Ludwig of Bavaria—but the staging is ultra-modern, and the concepts that lie behind the productions have their basis in ideas which might well make Wagner spin in his grave.

The fact that Wagner became a kind of totem for the Nazis must not be allowed to obscure the originality and significance of his works. The man himself lived a life that has created endless controversy, and it is difficult to disentangle that life and his vehemently held beliefs from the overwhelming effects of his music, but if a visitor to Germany wants to experience the best that Germany has to offer in terms of a modern approach to some of the great theatrical works of its past, he should attempt to see a Wagner performance at Bayreuth or one of the other major opera houses.

Romanticism, in a different form, marked the work of Wagner's contemporary Johannes Brahms (1833–97), who, like Beethoven, spent much of his life in Vienna. Unlike the music of Johann Strauss, who was the idol of Vienna at the same time, Brahms's music was closer to the somber, grave mainstream of German composition. Even today his works are slightly underrated. The last great flowering of Romanticism came with Richard Strauss (1864–1949). Inspired and influenced by Wagner and his follower Mahler, Strauss created work on an heroic scale, delving into the dark legends of ancient Greece for the plots of some of his operas, using other myths to fuel his symphonic poems, he was recognizably cast in the same Promethean mold. His mastery of, and influence on, orchestration made him one of the last of the great chain of composers nurtured on the Romantic ideal.

The twentieth century has produced several names in the front rank of modern composition. Arnold Schoneberg, Paul Hindemith, Carl Orff all kept Germany's name high among musical nations. Schoneberg, who emigrated to America towards the end of his life, became, by his experimental work, widely revered as the father of modern music. Hindemith, who was early associated with Richard Strauss and Schoneberg, established a humorous and adventurous style of his own. Carl Orff, too, created his own style, based on primary repeated rhythms which has proved very influential in the controversial arena of modern music.

Of the younger composers, one of the most celebrated is Karlheinz Stockhausen (born 1928). A pioneer of electronic music, his work has been consistently radical, volatile and provocative. Though it is difficult to approach, he has nonetheless aroused the approval of many experimental contemporaries. *Moments,* written for soprano, four choirs and thirteen instruments, is typical of his inventive and innovatory technique.

Carrying his dramatic, easily approached music to many international centers Hans Werner Henze (b. 1926) has made his mark, especially in the opera house. *The Bassarids, King Stag, Elegy for Young Lovers, The Young Lord* have been seen in places as far apart as London, New York, Sante Fé and San Diego.

Not only has Germany provided great composers to the world, but it is in the forefront of musical execution. The visitor to Germany will find orchestral and operatic performances of the highest quality in every city and most major towns. These events are held as a regular part of the cultural diet, but the country is also dotted with festivals throughout the year, which attract both German artists and the best international talent. One of the especial attractions of the festival scene is the holding of concerts in such lovely old buildings as the Baroque palaces at Nymphenburg, Schlessheim, Schwetzingen or the Brunnenhof of the Munich Residenz. Hearing the great music of the past—and present—by candlelight in such beautiful surroundings can provide a memory to treasure. As, too, can a visit to one of the great concert halls such as the home of the Berlin Philharmonic, a masterpiece of modern design.

Opera is one of the best ways for the theater-and-music-loving visitor to enjoy the best that Germany has to offer without having to struggle too much with a strange language. True, operas are mostly sung in German, but somehow that presents less of a problem than in the straight theater. The profusion of state opera houses has given Germany a richer operatic life than almost any other country. Production standards are high, and, as an added bonus for the visitor from the United States or Britain, many of the companies can boast young singers who have been unable to find training and employment in their own countries and have started their careers in Germany. As there are 72 state or municipally subsidized orchestra and opera houses, they have plenty of opportunity to develop.

Theater

Today's German theater is solidly built on its historic past. Unlike many other countries, Germany does not have any one single theatrical center, as Paris or London are, but a series of major focal points with many subsidiary ones. The original rulers of the states from which modern Germany evolved almost all maintained court theaters, and the tradition of these theaters has persisted into the present day. The buildings may not always be the same, the financial support now comes from the state and not from the ducal purse, but in essence the situation is similar. There are famous state or municipal complexes in most of the main centers, Stuttgart, Munich, Hamburg, Berlin, Cologne and Frankfurt among them.

One of the things that distinguishes these theaters is the fierce community support which they receive. Much as in other countries a community will support its ball team, in Germany the communities are behind their local theatrical enterprise all the way—not uncritically, but with regional pride riding high all the same. These regional theaters are supported by subscription schemes, a method of selling tickets often tried elsewhere in the Western world, but rarely as successfully as in Germany. Up to 90 percent of the tickets for any one season are sold by subscription, with the subscribers buying a block of tickets for 10 or 12 different performances. Nor does community involvement end there. There are organizations of theatergoers numbering many thousand members (one of them, the Christian-oriented Association of Theater Communities having around 13,000), who buy out complete performances.

One might think that this wholesale state and community support for the theater would act as a check to artistic enterprise, but the reverse seems to be the case. Germany for decades has produced many startlingly advanced and exciting approaches to the art of stage production. It has been helped, of course, by the fact that most of the buildings are fairly new, with excellent stage equipment. The destruction of theaters during World War II meant that, though they were sometimes rebuilt to reproduce their former design, they could be adapted to house the very latest in stage technology. It is an exactly parallel situation to German industry, which was able to move into the modern age with brand new factories, the most modern machinery and a completely new approach to work. Today, both the theater and industry are reaping the rewards of this enforced investment.

Although there are commercial theater enterprises, they form only a minor element in the general picture. Freedom from the need to create box office successes has meant that the state and municipal companies have had the chance to explore experimental avenues and to build tightly knit ensembles, a facet of theatrical art which is peculiarly suitable to the German artistic spirit. One of the great historical companies was that of the Duke of Saxe-Meiningen, who revolutionized Shakespearean production all over Europe during its tours in the 1880s, with its extreme realism and disciplined ensemble playing. This tradition of company participation still lives on.

Naturally, one has to be fairly expert in the German language to enjoy an evening at the theater, but since translations of popular modern and classic plays from other countries are favorite fare on German stages, it is often possible to find a play that one may already know in its original language. Shakespeare (whom the lunatic fringe sometimes claim to have been German) has long been near the top of the list. Shaw, Anouilh, Coward and other staples are frequently played. Most of the playwrights we have mentioned in the section on literature can be found and some of the other, newer writers whose works have been seen in America and Britain—Peter Weiss, Martin Walser, Peter Hacks among them—are also in the standard repertory companies' programs.

The other theatrical art form that is especially to be recommended to the visitor to Germany is ballet. Stuttgart, under the aegis of the Englishman, John Cranko, who tragically died in 1973 at the height of his powers, has developed into the ballet capital of Germany. The company is known in Britain and the States, and in other parts of the world, through its tours; and its blend of re-interpreted classics and daring original works has brought it to the forefront of the world's great dancing experiences. It is—once more—the product of an enlightened state theater, sharing its home with the opera and drama companies. Other cities have exciting ballet companies, among them Wuppertal, which has grown under the direction of Pina Bausch into a group to be seen by the devoted balletomane.

One last facet of theater which must be mentioned is typically German, indeed typical of artistic life in Berlin, are the cabaret-theaters. Berlin has long had a reputation for bitingly satirical revue, slashing at political and social targets with the unerring aim of circus knife-throwers. If one has a certain amount of German, naturally, the experience is more meaningful, but the atmosphere and sheer bravura of the performances can by themselves prove an eye-opener, even if a lot of the satire is missed.

Cinema

In spite of the social and political upheavals of this century Germany developed and, for the most part maintained, one of the most influential film industries in the world. At times thriving, as did Hollywood, in times of social distress, it has survived with its unique characteristics intact: a distinctly political flavor, tempered by a universal humanitarianism.

Prior to World War I a substantial film industry developed in relation to the popular theater, producing its fair share of romances and melodramas, culminating in the films of the writer, actor and director Paul Wegener (1874–1948); *The Student of Prague* (1913) and *The Golem* (1914, remade 1920) captured the Gothic atmosphere of 19th-century Romanticism and, in dealing with mythic and supernatural themes, prefigured many of the films of the 1920s.

In the years after World War I the industry flourished. Many of the films produced at the time have mistakenly been called Expressionist; there are a handful which in their imaginative and psychologically atmospheric use of sets, lighting and stylized acting can be allied with Expressionist painting, including Robert Weine's *The Cabinet of Dr. Caligari* (1919) and Arthur Robinson's *Warning Shadows* (1924). However, these represent a minute fraction of an industry which, centered around the UFA Studios in Berlin, maintained an annual output of over 200 films until 1930. Many of these show a greater concern for artistic quality and the creation of an intelligent cinema than was true of contemporary Hollywood.

The industry was characterized by the prevailing use of art directors to produce an overall, fluent style or "look" to each film, which matched the practice of allowing the directors to have total control over the production of their films, in contrast to Hollywood's factory production-line system. This was made possible by attracting an immense pool of talent drawn from culturally aspirant backgrounds from all over Europe. Most of the genres which have since dominated German cinema (many of which were later to develop in Hollywood) were established at this time, and can be found in the work of one of the most versatile of the early German directors, G.W. Pabst (1885–1967). In the space of six years he moved from the incisive social melodramas of *Joyless Street* (1925) and *Pandora's Box* (1928), through a grimly realistic view of the Great War, *Westfront 1918* (1930), the harsh satire of Brecht's *Threepenny Opera* (1931), to a more optimistic view of human relations in the dramatized documentary *Kameradschaft* (1931).

However, the two directors whose work dominated the period were F.W. Murnau (1889–1931) and Fritz Lang (1890–1976). Both their careers encompassed a wide range of subjects, realized with great visual inventiveness and narrative clarity. Murnau's classic vampire film *Nosferatu* (1922, remade by Herzog 1978) illustrated his sense of visual fluency and innovation, but only lightly touched his main concern, the drama of the everyday, of the common man, highlighted in *The Last Laugh* (1924) and in a film made after he was lured to Hollywood, *Sunrise* (1927).

Lang's themes were more grandiose; initially related to 19th-century Romaticism in the epic myths of *Destiny* (1921) and *Die Nibelungen* (1924), moving on to prophetic and pessimistic parables of disillusion with modern Germany in a series of films concerning a fictional arch-criminal dedicated to world domination, *Dr. Mabuse* (1922, '32, '60), a view furthered in his most famous film, the futuristic nightmare of *Metropolis* (1926). One of his last early German films, the dark study of criminality, *M* (1931) prefaced a Hollywood career mainly dedicated to taut urban thrillers.

A distaste for Nazism, and the lure of Hollywood's wealth led many filmmakers to leave Germany during the early 1930s. These included actors such as Conrad Veidt, Peter Lorre, Anton Walbrook, Hedy Lamarr, Marlene Dietrich and Garbo, and directors such as Billy Wilder, Ernst Lubitsch, Douglas Sirk and Alexander Korda, a dispersal of talent which led to an enrichment of other nation's cinematic cultures.

The Nazis were quick to realize the propaganda potential of films, and encouraged the industry to produce large numbers of historical epics (usually providing sweeping precedents for their policies) and modern dramas reflecting their own moral righteousness. These remained on the whole turgid and contrived, although a remarkably apt and original cinematic style was developed by the female director Leni Riefenstahl (b. 1902) in her documentaries of the Nurnberg Rally, *The Triumph of the Will* (1936) and of the Berlin Olympics, *Olympiad* (1938).

A decline succeeded World War II, relieved only by independent productions such as Peter Lorre's brilliant analysis of national guilt, *Der Verlorene* (1950). Film production was diverted to commercial collaborations with Italy and Spain, and to the development of television.

It was from the latter highly important source, and with the aid of public and government funds that the industry became re-established by the late 1950s, and although limited to commercial genres, it became strong enough to attract Lang back from America to realize two epic projects, The *Tiger of Ischnapur* and *The Indian Tomb* (both 1958).

Through the 1960s the film industry developed in tandem with the expanding German economy, and by the last quarter of the decade had produced a number of independent companies run by directors with international "art house" reputations, such as Volker Schlöndorff (1939–) and Jean-Marie Straub (1933–) whose *Anna Magdelena Bach* (1968) was the first masterpiece of modern German cinema.

This provided a background for a young generation of filmmakers, sprung from art colleges and avant-garde theater groups. Politically to the left, their tastes were influenced not only by their forerunners, but by the French New Wave critics, and by American films of the 1950s by Sirk, Samuel Fuller and Nicholas Ray.

The first to achieve international repute was R.W. Fassbinder (b. 1946) whose prolific output (over 15 films while still in his twenties) presented political conviction with formal originality. In films such as *Merchant of the Four Seasons* (1971) and *Fear Eats the Soul* (1973) he combined the immediacy of the theater with the economy of television production to create moving melodramas of everyday life, displaying remarkable compassion for his characters; by the mid-1970s his interest in melodrama seemed more stylized and academic (*Effi Briest*, 1974, *Chinese Roulette* (1976).

Werner Herzog (b. 1942–) proved more adventurous, although difficult to label. Initially making T.V. documentaries, by the 1970s he developed an apocalyptic visionary style culminating in the fabulous *Aguirre* (1972) more recently revealing Romantic leanings in his studies of innocence corrupted, *Kaspar Hauser* (1974), *Stroszek* (1977) and *Woyzek* (1978).

The search for national identity provided material for Wim Wenders' studies of the influence of American culture upon modern Germany in *Kings of the Road* (1976), and *The American Friend* (1977), and also for Syberberg, who has programmatically devoted miles of film to carefully staged analyses of dominant figures in German history, culminating in *Hitler* (1978).

The fecundity of modern German cinema may be ascribed to the collaborative contribution of writers such as Böll and Handke, to theatrical actors of the calibre of Bruno Ganz and Klaus Kinski, and to the common regard for defining a modern cultural and political identity. The maturity of the post-war generation has recently become marked in their discussions of current issues in the light of past events, illustrated by the reaction to the screening of the American T.V. film *Holocaust*. It has been consolidated in such ventures as Fassbinder's visual symposium of current left-wing politics, *Germany in Autumn* (1978), followed up by his *The Third Generation* (1979), which dealt with modern terrorism, as did Reinhard Hauff's *A Knife in the Head* (1978). Alexander Kluge's *Occasional Work of a Female Slave* (1974) and playwright Peter Handke's first feature *Left Handed Woman* (1978) examined feminism with uncompromising conviction.

All of these films have gained international acclaim, none more so than Schlöndorff's *The Tin Drum* (1979), based on Grass's controversial novel which significantly had to wait some 20 years until such an adaptation was feasible.

If the German cinema has now regained the vanguard of world film culture, then the best place for the visitor to see the latest work in its natural environment is at the Berlin International Film Festival, currently staged in April.

Literature

Until the 9th century, German hardly existed as a written language. Even after the appearance of a mystical text written in German in about 830 by an unknown monk, German remained a spoken language first and foremost. The differences between the tongues spoken by the various Germanic tribes and the highly successful efforts, presided over by Charlemagne, to collect, organize and recopy ancient classical texts, ensured that for some considerable time this remained the state of affairs. Consequently Latin continued as the exclusive language of literature until well into the Gothic period.

The earliest stirrings of a genuine German school of literature came with the Minnesingers, knight-poets who wandered from castle to castle and town to town singing their own verses in praise of the beauty of their ladies and the noble traditions of knighthood and chivalry. Walter von der Vogelweide (c.1160–1230) the best known, was not only a Minnesinger but a genuine poet who is widely considered the father of German lyric poetry. Two contemporaries of his, Wolfram von Eschenbach and Gottfried von Strassburg, continued his innovations and were largely responsible for the development of the epic poem of which the most important are *Parsifal* and *Tristan und Isolde*. It is no accident that Wagner chose the Minnesingers as the theme for one of his operas, *Tannhäuser,* which deals with the conflict between sacred and profane inspiration in art and in which von Eschenbach and von der Vogelweide appear as characters.

The Minnesingers were succeeded by the Mastersingers—another of Wagner's operatic subjects— artisans who formed guilds for the promotion of poetry and singing. But despite the relative sophistication of their literary forms and their awareness of their own significance, they produced, with one exception, little of any real literary importance. The exception was Hans Sachs (1494–1576). He was a humorous shoemaker-poet who wrote some 4,300 *Meisterlieder* and 300 plays. He was a vital figure who spanned the transition from the rigid forms of Gothic literature to the more naturalistic, humanist literature of the Renaissance.

Though much epic poetry, drama, satire, fables and even animal tales were produced in the following century—the 17th—of which the most renowned are *Till Eulenspiegel* and the *Adventures of Baron Munchhausen,* it was the 18th century that saw the full development of a mature German literature. Though mystical and religious works still continued to be written in verse—the most striking example is Jacob Böhme's *Signature of all Things,* a breathtaking work by any standard —the really central and significant shift in German literature was the development of a prose style. The background for this development was to some extent due to a number of scholars who—in collating and cataloguing German literature as it then was and, in translating other authors, particularly Shakespeare, into German—not only raised the level of consciousness of the native product but made available outstanding works from other countries.

The giant of the age was Wolfgang von Goethe (1749–1832). Like Beethoven, he was brought up in a Classical and rational age but he presided over the development of a literature that broke away from rigid cannons and espoused instead a more direct expression of the emotions, frequently those which would not have been considered suitable by those who were bound by the inflexible standards of "taste." But Goethe was a complex figure who cannot comfortably be placed in any one category, particularly one as vaguely defined as Romanticism. He was profoundly interested in the expanding awareness of the Ancient World that continuing excavations in Italy and Greece were propagating. In this sense he was as much a neo-Classicist as a Romantic. Nonetheless he was clearly the dominant influence on the flowering of Romantic German literature, and the enormous scope of his subject matter and the forms in which he worked expanded tremendously the repertoire of German writing. *Faust,* to mention only one example, a massive work, is a magnificently perceptive study of good and evil. It was astonishingly influential at the time and still exerts a powerful and mysterious fascination today.

Goethe also has many strong claims to be taken seriously as a philosopher—he wrote a number of studies on the nature of color that significantly altered the general understanding of the subject—and his boundless energy and curiosity also led him to practice law and indulge, for a time, in politics.

A more precisely Romantic writer was Friedrich Schiller (1759–1805). Schiller was a close friend of Goethe and shared many of his preoccupations, but his work is narrower in scope and more overtly Romantic in content. Though he wrote much lyric poetry, he is chiefly remembered today for his historical novels and dramas. Their themes are characteristic of the period and reveal a new interest in periods previously considered "dark" or "barbaric," namely the Middle Ages, and an identification with characters who suffer nobly and stirringly, all themes central to the development of the new Romantic sensibility. His most famous works are *The Robbers, Don Carlos, Wallenstein, The Maid of Orleans, Wilhelm Tell* and *Mary Stuart*—a favorite subject for

Romantic suffering. Similar concerns can also be seen by a number of other writers of the period, notably in poems and novels of Friedrich Hölderlin, Heinrich von Kleist (who wrote *Prince Heinrich von Homburg*) and in the fairy tales collected by the brothers Grimm, steeped in mysterious atmosphere.

Throughout most of the rest of the 19th century and even into the 20th, literature in Germany enjoyed a very close relationship with philosophy. Many of the finest writers of the period were in fact philosophers first and writers second. Consequently, the European discovery of the novel as the primary means of literary expression did not really include Germany. There was no internationally known German equivalent to Dickens, Zola or Flaubert. Rather German men of letters in the 19th century followed the models of Poe or Beaudelaire. They were men who, in varying literary forms—poems, essays, short stories—expressed opinions on social problems, championed their causes and argued for new sensibilities and perceptions.

While all of these men can be considered Romantics in their general stance, they nonetheless had widely differing views. On the one hand Arthur Schopenhauer (1788–1860) expressed profoundly pessimistic views, maintaining that conventional morality was meaningless and that life was an Odyssey of suffering. His influence was felt most strongly and with most effect in the work of Friedrich Nietzsche (1844–1900). Nietzsche's work has been consistently misunderstood and misrepresented. His pronouncements that a race of "Supermen" would be needed if the human race was to survive the traumas that faced it has been a consistent justification for Facism, when in fact Nietzsche was referring to spiritual rather than racial qualities. Nonetheless he highlights many of the darker and haunting qualities of Romanticism and all his writings contain a similar forceful and terrifying personality.

On the other hand, the Romantic cult of the hidden and invisible forces that motivate the world was put to much more positive use in the explorations of the Austrian Sigmund Freud (1856–1939). His pupil Carl Jung (1875–1967) continued and expanded Freud's work though attributing greater importance to dreams and their symbolic meaning. In this he echoed the mystical teachings of Oriental philosophers, and through him Chinese and other Eastern teachings were translated into both German and other European languages.

The mid-19th century produced a number of writers of note, among them the novelists Gustav Freytag (1816–95) and Wilhelm Raabe (1831–1910), both of whom rejected materialism and social hypocracies though never succumbing to the total pessimism of Nietzsche. In the world of the theater Friedrich Hebbel (1813–63) and Otto Luwig (1813–65) both wrote several interesting plays though nothing of outstanding merit.

It was only in Thomas Mann (1875–1955) that Germany eventually produced a novelist of real stature and talent. His work for the most part explores the Romantic preoccupation with the nature of the artist and in particular his relationship with society, especially a society that denies through its materialism the exotic, spiritual qualities that Mann saw in all artists. This is most brilliantly seen in *Death in Venice* (1911)—where the sick artist finds his spirituality in constant and irreconcilable opposition with the role imposed upon him by society— and the *Magic Mountain* (1927) for which he was awarded the Nobel Prize in 1929.

Mann was an ardent and forceful critic of the Nazi Party, and was eventually forced into exile in Switzerland, from where he continued to lambast the Nazis in a series of lectures and political essays. *Achtung Europa* (1938) is a typical example. After the war, his increasing pessimism about a rootless modern world, lacking real values and purpose, found its most potent outlet in *Doktor Faustus*. Nonetheless, for all his elegant, poignant despair, Mann never wholly abandoned—and this comes out most clearly in his delicate, ironic humor—the hope that tolerance and enlightenment were not impossible aims.

Lion Feuchtwanger (1884–1958) also dealt with the eternal conflict between the artist and society, as well as continuing the early Romantic interest in historical subjects, though reinterpreting them with modern psychological insight, including the inexhaustible Mary, Queen of Scots. However, his most famous novel demonstrates his basically liberal and tolerant stance. This was *Jew Süss* which dealt with the problem of a misfit Jew in a non-Jewish Germany. As it turned out, this was a very prophetic work. Feuchtwanger, like Mann, was exiled from Germany when the Nazis came to power and settled finally in America.

The tensions between the artist and society, the inequality of that society and the attempt to locate and define an ideal society continued as the leading themes throughout German literature in the middle years of this century, though the 19th–century concerns with fantasy and symbolism also remained prominent.

Gerhart Hauptmann (1862–1946) wrote two great novels on the plight of the ordinary citizen in an ever changing and inaccessible world, *Fuhrmann Henschel* and *The Great Dream*. His work was also characterized by what at the time was considered shocking and vulgar naturalism. Hauptmann was also a writer of great humor, though humor tinged with a terrible and timeless tragedy. His influence on later writers, though not great, continued to be felt for some time.

The dramas of Hauptmann were succeeded by those of the Marxist Bertold Brecht (1898–1956). Though essentially a poet, Brecht gained fame principally as a playwright. His polemical and provocative work set out to create a sense of alienation in his audience so that at any performance they would remain continually aware that they were merely watching a play, and consequently would not become emotionally involved. He hoped to achieve this by various devices such as obscuring his actors behind gauze curtains on which were flashed diagrams, headlines and so forth, accompanied by loud and distracting music. *The Threepenny Opera,* written in 1929 and with music by Kurt Weill, is a well-known and characteristic example. However, the imagination he consistently brought to his productions and writing ensured that his work was never merely didactic but, paradoxically, much more involving and moving than he intended.

The mystical and the spiritual in German literature are found in their most compelling form in the present century in Hermann Hesse (1877–1962), though the burning problem of the artist and his dealings with an imperfect and cramping world is never far away from his work. In *Der Steppenwolf,* Hesse, not without a great deal of humor, seemed to suggest that the artist should not adopt a position of isolation from reality as this inevitably leads to bitterness. But in his most famous novel, *The Glass Bead Game,* for which he received the Nobel Prize in 1946, Hesse proposed instead an ideal community of artists and thinkers who, cosseted from the bluff reality of the real world, impose an artificial order on its disorder. At the same time, the novel contends that this essentially artificial solution is not enough, that the artist has still not reconciled himself to the traumas of reality. Nonetheless, while no solution to this question may have been found by the writer, all his work is permeated by genuine and striking insight and a very real profundity and tolerance. Many of the same themes can also be found in the contemplative and spiritual poetry of Rainer Maria Rilke (1875–1926).

Though all these figures, from Mann onwards, suffered through— and were necessarily influenced by—the trauma and upheaval of World War I and its aftermath, none was a serving soldier and consequently none wrote of the war at first hand. This task fell, as it were, to a writer of really much lesser stature who nonetheless produced one striking and memorable work. This was Erich Maria Remarque (1898–19—). His novel, *All Quiet on the Western Front,* though lacking in subtlety, became an instant best seller. Its quiet, unemotional descriptions of the horror and endless suffering of ordinary soldiers' lives in the trenches and the sense of a new and futile order, beyond anyone's control, imposed on the world, is as moving today as when it was first published. Remarque never wrote anything as convincing or successful later, but is deservedly remembered today for this one striking achievement.

During the Nazi period and World War II, practically all German writers of significance left the country or were exiled by the Nazis as decadent and degenerate. So the Facist period and the war, while important themes in the work of Mann and Feuchtwanger for instance, were nonetheless dealt with at second hand. It was only after the war, when a new generation of writers appeared who had grown up under the Nazis, that the subject became a central topic in German literature. It is no understatement to say that the Third Reich seared and numbed the entire artistic consciousness of this generation.

Many, Hermann Kasack (1896–19—) is a fine example, wrote of the passing of a more refined and noble age. His novel, *The Town Across the Water,* reflects poignantly his despair at the grabbing, cruel modern world. Gerd Gaiser (b. 1908) dealt with the major crises facing the returning war hero in a land shattered both physically and mentally. His book *Ein Stimm Habt An* is a minor masterpiece of the genre. In a later work, *Schlussball,* he examines the moral dilemma posed by the post-war economic miracle which, whilst bringing material wealth, has not been so lavish with spiritual wealth.

In 1947 a group of younger writers who had grown up under the Third Reich formed themselves into a literary association called Gruppe 47. They rejected state institutions as a means of personal salvation championing instead the road of individual fulfillment—not by withdrawing into themselves but by facing up to the actual problems of the day. Among them were Gunther Grass, today Germany's leading novelist, Heinrich Böll and the poetess Ingeborg Bachman.

Böll's greatest gift is his dry and extremely sardonic humor which is masterly in *Entfernung von der Truppe.* Grass, by contrast, is more extravagant, even obscene, dragging all sacred rites and accepted conventions of morality into the gutter and exposing them mercilessly. *The Tin Drum* and *Cat and Mouse* are among his best-known satirical novels. While Bachmann is a lesser literary talent than either of the two novelists, she has nonetheless been a potent force in the German Feminist movement and one of its most ardent and articulate supporters.

Among younger playwrights, two stand out as exceptional talents, Rolf Hochuth and Peter Handke. Hochuth is a relentless exposer of the scandals of modern life, seen most effectively in plays such as *The Representative,* which examines the relationship of Pope Pius XII and the Nazis in wartime Rome, and *Soldier,* which is about Winston Churchill. Handke's star is still very much in the ascendant, particularly after the success of his early play, *Ride Over the Bodensee.*

Of the younger novelists, Uwe Johnson is now established for his novels on divided Germany while the Berliner Botto Strauss is gaining an increasingly large following for his psychological works, notably his play *Big and Little* and his novel *Rumor.*

Painting

The first stirrings of German painting occurred, like so much of German culture, under the benevolent guiding hand of Charlemagne in the 9th century. The "Palace School" at Aachen, Charlemagne's capital, produced a large and significant number of works. However, they were not paintings as we use the term today but illuminations—intricate, skillfull and extremely beautiful—used to decorate the vast collection of manuscripts that Charlemagne amassed and which formed the basis of the Carolingian Renaissance. The most splendid specimen extant today is the Bible of Charles the Great.

This tradition was continued in the following two hundred years, spreading far beyond the boundaries of Aaachen. Two of the finest examples are the Egbert Codex dating from about 980 and the Bible of Otto III, produced about 20 years later. Both came from the Monastery at Reichenau. At around the same time, the earliest church wall paintings were produced. Those in Reichenau's church of St. George date from around 950–975. A third type of visual decoration, stained glass, though again not painting in the strict sense of the word, makes up the trio that formed Germany's principal contribution to the visual arts in the early and mid-Middle Ages. The best examples are at Augsburg Cathedral, dating from the 12th century, and at the church of St. Elisabeth in Marburg.

It was not until the 14th century that the first paintings proper were produced in Germany. The outstanding painter of the period was Konrad Witz. Though a German by birth, most of his active life was spent in Switzerland. Despite this, the fact of his birth and the influence he was to have on later German painters qualifies him for inclusion here. In Switzerland he quickly developed a detailed and precise style that again owed much to Flanders. His major work, an altarpiece of the Redemption, indicates this clearly and is a powerful and mature painting. He was also a vital figure in the early development of landscape painting. His only signed work, *Christ Walking on the Water*, clearly uses as its model for the landscape a corner of the Lake of Geneva. This is an astonishingly precocious use of actual landscape in painting.

Despite his importance, Witz was nonetheless essentially a Medieval figure. But with the turn of the 15th century, a new and radically different approach was adopted under the influence of the Renaissance, casting its warm glow north through Europe.

The leading figure without a doubt was Albrecht Dürer (1471–1528). Dürer almost singlehandedly created the Renaissance in Germany. Like Leonardo in Italy, he was not merely a painter and engraver but a scholar, philosopher, mathematician and humanist—in short the Renaissance Universal Man. In this he was undoubtedly helped by his extensive travels in Italy, where he met many of the leading artistic figures. Probably due to this influence, he thereafter sought out the company of scholars rather than that of his fellow artisans, a radical step in the re-evaluation of the role of the artist. His principal achievement was in the graphic arts and his many prints, being easily accesible and easily reproduced, played a key role in spreading knowledge of the Renaissance in Germany and elsewhere in northern Europe. He not only raised the woodcut to an astonishingly high level of technical perfection but was a supreme master of copper engraving. To this technical virtuosity he added brilliant draftsmanship, great expressiveness and layer upon layer of learned allegorical meaning. Prime examples include the *Apocalypse* series and the *Sea Monster*. His paintings by contrast—examples of which can be seen in Augsburg, Berlin, Cologne, Frankfurt, Munich, Nurnberg and Weimar—still faintly echo the Middle Ages, though his inventiveness and purity of color make them unmistakably the work of a master. Perhaps the finest are his watercolor and gouache landscapes, painted with amazing delicacy and beautifully observed. Perhaps surprisingly he enjoyed relatively little influence, but his talent was such that really there was no one capable of following him. He is one of the giants of this or any other age.

Mathis Grünewald (1475–1553), though a contemporary of Dürer, could hardly have been more unlike him. Though certainly well aware of the new technical and conceptual language of the Renaissance which Dürer had imported into Germany, he made use of it to obtain exactly opposite effects. A well-known example is the *Isenheim Altar*—now in the Unterlinden Museum, Colmar, just across the French/German border in Alsace Lorraine. Here, Renaissance technical devices—color, light, space and perspective—are employed not to create balance and harmony but to exaggerate the emotional impact of a fundamentally Gothic vision. Unlike most of his contemporaries, he produced no graphic work.

The third great painter of the early Renaissance in Germany was Lucas Cranach (1472–1553). Like Grünewald, strong traces of the Gothic remain in work, but there is no sense of tension between them and his use of Italianate techniques. Rather they combine to produce a haunting and peculiar sense of mystery heightened by a characteristic enamel-like finish. This is most pronounced and vivid in his series of late full length female nudes, all of which are highly allegorical and extremely erotic. Though most of his early works were of religious subjects, the two developments for which he is principally remembered are his development of the full-length portrait, which antedates even the Italians—a superb example is his double portrait of Henry the

Pious of Saxony and his Duchess—and the use of landscape as a subject in its own right.

But the painter who took Cranach's interest in landscape to its logical conclusion was Albrecht Altdorfer (c1480–1538). Though the use of vivid and realistic landscape had been an important characteristic of German painting from Witz onward, it remained essentially no more than a background to the main subject of the painting itself. With Altdorfer, however, this process was reversed and the landscape itself became the subject. And though figures appear in his work, their purpose is simply to highlight the landscape and underline its emotional impact. This one development alone is enough to make Altdorfer a key figure in the history of Western art, and the father of the long tradition of pure landscape painting.

Hans Holbein the Younger (1498–1543) was the last of the great painters of this period. He was probably the most accomplished and penetrating portrait painter northern Europe has produced. Like Dürer he traveled in Italy as a young man, though not extensively. Nonetheless this brief immersion in the therapeutic waters of the Renaissance proved a key influence and thereafter all but the most superficial traces of the Late Gothic disappeared from his work. His conversion to and assimilation of Renaissance painting and the new Humanist spirit was cemented by his association in 1523 with Erasmus, the leading Humanist philosopher of the time. His three portraits of Erasmus marked his emergence as a major painter.

In 1526 the turmoil caused by the Reformation forced him to look outside Germany for employment and, like Handel in the 18th century, he came to England. It was here that the bulk of his exquisite portraits were produced. On his first visit he met Sir Thomas More and painted a large family-group portrait, unfortunately subsequently destroyed.

He returned to England in 1532 and entered the service of Henry VIII. Apart from several portraits of the king himself and a number of superb allegorical pictures illustrating his dynastic succession, he was responsible for a long and brilliant series of portraits of court notables. Henry also sent him abroad to paint Anne of Cleves, the only way the monarch could discover the beauty or otherwise of his prospective bride. Unfortunately Holbein excelled himself to such an extent that the king, falling in love with the portrait, was less than happy to find that Anne's beauty existed only on canvas. His delicacy of touch and shrewd yet sympathetic handling of his subjects has ensured Holbein a central role in the evolution of European portraiture. Sadly few of his paintings can be seen in Germany, most are in England, Austria, and America.

German painting after Holbein and in the 17th century failed to live up to the achievements of these giants of the Renaissance. This was partly the result of the Thirty Year War in the middle of the century which caused terrible devastation and made patronage impossible. Whatever the cause, the period produced no painters of genuine importance. The only two who can be singled out—Adam Elsheimer (1578–1610) and Johann Liss (1579–1630)—worked at the beginning of the century, before the war, and spent the majority of their working lives in Italy, both dying there. As such they really qualify more as Italian painters than German. Certainly neither had much influence on the development of German painting. Of the two, Elsheimer is the more interesting. He developed an idealized form of landscape—in which figures play only a minor role—painted with great delicacy and precision and using varied light sources.

In the 18th century, the story of German painting is rather different. Though again there were no truly important German painters a healthy native school nonetheless emerged. The first signs of this are seen in the work of the Austrian Johann Micheal Rottmayr (1654–1730). He spent thirteen years in Venice where he fell under the influence of the 16th-century painter Correggio. On his return to Vienna he worked mainly as a ceiling and fresco painter. His masterpiece is commonly held to be the ceiling of the splendid Karlskirche, full of swirling movement and grand heroic figures.

This essentially Baroque style was taken up by Cosmos Damian Asam (1686–1739). He was more, however, than just a painter. With his brother Egid Quirin, himself a sculptor of note, they decorated, designed, planned and built a score of south German churches. His paintings are best seen in the context of these remarkable buildings. For, by virtue of their multi-faceted talents, the Asams embodied the then current Italian concept of the *unisono* of the arts where architecture, sculpture, decoration and painting interact, the whole producing a splendidly theatrical effect. His best work is in the abbey church of Weltenburg and St John Nepomuk in Munich.

The middle of the 18th century saw two more German painters of stature though, as with Elsheimer and Liss, their fame rests principally on work done outside Germany. The first was Anton Raffael Mengs (1728–1779). His importance stems as much from his role in the development of neo-Classical aesthetics as from his achievements with his brush. Many today consider him a dry and arid painter more at home theorizing than painting. (Even here, though, he was not always fortunate. His treatise on *Beauty in Painting* was "borrowed" by an Englishman, Daniel Webb, in 1760 who then published it—very successfully—as his own work.) Nonetheless his association with Winckelmann, the foremost apologist of neo-Classicism, and his influence on the later French neo-Classicists, especially David, have ensured him an important position in the history of 18th-century painting.

The second figure is much more accessible to modern taste. This was Johann Zoffany (1725–1810). His early work in Germany looks back rather emptily and unsuccessfully to Baroque models, but in 1761 he went to England where he enjoyed his greatest success, again principally as a portrait painter. Mainly under the influence of Hogarth, he rapidly developed a new and much more intimate manner, most vividly seen in his series of Conversation Pieces, group portraits where the subjects are posed informally going about what, in the 18th century at any rate, passed for their everyday business. Despite the considerable success he had in England—he was patronized by Garrick and George III among others—in 1783 wanderlust struck again. He took the step, remarkable at the time, of going to India. The result was a series of astonishing portraits of princes, nabobs and landscapes which had a profound influence on the increasing interest in the East and things Oriental and exotic.

At the beginning of the 19th century, however, a German painter of real stature at last emerged. This was Caspar David Friedrich (1774–1840). He has strong claims to be considered the purest of all Romantic landscape painters; in this, a direct line links his work to that of Altdorfer. To Friedrich, landscape painting *was* painting. Consequently the human figure almost never intrudes in his work. Instead he concentrated exclusively on capturing the wild grandeur of the north German landscape, giving it a visionary quality that perfectly reflects the Romantic cult of feeling and a dark, haunted mystery. Many people have suggested that his work has a religious quality despite having no overtly religious references. And Friedrich himself seemed obliquely to support this attitude when he wrote, "The only true source of art is the heart, the language of the the pure and innocent soul. A painting which does not have its genesis therein can only be sleight of hand." The best collection of his work is in his native Dresden—unfortunately rather inaccessible today—including his famous *Cross in the Mountains* (1808).

German painting in the rest of the 19th century, though intermittently interesting, failed to live up to the standards set by Friedrich. A number of movements and groups appeared in fields as disparate as landscape and left-wing inspired social realism, many of them today considered very unlovely, but no painters of genuine importance materialized before the end of the century.

At the beginning of this century, painting in Germany enjoyed a sudden and striking renaissance. It originated in the work of Paula Modersohn-Becker (1867–1956) and Emile Nolde (1867–1956) who under the influence of Van Gogh and Gaugin and later of the Fauves, began to develop an exaggerated, idiosyncratic and forceful style using vivid, bright colors and simplified, bold forms, the whole creating an emotional and expressive style. It is tempting to see something of the spirit of Grünewald in this.

Nolde and Modershon-Becker's influence was taken up by two different groups Die Brücke (The Bridge) and Die Blaue Reiter (The Blue Rider). The first was wholly German in membership, consisting of Ernst Kirchner (1880–1938), Erich Heckel (1883–1970) and Karl Schmidt-Rottluf (1884–19—). The second group, though its leading members were not German, nonetheless made Munich the second artistic capital of Europe after Paris, and had a profound influence on later German painters. They can also claim to have laid the foundation stones of abstract art. Its guiding spirits were Paul Klee (1879–1940), Franz Marc (1880–1916) and Wassily Kandinsky (1866–1944), the latter in particular being a progenitor of "pure" abstraction. The group's unusual name came about because both Kandinsky and Marc liked blue, Marc liked horses and Kandinsky liked riders.

By 1920 Expressionism was more or less a spent force and in reaction to its growing respectability a new movement appeared in Germany. This was Neue Sachlichkeit (New Objectivity). Where Expressionism was confident and increasingly abstract, New Objectivity was realistic and largely concerned with social injustice and the detailed representation of every day objects. It did not remain a coherent group for long, but during its heyday its two prime movers were Otto Dix (1893–1959) and George Grosz (1893–1959). Dix is characterized by a relentlessly realistic style which, through its brilliantly pointed satire, hunted down and exposed social inequality, greed and bourgeois small mindedness. Grosz was a more complex figure. As one of the founders of Dada, the anti-art movement, Grosz epitomized its declared aim to shock and scandalize. He was fined on several occasions for insulting, among other things, the German army and public morality and was also tried for blasphemy. However, Grosz gradually abandoned Dada's more senseless manifestations in favor of vicious and startling social caricature. However, it was not until he left Germany in 1933 when the Nazis came to power that he began to enjoy wide success. He spent the majority of the rest of his life in America.

Painting in Germany today is as directionless and varied as it is throughout the world. Everything from pure abstraction to detailed realism abounds. Leading figures in the abstraction camp include Willi Baumeister, Fritz Winter and Theodor Werner. The principal figurative painters number such as Karl Hofer and Werner Scholz. The Bavarian, Wolf Reuther, by contrast, manages to have a foot in each camp simultaneously.

If you want to check up on the art of today—and perhaps even of tomorrow—the four leading museums are the National Gallerie in

Berlin, the Neuepinakothek in Munich, the Kunstammlung Nord-Rhein–Westfalen in Düsseldorf and the Museum Ludwig in Cologne.

Architecture

Almost inevitably the first German buildings of significance date from the time of Charlemagne. Though a few slightly earlier buildings exist, they seem very crude in comparison to the magnificent palaces and churches erected under the Emperor's sympathetic patronage. The best extant example is the palace chapel at Aachen, just over the Belgian border, dating from about 800.

However, the first real triumphs of German architecture came with the development of the amazingly fertile and inventive German Romanesque. The Romanesque was basically a style of ecclesiastical building which preceded the relatively more sophisticated Gothic. Its principal features are round, as opposed to pointed, arches and a general massiveness and weight allied to wonderful and intricate decorative details derived rather loosely from Roman architecture—hence the name.

The fully developed Romanesque is first found in Germany at St. Michael in Hildesheim (c. 1030). For the next two hundred years it was to remain the dominant style in Germany and to make the Germans the leading architectural nation in Europe. The climax of the style was in the great cathedrals of the Rhineland of which the most splendid is St.-Mary-in-Capitol in Cologne. Before the devastation caused by the Allied bombing of World War II, Cologne had more Romanesque buildings than any other city in Europe. Similarly severe and weighty masterpieces of Romanesque architecture are the cathedrals at Speyer and Trier, both also in the Rhineland.

Gothic, a lighter more vertical style imported from France, did not appear in Germany until about 1200. The earliest examples, nearly all in northern Germany, are basically imitative and not wholly successful. They were really no more than the first tentative attempts to emulate French masterpieces. But after these early experiments, German Gothic flowered suddenly and marvellously, developing into a mature and complete style which, though it owed much to France is nonetheless wholly German. Of the earliest churches, the finest is Cologne Cathedral, begun in 1248 though finally completed only in the last century. Over the next two hundred years the style spread and thrived throughout Germany. Its two most important characteristics are the development of the "hall" church—where the aisles and nave are approximately the same height—and, as an extension of this, astonishing height and lightness. At St. Sebalds in Nürnberg and Erfurt Cathedral in East Germany, both built in the 14th century, high, slim windows soar from floor to ceiling in one unbroken line, giving an almost ethereal lightness and delicacy.

From this time onwards, the names of architects, hitherto largely unknown, became more important, indicating their increasing status. The greatest of them all seems to have been Peter Parler who was appointed architect of Prague Cathedral by Emperor Charles IV. He came from a prolific family of architects. Heinrich Parler was responsible for the chancel of Schwäbisch Gmund in 1351, considered by many the most perfect of all Late Gothic buildings. Other outstanding architects of the period include Ulrich and Matthäus Ensinger, Konrad Heinzelmann who designed the fabulously beautiful chancel at Nürnberg Cathedral and Hans and Matthäus Boblinger. Matthäus Ensinger designed the west tower of Ulm Cathedral, at 530 feet the tallest church tower in Europe. It wasn't actually completed until the 19th century as at the time it was widely believed that it was recklessly high and, when cracks appeared in the fabric, poor Matthäus was forced to leave Ulm.

The architectural richness of the Late Gothic period was not confined exclusively to ecclesiastical building. Town halls, castles and, later, palaces abound. The castles tend to be overwhelming and massive; a good example is that at Tourn in Prussia built in the late 14th century for the Teutonic Knights. Town halls, particularly those in the north, on the other hand, are wonders of intricate and fantastic brickwork. Palaces, developed from castles as the need for defense became less acute, are equally fantastic and splendid. Largely because they were centers of courtly elegance, these Late Gothic palaces were among the first buildings to come under the influence of Italian Renaissance architecture. However, pure Renaissance classicism never established itself successfully in Germany. There are one or two early examples— the most famous is the Fugger chapel in Augsburg of c. 1509—but this style was quickly superseded by a native product, confused but highly attractive, halfway between the Gothic and the Renaissance. Leipzig town hall, built in the middle of the 16th century with gables, stubby columns and coarse rather Flemish decoration, is a perfect example.

As in both England and France, a real understanding of Renaissance architecture did not develop until the early 17th century. It is most perfectly seen in the work of Elias Höll, who traveled extensively in Italy before his appointment as city architect of Ausburg in 1602. His masterpiece is the town hall dating from 1615, which in both conception and execution is wholly classical.

However, the development of a native German classicism was brutally interrupted by the Thirty Year War which left the country devastated and whose effects were felt for many years. When building became possible again toward the end of the 17th century, the Baroque was the dominant European style and German buildings quickly began to reflect its exuberant and heroic qualities. Which is an understatement, for Germany assimilated Baroque, and later Rococo, styles rapidly and went on to produce many supreme examples.

Most of the important early developments in the revival of German architecture took place in the Catholic south of the country, and for a time many of the leading architects working there were Italian. Before long, however, a number of outstanding German architects appeared. Of the earliest, the most influential were Fischer von Erlach (1656–1723), Andreas Schülter (1660–1714) and Matthaeus Daniel Pöppleman (1662–1736). All, particularly von Erlach, with a wonderful mixture of bravado, fantasy and drama built some of the most imaginative edifices of the period. Perhaps the most remarkable building produced by these three is Pöppleman's Zwinger in Dresden, a fantasy playground that resembles nothing so much as a piece of gargantuan porcelain.

The dramatic and large-scale qualities of these Baroque architects, though they had enormous impact, did not last long. Instead, to some extent under the influence of the Austrian, Lukas von Hildebrandt, architecture became lighter and more playful, until the fully blown Rococo, extravagant, exuberant and intoxicating, came to occupy the central position of German architecture. While in France, where the Rococo developed, it was never more than a style of internal decoration; in Germany it became a fully developed and coherent architectural language. Two early examples, Frederick the Great's palace at Sanssouci dating from 1745 and the Amalienburg at Nymphenburg of 1734, show the style at its best in secular building. The Amalienburg is particularly amazing. It was built for the Elector Karl Albrecht of Bavaria as a hunting lodge by Francois Cuvilliés, who had previously enjoyed the position of court dwarf to the Elector. Though no more than an apparently simple single-story building, it is built and decorated with an elegant, frothy profusion of sculpture and painting unified by cool blue and yellow color schemes.

However, even this peak was surpassed shortly afterwards, for the real triumph of German Rococo was in ecclesiastical architecture. In this, though there were a number of architects of distinction, one name stands out above all others, Balthasar Neumann (1687–1753). He built a number of churches but far and away the most brilliant is the pilgrimage church of Vierzehnheiligen, northeast of Bamberg in Bavaria, begun in 1743. The foundations were laid out by a different architect, forcing Neumann to accommodate his design to a somewhat inconvenient ground plan. This, however, merely provided a spur to his genius, and the resulting design soared above and transformed the limitations of the site. It is based on a complex series of interlinking ovals that produce a permanent sensation of movement and elegance enhanced and exaggerated by the exquisite Rococo decoration. This is all the more striking as you enter the church because the exterior is plain to the point of dullness and gives no hint of the fabulous richness inside.

While this represented the high point of Rococo architecture, many other churches and palaces of almost equal sumptuousness were built at this time. Neumann himself was responsible for the grandest and most opulent, the Residenz at Würzburg, completed c. 1744. The centerpiece is a magnificent staircase, later decorated by Tiepolo. Of the other leading Rococo architects, the most important were the Asam brothers, Egid Quirin and Cosmos Damian—responsible for the marvelous church of St. John Nepomuk in Munich, completed 1746—Johann Michael Fischer who built the Benedictine abbey church at Ottobeuren, begun 1744, full of light and movement, and Dominikus Zimmerman. His masterpiece was the tiny church of Wies, completed 1754, a characteristic and scintillating piece of Rococo architectural trickery and charm.

These triumphs of devotional architecture and elegance took place mainly in the south of Germany. It was not surprising, therefore, when the inevitable reaction against the light and color of the Rococo came, that it took place chiefly in the Protestant north. Friedrich Gilly (1772–1800), though he died young, set the scene for an entirely new sensibility, that of neo-Classicism. His design for a monument to Frederick the Great, though never built, is severe and austere and strictly, even rigidly, classical with a minimum of ornamentation. However, despite this grand and impressive beginning, the Greek Revival did not find much favor in Germany though Gilly's pupil Karl Friedrich Schinkel (1781–1841) produced a number of buildings in that style. At the same time, following the lead provided by England, he was interested in the revival of Gothic architecture. Consequently this conflict of the styles —Classical and Gothic—precluded the development of one dominant architectural school. Instead the historicism inherent in the revival of Gothic continued and spread to include other types of architecture previously considered quite unsuitable for serious or prestigious building. The story of German 19th-century architecture is therefore rather muddled and confusing as first one style was revived and championed and then another, with endless arguments over their relative merits.

Gottfried Semper (1803–79), the leading architect of the mid-19th century, is an excellent example of this eclecticism. Though the majority of his buildings were derived from Italian models, his Dresden synagogue (1840) incorporates such unlikely and exotic features as Lombard, Byzantine, Moorish and Romanesque elements. Similarly, at the same time that Semper was continuing and expanding the vocabulary of Classical architecture by employing styles as fundamentally different as the neo-Renaissance and the neo-Baroque, so ambitious, rather Wagnerian, programs were undertaken to complete the Gothic cathedrals of Ulm and Cologne. Towards the end of the century there was an increasing use of decoration—Semper's second Dresden opera house (1871) is a case in point. This was built in an ornate and rather gaudy neo-Baroque manner in contrast to his first opera house which was a rather plain and elegant neo-Renaissance structure. But at the very same time, Ludwig von Hoffman was building the Leipzig Supreme Court in a neo-Classical style which is plain to the point of austerity.

At the beginning of this century an important and radical change took place. For the first time since before the Renaissance an architectural style was introduced that was completely modern in concept and which did not attempt to revive and re-interpret some older style. This has come to be known as International Modern and is, effectively, modern architecture—that is, buildings that are generally cubic in shape, asymetrical and white. It was developed largely in Germany.

The first truly modern building of this type was the AEG factory in Berlin, designed and built by Peter Behrens (1868–1940). Functional, stark and simple, and making much use of industrial materials, it has proved immensely influential and a key building in the development of modern architecture. Two of his pupils have since proved themselves among the leading figures of modernism. They are Walter Gropius and Mies van der Rohe. Though much of their best and most striking work was done in America, where they both emigrated after the Nazis assumed power, both produced important buildings in Germany itself, the most significant of which is the Bauhaus by Gropius, (1926). It is significant not only as a shining example of the functionalism and unexpected elegance of the new architecture but also for its role as the leading art school of the 20th century.

Since the war, the elegant functionalism of International Modern architecture has lost its leading role in the development of modern building to the architectural theories propounded by the Frenchman Le Corbusier. While his buildings are equally modern in spirit, they nonetheless constitute a distinctively different approach to the problems of contemporary architecture. Where Gropius and van der Rohe saw architecture as reflecting new demands and building techniques, but still as ultimately subsidiary to the demands and life style of those who had to live and work in it, Le Corbusier saw modern architecture as an artistic end in itself. People would have to accommodate themselves to these new buildings and not the other way around. Thus to Le Corbusier, modern architecture was a vision of the future which would radically and permanently change the way we live. His plan to demolish the center of Paris and build 18 giant skyscrapers in its place is typical of the bravado of his work but also of its brutal insensitivity.

Despite this potentially troublesome influence, Germany has nonetheless contrived to remain in the forefront of modern trends in building. To a very large extent, this is due to the devastation caused in the war when many cities were almost entirely obliterated and had to be largely rebuilt. Among the more adventurous contempory architects are Freidrich Kramer, who built the Verwaltungszentrum in Berlin, Gottfried Bohm, responsible for the Cologne Rathaus and Gunter Behnisch who designed the striking and daring stadium for the Munich Olympic games. Another outstanding building of post-war Germany is the Berlin Philharmonic Hall, completed in 1963 and the work of Hans Scharoun.

EATING IN GERMANY

Which is Mostly about Drinking

by
LEE CARSON

You've always heard that German food is heavy and doughy and uninspired, and you remember that in Grimm's fairy tales or some such book, they were always eating porridge. But what have you heard of the *Hase im Topf,* a divine rabbit *pâté,* or of *Spekulatius,* a delicate little cookie with its very special taste, or of *Rheinsalm,* the pale pink Rhine salmon, or of the famous Schwetzingen asparagus or the *Pumpernickel* bread from Münster and the cooled white wine of Meersburg? And what have you heard of the little *Gasthäuser,* perched on any high hill or nestled in every small town, where the low-ceilinged rooms are paneled in oak and the big round tables are darkened with age, where the beer steins are taller, the deer stews tastier, the atmosphere more *gemütlich* than any place you know on earth? Or at least that's what you'll think when you're there.

A Few Basic Remarks

But don't assume from this that you are likely to grow thinner in Germany. German food does put on poundage. To begin with, there is the matter of fat. You can classify schools of cooking by the basic fat used. Northern France and Belgium use butter. Southern France, Spain and Italy use olive oil. Germany uses lard.

There is also the matter of starch. In Germany everything which *can* be served with dumplings *is* served with dumplings. In addition, it sometimes seems that in this country the vegetable kingdom is represented (save for the cabbage) only by the potato.

Lastly, there is the size of the portions. You will get plenty to eat. Don't sit down and order a full course dinner from the start, as you might do in some countries. Take it stage by stage, testing your capacity as you progress.

If you don't go in for the gigantic meals you're served for lunch in Germany (but you'll be amazed how quickly you learn) you can find a bakery (*Bäckerei*) with little tables in the shop where you can order good coffee, a fresh roll or pastry just out of the oven. Or you can go to a dairy shop (*Mölkerei*), for a glass of fresh milk and a piece of cheese. This will cost you very little and it's fun.

There is always an *à la carte* menu in restaurants and most of them have fixed-price luncheon specials—soup, meat and vegetables, and sometimes dessert, for as little as 8 or 10 marks, as well as more elaborate meals at correspondingly more elaborate prices.

You are charged for every piece of bread you eat, except at the most deluxe restaurants, so if you're confronted with a question at the end of the meal, it's likely to mean the waitress wants to know how much bread to charge you for. It won't cost much.

Restaurants are usually either beer restaurants, where only beer is served with the food, or wine restaurants, which either serve wine from their own vineyards, or specialize in impressive collections of bottled wines from all over the country. More often, restaurants serve both. You aren't required to drink either; you can ask for *Wasser,* and you'll be brought a glass or a bottle of mineral water.

Beer comes in a small glass (*ein Kleines*) or a nice large glass (*ein Grosses*) or a stein (*ein Mass*). The best wines come in bottles, whereas usually only the lesser qualities are sold open, in carafe or by glass; but in Germany, white wines are almost always good, so you can safely get the wine of the house in a carafe. For one person, a quarterliter of wine is about right, so ask for a *Schoppen.* Cool Mosel wine comes in earthenware pitchers or, if you are in the Mosel area, ask for a *Pokal* of wine, when it will come to you in a delightful green-stemmed wine glass.

Cocktails are served only in bars, night clubs and in the international type restaurants and are very expensive. Substitute a glass of white wine or beer or a beer with a shot of Schnaps on the side, as the Germans do.

Particularly in the southern areas of Germany—except in top class restaurants—it is the custom for other people to sit down at your table. Tables are usually big, comfortably spaced, and it's no trial to have company. One always asks first for permission (*ist hier frei?*) and says good-bye when one leaves. You don't have to talk to them, but it's not at all bad manners in Germany if strangers at your table speak to you.

The regional variety of food in Germany is not quite as great as the menus might lead you to think. Many dishes have developed locally, but they have spread; you can find a Bavarian dish in a Hamburg restaurant, or a Rhineland dish in Passau. And some of the regional dishes to begin with were only local variants of some sort of food served throughout the country—like sauerkraut. We list in the regional chapters the dishes that originated there.

Introducing the Staples

All over the world, eating at its most elemental begins with one basic staple—some form of cereal—and there are three others which lend themselves to such subtle and intricate variation that cities honor themselves by naming their own creations in these lines after themselves. They are cheese, sausage and wine. Two of these three important divisions of the realm of foodstuffs are admirably served in Germany.

We might say a word also about the basic cereal. As children in America, we often read books about Europe in which the full horror of life on the low level of the peasants was rubbed in by the disclosure that they ate black bread—bread, in other words, made by bakers so benighted that they had not solved the problem of refining all the vitamins out of the flour so that they could put added vitamins back in. You will find a great deal of this vulgar bread with nothing but common natural vitamins in it in Germany, and if you call instead for white bread, you deserve what you get. White rolls (*Brötchen* or, in Bavaria, *Semmeln*) are good, but there's nothing like a slice of rye bread *(Roggen)* for sheer feeding power. Try also Westphalian *Pumpernickel,* a very rich, dark bread excellent with cheese.

Now for our three staples. In spite of the notoriety of Limburger (Limburg is a town in Hesse), Germany has not contributed greatly to the gamut of cheeses. But when we come to sausage, we enter a field in which the Germans are masters. *Frankfurters,* a sausage made from all parts of the pig, are eaten all over the world by people who never pause to think that their name derives from the city which invented them. Another sausage that goes generally by the name of the place it comes from is the *Regensburger,* a fat, heavily spiced pork sausage. Everyone knows *Leberwurst:* it is a specialty of Hesse (they call it *Zeppelinwurst* in Frankfurt, which is a great sausage city, producing also *Fleischwurst, Schwartenmagen, Gelbwurst* and *Rindswurst*). *Bratwurst,* the pork sausage of Nürnberg, usually served fried or, better, grilled, is so famous that you will find restaurants all over the country called "Bratwurststube" because they make a specialty of serving this particular type of sausage.

During the lively Munich Carnival celebration, the interruption of festivities by the entrance of *Weisswurst,* a delicate white sausage made from veal, calves' brains and spleen, means that midnight has just passed, for there is a tradition that Weisswurst should only be eaten between midnight and noon. A favorite between-meals snack in Mainz is *Weck, Worscht und Wein*—a roll, sausage and wine. Coburg serves sausages roasted; Soest, in Westphalia, bakes them in dough—Westphalia is the place for *Rinderwurst, Blutwurst,* and *Westfälischer Schinken*—beef sausage, blood sausage, and Westphalian ham. The *Bouillonwurst* of Hannover is served with mustard and horse radish; *Milzwurst,* a spleen sausage, found along the Danube; Stuttgart's *Saiten,* a juicy sausage served with lentils; and a whole panoply of them in Braunschweig. This is the city that gave cervelat sausage to the world, along with *Mettwurst* and *Knackwurst.*

This brief gastronomic note should not be concluded without a bow to the herring. If you are fond of herring, Germany has, and provides, your dish. The herring is consumed here in every imaginable form— fried fresh herring (called "green" herring in Germany); rolled up around pickles, cucumbers and onions, which makes it *Rollmops* or *Bismarck Hering;* sour pickled *Brathering,* served fried; *Matjeshering,* presented with potatoes boiled in their skins, and lots of butter; herring salad, with diced cucumbers, potatoes and much seasoning. In Emden, in fact, they'll give you a whole herring lunch, with hors d'oeuvre, main dish, and salad all provided by this protean fish.

First-Class Wines

When it comes to producing a fine wine, Germany takes second place to none, including France. True, Germany produces nothing like the quantity of wines France does, but within her range, she can provide bottles just as fine of their type as the best red Burgundy and equal to the best French white. For that matter, the range is not as limited as many outsiders believe. Some persons are under the impression that Germany produces nothing but white wines. Most German wines are. But there are also some reds. Others think that when you have spoken of Rhine wines, you have exhausted the German catalog. Not at all; there are a dozen wine-producing regions in Germany.

It is much more difficult to order wines in Germany than in France with any assurance of getting what you have in mind. Individual bottles vary widely, even when they bear the label of the same locality and the same year. This is partly because most wine holdings are small, and one winegrower in a given community may produce a much finer product than his next-door neighbor; but an even more important factor is the location of the vineyard: on the sunny side or in the shade, towards the north or south, high up on a steep slope or down towards the valley, and so on. So in Germany, it is well to consult the wine waiter.

A certain amount of protection against disappointment may be secured by ordering wines bottled by the grower (*Originalabfüllung* or *Originalabzug*) or by ordering *Kabinett* wines, a term which some growers use to designate their choicest productions.

You can also order certain special types of wine, whose quality is more or less guaranteed by the manner of their making. *Spätlese* (late harvest) is made from grapes picked after the normal harvest at a period when they are dead ripe. *Auslese* (selection) is made from grapes picked during the normal harvest time, but separately selected for special ripeness. Both *Spätlese* and *Auslese* are sweeter and more expensive than the normal types. Sweeter still is *Beerenauslese* (grape berries selection), made from grape berries culled from among the most mature. For *Trockenbeerenauslese* (dried grape berries selection), the grapes are allowed to stay on the vines in the sun until they are partly shriveled into naturally-dried raisins. Then the berries are picked one by one; the result is a rich heavy sweet wine suited particularly for drinking with dessert. It is comparatively rare and expensive.

White Wines

Pfalz or *Rheinpfalz* (*Palatinate*): The southernmost end of the Rhine wine region is Pfalz, on the west bank of the upper Rhine. The wine-growing area is located approximately in the center of this region, on the lowest eastern slopes of the Haardt mountains. The German Wine Road (*Deutsche Weinstrasse*) meanders through the wine-growing villages, among which Forst, Deidesheim, Wachenheim, Ruppertsberg, Kallstadt, Neustadt, Maikammer and Bad Dürkheim produce the best wines. Try *Forster Ungeheuer, Forster Jesuitengarten, Deidesheimer Herrgottsacker, Ruppertsberger Kreuz, Kallstadter Saumagen,* or *Dürkheimer Michelsberg*. Several good red wines are also grown in this region. The Pfalz white wines are well balanced, full-bodied, and perhaps a little heavier than other German white wines.

Rheinhessen (*Rhine Hesse*): Starts at Worms and runs north to the point where the Rhine swings around Mainz to flow west as far as Bingen before resuming its northerly course. Just below Worms is the Liebfrauenkirche, the Church of Our Lady, rising from the vineyards, which has given its name to a wine everyone has heard of—*Liebfraumilch* (Milk of the Blessed Mother). It is one of the best known names among people who order German wine abroad. However, Liebfraumilch apart from indicating that it comes from Rheinhessen, is not a place name, has no guarantee of quality, and is not legally protected as a wine name. It is a romantic appellation, originally given only to the wine growing in the vineyard around the Liebfrauenkirche, and later freely used by anyone else. If you want quality, you must select the wines from Rheinhessen according to the villages where they grow —Nierstein, Nackenheim, Oppenheim, Bingen, Bodenheim are the best. (Nierstein, Nackenheim, etc., is the name of the village, whereas *Niersteiner, Nackenheimer,* and so on—which you see on the bottle labels—is the name of the wine. One is the noun, the other the adjective, which is followed by a more specific local designation.) Rheinhessen wines are light, fruity, and soft. The interior types, however, which are grown in the interior away from the Rhine river, are quite good, and have a tang of the soil; these are usually sold abroad under the name of Liebfraumilch, without any further designation. Among the quality Rheinhessen white wines, try *Niersteiner Rehbach, Niersteiner Heiligenbaum, Nackenheimer Engelsberg, Oppenheimer Herrenberg, Binger Rosengarten, Binger Schlossberg, Bodenheimer Hoch, Bodenheimer Kapelle.*

Nahe Valley: Running into the Rhine from the south at Bingen (a city with a reputation for hard drinking, hence the English expression "go on a binge"), is the Nahe, a small river in whose valley grow some excellent smooth wines—try *Monzinger* (a favorite for several centuries), *Kreuznacher, Norheimer* and, if you want an unusual bottle, a *Schloss Böckelheimer Kupfergrube,* whose peculiar earthy black currant taste may be due to the copper in the soil.

Rheingau: Extends along the Rhine's right bank, from Bingen to Mainz, but across the river from them. This is the home of the finest German wines, which is to say some of the best wines in the world. *Johannisberger,* and its subdivision, *Schloss Johannisberger,* which was the label on the finest bottle of Rhine wine the writer has ever tasted herself, lies in this area. So does Hochheim, which gave the English language the word it applies indiscriminately to all Rhine wines—*Hock* —although Hochheim, being farthest east of the Rheingau towns, isn't on the Rhine at all, but on the Main. So does Rüdesheim, a quarter of whose vineyards were dug up by bombs which fell on them during the war, and whose wines are a little stronger than the other Rheingau wines, having a very golden color and an extraordinary full body; in good vintage years they are considered the best of the Rheingau. So does Markobrunn, which was Thomas Jefferson's favorite. So does Rauenthal, the most expensive of the Rheingau wines, and, many connoisseurs believe, justifiably so, for it is the fruitiest of all.

Middle Rhine: Here the situation becomes bewildering. There are hundreds of good wines, none of them so definitely outstanding among its fellows as to make it the undisputed champion. The best that can be done is to suggest a few good names—the wines of Bacharach (try a *Bacharacher Wolfshöhle*), and those of the nearby communities of Steeg, Oberdiebach and Engholl; *Bopparder Hamm,* a rather heady wine with a strong bouquet; and farther north the Linz and Königswinter vintages.

Mosel Wine-growing Region: Consists of the larger Mosel valley and of the smaller valleys of Saar and Ruwer, both of these two rivers flowing into the Mosel near Trier. For this reason, the region is known among the wine-growers, wine dealers, and wine drinkers as Mosel-Saar-Ruwer. But the vast majority of the superb white wines come from the vineyards of the Mosel valley proper. The Mosel region grapes make very dry and subtle wines, lighter and more delicate than those of the Rhine. They are probably the best dry white wines in the world. They possess also a perhaps less romantic quality, but one which was discovered, in the old days of sailing ships, to be highly useful—they prevent scurvy. If you find yourself in the Mosel region, by all means take precautions against this scourge. The best known of these medicines is probably *Bernkasteler Doktor,* which is grown in the central section of the Mosel valley (roughly halfway between Koblenz and Trier) above a colorful small town called Bernkastel. This central section produces the best Mosel wines; other top localities for it are Piesport, Graach, Wehlen, Zeltingen, Ürzig, Erden, Trittenheim, and several others. Anything you order from these vineyards will be excellent, provided that the wine was bottled by the grower. The best types will be quite expensive, even if you buy them where they are grown. The best Saar wines are those of Wiltingen, Oberemmel, Ockfen, and Ayl, and the best Ruwer wines are Maximin Grünhäuser, and various Eitelsbacher types.

Württemberg: Has a tendency to give playful names to wines, a practice which may cause doubts as to their qualities to arise among serious wine bibbers—such as *Lämmler* (little lamb), for a wine which comes from the Stuttgart region; *Sorgenbrecher* (care banisher); or *Elfinger,* whose name is explained by the story that the abbot of the monastery which grew it considered the wine so much too good for the

monks that he refused to let them drink it, but consented magnani-
mously to let them dip their fingers in it and suck them—which caused
the monks to wish that they had eleven (*elf*) fingers on their hands.

Baden: Has vineyards running the whole length of the Rhine, but
their produce, except for the wines of Kaiserstuhl area, does not equal
that of the opposite bank. The best Baden wines come from the south,
against the Swiss frontier, where there are two distinct regions—the
southwest corner of the country, against the Rhine, where only the
Kaiserstuhl area wines are outstanding—try *Ihringer Winklerberg* or
Edinger Steingrube—and the Bodensee region. The Lake wines are not
very strong, but have a good deal of body. *Meersburger* is as good as
any. The *Weissherbste* wines of this region have a curious pinkish tinge
showing through the white.

Franken (Franconia): There are some excellent dry wines in this
region, bottled in specially-shaped dark green flasks known as Bocksbeutel. The vineyards are located on the hilly banks of the middle Main
valley, and the principal growing centers are Würzburg, Escherndorf,
Iphofen, Roedelsee, Randersacker, Castell. Among the best wines, we
suggest *Würzburger Stein, Escherndorfer Lump, Escherndorfer Kirchberg, Iphöfer Julius-Echter-Berg, Ibhöfer Kronsberg* and *Roedelseer Kuchenmeister.*

Red Wines

Although red wine is rarer in Germany, there is still plenty of it. The
Ahr region, north of the Mosel, is red wine country and its produce
is made mostly from the Burgundy-type of grape; it is good, but inferior
to Burgundy; the *Walporzheimer Spätburgunder, Landskroner,* and
Marienthaler Berg are recommended. Since the Ahr is the farthest
north of any wine-producing region in the world, it is not astonishing
that its vintages are thin.

Some of the best German red wines come from the Rheingau—
Assmannshausen, which is smooth, slightly pungent and deceptively
strong—and as good as Burgundy, with which it is often compared. Try
Assmannshäuser Höllenberg. Other good red Rhine wines are *Ingel-
heimer,* from Rheinhessen, and *Dürkheimer Feuerberg,* from the Pfalz.
For a Württemberg red, *Schwaigern* may be recommended and from
Baden, *Oberrothweiler Kirchberg.*

Sekt: There are also German sparkling wines, called *Sekt,* from
various areas. Sparkling wines are not natural wines, and in Germany,
it is definitely the lesser wines that are converted into sparklers. Some
of them carry vineyard names on the labels, such as *Schloss Johannisberger* or *Steinberger,* while others derive their names from their producers, among the better ones *Henkell* (Henkell Privat being about tops

of this kind), *M.M.* (standing for Matheus Müller), *Deinhard, Söhnlein, Rheingold.* With the new prosperity, Sekt-drinking has become very popular, especially in areas where no wine is grown, and dozens of new brands have come out, often of low quality.

Beer and Schnaps

Beer. It is hardly necessary to remark that Germany is the greatest brewing country in the world and Munich the greatest brewing city. It is strictly a matter of taste whether you prefer the light Munich beer (*Helles*) or the dark (*dunkles*), the strong light (*Heller Bock*) or the strong dark (*Dunkler Bock*), the even stronger *Salvator* or perhaps one of the other similar beers that carry Latin names and are produced at the beginning of the spring, the *Wiesenbier* or *Märzenbier,* almost equally strong and made for *Oktoberfest,* or the lighter *Weizenbier* or *Weissbier* as it is known in Southern Germany, made from wheat.

For hot-weather refreshment, however, the Berliners have their own Weissbier specialty; ask for *eine Weisse mit Schuss* or *eine Weisse ohne Schuss,* depending on whether you want (or don't want) a shot of raspberry extract added. Unless you're strong on sweet drinks, you'll likely prefer it *ohne Schuss* (without).

Braunschweig (Brunswick) produces a dark bittersweet beer without hops called *Mumme,* about which some connoisseurs rave; but as others pour it into light beer, citing this as an improvement, one wonders if a beverage which is better when adulterated could have been really topnotch in the first place. Franconia goes to the opposite extreme and makes its beer extra rich in hops. Bamberg produces a "smoked beer" (*Rauchbier*); Bayreuth, "baker's" beer (*Bäckerbier*); Kulmbach, "frozen beer" (*Bayrisch G'frornes*), which is made from a frozen extract and is probably the beer with the highest percentage of alcohol made anywhere. The opposite to this is Cologne's low alcohol content *Kölsch* beer, which is almost white, while Düsseldorf produces an amber variant of it called *Altbier.* These are refreshing drinks on a hot day, light enough not to make you sleepy. Dortmund is a great brewing city, making a low alcohol content brown beer and tremendous quantities of light beer (66,000,000 gallons yearly). Hannover produces *Einbecker,* from which the term bock beer is derived; it was first brewed in the 14th century. The oldest beer in Germany is probably *Weihenstephan,* produced by the brewery of the School of Agriculture in Freising, Bavaria (for commercial purposes); this brewery was founded in 1040, and the school is a part—no wonder—of the University of Munich.

Distilled Drinks. It is the practice in many parts of Germany to drink *schnaps* and beer together, using the latter as a chaser. Schnaps is usually clear and strong. In Dortmund, a *Doppelstöckiger Münsterländ-er Korn* is usually tossed down before the beer, and you are not preserved from the danger of taking too many by inability to pronounce this long name when you shouldn't, because "Korn" will suffice. A similar drink is *Steinhäger.* In Schleswig-Holstein, the Korn will be flavored with juniper like gin. The Rhineland is fanciful in what it takes with its beer—*Bäs* made from juneberries, or *Fisternöllecken,* distilled from rye, and served with raisins and sugar. Amongst the German brandies Asbach is most recommendable. Both brands, *Asbach Uralt* and *Asbach Privat,* are tasty and mild.

If you like caraway seed flavor, try *Doppelkümmel* in Hamburg. Since you're getting up towards Scandinavia, you will also find plenty of Aquavit in this area. The Black Forest region goes in for fruit brandies—cherry (*Kirschwasser*), raspberry (*Himbeergeist*) or plum (*Zwetschgenwasser*). The Frisian Islanders have corn brandy—ask for *Doornkaat* or *Söpke.* They are also great tea drinkers, so in cold weather they reconcile their taste for strong drinks and for tea by producing *Teepunsch,* tea with rum in it. If you're in Hamburg in cold weather, ask for a *Steifer Grog*—rum, hot water and sugar. *Steif* means stiff, and it is—and so is German liquor in general.

SHOPPING

A Wealth of Craftsmanship

Germany is a consumer's paradise. From the sumptuous jewelry and fur shops along the fashionable city arcades to the humblest country gift shops, it is a land of plenty. However slender your means, you will always be able to afford some typically German mementos of your visit.

Craftsmanship is the universal quality. Here is a nation that likes to see things properly done, and has a high regard for the discipline that craft work needs. Clay, glass, metal, wood, cloth and leather, wax and even flowers have for centuries been transformed by German craftsmen into the finest—and often, the most intricate—household goods, clothes and works of art. Today they are combined with the latest synthetic materials but always with the same careful attention.

Porcelain

German ceramics have been famous for centuries. Perhaps the most celebrated have always been of porcelain, a smooth, pale clay which bakes to a dazzling white. The handmade dinner services of Meissen, Nymphenburg and Rosenthal have found their way to the tables of royalty throughout the Western world, but simpler handmade pieces are also to be found. Meissen is the oldest, always marked with a pair of tiny, blue, crossed swords. The best-known patterns are the Onion, the Vine-leaf and the Dragon, but they are expensive, so if you find what looks like Meissen offered cheap, beware: it is probably a forgery.

The Nymphenburg factory produces a smaller number of more easily recognizable designs, in particular the hand-painted figurines of famous characters in folklore. Cheaper than these, but no less beautiful, is the wide range of Rosenthal porcelain, marked with a crown between two crossed lines or roses.

Rougher Clays

There is also much ceramic work with stoneware and earthenware. Among the most popular with tourists are the stoneware beer and wine mugs, called *Krüge,* which are mostly made in the Rhineland—especially in the town of Mettlach—and are often ornately decorated and capped with a pewter lid. Their variety is matched by that of the beer-mats, which you will be welcome to take from your table at any restaurant or bar. Throughout the south, you will also find charming earthenware crockery—tiles, pitchers and human figures, hand-painted in a range of local styles. They are always cheaper than porcelain.

Glass

There is an ancient tradition of glass-blowing in Germany—particularly in Bavaria, where fine crystal plates, glasses, platters and jugs can be found. But they are expensive. If you want to enjoy the fruits of the craft, seek out one of the many small factories—like those around the Chiemsee Lake—where simple tableware is still handmade. It is fascinating to watch the subtle craft, each piece having some unique quality of its own, a personal touch which machine-made products cannot offer.

Lenses

Another branch of German glasswork is lense-making. Until recently, German cameras, binoculars and microscopes dominated the world market, but the rise of Oriental competitors—producing cheaper goods of equal quality—has changed this situation. Nevertheless, Zeiss and Leica cameras are still first-class, while binoculars by Leitz and Hensolt remain status symbols among horseracing and bird-watching pundits.

Clocks

Precision is very dear to the German heart, and nowhere more so than when it is a question of telling the time. Together with their neighbors, the Swiss, the Germans still make the world's finest timepieces. In some categories of clock, there are cheaper imported goods of equal quality, but two types remain typically German—the charmingly traditional cuckoo clock, housed in a miniature wooden chalet and hand-painted in attractive colors, and the 400-day clock, which needs winding only once a year. Both are made in the Black Forest region but can be bought relatively inexpensively throughout southern Germany.

Household Goods

The same fascination with precision in glass and metal can be found in a wide range of steel household goods. Knives, penknives and scissors; pocket manicure sets, beautifully finished and usually fitted into leather cases; high-quality car tools; medical and optical instruments; gracefully designed kitchen equipment, all are readily available. Among the best are those from the town of Solingen. Look out for the exquisite Solingen carving knives and forks, with forest scenes etched into the steel. Two other main manufacturers of steel goods are Menckels, always recognizable by the pair of tiny cubist twins stamped on the metal; and Württenbergische Metallwarenfabrik, stamped with the letters WMF in a tiny box.

Wood

Woodcarving has long been a native skill in Bavaria, and its ingenious products are to be found all over Germany. The most popular are the small religious statues, mostly of saints, although you will frequently find a Christmas Crib scene, complete with the Christ Child, Wise Men, assorted shepherds and barnyard animals. These can make a really delightful Christmas present to take home with you. Simple wooden toys are also mass-produced and are quite cheap. But for the visitor, perhaps the most interesting wooden gifts available are the musical boxes, called *spieldosen,* typically about seven inches high and crowned with tiny carved statues of mythical heroes, heroines and villains which circle to the tinkling music.

Dolls

Germany's most celebrated dolls have remained unchanged for over 50 years—the stuffed, cloth Käthe Kruse collection: their oil-painted faces and real hair, sewn strand by strand into their heads, are known to every German child and most of the adults too.

More recently, another collection—based on sketches of children by the nun Berta Hummel—have become equally well known. The Hummel family contains such favorites as the Little Wanderer, complete with bowler hat, carpet-bag and umbrella. The Trachten dolls, dressed in a variety of traditional costumes, are also popular: some are rendered more functional by making them into teapot warmers and egg cozies.

Toys

The best German toys are either simple and sturdy or else mechanically very complex. Among the former are excellent wooden toys for babies and small children—rattles, simple bricks and compact, colorful cars, animals and farmyard scenes. Among the latter are superbly constructed models of planes, boats and cars, often electric, sometimes clockwork. Märklin toy trains, in all their variety and accurate representation, are equal to any of their kind in the world, and are much cheaper to buy in Germany than elsewhere.

Clothes

Germans are smart and they like visitors to be equally well-attired. If your wardrobe needs replenishing, this is a splendid country to do it in. Prices are favorably comparable with other European marketplaces, and the quality is invariably good. This is especially true of children's clothes: the range of styles and colors, in all sizes, is admirable.

Of all the Germans, the Bavarians cling with tenacity to their traditions, and clothing plays an important part in this: some of the most famous typically "German" clothes hail from this area. Look out for the *Dirndl*—a prettily printed summer dress with leg-o'-mutton sleeves, a deep neckline and a contrasting colored apron; the *Lodenmantel*—a thick shepherd's cape made from waterproof Loden wool cut in a semi-circle and topped with a hood or high collar; the famous green, felt hunting hats, which usually sport a feather; the warm gray, elegantly cut folk-jackets, trimmed with green, which are often worn with *lederhosen*—gray suede leather breeches or shorts—sometimes with a wide pair of leather braces.

Leather

Leather clothes are popular throughout Germany, usually cut in modern styles, but no less solidly made than the Bavarian lederhosen. Overcoats, casual jackets, waistcoats and shirts, made from a wide range of leathers and suedes, can be found in every town. Leather shoes are also of the finest quality, sturdy and stylish, with as large a range for children as for the grown-ups. Leather luggage is also popular: from magnificent and expensive suites of matching suitcases to the humble handbag in all its myriad forms, this is a fine investment for any regular traveler. You should be warned, though, that however good the quality in leather goods, there are not that many real bargains to be found.

Furs

From the most expensive imported minks to cheaper furs from the local fox, there is a wide range of beautifully made fur clothes to be found in Germany. Frankfurt in particular is a great fur center, and the annual Fur Fair has brought many dealers to the city. The streets around the Central Station will provide you with the best value in high-quality furs in the country. In sports shops, you will also find imitation fur clothes and boots at very reasonable prices.

Sports Equipment

The Germans take their sports seriously and attach great importance to the proper clothes and equipment. In the south there is a plethora of mountaineering gear, wonderfully thick socks, breeches and jerseys; boots and crampons; ropes and pulleys; fly-weight tents and camping stoves. For the ski enthusiast there is the very best in clothing, skis of the most modern design and boots.

In the north, where yachting is a popular sport along the North Sea coast, you will find the sturdiest of windproof anoraks and sea-trousers as well as boats and boating gear.

In the Harz Mountains you will find everything conceivable for the happy hunter, and all over the country you will be able to get tracksuits and jogging shoes in astonishing variety, so that you can keep up the good work you started back home.

Music

Germany's great musical tradition has provided the makers of some of the world's finest instruments with plenty of employment. For the serious pianist there are the famous pianos of Blüthner and Bechstein. For less ambitious musicians there are splendid percussion instruments, drums, triangles, wooden xylophones, cymbals and the finest harmonicas and recorders, made by Hohner. Taking a grand piano back home as a memento is carrying things a bit far, but a classy penny-whistle might provide a happy winter evening by the fire. Germany is also the major sheet-music producer in Europe.

Books

A pleasant way of remembering a trip anywhere is to get one of the local picture books, even if you find the text tricky to follow. Germany is particularly good with this kind of book. They are available everywhere, even in the railway and filling stations you will find them, shelf upon shelf, alternating with a wide selection of maps—which the Germans love, in all their meticulous detail—and guide books. For those who enjoy high quality paper, there is also a fine range of personal and office stationery.

Wax

Being a sentimental people, the Germans love to celebrate anniversaries, religious and personal, and candles play an important part in the festivities. You will see shops which sell nothing but candles and wax sculpture. Some of the nicest are for children: Märchen candles, engraved with fairytale characters, and marathon birthday candles, marked off into sections which burn for three hours each, which are brought out each year at the birthday party.

For Christmas, there are the traditional red candles for the pine Advent wreath, lit each Sunday of the month before Christmas Day. You will also find candles molded like medieval sculpture, giants and dwarfs, modern candles, futuristic candles, Snoopy candles, in fact anything that can be reproduced in wax will have a candle to match.

Germany is also a major producer of charming Christmas tree decorations in wood, glass, paper and, of course, in wax.

Dried Flowers and Dried Fruit

Dried flowers are a specialty of the south; a small bouquet of alpine flowers, for example, makes an attractive lightweight gift to take home. Or there is dried food, from the vast array of the everlasting sausages, sold in strings to hang from your larder ceiling (though you might have some problem getting them through customs). A quiet wander in a grocery department will bring all sorts of goodies to light. Have you ever tried peppermint tea, for example? Candies are as good as anywhere in the world, and sometimes better.

Some Shopping Hints

Finally, a few hints on shopping in Germany. Prices are fixed in all but the open markets, so don't try to bargain; it's a waste of time.

Don't be afraid to ask questions, even in English, the Germans are a very hospitable people and many speak several European languages.

Don't assume that small specialist shops always have better quality goods than department stores. The latter, especially the Kaufhof, Horten and Karstadt chains, sell the finest goods available.

CENTRAL
GERMANY

CENTRAL GERMANY

The Historic Land

Central Germany consists of the modern states of Rhineland-Palatinate, Saar, Hesse and North-Rhine Westphalia. It is an area rich in history. The Romans knew this land, and after they had gone many tribes and races crossed and re-crossed it and fought over it during the days of the Völkerwanderung (the Great Migrations). Later the Holy Roman Empire of the German Nation sat enthroned here, and on this territory the pressures and counter pressures of kingdoms, principalities, duchies and free cities moved along their erratic course towards the consolidation of the many pieces of the mosaic that made up the German Empire.

Central Germany really means the Rhineland, not a state as such, but a large historically and geographically unified area that spreads east and west from the Rhine and embraces at least part of most of the states in the region.

To many the Rhineland is the most romantic name in the German gazetteer and the most potent symbol of Germany. It takes its name from the River Rhine, which flows north from Switzerland and into Germany at Basel, entering Central Germany at its most southerly point, the Rhineland-Palatinate. The eastern border of the state is the Rhine itself, its southern and north-western border France, with the tiny state of Saar nestling in its southwestern corner. To the north, Rhineland-Palatinate is bordered by Rhineland-Westphalia. The Saar is one of the gray areas of Germany, fought over and disputed for many years by France and Germany, both of whom wished to benefit from its rich and important coal fields. France claimed the Saar at the end of both World Wars, and, after the last, Germany was able to reclaim it only as late as 1959.

Continuing along the Rhine, north of Mainz, the river takes on its most famous and characteristic aspect. It winds between lovely hills, many of them thickly wooded and fortified with castles on their peaks, an indication that the river was for many years an important line of defense. But proof of the peace and prosperity that the region has also known is supplied by the terraced vineyards that stand on almost every slope and provide the fruity golden wines for which the Rhineland is most renowned.

This part of the Rhineland—still in the Palatinate—is the middle Rhine. It is Rhineland, in the best sense of the word, on both banks now. A little further north, at Koblenz, the Mosel Valley, also world-famous for its wines, joins the Rhine from the west. Above Koblenz, another heavily wooded region, the Westerwald, lies on the east bank. Opposite is the Eifel range, the only part of Germany of volcanic origin. The volcanos are long since extinct, but healing hot springs still bubble up. The basalt cones of the dead volcanos are still in evidence, and the region's many lakes (Maare) are their water-filled craters.

On the east bank, a little further north, is the Bergisch Land, another hilly area whose "singing, ringing" peaks rise as high as 1,500 feet. This is fertile, fruit-growing country, white with blossoms in the spring. The black-and-white frame houses seem designed for operas, not hard-working farmers.

East and north of this region is Hesse. It stretches away as far east as the western border of East Germany and is a castled and forested, mysterious land for the most part, quite different from the gorgeous valleys of the Rhine. However, the extreme southwestern corner is still in the Rhineland, and this area, the Rhinegau, produces the finest of all the Rhine wines. This magnificent liquid is produced in a country worthy of it. Bulwer-Lytton described it as the "most beautiful valley in the world."

Wiesbaden is the focal point of the Rhinegau. It introduces the second great attraction of Hesse—its spas. They swing in an arc from here to the east and north, offering cures for a wide variety of complaints. In the same south-west corner of Hesse is the Taunus, a region of wooded hills and valleys. A little further north, and at quite the opposite end of the scale, is Frankfurt-am-Main, the busiest and most cosmopolitan of all German cities. South of Frankfurt are Darmstadt, for many years one of Germany's principal intellectual centers, and the Odenwald forest.

The Lahn valley is in central Hesse. This area has many delightful and perfectly preserved old towns, foremost among them Limburg and Marburg. Upper Hesse, east of the Lahn valley, is equally quiet and undisturbed. Further north, Hesse assumes its most mysterious quality. It is still largely out of the tourist main stream, and its principal characteristics are its strange and romantic forests and castles. It was this region that provided the inspiration for the Brothers Grimm. The Reinhard Forest, north of Kassel, the area's principal city, was the setting for both *Little Red Riding Hood* and *The Sleeping Beauty*.

Rhineland-Westphalia is the largest and most northerly state in Central Germany. It presents an abrupt contrast to the vivacity of the Rhineland or the haunting mystery of northern Hesse. This is the industrial heart of the country. It contains the highly important cities of Essen and Dusseldorf, both lying in the Ruhr valley, as well as the nation's capital city, Bonn. They are north of Cologne in the Lower, or North, Rhine. The land is flat here, and the river spreads itself over it widely, following a series of grotesque twists and turns as the current becomes sluggish. In many ways it is similar to Holland, with which it shares a common border. On the east bank are the modern industrial cities which sprang up in the fifties and sixties to replace the almost complete destruction caused by the war. Banks of smoking chimneys and enormous modern factories combine to make up the "forge of Germany."

Westphalia is known as the Land of the Red Earth, not only because of the natural color of its soil, but because for centuries the area has been drenched with blood. It has been a harsh land, a land which has seen many battles throughout its history. It seems appropriate that the Ruhr is in its center.

North of the Ruhr is Münsterland, a wide plain dotted with moated castles. The Teutoburger Forest lies to the north east. In its dark depths the Roman legions of Varus met their defeat at the hands of Hermann, the commander of the Germans. This defeat halted the Roman advance and limited the border of their Empire to the eastern bank of the Rhine.

FRANKFURT

The Concrete Phoenix

Frankfurt-am-Main, not long ago a charming, largely medieval town, is now a rather graceless, modern city. Narrow cobbled streets have given way to broad, car-clogged urban highways; oak-beamed houses built higgledy-piggledy are replaced by concrete apartment buildings and massive highrise offices. Destroyed almost entirely by Allied bombers on the night of 22 March 1944, Frankfurt has risen like a phoenix from the ashes, with all the material optimism of the new Germany.

Yet, in many ways, the spirit of the city remains as it used to be. Situated in the middle of Germany, it was always a major crossroads, and is now not only at the heart of the post-war autobahn system but also a major air, ship and rail center. The new airport is one of the biggest and busiest in Europe; there are five large main-line railway stations, connecting the city with all parts of Europe; and the three harbors—connecting with the mighty river Rhine—comprise the largest inland port in the country.

A crossroads always attracts trade, and this has been true of Frankfurt since the Romans first built a bridge across the Main here 2000 years ago. The first customs house was built in the 11th century, providing a regular flow of trade taxes to the city coffers. By the 12th century the city was a major trading center, and the annual late Summer Fair has been held ever since 1240. The Spring Fair is relatively new, dating only from 1330.

Trade brings finance houses, to provide credit and to arrange transactions of money for traders who do not want to carry cash. Following the example of the Flemish in Antwerp, the Frankfurt City Fathers set up their first Stock Exchange (Börse) in 1595. Banking became an important business and the oldest banks are still functioning today: Lauteren and Co., Hauck, and Bethmann. The Frankfurt Jewish community, though confined to a ghetto within the old town walls, was to produce some of the world's greatest financiers, including the Rothschild Family, who opened their first bank in 1798. The bankers of Frankfurt played a part in the American Civil War when they financed the armies of the North at a time when Paris and London were helping the South. By one of the ironies of history, American bombs destroyed the Frankfurt Börse somewhat less than a century later. Today, Frankfurt is still the country's financial center and the city skyline is dominated by the major banks. Trade always goes hand in hand with political power. In the 9th century, Charlemagne set up court here and subsequently the German Emperors of the Holy Roman Empire were elected and crowned here. The city was politically independent for several centuries until this special status was abolished by Napoleon's occupying army in 1805, but it was later re-established within the confines of the German Union, which had its first all-German Parliament in Frankfurt. The City Fathers fought a political battle with the Prussian Monarchy for supremacy of the united Germany, but failed to win, and in 1866 Frankfurt's free status was finally abolished for good.

The political power is gone, but a cultural power lingers on, a spirit of liberalism which has survived several wars. Even in the early days of Hitler's Third Reich, the city's major newspaper, the *Frankfurter Zeitung,* was a spearhead of resistance: sadly, it was also an early victim. Publishing has for centuries been important to Frankfurt, perhaps sparked off by Johann Gutenberg, the inventor of movable type, who set up shop here in 1454. Within decades, the city became the printing center of Europe and the Annual Book Fair is the largest of its kind in the world.

By an odd coincidence, Germany's greatest writer, Goethe, was born here. The remains of his house, lovingly restored after the last war, are now open to the public (see under Old Town). Frankfurt has for many years offered a Goethe Prize for Literature, which has been won by such eminent authors as Gerhart Hauptmann, Sigmund Freud, Albert Schweitzer and Thomas Mann.

EXPLORING FRANKFURT

Frankfurt is not a tourist city: visitors usually have business here or are in transit for other destinations. Yet the city has a charm of its own, something that has survived the wholesale bombing and subsequent reconstruction work, something of the ancient spirit of Frankfurt. You may find it among the few streets that survived the war, or the painstaking reconstructions of major buildings, or—more simply and mysteriously—in one of the old teashops where Frankfurters still gather to read the newspapers and chew over a slice of traditional cake. In addition, the city boasts some excellent museums, art galleries, and one of the best municipal theater companies in Germany—enough to encourage the business visitor to extend his stay for a short period of tourism.

The Old Town

The medieval town (Altstadt) was enclosed by a semi-circular wall on the north bank of the river. It was almost entirely destroyed during the last war, but some of the more interesting buildings have been carefully reconstructed with as many of the original stones and as much of the ironwork as could be retrieved from the ruins.

The most pleasant approach is from the west along Main Kai, separated from the river by a small, grassy park. Just after the Eisernersteg turn left into the cobbled square called Römerberg, dominated by the 13th-century Nikolaikirche: the tower is a reconstruction but some of the interior remains intact. Its forty-bell carillon rings out four times a day. Opposite the church is a group of three gothic buildings, the Römer, for many years a symbol of Frankfurt. This was, for over 500 years, the City Hall, and it now houses a small museum. Outside, in the center of the square, which is the scene of great festivity on national holidays, is a fine 17th-century fountain topped by a statue of Justice, one of four city fountains to have survived the bombing.

Beside the Nikolaikirche is the main City Museum. Here you can see a perfect scale model of the Old Town, complete with every street, house and church, and—on the floor above—the astonishing city silver.

One piece in particular is worth examining, a vast table ornament in the shape of a ship, one meter high in solid silver, with a symbolic father at the helm, mother at the bow and two children trimming the gold-fringed sails. Carved across the waters is "Frankfurt als Freistadt," the free city.

Outside once more, you might take a little light refreshment before passing on east to the Cathedral. In the south-west corner of the Römerhof is a rebuilt 17th-century inn. Half houses a traditional Frankfurt-style teashop, and the other a beer-hall and restaurant. Schopënhauer, the philosopher, lived the last years of his life next door, in a house overlooking the river.

You will see the 300-foot, red sandstone tower of the Cathedral of St. Bartholomew as soon as you leave the Römerhof. Built between the 13th- and 15th-centuries, it survived the bombs of the last war, along with some 14th-century carved pews and 15th-century murals, which had been bricked up in anticipation of disaster. These treasures now add dignity to an otherwise unremarkable interior. The German Emperors used to be crowned here in days gone by. One of the most interesting features of the tower is the view from the top. This is no longer open though you might—during the low season—gain special access.

Behind the cathedral is the old Cloth Hall (Leinwandhaus), built in 1399 as a textile sample room for fairs. Later it became a court building and is now a small museum. Pass it on your right, and turn left towards Kurt-Schumacher Strasse, which will take you to the Karmeliter-kloster, faithfully reconstructed from pictures and plans of the original, which dated from the 14th and 15th centuries.

Now we turn left along Berlinerstrasse, passing the oval-topped Paulskirche, where the first all-German Parliament sat in 1848. A little further on is the oldest remaining building in the city, a 13th-century chapel once belonging to the palace constructed by Friedrich Barbarossa. Opposite stands the only wooden building to escape the British and American bombs, a fine half-timbered Renaissance house.

At the Kornmarkt, turn right and then left, which takes you onto the Grosser Hirschgraben, where the reconstruction of Goethe's house stands. Furnished and decorated in the 18th-century manner, it gives a good impression of how the great man's life-style might have been.

You are now outside the Old Town walls, and ready to embark on the next leg of your tour, which takes in the so-called New Town (Neustadt). If you are hungry, stop off at the marvelous delicatessen shop two short blocks north, in Grosse Brockenstrasse, before continuing on your way.

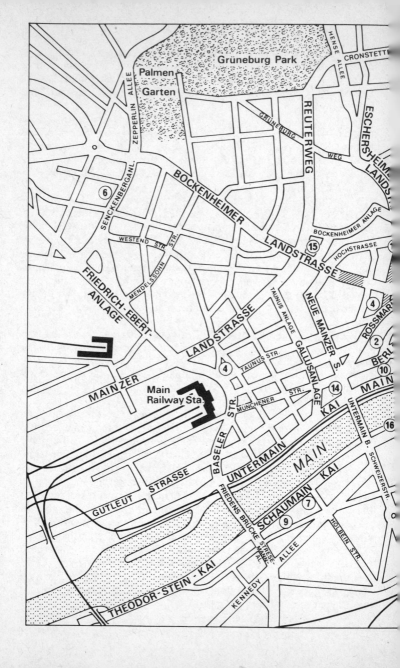

FRANKFURT

▨ Pedestrian Zone
1 Cathedral
2 Goethe's House
3 Romer (Old Town Hall)
4 Tourist Information
5 Post Office
6 Senckenberg Museum
7 Städel Museum
8 Applied Arts Museum
9 Sculpture Museum
10 St Leonard
11 St Katherine
12 St Paul
13 Eschenheim Tower
14 Theater
15 Opera
16 Flea Market

The New Town

There are two possible routes now. Following one of them, you can walk east along the Zeil, the city's largest pedestrian zone, lined with one department store after another, and the site of the old cattle market, which leads you out of the New Town at Alfred-Brehm Platz to the entrance of the Frankfurt Zoo.

The Zoo is one of the chief attractions of Frankfurt, the oldest in Germany, except for that in Berlin. Its remarkable collection includes a Bears' Castle, an Exotarium (aquarium plus reptiles) and an aviary, reputedly the largest in Europe, where many of the birds can be seen in a natural setting. As is generally the case in Germany, the Zoo is a recreational center where animals are not the sole attraction. Others include a restaurant, a café, and afternoon concerts during the summer, while its Kleines Theater im Zoo offers plays.

The second route will take you northwards towards the Eschenheimer Turm, passing—at the northern end of the Rossmarkt—Frankfurt's original place of execution. It was here that Faust's Marguerite was put to death for infanticide.

The area around the Turm has become the financial center, with vast new office buildings which tower over the entire city. Some are of great architectural interest—notably the Bayer-Haus and the Post Office Telecommunications Center—but they are frowned upon by many an old Frankfurter, resistant to change. As you walk west from the Turm, along the parkway that marks the site of the old ramparts, there is a sea of construction work on newer and even higher buildings. The most impressive, so far, is the greenish steel and glass Zurich-Haus, owned by an insurance company.

Walking south-west, you pass the old Opera House at Opernplatz, recently entirely renovated within the old walls, which were gutted by fire during the war. The new complex contains conference halls, theaters and a cinema. Further south, along Neue Mainzer Strasse is the Municipal Theater (Schauspielhaus), which also contains an opera house: the productions here are first-class. A few minutes further south is the Unter-Main Brücke and the river.

For a quieter stroll, turn east at the Turm instead of west, and follow the parkway along Eschenheimer Anlage and Friedberger Anlage. There is little to see but everyday life in Frankfurt, which to many a visitor provides as interesting a time as the more sensational round of buildings and statues. When you come to the river, you will be well positioned to start a short visit to Sachsenhausen, which is just across the Ober-Main Brücke.

Sachsenhausen

Formerly a village separate from Frankfurt, Sachsenhausen is said to have been established by a colony of Saxons conquered by Charlemagne and resettled here by the Main. It is now largely a residential area and—having suffered far less from the war than the city itself—it contains much of authentic historical interest. It is, of course, more recent, mostly dating back less than 200 years, but there are pockets of 16th- and 17th-century houses, which give a fine impression of what the Old Town must have been like.

Once over the river, turn half-right along Frankensteiner Strasse, which leads into the old nightlife quarter around the eastern end of Schulstrasse. Here you will find a charming assortment of old and new, with nightclubs, discos and restaurants scattered among the half-timbered houses and narrow alleyways. You might care to pick out a venue for the evening, returning after the theaters have closed. Then continue west along Kolb Strasse, past elegant 19th-century residential houses, into the busy shopping area of Schweitzerstrasse. This is where many working Frankfurters live. There are several old inns where the specialty is apple cider, which the locals call *appelwein,* a strong, tasty brew.

At the north end of the Schweizerstrasse you arrive at the river again. If you have time, there is a pleasant walk along the Schau-Main Kai, where you can enjoy the river traffic and a view of the busier northern part of the city across the water. On the left, you will see the Städel Art Institute, which contains a fine collection of paintings, including works by Dürer, Renoir, Monet and Vermeer, as well as Rembrandt, Rubens and other great masters.

A little further on is the charming 17th-century Liebeg-Haus, now administered by the Städel Institute to house their collection of classical, medieval and Renaissance sculpture. You can return to the northern bank of the river by way of the Friedens Brücke, which leads you, via Baseler Strasse, to the Main Station, at the heart of Frankfurt's West End.

The West End

From the Station (Hauptbahnhof) three avenues lead to central Frankfurt: Kaiserstrasse, Munchenerstrasse and Taunusstrasse. They are lined with shops, restaurants, strip clubs and cinemas, and once made up a lively and colorful district. Unfortunately, as in city playgrounds all over Europe, there is a rather desolate and unfriendly atmosphere here today, with blaring music and neon lights taking the place of the welcoming charm that once prevailed.

More interesting for the visitor on the lookout for something characteristic of Frankfurt, is to wander north along Friedrich-Ebert-Anlage
to the Messe, a vast complex of exhibition halls where some of the
world's greatest trade fairs are held. Apart from the two major fairs in
spring and late summer, there are several important smaller ones,
notably the Poultry Show in January, the Automobile Show in March,
the Fur Fair at Easter and the Book Fair in early fall.

Further north still, along Senckenberg-Anlage, is the delightful Pal-
men Garten, one of the most complete botanical gardens in Europe. It
includes a number of special collections—like the 2½-acre rock garden, the rose and rhododendron garden and a splendid cluster of
tropical and semi-tropical greenhouses, which contain over 800 species
of cactus and a magnificent Victoria Regia waterlily from the Amazon,
its six-foot leaves capable of supporting the weight of a child.

To the east of the Palmengarten is the Grüneberg Park, the former
Rothschild Estate which is now open to the public. It contains a sports
center and a magnificent office complex designed by the architect Hans
Pölzig in 1925. Originally a munitions factory, these offices were a
target which the Allied bombers missed: they destroyed the elegant
Rothschild mansion instead.

Excursions from Frankfurt

Höchst is Frankfurt's farthest western suburb, on the Main, and was
once a medieval town in its own right, governed from Mainz before
Frankfurt engulfed it. Thus it possesses buildings of the Middle Ages
which, since they remained undamaged, are worth seeing now that the
medieval part of Frankfurt itself has been laid waste. Its importance,
however, is largely industrial, almost all of its citizens being employed
in the machinery, electrical, shoe, and dye works of this quarter. The
last named is the most important, the Höchster Farbwerke being the
largest chemical plant in Germany; it produces not only the aniline
dyes of which Germany once had almost a monopoly, but also such
drugs as salvarsan and diphtheria serum. Höchst has long been a center
of manufactures. In the 18th century it was famous particularly for its
porcelain. This industry is now being revived after a lapse of 150 years,
by the Sudeten Germans who were expelled from Czechoslovakia.

Of the old buildings to be seen in this quarter, by far the most
interesting is the Justiniuskirche, older than anything remaining in
Frankfurt proper, since it goes back to the days of the Carolingians,
that is to say, the beginning of the 9th century. Its older part is early
Romanesque, while the 15th-century choir is Gothic. Some of the
ancient town walls are still in place along the river, together with the
customs tower; there are old timbered houses of the kind similar to

those wiped out by the air raid in Frankfurt, as you climb the hill from the river; and you can also see the ruins of the old castle and the magnificent Bolongaro Palast, once the home of a family of Italian snuff manufacturers who established themselves here in the 18th century. The view over river, fields, and woods from this château is alone worth the trip.

A supermodern contrast to these old buildings is the Höchst Centennial Hall with its huge round roof, designed for use as a concert hall, theater, convention hall and sports arena. Another contemporary addition on the western border of Frankfurt is the Main Taunus Zentrum, a colossal shopping center, the largest in Europe, located in the middle of meadows and woods and featuring some 80 specialized stores along with two supermarkets, several restaurants, many service establishments ranging from gas stations to a kindergarten, parking space for 3,000 cars, fountains and flower beds.

For a more rural ride, take a day trip to the southwest of the city, where you will find the Stadtwald, the City Forest, which is threaded with lovely bridle-paths and roads, as well as containing one of Germany's most beautiful sports stadiums. It was a big forest before the war, when it covered 1,000 acres, but the necessity of replanting 42 acres started the local authorities on a reforestation program that is adding 3,000 acres to the original area.

There are many tremendous old trees in the Stadtwald, not unsurprisingly, as it is the first place in Europe where trees were planted from seed (they were oaks, sown in 1398, while thirty years later evergreens were started in the same fashion). There are a number of good restaurants in the forest, and it would be difficult to imagine a pleasanter place to eat and linger.

Other interesting places that can be enjoyed by excursion from Frankfurt are:

Hofheim, lies 11 miles to the west, starting on the Wiesbaden road, no. 40, or thirty minutes by trains leaving every half hour from the central station; an old Roman town, with a parish church dating partly from the 15th century, a Kurhaus, trips to the beautifully located 17th-century Hofmeier Kapelle, ruins of an old fort, lookout tower and the old suburb of Marxheim. River and forest walks.

Königstein im Taunus, about 5 miles northwest of Soden, can be reached from there by car (alternate routes from Frankfurt are by the direct autobahn, or via Kronberg), or by bus (eight departures daily from the Soden railroad station). There are also four bus services daily from Frankfurt and direct train service hourly.

This is a favorite weekend spot with woods on three sides, and two mountains embracing the town. The old quarter contains many interesting buildings, and the town is dominated by the massive ruins of Königstein castle, usually floodlit during summer weekends.

Kronberg, 10 miles north, in the same direction as Königstein. A lovely old town with a very interesting castle, open 9–12 and 2–5:30. Also reached from Frankfurt by train (about ½ hr.). Less than 2 miles from Kronberg is **Falkenstein,** another small hilly summer resort, with ruins of 13th-century castle of the same name.

Eppstein im Taunus, same road or train as to Kronberg, 15 miles farther north. Chiefly for nature lovers, but there is also the 12th-century Eppstein castle and a 15th-century Protestant parish church.

Bad Soden, to the northwest, 9 miles by car, is reached by starting out on the Wiesbaden road; trains take about 35 minutes and leave the central station at intervals of about an hour. This is a spa with 26 hot salt springs, prettily located on the Sulzbach river. It has a Kurhaus, Kurpark and swimming pool.

Grosser Feldberg is reached by private car or bus from Königstein, by train from Frankfurt to Kronberg, where you shift to a bus. It's the highest of the Taunus Mountains, 2,890 feet, with a wonderful view.

You can visit the remains of a Roman fort at **Wellquelle,** or stay at one of the neighboring villages—in **Relfenberg** (Ober-Reifenberg at 2,000 feet is the highest settlement in the Taunus region, with the ruins of an old castle and an 18th-century chapel); in **Schmitten,** a resort village with a swimming pool; at **Arnoldshain,** where there is a ruined castle and a 12th-century church; or in **Glashütten.** Each of these villages has several pleasant, quiet, and low-priced hostelries.

While in the Grosser Feldberg neighborhood, you can climb the Altkönig to see the remains of Celtic fortifications there.

Bad Vilbel, to the northeast in the Nidda valley, has been a spa since Roman times. By car, leave Frankfurt on the Friedberg road; it's about 8 miles. It is also reached by 57 or 65 buses from the Nibelungenplatz or the railway bus to Lauterbach, or by frequent trains from the central station. Old buildings, pleasant walks in the parks and neighboring country. Kurhaus, swimming pool.

For further excursion possibilities from Frankfurt, see also the Taunus section in the next chapter.

Cheap day tickets on public transport to many of the attractive spots around Frankfurt are offered by the *Frankfurt Tourist Association.*

PRACTICAL INFORMATION FOR FRANKFURT

 WHEN TO GO. Take in folk festivals if you are in Frankfurt at the right times: Whit Tuesday, the Wäldschestag in the Stadtwald near the Oberforsthaus; end of July, the Volksfest am Main; during the summer, the fairs in the various suburbs; the "Dippemess" in September with its colorful crockery stalls and fairground; at Advent, the Christkindchesmarkt on the Römerberg; during Carnival season, the week ending Ash Wednesday, there are big dances in restaurants and public halls everywhere. May to September, try the two-hour steamer ride on the Main (right bank, Eiserner Steg and Untermain bridges) or the all-day trip up the Rhine as far as Rüdesheim (boats leave from Höchst).

Ask at any Lufthansa office, or your travel agent, about the Frankfurt "Stopover" plan: it offers 19 complementary services such as sightseeing, museum and historic site admissions, food and wine tastings, hotel and car rental reductions.

 HOTELS. Most of the larger Frankfurt hotels are located in the vicinity of the main railroad station, not far from the fair grounds. This fact, and because the principal airlines have their offices near the main station, makes it very practical to stay in that vicinity. But it also has its setbacks: the business center of the city is a long walk away (15–20 minutes) and at night some of the streets around the station have a noisy, unpleasant aspect, which doesn't improve very much by day. Since Frankfurt is a very busy commercial city, you are wise to reserve in advance; this becomes a must at the times of fairs, exhibitions, conventions, and so on, that occur frequently.

Do-it-yourself hotel reservation machines have been installed at Frankfurt's airport and the main railway station. It works this way: Arriving visitors push buttons to register their choice of accommodation, price range and length of stay. The computer responds by giving names of hotels that fit the bill and lights indicate their positions on a city map. You then decide on one hotel by pushing another button, insert a ten-mark note (about £2.50) and out comes written booking confirmation of your hotel together with its full address. Six marks constitute a deposit towards your hotel bill, the balance is the service charge due to the machine, already nicknamed "Hot Resy" by the locals. Instructions for its operation are multi-lingual; sixty-five hotels in Frankfurt are programmed into this computer.

Deluxe

CP Frankfurt Plaza, across square from Fair and exhibition grounds, with 1,182 beds, every amenity and superb views from all guest rooms.

Hessischer Hof, Friedrich-Ebert-Anlage 40, near the fair grounds. Modern, tastefully furnished. 160 beds, most rooms with bath, radio and TV. Cuisine of note. Meeting place of industrialists. 300-car garage.

Frankfurt Intercontinental, Wilhelm-Leuschnerstr. 43. Overlooks the Main River; 508 modern rooms on 20 floors, most with fine view, 65 suites and a 306-room, 18-floor annex. On the 21st floor you can dine and dance with a very fine view over Frankfurt: two other restaurants on the ground floor, a wine tavern in Old German style, extensive convention facilities, 500-car garage.

Parkhotel, Wiesenhüttenplatz 36–38, near the main station. 400 beds, almost all rooms with bath. Restaurant of note. Bar and TV room. Rooms in old section can be hot and noisy.

Ramada-Caravelle, in western suburb of Griesheim, a mile from exhibition halls and 10 mins. from airport; 236 rooms, most with bath, radio, TV, telephone; terrace, 3 restaurants, bars, pool, sauna, good parking.

Frankfurt Savoy, Wiesenhüttenstr. 42, near the main station, 151 rooms, modern. Restaurant specializes in grills, and there is dancing in *Le Tourbillon*.

Sheraton, right at airport. 560 rooms, 14 suites, all amenities, pool, sauna. Has direct access to central terminal building, thus to airport rail link service.

Steigenberger Hotel Frankfurter Hof, 17 Am Kaiserplatz. Fine central location. Vast and glittering; 460 rooms with bath. Plush suites. Restaurant and café with inviting outdoor terrace. *Lipizzaner Bar* for smart dancing; a French restaurant, the *Frankfurter Stubb.* A 360-car garage across the street.

Steigenberger Airport-Hotel, a half-mile from airport; 350 sound-proofed and airconditioned rooms. Glass-domed indoor pool on 9th floor with fine view, several restaurants, bars and a nightclub. Hotel bus shuttle service to the airport. Special overnight terms for air passenger arrivals.

Expensive

Arabella, Lyoner Str. 44, south of river in the suburb of Niederrad. 283 rooms with bath and all facilities, including pool. Charming surroundings.

Continental, Baseler Str. 56, not far from the station, an excellent choice, particularly if you wish to stay put for meals. 131 beds.

Euro-Crest Hotel, midway between airport and town, 312 rooms, all airconditioned.

Gravenbruch Kempinski, at Neu-Isenburg convenient for downtown, airport and for motorists. 170 beds, all rooms with bath or shower. Beautiful surroundings, excellent pool; tennis, riding, golf; separate restaurant *Forsthaus Gravenbruch.*

Holiday Inn, City Tower, 1½ miles from city center in Sachsenhausen. 11 miles from airport. 190 rooms include 66 2-story duplex suites.

Holiday Inn, in Sulzbach, at Main-Taunus-Zentrum trade center, halfway between Frankfurt and Rhein-Main airport; 300 rooms with bath, air-conditioning, indoor heated pool, two dining rooms.

National, Baseler Strasse 50, at the main station, 95 rooms with bath. Comfortable dining and unobtrusive professional service.

Savigny, Savignystr. 14–16, not far from main station, modern. 85 rooms, most with bath or shower, and balcony. Elegant and full of atmosphere.

Moderate

In the main station area: both upper (M) are—**Saloniki,** Moselstr. 46, 90 beds, and **Frankfurter Elbe,** Elbestr. 55, 65 beds, good value; both have most rooms with bath or shower.

All (M) are—**Terminus,** Munchener Str. 59, in a street of hotels, 42 rooms, about half with bath; **Westfälinger Hof** nearby at Düsseldorferstr. 10; **Wiesbaden,** Baseler Str. 52, on other side of station; **Atlantic,** Elbestr. 60; all breakfast only; **Excelsior-Monopol,** Mannheimer Str. 11–13, at the main rail station; 95 rooms, 65 with bath. Has reputation for good food.

Near Rathenauplatz there is the 55-room **Schwille,** Grosse Bockenheimerstr. 50. Also in a practical location not far from the Rathaus, is **Rex,** Berliner Str. 31, 60 beds. Smaller and newer, **Zentrum** at Rossmarkt 7.

Near zoo and East Station: Upper (M) are—**Luxor,** Allerheiligentor 2, good, 46 rooms. **Admiral,** Hölderlinstr. 25, 52 rooms, quiet.

(M) are—**Am Zoo,** Alfred-Brehm-Platz, 6, 85 rooms; **Jaguar** (garni), Theobald-Christ. Str. 17, 37 rooms, good facilities.

In the west section: **Schwille,** Grosse Bockenheimerstr. 50, 50 rooms; **Palmenhof** (garni), Bockenheimer Landstr. 91, 39 rooms, near the Palmergarten.

Inexpensive

Best of many are, near the main railroad station: **Ebel,** Taunusstr. 26; **Ambassador,** Moselstr. 12; **Württemberger Hof,** Karlstrasse 14; **Deutsches Haus,** in the same street at number 9; **Goldner Stern,** Karlsruher Strasse 8; **Gloria,** Munchener Str. 15.

In the center you might try the very small **Aida,** Schäfergasse 22, or the equally small **Martha,** Elefantengasse 1 (no restaurant), both pensions.

SUBURBS

In Sachsenhausen, near the apple wine district, are the **Maingau** (M), Schifferstr. 38, 83 rooms, and **Hübler** (M) (garni), Gr. Rittergasse 93, with 50 rooms, both moderate. In Höchst, the **Höchster Hof** (E), Mainberg 3, 140 rooms, most with bath or shower, first class reasonable. In Sprendlingen, 8 miles south, is the first class superior **Air Kongress Hotel im Park,** Eisenbahnstr. 200; central, useful for airport; 92 rooms with bath, out-door pool, sauna.

HOTELS AND RESTAURANTS IN EXCURSION POINTS FROM FRANKFURT

Bad Soden. (E) are **Türck** (garni), near the Eichwald, and **Europahof,** Königsteiner Str. 45. **Am Kurpark** (garni), Kronberger Str., and **Weisses Haus** are moderate.

Königstein im Taunus. The leading establishment is the expensive **Sonnenhof,** 80 beds, all rooms with bath and balcony, recently modernized and enlarged with the best restaurant in the area, also local-color tavern. For horseback riding drive out about 2½ miles to **Rettershof** country manor which also serves very good meals in its restaurant.

La Bonne Auberge is a pleasant French restaurant in Limburger Str., and so is the **Ratsstuben,** Hauptstr. 44, which specializes in seafood, including oysters in season.

For green surroundings, genuine country atmosphere, drive 5 miles to **Wirtshaus Reichenbachtal** in a hidden small quiet valley.

Kronberg. At the upper edge of the town is the super deluxe **Schlosshotel Kronberg,** a converted castle, in large private park with golf course (18 holes) and tennis courts; 54 rooms, 20 baths, suites, exquisite antique furnishings, outstanding cuisine (try lobster salad, woodcock flambé or roast duck), magnificent terrace; perhaps the best castle hotel in Germany.

Rather more intimate is the **Weinstube zur Kugel** (M), Mauerstr. 14, charming restaurant, good choice of food and pleasant wines.

 RESTAURANTS. The best known specialty of Frankfurt is, of course, the frankfurter, a sausage made from every part of the pig, but Frankfurt is also known for many other types of sausage, including a liver sausage known as *Zeppelinwurst.* The city's culinary specialty is *Rippchen mit Sauerkraut* which consists of pickled ribs of pork, nestled in Germany's best known vegetable dish. Frankfurt is also known for its cookies, *Bethmännchen* or *Brenten,* almond cookies flavored with rosewater or rum, particularly prevalent at Christmas, when the city produces its quince paste (*Quittenpaste*).

Its specialty in the way of drinks is *Apfelwein,* hard cider, which you will find especially on the south bank of the Main, in inns that display a green garland over the door to indicate that Apfelwein is on tap there.

Expensive

Among the leading hotel restaurants serving food in elegant surroundings are **Hessischer Hof, Parkhotel,** and **Frankfurt Savoy.**

One of the best of the hotel restaurants is the **Restaurant Francais,** (E), in the Steigenberger Hof. It has, naturally, fine French cooking and should be high on anyone's list for a good evening's dining. Also (E) is the **Frankfurter Stubb,** in the cellar of the same hotel but with a separate entrance near the corner of Bethmann Strasse, offers fine local specialties amidst the décor of mid-19th-century Frankfurt by waitresses in the same period dress. French cuisine of the highest class at **Maison Pierre,** Friedberger Landstr. 60, a small and very reputable restaurant.

Moderate

Ernos Bistro, Liebigstr. 15, moderate to fairly high prices but lavishly praised by gourmets. French cuisine, mostly traditional. In summer you can sit outside. Reservations essential.

For a fine view, try the **Henninger Turm** in Sachsenhausen across the river, a towerlike grain elevator belonging to Henninger Brewery, with two rotating restaurants at the top (about 400 ft.): the **Panorama** and the **Turntable** one floor above, revolving in opposite directions, and a beer tavern at ground level.

Gumpelmann, Am Salzhaus 4, very reasonable, roomy modern restaurant with quick service. Food is substantial and their specialties are pork dishes. **Dippegucker,** Eschenheimer Anlage 40, the name means "Pot Looker" but you'd do better to look at the menu's specialties and salads. Rustic and reasonable.

In the Steigenberger Hotel at the airport, try the **Rôtisserie 5 Continents** for a good grill. **Le Caveau,** Deutschherrnufer 29, is a pleasant restaurant with particularly good food at moderate prices.

There are **Mövenpick** restaurants with snack bars at Opernplatz 1, and in Sulzbach at the Main-Taunus trade center. The Opernplatz branch, called **Rôtisserie Baron de la Mouette,** is especially to be recommended.

WINE AND BEER RESTAURANTS

One of the best wine restaurants in Europe is the ancient **Brückenkeller (M),** Schützenstrasse 6, packed with medieval atmosphere; a huge barrel and antique statues of saints watch over the superior selection of German vintage wines and culinary delicacies. A very popular dining place. Open evenings, not Sunday.

Among the best reasonably priced wine restaurants are **Rheinpfalz-Weinstuben** near the City Theater and **Hahnhof,** Berliner Strasse 64, which have had wine and food from the Palatinate, as has the tiny, 1920-ish **Heyland's Weinstuben,** Kaiserhofst. 7, and the **Pfalzer Weinstube** near the cathedral.

Beer restaurants (you can also get wine) are inexpensive to moderate and serve hearty meals. These include:

Alt Nürnberg, Grosse Bockenheimer Strasse 19, near Rathenauplatz, with old-time décor, is open until 2 A.M. for beer, wine and Nürnberg sausages.

Restaurants specializing in regional dishes and wines (and also serving beer), are well worth while: **Schwarzwald-Stube** (Black Forest). Mainkurstr. 36; the pretty **Weinstube Zur Kugel.** Mauerstr. 14 in the Kronberg/Taunus district and the **Schwarzer Stern** in Kalbächer Gasse, for instance.

APFELWEIN TAVERNS

Frankfurt's Apfelwein taverns are a specialty of Alt-Sachsenhausen district south of the river. Here you drink your apple wine (or *Appelwoi* as it is called in the local dialect) in simple, old-style Stuben to the accompaniment of salt sticks, pretzels, baked river fish, succulent pork dishes, and particularly *Handkäs mit Musik,* which is a typical local treat composed of small pieces of cheese prepared with "music," represented in this case by oil, vinegar, and onions. A bit of real music is often added. You can enjoy Apfelwein, pretzels and music and also take in a roundtrip sightseeing tour with the colorful streetcar "Ebbelwei-Express". Departs Saturdays and Sundays, 1. P.M. and 6 P.M., from the Friedberger Anlage.

One of the better known Apfelwein-Wirtschaften is **Zum grauen Bock,** Grosse Rittergasse 30, a very basic, typical family restaurant for hungry people. Also the very old and atmospheric **Zum Gemalten Haus,** Schweizerstr. 67.

OPEN-AIR EATING

If you like to eat outdoors, there are good restaurants in the Palmengarten and the Zoo, and several beautifully located ones in the City Forest.

An excellent spot is **Hofgut Neuhof,** elegant antique furnishings indoors and country-style garden outside; expensive, located about 8 miles southeast of the city (drive through Neu-Isenburg). Also nearby, a bit east of Neu-Isenburg, is **Forsthaus Gravenbruch;** swimming and horseback riding facilities.

In Neu-Isenburg, at Frankfurter Strasse 1, is the first-class and atmospheric **Ammerländer Schinkenkrug,** which specializes in smoked eel, dry smoked ham and tea prepared in the East Frisian manner, with cream and candied fruit. Also at Neu-Isenburg is the **Alter Haferkasten,** serving, oddly enough, top-notch Italian food.

In Schwalbach, a northwest suburb, is **Haus Mutter Kraus,** renowned for its food since 1799.

FOREIGN FOOD

For an American-type steak try the **Steak House,** Hanauer Landstr. 41. Also **Maredo,** Gr. Bockenheimerstr. 24, serving juicy, charcoal-broiled Angus steaks and crunchy salads. Rather special in nationality and cuisine—especially the steaks—is the Argentinian **Churrasco,** Domplatz 6.

Lung Fung, in the Central hotel, Gutleutstr. 95, is probably leading in Chinese food, with **Tai-Tung,** Fürstenberger Str. 179, and **Peking,** Kaiserstr 15, runners up.

For Spanish, **Stadt Malaga,** Töngesgasse 11. Italian, **Da Bruno,** Elbestr. 15. Fondue and other Swiss dishes at **Schwyzer Hüsli,** Mendelssohnstrasse 56.

Balkan food: **Dalmatiner Stube,** Weissfrauenstr. 3, and **Dalmatia,** Escherheimer Landstr. 444.

Danish smörrebrod at **Alt Kopenhagen,** Steinweg-Passage, and for Russian borscht, **Troika,** Brönnerstr. 21.

CAFES AND PASTRIES

For good pastries **Schwille** in the hotel of the same name, as well as off the Hauptwache Square behind the Katharinen Church. **Hauptwache,** a 250-year old building, has courtyard and sidewalk sections, as well as a roof terrace overlooking the busy square of the same name. **Café Wipra,** Neue Kräme 27, has miniature zoo on the premises.

SHOPPING. Frankfurt's shopping center is on and around Rossmarkt, Goetheplatz, Rathenauplatz, along the Zeil (a pedestrian zone), Hauptwache (a square at the centre of the city's public transport network, where you can shop above and below ground level), and Kaiserstrasse, which leads to and from the main station. Berliner Strasse also has many attractive stores.

 TRANSPORTATION. Frankfurt and its suburbs are well served by tram and bus lines. For taxis dial 23001; there are also some 50 taxi stands in the downtown area. Fare from airport is about DM 25. Guided city bus tours start daily at 10 A.M. and 2:30 P.M. at the north side of the main railroad station from April 1 to end Oct. A roundtrip bus tour of Feldberg, Königstein, Kronberg begins daily at 2:30 from June 1 to Sept. 30 from the same place. Frankfurt is also served by a network of fast suburban electric trains (S-bahn) and the underground system (U-bahn), at present with five main lines.

From Airport. There is an excellent train service to the main station from the airport terminal. The journey takes about 15 minutes at a cost of DM 1.50. The taxi fare would be about DM 25, and the helicopter in to the fair DM 60.

Car hire. *Hertz,* at the airport and Mannheimerstr. 7–9; *Avis,* at the airport, Niddastr. 46, Intercontinental Hotel, Frankenallee 41 and Hanauer Landstr. 66; *Selbstfahrer Union,* in the arrival hall at the airport, at Schlosstr. 34 and Auto Sixt, represented in the U.S.A. by Auto Europe, 770 Lexington Avenue, N.Y. 10021; *Eurocar,* airport at Wiesenhuttenplatz.

Parking. *Parkhäuser* (parking garages) open day and night; *Am Theater,* from Bürgerstrasse, 750 cars; *Platz der Republik,* corner Mainzer Landstrasse and Westendstrasse, 1,000 cars; *Kaiserplatz,* entrance from Bethmannstrasse, 370 cars. About 20 attended outdoor parking lots in the downtown area.

 THEATER. Opera, drama and comedy are performed on the various stages of the ultramodern City Theater (*Städtische Bühnen*). Plays are given also at *Die Komödie,* Am Theaterplatz, in the *Kleines Theater im Zoo* (in the Zoo), and in several others. English-speaking theater Cafe Theater in Bruchstr. 9.

Die Schmiere, a literary-political cabaret theater which calls itself "the worst theater in the world," is in Karmeliterkloster at Seckbächer Gasse 1.

The tickets for the municipal theaters can be purchased at the *Frankfurter Verkehrsverein,* An der Hauptwache (B-level) (9–6:30, Sundays 10–12), or in the theaters themselves (11–1, Sundays 11–12, and one hour before the beginning of the performance). For other theaters at their ticket offices. All tickets also available at the ticket agencies: *Kartenvorverkauf Wagner,* Hauptwache (B-level); *Ludwig Schäfer,* Schweizerstrasse 28a; in Höchst: *Lotterie Beck,* Bolongarostrasse 134.

MUSIC. Frankfurt has three symphony orchestras, the *State Opera House and Museum Orchestra,* the *Hessian Philharmonic Orchestra* and the *Hessian Radio Symphony Orchestra.* There are also several choral societies, of which the most important are the *Cäcilienverein* and the *Singakademie.* Orchestral and choral concerts are given in the Great Hall of Radio Hesse, the City Theater, the halls of the Palmengarten or of the University, and in the *Hochschule für Musik,* Eschersheimer Landstrasse 33.

Organ concerts and concerts of sacred music are given in several churches, while both the British Centre and Amerika Haus give chamber music concerts.

 NIGHTLIFE. There are a number of nice dancing spots, among them: on the top floor of the Hotel Intercontinental (with good view); *Le Tourbillon* in Hotel Frankfurt Savoy; *Jimmy's Bar* in Hotel Hessischer Hof; *Park-Café Odeon* at Friedberger Anlage; *Le Clou* disco at the corner of Hamburgerallee; in *Paradieshof,* Paradiesgasse 23, in the colorful suburb of Sachsenhausen, and in *The Pub,* Dreieichstr. 34, also in Sachsenhausen. *Gemütlich* dinner-dancing to Austrian tunes at *Stadt Wien,* near the cathedral; and a disco at *Pony-Club,* Kaiserhofstr. 6.

The leading nightclub with floorshow is *Imperial,* Moselstrasse 46, with outstanding revues including name artists of the stage, screen and radio. Striptease is the main thing at *Pigalle,* Moselstr. 30; *Ellis Elliot,* Varrentrappstrasse 35: *Casino de Paris,* Kaiserstrasse 51, and many others, mainly in the vicinity of the main station, all crowded with dance hostesses.

For jazz: *Jazz-Haus,* Kleine Bockenheimerstr. 12; *Jazz-Keller,* Kleine Bockenheimer Strasse 18. For Bavarian brass-band type of entertainment: Maier Gustl's *Oberbayern,* Münchener Str. 57.

 MUSEUMS. *Städel Art Institute and Municipal Art Gallery,* Schaumainkai 63, Tues., Thurs., Sat., 10–1. A fine and large collection of old masters, though only a small representation of each one.

Liebieghaus, Schaumainkai 71, 10 A.M. to 5 P.M. Tuesdays through Sundays (Wednesdays until 12 noon). Operated in conjunction with the Städel Institute, this museum contains the city's collection of sculpture—Egyptian, Greek and Roman antique, German and French medieval, Italian Renaissance, baroque, and a small amount of Far Eastern sculpture.

Senckenberg Natural History Museum, Senckenberg-Anlage 25, 9–4 daily, Wed., Sat., and Sun. until 8. Paleontology, mineralogy, geology, botany but especially zoology. The most important single exhibit here, reversing the usual order of things, is an import from the United States—the only complete specimen in Europe of a diplodocus. This 66-foot prehistoric skeleton was found in Wyoming.

Ethnological Museum, Schaumainkai 29, Tues.-Sun., 10–5, Wed. to 8.

Goethe-Haus and Museum, Grosser Hirschgraben 23, near Hauptwache. Open 9–6 daily, 10–1 Sun. This is the house where Goethe was born, with collections of manuscripts, paintings, etc., from his times.

Museum of Artisan Art, Shaumainkai 29, contains furniture, porcelain, glass, silver and textiles from the 18th century.

Emperor Barbarossa Chapel in Saalhof. The Romanesque chapel is the oldest preserved structure in Frankfurt and is the only remnant of the Fortress-Palace built here by the Emperor Barbarossa in 1150–70

SPORTS. The Stadtwald (the City Forest) is the chief center for sports. There is a stadium with three **swimming** pools, 20 **tennis** courts, **archery** stand, **ice skating** rink in winter, and in the immediate vicinity an 18-hole golf course. There is a **horse race** course, with meetings from March to November.

Besides the stadium pools, you may swim in the open-air Brentano Parkbad at Rödelheim, in the northwestern sector of the city; at Heddernheim, north; and at Höchst, southwest, but north of the Main. Indoor pools are in Höchst in Melchiorstrasse (tram 12), in Fechenheim, Konstanzer Strasse 16 (tram 14, bus 64), and Stadtbad Mitte, Hochstrasse 4–8, in the center of the city.

Tennis courts at the Frankfurter Tennis club, at the Wald-Stadion (the stadium), and elsewhere.

Among other sports, you may see **soccer** matches at the stadium, **boxing** in the Festhalle or fairground halls, **motorcyle racing** over the hilly Grosser Feldberg course northwest of Frankfurt, **bicycle racing** in the stadium or in winter in the Festhalle, and **rowing races** on the Main during the June–July regatta.

USEFUL ADDRESSES. City and German travel information. *Frankfurter Verkehrsverein* (Frankfurt Tourist Association), main RR station, opposite track 23, tel. 23–11–08 and 23–22–18, has a special section for room reservations, open in winter 8 A.M. to 9 P.M. (Sundays 12 A.M. to 8 P.M.), in summer from 8 A.M. to 10 P.M. (Sundays from 9:30 A.M. to 8 P.M.). Their other information offices are in the underground shopping area at the Hauptwache subway station (B-level) and in the airport. *Deutsche Bundesbahn* (German Railroads), information about train schedules, in the main station opposite tracks 10 and 11. *City Streetcar and Bus Information,* Rathenauplatz 3. Official tourist organization for all Germany: *Deutsche Zentrale für Tourismus* (German National Tourist Office), Beethovenstr. 69.

Information for Motorists. For incoming motorists ADAC (German Automobile Club) maintains information offices at Schumannstr. 4 (tel. 74 30 1), Wiesbadener Str. and Walter-Kolb-Str. 9–11; here you can obtain information on Frankfurt, reserve a hotel room, change money and hire a driver-pilot to steer you through the city. A.v.D has offices at Lyonerstr. 16.

Travel Agencies. *American Express,* Steinweg 5, and several branches in American military installations throughout the city. Credit card head office in the Moselstr. 4. *Deutsches Reisebüro* (Official German travel agency), Eschersheimer Landstr. 25–27, with a branch at the main station. *Thomas Cook,* Kaiserstr. 11; *Hapag-Lloyd-Reisebüro,* Kaiserstr. 14.

Consulates. *United States,* Siesmayerstrasse 21, tel. 74–00–71. *Great Britain,* Bockenheimer Landstr. 51, tel. 72–04–06.

Business Organizations. *American Chamber of Commerce in Germany,* Rossmarkt 12. *U.S. Trade Center,* Bockenheimer Landstrasse 4.

American Services. *Amerika Haus,* Staufenstrasse 1. American information tel. 72–28–60 (mainly on matters concerning American installations in Frankfurt area).

Reading Matter. *American Book Center,* Reuterweg 80. *The British Bookshop,* Börsenstrasse 17. Wide selection of English-language newspapers and periodicals at various newsstands inside the main station.

Money Exchange. Before and after regular banking hours at the *Wechselstube* of the *Deutsche Verkers-Kredit-Bank* at the main railroad station, daily from 6 A.M. to 10 P.M., and at the airport, daily from 7:30 A.M. to 9:30 P.M.

Post Offices. Open day and night (including telegraph and telephone) are: *Hauptpostamt* (main post office), Zeil 108–110; *Postamt 9,* Poststrasse 16–20, near the main station, and the office inside the main station.

Lost and Found. *Eisenbahnfundstelle,* opposite track 1 inside the main station, for articles lost in trains and at the station, open day and night; *Strassenbahnfundbüro,* Rathenauplatz 3, for items lost in city streetcars and buses; for those lost while traveling by air there is an office at the airport; and the *Polizeifundbüro* is in Police Headquarters at Friedrich-Ebert-Anlage 11, Room 20.

St Boniface

HESSE–SPA COUNTRY

The Land of Healing Springs

This is a region of wooded uplands and peaceful river valleys, of half-timbered houses and fairy-tale castles, of medieval towns and modern commercial cities, where the past gently merges into the present and of vast areas of nature parks which cover one quarter of the state. It is a land bubbling with mineral springs, whose health-giving waters were valued even in Roman times. And today a score of famous watering places cluster along Hesse's chain of spas like beads on a string, while some of the best white wines in the world grow in its southwest corner, in the Rheingau. Also in the same corner are the forested Taunus hills. South of Frankfurt the fruit-scented Bergstrasse hill road takes you to the forest of Odenwald and to southern Germany beyond.

EXPLORING HESSE

The city of Frankfurt is located in Hesse and a number of interesting places east, south, north and west of Frankfurt can be most easily visited by taking short trips from this expanded metropolis, whose borders reach deep into the surrounding countryside.

Immediately east is Offenbach on the Main River, virtually a suburb of Frankfurt but a city in its own right with a long history going back to the 10th century. The landmark of Offenbach is the 16th-century Renaissance Isenburg Castle, today housing a technical school, but the city is perhaps even better known for its German Leather Museum, unique in the world, containing objects made of leather of all types, from all ages and from all over the world; naturally, there is a large section devoted to the history of shoes. It is located here because Offenbach is the center of the German leather industry, in addition to supporting important machine and chemical plants. Those interested in printing and the graphic arts will want to see the Klingspor Museum, where some of the best specimens of world-wide book production from 1890 to the present are displayed.

The chief sights of Hanau, a little further up the river, are the extensive baroque Schloss Philippsruhe and the half-timbered Goldsmith's House with exhibits of local jewelry for which this area is renowned. In the market square is a monument to the famous Grimm brothers, the collectors and writers of fairy tales and folk stories, who were born here (Jakob in 1785, Wilhelm in 1786); Jakob Grimm was also an outstanding philologist.

The Kinzig River flows into Main at Hanau, coming from the nearby Kinzig Valley whose soft meadows are protected by the forested slopes of Vogelsberg and Spessart hills. In the upper section of Kinzigtal are Steinau, where the Grimm brothers spent their childhood, and two small and quiet spas, Bad Orb and Bad Soden (not to be confused with the spa of the same name in the Taunus). At Gelnhausen, nearer to Hanau, you may visit the reddish and still impressive remnants of the 12th-century castle-fortress of Emperor Barbarossa. Philipp Reis, who invented the telephone in Germany at the same time Bell developed one independently in the United States, also lived in Gelnhausen.

A few miles up the Main from Hanau is Seligenstadt, where a Carolingian basilica, built about 825, rears one large and two small spires above the waters of the river. The town possesses many other old buildings and its city walls, with three watch towers and the water tower, are still standing.

Darmstadt and Odenwald

South of Frankfurt and overshadowed by its propinquity is Darmstadt. Yet it is a town with a long cultural history, and its picturesque artists' colony, in the neighborhood of the Wedding Tower and the Russian Chapel, is still the center of much intellectual activity. Its musicians have been better known abroad than its artists. Weber and Flotow lived here for some time—and holiday courses in modern music are given here. Among other prominent Darmstadt inhabitants of the past were the poet Stefan George, who went to school there, and the renowned 19th-century chemist, Justus von Liebig, founder of agricultural chemistry, who was born there. Intellectuals know it for the annual Darmstädter Gespräche, gatherings of prominent philosophers, artists and scientists for discussions on contemporary issues, open to the public, lasting a week and combined with art exhibits.

In addition to the old artists' colony houses and other buildings on Mathildenhöhe (there is also a new artists' colony on Rosenhöhe), the main points of interest are in downtown Darmstadt: the market square with the reconstructed Renaissance Rathaus, the Residence Palace and the White Tower, the Ludwig Column on Luisenplatz; the parish church and the remainder of the 14th-century city walls.

After Darmstadt, you are in the rolling hill country of the Odenwald —Odin's wood, named for the king of the gods of Teutonic mythology. Along its west slope runs the Bergstrasse—the Mountain Road, though it does not appear particularly mountainous, as the slope upward from the Rhine to the Odenwald is gentle enough. The peculiarity of the Bergstrasse is its freak climate. Fruit trees bloom here earlier than anywhere else in Germany, sometimes in March, for the Bergstrasse shares with Frankfurt a climate much warmer than that of the rest of the nation, even its most southerly parts, so not only is this great country for fruit, vegetables and asparagus, but it even grows tobacco. It is wine country too, as you will see for yourself as vineyard succeeds vineyard through Seeheim, Jugenheim, Bensheim and Heppenheim, the last two with especially beautiful half-timbered houses. In September Bensheim is the site of the picturesque and lively Bergstrasse Wine Festival. West of Bensheim is Lorsch with the Carolingian Kings' Hall, built in 774 and once part of a monastery.

Odenwald proper can be explored by two routes soaked in romantic sagas and memories of the past and appropriately named the Nibelungenstrasse and the Siegfriedstrasse. According to legend Siegfried was mortally wounded by Hagen's spear at a well in today's Gras-Ellenbach, reached via the Siegfried road from Heppenheim. The Nibelung Road, only a few miles to the north, crosses the Odenwald in a west-east direction: from Bensheim, passing Mount Melibokus, through Lindenfels, a delightful climatic resort from which you can wander through fields and forests, to Michelstadt with its half-timbered 15th-century Rathaus standing on wooden pillars and the Einhardbasilica built in 827 and of considerable architectural significance.

Less than two miles south of Michelstadt is Erbach with various historic structures ranging from 12th-century watch tower to the baroque palace of the Counts of Erbach-Erbach, housing an outstanding collection of medieval armor and an ivory museum. From here you might return to Darmstadt via Bad König (north of Michelstadt), with its ferrous waters and remainders of the Roman Limes; Neustadt dominated by the impressive Breuberg castle-fortress; Grosse-Umstadt, an island of vineyards in Odin's woods; and tiny Hering with the ancient Otzberg fort above it.

Taunus, Frankfurt's Playground

The wooded hills of Taunus, northwest of the city, are the outdoor playground of Frankfurt: the predilected destination for weekend trips to the small towns and villages hiding in its folds, for walks and hiking tours through its forests, for cross-country horseback riding and in winter for skiing. The excursions from Frankfurt—to Hofheim, Eppstein, Bad Soden, Kronberg, Königstein, Falkenstein, Grosser Feldberg, Reifenberg, Schmitten, Arnoldshain, Glashütten—are all within the Taunus. Oberursel, with its romantic old town streets containing the Gothic St. Ursula Church and the half-timbered Town Hall, is considered the gate to the Taunus. (See also the Frankfurt chapter.)

In the same northerly direction, still within the Taunus region and less than 12 miles from Frankfurt is Bad Homburg, one of Germany's loveliest spas. Its springs were known to the Romans, and from that time on the place has been frequented by health and fun seekers. A fashionable turn-of-the-century rendezvous, it was favored, among others, by pleasure-loving Edward VII, and it gave a name to the hat that is still popular in certain conventional circles.

Monte Carlo may today be the name most associated with roulette, but Bad Homburg preceded it. The French Blanc brothers, who opened the Casino there in 1841, only moved on to found the Monte Carlo Casino in 1866. Its fame as a gaming center caused Dostoevsky to use it as a background for his novel, *The Gambler*.

One of the greatest attractions of Bad Homburg is the beautiful Kurpark. The most popular spring it contains is the highly saline Elisabethbrunnen. Two of the park's features are a Siamese temple and a Russian chapel, mementos of two of Bad Homburg's distinguished visitors, King Chulalongkorn of Siam and Czar Nicholas II.

The chief sights of Bad Homburg are the 17th-century Schloss, the former residence of the Landgraves of Hesse-Homburg, whose state apartments are well worth visiting. The garden around the Schloss is famous for its two great cedars of Lebanon, now more than a century and a quarter old. The Weisser Turm, a 12th-century tower that remains from the castle's earliest form permits a good view of the sizable town of Homburg. The Church of the Redeemer has a rich marble and mosaic interior.

A unique attraction of Bad Homburg is not in the town itself, but four-and-a-half miles away, at Saalburg. Here you can see the best preserved Roman fort of the 342-mile-long Limes, the northern border of the Roman Empire and part of the wall of fortifications which the Romans built from the Rhine to the Danube. The earliest part of this fort is 2nd century and the Romans held it until the latter part of the 3rd century. The Roman structures were not only excavated when they were discovered, they were rebuilt, with the result that it is possible today to envisage the life of a Roman garrison outpost settlement by inspecting Saalburg, just as you can understand Roman civilian life by visiting Pompeii. In addition to the fortifications proper, you may see the administrative quarters, the granary (now a museum containing more than 30,000 relics of Roman times), the wells, armories, front and rear camps, the parade ground with its catapults, the houses, shops, baths, and temples of the village that sprang up around the fort during its long existence as a military center.

Bad Homburg lies on the "international promenade of spas" which stretches across Hesse from Wiesbaden near the Rhine to Bad Sooden-Allendorf at the East German border east of Kassel. At the northern tip of Taunus is Bad Nauheim, whose naturally warm carbonic acid springs are particularly beneficial in disorders of the heart and blood circulation. The beautifully-treed Kurpark contains a small lake, many flower beds, a golf course, tennis courts, a relaxing Kurhaus and a heart research institute in addition to cure installations.

Wiesbaden, Queen of Spas

On the shortest route Wiesbaden is only half-an-hour's ride west of Frankfurt, but taking a road closer to the Main river you first come to the village of Hochheim, submerged in vine leaves. Its fine Rhine wines, called Hochheimer, were so much in favor in England that all Rhine wines to this day are referred to as "hock," an abbreviated and anglicized version of Hochheimer.

One of the world's leading spas, Wiesbaden has long enjoyed international renown, and has always been a favorite with royalty. Crowned

heads are few and far between today, and Wiesbaden today houses the
European headquarters of the U.S. Air Force.

Even if it had not been for the healing qualities of its hot saline
springs, particularly efficacious against rheumatism, Wiesbaden was
bound to attract visitors, for the natural beauty of its situation is
combined with accessibility from big cities. It is in the Rheingau, one
of the loveliest stretches of the Rhine Valley, and the place where the
best wine grapes grow. It lies next to the autobahn, near Frankfurt and
across the Rhine from Mainz, the capital of Rhineland-Palatinate. The
city itself is set back from the river; its suburb of Biebrich fronts on it.
Here the river steamers stop and the baroque castle of the Dukes of
Nassau extends its imposing façade along the shore. Wiesbaden is noted
not only for its fine parks, especially the Kurpark, but also for the
beauty of the walks in its neighborhood.

Amid these ideal surroundings, activity goes on about the pillars of
the famous Brunnenkolonnade (Fountain Colonnade) and Theaterkolonnade (Theater Colonnade), mostly in the Hessian State Theater
and the neo-classical Kurhaus. World-renowned artists appear in operas and concerts, plays are given not only in German but occasionally
also in French or English, and the International May Festival presents
opera companies, ballet groups and theatrical troupes from many countries. And at all seasons, the roulette wheels spin and the baccarat shoe
circulates in the Kurhaus Casino.

Wiesbaden is also the capital of the State of Hesse, whose Landtag
(state parliament) sits in the former city palace of the Dukes of Nassau
on Schlossplatz. Not far away at the Kaiser Friedrich Baths is the
oldest structure in the city, a Roman Arch dating from A.D. 300, while
one of the newest, the airy and glass-walled Rhein-Main-Halle exhibition and convention hall is in the vicinity of the main station. On the
Neroberg elevation in the northern outskirts, reached by the oldest
German cable car, constructed in 1888 is another building connected
with the Nassau family: the Greek-Orthodox Chapel constructed over
a century ago as a memorial church for a romantic Russian-born
Duchess of Nassau who died in the flower of her youth.

From Rheingau to Lahn Valley

West of Wiesbaden the steep and sunny river slopes of the Rheingau
hills are covered with vineyards, whose grapes give some of the best and
most famous white wines in the world. Half-timbered and gabled wine-
producing villages, with many castles about them, are strung along the
right bank of the Rhine.

The best known and the most popular is Rüdesheim, chief center of
this most intensively cultivated part of the Rhine wine region. Rüdesheim is a name connoisseurs delight to see on a wine label and the

importance with which the town takes the art will be obvious if you visit one of the wine cellars where the great casks have elaborately and lovingly-carved heads, the Museum of Wine History in the old Brömserburg Castle, or attend the September wine festival. Stop off too at the old Drosselgasse, a small street lined with wine taverns. But Rüdesheim has other attractions than its wine (and brandy, for that is made here too, as well as Sekt, the German version of champagne). Few Rhine towns are richer in beautiful old houses, whose half-timbered walls are enriched by quaintly-shaped gables and turrets. And in addition to Brömserburg, which is the lower castle, there are Boosenburg, the upper castle, and soaring above the Rhine on a nearby hill, the mighty towers of the ruins of Ehrenfels; all three castles are from the 13th century, overgrown with moss and ivy.

Above Rüdesheim, on the elevation of Niederwald, stands a colossal statue erected in the 19th century to commemorate German unification. You can reach it from Rüdesheim by cabin chair lift, by a short motor road, or by lovely walks through vineyards and forests. Your reward will be a splendid view over this section of the Rhine.

Schloss Johannisberg, near Rüdesheim, is a beautiful wine-producing estate; its cellars can be visited (usually noon and afternoons), and there is a small restaurant.

Niederwald can be reached by a chair lift from the town of Assmannshausen, which has one of the most beautiful locations on the entire river. Assmannshausen is also a small spa and red wine is produced here, a rather rare occurrence on the Rhine. Further down the river is Lorch with the Renaissance Hilchenhaus and a masterfully-carved Gothic altar in St Martin Church.

From Lorch a scenic road through the narrow Wisper Valley leads away from the Rhine and wine to the Rheingau's quiet, forested heights, alive with game, and to Bad Schwalbach, an important spa with ferrous waters, which can be reached faster by a direct route from Wiesbaden. At Idstein, where the round Hexenturm (Witches' Tower) presides over the half-timbered houses, we are in the northern approaches of the Taunus. Further north in the Ems Valley is Camberg, an old town with 14th-century walls and gates and with Kneipp cold water cure installations.

The Ems flows into the Lahn a little above Limburg, an aged town whose seven-spired Cathedral of St. George, built in 1235, seemingly grows out of the cliff on which it stands and represents perhaps the best example of the transition from Romanesque to the Gothic style in Germany. It contains murals and other artistic treasures from the same period, while its majestic exterior can be best observed from the Lahn tower-gate bridge, constructed in 1315. Other main points of interest include a two-wing Gothic castle, two other churches which are even older than the cathedral, and many half-timbered houses.

The romantic Lahn Valley is lined by many old towns clustered under medieval castles. Some of the most remarkable sights upstream from Limburg include the powerful 12th-century fortress at Runkel, the Renaissance residential castle at Weilburg with rich furnishings, and the Braunfels castle-fortress, high up above the river, towered and turreted, with colossal walls, courtyards and four gateway tunnels. Wetzlar, at the confluence of the Lahn and Dill rivers, is a cathedral town and the place where Goethe sustained his hopeless love for Charlotte, the literary result of which was his *Werther*.

Further up the Lahn is Giessen, a university town. The university was founded in 1627 but today it possesses ultramodern installations and structures, such as the library building. Famous scientists taught here, among them Wilhelm Konrad Röntgen, who harnessed X-rays, and Justus Liebig, the founder of agricultural chemistry.

North of Giessen, after passing the 12th-century Staufenburg Castle, we come to Marburg, our last and most interesting stop on the Lahn River. Marburg is the home of the country's oldest Protestant University (it was founded in 1527). Its library, the largest in Germany, is a jewel of Gothic architecture. The 13th-century St. Elisabeth Church is one of the purest examples of Gothic in Europe; it was erected over the grave of St. Elisabeth, a Landgravine of nearby Thuringia and champion of the poor, and particularly outstanding among its many artistic treasures are the shrine of St. Elisabeth, the Landgrave's choir and the stained glass windows. The State of Hesse was founded in Marburg in 1256 and soon afterwards the ruling Landgraves constructed the massive, early Gothic castle, still standing on the hill above the town and reached either by a steep climb through the terraced streets, lined with half-timbered houses, or by driving up a narrow road. But when you reach the castle, the effort involved will be well repaid by the sight of its interiors, particularly the splendid Knights' Hall, a stroll in its park (summer performances on the outdoor stage) and the fine view of the town and the surrounding countryside. Other chief sights of Marburg are the old university building with the university church, the 16th-century town hall (its Trumpet of Justice is blown every hour) and the 14th-century Marienkirche.

Only about 60 scenic miles through the vast forests of Burgwald and Kellerwald, where stag, roe deer and wild boar roam, separate Marburg from Kassel, the principal city of Northern Hesse. First you come to Frankenberg whose landmark is the half-timbered Rathaus from 1509, playfully roofed with ten little spires. Bad Wildungen in Kellerwald, a noted spa, has picturesque old town streets and a beautiful

Kurpark with trees and flowers transplanted from all over the world. The 1,000-year-old Fritzlar has preserved 18 of its wall towers, the town hall is among the oldest in Germany and the 16-altar Romanesque cathedral was originally founded by St. Boniface in 732. The Eder river is dammed some 20 miles above Fritzlar, forming the 17-mile-long artificial lake of Endersee, the meeting point of fishing and boating enthusiasts and presided over by the Waldeck Castle, best reached from Bad Wildungen.

Upper Hesse to Kassel

Before visiting Kassel we shall travel through Upper Hesse, a region east of Marburg, Giessen and Bad Nauheim (the last two actually in Upper Hesse). In this land, as well as in the nearby section of northern Hesse, old folk dress and folklore customs have survived. Some of the best preserved folk dress can be seen at Alsfeld, a historic town southeast of Marburg; folklore performances are staged here on the medieval market square in the shadows of the 16th-century Rathaus (Town Hall), Weinhaus (Wine House), Hochzeitshaus (Bridal House) and the even older Walpurgis Church.

Another center of folk dress further southeast is Schlitz, a town with four castles (destined for tourist development, so see it now before things change). Schotten, located in the Vogelsberg mountains in the middle of Upper Hesse, has a famous Gothic wing altar in the Liebfrauenkirche but it is even better known for its mountain road race course.

West of Vogelsberg is Fulda, on the river of the same name, where a monastery was founded in the 8th century by Sturmius, a pupil of Anglo-Saxon St. Boniface whose body lies in the impressive early 18th-century cathedral, with its twin towers and central dome. The whole city is an object lesson in baroque architecture, none of it more involved than the intricate figures of the "Flora Vase," which stands outside the Orangery. The museum of Schloss Adolphseck, on the outskirts, contains a notable collection of ancient sculpture, porcelain, and glassware. The cathedral treasure includes Boniface and Sturmius reliquaries, episcopal staff of Boniface, and specimens of medieval sacred art. In contrast to the prevailing baroque style, the Carolingian St. Michael's Church has preserved its original form since 820 A.D.

East of Fulda are the Rhön mountains, the home of glider pilots and the source of the Fulda River. To the north in the Fulda Valley is Bad Hersfeld, a minor spa with the 1,200-year-old ruins of a monastery where plays are staged during summer. From here if speed is your object, you can drive to Kassel directly on the autobahn. If you want to loaf through the picturesque small towns on the way, take one of the two main roads east of the autobahn. One will lead you downstream to where the peaceful castle in Rotenburg is mirrored in the river and on to the richly half-timbered Melsungen. The other route will take you into Eschwege which also has many half-timbered houses, often enriched with wood carvings, while its castle has a fountain about which many legends have been spun; and to still another spa, Bad Sooden-Allendorf, a medieval town with brine baths. This is a good starting point for hikes to the region of the Hoher Meissner, a mountain in Grimm's fairy-tale country, for this was the abode of Lady Holle, who made snow on the earth by emptying her featherbeds from this height. These regions, along with Bad Sooden-Allendorf, are weekend playgrounds for Kassel.

Kassel, on the Fulda River, is the principal city in northern Hesse and makes a very good base for visiting the country round about. It is a big industrial center, producing such heavy manufactures as railroad rolling stock and locomotives, but it also has considerable attractions for visitors. One of the most important is the Staatliche Kunstsammlungen (Provincial Art Collection) housed in Schloss Wilhelmshöhe. This is in the beautiful Bergpark Wilhelmshöhe in the western outskirts of the city at Schöne Aussicht. The collection is one of Germany's very finest and has notable works by Rembrandt, Rubens, Hals, Jordaens, Van Dyck, Dürer, Altdorfer, Cranach, Baldung Grien, and others. The Neue Galerie has works by European artists from 1750 to the present day, but it also includes the world-famous Apollo of Kassel, a perfect Roman copy of a statue by the 15th-century B.C. Greek Phidias. The international *Documenta* art exhibitions take place in Museum Fridericianum on Friedrichs-Platz every four years.

In the same building as the Hessian State Museum (Hessische Landesmuseum) is the German Wallpaper Museum. This is perhaps the only museum of its kind in the world and has wallpapers that date back to the 16th century.

Kassel is also known as the city of parks. In the southern section of the city the Schönfeld Park contains a castle and the Botanical Garden. Spread along the left bank of the Fulda, the Karls-Aue with waterways, a lake, the Siebenbergen flower island, the Orangery and other attractions, reaches to the Rathaus and the State Theater in the center of the city. But the most outstanding is the Bergpark Wilhelmshöhe with fountains, pyramids, temples, Löwenburg Castle and a colossal monument of Hercules, the symbol of Kassel. The neo-classical Schloss Wilhelmshöhe forms the gate to this "park on the hill", as it is commonly known.

About eight miles to the north is the rococo Schloss Wilhelmstal with rich interiors. Several more castles can be seen north of Kassel, mainly along and near the route 83, which takes you to the Weser Hills area of Lower Saxony. The most famous among them is the romantic Schloss Sababurg, the legendary castle of the Sleeping Beauty in the midst of the thousand-year-old forest of Rheinhardswald. In Arolsen, west of Kassel, is the baroque palace of the Counts of Waldeck. From here there are only a few miles to Westphalia.

PRACTICAL INFORMATION FOR HESSE

 HOTELS AND RESTAURANTS. Hesse is well supplied with accommodations, most of them in the medium-priced and inexpensive categories. You will find *Rasthaus* lodgings along autobahns in this area.

Regional specialties. Almost any pork dish is a favorite in Hesse, just look for the word *Schweine* on the menu and you'll be safe: *Gepökelter Schweinekamm,* roasted salt pork, *Schweinekotelett,* breaded pork chop. In the north of Hesse, near Kassel, be sure to find *Weckewerk,* a rich mixture of pork, veal and bits of white rolls; as good eaten cold as it is hot. One of the best things you'll ever taste is the *Zwiebelkuchen*—a flat covered pastry flan filled with onions.

Assmannshausen. Hotels: *Krone* (100 rooms, 30 with bath), an inn since the 16th century, where Goethe used to stay. Enjoy its excellent cuisine and visit its cellars, hewn out of solid rock, where the produce of its own vineyards is kept. Pool. Expensive (some single rooms lower) but avoid rear rooms facing railway. Closed Nov.–mid-March. *Anker* (E), with Rhine-terrace and own vineyard; *Schön* (M).

Restaurant: The old and atmospheric restaurant *Ewige Lampe* now offers modernized rooms, inexpensive to moderate.

Bad Hersfeld. Romantik Hotel *Zum Stern* (M), Lingplatz 11, once belonged to the Benedictine monastery and dates back to 1622. Indoor pool, restaurant.

Bad Homburg. Hotels: *Steigenberger Ritters Parkhotel,* Kaiser-Friedrich Promenade 69 next to Kurpark, almost deluxe, has 150 rooms, most with bath, restaurant of note. *Prinz von Homburg,* Ludwigstr. 3, and the quiet *Hardtwald,* at the end of Philosophenweg, are (M). *Taunus,* (I). About 2 miles north the *Hollstein-Hotel im Taunus,* all rooms with bath, pool, is (E).

Restaurants: *Zum Silbernen Bein,* in the castle (seasonal opening only). Roulette and baccarat in the *Casino. Pfeffermühle* has grill. Evenings only.

Bad Nauheim. *Hilberts Parkhotel,* modern furnishings, almost deluxe; the *Hessenland am Kurhaus* (E), Burgallee 20, 50 beds, all rooms with bath.

Moderate are: *Rex,* Reinhardstr. 2, near the station, 20 beds, some rooms with bath; and the small and very comfortable *Grünewald* (garni), Terrassenstr. 10.

Bad Wildungen. Hotels: *Staatliches Badehotel* (E) in the Kurpark, 70 rooms; *Europäischer-Hof* (E), Langemarckstr. 3, smaller; *Post,* garni Brunnenstr. 54, (I–M).

Restaurant: *Astoria,* Brunnenstr. 60.

Darmstadt. Hotels: The 80-room *Parkhaus-Hotel* (E) is on the top two floors of a car park building. *Weinmichel* (E), with 74 rooms, Schleiermacherstr. 10. All rooms have bath or shower. Good value restaurant and colorful wine tavern.

Moderate are: the *City-Hotel,* garni, Adelungstr. 44. *Ernst Ludwig,* garni, Ernst-Ludwig-Str. 14, quiet location. *Hotel Mathildenhöhe,* Spessartring 53, garni.

The 16th-century hunting castle *Jagdschloss Kranichstein* (E), 4 miles distant, offers 20 beds, most rooms with bath or shower, period furnishing and a restaurant specializing in game dishes.

Restaurants: *Ratskeller,* Marktplatz 8, with wine restaurant upstairs, is (E). Moderate are *Altdeutsche Bierstube,* Bessunger Str. 93, and the garden restaurant *Datterich-Klause,* Steinacherstrasse 2.

Zum Goldenen Anker (M), Landgraf Georg Str. 25 is a brewery restaurant over 300 years old, in the center; several different rooms to choose to sit.

Fulda. Hotels: Moderate to inexpensive are *Kurfürst,* Schlossstrasse 2, *Lenz,* Leipzigerstrasse 122, with good restaurant. *Hotel zum Hirsch,* Löhrstr. 36, and *Hessischer Hof,* Nikolausstr. 22, 46 beds, near the station.

Restaurants: *Orangerie-Diana-Keller* in the Orangerie; *Hauptwache,* Bonifatiusplatz 2; and *Stiftskeller,* Borgiasplatz 1, are all moderate.

Quite different atmosphere is *Felsenkeller* (M), Leipziger Str. 12, a brewery restaurant with several atmospheric rooms, central, garden terrace.

Kassel. Hotels (all with restaurants): *Schlosshotel Wilhelmshöhe,* near Wilhelmshöhe Palace (E), modern, 60 rooms with bath, balconies, pleasant setting; also *Reiss,* near main station, 102 rooms, most with bath or shower, local color wine tavern; *Parkhotel Hessenland* (M) at the Rathaus, 148 rooms, pleasant roof terrace, dance-bar.

The *Holiday Inn* (M), 10 miles out of town at Autobahn exit Kassel-east, has 155 beds, indoor pool, solarium, sauna, bar, and color TV in all rooms.

Also (M) are *Excelsior,* Erzbergerstr. 2, all rooms with shower, excellent restaurant; the quiet *Am Rathaus; Hospiz* Treppenstrasse; and *Autobahn-Rasthaus,* at the autobahn exit in the Hannover direction.

Restaurants (other than those in hotels): Among the best are *Weinstuben St Elisabeth,* Oberste Gasse 6, *Henkel* in the main station, *Ratskeller* and *Kropfwirt* in the Obere Königstrasse. *Alt-Cassel,* Hotel Reiss, high quality, expensive.

(Lahn-)Giessen. Hotels: *Am Ludwigsplatz,* garni, Ludwigsplatz 8, has a pleasant restaurant and is moderate. *Motel an der Lahn,* garni, near the river is inexpensive.

Restaurants: *Schwaabs Weinstuben,* Seltersweg 11, and *Hessischer Hof,* Frankfurter Strasse 7.

In the vicinity (5 miles) is *Burggaststätte Gleiberg* in the castle of the same name, with fine view from the garden and historic décor.

Limburg. Hotels: *Dom-Hotel,* Grabenstr. 57, 50 rooms, very comfortable and quiet. *Huss,* garni, Bahnhofplatz 3, 31 rooms, bright and friendly, on quiet square; moderate.

About 6 miles southwest, via Diez, is *Hotel Waldecker Hof,* an annex of Schaumburg Castle above it, belonging to Fürst zu Waldeck und Pyrmont; 40 beds, moderate (rooms with bath higher), good table, swimming pool.

Restaurants: *Ratskeller* (from the 13th-century) with baroque and renaissance rooms, on the Fischmarkt.

Marburg. Hotels: *Europäischer Hof,* garni, Elisabethstr. 12, 68 rooms, near the famous Gothic church of the same name; and *Waldecker Hof,* Bahnhofstr. 23, are moderate. A little out of town in Wehrshausen on the banks of the Lahn is the old mill-house hotel-restaurant, *Dammühle* (M), with garden terrace and excellent food.

Restaurants: For local color try *Gasthaus zur Sonne,* in a historic, half-timbered house on the main old square, closed Mon., and *Altes Brauhaus,* Pilgrimstein 34, closed Sun.

Rüdesheim. Hotels: *Parkhotel Deutscher Hof* (E), Rheinstrasse 21–3, on river, 146 beds. Also in this category are *Rheinstein,* on the river with fine view, 78 beds, and the *Central,* Kirchstr., 60 beds but few private facilities. *Aumüller,* on the river, and *Rüdesheimer Hof,* with a rustic-style restaurant, are moderate. *Felsenkeller,* Oberstr. 41, 54 rooms, some with bath or shower, and *Lindenwirt* are inexpensive.

Jagdschloss Niederwald (M), above the town, is former hunting castle of the Prince-Bishops of Mainz; 33 rooms.

Restaurants: *Bauernstube Rüdesheim,* Geisenheimerstrasse 1, *Bergkeller,* Oberstrasse; *Niederwaldschänke,* at Niederwald Monument, reached by chair lift.

One of Germany's top attractions is the unbelievable double row of Weinhäuser in the Drosselgasse. This is *the* place for merry wine-drinking in the musical comedy tradition. The *Lindenwirt, Drosselhof,* and *Bei Hannelore* are the leaders.

Sababurg. A castle hotel and restaurant, *Burghotel Sababurg* (E), the legendary castle of the Sleeping Beauty, 13 rooms. About 10 miles from Hofgeismar north of Kassel.

Spangenberg. In the 13th-century castle *Jagdschloss Spangenberg* (E), there is a 19-room hotel and restaurant with fine view; very quiet.

Staufenberg. An inexpensive 25-bed hotel in the Gothic *Burg Staufenberg,* restaurant and park and panoramic views.

Trendelburg. *Burghotel Trendelburg* (M), near Hofgeismar (north of Kassel). Castle dating from 13th century. 70 beds available to guests, some rooms in the round corner tower. Dining indoors by candlelight, outdoors on the ramparts. Try "Trout Poacher's Art" served on hot brick.

Waldeck. *Schloss Waldeck* (M), above Eder Lake. Originally built 1120, walls and towers date from 16th–17th centuries. Beautiful view and location; 25 beds.

Wiesbaden Hotels: *Schwarzer Bock,* Kranzplatz 12, a hostelry since 1486, completely modernized, super deluxe; 185 rooms, suites, most rooms with period furniture; outstanding cuisine, roof garden with view; indoor thermal pool, baths, and treatment in the house.

(L) are: *Nassauer Hof,* Kaiser-Friedrich-Platz 3, suites, smart restaurants *Die Pfanne* and the exclusive *Ente vorn Lehel,* bar, thermal baths and treatment, 80-car garage; *Rose,* Kranzplatz 8, most rooms with bath, cuisine of note, indoor tennis court.

Expensive: *Hansa-Hotel,* Bahnhofstr. 23, 120 beds, some rooms with bath, is near rail station; *Blum,* Wilhelmstr. 44, has restaurant and a sidewalk café.

Moderate: *Hotel de France,* Taunus Str. 49, 22 rooms with bath or shower. *Oranien,* Platter Str. 2, 92 rooms with bath or shower; *Bären,* Bärenstr. 3, with thermal baths; *Fürstenhof-Esplanade,* Sonnenbergerstr. 32; *Central,* Bahnhofstr. 65; *Klee,* garni, Parkstr. 4.

Among the inexpensive is *Albany,* garni, Kapellenstr. 2, 20 rooms. *Goldenes Ross,* Goldgasse 7–9.

Restaurants: Some of the best and most expensive dining spots are in the leading hotels, especially in the elegant *Nassauer Hof* and *Schwarzer Bock* with its differently decorated rooms ranging from a Chinese salon to a rustic tavern.

Other top establishments: *Alte Krone* (E), Sonnenbergerstr. 82; *Le Gourmet,* Uhlandstr. 15, fine French cuisine; *Kurhaus,* J. F. Kennedy-Platz, with music.

Among the best moderate: *Schumacher,* Am Michelsberg 28 and *Cattle Baron,* an American steak-house in Büdingerstr. 4.

Inexpensive: *Ratskeller,* Schlossplatz 9; *Gambrinus,* Tempelhoferstr. and Kirschblütenstr.

Wine taverns with local color; *Uhrturm,* Marktstrasse 15; *Alt Prag* (Bohemian specialties), Taunusstr. 41; and half a dozen others. *Weinhaus Schreiner,* Rheinstrasse 38 (closed Mon.).

Mövenpick, Sonnenberger Str. 2, moderate.

In the outskirts: *Weinhaus Rheinterrassen,* wine restaurant at the ship station in Biebrich overlooking the Rhine. In the suburb of Sonnenberg: *Burg Sonnenberg* specializes in game and Rhine wine, and for steaks and beer try the Casino (*Spielbank Wiesbaden*), bus no. 6 from Wiesbaden.

Cafes. *Park* and *Blum* (in the *Hotel Blum*), in Wilhelmstrasse, have sidewalk terrace sections where you can observe the life on Wiesbaden's smartest artery. Nightclub also above *Park* café. *Opelbad* on Neroberg with fine view, also restaurant service.

Nightlife: Dancing at *Pavillon-Bar* in Kurhaus, in *Tabarin* (also show) and *Park-Café* in Wilhelmstrasse, and in the bar of Hotel Nassauer Hof. For spicy shows: *Parisiana,* Taunusstrasse 27 and several others. Roulette and baccarat daily after 3 P.M. in Kurhaus Casino.

 MUSIC AND THEATER. Outdoor and indoor concerts and theatrical performances throughout the summer season in all more important spas. Regular concert seasons in Kassel, Darmstadt, Marburg and Giessen, all of which have local symphony orchestras and choirs.

Opera, operetta and plays are performed: in Kassel, whose modern *Staatstheater* with two auditoriums rates as one of the most modern in the world; in *Landestheater* in Darmstadt and in *Theater der Stadt* in Giessen, Marburg has a permanent theatrical group appearing in the *Stadtsäle,* as well as an open-air theater in the castle park. Darmstadt now has a *National Theater* with two auditoria and underground garage parking for 400 cars.

Wiesbaden has a city symphony orchestra, the orchestra of the Hesse National Theater, and a municipal chorus. The fine *Hessisches Staatstheater* presents opera and major productions in its 1,300-seat large auditorium and small plays in its 300-seat smaller one. The 1,400 seat Kurhaus hall is also the setting for many theatrical events. The greatest yearly event is the International May Festival.

 MUSEUMS. Bad Homburg: *Castle of Landgraves* of Hesse-Homburg, conducted tours of state apartments; the Roman military town at Saalburg.

Darmstadt: *Hessisches Landesmuseum.* Friedensplatz 1, contains an excellent natural history collection, objects from prehistoric and Roman times, art objects from the Middle Ages, paintings by old Dutch and German masters, and displays from the copper engravings cabinet. *Porcelain Museum* in Prinz-Georg-Palais; *Hunting Museum,* in Kranichstein Castle.

Fulda: *Dom-Museum,* conducted tours, Boniface and Sturmius reliquaries, sacred art; *Schlossmuseum Adolphseck,* ancient sculpture, porcelain and glassware.

Kassel: *Staatliche Kunstsammlungen* in Schloss Wilhelmshöhe; old masters including 17 Rembrandts, and *Neue Galerie* with famous European works; *Landesmuseum* early and prehistoric history of Hesse, also houses *Tapeten-Museum,* which has wallpaper of all kinds with a constantly up-dated section showing contemporary trends; *Brothers Grimm Museum,* manuscripts and mementos of the famous authors.

Marburg: *Universitätsmuseum,* cultural and art history; art treasures in St Elisabeth Church.

Rüdesheim: Musical boxes, early gramophones, hurdy-gurdys, etc., *Bromserhof* in the famous Drosselgasse.

Wiesbaden: *Städtisches Museum* (City Museum), Friedrich-Ebert-Allee, entrance free, noted gallery of modern painting, prehistoric and Roman finds, natural history collections with aquarium. *Schloss Biebrich,* baroque palace with large park on the Rhine.

 SPORTS. Tennis courts and swimming abound. **Golf** links at Kronberg, Kassel, Bad Homburg, Bad Nauheim, Bad Wildungen and Hanau. Wiesbaden has an 8-hole course (Chausseehaus) and an 18-hole (Dotzheim-Nerotal). Many facilities for **horseback riding** especially at Landgut Ebental, Rüdesheim, on Shetland, Bosnian and Haflinger ponies. Wiesbaden has two stables; riding and jumping meet at the Biebrich Palace park at Whitsun.

Sailing and **rowing** on the artificial Eder Lake and on the Rhine in Rheingau. **Kayaking** on the rivers Eder, Fulda, and especially scenic and not difficult on the Lahn frm Marburg to the Rhine (110 miles, slow current, about a week). **Gliding** at Rohn near Fulda and Dornberg near Kassel.

Hunting especially in northern Hesse, mostly for stag, roe deer and wild boar. **Fishing** in Eder Lake and in Eder and Lahn rivers, primarily for pike, salmon, trout, eel, perch and tench.

Skiing on Taunus, Rhön, Meissner and Waldekisches Upland, where the main center is Willingen (2 ski lifts, 2 ski jumps, ski school); medium to easy terrains, particularly recommended for beginners.

Walking Tours in Hesse. There is a special brochure listing all special package deals for hiking tours which can be obtained from the tourist office at the *Landeszentrale für Fremdenverkehr,* A. Lincoln Str. 38–42, 6200 Wiesbaden.

Nature Parks in Hesse include those at Bergstrasse-Odenwald; Diemelsee; Habichtswald; Hessische Rhön; Hessischer Spessart; Hochtaunus; Hoher Vogelsberg; Meissner-Kaufunger-Wald; Rhein-Taunus. For information write to: *Arbeitsgemeinschaft,* Hessischer Naturparkträger, Gräffstr. 5, 6148 Heppenheim 1.

 TOURS. Sightseeing flights over thirty of the most picturesque miles of the Rhine Valley are now being operated by Rheingau Air Service, using Dornier Do-27 high wing aircraft. Flying from Ruedesheim airport, an English-speaking commentary is offered and the bird's eye view of castles, vineyards, villages and river traffic makes it ideal for photographers.

HESSE BY CAR. Any legendary figures that have escaped the Rhine will surely be found in Oldenwald, the wooded mountains of Hesse found just north of Heidelberg, or in the Bergstrasse, slightly further north again. Taking Heidelberg as the point of entry it can be reached from Belgium on A 61, or from Luxembourg on A 6, after which there are two tourist routes to explore—the Siegfriedstrasse and the Nibelungenstrasse which will, of course, have their fair share of traffic on them. There are also the Castle and Hillside routes. But apart from the Grimm industry, this is a very elegant area just made for gentle touring and enlivened by fascinating old villages, stately homes and roads which have a genius for providing the good view, often high above some of the most famous vineyards in the country. One should always aim to look down on vineyards, rather than drive among them.

 USEFUL ADDRESSES. Local Tourist Offices: *Bad Homburg:* Kurverwaltung, Ludwigstrasse 3; *Bad Nauheim:* Kurverwaltung, Friedrichstr. 3; *Darmstadt:* Verkehrsamt, Luisenplatz 5; *Fulda:* Städtisches Verkehrsbüro, Schlosstr. 1; *Giessen;* Verkehrsamt, Berliner Platz 2; *Kassel:* Verkehrsamt, Obere Königstr.8; *Marburg:* Verkehrsamt Neue Kasseler Str.1. *Wiesbaden:* city information offices in Brunnenkolonnade at Wilhelmstrasse and in the main station (open until 11 P.M.)

Other Wiesbaden information *Sightseeing by bus:* Blaue Kurautobusse, Theaterkolonnade, and Kirchgasse 2; Rheinland, Wilhelmstrasse 58. *River steamer trips:* Köln-Düsseldorfer Rheindampfschiffahrt, Rheingaustrasse 145 in Biebrich. *General travel:* American Express, Wilhelmstrasse 30. *Airport bus:* every hour on the hour from the main station to the Frankfurt airport between 6 A.M. and 10 P.M. and from the airport to Wiesbaden between 7 A.M. and 11 P.M.: the trip takes 35 minutes. *Car hire:* Avis, Gustav-Stresemann-Ring 1; Hertz, Burgstr. 3.

CASTLED WESTPHALIA

The Forge of Germany

Westphalia is approximately that territory lying between the Weser and the Rhine, so that if we head northwest out of Kassel we soon find ourselves in this province whose name is best known throughout the world in connection with a ham. Westphalian ham, and for that matter, bacon, is supremely good because the oak forests of this country have for ages provided its pigs with luscious acorns, which they have converted into even more luscious meat. The farm areas are found particularly in the region between the Lippe and Ems rivers, dotted with castles and called Münsterland after the principal city of Münster, and to the northeast of it, in the hilly Teutoburger Wald and Lippisches Bergland, sprinkled with spas and extending between the upper courses of Ems and Weser.

Converting raw materials into machines and tools for industry is another string to Westphalia's bow. For between the Lippe and the

Ruhr rivers stretches the mighty Ruhr district, industrial heart of Germany. South of the Lippe river is the forested and mountainous Sauerland with Siegerland which represents the southernmost tip of Westphalia.

EXPLORING WESTPHALIA

West of northern Hesse lies Sauerland which, together with Siegerland, forms the southern section of Westphalia. This "land of a thousand hills," as it is called, is actually a succession of green plateaus cut by deep valleys and offers a great contrast to the smoking chimneys of the Ruhr, less than two hours' drive away. Its thick forests embrace some of the quietest vacation spots in all Germany, many of its rivers have been dammed into artificial lakes, its undersoil is hollowed by huge stalactite caves and its small towns trace their history into the early Middle Ages.

Entering Sauerland west of Kassel we first come to Brilon, a winter and summer resort with the nearby Diemel artificial lake. Less than 20 miles south of Brilon is the village of Winterberg, the leading winter sports center in Westphalia, located on the slopes of green Kahler Asten whose 2,760 feet make it the highest elevation in Westphalia. On the other side of Kahler Asten tiny Alt-Astenberg, the highest village in northwestern Germany (2,560 ft.), is also well known to skiers. In Berleburg, in the vicinity, you may visit the 18th-century castle, the façade of which is coated with cut stones, many of them semi-precious, encrusted in the wall.

Further south is Siegen, the center of Siegerland, birthplace of Peter Paul Rubens, whose parents lived here as refugees, and the former residence of the Princes of Nassau-Orange, whose bodies rest in their crypt in the Lower Castle. The Upper Castle contains the works of Rubens, along with a 2,000-year-old iron melting furnace. Less than 40 miles south of Siegen you can reach Limburg in Hesse and the Frankfurt-Cologne autobahn. North of Siegen is Attendorn with its Sauerland Cathedral and several lakes in the middle of the Ebbegebirge Nature Park, Schnellenberg Castle and the huge Atta stalactite cave in the vicinity; Altena with its castle overlooking the Lenne river; and the old streets, towers, and fortifications of Arnsberg, called "the pearl of Sauerland." East of Arnsberg we come to Meschede, with a Carolingian crypt in the parish church and the Henne Dam nearby, and complete our circular tour of Sauerland back in Brilon.

Teutoburg Forest

Paderborn, the gate to the Teutoburger Wald, can best be reached from Kassel via Warburg in the Diemel valley. Warburg, a small town but once a member of the Hanseatic League, has preserved some of its medieval fortifications, houses and churches. Paderborn is a city with a long history; here Charles the Great met Pope Leo III in 799 and Paderborn has been a bishopric since 805. The first cathedral was built by Charles the Great in the 8th century, but the present monumental structure with the famous Paradiespforte (Paradise Portal) dates from the 11th–13th centuries. Other main sights include the Town Hall dating from 1620, half-timbered houses from about the same period, the Diocesan Museum with the Imad Madonna from about 1060, and over 200 small bubbling springs in the cathedral area giving birth to the Pader river (hence the name of the city).

Nearby to the east is Bad Driburg, an elegant spa set among thickly wooded parks. The road north from Paderborn takes you to the Teutoburg Forest. Passing through the spas of Bad Lippspringe and Bad Meinberg, we come to Detmold, in the region known as Lippe. This is a good starting point for trips into the rolling country of the Lippisches Land and the Ravensberger Land, filled with traces of centuries of habitation running all the way back to prehistoric times—which accounts for the wealth of Stone Age, Bronze Age and Iron Age relics in the Lippisches Landesmuseum of Detmold. In the vicinity, near the town of Horn (about 7 miles from Detmold), are the famous Extern Stones, carrying an early Romanesque bas-relief of the Descent from the Cross. Even closer to Detmold (4 miles), high on a mountain, is the colossal monument to Hermann (Armin), the hero of early German history, who defeated the Romans in this area in the year 9 A.D. and stopped their penetration into Germany. From the monument there is also an excellent view over the surrounding region; nearby are the walls of an old Germanic fort. Both these localities are only a few miles from each other and are within easy reach from Paderborn (about 16 miles). Also near Detmold are several small towns, such as Lemgo, Blomberg, Schwalenberg, which have preserved their medieval aspect.

The road continues through Bielefeld, whose industrial nature is symbolized by the pipe-smoking figure of the Linenweaver's Fountain, and with Sparrenberg Castle, containing a playing card museum, as well as with several interesting buildings in the old town section; then to Halle, with its steep-roofed, half-timbered old houses and the Tatenhausen water castle. From Halle we can either continue in the same direction through the scenic Teutoburger Wald and then descend west to Münster, or we can cut across a tongue of Lower Saxony that thrusts itself here into Westphalia, perhaps visiting at the same time Osnabrück, in Lower Saxony. Embarking on the latter course we come close to the northern border of Westphalia at Lübbecke—with its fine 16th-century town hall, its 14th-century St. Andrew's church and other old buildings—and at Minden. An unusual spectacle in this old Hanseatic city is one stream crossing another on a bridge; the Mittelland Canal passes over the Weser River here, the only such crossing in all Germany.

From Minden you can pay a visit to one of the chief sights of the region, a natural geological exhibit—the Westphalian Gap, through which the Weser, in prehistoric times, broke through the mountain barrier northward, leaving to this day the traces of this revolution of nature. A remarkable view through the Gap is provided from the monument of Kaiser Wilhelm on one of its flanking hills and from the Bismarck statue on another hill across the river.

To the southwest are Bad Oeynhausen, a pleasant spa, and Herford, with its beautiful specimens of medieval architecture, including the 13th-century Minster, and several 14th-century churches. Another spa lies east of the main road after we pass Herford, Bad Salzuflen, with its large Kurpark, 16th-century Rathaus (Town Hall), half-timbered houses, restaurants, numerous pensions and small hotels. If you haven't witnessed the spectacle of true spa believers recovering their health, spas are the place for a rather unkind giggle. They are often to be found throughout central, southern and eastern Europe. They began in order to help the rich overcome the results of their self-indulgence, but no one would describe them thus today. They are there to combat the stresses and strains of overwork and modern life. And if you don't die of boredom, you will probably recover, through their machinations, plus the excellent air and surroundings. Foreigners are very welcome and there are even inclusive holidays arranged for the purpose. Bad Salzuflen is within an hour's drive of Hannover airport.

Southwest of the Teutoberg Forest is the broad plain of Münsterland, a region of moated castles and old manors, and of fertile countryside against which the red brick wide-gabled farm houses shine like garnets on green velvet. Münster itself, the center of this region, can be reached from Paderborn direct, or from Bielefeld, Halle, and Osnabrück.

Trips from Münster

Münster, the regional capital and a bishopric for more than 1,100 years, has an old, medieval center. Together with Osnabrück it was host to the treaty of Westphalia, which ended the Thirty Year War. The period portraits of the treaty signers can be seen in the Peace Hall of the Gothic Rathaus, faithfully reconstructed after World War II destruction. The Romanesque cathedral, the largest in Westphalia, also badly damaged during the air raids and mostly rebuilt again, has a portal hall with big 13th-century carved figures of the apostles and saints and an astronomical clock with a Glockenspiel playing at noon. The Gothic St. Lamberti Church with interesting sculptures, the arch-windowed and arcaded houses in Prinzipalmarkt and several moated castles in the vicinity, among them particularly Burg Vischering in Lüdinghausen (about 18 miles away) and Wasserschloss Rüschhaus (5 miles), are other top sights. The city has also a lively cultural life—the Westphalian University is here, housed in the baroque residence palace of the former prince-bishops—and there are frequent theatrical and musical performances in the city theater.

Münster is a good center for visits to the picturesque places in which this section abounds: Freckenhorst, to the southeast, where there is a fine medieval Romanesque church; to the northwest, Burgsteinfurt, with an important moated castle; Rheine, for St. Anthony's basilica; and west to Coesfeld, a Hanseatic city with its old walls and gates still standing; Borken with a 12th-century tower and the 15th-century Church of the Holy Ghost, among others, and Bocholt, an important center for more than a thousand years, with many interesting buildings, of which the 17th-century Rathaus, in the Renaissance style, though far from the oldest, is one of the most pleasing.

Southwest of Münster, reached via Lüdinghausen, is Nordkirchen with a baroque castle, or rather group of castles, on an artificial island surrounded by a moat. Southeast is Soest, a medieval Hanseatic city with preserved walls and gates, among them the massive Osthofentor, containing a notable collection of weapons. The mighty tower of the Romanesque St Patroclus Church was used not only for ecclesiastical purposes but served also as the armory for Soest citizens. St. Peter's Church, from the same period, contains important 13th-century murals. In the Gothic Wiesenkirche is a 16th-century stained glass window representing the Last Supper—with the menu composed of Westphalian ham, pumpernickel, and beer. South of Soest is Möhne Dam on the Ruhr river on the northern approaches to Sauerland. West are the chimney forests of the Ruhr.

Industrial Cities

When we arrive in Dortmund, we have reached "the forge of Germany," the industrial Ruhr, the empire of coal and steel. As such, it was subjected to heavy bombing during the war, but it is booming again as never before.

Dortmund is the largest city of Westphalia and as befits an industrial center, takes pride in its modern achievements rather than in those of the past. It is proudest of all of its tall TV tower with a rotating restaurant and magnificent view, and of the Westfalenhalle, the largest congress and sports hall in Europe, an oval building that appears from the outside to be made exclusively of glass, which has a capacity of 230,000 persons. Dortmund is, after Munich, the greatest brewing center in Germany—and it also turns out liqueurs. The industry is of respectable antiquity: St. Mary's Church has a medieval drawing of a man drinking from a cask of beer. The Ostwall Museum has a fine collection of modern German artists.

Bochum is an important center of mining, steelworks, and of the automobile, machine, chemical and electronic industries. It has very little to offer the ordinary tourist. The city is characterized by the heavy solid mass of its modern city hall, impressive by sheer size, harmonious in its proportions (except perhaps for an appendage recalling a railroad control tower tacked to one side of it), but without grace. Yet it is not completely without reminders of the past. The Evangelical Church in Bochum-Stiepel contains some first-rate medieval frescos. Bochum also harbors in its Bergbau Museum a unique exhibit, the model of a coal mine. The grimness sometimes characteristic of industrial cities is here relieved by four major parks, of which the Stadtpark is the largest in the Ruhr.

South of Bochum is Hagen, more industry and a nice location on the northern slopes of Sauerland, and to the north is smaller Recklinghausen, known particularly for its annual Ruhr Festival featuring orchestras, opera companies and theatrical groups from all over Germany as well as art exhibitions.

Gelsenkirchen is the second-largest city in Westphalia, one of the greatest industrial centers in the world and located next door to Essen in Northern Rhineland. But Gelsenkirchen is also known for its green parks, including the Ruhr Zoo, and several castles in the suburbs, for the quality of its musical and theatrical performances, and for the fact that it possesses two of the best horserace tracks in Germany. It is approximately one hour on the autobahn from Cologne airport and less than half an hour from Düsseldorf.

PRACTICAL INFORMATION FOR WESTPHALIA

 HOTELS AND RESTAURANTS. Westphalian hams sometimes weigh as much as 33 pounds, and for breakfast a huge slice of it is served on a wooden board with rich dark pumpernickel which has been baked 20 hours, and a glass of strong *Steinhäger*. Bacon, as much in favor as ham, is served with giant beans and a good thick gravy. *Pfefferpotthast* is a deliciously spicy dish of pieces of beef boiled with bay leaves, cloves and a pound of onions for every pound of meat, all mixed with breadcrumbs and spiced with peppercorns.

Münster, the capital of Westphalia, has an equally highly seasoned stew called *Töttchen*, and in Soest you must try the similar *Wamme* which must be consumed with *Braune Ecke*, a rye bread roll. A dish to look out for in the Teutoburg Forest area is *Pickert*, a dough made of grated potatoes and buckwheat flour and fried in a skillet. Another Westphalian specialty is a type of sausage baked in dough.

Attendorn. In Sauerland. *Burg Schnellenberg* (M), a castle hotel dating from the 13th century; 30 rooms, most with bath; tennis, riding, hunting, fishing.

Bad Driburg. Hotels: *Gräfliches Kurhaus* (M), in Kurpark, 180 beds, restaurant, outdoor café, horseback riding.
Teutoburger Hof (M–I), Brunnenstr. 2, 20 rooms.

Bad Salzuflen. Hotels: Leading is *Maritim Staatsbad*, 200 rooms, indoor pool, private facilities, deluxe. Excellent restaurant.
The *Schwaghof* (M), 2 miles outside and very quietly located, 70 beds, all rooms with bath or shower, good food. *Lippischer Hof* (M), Mauerstr. 1, is the same size, and in town is *Kurhotel Menz* with a roof terrace.

Bochum. Hotels: *Novotel*, upper (M) am Stadionring; 118 rooms, heated pool, good-value restaurant.
The *Plaza* (M), 36 rooms, all with radio, TV, beverage refrigerator and grill specialties in *Torkelkeller*, is near main station. Nearby is the *Savoy* (M), 60 rooms with bath or shower, no restaurant; the *Bundesbahn-Hotel*, at the main station, is slightly cheaper, 56 beds, some with bath or shower. In nearby Wattenscheid, *Hotel George* (M), Höntropper Str. 10, near station; 20 beds, all with bath/WC. Sporting facilities, international cuisine, wine *stüberl*, beer cellar.
Restaurants: *Parkhaus* in city park, expensive; reasonable with fine meals are *Haus Wenderoth*, Castroper Str. 178, close to the Planetarium, open 11 till 11, and *Schlegel-Bräu*, Rathausplatz 5, belonging to the brewery of that name.

Detmold. Hotels: *Detmolder Hof* (M), Lange Strasse 19; *Kanne* (M), Paderborner Str. 155, on outskirts at Berlebeck. Also at Berlebeck, inexpensive *Zur Forelle,* No. 131 on same street. Both inexpensive.

Burghotel, 13 miles out, is pleasant, part of the former castle of the Counts of Lippe.

Restaurants: *Alte Mühle,* moderate to expensive; *Fürst Leopold,* inexpensive; the colorful *Westfälisches Haus* at the corner of Lange and Krumme streets; and for view, *Turmgaststäett* at Papenbergweg 45.

Dortmund. Hotels: All (M) are— *Römischer Kaiser,* Olpe 2, with 175 beds, all rooms with bath or shower and radio, airconditioned, first-class restaurant and café. *Esplanade,* garni, 65 beds, most rooms with shower, at Bornstr. 4, and *Westfalenhalle,* 130 beds, most rooms with bath or shower, good cuisine, at Rheinlanddamm 200.

Restaurants: *Zum Ritter,* Osten Hellweg 3, enjoys high reputation, expensive, as is *Union-Bräu,* Hoher Wall 38.

Krone, Markt 10, is known for good cuisine, moderate. *Zum Alten Bergamt,* Markt 6, is colorful.

The slowly-rotating *Turmrestaurant* on top of the TV tower has a fine view.

Gelsenkirchen-Buehr. Hotels: *Maritim,* 225 rooms, private facilities, is deluxe, with 265 rooms and apartments, sauna, swimpool, nightclub, bars; first-class service, fresh, imaginative food, accent on business rather than tourism.

* **Restaurants:** *Schloss Berg,* a moated castle, has a spacious indoor and outdoor restaurant and is a favored excursion point. A Mövenpick establishment.

Minden. Hotels: (I) are *Kruses Park-Hotel,* Marienstr. 108, and *Bad Minden,* Porta Strasse 36.

Restaurant: *Ratskeller* on Markt has wide reputation and two sections, an expensive wine restaurant and an atmospheric, moderate beer tavern.

Münster. Hotels: *Kaiserhof,* garni, Bahnhofstr. 14, 125 beds, most rooms with bath, music in the café, (E) but some rooms lower; *Conti,* garni, at the main station is moderate.

Among the many inexpensive hotels are *Horstmann,* garni, Windthorststr. 12, and the picturesque *Überwasserhof,* Überwasserstr. 3.

Just out of town, at Steinfurterstr. 374, is the castle-hotel *Schloss Wilkinghege* (M–E) in park-like surroundings, with castle tavern and restaurant of note.

Also just outside, *Hohenfeld Schlosshotel,* 78 beds, all rooms with bath, is moderate.

Restaurants: Eating and drinking places with local color include *Rietkötter Schinkenstübchen* (ask for Töttchen here), and *Stuhlmacher,* both moderate.

Altes Gasthaus Leve, over 350 years old, is inexpensive.

Paderborn. Hotels: *Arosa,* Westernmauer 38, 150 beds, all rooms with bath, good swimming, is (M) as is *Hotel zur Mühle,* Mühlenstr, with restaurant *Au Cygne Noir.*

Krawinkel, on Karlsplatz, and *Deutscher Hof,* Bahnhofstr. 14, inexpensive. Best **restaurants** are *Ratskeller,* in the Town Hall, and *Schweizer Haus* on Warburgerstr.

Recklinghausen. Hotel: *Park-hotel Engelsburg* (M), Augustinessenstr. 10, small, comfortable and quiet, fine food, with atmospheric *Burgklause* tavern.
Restaurants: *Ratskeller* in the City Hall, *Schweizer Haus,* Warburgerstr. 99. Both (M).

Soest. Hotels: (M–E) is *Stadt Soest,* Brüderstr. 50. The moderate *Andernach zur Börse* has good food in its colorful restaurant and so has inexpensive *Haus zur Börde,* Nöttenstr. 1.
Im Wilden Mann (E), "Romantik Hotel", Am Markt 11, tel: 2595. In the center of town, a picturesque half-timbered house with an original beer parlour and elegant restaurant specializing in fish and game dishes as well as traditional Westphalian recipes. Reservations essential as hotel is small with only 11 beds.

Willingen. Just outside Westphalia and into Hesse, this prominent winter sports resort has several small moderate hotels. Leader, however, is the super, all-amenities *Sauerland Stern* (E), 500 rooms.

 WESTPHALIA BY CAR. If one approaches Germany from England on the Belgian motorways one arrives, unfortunately, bang in the middle of Westphalia's industrial area, better known as the Ruhr. It is intimidating. A pair of autobahen run through it north-south and others feed into it from either side. Driving on them is not restful, even though it may be fast. Germany is the only country in Europe which has no speed limit on its motorways, and German drivers take full advantage of this fact. About 40 miles east of Cologne one can, however, escape from A4 into the peaceful, smallish Siegerland of medium-altitude mountains, forests and lakes knitted together by the stringy roads which are such a feature of the more solitary parts of Germany. One can avoid the Ruhr somewhat by coming into north Westphalia through Holland, but this Münsterland district is flat farmland with hedges which does not make good touring ground.

 MUSEUMS. B̈ielefeld: *Deutsches Spielkartenmuseum,* in Sparrenberg Castle, playing cards. **Bochum:** *Railway Museum,* open Sunday A.M., largest in Germany; *Bergbau-Museum,* Vödestr. 28, mining museum including an underground mine maintained for exhibition purposes.
Bünde (near Herford): *Zigarrenmuseum,* Fünfhäuserstr. 12, tobacco articles, among them the biggest cigar in the world.

Dortmund: *City Museum of Art and Cultural History,* located in Cappenberg Castle in the outskirts, a good collection of old German and modern art; *Geschichtliches Museum,* Ritterhausstr. 34, Roman gold coins; *Museum am Ostwall,* Ostwall 7, modern art; *Museum für Naturkunde,* Balkenstrasse 40, natural history; *Museum am Ostwall,* modern art.

Münster: *Provincial Museum of Art and Cultural History,* Domplatz 10, medieval and modern art; Diocesan Museum, Domplatz 25, religious art.

Paderborn: *Diocesan Museum,* Domplatz 3, medieval church art.

Recklinghausen: *Icon Museum,* in Propstei at Kirchplatz, the only one of its kind in Western Europe.

Siegen: *Museum des Siegerlands,* in Upper Castle (Oberes Schloss), local history and culture, including paintings and drawings by Rubens who lived here.

Soest: *Burghofmuseum,* local history.

 MUSIC AND THEATER. A major event is the annual Ruhr Festival featuring concerts, opera, and drama and taking place in Recklinghausen from mid-May through June. The most important symphonic orchestras are the *City Orchestras* of Dortmund, Bochum, Gelsenkirchen and Münster. Other orchestras as well as choral groups in every larger city and some spas, notably Bad Sulzuflen.

Regular seasons for opera, operetta and plays: *Städtische Bühnen* (city theaters) in Dortmund, Gelsenkirchen, Hagen, Münster, Bielefeld; and *Landestheater* in Detmold. The *Kurtheater* of Bad Sulzuflen has a rich program especially during the summer season.

 SPORTS. Westphalia is particularly fond of **horseracing** and many international and national galloping and trotting events are scheduled especially in Gelsenkirchen, Dortmund, Recklinghausen, and riding tournaments in Dortmund, Münster, and Herborn. Bochum has a riding stadium. **Horseback riding** schools and facilities in Münster, Warendorf and several other localities. **Golf** courses exist at Dortmund, Neheim-Hüsten near Möhne lake, Bad Salzuflen and Burgsteinfurt. There are **tennis** courts in all spas and all larger cities.

Swimming in the many artificial lakes: in the swimming stadium and other pools of Dortmund; in the very modern pool at Wittenerstrasse in Bochum, and in numerous other pools scattered throughout the region. **Gliding** at Borkenberge near Haltern, Oerlinghausen near Bielefeld and at Arnsberg.

The main **winter sports** resorts include Winterberg, Alt-Astenberg, Fredeburg and Willingen, with between them some 40 ski jumps, 100 ski lifts, 1,000 miles of marked ski trails, 18 ski schools, etc. Full details from the Dortmund regional tourist office (see below).

USEFUL ADDRESSES. Parking garages: *Bochum:* Dr Ruer-Platz underground garage and Auto-Einstellhaus, Kortumstr. 2; *Münster:* Parkhaus, Stubengasse 22.

Tourist Information; *Bad Driburg,* Verkehrsamt, Lange Str. 140; *Bad Salzuflen,* Verkehrsamt, Am Schliepsteiner Tor 5; *Bochum:* Verkehrsverein, in Rathaus and main station; *Detmold,* Verkehrsamt in Rathaus; *Dortmund:* several offices for city, regional (Westphalia) information at Balkenstr. 4; *Gelsenkirchen:* Verkehrsamt, Ebertstr. 11; *Minden:* Verkehrsamt, Ritterstr. 31; *Paderborn:* Verkehrsverein, Marienplatz 2a; *Recklinghausen:* Verkehrsamt, in the Rathaus; *Soest:* in the Rathaus.

THE NORTHERN RHINELAND

The Realm of Charlemagne

The A, B, C and D of Northern Rhineland cities are Aachen, Bonn, Cologne, and Düsseldorf. To these we might add an E for Essen, Ruhr industrial center and the largest city of the region. But cities alone represent only a small part of the regional story, which boasts as well a wealth of art treasures, historical interest, and natural beauty.

EXPLORING THE RUHR AND NORTHERN

RHINELAND

Essen is the center of the Ruhr and the largest city in the region, known the world over as the capital of the powerful Krupp industrial concern. It boasts the tallest and largest Town Hall in West Germany, over 300 feet high and completed in 1979. With its modern business buildings, busy streets, underground railway, and immense industrial plants in the outskirts, Essen does not at first glance appear to have much relation to old Germany or to the legendary country of the Rhine. But its cathedral dates from 852, while the abbey in the suburb of Werden goes back to the 8th century. The treasury of the cathedral is famous for the valuable and unique examples of Romanesque goldsmith's art, including three crosses of the Abbess Mathilde and numerous reliquaries. The Golden Madonna (originating around 1000) is the oldest preserved statue of the Madonna in the West. Two other churches are worth visiting: the 11th-century Market Church, scene of the Reformation in Essen in 1561, located in the center; and St. Lucius Church, the oldest German parish church founded in 995 and located near the abbey in the Werden suburb. The 13th-century Borbeck Castle, in a large forest-park in a northwestern suburb, was formerly the residence of the princess-abbesses of Essen.

Another Essen treasure is the modern Folkwang Museum with its excellent collection of 19th- and 20th-century art. You can see an exhibition of the building industry in the exhibition hall of Bauzentrum, in itself an example of modern building skill, while Haus Industrieform has a permanent display of industrial design. Other outstanding examples of contemporary architecture include the Städtischer Saalbau, where concerts and congresses are held, as well as many buildings on the Huyssenallee and on the Freiheit square. Of particular interest is the Grugahalle, a harmonious composition in steel and glass, perched like a bird with lifted wings in the beautiful gardens of the Gruga Park, a recreational area including an aquarium, sports installations and an outstanding Botanical Garden. Grugahalle, in its various sections, plays host to congresses, conventions, musical and special programs, exhibitions and sports.

The suburb of Werden is located at Baldeney Lake, the Essen summer playground for sailing, swimming and boating. Presiding over the lake is the Villa Hügel, former residence of the Krupp family and since 1953 made available by them for concerts, exhibitions and representational needs of the city. Among other items of interest in the villa are the Flemish tapestries and the Krupp collection of the history of German industry. The large park is also open to the public.

Essen and music, particularly choir music, are as well mated as Krupp and steel. There are around 100 choirs, of which nine are more than 100 years old, and many choir festivals are held to display their internationally-known talent. One choral rarity is the famous Johannes-Damascenus-Chor, which sings Eastern Orthodox liturgy in the original Church Slavic. Further evidence of Essen's love of music are its several orchestras and the Folkwang School of Music, Theater and Dance. From October through December, Essen bursts out in full glory during the Weeks of Light, an annual event in which the shopping center is illuminated with a hundred thousand electric bulbs.

Mülheim an der Ruhr has everything. A large city on both banks of the Ruhr River, it has managed to keep its industry (served by a river port) in a section entirely separate from the rest of the town. The town itself comprises both a bustling up-to-date modern section and some old buildings, particularly in the outskirts, that escaped the bomb damage that leveled others—notably Schloss Broich, parts of which date from 1000 A.D. and one of the strongest fortresses on the Lower Rhine, and the Convent Church in Saarn, a Romanesque church from the 13th century. Although almost completely destroyed in the last war, St. Peter's Church, the symbol of Mülheim and its oldest church (11th century), has been rebuilt exactly as it was. Around St. Peter's are many old half-timbered houses, notably the Tersteegenhaus, offering a glimpse of 18th-century life in the house of the preacher and church song-writer Gerhard Tersteegen.

The suburbs straggle along both river banks, so that Mülheim appears to be more a federation of separate settlements than a single integrated community. This peculiarity has led to the laying out of many long avenues linking different sections of the associated Mülheims, and there are also limitless possibilities for trips to the surrounding countryside. If you prefer to do your promenading on the water instead of on land, steamers take off from the attractive Wasserbahnhof (Water Station) on the lock island in the Ruhr. Mülheim also has its own private spa in Solbad Raffelberg, another of its many suburbs, with a lovely Kurpark.

Whether Duisburg, a city at the junction of the Ruhr and the Rhine, is the largest inland port in the world, as local enthusiasts claim, or not, it is one of the largest inland ports in Europe, and a visit to its river harbor is well worth while. In its Gothic Salvatorkirche you may see the gravestone of Gerhard Mercator, the famous maker of maps, for whom a concert and congress hall has been named (Mercatorhalle). The Lehmbruck Museum honors the famed local sculptor Wilhelm Lehmbruck with a comprehensive collection of his works, as well as recent additions of other modern sculpture and post-Expressionist German painters.

Just north of Duisburg is Oberhausen, a modern industrial city of coal, iron and steel, where the first iron works in the Ruhr (the St Anthony Iron Works) were founded more than 200 years ago and thus known as "the cradle of the Ruhr industry." The main attraction is Schloss Oberhausen, housing the Municipal Gallery with modern art and an unusual collection of 20th-century glass. There is also an interesting newly created stained glass wall in the 14th-century Holtener Church and don't miss the 16th-century Vondern Castle, a small red brick structure typical of this area, in the Osterfeld part of the city. In contrast to these works of the past, stands the ultramodern Stadthalle, offering stages and halls for theater, concerts and congresses. Like so many cities in the Rhineland, Oberhausen enjoys many choirs.

From Blast Furnaces to Windmills

From Oberhausen it is possible to take off on a little circular tour of the northwestern corner of the Rhineland, through the former Hanseatic strongholds of Wesel, Rees and Emmerich, on the right bank of the Rhine, where the scenery evokes Holland rather than Germany. Here the hills fade away, the Rhine becomes broader, the river is busy with boats and barges crossing the nearby Dutch frontier and the landscape is peppered not only with little old redbrick towns but also with lazily turning windmills.

Crossing to the left bank, we arrive in the old city of Kleve, associated in legend with Lohengrin, whose Schwanenburg Castle, the former home of the Dukes of Kleve, stands on a cliff over the Rhine and which you might want to visit. It is also known as the home of Anne of Cleves, fourth wife of Henry VIII.

Swinging back to the south, we come first to Kalkar, where you must not fail to stop to see the beautifully carved altars of the St. Nicholas Church. The Mary Magdalene alone justifies this whole detour. Xanten is another town in which the past speaks eloquently. Well-preserved examples of medieval architecture include the impressive and massive Kleve Tower Gate, the Town Mill, remains of the city walls and towers, all from the 14th–15th centuries, and most particularly the Gothic Cathedral of St. Viktor, begun in the 12th century with a beautiful cloister and containing notable works of art. Once a Roman garrison town, a colony of Trajan, Xanten has excavated an amphitheater and drama and comedies from classical and modern playwrights are performed here during the summer. The Roman reconstruction is in what is now an archeological park and is reached on the B57 between Moers and Kleve. They even serve Roman food here! Continuing through Kevelaer, whose Gnadenkapelle (Chapel of Graces) is a pilgrimage center, we reach Krefeld.

Capital of silk and velvet making (along with nearby Ürdingen), Krefeld is also the center of the clothing industry; and if you see a group of young people sitting in the sun on a fine day, working busily away on sketching pads, it is a safe guess that they are students of dress design in the local fashion school. There is a textile museum in the Textile Engineers' School at Ürdingen, while Krefeld's Kaiser Wilhelm

Museum specializes in Lower Rhineland and Italian art. Krefeld's prosperity is not due to silk alone. It is also a city of heavy industry, with iron and steel works, and the principal agricultural center in this area, with important agricultural experimental institutes. While you are in Krefeld, you could make a trip to Linn Castle, surrounded by a moat, where there is a fascinating folklore museum.

Turning west we come to Süchteln, with an interesting Heimat Museum in the 18th-century house known as Jakobsgut, the Romanesque St. Clemens Church and sand quarries of value to the steel and iron industry. The nearby city of Viersen is known primarily as the cultural center of this border area, with an unusually large number of concerts and stage presentations by important international and German ensembles, and spectators coming also from neighboring Holland. The tall Gothic St. Remigius Church, the symbol of Viersen, presides over the parks, gardens and tree islands of this quiet town, surrounded by unspoiled countryside. Immediately south is Mönchengladbach, a busy textile center, which not only manufactures cloth and maintains technical schools on textile production, but is also an important producer of textile machinery. The town possesses many notable old buildings, among them the 13th-century cathedral, the baroque Rathaus and the former Benedictine Abbey Neuwerk.

Mönchengladbach is proud of its reputation as the German capital of male chorus singing and of its soccer team. The surrounding countryside is pleasant—two small streams, the Schwalm and the Nette, with their lakes, provide a cheerful natural background for picturesque water mills and moated castles. One side trip from here might be to Rheydt, with a Renaissance castle noted for its arcaded courtyard and also containing a museum.

Returning to the Rhine we reach Neuss, one of the oldest (nearly 2,000 years old) German towns, which was probably a thriving settlement during the Stone Age. A Roman garrison and town here was known as Novaesium and recent discoveries have unearthed early Christian graves and relics and an early Christian chapel under the St. Quirinus Cathedral, whose round dome and square tower are the landmarks of Neuss. In 1956 an early 4th-century baptismal cellar of the Cybele cult, at that time a great rival to Christianity, was discovered, the only such cellar, except for the one in Ostia near Rome, which has been found within the boundaries of the former Roman Empire. The Obertor, a massive medieval gate, housing a museum, should not be missed. Visit also the Dreikönigenkirche with interesting stained glass windows, and the old town houses, including the historic inn *Em Schwatte Päd*. The modern St. Konrad Church has an unusual stained glass window-wall. A short jump across the Rhine is Düsseldorf.

Tour of Bergisch Land

From Düsseldorf, the most direct route for the exploration of the Rhine Valley would be straight south to Cologne. But for the more leisurely traveler, there is an opportunity here for a circular swing through the territory east of the Rhine. The key to this area, known as Bergisch Land, is Velbert, the center of the German lock industry since the 16th century and the home of the German Museum for Locks and Keys. This amazing collection includes 4,000 examples from all over the world and from the earliest times (such as an Assyrian wooden lock from 5000 B.C.) to the latest devices of the modern age.

Wuppertal is a city that should interest engineers, as a pioneering center of their art. Not only are there several dams in its vicinity, but among them is the oldest one in Germany; and one of its sights is an elevated railway, invented by a Wuppertal engineer and built in 1900, that hangs suspended from an overhead rail like a mechanical sloth. Always a patron of the arts, Wuppertal has a fine collection of paintings from the 17th to 19th centuries in its Städtisches Museum and modern art in its Studio für Neue Kunst section. The Clock Museum, with a Glockenspiel, displays a long line of historic time-measuring devices, beginning with an Egyptian water clock dating from around 1400 B.C. A beautifully landscaped zoo contains several thousand exotic animals and it blossoms in the spring with innumerable flowers. Among the many examples of modern architecture, particular mention should be made of Stadtbad Johannisberg, an elegant glass structure, in a park, which houses several swimming pools.

Proceeding south from Wuppertal, the chief city of the Bergisch Land, we continue through Remscheid, the German center for the manufacture of machine tools. Its local museum is a beautiful example of the patrician houses of this region. It is here also that you will see the oldest of German dams, mentioned above. Röntgen, the discoverer of X-rays, was born here and in the suburb of Lennep is a museum devoted to him and his discovery.

Passing the symbol of the Bergisch Land, Schloss Burg, one of the biggest fortresses in western Germany, we come to Solingen, a city of workshops famous for cutlery. Solingen's predominant architecture is typical—roomy, two-story houses with slate roofs, white windowsills, and green shutters. Some of the old workshops along the Wupper are of half-timbered construction.

From Solingen we can make a lazy swing around the eastern edge of Bergisch Land, moving from ploughed fields to slowly rising, thickly forested hills. We come first to Wipperfürth, not far from the Neye Dam; there are several other dams farther east and north, as well as—even more important to a summer tourist—the artificial lakes created by them. This is also an area of underground caves, spreading from here in an easterly direction through the rest of Bergisch Land and through Sauerland. Two caves of note are Aggertal Cave near Ründeroth, and a stalactite cavern, near Wiehl. Also nearby is Marienhagen, one of the best-preserved medieval villages in the whole area: a wealth of half-timbered houses and a small Gothic church known as the Bunte Kirche (Church of Colors), which has valuable Gothic frescos and carved doors.

From Ründeroth a very scenic stretch of road takes us to Gummersbach and the nearby Aggertal Dam and artificial lake. From here we may proceed directly south through Denklingen and Waldbröl to reach the scenic Sieg valley, and stop off in Siegburg, whose 11th-century Benedictine Abbey on Michaelsberg commands a magnificent view over the surrounding hills. The Servatiuskirche has a famous Romanesque treasury, with masterpieces of the goldsmiths' art. Siegburg was a well-known pottery center of the Middle Ages, as the collection of pottery and ceramics in the Heimat Museum shows. Don't miss the pillory on the Market Square and the historic 15th-century Weinhaus "Auf der Arken." Also visit the building which now houses the Magistrate's Court, birthplace of composer Engelbert Humperdinck.

Continuing north we come to Bensberg, with the old castle and the baroque palace of the Counts of Berg. Eight miles northwest is the early Gothic Altenberg Cathedral, offering the effect of a great church surrounded, not by shops and houses but by a forest.

Leverkusen, virtually a suburb of Cologne and the home of aspirin, offers the 400-ft.-high Bayer skyscraper, the Bayer plant with a Japanese garden, a host of modern structures and a bit outside, Morsbroich Castle with a city museum. Across the Rhine stands Cologne.

Aachen—Charlemagne's City

About nine miles south of Cologne is Brühl, where the baroque castle of Augustusberg, with a famous stairway by Balthasar Neumann, is set in magnificent gardens. Here, too, is Phantasialand, a 60-acre leisure park, with bob-sled runs, monorail and boat trips.

West of Cologne, a bit more than an hour's drive via the autobahn, is Aachen, founded in 795. Aachen—or if you use the French name for it, Aix-la-Chapelle—is also known as Bad Aachen, for while this is by no means its main claim to fame, Aachen is a noted spa, with the hottest springs in northwest Europe.

The French name refers to the early 9th-century Imperial Chapel, once a part of the imperial palace and later enlarged into the present cathedral, whose importance was due to the fact that Aachen was

Charlemagne's capital and long his residence. Thirty-two of the Holy Roman Emperors of the German nation were crowned in the cathedral whose most admired central section, the Carolingian-style Oktogon, was built around 800 under Charlemagne. From 1349 to 1531, the coronation dinners were held in the Reichssaal of the Gothic Rathaus, built in the 14th century on the foundations of the former Carolingian palace; two towers, however, Granusturm and Marktturm, have remained from the Carolingian times. The marble throne of Charlemagne may still be seen in the upper section of the cathedral and his remains lie in the richly-ornamented and sculptured Karlsschrein, located today on the main altar in the Gothic choir of the cathedral. The choir has enormous stained glass windows and presents a brilliant spectacle.

Another great treasure, located presently on the altar of the St. Nicholas Chapel, is the Shrine of Mary, an intricately and richly sculptured gold and silver reliquary, finished in 1237, designed to hold the four holy relics of the city—possibly the finest medieval reliquary in Germany where there are many fine ones. In the treasury of the cathedral, you can see a host of other jeweled objects, many of gold and silver, such as the bust of Charlemagne, dating from 1350 and containing part of his cranium; the 10th-century Lothar Cross; the Bible of Charlemagne from about 800; the Bible of Otto III from about 1000.

Since 1950, in the Coronation Chamber of the City Hall, the International Prize of the City of Aachen has been awarded for special services contributing to the unification of Europe. Among those prizewinners of the last quarter-century are such names as Konrad Adenauer, Sir Winston Churchill and Robert Schumann.

Other principal sights include the city gates, Marschiertor and Ponttor; two fountain statues, the "Chicken Thief" on the Hühnermarkt (Chicken Market Square), and Marktbrunnen with Charlemagne's statue on the Rathaus square; Suermondt-Museum for old Dutch, Flemish, and German paintings, Couven Museum in Haus Monheim for rococo and Biedermeier patrician furnishings, with its Neue-Galeric Sammlung Ludwig, housing Germany's most comprehensive collection of 20th-century art and specializing particularly in post-1970 works. There is also an International Press Museum, a unique collection of newspapers from all over the world, housed in the oldest (1495) burgher's house in Aachen. For further old-world atmosphere, wander through the old Körbergäschen; for spa atmosphere and water the Kurhaus and Kurgarten, and Elisenbrunnen. For those looking for a different kind of excitement, Aachen has a modern casino.

Markets in Aachen are a great attraction: inquiry at the local tourist office will indicate what is currently on, but they include good craft and art, a flea market, flowers, and sometimes a peddlers' market with the sellers in traditional costumes and traveling players to entertain.

Northeast of Aachen is the old town of Jülich, once the granary of the Holy Roman Empire. The 13th-century Witches' Tower and the 16th-century Citadel are worth a visit.

At Aachen you are at the beginning of the Eifel mountain region, noted for its natural beauty, which extends south of this point, west of the Rhine. We plunge southward into this attractive country and come immediately to Monschau, squeezed into the narrow rocky valley of the Ruhr, which chatters noisily through the town. Local sports enthusiasts enjoy going over a dam on the river in a "canoe slalom." Narrow steep-roofed, half-timbered houses, often perched on stone foundations rising three or four stories from the river in apparently perilous equilibrium, line both shores. Monschau looks just as it did in the 18th century.

Penetrating deeper into the Nord Eifel, we pass through the Hürtgen forest; by the Castle of Nideggen; on to the climatic resort of Gemünd, where the Urft and Olef flow together; where you are in the Eifel lake district and where you can see the Rur Dam, about six miles from Gemünd; through Steinfeld, with its monastery and the Eifel Cathedral; through Schleiden, a resort in forested mountains whose Gothic church has famous stained glass windows and the 14th-century King's Organ and where there is also a 12th-century palace, to Blankenheim, above which towers a castle, another climatic station at the source of the Ahr River; and then, swinging northward on the return loop, to Münstereifel.

This town, with its medieval city walls, towers and gates well preserved, offers many prizes for the admirer of the Middle Ages: a Romanesque Stiftskirche with crypt from Carolingian times; old patrician houses (half-timbered and gabled), such as Windeck-Haus; one of the few Romanesque private houses north of the Alps at Langenhecke No. 6 and a few Gothic houses, among them the Rathaus. From this stronghold of the Middle Ages we return to the Rhine.

Bonn, the Capital

Bonn, gateway to the romantic Rhine Valley, is much more than the capital of the German Federal Republic—its history stretches back for 2,000 eventful years. Under the name of *Castra Bonnensia* it was an important link in the Roman defense line along the Rhine. In 253 A.D. two Roman soldiers, Cassius and Florentius, were put to death because of their Christian beliefs. One of the first Christian shrines arose over their graves, the place where the cathedral stands today.

In the 13th century, the powerful Prince Electors of Cologne moved to Bonn and built up the city as a worthy capital of their domain. They put up monuments, laid out parks and avenues, and erected a palace (today the home of Bonn's university, completed in 1725 in a late Baroque manner), Poppelsdorfer Castle and the city hall. The castle and university are joined by the Poppelsdorfer Allee.

A more modern point of pilgrimage, however, is the house at Bonngasse 20, today a museum, where Beethoven was born in 1770. The house contains many relics of the great man, including the sad eartrumpet, and his piano, once equipped with an equally pathetic sounding-board, that could not help overcome his deafness. In his honor, an annual music festival is held in the Beethovenhalle, a modern concert and congress building consisting of several halls of varying sizes, all with excellent acoustics and outfitted with the latest technical devices. Near Beethoven's house is the Gothic-style Remigius Church. The top attraction among the churches is the late Romanesque cathedral with very fine cloister colonnade.

Among Bonn's other attractions, the "Alter Zoll," a mighty bastion overlooking the Rhine, is doubtless the most beautiful. An attractive promenade extends along the banks of the Rhine from the Alter Zoll to the Bundeshaus, the German Parliament. For another pleasant view, walk up to Venusberg.

South of Bonn and virtually a diplomatic suburb, is Bad Godesberg, one of Germany's oldest spas. This is the site of the Godesburg, a 96-foot-high watch tower. It was built in 1210 and, amazingly, in 1583 the hill on which it stands was blown up but the tower itself survived. Its 18th-century Redoute Kurhaus is today the center of diplomatic social activities in Germany. Across the Rhine at Königswinter are the Siebengebirge (Seven Mountains), a natural preserve of forested hills, magnificent views over the Rhine and the Eifel mountains, very good wine (the famous Dragon's Blood), and a legend lurking around every craggy peak. It is an intriguing thought that the bath of blood which made Siegfried invincible might have been nothing more than a vat of extra-special vintage wine.

The top of Drachenfels (Dragon's Crag), the most famous of the seven with the ruins of an old castle, can be reached via easy footpaths and a cogwheel railroad (the first and oldest in Germany—built in 1883). Earlier the Seven Mountains were noted for their quarries, which provided stone for most of the surrounding castles and churches, including Cologne Cathedral, but since being declared a national park in 1889, the quarries are no longer worked. Do not be confused by the name Königswinter, for it has nothing to do with winter, but derives from the Latin *Vinitorium (Vintra)* meaning King's Vineyards, a name in existence since the 14th century and acknowledging the fact that many of the vineyards were in the possession of the kings of Germany.

From this romantic vantage point we leave the Northern Rhineland to continue upstream to the Rhineland-Palatinate.

PRACTICAL INFORMATION FOR THE
NORTHERN RHINELAND

HOTELS AND RESTAURANTS. You mustn't leave the Rhineland without eating *Hase im Topf,* a pâté made of rabbit, pork, Madeira, brandy and red wine, highly flavored and baked for hours in an earthenware pot. You should try the wonderful white beans cooked with bacon which is served with the famous *Neusser Sauerkraut* of Neuss, but it's also a meal in itself. *Himmel und Erde,* heaven and earth, is a dish of potatoes and apples cooked together and mashed. A specialty on the Lower Rhine and in Bergisch Land is *Panhas,* a meat paste prepared with sausage gravy, blood, and buckwheat meal.

In Cologne you should not get mixed up with your usual terminology: *Kölscher Kaviar mit Musik* here means a rye bread roll *(Röggelchen)* with blood sausage and onions; *Halver Huhn* is not half chicken as the name would imply but half Röggelchen with old Dutch cheese and strong Düsseldorf mustard; *Forelle Blau* in the Cologne tavern dialect is pickled herring.

Lighter and more delicate fare is a delicious eel dish called *Gebackener Aal,* trout fixed in a special way that involves cooking in paper and called *Forelle in Papierhülle,* and *Moselhecht,* Mosel pike cooked with cream and grated cheese.

If you like sweets, try *Muzenmändelchen* and *Mandelspekulatius,* both almond cookies, or *Printen,* Aachen's honey cookies.

Aachen (Aix). Hotels: *Parkhotel Quellenhof,* Monheimsallee 52, at the Kurpark, 220 beds and 80 baths, indoor thermal swimming pool, luxurious top establishment in town; *Novotel* (E), Europaplatz, new 1980, 238 beds, pool, restaurant, central location; the smaller *Brüls am Dom* (M), Hühnermarkt. Most rooms with bath or shower. *3 Türme* (M), Ludwigsallee 25. A small hotel near the Veltmanplatz gardens. Some rooms can be noisy.

Restaurants: One of the most interesting eating and drinking taverns in this part of Germany is the historic *Ratskeller* (M–E) in Rathaus. The tower restaurant on Nussberg offers a magnificent view of the city.

Noted for cuisine: *Elisenbrunnen* (M), on Friedrich-Wilhelm-Platz, with glass front facing its garden and café terrace. *Gala im Casino* (E), highly recommended. Monheimsallee 44. *Gut Schwarzenbruch* (M), 5 miles outside in a former stable for noble horses, with game as specialty. For an (I) selection, try *Haus des Deutschen Ostens,* Franzstr. 74.

Bad Godesberg. The modern *Parkhotel,* garni, Am Kurpark, 54 rooms, with Chinese restaurant attached, *Rheinhotel Dreesen,* Rheinaustr. 1, 90 rooms, indoor seawater pool, *Insel,* Theaterplatz 5, modern, are all (E).

All (M) are—Two tradition-filled establishments are *Zum Adler*, garni, Koblenzer Str. 60, first class superior, small, antique-furnished, with an excellent restaurant, and *Schaumburger Hof*, at Plittersdorf on the river, with garden. *Rheinland*, Rheinallee 17, quiet, good cuisine.

Drachenfels, on the river in Mehlem, is (M). Quiet.

Godesburg-Hotel (L), an ultramodern attachment to the medieval Godesburg Castle ruins; the combination is of doubtful esthetic appearance, but the small hotel (30 beds) is very comfortable (all rooms with bath and shower) and there is a nice view from the restaurant terrace.

Bonn. The hotel situation here has now eased up considerably, but advance reservations are still recommended. **Hotels:** *Königshof* (L), Adenauerallee 9, modern, 120 beds, all rooms with bath or shower, half of the rooms with view of the river, suites available, excellent cuisine and wine cellar.

Expensive are the *Steigenberger*, Am Bundeskanzlerplatz, 160 rooms, two restaurants and club on the 18th floor; the *Schlosspark-Hotel*, very quiet position at Venusbergweg 27, 67 rooms, indoor pool, sauna, and *Bristol*, 120 rooms; very comfortable; first class cuisine. The *Sternhotel*, Markt 8, 65 rooms; *Bergischer Hof*, Münsterplatz 23.

Moderate are—Smaller *Eden*, Am Hofgarten 6, and *Muskewitz*, Dechenstr. 5. *Savoy*, Berliner Freiheit 17, and the *Rheinland*, 30 rooms with shower, near the Rhine Bridge.

Restaurants: *Ambassador*, 18th floor of Steigenberger Hotel; *Am Tulpenfeld*, An der Heuss-Allee 2; *Ristorante Grand Italia*, Bischofsplatz 1, with outstanding Italian cuisine, *Chez Loup*, Oxford Str. 18; all expensive.

Moderate are the colorful *Weinhaus Jacobs*, Friedrichstr. 23 with excellent wine cellar; *Hansa-Keller*, Kaiserplatz; *Beethovenhalle*, Erzberger Ufer, with view of the river; the *Im Stiefel*, Bonngasse 30; and *Im Bären*, Acherstr. 1.

Duisburg. **Hotels:** *Steigenberger Hotel Duisburger Hof* (L), König Heinrich Platz, 128 rooms with bath or shower, restaurant, café with music, bar.

Moderate are—*Rheingarten*, Konigstr. 7, in Homburg suburb; *am Stadion*, Kalkweg 26; *Ideal*, Realschulstr. 20. *Haus Reinhard*, garni, Fuldastr. 31; small, 18 rooms, all with bath, very comfortable and quiet.

Mercator (I), garni, Mercatorstr. 92.

Restaurants: Medium-priced are *Börsenstuben*, Dammstr. 28a, and the roof garden restaurant in the *Priel* store.

Dürscheid, east of Cologne. Nearby *Schloss Georgshausen* (M) is run by the owner, Baron von Landsberg. All period-furnished, including the first-class restaurant and the deep wine cellar tavern.

Essen. **Hotels:** The *Arosa*, in the Rüttenscheid sector, is deluxe; 120 air-conditioned rooms, all with bath or shower, 2 restaurants and bar.

Handelshof (E), 300 beds, at main station. The 150-bed *Essener Hof* (formerly *Vereinshaus*) in Teichstr. 2; the *Scheidegg*, Am Waldhausenpark 7, and the

Hotel-Restaurant Parkhaus Hügel, on the lakeside at Baldeneysee, Freiherr-von-Steinstr. 209, small, are all (M).

Hotel Heihoff, Essener Str. 36, 17 beds, some rooms with bath, is inexpensive.

Motel: *Touring Hotel,* garni, Frankenstr. 379, quiet location in Bredeney section, 65 beds, first class reasonable.

Restaurants: Best, and expensive are *Burghof,* Kettwiger Strasse 36; *Blumenhof* and *Silberkuhlshof,* both with outdoor terraces, at the Gruga Park; *Strothe,* in main rail station; *Mathäserbräu* in Hotel Handelshof, with music; *Schwarze Lene,* overlooking the Baldeney Lake, and; in Rellinghausen suburb, *Kockshusen,* Pilgrimsteig 51; a 17th-century house in Schellenberg Forest.

(M) are *Pilsstuben* (Hotel Handelshof) at the main station and *Clubhaus Wilmes,* Moltkeplatz.

Foreign food with good reputation: *Asia,* Kreuzeskirchstr. (Passage), for Chinese food; *Dalmatien-Grill,* Hohenzollernstr. 34, Balkan; *Pizzeria Taormina,* Rüttenscheider Str. 143, Italian.

Kettwig. *Schloss Hugenpoet* (L) near Kettwig southwest of Essen; 23 rooms, some suites; outstanding restaurant. Riding and tennis: hunting and fishing.

In town, *Schmachtenbergshof,* Gasthaus since 1726, most rooms with bath.

Restaurant: *Rôtisserie Ange d'Or* (E), Bahnhofstr. 133, excellent.

Königswinter, across the river from Bad Godesberg. *Zum Anker,* Am Rheinufer 102 and *Rheingold,* Drachenfelsstr. 36, 47 beds. Both (M).

Restaurants: Leading for food and comfort are *Haus Maternus,* Poststr. 3; *Wirtshaus St. Michael,* Brunnenallee 26; *Stadthalle,* Koblenzerstr. 80; *Mehlemer Eck,* Mainzerstr. 151, modern, has 120 beds; *Wirtin,* locally known as "Ännchen", at Ännchenplatz 1, is a 300-year-old student inn. *Rheinterrasse* at the ship station, overlooks the river.

Worth investigating is *Da Roberto,* for trattoria atmosphere and excellent Italian cooking. Moderate.

Krefeld. Hotels: *Parkhotel Krefelder Hof* (L), Ürdinger Str. 245, good food in restaurant *L'Escargot. Haus Schüten* (E), Ürdinger Str. 145, garden restaurant.

Both (M)—*Niederrheinischer Hof,* Hülser Str. 398, 27 rooms; *Haus Fänsen,* Krüllsdyk 25, 8 rooms, quiet location.

Restaurants: Tops are *Korff zum Königshof* (M), Kölner Str. 256 and *La Capannina,* Uerdingerstr. 552, fine Italian specialties; book ahead.

Tivoli-Haus (I), Rheinstr. 89, for good food at good prices.

Mönchengladbach. Hotels: The *Dorint* (E), Hohenzollernstr. 5, tops the list; 172 beds, all rooms with bath, suites with TV, international cuisine.

Holiday Inn (E), am Geroplatz, 128 double rooms with bath, heated indoor pool, sauna, and local specialties in restaurant.

Möller (M), Hindenburgstr. 175, garni, handy to the main rail station.

Restaurants: *Dortmunder Hof,* Bismarckstr. 21; and particularly the old and colorful *Sankt Vith* at Alter Markt 6. *Kaiser-Friedrich-Halle,* Hohenzollernstr. 15, with terrace.

Mülheim an der Ruhr.
Hotels: *Noy* (E), Schloss Strasse 28, 55 beds, smart restaurant; the *Euro-Hotel,* Duisburger Strasse 486, has 40 beds and is moderate; 140-bed *Handelshof,* Friedrichstr. 15, is inexpensive.

Restaurants: *Fuente* (E), Gracht 209, high-class French cuisine; specialties: *kohlrabi soufflé* with crayfish, lamb-filet in pastry; *Wasserbahnhof-Mintard* with view of river traffic; cozy *Becker-Eichbaum,* Obere Saarlandstr. 5; *Sassenhof* in Spelldorf suburb with rustic décor and Westphalian ham.

Solingen.
Turmhotel (M), Kölner Str. 99, garni.

Restaurant: *Theaterrestaurant* (I), Hauptstr. 255, good food at a reasonable price.

About 2½ miles south is *Burg Hohenscheid,* a castle with 40 beds (all rooms with bath or shower); lovely setting, moderately acceptable hotel, adequate food, limited wine list.

Wahlscheid,
east of Cologne, autobahn exit at Siegburg. Nearby *Schloss Auel* (E) dates from 1391. Riding, trout fishing; 40 beds. Worth seeking out.

Wuppertal.
The city consists of two main districts: Elberfeld to the west, and Barmen to the east. When selecting a hotel, be sure that it is located in the section you prefer.

Hotels: *Kaiserhof* (E), at railroad station in Elberfeld, 110 beds, 80 baths. *Hotel Haus Juliana* (E), Mollenkötten 195, in the Barmen section. *Zur Post* with music and dancing in its café is moderate while *Trierer Hof* is inexpensive, both in Elberfeld.

Restaurants: Hotel restaurants are the best bet hereabouts (for plain reliability). Hotel *Kaiserhof* has a good restaurant; *Ratskeller* (I) in Elberfeld, Neumarkt; *Donau-Stuben* in Barmen, Concordienstr. 4; the pleasant *Zoo-Gaststätten,* also café with music and dancing, at the zoo; *Zum Alten Kuhstall* in Elberfeld, Böttingerweg 3, for local color.

The *Turmrestaurant im Sparkassenhochhaus* (M), is a tower eating spot with an excellent view.

A rewarding place to visit is the Schloss Lüntenbeck where *Il Castello* (M), provides fine Italian cooking in atmospheric surroundings. It's a little outside town, just off the route to Düsseldorf.

NIGHTLIFE. Bonn: Show and dancing in *CD-Night-Club* Rheingasse 14; *Club Populaire* (Jazz club), Kasernenstr. 28; *Carlton* (cabaret), Wilhelmstr. 1.

Essen: Cabaret, variety, striptease: *Studio-Kabarett,* Friedrich-Ebert Str. 70; *Zur Silbermine* and *Whisky Bar,* both at Kleine Kronenstr. 3 (corner of Rottstr.); *Zillertal,* Rottstr. 28; *Club David,* Bachstr. 9 (very theatrical).

Mostly for dancing; *Ball der einsamen Herzen* (lonely hearts, 'real' dancing), Schützenbahn 19; *San Francisco* and *Essen City,* both Dellbrugge 5; *Mississippi* in Handelshof hotel. Outdoor dancing in summer; *Städtischer Saalbau* and *Stadtgarten-Saalbau* in Steele district. Wine, songs and dancing: *Burgplatz-Weinstuben,* Kettwigerstr. 36; *Pony,* Alfredstr. 41; *Spiegel-Bar,* Kastainenallee 28.

Wuppertal: Cabaret: *Maxim-Bar,* Burgstr. 9; *La Femme,* Friedrich-Ebert-Str. 26.

MUSIC AND THEATER. All cities with their own musical groups and theaters have rich concert and theater seasons. Many other cities also schedule regular programs by inviting guest performing groups. The most important symphonic orchestras are the *City Orchestras* of Aachen, Bonn, Duisburg, Essen, Krefeld-Mönchengladbach, Oberhausen, Remscheid, Solingen and Wuppertal. Many other musical groups exist in Rhineland, notably a tremendous number of choirs. Mönchengladbach reputed to be the capital of male choral singing in Germany and Essen, for instance, counts 110 choirs.

Opera, operetta, ballet and plays are performed by *Städtische Bühnen* of Essen, Krefeld-Mönchengladbach, Oberhausen, and Wuppertal-Solingen; by *Stadttheater* of Aachen and Rheydt; by *Theater der Stadt* in Bonn; and by *Remscheider Bühne* in Remscheid. Most of these cities have new and very modern theater buildings and concert halls, such as the remarkable theater building and the *Beethovenhalle* in Bonn, the *Opernhaus* and *Städtischer Saalbau* in Essen, *Mercatorhalle* in Duisburg and the *Stadthalle* in Oberhausen.

MUSEUMS. Aachen: *Suermondt-Museum,* Wilhelmstr. 18, 15th–17th-century paintings and old wcodcarved sculptures, also includes the Ludwig Collection of modern art which is in the Neue Galerie; *Couven-Museum,* Hühnermarkt 17, old patrician furniture; *Cathedral Treasury,* the most outstanding north of the Alps; *International Press Museum,* Pontstr. 13, 80,000 press publications of all ages in 30 languages.

Bonn: *Rheinisches Landesmuseum,* Colmantstr. 14, prehistoric relics (including the skull of Neanderthal Man, said to be Europe's "oldest inhabitant"— 60,000 years old), Roman and Frankish antiquities, old German and Dutch paintings; *Zoological Museum,* Adenauerallee 150, one of the world's largest. *City Art Collection,* Rathausgasse 5, 18th–20th-century German paintings; *Beethoven-Haus,* Bonngasse 20, recently restored birthplace of Beethoven.

Essen: *Folkwang Museum,* Bismarckstr. 66, noted collection of 19th–20th century art. *Münsterschatz,* Am Burgplatz, large collection of early Romanesque church treasures. *German Poster Museum,* Steeler Str. 29, international posters from 19th century on. *Ruhrland- und Heimatmuseum,* Goethestr. 41, local and natural history.

Krefeld: *Kaiser-Wilhelm-Museum,* Karlsplatz 35, art and cultural history, artistic crafts, Italian Renaissance art.

Neuss: *Clemens-Sels-Museum* in Obertor, Roman relics, medieval paintings and sculpture, local history and customs.

Remscheid: *Heimatmuseum,* history, economy and culture of Bergisch Land; *Deutches Röntgenmuseum* in Lennep, discovery, development and application of X-rays.

Solingen: *Deutsches Klingenmuseum* in Gräfrath, blades and steel tableware.

Velbert: *German Locks and Keys Museum,* in the Rathaus.

SPORTS. Horseracing is very popular: important international events are staged every year, particularly in Mülheim, Krefeld and Mönchengladbach. The Aachen Week, one of the top international riding tournaments, is a yearly affair in late June or early July. **Horseback riding** facilities in all the principal cities; in Essen in Stadtwald. One of the peak **bicycle** competitions is the 6-day indoor race in Essen during winter. **Golf** courses exist in Aachen, Duisburg, Krefeld, Bensberg, Neviges and Gummersbach. Important golf tournaments take place every year at Duisburg, Krefeld and Neviges. There are **tennis** courts in all larger towns.

Baldeney Lake is the center for **sailing** as well as **rowing** and the site of several regattas every year. **Motor boating** competitions also take place here. Sailing is also popular on the lower Rhine. Essen has about a dozen indoor and outdoor **swimming** places—including Baldeney Lake. Indoor and outdoor facilities also at Bonn, Duisburg (4 indoor pools), Krefeld, Mülheim, Oberhausen, Remscheid (3 indoor pools), Wuppertal and elsewhere.

The main **skiing** centers are Hellenthal-Hollerath, Udenbreth, Monschau, Kalterherberg, Höfen, Blankenhelm and Gemünd, all in the Eifel; also several places in Bergisch Land and Siebengebirge. Artificial **ice skating** rinks in Essen and Krefeld.

USEFUL ADDRESSES. Parking: *Bonn:* City-Parkgaragen, Annagraben; Scheben, Königstr. 77; Bieber Weberstr. 60. *Duisburg;* Parkhaus Mercatorhalle, Averdunkstr.; Tiefgarage Karstadt, König-Heinrich-Platz. *Essen:* Parkhaus Rüttenscheider Stern, Bertoldstr. 15 and Waldhausenpark, Hindenburgstr. 35. *Mönchengladbach:* at the main station. *Wuppertal:* Alte Freiheit, Hofaue 90 in Elberfeld. All other cities have at least one parking garage.

Tourist Information: *Aachen:* Kur and Verkehrsamt, Markt 39–41; *Bad Godesberg:* Moltkestr. 66; *Bonn:* Information pavilion at Munsterstr. 20; *Duis-*

burg: Verkehrsverein, Hochhaus at main station; *Essen:* Amt für Wirtschafts- und Verkehrsförderung in Rathaus and Verkehrsverein in Haus der Technik at main station (room reservations weekdays 8 A.M. to 10 P.M., Sundays 10–12); *Krefeld:* Verkehrsverein in Hansahaus at main station and Informationszentrum, Theaterplatz 1; *Mönchengladbach:* Verkehrs- und Werbeamt in Rathaus and Verkehrsverein at main station; *Mülheim an der Ruhr:* in Rathaus; *Wuppertal:* Informationszentrum in Pavillon Döppersberg near Elberfeld railroad station.

Embassies: United States, Mehlemer Ave. in Bad Godesberg; Canada, Friedrich-Wilhelmstr. 18, Bonn; Great Britain, Friedrich-Ebert-Allee 77, Bonn.

COLOGNE AND DÜSSELDORF

Great Cities on the Rhine

The two most important centers of culture, trade and industry on the Rhine are historic Cologne and Düsseldorf, less than 35 miles apart. One on the left bank and the other on the right, they are both cities with a rich history and an even richer present. We are devoting a chapter to them, since a comparison is easily made on the spot and will provide many glimpses into the way that Germany has brought her history into contemporary focus.

COLOGNE

Cologne (Köln in German), with a population of about a million, is the largest city in the Rhineland, and the fourth largest—after Berlin,

Hamburg and Munich—in Germany. Known throughout the world for its scented waters, Eau de Cologne, first produced over a century ago, the city is now a major commercial center. Many visitors come for one of the numerous trade fairs, rather than as mere tourists and Cologne is ready for them. On the Deutzer side of the Rhine there are fourteen massive exhibition halls, where over twenty international events are held yearly.

But the city is also a great cultural center: the University, founded in 1388, and numerous technical colleges, the large number of theaters, concert halls, the headquarters of the West German Radio and the impressive range of museums, all bear witness to the rich intellectual life of the city—as well as to the depth of its financial resources. Cologne's greatest heritage comes from its history, which is embodied in a remarkable range of buildings, dating as far back as the Romans.

Not that the city was founded by the Romans. The Celts had already occupied the site, but the Romans were the first to circle it with walls, and there are many relics of their adventurous civil engineering. The Rhine was as far as the Romans penetrated to the north-east, and Cologne's name reflects its status in the Empire. It means "colony," an outpost, and the Romans were able to hold it for more than 400 years, before being ousted by the Franks and other Germanic tribes.

During the Roman period, some 20,000 people lived in Cologne. Flourishing trade increased this number over the following centuries— 35,000 in the 13th century, 800,000 by the beginning of World War II. But the number had dropped to only 40,000 when the Allies arrived in 1945. Now only half the population is locally born and one in ten is not even German. Despite this, the local dialect and many local traditions have survived in the older neighborhoods, in the traditional Millowitsch Theater and, of course, in the Cologne Carnival.

Many famous people have lived here: Marie de Medici, wife of Henri IV of France, who died here in exile in 1642; Peter Paul Reubens, who spent his childhood here in the 1570s; the physicist G.S. Ohm, whose name was given to the electrical unit; and Konrad Adenauer, a Lord Mayor who went on to become Chancellor of Germany.

Although the city's historical heritage is vast, there are magnificent new structures to match the aging grace of earlier buildings. The Gerling Versicherung, the ultra-modern Opera House, the new Chamber of Commerce and whole streets like Schildergasse, as well as many pedestrian precincts, have all helped to give Cologne a bright new face.

EXPLORING COLOGNE

At the heart of the ancient city of Cologne stands the magnificent cathedral of St. Peter and St. Mary. Largely untouched by the devastating bombing of the last war, its soaring stone spires, carved like lace, are a symbol of the city's proud spirit. They are surrounded by post-war structures—like the glass-walled Central Station next door—but these only serve to accentuate the cathedral's gothic splendor. Our two tours of the city will start and end here.

Built between 1248 and the middle of the 16th century, the cathedral was designed to be the largest in Europe. From the outside, it is a mass of buttresses and flying buttresses, which can be viewed with ease from the broad pedestrian terrace. Inside, there are finely carved choir stalls, tombstones of archbishops, religious paintings and stained-glass windows of breathtaking beauty. The high altar dates from 1330 and the golden, jeweled shrine to the Three Kings from 1220. The crypt is still being excavated and all sorts of discoveries are being made, including Roman remains and the tomb of a young knight in armor. It is worth climbing the spire nearly 100 meters from the ground, where you will be rewarded with a superb view of Cologne and the distant mountains. Survey the city: our first, and longer, tour takes you south as far as the towers of St. Severin, beyond the second bridge, on the western side of the Rhine.

South of the Cathedral

As a reminder that great builders occupied the site of Cologne long before the cathedral was built, you might like to start with the Romanic-German Museum on the south side of the cathedral terrace. Opened in 1974, it contains the famous Dionysus mosaic, as well as a collection of Roman tombstones, glass, coins and jewelry. At the gate, you can hire a portable cassette player, complete with guide cassette, which brings the exhibition poignantly to life.

South of the museum, at the corner of Am Hof and Unter Taschenmacher is the Saaleck House, dating from the 15th century. The whole street once looked as grand, but now it is rather dull, so pass on down Taschenmacher to Kleine Budengasse, where the new City Hall stands. Underneath it is the Prätorium Museum, which contains a 1st-century excavation of walls once belonging to the residence of the Roman Viceroy.

Retracing your steps, walk south along Burgerstrasse to the Old Market (Altermarkt), once the throbbing center of the old city. You can imagine the scene here 300 years ago, with jugglers, bears on chains, chickens and pigs for sale, horses tethered along the stone walls. Most of the buildings were destroyed in the war, and traffic has taken the place of the horses, but the twin houses "Zur Bretzel" and "Zum Dom," numbers 20–22, have retained their original 16th-century style.

Just south-west of the market-place is the old City Hall (Rathaus), an impressive ensemble of buildings from several different periods: look out for the 14th-century Hansa Hall, the 15th-century tower with a tuneful peal of bells, and the 16th-century entrance hall, a fine example of Renaissance architecture. Outside stands the famous sculpture of the Apes of Palestrina, dating from the 3rd century.

South-west again is Gulichplatz, where you can see the remains of a 12th-century synagogue, with its ritual bath or *mikwe*. Outside it stands the Carnival Fountain, designed by Grasegger early this century. This is a pretty little square, and there are benches to rest a while and enjoy the local life milling about you. One of the first producers of eau-de-Cologne, Johann Farina, had his factory here, in a small residential house. Production is now carried on outside the city in vast factories.

One block further south is the Gürzenich, built as a place for dancing and other festivities in the 15th century. It is still used for this purpose when Cologne holds its carnival in February. During its reconstruction after the war, it was extended by a modern section as far as the ruins of St. Albans opposite. These ruins are all that remains of a 10th-century Gothic church and its 14th-century tower, and are now kept as a memorial for the city's victims of the war. It contains Matare's copy of the touching *Sorrowing Parents* by the great German sculptress Kathe Kollwitz. Oddly enough, there is another fine sculpture of mourning in the church of St. Maria in the Kapitol, a 12th-century building in Pipinstrasse, just south-west of the Heu Market. Called *The Sorrowful Women*, it was created by Gerhard Marcks in the 1940s, and now stands in the south-west cloister of the church. The building itself, particularly well preserved inside, has a fine nave and crypt and splendidly intricate leaf doors, dating from the 12th century.

Returning towards the river and heading south, you come to the Rheingasse, which contains the Industrial Arts Museum—in the last remaining Romanesque house in Cologne, Oberstolzen Haus, built in 1225. Just south, along Holzmarkt, by the river, is St. Maria Lyskirchen, a small seamen's church of the same period: inside are some important frescos of the 13th century, stained glass work of the 15th century and a beautiful 14th-century Blessed Virgin.

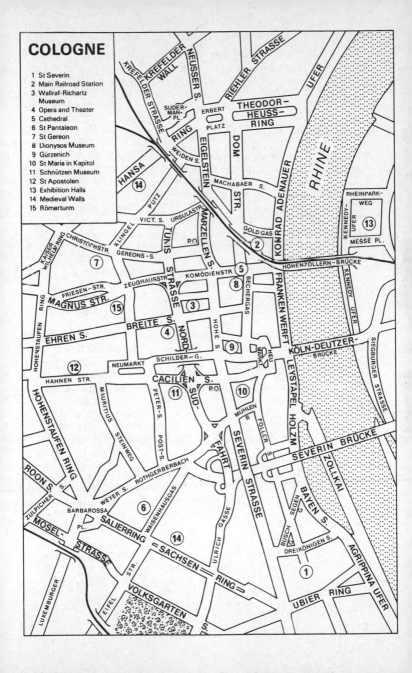

COLOGNE

1 St Severin
2 Main Railroad Station
3 Wallraf-Richartz Museum
4 Opera and Theater
5 Cathedral
6 St Pantaleon
7 St Gereon
8 Dionysos Museum
9 Gürzenich
10 St Maria in Kapitol
11 Schnützen Museum
12 St Apostolen
13 Exhibition Halls
14 Medieval Walls
15 Römerturm

Now leave the river, and take Witschgasse through to the bustling Waidmarkt, where St. George's Basilica stands, the only 11th-century building of its kind left in the Rhineland. Outside stands the Hermann-Joseph Fountain, dating from the turn of the last century. From this square, Severinstrasse leads straight south, a typical old city thoroughfare. The Balchem House at number 15, with its gables and bay windows is characteristic of the 17th-century architecture that once filled the street.

Several blocks down is one of the city's oldest and greatest churches, St. Severin, built on the site of early pagan and Christian graves. Severin was Bishop of Cologne in the 5th century and his shrine, in the upper church, contains exquisitely carved stalls. There is also a 13th-century Madonna in chalk, and many wall hangings worth seeing. The church marked the southern limit of the old city and marks the limit of this part of our tour. It would be a good idea to stop off at one of the many old taverns in the neighborhood, to get up the strength to turn north again.

The southwest wall of the medieval city still stands at one or two spots, and the best place to see them is at Kartäuserwall, just north of the busy Sachsen-Ring. (All the roads whose names end in "Ring" follow the course of the old walls. From here it is only a stone's throw to the remarkable Church of St. Pantaleon off Waisenhaus Gasse. The west wing is particularly curious. It was the gift of Archbishop Bruno, brother of Otto the Great, and both Bruno and Otto's step-daughter, Queen Theophanu, were buried here. A marble sarcophagus commemorates the queen, among other more ancient figures.

North-west, along Mauritius-Stein Weg, we come to the ruins of the 19th-century neo-Gothic church of St. Mauritius, now restored in a modern style by the architect Fritz Schaller. Inside is a 15th-century crucifix. If you continue north-west, you come to the western city gate, the Hahnentorburg, two weighty round towers with vaulted entrances, but you can equally well continue north along Mauritius-stein Weg to the church of St. Aposteln, at the west end of the New Market (Neumarkt). Here we are once again on the edge of the inner city. If you walk along Cäcilianstrasse, you come to some of the city's finest museums, notably the Art Gallery, the Art Union and the Schnütgen Museum of Church Art, attached to the Church of St. Cäcilian (Cecilia), one of the most richly endowed in Germany. This group of museums really require a fair amount of time to visit properly and, if you are interested in religious art, set aside several hours for them.

From this point you can return to the cathedral by way of Hohe Strasse, where, on the north side of the terrace, there are some attractive traditional coffeehouses. This is now a pedestrian precinct and a good spot to find good shopping and reasonably priced restaurants.

North of the Cathedral

Komödien Strasse runs west from the cathedral terrace, and a few steps along it you can see the charming St. Andreas (St. Andrew) church, dating from the 13th century. Inside is a Roman sarcophagus and, in the crypt, the remains of Albertus Magnus—a medieval philosopher and bishop, who figures largely in the history of the occult. Two blocks south, and in great contrast to this early stone building, is the massive, modern West German Radio Station on the Rechtschule. Next door to it is the Wallraf-Richartz-Museum, the largest picture gallery in the Rhineland, with an interesting collection of local and international works, ranging from Gothic pieces to modern works by such artists as Picasso and Andy Warhol.

Returning to Komödien Strasse, and passing a round tower which remains from the Roman city wall, continue onto the Zeughaus Strasse. On the left is the original city arsenal, built on the remains of the Roman wall, which houses the Cologne City Museum: the collection of weapons, documents, armour, paintings and furniture here is well worth a visit. A little further on, across Auf dem Berlich, the corner tower of the Roman wall still stands, with its ornamentation of colored tiles.

Now turn north, along Steinfeldergasse, to one of the most impressive buildings remaining from medieval times, the twin-towered church of St. Gereon. The nucleus is 4th-century, and dedicated to the early Christian martyrs called the Theban Legion, some of whom are buried in the crypt, which, with the nave and the decagon (in between the two towers) were added later. In the choir there is a lovely carved sacristy door. The church has other interesting carvings, an Aubusson tapestry and early frescos.

Following Klingel Putz, turn right along Ursula Strasse, where, just before the road passes under the railway, you will find the magnificent tower of St. Ursula's Church, which contains the marble grave of the saint. A peculiarity inside is the gold closet (Treasury) which contains some valuable relics and liturgical vessels.

Eigelstein leads you north to Ebertplatz, where the northern exit from the medieval city was. The remains of the 13th-century gate still stand there, amid the bustle of modern-day traffic passing between the city and the vast suburbs which lie beyond. From here you can stroll through the gardens of the Theodor-Heuss-Ring to the river, before returning south again. There is a famous restaurant here called The Bastei, built on the plinth of a fortress tower and offering a fine view over the Rhine.

On your return southward, you will pass the Church of St. Kunibert, built between 1215 and 1247, the last Romanesque church in Cologne with some signs of Gothic architecture. The choir windows are exceptional, and the altar paintings and wall tabernacle are worth seeing. Afterwards, turn right along Machabäer Strasse, past the 18th-century Ursuline church on your right, to the Nord-Süd-Fahrt, a busy main street which takes you quickly back to the cathedral again.

EXPLORING DÜSSELDORF

One of the greatest cities in this most industrialized region of Germany, Düsseldorf is also the capital of the State of Northern Rhineland-Westphalia. It is an important cultural center, one whose eminence in this field is not new. The artist, Peter Cornelius, and the poet, Heinrich Heine, were born here. Johannes Brahms, Robert Schumann, and Goethe lived here. The city is reputed today to present some of the finest theatrical performances in all Germany and a film distributing center has sprung up here, as well as another German venture that lies halfway between art and trade—press designing. Its excellent Academy of Fine Arts has helped attract many artists, and the Robert Schumann Conservatory has encouraged musical talent. Rich collections from the fields of art, literature and science are housed in many museums (for details consult *Practical Information*).

When you walk on the streets of Düsseldorf, particularly on the main Königsallee, little boys may turn cartwheels in front of you; they are called *Radschläger* and will expect you to give them a few pfennigs as a reward. It is an old tradition going back to the wedding of Elector Johann Wilhelm, Düsseldorf's beloved ruler in the 17th century, when during the great procession a wheel of the wedding coach became loose and a ten-year-old boy saved the situation by attaching himself to the wheel, gripping the hub, and "cartwheeling" with it to the end of the parade, at which point Johann Wilhelm rewarded him with a golden ducat. The little *Radschläger* come mostly from a nearby school in the Old Town where cartwheel turning is part of the physical culture program, and every year there is a competition with the winner receiving a savings book from the Lord Mayor.

"Jan Wellem," as Johann Wilhelm II, Elector of Palatinate, has been affectionately called by Düsseldorfers, greatly contributed to the cultural development of Düsseldorf and the grateful citizens erected a monument to him in 1711, five years before his death. This baroque equestrian statue stands next to the 16th-century City Hall, rebuilt after the last war. Here we are in the center of the Old Town between the Oberkasseler bridge and the Rheinkaie bridge and flanked by the Hofgarten, with its two landmarks overlooking the Rhine: the twisted spire of the Gothic St. Lambertus Church and the round Castle Tower, the only remainder of the 13th-century city castle; in its shadow is the postwar Cartwheelers' Fountain and the Rhine excursion steamers make their station here. In addition to the three-naved St. Lambertus, which contains a remarkable late Gothic tabernacle, the Renaissance tomb of the 16th-century Duke Wilhelm the Rich, the bronze door by the German sculptor Edward Mataré and a rich treasury. There are several other churches, notably Neanderkirche and St. Andreas with the sarcophagus of "Jan Wellem," and a glockenspiel in the picturesque Wibbel street.

On the southern edge of the Old Town the 24-story Mannesmann Building, a slender masterpiece of glass and steel, soars above the Rhine and on the other side is mirrored in the Spee Graben, one of the many small lakes which, together with the parks surrounding them, keep the city air fresh and provide an element of relaxation from the daily razzle-dazzle of this busy metropolis.

The heart of Düsseldorf is Königsallee, nicknamed "Kö," a 275-foot-wide park-boulevard dating from the early 19th century and split in the middle by a many-bridged waterway and lined on one side with café terraces and some of the most elegant stores in Germany. Here you sip your apéritif or coffee, or promenade under the trees and feel the pulse of the city. The "Kö" melts into further green surfaces on both sides. At one end is Graf Adolf Square with a botanical garden and not far from it the Schwanenspiegel (Swans' Pond) and the Landtag (State Legislature). At the other, northern, end, past the Cornelius Square fountain, the expanded Hofgarten area begins with more swans, statues (including one by Maillol, commemorating Heine), the baroque Jägerhof Castle, another castle called appropriately Malkasten ("Paintbox" —the seat of the local artists' association), and the neo-classical Ratinger Tor entrance. Above it all rules the 26-story Thyssen building, built in 1957 as an early portent of German regeneration, superbly elegant in its simplicity. At its foot the "Centipede," an elevated motor road standing on pillars, arches its course over bustling shopping streets.

Congress, conventions, trade fairs and other business gatherings follow each other practically throughout the year and play an important role in Düsseldorf's tradition. The first trade exhibition was staged here in 1811 and its most prominent visitor was Napoleon. The well-equipped exhibition grounds, located on the northern edge of Hofgarten, extend from the right bank of the Rhine to Fischerstrasse and contain several halls, particularly the ultramodern Messehalle. A pleasant walk along the river banks will take you from the exhibition grounds through the Rheinpark to the Theodor Heuss Bridge (three more bridges span the river within the city limits) and the yacht harbor. Further downstream is Nordpark with fountains, flower gardens, including the famous Japanese gardens, and sculptures.

In fact gardens and lakes characterize much of the town. From the Nordpark you walk through a green belt as far as the Trade Fair complex while in southern Düsseldorf, peace and relaxation can be found at the Castle Benrath, a marvellous late-Baroque chateau, with 157 acres of parkland and lakes. The Zoo district and the districts of Grafenberg and Kaiserswerth were never other than green. Other excursion spots are village-like Niederkassel and Hamm, or north to Grafenberg Forest with its wild-game park.

A university was opened in Düsseldorf in 1965. Today it has 13,000 students. In the grounds of the University are the Botanical Garden and the hemispherical 18-meter-high greenhouse, open to the public every day from 8 A.M. to 8 P.M.

The interior of the Church at Wies, Bavaria
a wonder of rococo decoration

The Schloss Herrenchiemsee on an island in Lake Chiemsee. In contrast, the medieval atmosphere of Rothenburg ob der Tauber

The 13th-century statue of a Knight
in Bamberg Cathedral

Two scenes in Oberammergau; a street,
with its characteristic painted houses, and
a performance of the Passion Play

PRACTICAL INFORMATION FOR COLOGNE AND DÜSSELDORF

 WHEN TO COME. Cologne. The most important and exciting time is Fasching (carnival season)—also called Karneval—which here reaches even livelier proportions than in Munich. Officially it opens on 11 *November,* with the end of the year being its first important date; hundreds of masked balls during *January* and *February,* with peak days on the Thursday and Saturday before Shrove Tuesday, on Shrove Sunday and Rose-Monday (with a great carnival parade). The principal halls for carnival events are in Gürzenich, Sartory, Flora at the Botanical Garden, and the halls of the fair exhibition grounds, as well as the principal hotels. On Corpus Christi day there is a great religious procession together with Mühlheimer Gottestracht, a colorful boat procession on the Rhine.

In **Düsseldorf** the fun period is the carnival season with a tradition going back to 1440 when Shrove Tuesday was first celebrated. *Fasching* reaches its climax during the last three days before Lent, especially with *Rosenmontagszug,* a procession of thousands of costumed merrymakers, decorated floats and brass bands on Shrove Monday. *June* is the month of the Düsseldorf Musical Weeks.

A week-long marksmen's folk festival *(Schützen-und Volkfest)* is celebrated during the second half of *July* to the tune of brass bands, lively parades, rifle competitions and fireworks. *November* is the month of *Martinsfest,* a centuries-old children's festival reaching its peak on November 10, the eve of St. Martin's Day, when some 50,000 children with lighted picturesque self-made lanterns participate in the symbolic St. Martin's Procession.

Trade Fairs: Both cities are host to important trade fairs throughout the year. The Central Committee for Exhibitions and Trade Fairs of German Industry and Commerce (AUMA), Lindenstr. 8, Cologne, publishes regular lists of forthcoming events, together with organizers' addresses and accommodation booking information. Inclusive travel arrangements can usually be made.

HOTELS. Hotel prices in Cologne, like those of Düsseldorf, are a little above the German average.

COLOGNE

Deluxe

Heading the list is the palatial and constantly renovated **Excelsior Hotel Ernst,** on the cathedral square (Domplatz), 250 beds, all rooms with bath, several suites, fine grill room, the international *Hanse-Stube.*

Dom-Hotel, Domkloster 2a, 135 rooms with bath; restaurant of note with music in the evening, outdoor café with view of the cathedral, altogether a palatial establishment.

In the same category is the 12-storied **Intercontinental,** Helenenstr. 14, 300 rooms, several bars and restaurants, including on roof, heated pool.

Expensive

Senats-Hotel, Unter Goldschmied 9–17 at the City Hall, 100 beds, all rooms with bath, fine restaurant, bowling, very modern.

Consul, Belfortstr. 9, 80 rooms with bath or shower, has indoor pool, sauna.

Mondial, Bechergasse 10, 200 rooms, useful restaurant, close by the Roman-Germanic Museum.

Regent, at Melatengurtel 15 in the western suburb of Braunsfeld, convenient for motorists, with large garage and parking space, 200 beds, all rooms with bath or shower, nice view from the roof terrace.

Euro-Crest Hotel, Dürener Strasse 287 in Lindenthal section, has 152 rooms with bath or shower, two restaurants and bar, located in a park on a lake.

Moderate

Haus Lyskirchen, Filzengraben 28, most rooms with bath, indoor pool.

Berlin, Domstr. 10, 150 beds, half of rooms with bath or shower, wine restaurant.

Holiday Inn, 120 soundproofed, airconditioned rooms with bath, good views, solarium. Near the Cologne/Bonn Airport, and junction of Hannover-Frankfurt motor way.

Engelbertz, Obenmarspforten 1, most rooms with bath and radio.

Kaiser, Genovevastr 10, in Mülheim across the river, all rooms with bath.

Am Augustinerplatz, Hohe Str. 30. 60 rooms, and **Esplanade,** Hohenstaufenring 56, 33 rooms, both garni.

If you prefer a colorful old-Cologne inn, the **Stapelhäuschen,** Fischmarkt 1, 30 rooms.

Inexpensive

Lenz, Ursulaplatz 9, 140 beds, wine restaurant; *3 Könige,* Marzellenstr. 58, 50 beds, nice and central. Or try one of a dozen family hotels near the main station such as the *Berg,* Brandenburgstr. 6.

Spiegel (I–M), Hermann-Löns-Str. 122, 19 rooms and good open-air eating, is about 7 miles out on the way to the airport.

DÜSSELDORF

As befits the richest city in the Federal Republic, Düsseldorf has outstandingly good hotels. It also follows that because of the great business activity prices here are a bit higher than elsewhere.

Deluxe

The two best hotels, both palatial and super deluxe, are 160-room **Breidenbacher Hof,** Heinrich-Heine-Allee 36, with suites, artistic and antique furnishings, completely air-conditioned, one of the top hostelries in Germany, and 140-room **Steigenberger Park Hotel,** Corneliusplatz 1, with view of the Hofgarten park and elegant, modern interiors behind the old-world façade.

The **Intercontinental Düsseldorf,** Karl Arnold Platz 5, has 316 deluxe rooms, air-conditioned, roof restaurant and bar with fine view, several other restaurants and bars, heated pool and golf course.

The **Düsseldorf Hilton,** between Kennedy Damm and the Rhine, 383 rooms, offers similar deluxe amenities, as well as the steakhouse *San Francisco.*

The **Holiday Inn,** Königsallee, new in 1978, all facilities.

The **Rheinstern Penta,** Emanuel-Leutze-Str. 17, 10 mins. by taxi from airport and center, has 332 beds and every facility, as has the **Ramada,** Am Seestern 16, across the river in Oberkassel sector, with 222 rooms.

Expensive

Eden, Adersstr. 29, 160 beds, suites, restaurant.

Graf Adolf Hospiz, Stresemannplatz 1; garni, 100 rooms, parking nearby.

Uebachs, Leopoldstr. 3, 110 beds, most with bath, very comfortably furnished, restaurant.

Moderate

Near the main station: small **Germania,** Freiligrathstr. 21; **Bahn,** Karlstr. 74; **Monopol,** Oststr. 135, some rooms with bath; **City,** Bismarckstr. 73, garni.

Near Königssallee, the **Central,** Luisenstr. 42, has half of rooms with bath, garni; **Stadt München,** Pionierstr. 6, modern, 45 rooms, is quiet, central.

Royal, Gartenstr. 30, 43 rooms, some rooms with bath, and **Regina,** Scheurenstr. 3, 35 rooms, are both garni.

Wurms, Scheurenstr. 23, garni, 30 rooms.

A little out of the center is **Haus Leonhard,** Kaiserwerther Str. 265, 25 rooms, garni.

Inexpensive

Nizza, Ackerstr. 8, and *Astor,* Kurfürstenstr. 23, both near the main station.

Berger, Worringer Str. 6, 36 rooms, garni. A bit far out, but good value.

Waldesruh, Am Wald 6, 29 simple rooms, again a long way out at Benrath, but worth it for the value.

Flughafenhotel, right at airport, is amazingly cheap if you can make do with utter simplicity; some rooms with shower, but no restaurant.

 RESTAURANTS. Really outstanding opportunities are offered for eating and drinking; they range from top German and international dishes and old vintage selections to the spicy river boatman's fare washed down with *Kölsch,* as the light local beer is called.

The Cologne Tourist Office, opposite the main entrance of the Cathedral, gives a complete list of restaurants, bars and places of entertainment and is a good little guide to "dining and wining" in Cologne.

COLOGNE

Expensive

For the gourmet: **Chez Alex,** Mühlengasse 1–3; **Poêle d'Or,** Komödienstr. 50; **Hansestuben,** at Excelsior Hotel.

Almost as expensive but with beautiful view and/or delightful atmosphere included: **Die Bastei,** Konrad-Adenauer-Ufer; *Schweizer Stuben,* on the south side of the Cathedral, and the country-style **Landhaus Kuckuck,** Olympiaweg 2, Im Stadtwald.

For a really special meal try the **Weinhaus in Walfisch,** Salzgasse 13, tucked away between the Heumarkt and the river. Can be (M) if you choose carefully.

Moderate

Less expensive and especially recommended for lunch: **La Lavallier,** opposite the south entrance of the Cathedral, **Dionysos-Restaurant,** next to the Roman Museum, and **Opernterrassen,** Offenbachplatz.

Auberge de la Charrue d'Or, Habsburger Ring 16, close by the Hahnentor, is a good bet for that half-way stop on your walking tour.

Sigi's Bistro, Kleiner Griechenmarkt 23, a really worthwhile spot to find.

Inexpensive

For local atmosphere: the restaurants of the breweries, **Früh,** am Hof 12, or **Brauhaus Sion,** Unter Taschenmacher—or **Alt Köln,** Trankgasse 7, opposite the Cathedral.

Cafes

Kranzler, Offenbachplatz; **Franck,** Rudolfplatz 12; **Zimmermann,** Herzogstr. 11–13—all famous for their pastries.

Reichard am Dom, only one with outdoor terrace; faces Cathedral.

DÜSSELDORF

Expensive

The **Altstadt** is for good, plain food at reasonable prices (*haxe,* shin of pork; *sauerbraten,* stewed marinated beef; or grilled *bratwürst*), washed down with Düsseldorfer Altbier; or if you prefer haute cuisine, try one of the countless international eating establishments with international prices.

Düsseldorf's cuisine has a strong international accent. In addition to the renowned and expensive restaurants in the hotels **Breidenbacher Hof** and **Park-Hotel,** and, most notably, the **San Francisco** in the *Hilton,* Düsseldorf boasts a long line of other outstanding establishments in the higher price category.

At **M & F** *(Müllers & Fest)* with smaller **KD** *(Königsallee-Diele)* and an outdoor terrace, Königsallee 12–16, 24 cooks prepare each order individually.

The colorful **Schneider-Wibbel-Stuben,** Schneider-Wibbel-Gasse in the Old Town, specializes in steak, lobster, sweetwater fish and original Pilsener beer.

Walliser Stuben, Adersstr. 46, is another very atmospheric spot, with excellent game in season and Swiss specialties.

Fischer-Stuben, Rotterdamer Strasse 15, with garden and accent on fish, and **Golzheimer Krug,** Karl-Kleppe-Strasse 20, are both in the Golzheim section.

Bateau Ivre, Kurze Strasse 11, offers French cuisine and ship atmosphere. One of the most historic local inns, dating originally from the 17th century, is the **Weinhaus Tante Anna,** Andreasstr. 2, which has a fine variety of food and wine and is open till 3 A.M.

Alt-Düsseldorf, a well-liked establishment, is rebuilt in the style of old pre-war Düsseldorf and is under new management. It maintains the atmosphere, and choice is as good as ever. In Oberkassel, on the left bank of the Rhine, there is a restaurant that enjoys international renown, **Robert's Restaurant,** Oberkasseler Str. 100. Average cost of a main course is over DM35.

In the northern outskirts is **Flughafenrestaurant** at the airport with Indonesian food and music in the evening.

Moderate

La Vieille Auberge, Münsterstr. corner of Heinrichstr. which is to be recommended for traditional French dishes.

When venison is in season, some of the best is found at the **Heinrich Heine Stuben,** in the old part of the city, opposite the poet's birthplace.

Rheinterrasse, a vast establishment on the river bank at the exhibition grounds, with music.

Victorian, Konigstrasse 3A (upstairs), a few steps from the Kö.

Inexpensive

A number of inexpensive taverns serve *Obergäriger,* a dry, dark, very still and aged beer, along with typical local dishes fortified by the famous sharp Düsseldorf mustard, in a lively atmosphere created by fast-joking natives who love to crowd these picturesque outlets of small home breweries.

Among them are: **Zum Schiffchen,** Hafenstr. 5, in existence since 1628; **Zum Schlüssel,** Bolkerstr. 45, and **Im Goldenen Kessel,** across the street.

A dozen or so **Dieterich** brewery restaurants, spread all over the city, serve their beer and hearty fare.

Also very reasonably priced are **Zum Burggrafen,** a large beer restaurant with garden on the corner of Hüttenstrasse and Graf-Adolf-Strasse and at the next corner on Berliner Allee is **Löwenbrauhof.**

Cafes

Rathaus-Café Funke-Kaiser, Markt 6 (arcades). **Bierhoff,** glittering café in Savoy Hotel, known for its excellent pastry for over 100 years.

Bittner, Königsallee 44, with several branches and pleasant sidewalk terrace. The nearby **Hemesath** has a terrace on "Kö," and dancing at its other branch at Graf-Adolf-Strasse 14.

Schubert, Friedrichstr. 2, has musical entertainment in the evening.

Café Stockheim, Grabenstr. 17.

TRANSPORTATION. COLOGNE. The city is well served by **streetcars** and **buses.** Taxi stands are at the main railroad station and in all more important squares; if you get stuck, call 31–0–31. A small local electric railroad *(Rheinuferbahn)* operates frequent service between Cologne and Bonn; the Cologne station is on the Kaiser-Friedrich-Ufer below the main railroad station. The main bus station for out-of-town lines is between the cathedral and the river. River passenger ships leave from Frankenwerft nearby. Day **boat** cruises and moonlight cruises (summer months) from the vicinity of Hohenzollern and Deutzer bridges.

Guided **bus tours** leave twice daily May 1–September 30 from the city tourist office at the cathedral square (Domplatz). Air terminal is at the main bus station with half-hourly coach service to the airport from 7 A.M. to 9 P.M. Sightseeing flights over the city and over the nearby area on fine days.

Car hire: *Interrent,* Luxemburgerstr. 163 and Neusser Str. 363; *Avis,* Clemensstr. 25 and at the airport; Hertz, Bechergasse 10 (Mondial hotel) and airport. Auto Sixt, a German company, can also be located in the U.S.A. through Auto Europe, 770 Lexington Avenue, N.Y. 10021.

Parking garages, central (open day and night): On Cäcilienstr., Kaufhaus-Parkhaus, and BP-Parkhaus; on Von Werthstr., Hochgarage Gerling, and Auto-silo; on Wolfstr., Parkhaus, and Kreissparkasse; ARAL-Parkhaus, Augustinerplatz; Theater-Parkhaus, Krebsgasse; Parkhaus Hohenzollernring/Masstrichterstr.; Magnusstr./Alte Wallgasse; Karstadt, Zeppelinstr.; Ladenstadt, Glockengasse; Grosse Budengasse; Parkhaus Brückenstr.; BP-Parkhaus, Lungengasse; Parkhaus a.d. Börse, Enggasse.

DÜSSELDORF. The city and suburbs are well served by **streetcars, buses,** suburban (S-Bahn) **railway** and **underground** (U-Bahn). For **taxi** call 33–33 day and night. If for some reason or other you don't feel in shape to drive your own car call the same number and your car will be driven wherever you want at a 20% higher than regular taxi tariff. River steamer station is near the City Hall. Rheinische Bahngesellschaft organizes full-day and half-day excursions by bus and **steamer.** Airport: Suburban (S-Bahn) trains to city (15 mins.) leave half-hourly, 5.45 A.M. to 11.15 P.M.

Car hire: Selbstfahrer-Union, Charlottenstr. 50 and at airport; Hertz, Immermannstr. 48 and airport; Avis, Berliner Allee 32, Am Hauptbahnhof, at the Hilton and airport.

Parking garages in the downtown area: Parkhaus Kaufhof, Heinrich Heine Allee; Stadtgaragen, Jahnstr. 10; Parkhaus, corner Tal and Luisenstrasse; City-Park-hochhaus, Bendemannstr. 5; Parkhochhaus Nowea, Fischerstr, 2, Parkhaus Charlottenstr. 62, by the main station and several others.

NIGHTLIFE. COLOGNE. We would only reluctantly *recommend* any of the nightclubs (they are listed in Tourist Office publications), and it may be sufficient to give the areas where most of them are located: again, the area around Intercontinental: Friesenstrasse, Friesenwall, Hildeboldplatz and near Hohenzollernring: Maastrichterstrasse (some between Hohe Str. and City Hall).

For sound evening entertainment, pubs, bars and discos: Altstadt: area between Alter Markt and Frankenwerft.

From May to September: attractions, shows and open-air dancing in *Tanzbrunnen*. Program available at Tourist Office.

DÜSSELDORF. Night bars, usually small, sometimes combined with restaurant, sometimes with dancing, sometimes with both, and sometimes with neither, appear to be the evening-out preference of the Düsseldorfer. For elegant dancing with supper visit *Palette* in Hotel Breidenbacher Hof and *Etoile* in Park-Hotel. The mortality rate among clubs which provide recommendable food, reasonable drinks, and spicy shows is currently fairly high. Locals like *Lord Nelson*, Bolkerstr. 18, but people who favored the old *Flohmarkt* may be disappointed (or glad)! to find a pizzatoria on the same street at No. 4.

For outdoor dancing: *Rheinterrasse*, overlooking the river at exhibition grounds. Brass band program and dancing. Special character: *Fatty's Atelier*, Hunsrückenstr. 13, artists' locale with food and drinks until 3 A.M.

 THEATER AND MUSIC. COLOGNE. For opera and ballet: *Opernhaus*, Offenbachplatz, one of the world's most modern opera buildings. For drama and comedy: *Schauspielhaus*, next to the opera. *Theater am Dom*, Kölner Ladenstadt, Glöckengasse, mostly for modern plays; *Der Keller*, Kleingedankstr. 6, experimental type; *Millowitsch-Heimatbühne*, Aachener Strasse 5, folk plays.

Concert halls in Gürzenich, Funkhaus, and in the hall of the School of Music. The main orchestras are *Gürzenich Cologne City Orchestra; Broadcasting Symphony Orchestra* of the Cologne radio station. There are five major choral societies.

Stadtische Puppenspiele, Eisenmarkt—this is something special, a famous marionette theater, where you will hear the old Cologne dialect.

DÜSSELDORF. For opera, operetta and ballet: *Deutsche Oper am Rhein*, Heinrich-Heine-Allee 16-a. For drama and comedy: *Schauspielhaus*, Gustaf-Gründgens Platz; *Kammerspiele*, Jahnstr. 3. *Theater an der Berliner Allee* with two stages, *Grosses Haus* and *Kleines Haus*.

Literary cabaret (you have to understand German very well): *Das Kom-(m)ödchen*, Hunsrückenstr. 12-b, in the Kuntshalle.

Marionettes: *Theater Rheinischer Marionetten*, Bilkerstr. 7.

The best concert orchestras are *Düsseldorf Symphony Orchestra* and *Düsseldorf City Orchestra*. Concerts are given mainly in the *Robert-Schumann-Saal* and in the *Rheinhalle*.

MUSEUMS. COLOGNE. *Wallraf-Richartz-Museum,* An der Rechtschule, in its interesting new building near the cathedral, famous particularly for its old Dutch and Flemish paintings, old and modern German paintings, some French impressionists; excellent collection of modern paintings.

Dionysos Mosaic, in the *Roman–Germanic Museum,* next to the cathedral, is in the same place where it was discovered during the last war. 70-square-yard Roman mosaic, composed of 1¼ million individual stones, showing 31 pictures. The museum has a world-famous collection of Roman glass and of art from the period of the migration of Germanic and other peoples.

Rautenstrauch-Joest-Museum für Völkerkunde, Ubierring 45, an exceptional ethnological museum; collections from Africa, Polynesia and Indonesia.

Schnütgen in St. Cecilia's Church near Neumarkt, religious art from the Middle Ages to baroque. Crypt now open.

Cologne City Museum, history of Cologne, located at Zeughausstrasse in the 17th-century Zeughaus.

Kunst-Bibliothek, a public art library and largest in the North Rhineland-Westphalia region, is located in Wallraf-Richartz-Museum.

Art exhibitions are held at Wallraf-Richartz-Museum, Hahnentorburg, and Eigelsteintorburg.

Arts and Crafts Museum in Eigelsteintorburg; arts and crafts from medieval times until present including pottery collections and a very complete collection of German faience. Museum of East Asian Art at Aschener Weiher is new and Japanese designed.

DÜSSELDORF. *Municipal Art Museum,* Ehrenhof 5, has a particularly fine collection of medieval, baroque and contemporary sculpture, arts and crafts and of 16th- and 20th-century paintings (among them Rubens' *Venus and Adonis*).

In the *Hetjens Museum,* Palais Nesselrode, Schulstr. 4, is a remarkable exhibit of ceramics dating from the late Stone Age to the present.

Kunstsammlung Nordrhein-Westfalen in Schloss Jägerhof, Jacobistr. 2, contains 20th-century art, especially the Paul Klee Collection. The same castle houses an excellent collection of early Meissen porcelain.

Also in Hofgarten, Jägerhofstr. 1, is the *Goethe Museum* with more than 30,000 manuscripts, first editions, paintings, sculptures and medals.

Kunsthalle, Grabbeplatz 4, periodic exhibitions staged by the Artists' Association of Rhineland and Westphalia.

City Museum in Spee Palace at Bäckerstr. 9, for local history and culture.

In the Museumbunker am Zoo are the *Löbbecke Museum* of natural history and *Aquarium.*

SPORTS. COLOGNE is richly endowed with parks, equipped for sports activities of all kinds, with one tremendous sports center on the Aachenerstrasse, which is a dozen or so playing fields of different kinds rolled into one: swimming pool, football field, tennis courts, running track, bridle paths, etc.

A **swimming** pool in summer, **ice hockey** rink in winter, is the Eis- und Schwimmstadion, in Lentstrasse. Indoor swimming pools in Deutz and Ehrenfeld districts, as well as the Agrippa-Hallenbad near Neumarkt in the center.

Golf courses at Refrath (18 holes) and Marienburg (9 holes); **horseracing** at Weidenpesch. For information about sports, dates of sporting events, inquire: Sportamt der Stadt Köln, Aachnerstrasse, Stadion, D5000 Köln 41, tel. 49831.

Düsseldorf The largest sports center is the Rhine stadium in Stockum near the Nordpark with several **tennis** courts and a **swimming** pool. Outdoor pools: Freie Schwimmer, Flinger Broich; Strandbad Lörick; Strandbad Unterbacker See. Indoor pools: Kettwiger Str. 50; Münsterstr. 13, in Derendorf; Benrath; Oberkassel; Unterrath; Gerresheim.

For **horseback riding** contact Reitinstitut Rumstich, Jägerhofstr. 10, Düsseldorfer Reiter und Rennverein e.V., Wagnerstr. 26, or Reitinstitut Schmitt, Am Dammsteg 99. **Horseracing** at Grafenberg; annual international events include the Grand Prix of Northern Rhineland-Westphalia (July.) and the Grand Prix of Industry and Commerce (Oct.).

Two **golf** courses are available belonging respectively to the Düsseldorfer Golf Club and to the Land und Golf Club Düsseldorf. **Yachting** and **motor boating** on the Rhine, contact the yacht harbor administration at Rotterdamer Strasse 30. Two **ice skating** rinks are at Brehmstr. 27.

 EXCURSIONS FROM DÜSSELDORF. Schloss Benrath, the most beautiful rococo castle in Northern Rhineland in a large park. The western wing houses the local natural history museum. Reached by streetcars 1 and 18.

Grafenberg and Aaper Woods. Very pleasant walks. In Grafenberg Wood is the horserace track and a natural game park with red and fallow deer, roe and wild boar. Several restaurants deep in the woods. Streetcars 3, 9 and 12.

Kaiserswerth. North of the city on the Rhine, reached by streetcars 11 and D and in summer also by river boat. Ruins of the palace built by Emperor Barbarossa. Suitbertus Cathedral dating from 1000 with 13th-century works of the Cologne Goldsmiths' School and with the shrine containing the mortal remains of Suitbertus, the Anglo-Saxon missionary active in this area around 700. Baroque gabled houses.

Neanderthal. Famed as the place where the remains of a Glacial Age man, since then called Neanderthal Man, were found in 1856. The museum shows the life of the glacial period, the Neanderthal Man is reconstructed in the place where he was discovered, and there is a preserve stocked with animals of the glacial era: bison, wild horses and wild cattle. About 10 miles from Düsseldorf, bus 43 from the main station.

Zons, the only town on Lower Rhine, a bit upstream from Düsseldorf, with fully preserved walls, gates and towers. Bus line 2242/18 or river boat during summer.

Minidomm, 15 minutes from Düsseldorf Hilton, a Lilliputian town covering 27 square miles, open all year round; shows landmarks from all over Germany.

CITY TOURS. Daily coach tours from 15th April to 15th October, for the rest of the year there are tours on Saturdays only. Departures at 2:30 P.M. from the bus stop opposite the Central Railway Station. Special tours and bilingual guides can also be taken on conducted tours by tram with buffet car. For details, contact the Verkehrsverein (tourist office), tel: 35 05 05.

USEFUL ADDRESSES. COLOGNE. Tourist Information: Verkehrsamt der Stadt Köln (city tourist office), across the square from the main portal of the cathedral, tel. 221–33–40, also has a room reservation section open daily 8 A.M. to 10:30 P.M., Sundays and holidays 9 A.M. to 10:30 P.M. (during winter from 2 P.M.), tel. 221–33–45. KD (German Rhine Line), Frankenwerft 15.

Money Exchange: Regular banking hours until 5 P.M., Fridays until 6:30 P.M., closed on Saturdays and Sundays. The exchange office inside the main station is open from 7 A.M. (Sundays from 8 A.M.) until 11 P.M.

DÜSSELDORF. Tourist information: Amt für Fremdenverkehr und Wirtschaftsförderung (City Office for Tourism and Business Promotion), Ehrenhof. 3, Monday through Fri., 8–5, Sat., 8–1, Sun., closed. Verkehrsverein Düsseldorf, Konrad-Adenauer-Platz, with room reservation office in the main rail station open 8–11, Sun. and holidays 4–10; Rheinische Bahngesellschaft, Konrad-Adenauer-Platz 3, for river steamer and other excursions. Deutsche Bundesbahn, general train information tel. 88–44–44.

Information for Motorists: ADAC (General German Automobile Club), Kaiser Wertherstr. 207; AvD (Automobile Club of Germany), Heinrichstr. 155.

Consulates: United States, Cecilienallee 5, tel. 49–00–81; Canada, Immermannstr. 3, tel. 35–34–71; Great Britain, Georg-Glock Str. 14, Nordstern Haus.

St Ursula

THE RHINELAND-PALATINATE

A River of Wine

It is above Cologne that the Rhine becomes most like the popular idea of the river, and it is from this point southward that the tourist who has no time for a longer voyage should try a leisurely cruise along this famous river in the comfortable, efficiently-operated river steamers which ply up and down it, making frequent stops, so that you can fit the boat ride into any itinerary you may have planned along the river.

As you mount the stream, it winds between lovely hills, some of which are thickly wooded, while others rise, step on step, in a terraced pattern of the vineyards which produce the fruity golden wines of the Rhine. Massive stone castles, or the ruins of castles, crown almost every hill. Charming villages lie scattered along the shore.

Above Koblenz, the Rhine swings around a sharp curve at St. Goar, forced out of a more direct path by a sheer mountain of rock to whose sides only sparse vegetation has been able to cling. You can readily

193

understand how, in an age when river boats were less powerful, strong winds and tricky currents could dash them against this forbidding crag. Legend turned this dangerous rock into either a scaly hideous monster or, more effectively, a beautiful siren who lured boatmen to death by bewitching them with song; for this is the Lorelei, not, as you see it with the skeptical modern eyes, a lovely mermaid, but, disappointingly, an unfeminine and massive chunk of mountain, the triumph of geology over legend. Or is it? Even today, the river boats have to tack from one side of the narrow gorge to the other, and pleasure boats put on the recorded Lorelei song in which everybody who knows it joins, until the danger is passed.

Farther south, the river takes a major curve eastward, by Rüdesheim, the center of Rhine wine-growing on the right bank and, on the left, by Bingen, where the river Nahe joins the Rhine.

EXPLORING THE RHINELAND-PALATINATE

Traveling on the Rhine south from Bonn and Bad Godesberg, the first landmark which greets us in the state of Rheinland-Pfalz is Rolandsbogen (Roland's Arch), the only remains of the castle of Knight Roland, destroyed in 1475. It stands on the slope of the Roddersberg. This peak is an inactive volcano, for the Eifel below this point is an ancient volcanic region of which the Roddersberg is the northernmost peak—a fact that accounts for the prevalence of hot springs in this country. A little further upstream and across the river on the right bank is the pleasant summer resort of Unkel, framed by vineyards. Southward on the left bank Remagen, a small town of Roman origin, lies near the confluence of the Ahr and the Rhine.

This could be the starting point for a westerly swing from the Rhine, with Trier as its main objective. The first stop would be Bad Neuenahr, an internationally-known spa with the largest gambling casino in Germany. This was for six years the place Beethoven chose for his summer vacation, staying with a private family in a dwelling that is now known locally as the Beethovenhaus.

Passing up the lovely valley of the Ahr, pinched tightly between hills with terraced vineyards rising up their slopes and producing most of the German red wine, we reach medieval Ahrweiler with massive tower gates and Altenahr, where stand the ruins of the castle of the 12th-century Archbishop of Cologne, Konrad von Hochstaden, who was responsible for the building of Cologne Cathedral. Next comes Adenau, whose attraction is much more modern. Here you are at the Nürburgring, a world famous track over which international automobile and motorcycle races are held yearly. If you drive through here when there are no races scheduled, you can try the course yourself—170 curves in seventeen miles, in the shade of the Hohe Acht, the highest point in the Eifel (2,450 feet).

Daun is a climatic resort with a mineral water source, in whose vicinity there are three crater lakes (for we are now in really ex-volcanic territory); from there we take a side road through Manderscheid (castle ruins; excursion to Mosenberg, the best preserved former volcanic hill in Eifel, with four craters) to the 12th-century Abbey Himmerod, rebuilt in baroque style. A little farther to the west is Kyllburg, a small resort town picturesquely located above the Kyll River, with a 13th-century watch tower and 14th-century church.

Trier and the Mosel Valley

The oldest city in Germany, Trier is also one of the most interesting. Situated between the points where the Saar and the Ruwer flow into the Mosel, the city is a museum of the European history of which it was for so long an important part—for Trier was the Rome of the north, the point from which western Europe was governed by the Roman emperors who made it their northern capital—Constantine, Valentinian and Gratianus all had residences here in the 4th century. Later the Archbishop of Trier was one of the three ecclesiastical princes of the realm (the other two were the Archbishops of Mainz and Cologne) and was made one of the seven Electors of the Empire by the Golden Bull of 1356.

Just how old Trier is no one really knows. The historical date given for the official founding of the city by the Emperor Augustus was 15 B.C. But though the Romans chose to regard this as the official starting date for Trier, it was obvious that there must have been something there already for Julius Caesar to conquer in 58 B.C. It is indeed known that there was a Celtic settlement dating from about 400 B.C., of a tribe known as the Treveri, but they did not give their name to the city—on the contrary. For legend, going back more than 2,000 years, ascribes the founding of Trier to Assyrian Prince Trebeta, who gave it his name, in 2053 B.C. Other German towns have a Roman history, but this is the only one to claim Assyrian ancestry; yet even this does not finish the story, for traces of human occupation have been found going back to about the year 2500 B.C.

There are no Assyrian winged bulls in Trier, but from the time of the Romans onwards, the city has preserved monuments of all its periods. Rome left behind a bridge across the Mosel; two bathing establishments (the Barbara baths, dating from about 150 A.D., the

Imperial Baths, from about 300) now in ruins; an amphitheater built about 100 A.D.; the Basilica, which was the palace of the Roman Emperors; and the Porta Nigra, the pride of Trier. The Porta Nigra is indeed a massive structure, worthy of the admiration even of those who have seen the finest of the edifices of the Roman Empire. Now fully restored, it is open to the public. The citizens of Trier explain its uniqueness by pointing out that it was not a mere gate to a city but the northern gate to the Roman Empire. Climbing up on to the Petrisberg, about a quarter of a mile away, you get an impressive view of the city.

From the Middle Ages the city has preserved its impressive church-es; the Romanesque cathedral (with later-style additions) whose oldest part dates from the 4th century; Liebfrauenkirche, next to the cathedral and forming one group of buildings with it, is one of the oldest Gothic churches in Germany; the imposing and uniquely designed St. Mat-thew Church, Romanesque but with additions from later periods, a very well-known pilgrimage church because in a golden shrine in the choir it houses the earthly remains of Apostle St. Matthew, and thus possesses the only grave of an apostle north of the Alps. The cathedral has a rich treasury, including a seamless cloak that Christ is believed to have worn; called the "Holy Robe," it is supposed to have been given as a present to the Bishop of Trier, in the 4th century by the mother of Constantine the Great, and she is said to have brought it personally from Palestine. This relic is very rarely displayed to the public. Of more recent vintage is the baroque St. Paulinus Church, one of the finest examples of this style in Rhineland.

Nor does Trier live only in the past, it is the commercial center for wine grown along the banks of the three rivers converging in this area, known among the wine merchants and connoisseurs as the Mosel-Saar-Ruwer wine region. Foremost examples of German wine cultivation are the old cellars of the *Hohe Domkirche,* the *Priesterseminar,* the *Bischöfliches Konvikt,* and the *Vereinigte Hospizien* with cross-shaped vaults, artistically carved tuns, and old tankards. Altogether almost 8 million gallons of wine can be stored in the subterranean cellars extend-ing under the buildings and streets of the city. The Trier Tourist Office arranges conducted tours of the cellars with wine tasting included.

Upstream from Trier, in the Saar Valley, is Saarburg surrounded by some fine vineyards. It rings, picturesquely, a steep hill crowned, equal-ly picturesquely, with the ruins of a castle; it offers the spectacle of the 63-ft.-high Leuk waterfall; and if you are curious about how bells are cast, you might visit the local foundry and watch the craftsmen at work.

One way back to the Rhine from either Saarburg or Trier would be the excellent Hunsrück mountain road, leading through thick woods over a high plateau, and disclosing from its curves a view of the Mosel

Valley to the north and the Nahe Valley to the south. It begins at Niederzerf, a village east of Saarburg or south of Trier (the better approach), and ends at Koblenz. Another even newer and faster road beginning at Schweich near Trier takes you to Koblenz across the southern slopes of Eifel.

But if you have only enough time to make this trip in only one direction, it is more rewarding to return to the Rhine via the lovely Mosel Valley. This route takes us through Pfalzel, a small town with an old Romanesque church and once the residence of Merovingian kings, and through the renowned wine villages of Trittenheim and Piesport to Bernkastel, the best known of them all.

Bernkastel, with its suburb of Kues across the river, is a colorful town with half-timbered houses, steep vineyard slopes, crowned by Landshut Castle, and a romantic story-book Rathaus square. The 15th-century scientist-philosopher Nicolaus Cusanus was born here; and in the Middle Ages a Prince Bishop of Trier lay seriously ill at his castle overlooking Bernkastel—the Burg Landshut—and his physicians could seemingly do no more to help him. However, one of the bishop's wine-growing tenants, hearing of his master's illness, brought him some wine from one of his best vineyards. A few sips, then a whole glass, and finally a bottle or two are said to have effected a cure; whereupon the Prince Bishop blessed the elixir and decreed that the vineyard should be named "Doktor." Hence, Bernkasteler Doktor, an excellent white wine with a world-wide reputation.

From here on, if you are a wine drinker, you will recognize the name of almost every town and village, for at one time or another you will have seen it on one or another bottle label. Graach, Wehlen, Zeltingen, Ürzig, Kröv are some of them. Traben-Trarbach, with the ruins of Grevenburg Castle above it, is the center of the wine trade in the middle Mosel Valley. Near Traben-Trarbach in the Kautenbach Valley is the beautifully situated Bad Wildstein, with warm radioactive springs. Farther down the Mosel River is Zell, another renowned wine-growing town, with the former castle of the Elector of Trier. Not far from Zell is Alf, at the foot of Marienburg and Arras castles.

This is also the place where you can slip up a side valley to the northwest for Bad Bertrich, a tiny spa with a reputation much greater than its size—it has been known since Roman times, and it is referred to as "the mild Karlsbad" because its waters, the only warm sulphate of soda springs in Germany, are almost the same as those of the Czech town of Karlovy Vary, formerly Karlsbad.

The way back to the Rhine continues through Cochem, a lovely town on the Mosel, whose vineyards rise in a checkerboard of terraces to the splendid castle above; Moselkern, from where there are less than three miles to the romantic Eltz Castle, one of the finest in Germany. The Mosel flows into the Rhine at Koblenz.

Across the Rhine from Remagen, where we had left the Rhine for our trip west to the Eifel Mountains, Trier, and the Mosel Valley, is the old town of Linz with half-timbered houses and remains of town walls. South of Remagen, on the left bank, are Bad Niederbreisig with thermal springs and the Rheineck Castle in the vicinity, which can be reached by a chair lift; Brohl, near the largest of the crater lakes of the Eifel, the beautiful Laachersee, on whose shores stand the 11th-century Maria Laach Abbey and the abbey church, the latter a surpassingly satisfying Romanesque structure dating from the 12th century; and the walled town of Andernach with its Round Tower, the 13th-century Liebfrauen Church which has an exquisitely arcaded façade, and an ancient crane which was in use until 1911. Maria Laach Abbey can also be visited from Andernach, by a road a little beyond the fork for Maria Laach that takes us also to the medieval town of Mayen, with 13th-century walls and castle, and the nearby powerful Bürresheim Castle.

Koblenz and the Middle Rhine

Located at a geographical nexus known as "the corner of Germany," Koblenz is the heart of the middle Rhine region. Rivers and mountains both converge here. Koblenz stands where the Mosel runs into the Rhine, and just south the Lahn enters it from the opposite side. Three mountain ridges intersect at Koblenz. West of the Rhine are the Eifel Mountains north of the Mosel, and the Hunsrück ridge south of it. East of the Rhine the undulating plateaus of Westerwald hide among their forests many small and quiet climatic resorts and towns, such as Rengsdorf, Flammersfeld, Marienburg, Westerburg and many others. Koblenz is the gateway to the most romantic section of the Rhine. If you resisted the lure of a Rhine trip at Cologne (or even if you didn't), succumb to it at Koblenz and sail southward. Here the Rhine has cut deeply between the heights on either side. Little wine villages line the shores and castles (or ruins) stand on every hill. If what you prefer is a quiet vacation, pick any of the riverside towns here.

Koblenz is the cultural, administrative and business center of the middle Rhine area. Its position at the confluence of two rivers bustling with steamers, barges, tugs and every other kind of river boat makes it also one of the most important traffic points on the Rhine. Through the construction of a series of locks and dams the Mosel has become navigable all the way to Luxembourg and France. A bridge across the Rhine and a new autobahn link connect Koblenz directly with the autobahn net of Germany.

Koblenz was founded by the Romans and its history goes back 2,000 years. The city suffered severely from air raids during the last war (85 percent of the buildings destroyed) but some of the most architecturally valuable buildings partially remained and have been reconstructed. The most interesting churches include the 9th-century Romanesque basilica of St. Kastor, the 12th-century Romanesque Liebfrauenkirche with a Gothic choir, and the 11th-century St. Florin's, erected on Roman foundations. Alte Burg (Old Castle) originates from the 13th century and now houses the City Library, while next to it the Balduin Bridge across the Mosel is about a hundred years younger. The Rathaus (1700), formerly a Jesuit college, is baroque, whereas the large and monumental Schloss, the former palace of the Prince Electors, is neo-classic. Outstanding among the examples of contemporary architecture is the ultramodern Rhein-Mosel-Halle containing several halls for theatrical performances, concerts, conventions, congresses, balls and other events. The lovely promenade along the Rhine extends from the outdoor water stage where operettas are performed during summer to the point where the Mosel flows into the Rhine, called Deutsches Eck (the corner of Germany) because it was here that the German Order of Knights (Deutscher Orden) established its first post on German soil in 1216.

Across the Rhine the powerful Ehrenbreitstein Fortress towers above the city; it can be reached by chair lift. For another fine view walk up the wooded path or take the city bus to Rittersturz hill on the left bank.

Just east of Koblenz is the internationally known spa of Bad Ems, which was for twenty years (1867–87) the spot Kaiser Wilhelm chose for his yearly cure. Bad Ems has never forgotten this fact, and there is a monument to Wilhelm in the spa. Pleasantly laid out along both banks of the Lahn River, Bad Ems provides all the amenities of a modern spa. Further up the Lahn Valley is Nassau, a climatic health resort with the ancestral castle of the house of Orange-Nassau, now the reigning dynasty in Holland.

We have already remarked that from Koblenz upstream all the settlements are jewels, but here we must limit ourselves to mention briefly only the principal communities:

Oberlahnstein, east bank: at the confluence of Lahn River with Rhine with some of the old fortifications preserved; above it is Lahneck Castle with a pentagonal tower and beautiful view over Lahn Valley.

Braubach, east bank: St. Barbara Church dates from 1300; above it is the magnificent Marksburg, the best-preserved medieval castle on the Rhine with outstanding interiors, particularly the Knights' Hall.

Boppard, west bank: a wine-producing town, located on a wide bend of the Rhine, along which are two miles of pleasure grounds. There is also a fine municipal forest.

St. Goar, west bank: founded in 570 by Irish monk St. Goar; above it the remains of the Rheinfels Fortress, once the strongest on the Rhine.

St. Goarshausen, east bank: above it Burg Katz (Cat Castle) and a bit away Burg Maus (Mouse Castle); the name of the latter was allegedly given by the owner of the former out of spite.

Lorelei, east bank: the cliff connected with the Lorelei tale mentioned at the beginning of this chapter; if you haven't viewed it from the river steamer, the next best view is from the road on the west bank of the river. You can drive up the Lorelei by a back road, and enjoy the view of the Rhine from its top.

Oberwesel, west bank: a small town surrounded by vineyards, much frequented by those interested in architecture (Schönburg Castle on the hill, below the medieval walls and towers, Our Lady's Church, St. Martin's Church, St. Werner's Chapel) and nature (Rhineside promenade, excursions into the Hunsrück hills).

Kaub, east bank: here, in the middle of the river, on an island, stands a small but famous castle, the Pfalz. This was a toll house, where in medieval times boats using the river had to pay tribute. Above the town is Gutenfels Castle-Fortress which was garrisoned as late as 1806, now also an exquisite, tiny, castle hotel which serves an enormous breakfast.

Bacharach, west bank: a particularly beautiful town. Above it is Stahleck Castle with its unique youth hostel. And there are half-a-dozen other castles on this bank before getting to Bingen, where the Rhine makes a big turn from a roughly south–north course to an east–west one. On the right bank are Rüdesheim and other vineyard towns of Rheingau, all part of Hesse.

Bingen, on the other side of the Rhine, at the confluence of Nahe and Rhine, is an important river port, and its principal attractions are the Klopp Castle, Mäuseturm (Mouse Tower) on a tiny island in the river, and St. Rochus Chapel on a nearby hill. Around this small church the 300-year-old Rochus Festival is held. It commemorates the saving of the town from the Black Death. St. Rochus was the protector against pestilence, and the chapel erected to him at that time has become an important pilgrimage goal; the festival occurs at the end of August.

Pfalz (The Palatinate)

From Bingen we can proceed straight to Mainz, the capital of the state of Rhineland-Palatinate, where with another turn the Rhine again resumes its south–north course. But in order to make a tour of the Pfalz section of this hyphenated state, we turn at Bingen up the Nahe River.

Bad Kreuznach, a good-sized radium spa, also grows wine, and is locally called the "town of roses and nightingales," both of which are to be found in abundance in its well-kept parks. The most picturesque of its relics of the past are the 15th-century houses built on its bridge. One of its historic houses is reputed to have been the home of Dr. Faust. Bad Münster am Stein, another spa, is dwarfed by the tremendous towering crag of the Rheingrafenstein that rises above it. Less than a mile from here is Ebernburg with its castle, where Franz von Sickingen, the aristocratic propagator of Reformation, was born; the castle has an interesting Knights' Hall, museum, and historic inn. The double town of Idar-Oberstein is dominated by the ruins of two castles and by a unique "rock church" built in 1482 halfway up the cliff; but the town is even better known for agate grinding and for the manufacture of other precious and semi-precious jewelry; there is a permanent exhibition of jewelry in the Gewerbehalle, the hall of the local business organization.

South of Bad Kreuznach is Donnersberg, the highest mountain in Pfalz, in whose eastern approaches lies Kirchheimbolanden, a town founded in Carolingian times, with a few wall towers and two gates preserved from the Middle Ages. From Bockenheim, located at one end of the Weinstrasse (Wine Road), the road is lined with vineyards and the towns of wine growers, the most important among which are (north to south): Bad Dürkheim, the largest wine-growing commune in Germany, and also a notable spa with a lovely park and casino; Wachenheim, with old patrician houses and Gothic parish church; Deidesheim and its medieval main square; Neustadt, the wine-trade center of the area, with the Gothic Stiftskirche, interesting Rathaus, and nearby Hambacher Schloss, also called Maxburg, with a fine view and at Hassloch, Germany's largest holiday park, including a magnificent giant model railway; Maikammer, with half-timbered houses; Leinsweiler, also with half-timbered houses and the Neukastel Castle ruins.

Not far away are Landau, with it lovely parks, and Annweiler, with the imposing Trifels Castle-Fortress that belonged to the early German emperors. Farther south on the Wine Road are Bergzabern, with its Renaissance Schloss, and Schweigen, with a "Wine Gate" marking the other end of the Wine Road, and the French border beyond.

To continue our tour of Pfalz, we return to Bergzabern and from there take the extremely scenic road through Wasgau to the small town of Dahn. Wasgau is the name of the southernmost section of Pfalz, with romantic, unspoiled scenery, castle-forts built on sharp cliffs, unusual rock formations, trout streams, and hundreds of hiking paths. Bergzabern and Dahn are the main points for the exploration of this area. Near

Dahn are the interesting Altdahn Castle ruins as well as many strange rock formations.

At Hinterweidenthal, we join the main road coming from Landau and leading to the cities of Pirmasens and Zweibrücken, and to Saarland. Pirmasens is the center of German shoe manufacturing while Zweibrücken is known particularly for horse breeding and for its extraordinary Rose Garden with 70,000 rose bushes; there are also the ruins of the Residenz Palace, Alexander Church, and the historic Zum Hirsch inn, the oldest house in the city (built around 1600).

Kaiserslautern is the district capital. Founded by Emperor Barbarossa, it is an important industrial center, and its chief sights include the 13th-century Abbey Church and St. Martin's Church from the same period; a few miles southwest of the city is Lake Gelterswoog.

In order to explore the little-visited, scenically beautiful area to the north of Kaiserslautern, take the road through Wolfstein to the Glan Valley and end at Idar-Oberstein. The main road for Saarland also leads through Kaiserslautern, in a westerly direction. To the east, it leads across the green landscape of Pfälzer Wald (Palatine Forest), back to Neustadt on the Wine Road, and from there to Speyer.

From Speyer to Mainz

Speyer is believed to have originated some 3,000 years ago as an early Celtic settlement; traces of Celtic tribes dating back to the 2nd century B.C. have been discovered. It is also one of the old cities of the Holy Roman Empire, and in its cathedral, the largest Romanesque church in Europe, begun in 1030 by Conrad II, no less than eight emperors are buried. Conrad II's grandson, Heinrich IV, left from here in 1076 on his long walk of repentance to Canossa, now in northern Italy, to seek forgiveness and the blessing of the Pope who had excommunicated him. There is also an important Protestant Memorial Church, the 18th-century Trinity Church, remains of the city walls and Altpörtel, an imposing tower-gate from 1230. The Palatine Historical Museum has fine collections of prehistoric and Roman relics and medieval art. Furthermore it includes a very interesting Wine Museum with priceless articles, such as a Greco-Roman vintner's knife dating from 260 A.D. and a sealed glass case containing the world's oldest (from 300 A.D.) wine preserved in liquid state.

Descending the Rhine from Speyer, we come to a pair of cities facing each other across the stream. Ludwigshafen, on the west bank, and Mannheim, on the east bank, are actually twin cities. But while the first is in the Rhineland-Palatinate, the latter belongs to Baden-Württemberg, the Rhine being the border between these two states. Ludwigshafen is the center of the German chemical industry and one of its biggest river ports.

Worms has played an important part in the history of Europe. Its early beginnings are reflected in the fine historic collections of the Municipal Museum with objects from 3000 B.C., and in Hagen's Monument on the bank of the Rhine showing this mythical hero of ancient German sagas throwing the famous Nibelungen hoard into the river; and it is from Worms that the Nibelungs were supposed to strike towards the east, hence the "Nibelungen Road" begins here. The remains of medieval walls remind us of later times when the Imperial Diet sat here, when the Emperor and the Pope in 1122 reached agreement about the roles of spiritual and secular power, beginning a new era in the political development of Europe, and when the edict of Worms in 1521 condemned Martin Luther. Worms has since then become two-thirds Protestant and has erected an impressive Reformation Monument, reputed to be the greatest in the world. But the city is presently best known for its magnificent 12th-century cathedral (Dom St. Peter), whose exteriors are in the purest Romanesque style to be found in Germany. Heylshof Museum contains 15th–19th century art and outstanding exhibits of porcelain and glass painting. The Gothic Liebfrauenkirche in the middle of vineyards has given the name to Liebfraumilch, the famous white wine.

Mainz is the capital of Rhineland-Palatinate. A bridge across the Rhine connects it with the suburb of Kastel and from here there are only about eight miles to Wiesbaden. Mainz is an ancient city, whose Romanesque cathedral, an imposing structure with a heavy central tower flanked by two light ones, is a thousand years old. Its interior contains perhaps the finest collection of works of art of any German cathedral. Note the rococo choir stalls, the Gothic cloister colonnade, and the Diocesan Museum with its famous medieval sculpture that includes works by the unknown Master of Naumburg. Mainz was the seat of a Prince Elector, and the birthplace (1397) of one of the world's most famous citizens—Johannes Gutenberg, inventor of movable type, who died here in 1468.

Although ancient Mainz, which celebrated its 2000th anniversary in 1962, lost most of its old buildings during World War II, some have now been reconstructed including the Renaissance Palace of the Prince Electors with the Roman-Germanic Museum; the former Elector's Stables which now contain the Museum of Antiquity and the City Art Gallery; portions of the former Clarissen Convent (presently the Natural History Museum); and the Renaissance-style "Römischer Kaiser" with a modern annex—both housing the Gutenberg Museum with such rare works as the 42-line Bible and the Book of Hours of Charles the Bold.

Other sights include: The Gutenberg Monument on Gutenberg Square; the citadel with Drusus Monument; the market square fountain; the lovely promenade along the Rhine; the old houses in the Kirschgarten; the university named for Gutenberg; and the busy river harbor. The colorful market is held Tuesdays, Fridays and Saturdays from 7 A.M. to 1 P.M.

Mainz is at its liveliest at Mardi Gras, when it holds a famous festival, and during the August–September Wine Market, for the city plays a leading role in the German wine trade. It is also a good point from which to take a boat for a trip on the Rhine—or for that matter on the Main, which joins the Rhine here, to Frankfurt.

Saarland

Following an agreement between Germany and France, the Saar, or Saarland, was politically reunited with the former country in 1957. Economic reintegration followed in 1959, the German Mark became once more the currency of Saarland, and this entirely German-speaking province again forms an integral part of Germany as it had in previous centuries.

The capital of Saarland, Saarbrücken, is best reached from Frankfurt via Mannheim and Kaiserslautern, or via Mainz and Kaiserslautern. Saarland is usually associated with the coal and iron industry of which it is an important center; less well known is the fact that its countryside offers lovely rural landscape, and that certain sections of the winding Saar River are of outstanding natural beauty. One-third of Saarland is covered by forests and more than one-half of it is cultivated land. Industry is concentrated in the southern part of the province where Saarbrücken is located.

Saarbrücken is not only the business but also the cultural center of this state. There is a university whose modern buildings are quietly located in a suburban forest; opera, operetta, ballet, and drama are performed in the city theater; and there is also a symphony orchestra. The principal sights include: the baroque Elector's Palace and gardens; the Protestant Ludwigskirche also in baroque style and built by Stengel, who came here from Fulda, developed his own version of baroque, and became the master builder in this area; the Gothic Abbey Church of St. Arnual, located in the city district of the same name; the Saarland Museum and the Rathaus.

Since Saarland is small, all the points of interest can easily be reached from Saarbrücken. The road along the Saar River, through the industrial centers of Völkingen and Saarlouis, offers particularly beautiful, unspoiled landscape after Merzig (St. Peter's Church) through the picturesque Mettlach ("Alter Turm" from the year 987, the remains of the old abbey) and continues to Saarburg and Trier.

At Orscholz the Saar flows in a magnificent horseshoe bend. A few miles west is the village of Nennig, with its vineyards and Roman villa boasting an extraordinarily well preserved Roman mosaic.

Starting out north of Saarbrücken, you can make a round trip taking us through: Lebach, with a castle, 1,000-year-old oak tree, and Gothic church; Tholey, with the 13th-century Benedictine Abbey; the climatic resort of Nonnweiler in the mountains of Schwarzwalder Hochwald, with nearby Hunnenring, a huge fortification from Celtic times; St. Wendel, with the Gothic Wendlinus Church; the medieval Ottweiler; and the industrial town of Neunkirchen.

PRACTICAL INFORMATION FOR THE
RHINELAND-PALATINATE

 HOTELS AND RESTAURANTS. Accommodations in this area are plentiful. Hotels are heavily booked up during the spring and summer season, however, and it is better to make advance reservations. Otherwise consult the local tourist offices.

Alf, in Mosel Valley. *Gasthaus Alte Post* (I) is a small hostelry but great on the menu and has existed since 1795. *Burg Arras* (I), in the outskirts, is a small castle hotel with fine view.

Altenahr, in Ahr Valley. Several (I) hotels, among them *Zum Schwarzen Kreuz,* an historic house with its own vineyard. In the vicinity the *Lochmühle* (M), located among vineyards, offers outstanding cuisine.

Restaurant: *Bellevue,* reached by chair lift, has a garden terrace with splendid view.

Andernach. Hotels facing Rhine; *Rhein-Hotel* and *Traube,* smaller but reputed for good food, are (M).

Bad Dürkheim, on the Wine Road. **Hotels:** *Heusser,* garni, 85 rooms, all with bath or shower, many balconies, garden location, swimming pool; *Kurpark-Hotel,* 70 rooms, about one-third with bath, bar: Both (M).

Restaurants: Colorful wine restaurants in the vicinity: *Kasbüro* in Seebach, *Kanne* in Deidesheim, *Henninger* in Kallstadt; in Dürkheim: *Dürkheimer Fass,* the tavern inside a huge barrel. *Zum Winzer,* Kaiserslautere Str. 12, is nice if you are a larger group.

Bad Ems, in Lahn Valley. **Hotels:** *Staatliches Kurhaus,* and *Kuckenbergs Hotel,* both (E).

Parkhotel Guttenberg, and the smaller *Russischer Hof,* both (M). Czar Nicholas II stayed here. All seasonal. Open all year.

Hotel Quisisana (E), beautiful position and restaurants.

Restaurants: *Kursaal* and the *Delphin,* also a cafe. Cafés: *Kurgarten* (music); *Maxeiner,* Römerstr. 37; *Wien,* Lahnstr. 6; cafés of Bad Ems are famous for pastries. Pleasant *weinstube* in Römerstr. 8 is the *Domänen.*

Bad Kreuznach, in Nahe Valley. Hotels: *Steigenberger Kurhaus* (L), completely remodelled. 200 beds, 2 restaurants, café, wine tavern. *Caravelle Kurhotel* (L), 180 beds, all rooms with bath; open-air pool, sauna.

Oranienhof (M), 37 beds. *Grüner Baum,* Kreuznacher Str. 33, first-rate quality and less expensive than the others.

Restaurants: *Die Kauzenburg,* sited in old castle ruins, fine views; long wine list, medieval dining on advance ordering. *Dr. Faust-Haus,* good cuisine and wine list, dates from 1492.

Bad Neuenahr, in Ahr Valley. Hotels: *Steigenberger Kurhotel* (L), in spa park, 240 rooms, thermal baths in house and fine *Pfeffermühle* restaurant. *Hamburger Hof* and *Pfäffle,* both (M).

Restaurants: *Kurhaus* with music and *Casinobar* with dancing, both in Kurhaus; *Ratskeller* in Rathaus; *Zum Klausner,* very reasonable.

Bad Niederbreisig, on the Rhine. Hotels: *Alte Post* (M), 69 beds.

Zum Weissen Ross (I), is known primarily for its outstanding cuisine. *Rheinischer Hof,* 67 beds, simple and inexpensive.

Restaurants: *Kunibert der Fiese,* also small hotel; *Künstlerklause,* wine tavern; *Burg Rheineck,* in vicinity, castle restaurant with good food and fine view.

Bad Bergzabern, on the Wine Road. Hotels: *Kurhotel Westenhöfer* (M), 70 beds, cold water cures in house; more expensive is the *Parkhotel,* in a park with swimming pool.

Rössel (I), is great on food served amid regional décor.

About 7 miles south, near German-French border: *Kurhaus St. Germanshof* (I), garden, fishing and hunting. Historic inn: *Gasthaus zum Engel.*

Watch out for Ruhetag (roo-er-targ), meaning quiet day, when places are closed. Usually Mon. but can be Tues. or Thursday.

Inexpensive cafes in Bad Bergzabern itself include *Herzog,* Marktstr. 48, *Bacchuskeller,* Weinstr. 58, *Weinstube Koch,* Am Plätzl and *Weinstube Boch,* Weinstr. 17.

Bernkastel-Kues, in the heart of Mosel Valley. Hotels: *Drei Könige* (M) at bridge on Kues side, atmospheric, rooms on river with balconies and fine view, outdoor terrace restaurant.

Römischer Kaiser (M), at bridge on right bank, good table. Next door, *Burg Landshut.* Not far away is old, picturesque *Zur Post,* only a few rooms, but long menu of outstanding dishes; reserve ahead. Last two establishments are (I).

The *Haus Behrens,* with large sun terraces, and old *Bernkasteler Hof,* in heart of old town section, are (I).

In summer, particularly on weekends, reserve at least a few days in advance—the town, because of its excellent wine and medieval atmosphere, is popular.

Restaurants: Old wine taverns (with food): *Ratskeller* in Rathaus (with music); *Brunnenstuben,* Moselstr. 5, and *Huwer,* Römerstr. 35, 15 beds.

Restaurant at Landshut Castle in courtyard, fine view.

Bacchus Keller, Gestade 2 in Kues section is a romantic restaurant with good choice and grill. Cheaper is *Pizzeria-Restaurant Sole d'Oro,* Schwanenstr. 9. No prizes for guessing their specialty.

Bingen, on the Rhine. **Hotel, restaurants:** *Starkenburger Hof* (M), facing the river; *Römerhof* and *Weinstube Schinderhannes,* in the suburb of Bingerbrück.
About 5 miles down the river, above Trechtingshausen, the 11th-century castle *Reichenstein* is now a 12-room hotel with a Knight's Room and converted horse stable restaurant; concerts in the crystal-chandeliered festivity hall.

Boppard, on the Rhine. **Hotels:** *Bellevue,* 88 rooms, pool, sauna, tennis and good restaurant; and modern *Motel am Ebertor,* 48 rooms with shower; both (M).
Rheinhotel Spiegel (M).
Above Boppard, the *Jakobsberghof,* 39 rooms, with riding facilities, indoor pool, wild game park and even a wedding chapel. Restaurant is (E) and is something rather special.

Buchholz, in Hunsrück mountain range. Nearby in a beautiful location above the Ehr valley is *Schloss Schöneck* (M), a castle first built in the 11th century. 16 beds, fine view. Open summer only.

Cochem, in Mosel Valley. **Hotel-restaurants—**all (M–I): *Germania,* 31 rooms, bar, terrace, eel is specialty; *Alte Thorschenke,* historic inn since 1332, atmospheric wine tavern, hunting possibilities and own vineyard. *Brixiade* in Cond section on Uferstr. 13, with a fine view over the Mosel and Cochem from the terrace restaurant. Can be noisy.
Charming spot for coffee and cakes is *Lohner,* Oberbachstr. 26, near market place. Also bakery and has some rooms.

Daun, in rural, unspoiled rock-and-stream countryside, the *Hotel Wasgauland* (M) with good private facilities, pool, sauna and family rooms. Ideal for combining business in Pirmasens with rural peace. 200 beds, 78 rooms.

Deidesheim, on the Wine Road: **Hotels:** the *Haardt* (M), 84 rooms with bath or shower, thermal treatment, pool. *Reichsrat von Buhl* (M), 80 rooms, with wine tavern.
Restaurant: *Zur Kanne,* 12th-cent. house with own vineyard; French cuisine.

Ebernburg, in Nahe Valley not far from Bad Kreuznach. Small castle-hotel *Reichsgräfin von Sickingen* (M), in the rejuvenated former manor house of the Counts of Sickingen; the historic cellar of the old castle has remained and is now a wine tavern called *Schwarze Katze* (Black Cat).

Kaiserslautern. Hotels: *Dorint Hotel Pfalzerwald* (E), St. Quentin-Ring, 1. 226 beds, all rooms with private facilities, ice-box, radio, TV, swimpool.

Bonk (M), Riesenstr. 13, (garni) 39 beds. *Pfälzer Hof,* Fruchthallstr. 15, and *Reitz,* G-M-Pfaff-Platz 1, both (M).

Restaurants: *Haus Hexenbäcker* (E), Pariser Str. 2. *Pfalzkeller,* Am Altenhof 14 and the *Spinrädl* wine tavern in a 16th-cent. half-timbered house at Schillerstr. 1. Both (M).

Kobern-Gondorf, near Kobern on the Mosel. *Schloss Liebieg* (M), a small castle hotel, with antique furnishings and the watchtower originating from Roman times; wines from own vineyards, swimming pool; under personal management of Uta Freifrau von Liebieg.

Koblenz. Hotels: Near the main station, the 50-bed *Brenner* (garni), attractively furnished and with small garden-terrace, and the 35-room *Höhmann* with beer and wine tavern are both (M); the 68-room *Hohenstaufen* is also (M).

Facing the Rhine are *Kleiner Riesen,* 22 rooms, on city bank and *Diehls Hotel Rheinterrasse,* 64 rooms, on Ehrenbreitstein bank, both (M).

Facing the landing stages for Rhine and Mosel boats is the *Haus Morjan,* 37 rooms, most with bath or shower, gaily-decorated balconies. The 70-room *Union,* Löhrstr. 73, is (I); *Trierer Hof,* Deinhardplatz, 1 is (M).

Restaurants: All (M) are—*Metro,* Alte Heerstr. 130, also discothèque, cabaret and nightclub; *Rhein-Mosel-Halle* in the building of the same name and *Rheinland-Pfalz-Stuben,* Bahnhofsplatz 9, both modern.

Weinhaus Hubertus, Florinsmarkt 6, hunting atmosphere, an inn since 1689; *Balkan Grill* in the small Christo Bajew hotel; *Café Rheinanlagen,* with terrace, are also all (M).

Weinhaus Merkelbach, in Pfaffendorf, inexpensive; *Weindorf* at the Rhine bridge, a colorful group of wine taverns. Inexpensive is *Binding Fass,* in Löhrstrasse.

Linz, on the Rhine. *Burg Ockenfels* (M) is a castle hotel, 23 rooms, first class reasonable. Magnificent views over the Rhine and Ahr rivers, gardens, riding school.

In town, *Weinstock* (M), 38 rooms, pleasant terrace.

Ludwigshafen, on the Rhine. **Hotels:** The *Pfalzhotel Excelsior,* 160 rooms, and *Ramada,* 204 rooms, are (E); both have good restaurants, sauna, pool.

Viktoria (M), Bahnhofstr. 1b, 100 beds. *Parkpension Speichermann* (I), Luitpoldstr. 150, 32 beds.

Restaurants: *Inselbastei,* Parkstr. 70, with very fine view of the Rhine, *Pfalzbau,* Berliner Str. 30, and *Treiber,* Altstadtplatz 15.

Mainz. Hotels: Deluxe are the 240-room *Mainz Hilton* on the Rhine bank, with attractive restaurant, wine tavern and two bars, and the *Mainzer Hof,* Kaiserstr. 98, 75 rooms, very elegant, with panoramic restaurant.

All (E) are—*Europa-Hotel,* Kaiserstr. 7, very modern, all rooms with bath, restaurant with grill specialties; *Moguntia* (garni), Nackstr. 48; also, the *Hotel am Hechenberg* (garni), Am Schinnergraben 82, equidistant from town and airport.

(M) are—*Hammer,* Bahnhofplatz 6, 31 rooms, all with bath; *Am Römerwall,* Römerwall 53. Both garni.

Restaurants: *Haus des Deutschen Weines* (House of German Wine) in Gutenbergplatz serves over 350 different German wines in its several cozy rooms (M). *Eden,* excellent restaurant in Central-Hotel Eden at station.

For outdoor dining try *Stadtpark-Restaurant,* better known as *An der Favorite Rats-und Zunftstuben. Heilig Geist* (Holy Ghost), the only remaining medieval building, is now an excellent restaurant, near Rheinstrasse, opposite City Hall (M).

For foreign dishes, *Bei Luigi,* Am Stiftswingert 4 (Italian); *China Restaurant,* Gutenbergplatz 2.

Oberwesel, on the Rhine. Above town, beautiful view, castle hotel *Schönburg* (M). Very romantic and authentic. Only a few rooms, all with bath.

Rengsdorf, climatic resort in Westerwald. **Hotel-restaurants:** *Obere-Mühle,* an der Strasse nach Hardert, 50 beds, terrace-restaurant and park; *Zur Linde,* Westerwalderstr. 35, also 80 beds, both (M). *Rengsdorfer Hof* is (I).

Saarbrücken. (Most rooms with bath or shower): *Haus Berlin* in Faktoreistr., 65 rooms, and *Zum Kurfürsten* restaurant. *Am Triller,* Trillerweg 57, 130 rooms. Both (E).

Christine. Gersweiler Strasse 39, with the fine *Rotisserie* grill-restaurant and *Wien,* Gutenbergstr. 29, are (M).

Restaurants: *Ratskeller,* Rathausplatz; *Weinhaus Rebstock,* St Johanner Markt; *Bastei,* Saaruferstr. 16; *Schlossgarten,* on Schlossplatz; *Welsch,* Breite Str. 12, in the Tivoli House, specializes in charcoal grills.

Southeast of city, *Schloss Halberg,* excellent restaurant; (E); has 6 rooms.

St. Goar-Hausen. On Burg Rheinfels is the 27-room *Schlosshotel,* superb views, heated pool. (Day package trips arranged through St. Goar Tourist Office.) Can be crowded and noisy at weekends.

Speyer. Hotels: *Kurpfalz,* Mühlturmstr. 5, and *Goldener Engel,* at Postplatz, both garni, and (M).

Across the Rhine, near bridge, is *Luxhof* (M) small country hotel, with delicious cuisine, fishing and hunting.

Restaurants: *Siedlerschenke,* Birkenweg 2; *Stadthalle,* Obere Langgasse 11; both (M).

Trier. Hotels: At the Porta Nigra, deluxe *Porta Nigra,* 67 rooms, with bath, restaurants, 350-car underground garage.

Holiday Inn (E), 2 minutes from the station, is an upgraded version of the former *Merian Hotel.* Heated indoor pool and all top-grade facilities.

All (M) are—*Parkhotel Bürgerverein,* Viehmarkt 14, 80 rooms, good restaurant, and the *Petrisburg,* Sickingenstr. 11, 18 rooms, garni, fairly near the railroad station. *Monopol,* near station; and *Christophel,* near Porta Nigra. The 90-room *Deutscher Hof,* Südallee 25, is (I).

Restaurants: Top are *Pfeffermühle,* Zurlaubener Ufer 76 (reservations advised) and *Lion d'Or,* Glockenstr. 7, both French cuisine.

Zum Domstein, Hauptmarkt 5, attractive; consists of several small taverns and courtyards and has 170 wines from its old Roman wine cellar. Wine tasting from DM3 per person, good food. *Krokodil,* Böhmerstr. 10, local color, inexpensive.

The hotel restaurants of *Zur Post,* Ruwerer Str. 18 and *Zum Zewener Turn,* Wasserbilliger Str. 59 are reliable and good.

Waldrach near Trier, in the Ruwer Valley. *Gasthof Schenk-Oster,* 27 rooms, garni. It's also a good *weinstube,* so you kill two birds with one stone, and get excellent wine and local color.

Walporzheim, idyllic vineyard village in Ahr Valley. Colorful old country inns: *Sankt Peter,* trout from the Ahr and own red sparkling wine are specialties, a wine estate since 1246; *Bunte Kuh,* near a gorge of the Ahr, garden with view; *Zum Sänger,* also outside the village, framed by vineyards and rocky slopes, outdoor terraces, evening music and dancing.

Worms. Hotels: *Domhotel* (M), Obermarkt 10, 60 rooms, all with bath or shower. *Europäischer Hof* (M), Bahnhofstr. 28.

Restaurants: *Kriemhilde,* at cathedral, Hofgasse 2; *Domschänke,* also nearby in Stephansgasse 16; also noted for food is *Bahnhofshotel* at station, inexpensive; likewise *Rheinischer Hof,* quiet position on river, also has a few rooms.

Zell. *Schloss Zell* (M), dating from 1220. "Zeller Schwarze Katz," the famous Mosel wine, comes from its vineyards. Period-furnished 12-room hotel, honeymooners' guest room in one of the towers. Avoid weekends preferably.

RHINELAND-PALATINATE. By Car. When we think of Germany we think of the Rhine. Everybody does, from all nations, and they are *all* there—which doesn't make for good motoring or easy parking. Scenically the best part of the Rhine is from Koblenz to Mainz. There is a road on either side, the larger being on the west, near which there is also an autobahn, A 61. In spite of this, the river roads are crowded, and it has been said that if you drive either of them all you see is the back of the vehicle in front of you. Even without the traffic one sees very little of the river—as is so often the case with rivers—and the delectable little villages along it have difficulty in accommodating the tourists who flood them. The only satisfactory way to see the river is to go along it by boat, taking your car with you. But get off at Bingen and drive up the Nahe River, or follow the enchanting Weinstrasse which ends near the French border. No marked road will, naturally, be without traffic, but it will be preferable to the Rhine roads.

 NIGHTLIFE. Bernkastel. Music and dancing: *Kaiserkeller* in Hotel Römischer Kaiser; *Zum Kurfürst* in Hotel Burg Landshut; *Bernkasteler Hof; Casparybräu.* **Ludwigshafen.** Dancing: *Wintergarten* in Europa-Hotel.

Koblenz. Cabaret: *Kosmopolit,* Löhrstr. 107. Dancing: *Butterfly,* Schulgasse 9; *Kellers-Künstler-Keller,* Schlosstrasse; *Trierer Hof,* Deinhardplatz 1. Merry Rhenish tunes and dancing: *Weindorf.* Bavarian brass-band-type and dancing: *Mata Hari,* Gorresplatz 18. Gypsy music: *Puszta-Keller* in Hotel Christo Bajew.

Mainz. Variety: *Palast-Betriebe.* Intimate bars in Europa-Hotel and Central-Hotel.

Casinos in **Bad Neuenahr** and **Bad Dürkhelm.**

 **MUSIC AND THEATER.** Indoor and outdoor concerts in all the spas during the summer season. Important symphonic orchestras include the Rhine Philharmonic Orchestra of Koblenz and the City Orchestras of Mainz and Trier. Opera, operetta and plays are performed in the City Theaters of Koblenz, Mainz, Saarbrücken and Trier. During the summer festival Koblenz has outdoor performances of operetta on the famed water stage and of opera and concerts in Blumenhof.

 MUSEUMS (consult also the descriptive text on individual cities). **Koblenz:** *Middle Rhine Museum* in Florinsmarkt, with collections of prehistory, ancient history, art from the Middle Ages to present, city history; *Rhine Museum,* in Ehrenbreitstein Fortress, natural history and Rhine shipping. Also, the house in Ehrenbreitstein where Beethoven's mother was born is now a museum of Beethoven memorabilia hitherto unavailable to the public, as the exhibits stem mostly from the Deinhard family of wine shippers, who bought the house. *Marksburg Castle* above Braubach near Koblenz contains rooms depicting medieval castle life, plus a library of publications on castles.

Mainz: *Roman–Germanic Central Museum,* Ernst-Ludwig-Platz 2; *World Museum of Printing,* Liebfrauenplatz 5; *Museum of Antiquity and City Art Gallery* in former Elector's Stables; *Natural History Museum,* Mitternacht; *Diocesan Museum,* Domstr., important medieval sculptures. All museums are closed on Mondays.

Saarbrucken: *Saarland Museum,* regional history, culture and art. **Speyer:** *Palatine Historical Museum* with *Wine Museum.*

Trier: *Provincial,* Ostallee 44, prehistoric; Roman and early medieval art (see especially the 4th-century Roman glass), *Bischöfliches Museum,* Banthusstr. 6, exhibits from the time of Constantine; *City Museum,* Simeon Monastery, valuable medieval sculptures; *Cathedral,* treasury; *City Library,* Weberbach 25, remarkable illuminated mss. (see particularly the jewel-set binding of the Ada manuscript and the Egbert Codex, painted in 980 in the Monastery School of Reichenau); the *Porta Nigra* itself.

Worms: *Andreasstift,* antiquities from Rhineland; *Kunsthaus Heylshof,* 15th–19th-cent. art, porcelain and glass painting.

 SPORTS. Horseback riding is very popular in this area and riding schools exist among other places in Mainz, Koblenz, Trier, Ludwigsburg, Bad Ems, Ehlscheid near Rengsdorf, Montabaur and Idar-Oberstein. Saddle horses can be hired in many localities. International riding tournaments in Trier and Bad Ems.

Golf courses in Bad Ems, Traben-Trarbach and Ramstein; and golf tournaments at Bad Ems. There are **tennis** courts in all spas and larger towns and international tennis meets are held in Trier.

Swimming pools, both indoor and outdoor, abound. Thermal pools in Niederbreisig (indoor and outdoor), Hönningen and Bodendorf. The numerous rivers afford opportunities for **kayaking** along long stretches of unspoiled scenery. The Mosel between Trier and Koblenz (120 miles, moderately swift current, requires about a week) is scenically one of the finest. **Sailing,** mostly on the Rhine. **Rowing** meets in Trier and Koblenz. World and European champion **motorboat** races take place yearly in Traben-Trarbach.

The Nürburgring twisting course in the Eifel Mountains is famed for **motor racing,** including such annual events as the Grand Prix of Germany. Other International yearly competitions include the Eifel Race, Trier Airport Race and the Rhineland-Palatinate Hill Climb.

The principal **winter sports** centers in the Eifel include Nürburg-Hohe Acht (2 ski lifts, 2 ski jumps), Hollerath (ski school, ski lift, ski jump), Daun, Hellenthal and Monschau. Skiing also in Westerwald and Hunsrück.

Fishing in Mosel, Saar, Ahr and Rhine, especially for trout, pike, perch, carp and eel. **Hunting** particularly in Westerwald. **Gliding** at Boppstätten near Birkenfeld, Idar-Oberstein, Kirn, Langenlonsheim-Sobernheim.

 USEFUL ADDRESSES. Tourist Information: Bad Dürkheim, Kurverwaltung in Kurmittelhaus and Verkehrsamt at station. Bad Ems, Kurverwaltung and Verkehrsverein, Lahnstr; Bad Neuenahr, Kur- und Verkehrsverein at main station. Bergzabern, Kurverwaltung, Kurtalstr. 25; Bernkastel, Tourist Information, Gestade 5. Kaiserslautern, Verkehrsverein at Stiftsplatz. Koblenz, Verkehrsamt opposite main station. Mainz, Verkehrsverein, Bahnhofplatz 2. Saarbrücken, Verkehrsamt, Rathaus St. Johann. Speyer,

Verkehrsamt, Maximilianstrasse 11. Trier, Verkehrsverein at Porta Nigra. Worms, Verkehrsverein, Neumarkt 14.

SOUTHWEST GERMANY

SOUTHWEST GERMANY

The Picturesque Land

This area is very largely that of the state of Baden-Würtemburg. It is bordered on the east by the Rhine, which also forms the German-French frontier, and on the north by Hesse. Switzerland and Lake Constance (Bodensee) lie on its southern border, and Bavaria its eastern border.

The highest mountains are in the extreme southeastern corner in the Allgäu, just over the Bavarian border. This is skiing and mountain-climbing country. North-west of the Allgäu is Upper Swabia (Oberschwaben), still hill country. Its southern border is the broad expanse of Lake Constance lying between Germany, Switzerland and a tiny bit of Austria.

The Black Forest (Schwarzwald) is perhaps the most famous and evocative mountain range in Germany. It runs north-south from Basel and Lake Constance where France, Germany and Switzerland meet, with the Rhine flowing along its eastern side. It is a quiet and remote area still, with fresh and lovely woods and streams, and deep, dark hollows where the houses shelter beneath immense roofs. Its valleys cut deeply into the evergreen-clothed mountains whose smoothly rounded tops give magnificent views of the alps away to the south.

A little to the northeast of Basel in the Hengau region, and running off in a north easterly direction, are the Swabian mountains (Schwäbische Alb). The Upper Danube runs along their southern slopes where the peaks rise up in great domes of basalt. Water eating away at their interiors has produced at least seventy known caves decorated with fantastic stalactites and stalagmites. And between the diverging heights of the Black Forest and the Swabian mountains, the river Neckar flows northward.

To the north of both the Black Forest and the Swabian mountains is the Swabian Forest (Schwäbischer Wald). It pushes its appealing and wild hills as far west as the Neckar, but not far enough to divert its course. It is still a rugged and barren area, with a harsh climate. In many places, mountains detach themselves from the main block to form great natural fortresses which were chosen as castle sites by families, such as the Hohenstaufens and Hohenzollerns, that were to acquire great glory and dynastic status.

North again from the Swabian Forest is Hohenloe, still hill country, though appreciably lower. The region is most mountainous where the Jagst and Kocher rivers sweep westward between steeply rising banks to join the Neckar north of Stuttgart. It is a traditional and profoundly rural area. Even German visitors sometimes have difficulty understanding the local speech. Along the Neckar, between Heilbronn and Heidelburg—the romantic capital of the region—the heights along both banks are dotted with one of the most beautiful collections of castles in Germany, which rise above the vine-planted slopes.

Northwest of the Hohenloe, the densely wooded heights of the Odenwald finally turn the Neckar westward to the twin industrial cities of Mannheim and Ludwigshafen—the first in Baden-Würtemburg, the second in Rhineland-Palatinate—where it empties into the Rhine.

THE COUNTRY OF THE NECKAR

Old Heidelberg and its Castle

Starting our tour of southwestern Germany from Frankfurt, we strike out through southern Hesse to Heidelberg and the valley of the Neckar. Here, in its meandering waters, the river mirrors an entrancing succession of feudal castles and free towns, of vineyards, cathedrals, and princely homes. To the east are the low hills of the Swabian Forests and Hohenlohe, dotted with half-timbered villages and more castles, and to the south is the city of Karlsruhe, a busy industrial center and the northern gate to the Black Forest.

219

EXPLORING THE NECKAR COUNTRY

Traveling south of Frankfurt on the Bergstrasse we cross into the State of Baden-Württemberg at the pleasant town of Weinheim, "the home of wine" as its name implies. A 185-year-old cedar tree, the tallest in Germany, grows in its carefully-tended downtown castle park while two more castles, Wachenburg and Windeck, the latter in ruins, look down upon it from the heights.

We meet the Neckar River at Mannheim where it flows into the Rhine. Mannheim is considerably larger than Ludwigshafen, its twin neighbor across the Rhine, which is located in Rhineland-Palatinate. But in spite of its size, a stranger need ask no directions in Mannheim to find his way about the center. It was laid out in the 17th century on a gridiron pattern within a roughly oval frame, lying between the Rhine and the Neckar, with the streets parallel to the two rivers lettered (from the Rhine to the Neckar) A to K for the west half, L to U for the east half. The cross streets are numbered, with the numbers running from the center outwards in both directions, and each block thus has a different name—so if your hotel's address is given as B 2, you know that it is in the second block from the Rhine and the second block to the west of the center.

The Elector's Palace, once the residence of the Prince Electors of Palatinate, is one of the most important and one of the largest baroque buildings in Europe. Other outstanding examples of the baroque style include the Jesuit Church with an ornately sculptured façade and an exquisite wrought-iron gate, as well as the twin buildings of the Old Tower Hall and the Parish Church on the market square. A profiled landmark of the city is the Water Tower in whose vicinity stands the Kunsthalle, containing a very fine gallery of 19th- and 20th-century paintings and sculpture. The Dalberg House, an 18th-century patrician home, is named after Freiherr Wolfgang Heribert von Dalberg, who lived in it after 1782 and who was the first manager of Mannheim's National Theater; today it houses the city library. The National Theater, rebuilt in 1957 after destruction during the last war of its original 18th-century home, is one of the most attractive examples of modern architecture in the city.

In addition to being a great industrial center and the second largest river port in Europe (boat tours during the summer), Mannheim has also distinguished itself as the place of great inventions in the transportation field: Baron von Drais constructed the first bicycle here in 1817,

Benz the first automobile in 1885, and Dr. Huber the first "Bulldog" tractor in 1921. Apart from its busy river traffic, the city is also a very important railroad junction, the meeting point of several autobahns, and a very good point of departure for trips to the Palatinate and to the Neckar Valley and Heidelberg.

Old Heidelberg

About 11 miles from Mannheim, on Autobahn A656 is Heidelberg. With its castle rising above the town and river, and its wooded hills rising above the castle in an incredible backdrop, Heidelberg resembles a stage set for an operetta. It looks even more unbelievably theatrical in summer, when the traditional illumination of bridge and castle takes place, with accompanying storms of fireworks. But it is real and it is here, no paint and canvas scenery, but extremely hard and solid rock.

The castle is a ruin, but it was in the battles of the 17th century that it was destroyed. The castle is a flourishing ruin; there was so much of it that what is left remains exceedingly imposing, and the architectural styles in which its various parts were constructed during the 700 years of its building and rebuilding are still evident. [Part of it has also been echoed in the elaborately adorned Ritter House in the center of the town, which was built in imitation of the Otto Heinrich building of the castle.] Enough remains also to house the famous Heidelberg Tun, that tremendous vat which is so big that it has a stairway built up one side to permit reaching its top (and it is lying on its side, at that). However, the Heidelberg Tun was not so big that its guardian, a dwarf named Perkeo, did not succeed in draining it to the last drop.

There is a great deal to be seen in the castle and gardens, and a great many people visit it each year, turning the place into a kind of real-life Disneyland. If you aren't happy with crowds, try to get there out of the rush hour. You may reach the castle on foot, by car, by a 290-ft.-long escalator, or by cable railway. The latter will also take you even further, to the Königsstuhl (King's Seat), nearly 2,000 feet high, with a superb view over the Neckar Valley.

On the other bank of the river, the view is combined with a pleasant stroll. A long pathway, or complex of pathways, winds about the landscaped slope. One of them, known as the Philosopher's Way—perhaps because its view is conducive to meditation—leads to the Bismarck Monument; from there you can take the Upper Philosopher's Way, combined with other pathways, to the observation tower on Heiligenberg, and past the remains of a Celtic fort to the ruins of 9th-century St. Michael's Basilica and monastery.

The Student Quarter

The university may well be the first thing that comes to mind when you think of Heidelberg, for *The Student Prince* borrowed this university, founded in 1386 and Germany's oldest, as its setting. Although the old buildings—among them the notable Aula built in the 19th century —are still in use, a new building was added in 1930–32. Most of the funds for this building were collected in the United States by Jacob Gould Schurman, onetime American Ambassador to Germany and former student at the university, for whom the city has named a street along the river.

But it is the old university which is responsible for the reminders of student life that visitors find so picturesque—the student prison (the university did its own disciplining, and no joking about it) and the student inns, can be visited down in the narrow streets of the old town, which remains today just as it was when it was rebuilt in the 17th century after those wars which were so hard on the castle.

"Eternally young and beautiful," one admirer of Heidelberg described the city, but while it remains eternally beautiful, it definitely looks old. That is what visitors like about it. And there are numerous unexpected vistas that greet you everywhere you turn in the streets of this baroque city built on its Renaissance and Gothic foundations (make a special point of looking at the old bridge, the Church of the Holy Ghost and the Jesuit Church).

You may be urged to visit in Heidelberg the house of the poet Scheffel, but it is less likely that anyone will inform you that this is the birthplace (and the burial-place) of a German much more universally known—the first President of Germany, Friedrich Ebert, who headed the Weimar Republic after World War I. Another very important native of Heidelberg was the astronomer Max Wolf, the founder of astrophotography. You can see another first citizen of Heidelberg, the very first, for he is prehistoric. You may recall, among the few examples of early man, or near-man, that there is one known as Heidelberg Man. You will not get a very complete idea of what this particular prehistoric man looked like, for this precious fragment, to which savants have devoted years of study, consists only of a lower jaw (there's a cast of it in the Electoral Palatinate Museum, along with some more attractive exhibits).

A more complete relic of the past, one that you should on no account miss, will be found in Kurpfälzisches Museum. This is the Twelve Apostles Altar, an unexcelled example of the woodcarver's art and one of the top masterpieces of Tilman Riemenschneider, the greath 15th–16th-century woodcarver of Würzburg. This particular piece, completed in 1509, had been in a church in Windsheim and when that city burned down in 1730, the altar was presumed to have been lost. But it was eventually discovered—in the Heidelberg Museum! In the middle of the last century, it had been daubed thickly with paint, which had concealed all the fine details of the figures, and in that condition it had been exhibited as a more or less nondescript offshoot of the art of its period. Removal of the paint restored not only its original beauty but its identity as well.

The Neckar Valley

From Heidelberg eastward the beautiful Neckar Valley is a gorge between high wooded hills on either side, providing some of the most romantic scenery in Germany, especially by moonlight. (The most scenic road is that along the north bank, especially beyond Neckargemünd.)

Progressing up the Neckar Valley, we pass through these places:

Neckargemünd (south bank), whose church steeple, seen from the water, rises with calm dignity above the old houses, while geese graze along the shore. Here you cross to the north bank, if you left Heidelberg on the southern shore.

Neckarsteinach, which has four castles of its own, and also provides a long-distance vista of Heidelberg's castle. Across the Neckar, high up on the hill, is the walled fortress town of Dilsberg.

Hirschhorn, on the north bank, an old (773) town with Carmelite church, remains of the town walls and an impressive castle-fortress. The best view of it is from the historic Ersheimer Chapel across the river.

Eberbach, whose buildings are clustered thickly about a bridge crossing the Neckar, beyond which long, curving, thickly-wooded slopes rise from the water. (Another Eberbach, in Hesse (Rheingau), has an historic Cistercian monastery.)

Zwingenberg, whose castle rises unexpectedly from the depths of the thick woods about it.

Neckarelz, where lovely old houses and oddly spired churches rise beyond a little stone bridge.

Mosbach, a short distance inland from Neckarelz and a wonderful city with whole streets of old half-timbered houses.

Neckarzimmern, the site of Hornberg Castle, where Götz von Berlichingen, the knight who had an iron hand, the hero of one of Goethe's plays, spent the last years of his life. Across the river is Guttenberg Castle with its historic restaurant.

Bad Friedrichshall, a small spa located at the junction of the Neckar and the Kocher. Just before Bad Friedrichshall another river, the Jagst, joins the Neckar; you can follow it to Jagsthausen, in whose Götzen-burg Castle Götz von Berlichingen was born.

Bad Wimpfen (back from the river, on the south bank), which specializes in asthma cures, an old imperial free town, with a tight cluster of old houses, and the remains of the 12th-century castle, with its so-called Blue Tower. A town worth visiting.

This brings us to Heilbronn, another imperial town, today a flourishing community. There are many interesting buildings in this city, which boasts that the tower of its Kilians Church represents the first appearance in Germany of Renaissance architecture; the tower was started in 1513, while parts of the church go back to the 13th century. Other historic buildings include: Götz Tower, named after the famous knight Götz von Berlichingen of the iron hand fame; Bollwerks Tower (Götz slept here); the Gothic Rathaus with 16th-century Renaissance modifications; Kätchenhaus, a patrician dwelling from Heilbronn's most flourishing period; and the baroque Hafenmarkt Tower. Heilbronn is the largest wine center of the Neckar Valley.

The Swabian Forest

Now for a short circular tour of the Swabian Forest (Schwäbischer Wald) and Hohenlohe, an area delineated approximately by the Rems, middle Neckar, lower Jagst, and upper Kocher rivers. This is a lovely region worth visiting for its natural beauty, its castles, and its unspoiled old towns. From Heilbronn we continue along the Burgenstrasse (Castle Road), through Weinsberg, harboring castle ruins; Öhringen, with the 15th-century abbey church; Künzelsau and its half-timbered houses; to Langenburg, with its castle.

Here we turn south to Schwäbisch Hall, the most picturesque town of the entire region. Visit it for its half-timbered houses, two romantic wooden bridges spanning the river, 15th-century parish church atop a broad 18th-century staircase, rococo Rathaus, and the nearby powerful abbey-fortress of Comburg (Grosskomburg). From Schwäbisch Hall we can proceed south to Gaildorf, with an interesting castle and Rathaus, then west to Murrhardt, for its Romanesque Walterich Chapel and Carl-Schweizer-Museum, and then return via Mainhardt, where remains of a Roman fort can be seen, to Heilbronn and to Heidelberg.

From Heidelberg let us travel a few miles west to Schwetzingen (also reached by tram) before heading south, to admire the interior of the castle and particularly the 200-year-old castle park, with its statues, famous rococo theater. This is also asparagus country and in May and June the roads are lined with stalls selling deliciously fresh asparagus. Hockenheim boasts an internationally-famed motor racing track, and Wiesloch, the wine center at the southern end of the Bergstrasse, an interesting local museum. Bruchsal's rococo palace, the most beautiful example of this style in all Germany, was destroyed during the last war but has now been fully restored.

Bretten has many old buildings that have remained unchanged since the early 16th century, when Luther's friend, the scholar and religious reformer, Melanchthon, lived there; while Maulbronn's monastery provides an object lesson on the way in which early Romanesque architecture developed into late Gothic. If medieval monastic life interests you, this is a good place to visit, as it is very well-preserved, and it is easy to imagine what it must have been like in the days of its glory.

Karlsruhe

One of the large cities of Germany, Karlsruhe is a busy industrial center and a major rail nexus as well as an important inland harbor, although the city proper is not quite on the Rhine, but somewhat east of it. It is also an important brewery town, where half a dozen leading brands of beer are made.

Karlsruhe (founded around 1715) is a comparatively late German city and its pattern, more original than the gridiron plan of Mannheim, is in the shape of a fan. This arrangement was due to the Margrave Karl Wilhelm, who conceived the idea in 1715, when he began building a new residential palace for himself at this spot. The completion of his design took place 66 years later under Grand Duke of Baden Karl Friedrich by architect Friedrich Weinbrenner, a native of Karlsruhe.

The handle of the fan is provided by the palace, whose two wings, leaving its central portion at obtuse angles, started the side of the fan, while long rows of impressive buildings housing the Margrave's ministries continued the outer edges to the point where they were joined by a third curving line of structures which constituted its top. In spite of the changes wrought by time, this basic plan is still traceable, and there is virtually no change at all in what lies to the other side of the fan and the palace—the palace park and beyond that an extensive wooded area which also presents a fanlike aspect, because of the long avenues radiating outward like the spokes of a wheel of which the castle is the hub, while two concentric half-circle avenues with the castle as their center complete the pattern.

There are German cities whose dominant style is Gothic, Romanesque, Renaissance, baroque, rococo; Karlsruhe is a one-style city also, and the style is neo-classic, for which Weinbrenner was largely responsible. The city was badly bombed during World War II but enough of its important buildings remain to retain the general impression. The Ducal Palace has been rebuilt and some structures have been replaced or repaired, but in other cases, as with the Baden provincial theater, the attempt to restore what was lost has been abandoned. Yet Karlsruhe still remains a monumental city of imposing structures, standing in a setting of noble parks and avenues. Perhaps it was for this reason that the Supreme Constitutional Court of the Federal Republic was established here in 1951, housed in the former Prinz-Max-Palais.

An interesting sight is the pyramid on the large market square which is flanked by the neo-classic Town Hall and the Protestant City Church, both designed by Weinbrenner. An outstanding contemporary building is the supermodern, multi-purpose Schwarzwaldhalle (Black Forest Hall), used for concerts, congresses, grand balls and the like. The extensive and pleasant Stadtgarten (city park) includes a zoo and a botanical garden, whose special attractions are the Japanese and Rose Gardens.

PRACTICAL INFORMATION FOR THE NECKAR COUNTRY

 HOTELS AND RESTAURANTS. Except for the larger cities (Mannheim, Karlsruhe) and the tourist Mecca of Heidelberg, prices in the charming old towns and castle-studded hills of this area are generally 10–20% lower than in similar areas along the Rhine.

Bad Friedrichshall. *Schloss Lehen* (M), built in 1553, large park, 45 beds, castle hotel garni.

Heidelberg. Hotels: The choice is wide. The newest and most comfortable is the *Europäischer Hof* (E), Friedrich-Ebert-Anlage, large, with excellent restaurant, wood-paneled *Kurfürstenstube* wine tavern, bar.

Crest (E), halfway between autobahn and city center, in Pleikartsförster Str. Also (E) are—*Stiftsmühle,* Heidelberger Str. 129, in a remodeled mill formerly belonging to Neuberg Abbey, 100 beds, 30 baths, on river just outside city. *Schrieder,* Kurfürsten-Anlage, good restaurant, bar.

Parkhotel-Atlantik-Schlosshotel, in a quiet location beyond the castle at Wolfsbrunnenweg 23, garni.

(M) are—*Zum Ritter,* Hauptstr. 178, a 16th-cent. inn, has retained its atmosphere in the beautiful Renaissance façade and colorful old restaurant.

Haarlass, Heidelberger Str. 2, on right bank of river about 2 miles east of city, fine terrace restaurant and café.

Tannhäuser, Bismarckplatz, 34 rooms.

Palmbräuhaus, Hauptstr. 187, small, all rooms with shower.

Regina, Luisenstr. 6, most rooms with bath.

Alt Heidelberg, Rohrbacher Str. 29, garni.

Neckar, Bismarckstr. 19, garni, is modern.

Also (M) are—*Monpti,* Friedrich-Ebert-Anlage 57; *Hackteufel,* Steingasse 7, small. There are many colorful old inns with inexpensive rooms.

About 2 miles east on the river, *Neckarschlössl* has a superb view and is (M).

If you are motorized, there are two excellent hotels about 10 miles south near the autobahn at Walldorf: *Holiday Inn* (E) large, all rooms with bath, radio and TV, air conditioned, heated pool, bar. *Vorfelder* (E), smaller, all rooms with bath or shower, top restaurant.

Restaurants: *Perkeo* (E), Hauptstr. 75, has been serving fine food with atmosphere since 1701. *Kupferkanne* (M), Hauptstr. 127.

Atmospheric wine restaurants: *Weinstube Schloss-Heidelburg,* (E), in the castle; *Kurpfälzische Weinstube* (E), in museum at Hauptstr. 97; *Altdeutsche Weinstube* (M), Hauptstr. 224. Excursion restaurants with terraces and magnificent views are *Molkenkur* (E), reopening 1982 after extensive renovation; about half-way up mountain. *Königstuhl* (M), at the upper end of the cable railway.

Historic students' taverns (also food): *Schnookeloch,* Haspelg. 8, since 1407; *Zur Hirschgasse,* Hirschg. 3, since 1472; *Zum Seppl,* Hauptstr. 213, since 1634; *Roter Ochsen,* Hauptstr. 217, since 1703; *Zwicker-Stub,* Steing. 2, since 1717.

Others are: *Knösel,* Untere Str. 37 (since 1865); *Schnitzelbank,* Bauamtsgasse 7; beer-drinking is traditional here and there are *Bierbrunnen* (beer "fountains") selling six different draught beers at Kettengasse 21 and Kranchiweg 15; four special draught beers come from the *Bierstubl* at Bluntschlistr. 31 and *Zwitscher-Stube,* corner of Blumen and Kleinschm. Str.

Wine restaurants which do not fall quite into either of these brackets are *Kurfürstenstube,* Friedrich-Ebert Anlage 1, *Zum Ritter,* Hauptstr. 178 and the very charming, atmospheric *Weinkrüger,* Hauptstr. 185.

Heilbronn. Hotels: *Insel* (M), Friedrich-Ebert-Brücke, on small island in river, large, most rooms with bath, good restaurant, café terrace and roof garden, indoor pool and sauna.

Near the railroad station are *Kronprinz, Beck,* (garni), 25 rooms, both (M), and *Paulinenhof* (I).

Restaurants: *Ratskeller* (M), in Rathaus; *Harmonie* (M), with garden terrace; *Schwabenbräu* (I); *Burgerbräu* (I); *Wartberg* (M–I), 3 miles out, with good view.

Heinsheim. *Schlosshotel* (M–E), castle hotel, 40 rooms, lovely park, swimpool, top restaurant with own wine.

Hirschhorn. Hotel: A section of *Schloss Hirschhorn* (I), above the town, is an up-to-date 30-bed castle hotel, retaining its medieval appearance. Fine view and good cuisine.

Jagsthausen. *Götzenburg* (M), medieval castle-fortress, birthplace of the famous knight Götz von Berlichingen and still owned by Berlichingen family; 25 beds, excellent food and wines. Open Apr. through Oct.

In town, the very simple 12-room *Zur Krone.*

Karlsruhe. Hotels: *Parkhotel* (E), Ettlinger Str. 23, large, all rooms with bath or shower, good restaurant on 10th floor, with grill specialties and view over the city, wine tavern, café.

Also (E) are—*Schloss-Hotel,* Bahnhofplatz 2, 130 beds, 50 baths, with *Schwarzwaldstube; Kaiserhof,* Am Marktplatz, small, most rooms with bath; and *Eden,* Bahnhofstr. 17, 80 beds.

All (M) are—*Am Theater,* Rüppurer Str. 2, small, all rooms with bath or shower; and *Greif,* Ebertstr. 17 (7-foot beds for 6-footers available on request).

Also (M) are—*Kübler* (garni), Bismarckstr. 39; *Erbprinzenhof* (garni), Erbprinzenstr. 26; *National,* Kriegstr. 90. *Central* (garni), Hirschstr. 81, is (I).

In the Durlach suburb, *Maison Suisse* (M), Hildebrandstr. 24, small, all rooms with refrigerator.

In Ettlingen (5 miles south) is pleasant *Hotel Erbprinz* (E), 75 rooms, all with bath, several suites; one of the top restaurants in Germany; garden terrace.

Restaurants: *Unter den Linden* (M), Kaiserallee 71; *Stadthallen* (M), in the Stadthalle; *Goldenes Kreuz* (I), Karlstr. 21; *Neuer Kaiserhof* (M), Gartenstr. 68, grill dishes; *Kupferpfanne* (M), Beiertheimer Allee 18.

In the Daxlanden suburb, *Gasthof Krone* (M), Pfarrstr. 18, with garden and good food, has been in the same family since 1859.

Oberländer Weinstube, Akademiestr. 7, specializes in regional dishes.

Among several worthy beer and wine bars, with food, are *Eselshaut,* Lessingstr. 70 and Hecker-Klause, *Kaiserstr.* 65, both beer places with music; and of the wine restaurants *Badische Weinstuben* in the botanical garden is particularly pleasant and *Pfälzer Weinstube,* Wilhelm Str. 17 too.

Book lovers who have enjoyed the many works to come from the famous publishing house of Gollancz may care to call at Viktor Gollancz Str. 1 where the *Albtalstüble* is a good place to take a glass of local wine and reminisce.

Mannheim. **Hotels:** *Steigenberger-Hotel Mannheimer-Hof* (E), Augusta-Anlage 4–8, 200 rooms, most with bath; smart restaurant, bar, colorful *Holzkistl* tavern.

Augusta-Hotel (E), Leibnitzstr. 1, 150 beds, most rooms with bath, comfortable, good restaurant and *Badische Weinklause* tavern.

All (M) are—*Wartburg-Hospiz,* near Rathaus, 163 rooms. *Parkhotel,* Friedrichsplatz 2, and *Holländer Hof* (garni), U1, all rooms with shower, radio, TV and small refrigerator; the 130-bed *Mack* (garni), Mozartstr. 14, and *Basler Hof,* (garni), Tattersallstr. 27, at the main railroad station.

In nearby Viernheim, near north Autobahn, the 124-room *Holiday Inn* offers motorists superior facilities, indoor pool, good restaurant.

Restaurants: Among the best, all (E), are *L'Epi d'Or* at A1, high class French cuisine; *Alte Munz,* P7, 1; *Amicitia,* Paul-Martin-Ufer 3, also a very nice dance café; *Rosengarten,* in the Stadthalle; *Zeppelin,* rotating view in new TV tower.

Habereckl am Ring (M), U6, is a little more relaxed, with view.

Beer restaurants: *Eichbaum-Stammhaus* at P5, 9; *Parkbrau,* Hauptstr. 114; *Habereckl-Braustüble,* Q4, 13, has good fare; *Rheinterrasse,* Rheinpromenade 15, a pleasant terrace restaurant on the Rhine; all (M).

Cafés: *Schuler,* Luisenpark, with music and dancing. *Rhein-Café,* Schwarzwaldstr. 38, with terrace overlooking the Rhine, is an (I) restaurant and has a few (I) beds; *Kiemle,* Plankenhof-Passage, has Mannheim specialties.

Neckarelz. Nearby is *Schloss-hotel Hochhausen* (M), country castle. The original medieval castle was rebuilt in baroque style in 1752, owned by Counts of Helmstatt; 20 beds, good restaurant with wines from Baden.

About a mile away in Obrigheim is another (M) castle hotel, *Schloss Neuburg,* with a particularly good restaurant and lots of atmosphere.

Neckargemünd. *Hotel Zum Ritter* (M), historic inn (since 1579), with 200-year-old lilac tree in the garden, has a colorful restaurant serving top food—including a special Knights' Fare (*Ritterliche Mahl*), a specialty of the house that must be ordered in advance—terrace, dancing on summer evenings.

Neckarmühlbach. The castle tavern of *Burg Guttenberg* (E) offers own wine and Swabian specialties. Open March through October.

Neckarzimmern. *Schloss Hornberg* (M), a real medieval castle-fort dating from 1040, beautiful view, museum, café *Im Alten Marstall* and spit-roasts in the large terrace-restaurant *Götzengrill,* own wines.

Öhringen. 4 miles north in an elevated location at the edge of magnificent forests is *Schlosshotel Friedrichsruhe* (L) with 23 rooms in the castle proper and 40 in the *Waldhotel,* owned by the Princes of Hohenlohe-Öhringen; outstanding food, own wines; small heated swimming pool and golf course.

Schwäbisch Hall. Hotels: The half-timbered *Goldener Adler* on the Markt, an inn since 1586; and the *Ratskeller* next door on the same square, with annex and good restaurant are both (M).

Across the river at Weilertor 14, the *Hohenlohe* (M) has a magnificent view of the old city from its riverside rooms and from the restaurant and roof garden café. There are some very pleasant coffee houses and patisseries here: *Ableitner,* Bahnhofstr. 5, and *Hammel,* Schulstr. 1, are good examples.

Schwaigern, about 8 miles west of Heilbronn. Gasthof and wine tavern *Zum Alten Rentamt,* former administrative seat of the Counts of Neipperg, who still oversee the high standards of food and vintage wines in its restaurant. A few (M) beds in period-furnished rooms.

 THE NECKAR. By Car. Between Mannheim, where the Neckar empties into the Rhine, and Heidelberg there are no less than three autobahnen, followed by a little spur out of Heidelberg to Neckargemünd, where the interesting part of the Neckar valley begins. No one doubts any longer that motorways generate motor traffic, so it would be absurd to suppose that this area will be one for relaxed driving. The valley itself, of around 60 miles, is very attractive, although much of it is serviced by a main road. From Neckarelz southwards, however, there is a small road on the west side which would be worth seeking out.

MUSIC AND THEATER. Heidelberg. *Städtische Bühne* (city theater) for opera, operetta and plays. A city orchestra and choral society give winter concerts in Stadthallel, summer concerts and performances of "The Student Prince" in the castle courtyard.

Karlsruhe. *Badisches Staatstheater* (Baden State Theater) performs opera, operetta, ballet and plays. The principal symphonic orchestra is *Staatskapelle Karlsruhe.* Regular theater and concert season.

Mannheim. *National Theater* has played a large part in the history of German dramatic art and though its fine 18th-century building was destroyed during the war, it maintains its traditions in new quarters (Goethe Platz) with outstanding productions of opera, drama, operetta, and comedy. Concerts by the National Theater Orchestra, founded in 1779.

MUSEUMS. Heidelberg. *Kurpfälzisches Museum,* Hauptstr. 97; old German art including the Twelve Apostles Altar by Tilman Riemenschneider. Frankenthal porcelain, paintings of the German Romantic School. *University Library,* Plöck 107–9, significant collection of medieval manuscripts. *Ethnological Museum,* Hauptstr. 235, folk art and customs, local and foreign (America Asia, Oceania, Africa). Castle interiors can be visited only in guided groups formed at castle ticket office.

Heilbronn. *Historisches Museum* in a 16th-century building; local history and culture.

Karlsruhe. *Kunsthalle,* Hans-Thomas-Strasse 2, paintings from the Middle Ages to the present, including Grünewald, Rembrandt, Holbein, and many Impressionists. *Badisches Landesmuseum* (Baden Provincial Museum), in the former Grand Ducal Palace, excellent collection of prehistoric finds, antique Greek and Roman and early Germanic art, and medieval to classicist sculpture.

Mannheim. *Kunsthalle,* Moltkestr. 9, a representative gallery of 19th–20th-century art, particularly French Impressionists. *Residenzschloss* (Palace of Prince-Electors), one of the largest baroque palaces in Europe; particularly interesting are the staircase, Knights' Hall, library and the chapel with the crypt of the Prince-Electors. *Reiss-Museum* in the former Elector's Armory; art, crafts, Frankenthal porcelain, local history, culture and ethnography.

Schwäbisch Hall. *Keckenburg Museum,* in a medieval town mansion, local history. Rathaus, baroque town hall, the interiors can be visited.

Comburg, nearby fortified abbey, guided tours of the church and Schenkenkapelle.

SPORTS. Swimming in the polluted Rhine is no longer recommended, although not so bad here as further north; many outdoor pools; indoors at Mannheim (with 3 pools), Karlsruhe and Heidelberg; the latter also has a thermal water pool. **High diving** school in Mannheim where many swimming competitions and important international **rowing** regattas take place. Rowing is also extensively practised at Heidelberg. **Tennis** courts in Mannheim (also important competitions), Heidelberg, Karlsruhe, Schwäbisch Hall and elsewhere.

Golf courses at Mannheim, Heilbronn and Heidelberg. **Horseback riding** facilities in all larger towns; important **horse races** are staged in Mannheim (especially during May Market) and Karlsruhe. **Motor racing** events are held at the Hockenheimring near Heidelberg.

There are **skiing** terrains in the Swabian Forest, and Mannheim, with its modern ice stadium (capacity 10,000 spectators) is the center of **ice skating** and **ice hockey,** including important international competitions.

Fishing for trout, pike, carp and eel mainly in Jagst and Kocher rivers, in Neckar for mullet, and in Rhine for perch and tench but no trout. For **kayaking** try the Neckar from Stuttgart to Heidelberg (100 miles, slow current, 6 days, very scenic). **Gliding** facilities, with instructors exist at Schwäbisch Hall.

USEFUL ADDRESSES. Tourist information (also local room reservations and sightseeing tours): Heidelberg, Verkehrsverein, pavilion at main station and at Kornmarkt in summer; American Express, Friedrich-Ebert-Allee 16. For the whole area: Landesfremdenverkehrsverband Baden-Württemberg, D7 Stuttgart, Charlottenplatz 17.

Parking garages: Heidelberg, in Bahnhofstrasse and Plöck; Karlsruhe, Autosilo, Amilienstrasse 55; Mannheim, Parkhaus (day and night), R5.

THE SWABIAN MOUNTAINS

Gliders, Caves and Woods

The Swabian Forest (Schwäbischer Wald) runs northwest to southeast, with the latter extremity about at Aalen. If you consider Aalen as the point of the letter V, of which the Swabian Forest is one side, imagine the other side of the V, running from the northeast at Aalen to the southwest at say, Tuttlingen, and you have the area known as the Swabian Mountains, or Schwäbische Alb.

Throughout this area, the air currents that rise from the mountains are ideal for hang-gliding. Even if you don't leave terra firma you can still feel out of the world in the Swabian Mountains. There are marvelous caves, rocks, castles, endless woods, and 7,000 miles of marked hiking routes.

To the east the Swabian Mountains are flanked by the Danube and to the west by the Neckar, both still young rivers. The Danube flows here through the cathedral city of Ulm, while the Neckar passes through the old university town of Tübingen and through the great metropolis of Stuttgart, the capital of Baden-Württemberg.

To reach the Swabian mountain region from Karlsruhe we strike southeastward, and the first place of importance through which we pass is Pforzheim, long famous as a center of the goldsmith's art, with some interesting churches—700-year-old St. Michael's, where the Margraves of Baden are buried; the Barfüsserkirche, whose choir goes back to the same period; and the Altenstädter Church, with its medieval frescos.

Stuttgart

Stuttgart is an important railroad junction, river port and a great industrial city, producing among other things electrical equipment (Bosch), automobiles (Mercedes-Benz, Porsche), cameras and optical instruments (Zeiss-Ikon, Kodak), machines of all kinds, textiles (among the leading is Bleyle with branch companies in U.S.) and clothing. Two companies particularly are of prime importance for the Baden-Württemberg economy, Daimler-Benz and Bosch with survival histories against incredible odds. Every twentieth worker in the province works for them and they have under-pinned the economic well-being of numerous component manufacturers. Bosch is the largest supplier which in turn employs some 60% of its West German workforce in the state. President Heuss, West Germany's first President, said the locals drew their character from a blend of speculative imagination plus a rather pedantic thirst for accuracy and some say that these qualities account for the province's success in industry. People from other parts of Germany mock them and call them conservative, but their innate brand of conservatism is one that regions with a more erratic record might well envy.

Stuttgart is not thought of as a spa, but in its Bad Cannstatt and Berg sections it has 18 mineral springs and is Europe's second biggest (after Budapest) source of mineral water. Some of the springs feed the three mineral water swimpools and the extensive cure facilities. It is also not usually thought of as a wine and fruit center but Stuttgart is one of the biggest wine-producing communes in Germany, possessing some 1,100 acres of vineyards actually inside the city limits, and the biggest orchard community in Germany with eight million fruit trees growing within a 20-mile radius from the city center. Better known is the leading role of Stuttgart in the field of publishing: about 200 publishers are established here (among them such veterans as Cotta, the original publisher of Goethe and Schiller, and Württembergische Bibelanstalt, the oldest and still the biggest bible publisher in Germany), along with 160 printing establishments, 300 bookbinderies and 20 graphic art firms.

EXPLORING STUTTGART

The city traces its name back to the middle of the 10th century when the Alemannic Duke Luitolf set up here his *Stutgarten,* a "stud garden" or stud farm, hence the horse in the Stuttgart coat-of-arms. It took a while and another coincidence before Stuttgart came of age. In 1311 the Counts of the nearby "Wirtenberg" saw their castle destroyed by the not very neighborly citizens of Esslingen and decided to move their seat to Stuttgart. When its rulers were promoted to Dukes in 1495, Stuttgart became the capital of the Duchy of Württemberg and in 1806, in the same manner, capital of the Kingdom of Württemberg.

Its history is reflected in the city's old buildings, restored after severe damage during the last war. The Altes Schloss, originally a 13th-century moated castle, was enlarged and remodeled for the Dukes of Württemberg in the 16th century in Renaissance style. Today it houses the Landesmuseum. Its splendidly arcaded courtyard once served as the ground for tournaments of armored knights. Next to the Old Castle, across the Schiller Square, stands the Gothic Stiftskirche (collegiate church), exactly reconstructed after the last war. Today it is the parish church of the Old Town but it has been called Stiftskirche since the time when the Counts of Württemberg moved to Stuttgart and brought along their canons as well as their dead ancestors; the canons were then installed and the ancestors re buried in this church.

Schillerplatz, whose other sides are framed by the Prinzenbau (once the residence of the Crown Princes) and Alte Kanzlei (formerly the royal chancellery), is presided over by the Schiller statute and offers an lively, colorful picture on Tuesdays, Thursdays and Saturdays when it becomes the flower and vegetable market. Beyond the Stiftskirche you can see the tall clock tower of the modern, postwar Rathaus, where a Glockenspiel plays different folksongs several times a day and even performs concert programs during the summer. Not far away, on Leonhardsplatz, is the late Gothic Leonhard Church constructed by Aberlin Jörg, the house architect of the Württemberg rulers in the 15th century. In the narrow streets south of the City Hall you can still find a few Old Town houses which remained intact after the last war and the graceful wrought-iron Hans-im-Glück Fountain in a dreamy corner in the Geiss Strasse.

Neues Schloss

On the north side of Altes Schloss is the baroque Neues Schloss, a vast palace which served as the residence for the Kings of Württemberg. It has been painstakingly restored after World War II and its state rooms with marble walls, frescos, crystal chandeliers and Empire furniture are now used by the government of Baden-Württemberg for glittering receptions. Neues Schloss faces the great park-like Schloss Square, with a 200-ft. granite column monument from 1846 commemorating the rule of King Wilhelm I of Württemberg, and flanked on the opposite side by the neo-classic Königsbau building along Königstrasse, the main business artery of Stuttgart.

To the north of Neues Schloss is the beginning of the large Schlossgarten park. Here is the lovely Theater Lake with the cupola-crowned Kunstgebäude (house of art) on one side, while the other side is lined with the glass and cubic Landtag (state parliament), the turn-of-the-century Grosses Haus (opera house) and the ultramodern, hexagonal Kleines Haus (drama and comedy). This might well be the goal for any visitor to Stuttgart interested in the performing arts, for the state companies are internationally famous, and especially the ballet company. In fact, Stuttgart serves as the ideal example of state-subsidized theater. Most provincial centers in Germany have resident drama, opera and ballet companies with enviable standards, but the Stuttgart Ballet Company has reached a position of eminence on the world scene that would make a visit to their home town worthwhile to see one of their performances alone.

Even before the war Stuttgart was known for its advanced designs in contemporary building and such great architects as Ludwig Mies van der Rohe, Walter Gropius, Le Corbusier and Hans Scharoun, among many others, collaborated on the construction of the famous Weissenhof colony of apartment houses. War destruction brought the necessity of reconstruction and with it the realization of the most advanced architectural plans, encouraged by the city fathers. In addition to the Landtag and Kleines Haus mentioned earlier, some of the newest, most outstanding examples of contemporary architecture include: the asymmetrical and wavy-lined Liederhalle by Rolf Gutbrod and Adolf Abel, with superior acoustics in its three concert halls (guided tours on certain weekdays); the twin skyscrapers and the library of the Technical University; the 700-ft. television tower designed by Dr. Fritz Leonhardt and the first of its kind in the world located on the Bopser hill and revealing a fine panoramic view from its observation platforms (on a very clear day you can see the Alps). Of particular note among the new suburban housing developments are, to the north,

Freiberg and Rot, the latter with two buildings popularly called "Romeo and Juliet"; Fasanenhof to the south, near the autobahn, with another "apartment-skyscraper" by Scharoun; Lauchhau in the west; and Heumaden to the southeast of the TV tower.

The Garden City

In view of all its industry and 20th-century building, one might expect Stuttgart to be, like too many modern cities, a prison of steel and cement. Actually, it is a garden city. Only 25 percent of its area is built over; 50 percent consists of parks, vineyards, orchards, gardens, meadows and fields, while 25 percent is covered by woods. In suburbs you can still see genuine farmhouses with cattle in the pastures, and the vineyards reach almost downtown. The finest laid-out park on the heights is Killesberg and you can also enjoy an exceptional view of the city from such vantage points as the Zeppelin-Aussichtsplatte on Zeppelin Strasse in the northwest, Eugenplatz and Haussmann Strasse above the Schlossgarten to the east, from the upper sections of Alte Weinsteige to the south and Hasenbergsteige in the southwest area.

On the right bank of the Neckar is the suburb of Untertürkheim, the home of Daimler-Benz, oldest automobile factory in the world, which produces Mercedes cars and exports half of the yearly production to practically every country in the world. The impressive automobile museum belonging to the factory is now housed in a new building, while in Bad Cannstatt, located next door to the northwest, you can visit the original workshop of Gottlieb Daimler at Taubenheim Strasse 13.

The suburb of Bad Cannstatt is a spa in its own right with a neo-classic Kursaal in a lovely Kurpark. It is best known, however, for the lively Cannstatt Folk Festival, a 16-day yearly event in late September and early October, which was celebrated for the first time in 1818 in thanksgiving for a good crop after years of poor harvests and famine. The festival, which has retained its basic agricultural character, is staged on the Cannstatter Wiesen (Cannstatt Meadows) along the right bank of the Neckar and its salient points are the great parade on the first Sunday, with Swabians from all the Swabian areas participating (also from the U.S.A. by special charter flights), and great fireworks displays, usually taking place towards the end of the first week. The festival is also celebrated in six American cities, for Swabians have accounted for a great deal of the German immigration to America.

At Ludwigsburg, just north of Stuttgart, everything centers about the castle-palace. The Ludwigsburger Schloss, inspired by Versailles, is the largest baroque palace in Germany, with a fine park, its own theater, a baroque and a rococo chapel, and a huge barrel in its cellars. It also has one of Germany's finest collections of baroque art.

April to October it is the background for illuminations and firework displays. Ludwigsburg, noted also for its concerts and garden show, is another point from which to visit the Maulbronn Monastery, as well as nearby Marbach, birthplace of the great German poet, Schiller; here you may visit the Schiller Museum and the house where he was born.

Other principal sights in the outskirts of the city include the rococo Solitude Castle on the forested heights to the west; Schloss Hohenheim to the south with the University of Agriculture and a botanical garden; in the southeast, the old imperial free town of Esslingen, with its old fortress, outstanding Gothic Frauenkirche and parish church, and half-timbered houses, among them particularly the Rathaus and the one where Hofzirrer, the explorer of New Zealand, was born.

Through Northern Alb to Ulm

From Esslingen we proceed through Göppingen, with modern spa installations and a Renaissance castle, and the climatic resort of Hohenstaufen at the foot of Hohenstaufen Mountain (where there is a wonderful vista over mile after mile of typical Swabian countryside) to Schwäbisch Gmünd. This is another famous center for goldsmiths' work and jewelry, and it is also the site of a fine Gothic cathedral with exquisite portals and stained glass windows, and the Church of St. John in an unusual Romanesque style with richly decorated exterior. Lorch, in the Rems Valley, has an early 12th-century abbey church located in the woods. At Hornberg, a high plateau (about 2,300 feet) there is a good view over hilly Swabia and gliders take off and land all the time, since it is here that one of the best German gliding schools is situated.

Aalen will be the starting point for our circumnavigation of the Swabian Mountains proper, for we shall run along their southeastern side and then return up the northwestern slope, describing a flat oval around them. For scenery and picturesque small villages, you can turn off from our route and penetrate into the heights anywhere, at random, and the result will be much the same. Everywhere you will find beautiful mountain country, little towns with half-timbered steep-roofed gabled houses, dignified old churches and castles.

From Aalen, a former free imperial town with an old Town Hall, a new Town Hall and many venerable houses, you might want to take a side trip to the southeast to see the grandiose baroque abbey church at Neresheim and the nearby Katzenstein Castle. South of Aalen on the Swabian Mountain Road is Heidenheim, dominated by the Hellenstein Castle. A few miles southeast is Giengen, home of the famous Steiff toy animals. A bust of President Theodore Roosevelt was unveiled here in

1958 to celebrate the 100th anniversary of his birth, for it was in Giengen, in 1903, that the original Teddy Bear was made and named after him.

Ulm, on the Danube, possesses one of the most beautiful cathedrals in Germany, a 14th-century Gothic structure whose 528-foot tower is the highest church tower in the world. Inside the cathedral are some wonderfully-carved choir stalls by Jörg Syrlin, a 15th-century master, which are as spectacular in their way as the cathedral is as a whole. The old city walls, with their gates and towers, the old town houses, the Rathaus, and the museums are also worth seeing. Finally, Ulm has a more modern claim to fame—it was the birthplace of Albert Einstein.

The Hochschule für Gestaltung (School of Design) is situated at Ulm. It is the successor to the famous Dessauer Bauhaus, which originated the movement to integrate the arts into commercial and industrial fields. It also created a new form of modern design and architecture. The two famous heads of the Bauhaus, Mies van der Rohe and Walter Gropius, emigrated to the United States before World War II.

At Ulm one of the first attempts at flying was made as long ago as 1811 by Albrecht Ludwig Berblinger, known to posterity as the "Flying Tailor of Ulm." The poor but proud tailor devised some sort of homemade wings that fastened over each arm, and announced that he would make a flight over the Danube in honor of a state visit to Ulm by the King of Württemberg. Watched by some 10,000 onlookers, Berblinger leaped from the town wall with his weird-looking wings and plummeted like a stone into the Danube. His wife later sold the wings to an umbrella maker who used the silk for parasols.

Ulm is a good starting point for explorations directly south, to the Allgäu region, or west southwest into the Swabian Mountains; sightseeing excursions can be arranged by the Ulm Tourist Office.

Stalactites and Scholars

Southwestward of Ulm lies Blaubeuren, with more of Syrlin's superb carvings in the Benedictine monastery, and Zwiefalten, with the Benedictine church, one of the best examples of late baroque in South Germany. In the vicinity is the Friedrichshöhle, an interesting cave. South is Riedlingen in the upper Danube Valley, with 14th-century frescos in St. George's Church, picturesquely built over the river.

Following the Danube upstream we come to Sigmaringen with the impressive castle of the Princes of Hohenzollern, housing a very fine museum and gallery of paintings; Hausen, with Werenwag Castle on top of a rocky hill and two more castles in the vicinity; Beuron, with the famous Benedictine abbey which has fostered arts and choral singing since 1077 and whose present church is a fine example of the baroque style; the small industrial town of Tuttlingen amid beautiful woods, with Honberg castle ruins and a fine view from the top of the nearby Witthoh (2,800 ft.).

From Tuttlingen we cross the southwestern end of the Schwäbische Alb to Rottweil, passing through the summer and winter resort of Spaichingen at the foot of the Dreifaltigkeitsberg, known particularly as one of the finest gliding centers. Rottweil on the Neckar, once a free imperial town, has preserved several of its medieval gates, towers, walls, patrician houses and churches, and has recently restored its "Roman Baths," built between 110 and 130 A.D. Traveling downstream along the Neckar we reach Tübingen through Balingen with an old Zollern castle with water tower and Hechingen which has preserved some of its fortifications and two castles.

Four miles south of Hechingen, on a high elevation, is Hohenzollern Castle, the original family seat of Hohenzollern, the royal and later imperial house of Germany, and a magnificent structure with many artistic treasures. This is a castle straight from medieval legend, worth seeing for itself and for the tremendous view from the battlements.

East of Hechingen, along the Schwäbische Albstrasse, we come to a speleologist's heaven. For there are some seventy fantastic stalactite caverns inside these mountains, particularly at Erpfingen, where the Karlshöhle and Bärenhöhle are located, and near Lichtenstein Castle (worth visiting for its own sake) where the Nebelhöhle, a complex labyrinth of caves, is to be found. At the foot of Lichtenstein Castle, which stands on a 760-foot cliff above the valley, is the pleasant little town and summer vacation spot of Honau.

Further northeast on the Swabian Mountain Road in a deep valley is Urach, a climatic spa resort with a half-timbered main square and some notable waterfalls about two miles away. West of Urach or northwest of Honau you can reach Tübingen via Reutlingen, another former imperial town, which has an outstanding Gothic church, St. Mary's, with valuable interiors and the most singular Gothic towers in all South Germany; there is also the Friedrich List Museum, commemorating the great economist, who was born there.

Tübingen is not only another of the former imperial free towns along the Neckar, but a famous university town as well, which accounts for the large number of eminent intellectuals who have lived here—the poet Hölderlin, the philosophers Hegel and Friedrich von Schelling. The university, founded in 1477, is one of the oldest educational institutions in Europe. Melanchthon, the famous theologian and author, and Johannes Kepler, Germany's well-known astronomer, both studied here. It possesses many fine buildings—the Gothic Collegiate Church, the massive Pfalzgrafen Castle, the old houses clustered around the market square, including the 15th-century Rathaus, the late Gothic

Stiftskirche, and the 16th-century *Alte Aula,* part of the old university, with its students' prison. It is a pleasant place to spend a few days, and one where admirers of Neckar Valley scenery can take their choice of the river in two moods—upstream from Tübingen it is turbulent and rapid; downstream from the same point it becomes calmer and flows sedately around great sweeping curves on its way to Stuttgart, Heidelberg, Mannheim, and the Rhine.

PRACTICAL INFORMATION FOR THE SWABIAN MOUNTAINS

 WHEN TO VISIT STUTTGART. As befits a busy industrial center with great cultural interests Stuttgart begins its year with sample exhibitions of arts and crafts, ceramics, porcelain and glass in **January** and the Stuttgart rare book dealers' fair, the most important in Europe, in **February.** The latest fashions are shown during the Ladies' Outerwear Week (DOB) in **March.** The Killesberg Garden show begins in **April** and lasts through fall. End-March or **April** is also the time for the confectioners' sample fair (SUFA) and of the International Fair for Oil and Gas Fuels (INTHERM). The Ballet Week of the Württemberg State Ballet is usually scheduled in the second half of **May,** followed by the International Ballet Festival in **June,** during which the best ensembles from the East and West perform here.

The Beethoven Days of the Stuttgart Philharmonic Orchestra usually take place during **July** and about the middle of the same month some of the world's best drivers test their skills and cars on the Solitude race course. Rowing regattas, motorboat races and other sports events are scheduled throughout the summer months and especially in **August.** A short Mozart Festival occurs during **September.**

The Cannstatt Folk Festival, with considerable attendance by Americans of Swabian descent, opens its doors in late September and continues celebrations through the first week of **October.** The Light Music Week, with international participation, is staged during October. During late October or early **November** the second yearly DOB-Week confirms Stuttgart's position as the leading sales outlet for ladies' clothing in South Germany. The Great Stuttgart Book Exhibition is usually dated from late November through the first two weeks of **December,** which is also the month of the Stuttgart Christmas Market.

 HOTELS AND RESTAURANTS. You will find quality accommodations in this area often at below-the-usual prices.

Regional cuisine: In Württemberg, in and around Stuttgart, a specialty is *Spätzle,* a little ball of flour and egg cooked in water, with infinite variations. You'll have it in soup, with liver, with ham or sauerkraut, *Spätzle* fried richly brown, served with roast meat or mixed with mushrooms. In the same neighborhood you'll find a local version of the *Schlachtplatte,* which has a wonderfully unusual taste and its own capacity to fill you up: it's made of sauerkraut, *Spätzle,* mashed peas, liver sausage, and bits of boiled pork. If you don't try this sort of dish while in Germany, you'll miss one of the tastiest treats of your trip.

Another specialty of the Swabian country, is the *Käseflädle,* a sort of pancake made with rich Allgäu cheese or fried separately and folded over the cheese. Typical also are *Maultaschen,* which are similar to Italian ravioli. Try all the soups: *Flädle-Suppe, Riebele-Suppe, Brisle-Suppe,* and *Klössle-Suppe.* In Stuttgart, taste their *Saiten*—juicy sausage served with lentils and *Spätzle,* and a wonderful soup of thin slices of potatoes, beef and *Spätzle.*

Württemberg, and for that matter the city of Stuttgart itself, produces very good white wines, a fact little known outside of Germany. When in the Stuttgart area try the *Untertürkheimer, Cannstatter, Uhlbacher* or *Rotenberger.*

Aalen. In Unterkochen, 2½ miles out, *Kälber* (M), with panoramic view.

Burg Hohenzollern. The *Burgschenke* restaurant in this magnificent castle has several sections: *Berliner Stube* with large windows overlooking the valley, the wood-paneled *Zollerklause* and a large outdoor terrace on the ramparts. Good food and wines.

Honau. *Alb-Hotel Traifelberg* (M), near Lichtenstein Castle, in a quiet location with garden, good restaurant. Has 23 rooms.

Ludwigsburg. Hotels: *Heim,* (garni), at the railroad station and *Schiller-Hospiz,* Gartenstr. 17, are both modern and (M).

About 2½ miles north is *Schloss Monrepos* (E), a castle hotel, all its 83 rooms with bath, located in a lovely park, noted restaurant with Swabian specialties and Württemberg wines on the large wine list, pool.

Restaurants: *Alte Sonne* (E), am Marktplatz; *Ratskeller* (M), Wilhelmstr. 13, garden; *Post-Cantz* (I), Eberhardstr. 6.

Pforzheim. Hotels: *Ruf* (M), opposite the railroad station, about 40 rooms, more than half with bath, fine food with Black Forest game as specialty, bar.

Smaller and all (M) are *City-Hotel* (garni), near the station, about half of rooms with bath, all with radio; and *Schlosshotel,* Lindenstr. 2, bar and restaurant *Bijou. Schwarzwaldhotel,* Schlossgatterweg 7, is moderate.

Restaurants: *Goldener Adler* (M), Westliche Karl Friedrichstr. 35; *Kupferhammer* (M), Am Kupferhammer 1; *Ketterers Schlosskeller* (I), on station square; *Rotisserie La Canard* in Hotel Gute Hoffung, Dillsteinerstr. 9.

Reutlingen. Hotels: All (E) are—*Achalm,* Auf der Achalm; *Ernst,* Leonhardsplatz, most rooms with bath, terrace café, bar and the pleasant *Herzog Ulrich* restaurant.

All (M) are—the *Württemberger Hof,* Kaiserstr. 3 and the *Reutlinger Hof* at No. 33.

There are several inexpensive *gasthöfe.*

Restaurants: *Stadt Reutlingen* (E), Karlstr. 55. *Ratskeller* (M), in the Rathaus. Outside on the Achalm mountain, *Höhengaststätte Achalm* (M), has a fine view from its terrace.

Schwäbisch Gmünd. Hotels: All (M) are—*Pelikan,* Freudental 26, quiet, small, with good restaurant, has a large annex; *Bahnhofshotel,* at the station, 20 rooms and also fine restaurant; *Weber* (garni), Ledergasse 14, most rooms with bath.

From the terrace of *Höhengaststätte Hornberg,* a restaurant and hostelry on the 8-mile distant mountain of the same name, you can watch the gliders, which have their airport here.

STUTTGART

HOTELS: The city has some 200 hostelries ranging from luxurious hotels to simple but adequate and proverbially clean rooms in small guest houses. Because of numerous cultural and business events scheduled throughout the year it is advisable to reserve rooms in advance, particularly in the better establishments.

Deluxe

Heading the list is the super deluxe **Steinberger Hotel Graf Zeppelin,** opposite the main station, with 280 noise-proof, air-conditioned rooms and suites (color TV on request, and AFN—American Forces Network—reception), two top restaurants (*Grill Room* and *Zeppelin Stüble,* the latter offering Swabian specialties amid Swabian décor), American bar, nightclub, indoor pool, garage.

The 125-room **Hotel Am Schlossgarten,** Schillerstr. 23, in the large Schlossgarten park near the main railroad station; smart restaurant and Swabian-style tavern, 2-floor café with terrace, American drinks in the bar.

Stuttgart International, situated at Möhringen about halfway between airport and city near the autobahn Degerloch exit; 160 rooms, indoor pool, sauna, 4 restaurants, bar, café, nightclub and, in summer, a Viennese-style garden café.

Expensive

Parkhotel, Villastr. 21 in Berg section, 110 beds, 50 baths, quiet location and good food.

Royal, Sophienstr. 35, in center but quiet location, 90 rooms, an elegant restaurant with excellent cuisine, bar, TV in most rooms.

Intercity-Hotel, Arnulf-Klettstr. 2, 135 beds, is located within the main railroad station, with restaurant.

Moderate

The modern **Rieker,** opposite the station, all rooms with shower or bath. **Unger,** Kronenstr. 17, most rooms with bath or shower. **Azenberg,** Seestr. 114, quiet location, indoor pool and sauna; all garni. **Kronen-Hotel,** Kronenstr. 48; **Herzog Christoph,** Büchsenstr. 37; **Buchenhof,** Hasenbergsteige 90, on the heights with beautiful view of the city, woods right behind, garni.

Inexpensive

Erika (garni), Rötestr. 67a, nice location away from downtown traffic; **Marktplatz,** an underground hotel at Marktplatz 22.

SUBURBS AND OUTSKIRTS

The modern **Flughafen-Hotel Stuttgart**, at airport, all rooms with bath and radio, bar, terrace; and the *Holiday Inn,* in Sindelfingen, 6 miles southwest, large, similar facilities; both (E).

Schlosshotel Solitude (M), in a wing of the castle, 50 beds, first class reasonable.

Waldhotel Schatten (E), in the woods near Solitude race ring, 55 beds, most rooms with bath, rustic décor, fine food. **Novotel** in Untertürkheim, Korntaler Str. 207, 234 beds.

Rotenberg (M), in the Untertürkheim-Rotenberg suburb, in vineyards.

RESTAURANTS: Mainly French and exquisite cuisine is, logically enough, to be had at **Exquisit Restaurant** (E), Marktstr. 3, entrance on Karlstr.

Alte-Post-Stiftsstube (E), Friedrichstr. 43, is noted for cuisine and cozy, ye-olde-inn décor.

Schäffelstuben (E), Hausmannstr. 5, and the tradition-filled **Alte Kanzlei** (E), Schillerplatz 5, are noted for excellent food and pleasant atmosphere.

Swabian specialties at their best at **Zeppelin Stüble** (E) of Graf Zeppelin hotel and the **Schwobastub** (M), opposite the main station.

Swabian specialties at moderate and low prices are the main feature in **Ratskeller**, Marktplatz 1 (also in Rathaus); **Börse**, Heustr. 1; **Bäckerschmiede**, Schurwaldstr. 44; **Arche**, Bärenstr. 1; **Kiste**, Kanalstr. 2; **Bäcka-Metzger**, Aachener Str. 20 in Bad Cannstatt; **Weinhaus König**, Kronprinzstr. 6, popular wine-cellar in heart of the city, choice of five bars; **Weinstube Hasen**, Innsbruckerstr. 5, good restaurant; **Weinstube Paule** in suburb of Obertürkheim, Augsburgerstr. 643; all of them also have good local wines from Stuttgart and vicinity, which are among the best in Württemberg. **Eulenspiegel,** Bärenstr. 3, has mountain-lodge-like interiors and candlelight until 2 A.M. (many come mainly to drink).

The **Mövenpick Rôtisserie** (E), Kleiner Schlossplatz 11 in pedestrian zone (entrance Theodor-Heuss-Str.) also has a snack bar (M–I).

BEER RESTAURANTS (M–I): **König**, Königstr. 18 (with music); **Mathäser,** Geisstr. 12; **Oberbayern**, Marktstr. 2 (music); **Alt-Berlin**, Calwerstr. 48.

FOR VIEW: Killesberg (M), on the edge of the park of the same name, with heated terrace and music in the evening. For something out of the ordinary you might enjoy the panorama, and the cooking, in the "crow's nest" restaurant almost 500 feet up the 700-ft. *television tower* on Bopser hill in the outskirts.

FOREIGN FOOD: Maredo (M), Friedrichstr. 35, Argentine steaks; **Walliser Stuben** (M–E), Lange Strasse 35, Swiss; **Santa Lucia** (M), Steinstr. 3, Italian; **Lotos** (E), Königstr. 17, Chinese; **Les deux Pierres** (E), Feuerbacher Weg 101 in Killesberg, French; **Los Corales** (M), Kriegsbergstr. 28, Spanish.

CAFÉS AND PASTRIES: Large café in **Hotel Am Schlossgarten** overlooking the park, **Greiner,** opposite the main station, good pastries, also serves food. **Sommer,** Charlottenplatz, quiet, Viennese-style with plenty of newspapers available. **Königsbau,** Königstr. 28. **Reinsburg,** corner Marienstr.–Paulinenstr., mainly for pastries. **Schweickhardt** is in Bad Cannstatt, Marktstr. 24.

Tübingen. Hotels: *Krone* (M), Uhlandstr. 1, with colorful restaurant and *Uhlandstube* wine tavern. *Hospiz,* Neckarhalde 2; and *Barbarina,* Wilhelmstr. 94, are (M). *Hotel am Schloss* (no restaurant), Burgsteige 18, and *Gasthof Ritter,* Grabenstr. 25, are (I).

Restaurants: Swabian specialties in *Hölderlinsturm* (M), Bursagasse 4, *Alpirsbacher Schindelstube* (M), Brunnenstr. 9. Charcoal grill in *Schlosskeller* (M), Burgsteige 7. Large café-restaurant *Museum* (M), Wilhelmstr. 3.

Wine taverns (I–M): *Rebstock,* Ammerg. 12; *Forelle,* Kronenstr. 8. Student taverns: *Bierkeller La Cave,* Kirchgasse 6; and a few in the Haaggasse.

Ulm. Hotels: All (M) and all garni are—*Neutor-Hospiz,* Neuer Graben 23; *Stern,* Sterng. 17, 55 beds; *Am Rathaus,* Kroneng. 8, 90 beds with the colorful *Reblaus* annex; *Ulmer Spatz,* Münsterplatz 27, 45 beds.

Bäumle, Kohlg. 6, is (I).

About 30 km southwest in Allmendigen, is the small and pleasant Gasthaus *Zur Schweiz* (I–M).

Restaurants: *Forelle* (M), Fischerg. 25, in an old fisherman's house, small terrace on the Blau river; *Florian-Stuben* (E), Keplerstr. 26; *Pflugmerzler* (M), Pflugg. 6; *Höhengaststätte Oberberghof* (M), Oberer Eselsberg, about 3 miles northwest, with view from terrace; *Kornhauskeller* (M), Hafeng. 19, wrought-iron décor; restaurant in *Hotel Neutor-Hospiz* (M), opposite the new theater; *Herrenkeller* (M), Herrenkellerg. 4.

In the new University Center building are *Penthouse* (E) on the 22nd floor, with bar and café, and *Placa* (M), on the 2nd floor, also with café and grillbar.

Urach. *Hotel am Berg,* a little above town with view, 50 beds, good food and pleasant outdoor terrace; and *Vier Jahreszeiten,* indoor pool, are (I).

Weitenburg. On a hill high above Neckar River, the 11th-century *Schloss Weitenberg* (M) castle hotel with elegant dining, park, pool, horse riding.

TRANSPORTATION IN STUTTGART. Sightseeing. By bus: short tour in the morning, long tour in the afternoon, starting point at Schlossplatz near Dresdner Bank, daily April–October; from November to March, Sundays only. By boat: April through October, from the Wilhelma landing stage on the Neckar (at the zoo), a tour of the port and longer trips downstream as far as Heilbronn. By plane: sightseeing flights from the airport.

Public transportation. An efficient streetcar and bus net connects all the important points in the city and the suburbs. The central bus station is on the east side (Cannstatter Strasse) of the main railroad station. For the airport take bus line A. Taxi stands are in all strategic downtown locations or call Taxi-Auto-Zentrale, tel. 56–60–61. The new subway now has several lines in operation; the main subway station is located under the main railroad station square. Visitors to Stuttgart should buy a 24-hour ticket. This is valid on all public transport within the city environs.

Car hire: Autohansa, Hegelstr. 25; Avis, Katharinenstr. 18; Hertz, Hohenstaufenstr. 18; InterRent, Frankenstr. 3; all also at airport.

Parking: Many downtown streets have 1-hr. parking meters and there are a few attended parking lots in the center: at Rotebühlplatz, Karlsplatz and Fritz-Elsas-Str., among others. Parking garages open day and night are: Hauptbahnhof, Jägerstr. 17; Königshof, Stephansstr.; Kronengarage, Kronenstr.; Landtags-Tiefgarage, Konrad-Adenauer-Str. 3; Tiefgarage Österreichischer Platz, Tübinger Str.; Parkhotel, corner of Neckar and Kuhnstr.; Schlossgarten, opposite main station; Tiefgarage, Kronprinzstr.

City Air terminal: Lautenschlagerstr. 14, near main station. Departure point of airport bus, large waiting room and tourist information. Airport 13 km south of center. Buses every 30 mins, 5.30 A.M. till 11 P.M., cost DM3.50; taxi DM30.

THE SWABIAN MOUNTAINS. By Car. For the motorist the Swabian Mountains could be regarded as a smaller and milder edition of the Black Forest. They have the same hysterical-looking little roads on the map, only fewer, and are guarded, so to speak, on the east and west by the trunk roads Nos 311 and 27. There is also the autobahn A8 (Stuttgart-Munich), cutting across their upper end. Since Stuttgart, Gmund, Tübingen, Reutlingen and Ulm are ranged round these mountains, traffic is likely to be denser than in the Black Forest.

MUSIC AND THEATER. Regional: Opera, operetta, ballet and plays are performed by *Städtische Bühne* in Ulm (with two theaters), *Stadttheater* in Pforzheim and in *Württemberg-Hohenzollern Theater* in Tübingen. Württembergische Landesbühne gives guest performances in the *Stadthalle* in Ludwigsburg during winter. Ulm, Tübingen and Pforzheim have city symphonic orchestras as well as chamber orchestras, many choirs and concert seasons from fall through spring.

The Ludwigsburg Summer Festival, usually lasting from May to October, features opera and drama in the Baroque Theater of the castle-palace, symphonic and chamber concerts in the Ordenssaal and outdoor serenade concerts in the courtyard; concerts in the Ordenssaal continue through September while outdoor light music and ballet performances are staged in the palace gardens during the "Blossoming Baroque" garden show.

Stuttgart has rich, year-round theatrical and concert programs. Opera, operetta and ballet are performed in the *Staatsoper.* At Schlossgarten, the "big house" of the *Württemberg State Theater,* which enjoys an international reputation and which has given guest performances on the opera stages of Milan, Rome and Paris. Closely related to it is the *State Theater Ballet,* which during recent years has become one of the world's most famous ballet companies.

Ulm also has the smallest theater in the world, the *Theater in der Westentasche* (theater in a waistcoat pocket). It is in the Herrenkellergasse.

Plays are performed in the Staatsschauspiel, the "small house" of the State Theater, in *Komödie im Marquardt,* Bolzstr. 4, and in *Theater der Altstadt,* at the Charlottenplatz subway station. *Kleines Renitenztheater,* Königstr. 17, is a literary cabaret. *Stuttgarter Marionettentheater* in Wanner Saal of Linden-museum presents puppet shows.

Stuttgart is an important musical center with a State Academy of Music, and four renowned orchestras: *Württemberg State Orchestra, Stuttgart Philharmonic Orchestra, Symphonic Orchestra* of the South German Radio, and the *Stuttgart Chamber Orchestra* which has toured North and South America and Japan in addition to Western Europe. Most outstanding among many choirs are the *Stuttgart Philharmonic Choir* and *Hymnus-Chorknaben,* a boys' choir.

Concerts are given mainly in the Beethoven Hall, Mozart Hall and Silcher Hall of the ultramodern *Liederhalle,* in *Gustav-Siegle-Haus,* and in the halls of *Süddeutscher Rundfunk* and of the *Hochschule für Musik.* Church concerts are scheduled mainly in Stiftskirche and Markuskirche. Outdoor serenade concerts are performed during summer in Hospitalhof and Paul-Gerhardt-Hof and light music on summer weekends in Killesberg Park, on Schlossplatz and in the Kurpark of Bad Cannstatt.

MUSEUMS. Ludwigsburg: The *Schloss* (castle-palace) interior can be visited in guided groups formed at the ticket office. *Württemberg State Museum*—the section of this museum devoted to baroque art is located in Schloss Ludwigsburg.

Kirchheim (autobahn exit between Stuttgart and Ulm): in nearby Holzmaden is *Dr. Hauff Museum* with very interesting prehistoric finds.

Pforzheim: *Schmuckmuseum* in the very modern Reuchlin House, unique jewelry museum with fine examples of the goldsmiths' art from past through present, the oldest pieces from 4th and 3rd century B.C.

Schwäbisch Gmünd: *Städtische Sammlungen,* Olgastr. 100; a building containing Altertümersammlung, a collection dealing with all periods of local history, and Edelmetall- und Glasmuseum, old and new gold, silver and glass arts and crafts.

Stuttgart: *Staatsgalerie Stuttgart,* Konrad-Adenauer-Str. 32. An outstanding collection of paintings from the Middle Ages until today, including among many others Holbein, Cranach *(Lucretia),* Maulbertsch, Memling *(Bathsheba Bathing),* Rembrandt *(Self-portrait with Red Hat),* Frans Hals, Tintoretto, Tiepolo, Menzel, Leibl, Renoir, Monet, Cézanne, Corinth, Klee, Modigliani, Picasso, Beckmann.

Galerie der Stadt Stuttgart, in Kunstgebäude (house of art) on Schlossplatz; a very good collection of 19th–20th-century paintings by artists originating from the State of Baden-Württemberg. Periodic exhibitions organized by the *Württembergischer Kunstverein* in the halls on the other side of the same building.

Württembergisches Landesmuseum in Altes Schloss (Old Castle). History, culture and art in Württemberg and other Swabian lands from the Stone Age to the turn of the century.

Lindenmuseum, Hegelplatz 1, one of the largest ethnological museums in Germany; 120,000 objects ranging from golden masks of Peru to puppet figures from Java. Currently closed for renovation.

Museum für Naturkunde in Rosenstein Castle. Worthwhile exhibition of animal groups from various lands, displayed in their natural surroundings.

Stadtisches Lapidarium, Mörikestr. 24, in a garden. Antiquities, statues, gravestones, architecturally interesting remains of old buildings.

Bibelmuseum, belonging to the Bibelanstalt, Haupstätter Strasse 51b. 3,000 bibles in all languages and from four centuries, including the Luther Bible of 1545 with wood-carved covers from the workshop of Lucas Cranach.

Daimler-Benz-Museum in Mercedes-Benz Works in Untertürkheim (special bus D from the bus station). Motors, motorcycles, automobiles and racing cars, including the first motorcycle constructed by Daimler and Maybach, the first motorboat, the first aircraft engine and the first cars by Benz and Daimler.

Tübingen: City Museum, antiquities, archeology, zoology folklore.

Ulm: Ulmer Museum, Neue Strasse 92, old German art, history of art and modern paintings. Deutsches Brotmuseum, Fürsteneckerstr. 17, history of bread and baking.

 NIGHTLIFE IN STUTTGART. Show (mostly or exclusively striptease): *Balzac,* Hirschstr. 16; *Imperial,* Rathauspassage 7; *Evergreen,* Kronprinzstr. 6; *Excelsior,* Königstr. 54a. *Madeleine,* Eberhardstr. 39; *Four Roses,* Leonhardplatz 24.

Night bars: *Apéritif-Bar* in Hotel Graf Zeppelin; *Big Ben,* Kriegsbergstr. 11; *The Pub,* Bolzstr. 7.

Dancing: *Restaurant Killesberg* at the park; *Tanzcafe Marquardt,* Bolzstr. 2; the elegant *Scotch Club* in Graf. Zeppelin hotel.

 SPORTS. Regional: The air currents in the Swabian Mountains are particularly favorable for **gliding** (*Segelfliegen*) and hang-gliding (*Drachenfliegen*). The best gliding facilities exist on Hornberg near Schwäbisch Gmünd (also gliding school) and on Dreifaltigkeitsberg north of Tuttlingen. Around Ulm there are two hang-gliding schools: *Drachenfliegen Albrecht Berblinger,* Neue Str. 6 in Berghülen, and *Drachenflugschule Erbach* in nearby Erbach.

Hiking is another specialty of this region, which has some 7,000 miles of well-marked trails. Enquire at the *Deutscher Alpenverein,* Glöckerstr. 5. **Horseback riding** is also widely practised and saddle horses, often with instructors if desired, are available at Balingen, Ebingen, Esslingen, Göppingen, Ludwigsburg, Marbach on Lauter (state stud farm), Pforzheim, Reutlingen, Rottweil, Tübingen, Tuttlingen, Ulm, Urach, Schwäbisch Gmünd and elsewhere. Important riding tournaments take place in Ludwigsburg.

Fishing licenses can be obtained in Blaubeuren, Esslingen, Gammertingen, Ludwigsburg, Pforzheim, Rottweil, Sigmaringen, Tuttlingen and Ulm.

Ulm has a **swimming** stadium in addition to an indoor pool and Danube beaches. International swimming meets take place here as well as in Ludwigsburg and Schwäbisch Gmünd. Ulm is known for its **rowing** regattas. **Kayaking** on the Danube from Beuron to Ulm (85 miles) through a very attractive landscape but somewhat strenuous for paddling. **Tennis** courts are in all larger towns and **golf** courses exist at Hechingen and Göppingen.

Stuttgart: The largest sports installation is the Neckar Stadium in Bad Cannstatt, which can accommodate 75,000 spectators. **Soccer** games and **track and field** competitions take place here. It also has 16 **tennis** courts while other courts are available at half a dozen or so tennis clubs spread around the city; a tennis school exists at Sonnenberg. The Neckar Stadium also includes a section for **horseback riding** tournaments. For saddle horses and riding instructors contact Reitverein, Am Kräherwald 101, or Reitschule Hölzel in Möhringen.

Golf course is on Engelberg near Schloss Solitude, for details contact Stuttgarter Golfclub, Böblinger Strasse 72. For **swimming** you have a choice of mineral and regular water pools. Among several mineral water pools: Heilbad, Leuze, König-Karls-Brücke; Heilbad Berg, Neckarstr. 260; Mineralbad Breuninger, on roof of Breuninger Kaufhaus; Heilbad Canstatt, Sulzerrainstr. 4. Numerous outdoor pools include one on Killesberg. **Rowing and sailing** is practised on the Neckar, boats can be rented on the Neckar bank in Bad Cannstatt between Gaisburger and König-Karls-Brücke. **Ice skating** at Königsträssel in Degerloch. For **motor races** there is the famous Solitude course.

WINTER SPORTS. There is a steadily increasing number of ski resorts in the Swabian Mountains and, to a lesser extent, in the Swabian Forest. The terrain is more rolling than the Alps and perhaps not as dramatic, but it nevertheless offers good skiing possibilities, and throughout this area there is an unusually large number of ski jumps. Accommodations in these resorts are for the most part moderate and inexpensive.

Degenfeld. 1,748–2,560 ft. Chairlift, 2 ski lifts, 3 ski jumps, instructors.

Königsbronn. 1,640 ft. Two ski jumps (one illuminated for night jumping, with international tournaments), 5 ski schools, ice skating, horse sleighs.

Heidenheim, 1,567–2,115 ft. In the area, 3 ski lifts, ice skating.

Messtetten, 2,492–3,178 ft. Three ski jumps, ski lift, ski tours.

Welzheim, 1,705 ft. Two ski lifts, tours, ice skating, horse sleighs.

Westerheim, 2,722 ft. Six ski lifts, horse sleighs, ski jump, ski school, tours, winter camping site.

USEFUL ADDRESSES. Regional—Tourist Information: Ludwigsburg Verkehrsamt, Wilhelmstr. 24; Pforzheim, Stadtinformation, Marktplatz 1; Reutlingen, Verkehrsbüro, in Parkhotel in Listplatz; Schwäbisch Gmünd, Städt. Verkehrsamt, Im Prediger; Tübingen, Verkehrsverein, at the Neckar Bridge; Ulm, *Tourist-Zentrum "i-Punkt"*, Munsterplatz 51, in front of the Cathedral.

open Mon.–Sat. 8:30 A.M. to 10 P.M.; Sundays and holidays 11 A.M. to 8 P.M. Bundesbahn train information office in the main station, open daily 6 A.M. to 11 P.M.

General tourist information: American Express, Lautenschlagerstr. 3; Hapag-Lloyd, Königstr. 21; Wagons Lits/Cook, Königstr. 45. **For motorists:** ADAC, Richard-Wagner-Str. 53 and Theodor-Heuss-Str. 15. Breakdown service. tel. 28–00–11.

Consulates: United States, Urbanstr. 7, tel. 21–02–21; Great Britain, Kriegsbergstr. 28, tel. 29–32–16. **Other official:** Amerika-Haus, Friedrichstr. 32a.

Money exchange: Regular banking hours are Monday through Friday 8:30–12:30 and 1:30–4 (Thurs. until 5:30); at the exchange office inside the railroad station weekdays 8 A.M. to 9 P.M. and at airport till 10 P.M.

THE BLACK FOREST

Stronghold of Folklore

The Black Forest, or Schwarzwald, is one of those magic names that evoke for everyone a vague feeling of romance. If it conjures up for you a somewhat sinister image, a formidable wilderness of twisted growth below and matted foliage above, through which the sun never pierces, you are all wrong. The Black Forest isn't black in that sense. It isn't even forest in that sense. It's not easy to find much in the way of underbrush in this region. The dark evergreens that help to give the forest its name rise from soil so free of tangle that you would be excused for wondering whether landscape gardeners are not responsible for keeping it so neat and clean.

Nor does the forest extend unbroken. Conifers clothe the slopes of the mountains (they are not overpowering mountains, though they do have their moments of pride—the 3,824-foot Hornisgrinde in the north, the 4,065-foot Kandel in the central section, the 4,637-foot Belchen in

252

the south, and its neighbor, the region's highest, the 4,897-foot Feldberg), but the valleys are green with open fields. Your chief impression of the region will be picturesqueness—a much abused word, but one that describes the farmhouses, with their high-pitched thatched roofs, and the farm people, who still wear the regional costumes, not only on Sundays or on holidays, as is the custom in so many other places, but often weekdays as well.

EXPLORING THE BLACK FOREST

The Black Forest lies along the east bank of the Rhine, starting at the Swiss frontier and extending north as far as Karlsruhe. Heading southward from Karlsruhe takes you through its suburb of Ettlingen, an interesting old town going back to Roman days, which has preserved many of the buildings of its past in their pleasant location in the Alb Valley. Further up towards the end of the same valley is Herrenalb, a reputed climatic resort in an exquisitely tranquil green spot surrounded by waves of forested ridges. Southeast from here, most easily reached from Pforzheim, is the well-known spa Wildbad in the Enz Valley, with a mountain railway to Sommerberg, the charming resort of Enzklösterle, and Bad Liebenzell in the Nagold Valley, with an 11th-century castle-fortress nearby. At the western edge of the Black Forest is Rastatt, a sizable town centered around a large baroque palace.

Fashionable Baden-Baden

In an age of informality, Baden-Baden continues to operate as in the 19th-century days of its glory, when the very wealthy and the very noble considered that they owed it to themselves never to miss the season at this noted spa. It is, in the evening, a soft-music-and-champagne-in-a-silver-bucket sort of place and in the daytime a horseback-riding-in-the-bridlepaths haunt—for that matter, you can go riding in a coach and pair if you feel like it. There's no place in the world more likely to make you feel like it.

If all this makes Baden-Baden sound somewhat like an anachronism, banish the thought. A comprehensive plan is underway for conversion to a model spa resort, with modern facilities nicely balancing the Belle Epoque splendors. In tune with the times "anti-stress" cures are already offered, a sure sign that Baden-Baden is here to stay. Indeed, it has already lasted for some considerable time, due to its healing springs. The Romans started using them first (you can still see the remains of their bathing establishment) and they are still going strong. There are radioactive, chloride, and hot springs, whose waters one may drink, lie in, combine with soil for mud baths, or inhale. One may also ignore the springs entirely and concentrate on the casino.

Baden-Baden, although its wide streets and pretty river-side hotels are beautifully planned, is not much of a town for sightseeing. People come here to take life easy amid the pleasant surroundings of the parks and wooded avenues of a peaceful city. But if you do want to look at the sights, you will find that they are conveniently grouped in three clusters, the largest being the bathing establishments—the massive Friedrichsbad and the Landesbad, the state hospital. The Friedrichsbad, old on the outside but with the latest equipment inside, is well supplemented by the modern, 7-story, glass-walled Augustabad. Under the Römerplatz are the ruins of the Roman baths. Three ecclesiastical buildings are tucked in among the baths—the Kloster; the Stiftskirche; and the Spitalkirche, which houses Baden-Baden's most notable art object, a 15th-century crucifix by Nikolaus von Leyden. Across from these buildings is the 14th-century New Castle and its fine gardens. For the ruins of the Old Castle, begun by the Margraves of Baden in 1102, and also for a remarkable view from the tower, you start from the New Castle via the Altschlossweg. The Baden Historical Museum is in the New Castle.

A pedestrian mall leisurely brings you to the second group of buildings clustered around the Kurhaus (Casino) on the banks of the Oos, the lively little stream that flows so pleasantly through the heart of town. The Trinkhalle, where you drink the waters, stands behind the Kurhaus, and on the other side are the Municipal Theater and the Art Museum. Across the river are the new Haus des Kurgastes, "House of the Spa Guest," with a series of recreation rooms, and the ultra-modern Kongresshaus. Baden-Baden has moved into the modern world with a vengeance, and important international conferences are held here.

The third point of interest is farther along the Oos, where the swimming pool is located. There are tennis courts on one side of the stream here and on the other side a varied collection of churches—the Evangelical Church, the English Church and the Russian Church.

The time to come to Baden-Baden is definitely the summer. August is the big month, and its last week the big week. The attraction is the horseracing at Iffezheim, which, back in the 19th century, used to attract such giants of the literary world as Victor Hugo and Turgenev.

The Black Forest Scenic Roads

Baden-Baden is the starting point of the Black Forest High Road (Schwarzwald Hochstrasse) that runs through a succession of charm-

ing little resorts, all of which share the same delightful natural settings
—Bühlerhöhe, Plättig, Sand, Unterstmatt, Mummelsee (near that high
peak already mentioned, the Hornisgrinde), Ruherstein, Allerheiligen
(monastery ruins and the Bütten waterfalls), Oppenau, Bad Peterstal
and Bad Griesbach, Kniebis and Freudenstadt.

Two other scenic drives, parallel to the High Road, run through the
northern half of the Black Forest in a north–south direction. The one
to the east is the Black Forest Low Road (Schwarzwald Tälerstrasse),
beginning at Rastatt and continuing through Gernsbach (interesting St.
Jacob's Church and three castles in the vicinity); Forbach, with an old
wooden bridge and a notable parish church; and Baiersbronn (Sanken-
bach waterfalls in the vicinity) to Freudenstadt. The one to the west
is the Baden Wine Road (Badische Weinstrasse), starting in Baden-
Baden and proceeding through the picturesque wine villages on the
slopes of the Black Forest to Offenburg, once a free imperial town, and
to Gengenbach in the Kinzig Valley, from where you can continue
either to Triberg or to Freiburg. The Kinzig River flows into Rhine at
Kehl, just across the bridge from Strasbourg, the capital of Alsace (in
France).

Freudenstadt was founded in 1599 by the Duke of Württemberg to
house the local silver miners. The residents are still mining silver, but
not from the earth. It comes from tourists now, who seem to provide
richer pickings. Freudenstadt's Number One claim to distinction is that
it enjoys more hours of sunshine during the year than any other German resort. It lies in beautiful country, so the great sport here is
walking, and there are approximately 100 miles of well-tended paths
in the vicinity for that purpose. There is also good fishing and hunting.
If you get bored with nature, you can while away the time in the
tremendous town square, surrounded by Renaissance arches and good
shops.

Continuing southward, we pass through Alpirsbach, another climatic health resort with a fine Romanesque monastery church; Schiltach,
where there is a pleasant marketplace; Wolfach (the castle and the town
gate are to be noted); Gutachtal, for local color (you'll see regional
costumes worn and pass some rather impressive peasant houses); Hornberg, where there is a castle; and thus come to Triberg, a highly popular
health resort. Its waterfalls and the local museum are given as special
attractions, and, indeed, the waterfalls (take the path from the Gutach
bridge through Kurpark) are among the most beautiful in Germany;
the water drops 535 feet in seven steps. Triberg is also a good central
point for excursions through the area, especially to some of the peaks
in the region.

We are now deep in cuckoo-clock country. To prove it, there is at
Furtwangen a really remarkable historical clock collection. East of

Furtwangen and southeast of Triberg we come through the climatic and cold water (Kneipp) resort of Villingen, a 1,000-year-old town with a 12th-century church and some of the gates still standing; Schwenningen, in whose vicinity the Neckar has its source; Bad Dürrheim with its chloride brine baths; and finally to Donaueschingen, with its old church thrusting aloft twin onion towers and its castle-palace, housing very valuable collections and beautifully set in a park where you can watch the birth of the Danube, which, formed by underground sources that surface here and by the river Brigach, flows almost 1,800 miles to the Black Sea. Donaueschingen lies on the main road connecting Bodensee with Freiburg.

Freiburg—Capital of the Black Forest

The largest city of this region and its capital, Freiburg im Breisgau is the gateway to the southernmost part of the Black Forest, where its mountains are highest (Freiburg itself is backed by a wall of them). It was badly damaged in the war, but was fortunate in that its most spectacular buildings, such as the cathedral and the Kaufhaus, escaped. Those that were destroyed have been mostly replaced by new structures, which, for all their modernity are inspired by motifs borrowed from the medieval houses about them, so that the new and the old will blend harmoniously as soon as the new has had time to mellow.

The view of the city from the surrounding hills is dominated by the cathedral, whose roof rises as high as many of the steeples of the other churches of the town, while its own open lacework steeple soars still higher—to 370 feet, to be exact. Among its eight bells is a 5-ton bell, cast in the 13th century and called Hosanna, or in popular version, Susanne.

Freiburg's cathedral was started about 1200 and finished some three centuries later; its steeple has been called the most beautiful tower of Christianity's finest period. The 13th- to 16th-century stained glass windows are remarkably good (some have been removed to Augustiner Museum for protection), the main altar painting is by Hans Baldung Grien and dates from between 1512–16. There are also several woodcarvings by Hans Wydyz; a painting by Lukas Cranach the Elder in the sacristy; an altar painting by Holbein the Younger in one of the choir chapels; precious 17th-century Gobelin tapestries; a 12th-century Romanesque cross; and many other treasures.

The rest of the square in which the cathedral stands is also interesting. On its south side is one of the most fascinating buildings in the town, the Kaufhaus, in front of which, if you pick the right time, you may watch the colorful open-air market carrying on its busy trade. It could hardly have a more picturesque background. Four great arches at the base of the Kaufhaus curve over the sidewalk; at the next level, four statues of Habsburg monarchs stand against the wall between cunningly-shaped windows; above, the steep roof rises so sharply that its height seems to equal that of all the building beneath it, and from its slope, tiny windows peer out of gables like eyes half-covered by sleepy eyelids. And at the two corners, standing above the outermost columns of the arches, as though balanced on a single stilt, are two pulpit-like excrescences wearing high conical pointed hats. As though this were not enough for one square, it also contains the Wenzinger Palace, a gem of 18th-century architecture.

A good many other sights might be mentioned in Freiburg, but we will restrict ourselves to two other squares. One is the Rathaus square, in which you will see the City Hall, made by joining together two 16th-century patrician houses, complete with Renaissance gables and oriels. Of the latter, the southern one, built in 1545 carries a much admired bas-relief, *The Maiden and the Unicorn.* Chimes ring at noon from the City Hall tower. The 13th-century church of St. Martin stands opposite the façade of the old City Hall; if you wish to see it at its best, come at night, when the Gothic cloisters are lighted. The other square you should not miss is Oberlinden, for its medieval burgher houses, one of the oldest inns in Germany, Zum Roten Bären (Red Bear), and towering above the square's end the 13th-century Swabian Gate.

You might also visit the university, founded in 1457, one of the most important in Germany, whose buildings are conveniently located in the heart of the city. Freiburg is the cultural as well as the commercial center of this region, and the university is at once part of the cause and part of the result of this circumstance. American visitors to Freiburg should pause to pay their respect to Martin Waldseemüller's birthplace —for they owe their name to him. It was this geographer who for the first time put upon a map the word America. On other maps the country was being called a variety of names, but this one stuck.

Excursions from Freiburg

The nearest excursion takes you in 45 minutes from the city itself up to the top of the 4,200-foot Schauinsland Mountain by streetcar, bus, and suspended cable car. You can also drive up on a very interesting curved mountain road, which is used for car races. If you are driving, you can carry on from Schauinsland to the summer and winter resorts of Todtnauberg and Todtnau, as well as to Feldberg and Titisee. Another pleasant trip is to a small spa north of Freiburg, Glotterbad, the home town of the Black Forest Girls' Choir whose broadcasts have made it famous all over Germany.

You might also go west to the Kaiserstuhl, a height near the banks of the Rhine, which stands as a sort of advance guard of the Black Forest mountains, for at Freiburg the wall ends abruptly, and the level plain of the Rhine succeeds it. This is famous wine country, and the towns in the Kaiserstuhl region—you might select Ihringen as typical —are devoted to the cultivation of the grape.

Just beyond Ihringen, on the Rhine and on the French border, is Breisach, whose St. Stephen's Cathedral is worth the trip. It is a massive 14th-century structure perched above the river on a height which it seems to cover completely, whose high altar and frescos are immensely interesting. Breisach also encloses remains from Roman times and old city gates, among the latter notably the Rheintor. The views from Breisach are quite stunning, and you will easily see why its position made it highly sought-after by various warring factions across the centuries.

Traveling east from Freiburg, the main road traverses the Höllental (Hell Valley), a wild and rocky gorge, and leads to the lovely resort town of Hinterzarten, the highest point on the Freiburg–Donaueschingen road and about 800 years old. Some buildings date back to the 12th century; the Oswald Church, for example, is dated 1148. About three miles away lies Titisee, a rare jewel among lakes, set in a mighty forest; the only settlement on the lake, also called Titisee, was built primarily for summer vacationists and winter sports enthusiasts. There are more than 60 miles of signposted walks around the village.

Titisee, like Todtnau, is a good base from which to visit Feldberg, the highest mountain of the Black Forest. Halfway between Titisee and Todtnau (about seven miles from each) lies the highest point on this road, the Feldbergsattel. From here it is an easy walk to the summit of Feldberg, and a most rewarding one, for the mountain flora is abundant and fascinating. Skiers flock here in winter.

A few miles south of Titisee is Schluchsee, another beautiful lake in a green setting; this is, however, an artificial lake and at its lower end you can observe the mighty dam holding back its waters. It, too, is a popular summer vacation spot.

On the Upper Rhine

South of Schluchsee is St. Blasien, possessing a magnificently decorated church with a mighty dome that seems incongruous in these surroundings, the legacy of a former Benedictine abbey. From St. Blasien there is an interesting little circular swing into the extreme southwestern tip of Germany, delineated by the upper Rhine, which flows in an east–west direction as far as Basel where it makes a right angle continuing north. This is chiefly a scenic trip. It will take us through the picturesque mountain valley town of Bernau; Schönau, from which one may ascend the 4,637-foot Belchen; Badenweiler, which claims to have been a spa for at least 1,900 years (the Romans took over from predecessors going back to the Stone Age). Müllheim to the west, if you don't mind retracing your route to Badenweiler afterwards, for the sake of visiting the Markgräflerland wine country of which this town is the center (southward from Müllheim the road will land you in Basel, Switzerland); back on our main loop, Kandern, a resort famous for its bakery specialties; Lörrach, the site of Rötteln Castle, only a few miles from Basel; and then either through Schopfheim or through the historic town of Säckingen (almost as much Swiss as German) and the Wehra Valley to Todtmoos, a climatic health resort with a famous pilgrimage church, and thus back to St. Blasien.

The road continues southward through the Albtal, a deep rocky valley; where it is necessary to dodge continuously in and out of tunnels hewn through the rock. At Albbruck we reach the Rhine, whose left bank is in Switzerland, and then turn east to Waldshut, another storybook town, with a tower straddling one of its streets. We pass through Tiengen, with its old castle and suddenly, in front of us, is Switzerland again.

PRACTICAL INFORMATION FOR THE BLACK FOREST

 HOTELS AND RESTAURANTS. Baden-Baden and Freiburg are particularly well-off for accommodations in all categories. In summer Schluchsee and Titisee are apt to be crowded, so it is best to reserve well ahead.

In the northern part of the Black Forest, in the Baden area, there's a heavy meat dish so tasty that you can hardly believe *Badisches Ochsenfleisch* translates into simple boiled beef, with a horse radish sauce. A salad often served with this, but good all by itself, is made of the wonderfully unlikely mixture of shredded Swiss cheese, little pickles, bits of melon, cherries, plums, and cranberries. Just try it.

Other special dishes in this region are breast of veal stuffed with egg yolks and *Eingemachtes Kalbfleisch,* veal stew with white sauce and capers. Favorites with the local Baden-ites are all the different little *Küchle,* cookies, made of such interesting things as rose leaves, wild berries or nuts, dipped in batter and fried in deep fat. The roseleaf one is *Rosenküchle;* try the delicate *Frauenschenkeli,* too.

The Black Forest is also partial to the *Veschperle*—a little "snack," or second breakfast which you have at mid-morning (for the Germans, usually around 9 o'clock)—a piece of smoked bacon with dark rye bread and a glass of *Kirschwasser* (a schnaps distilled from cherries and not to be confused with cherry brandy liqueur). Making this your first course at lunch might fit your plans better.

A good Black Forest cold lunch, or a first course, is the *Eiersalätle* (egg salad) which, in all its varieties, is wonderful. And if you like fish, this, too, is your part of the world: Black Forest trout, pike, and a sort of carp; eel (which is delicious); salmon from the Rhine, served with steamed onions; snails and frogs' legs; for dessert have a *Schwarzwälder Kirschtorte*—a formidable cherry cake.

Bad Dürrheim. *Kür und Sporthotel Hänslehof,* Hofstr. 13, 220 beds, rustic-style decor, sauna, indoor pool, tennis and the fine *Hänslehof* restaurant, and *Am Salinensee,* quiet location on the lake, small, with good restaurant and terrace, are both (M). *Krone* (I), even smaller, but just as good a restaurant, is expensive.

Baden-Baden. Many accommodations in all categories; also numerous low-priced rooms in private houses. The hotels mentioned are open all year unless otherwise specified.

Deluxe: Heading the list is the internationally famed *Brenner's Parkhotel* (in Lichtentaler Allee), frequented by kings and maharajas; large and glittering, with superb cuisine, elegant bar, garden terrace opening on to large park, new indoor pool in Roman-style surroundings:

Bellevue, in beautiful private park in Lichtentaler Allee, 105 rooms, excellent restaurant and bar, open Apr.–Oct.

Two Steigenberger hotels: *Europäischer Hof,* Kaiserallee 2, facing casino on river bank, and *Badhotel Badischer Hof,* Langestr. 47, thermal water in rooms with bath.

Expensive: Golfhotel, Fremersbergstr. 113, near the golf course, 80 beds, indoor and heated outdoor pools, garden terrace, open Mar.–Oct.

Zum Hirsch, Hirschstr. 1, large, thermal baths in hotel.

Waldhotel Der Selighof, Fremersbergstr. 125, also near golf course, 58 rooms, indoor and heated outdoor pools, illuminated tennis courts, fine food in restaurant, open Easter–Oct.

Moderate: Tannenhof, Hans-Bredow-Str. 20, excellent restaurant, heated pool.

Atlantic, Lichtentaler Allee, garni.

Parkvilla Kossmann, Kaiser-Wilhelm-Str. 3, small and quiet.

Holland, Sofienstr. 14, 60 rooms, with indoor pool and garden terrace.

Also (M) are—*Haus Reichert,* Sofienstr. 4; *Müller,* Lange Str. 34; *Bären,* Hauptstr. 36, open April–Nov.; *Haus Tanneck,* Werderstr. 14; garni, quiet.

Inexpensive: Am Markt, Markt-platz 18, near Stiftskirche, small, attractive, with good restaurant; *Vier Jahreszeiten,* Lange Str. 49; *Merkur,* small, on top of Merkur Hill (cable railway).

On the heights above the town, near and along the Black Forest High Road, there are a number of scenically and quietly located hotels, at a height of 2,300 to 3,300 ft, including *Bühlerhöhe* (L), large, with park, indoor pool, beautiful location. *Plättig,* smaller, excellent restaurant and bar, indoor pool, is (M). *Zuflucht,* good food and quiet location, and *Rote Lache,* are (M); *Sand* is (I).

Restaurants (in addition to those of hotels): *Stahlbad* (E), Augustaplatz, superb cuisine in pleasant surroundings. *Kurhaus* (E), in spa establishment, with terrace, wine tavern, and dance-bar. *Sinner Eck* (M), Luisenstr. 2.

The *Krokodil* (I), Mühleng. 2. *Café König* (M), Lichtentaler Str. 12, smart, with very good pastries, also limited restaurant service.

Badenweiler. Hotels: Top of the list is *Römerbad* (L), 170 beds, excellent restaurant, bar, thermal baths in house, thermal water outdoor and indoor pools.

Parkhotel (L), 120 beds, in quiet location with pleasant view, fine grill dishes and other specialties in the attractive *Parkstüble* restaurant, thermal baths. *Eckerlin* and *Schwarzmatt,* both in quiet, pleasant locations and with heated pools, are (E).

All (M) are—*Post,* small, attractive and quiet, with good food and indoor pool; *Sonne,* also in a quiet location; fine food in the colorful *Altdeutsche Weinstube.*

About 5 miles southeast, *Berghotel Hochblauen* (I), (3,820 ft.) is a pleasant inn with good view.

Bad Herrenalb. *Mönchs Post-hotel* (E), with 90 beds, fine cuisine, renowned original old tavern called *Klosterschänke,* hunting and fishing opportunities, heated pool. *Landhaus Jäger,* small, quiet, and *Kull,* 65 beds, both with indoor pools, are (M). A bit outside is the (I) and pleasantly located *Waldschlösschen,* 17 rooms.

Bad Liebenzell. *Kronen-Hotel* (M), 60 beds, all rooms with bath or shower, noted restaurant (try their 10-year-old Kirschwasser). *Ochsen,* all rooms with bath or shower in the annex, good restaurant, *Litz,* comfortable, both (M).

Bellingen. Thermal resort. *Burgund und Rebland,* garni, heated pool; *Kurhotel Paracelsus,* small and quiet; *Dreiländereck,* garni; all (M). *Gasthof Schwanen* (I), with asparagus specialties and own wine in its excellent restaurant.

Bühl. Nearby is *Burg Windeck* (E), a partially restored castle-fortress, with fine restaurant and view; also a few inexpensive rooms.
In town, *Grüne Bettlad* (M) is another atmospheric inn with good food.
In nearby Bühlertal, the hotel *Wiedenfelsen* is (I).

Enzklösterle. Hotels: *"Romantik Hotel" Waldhorn-Post,* in same family since 1766; 104 beds, sauna, tennis, restaurant with fine game specialties from own estate; *Enztalhotel,* both with indoor pools, and *Hetschelhof,* in quiet location, are (M).

Feldberg. Hotels: The *Sporthotel Dorint Feldberger Hof,* Am Seebuck 12, indoor pool, sauna, ski school, lifts, also apartments, is (M). *Berghotel Schlager,* pleasant inn, nice view, and *Albquelle,* with bar and terrace, are (M).
Gasthof Todtnauer Hütte (I), with colorful restaurant, bar, garden, ski lift.
In nearby Bärental, *Tannhof,* most rooms with bath, indoor pool, tennis, is (M). *Berghotel Pony,* with *Pony Bar* and Iceland ponies for riding (I).

Freiburg. Hotels: All (E) are—*Colombi,* Rotteckring 16, 80 balconied rooms, many with bath, restaurant, bar, wine tavern. *Novotal,* Karlsplatz, large and modern, all rooms with bath, radio and refrigerator, restaurant, bar.
Bad-Hotel Jägerhäusle in Herden suburb, primarily for weight-reducing cures; indoor pool, sauna.
In the Betzenhausen suburb, *Kühler Krug,* Torpfatz 1, in Günterstal district, and *Victoria,* near station at Eisenbahnstr. 54, 40 rooms, good restaurant.
All (M), some rooms higher are—*Rappen,* Münsterplatz 13, of recent vintage, with traditional Black Forest furniture in reception rooms. *City,* Wasserstr. 2, 130 beds. *Hotel Alleehaus,* Marienstr. 7, garni, quiet, nice view, terrace.
The colorful *Zum Roten Bären,* Oberlinden 12, is reputed to be Germany's oldest (1311) inn, atmospheric restaurant with Black Forest specialties, wine tavern. *Hotel Rheingold,* Eisenbahnstr. 47, near station, 40 beds, garni.
All (I) are—*Stephanie,* Poststr. 3, and *Barbara,* Poststr. 4, are both small, quiet hotels, garni; *Schwarzwälder Hof,* Herrenstr. 43, delightful Weinstube.

Gasthaus Kybfelsen, with good food, is in Güntersal suburb but on tram line to city.

Restaurants (in addition to those mentioned above): *Oberkirchs Weinstuben* (E), near Kaufhaus, attractive, with own wines, also moderate hotel. *Weinkrüger* (M), Schusterstr. 30.

Falken (E), near Rathaus, old furnishings, specialized cuisine and excellent wines, also a moderate hotel.

Eichhalde (M), Stadtstr. 91. *Alte Burse* (M), Rathausplatz, with music on Saturday evenings. *Zum Roten Eber* (M), Münsterplatz 18. *Zum Storchen* (M), am Schwaben Tor.

Ratskeller (E) in the restored Kornhaus (1498) on Münsterplatz.

Somewhat cheaper are *Pizzeria Wolfshöhle* in the old town in Konviktstr., and *Pizzeria am Siegesdenkmal,* Friedrichsring 5.

On Schlossberg: *Dattler* (M) and *Greiffenegg-Schlössle* (M), have magnificent views. A fine view of the city can be had from *Wappen von Freiburg* (M) on the Lorettoberg.

Freudenstadt. All (E) are—*Steigenberger Park-Hostellerie* (E), Karl von Hahn Str. 1, luxurious hotel with 230 beds, all amenities and two restaurants, *Zum Jagdhorn* and the cozier *Schokeloch. Waldeck,* Strassburger Str. 60, about 100 rooms, many with balconies, fine restaurant; *Kurhotel Eden,* Im Nickentäle 5, a bit outside in quiet location, all rooms with bath or shower, radio; bar, terrace, and indoor pool; and *Waldhotel Stockinger,* about a mile south, also in beautiful, quiet spot, excellent food, indoor pool, own ski lift.

All (M) are—*Sonne,* Turnhallestr. 63, 70 beds, most rooms with bath, indoor pool; *Post,* Stuttgarter Str. 5, 35 rooms, many with bath, terrace; *Württemburger Hof,* garni, Lauterbadstr. 10, small rooms, riding, indoor pool.

All (I) are—*Bären,* Lange Str. 30, with good restaurant; *Zur Stadt,* Lossburger Str. 19, quiet location.

In nearby Baiersbronn (about 4½ miles south) are the (M) *Am Kurgarten,* with fine food, and *Eurotel,* 128 apartments. *Kurhotel Mitteltal* (M), 5 km northwest, has a noted restaurant. All have indoor pools and water cures.

Restaurants: the colorful *Ratskeller,* Marktplatz 8.

Hinterzarten. Hotels: *Parkhotel Adler* (L), owned by the same family since 1446, located in own park, 80 rooms (all with baths), wood paneling and antique furnishings, good cuisine (try the salmon sautée in wine), dancing, indoor pool, tennis courts.

All (M) are—*Weisses Rössle,* also park location, 67 rooms, attractive restaurant, indoor pool, tennis; *Kesslermühle,* 27 beds, all rooms with bath, quiet location, indoor pool, sauna and solarium; *Sassenhof,* garni, small and pleasant, indoor pool.

Hornberg. *Hotel Adler,* near station, 24 beds, half of the rooms with bath, newly renovated (M).

Kehl, on the Rhine, connected by bridge with Strasbourg in Alsace. The modern *Europa Hotel,* 80 beds, most rooms with bath, and the recent *Astoria,* with similar amenities, are both (M).

Restaurant: *Traube* (M), French cuisine, also has a few inexpensive beds.

Mummelsee, on the Black Forest High Road, near the high peak of Hornisgrinde. *Berghotel Mummelsee* (I), in quiet location,

Nagold. Hotels: "Romantik" *Hotel Post* (M), in a half-timbered town house with 400 years of tradition; King of Württemberg was among restaurant guests, trout and apple cake are specialties.

Nearby is *Schloss Sindlingen* (M), dating from 1100. Castle-hotel with 40 beds, park, swimming pool, horseback riding.

Schauinsland. Hotels: *Halde-Hotel* (M), indoor pool, ski lift.

Considerably cheaper and half the size is the *Hof,* Silberbergstr. 21 and there are two smaller still and cheaper *gasthöfe,* the *Liftstüble* and *Schwarzwaldhaus,* as well as several pensions.

Schluchsee. Hotels: *Hetzel-Hotel Hochschwarzwald* (E), new and with Kneipp cures. All (M) are: *Glöcklehof,* 2 indoor pools, horseback riding, *Parkhotel Flora,* small, all rooms with bath or shower and balcony, indoor pool; and *Schiff,* 32 rooms, indoor pool, colorful *Blasiwälder Hof.*

Stoll-Sternen, 45 rooms, attractive restaurant (I).

Titisee. Hotels: *Schwarzwald-Hotel* (E), terraces overlooking the lake, 94 rooms, excellent food, tennis courts, indoor pool, private beach.

All (M) are—*Kurhotel Brugger,* with lakeside terrace and own beach. *Villa Tannfried,* own beach; and *Seehotel Wiesler,* all rooms with bath or shower, indoor pool.

Bären, Waldlust, and *Pension Seestern* are (I).

In Neustadt suburb the "Romantik Hotel" *Adler-Post* (M), Hauptstr. 16, 65 beds, some apartments; 400-year-old coaching inn with atmospheric *Posthalterei Stuben* and *Rotisserie Postillion* restaurants.

Triberg. Hotels: *Parkhotel Wehrle* with *Park-Villa,* 60 rooms (all rooms in Park-Villa with bath), quaint period furnishings, atmospheric restaurant with excellent trout, heated pool. Both (M).

Adler and the quiet *Gasthof Sonne-Post* are (I).

Villingen. Hotels: *Parkhotel* (M), small, all rooms with bath, good food, bar. The quiet *Haus Diegner,* terrace café, is (M); *Gasthof Bären* (I).

In the six-mile-distant Königsfeld is the villa-like *Schwarzwald-Hotel* (M), 56 rooms, about half with bath, fine eating in the colorful *Fässle* restaurant, particularly noted for trout dishes.

THE BLACK FOREST 265

Wildbad. Hotels: All (E) are *Badhotel,* on the Kurplatz with an arcaded inner court, 120 beds, 60 baths, thermal baths; and *Kurhotel Rassman,* Olgastr. 11–13, 43 beds, 15 rooms with bath, excellent restaurant, thermal baths.

All (M) are—*Bergfrieden,* Bätznerstr. 78, and *Post,* Kurplatz 2, with indoor pool; *Hotel Rosenau,* Wilhelmstr. 93.

On Sommerberg (cable railway) is the *Sommerberg* (L) in modern semi-circular form, 130 beds, all rooms with bath and balcony offering fine view. Black Forest-style décor, terrace café, tennis, indoor pool.

THE BLACK FOREST. By Car. This is splendid holiday motoring country—the only thing against it being that so many people think so. Like the English Lake District it is no place for anyone in a hurry. Flanked in the west by A5 and in the east by the incomplete A81, it is crossed laterally by two main roads, Nos B28 and B31 which take all the serious traffic leaving a mass of small, wiggly up-and-down roads for the locals and tourists. Drivers approaching Germany from France are fortunate that the Black Forest is what they are most likely to see first.

NIGHTLIFE. Baden-Baden. Gambling: roulette, baccarat and blackjack from 2 P.M. until 2 A.M. in the splendidly decorated halls of the 200-year-old *Casino* (in a wing of the Kurhaus), the most elegant in Europe, the oldest in Germany, and the only one where solid gold and silver chips are used on weekends and holidays in *Salon Pompadour.* Shows and dancing: *Jockey Bar Pigalle,* Lange Strasse 68; and *Barberina,* Luisenstr. 1a. Dancing during summer in *Kurhaus-Bar,* Kurhaus.

Freiburg. *Playboy,* Moltkestr. 3, dancing and swimming; *Georgs Klause,* in the Kornhaus on Münsterplatz, for dancing. Cabaret and dancing: *Mon Cheri,* Grünwälderstr. 6–8, and *Arena,* Schwarzwaldstr. 2.

MUSIC AND THEATER. Opera, operetta and plays are performed in *Stadttheater* in Freiburg. The city has two other, but smaller, theaters for plays, which are also given during summer in the Rathaus courtyard.

Guest performances of opera and operetta in Baden-Baden which has its own drama company in *Theater der Stadt Baden Baden.* Guest performances are staged in the modern *Theater am Ring* in Villingen and in *Kurtheater* in Freudenstadt. Theatrical performances are a regular feature in Donaueschingen and a seasonal feature in Badenweiler.

Hornberg has an open-air theater where the summer festival play "Das Hornberger Schiessen" is given every year. Freiburg has its *Städtisches Orchester* and Baden-Baden its *Symphonie- und Kurorchester;* both have regular concert seasons. Baden-Baden also has much indoor and outdoor music during the summer spa season.

Badenweiler offers periodic symphonic and chamber music concerts and three light music concerts daily in the Kurpark during the summer season. Light music is also a summer feature in Triberg, Titisee, Villingen, Hornberg and several other resorts. Donaueschingen has a lively musical activity and Contemporary Music Days every year in October.

MUSEUMS. Baden-Baden: *Zähringer Museum* in the Neues Schloss, local history and art; Staatliche Kunsthalle, Lichtentaler Allee 8a, periodic art exhibitions.

Badenweiler: The best preserved remains of Roman baths north of the Alps, built by Emperor Vespasian in 1st century A.D.

Donaueschingen: *Fürstenbergisches Museum* in the Residence Palace contains an outstanding gallery of old German masters (including Grünewald, Holbein, Cranach), important prehistoric and geologic collections and a library with a large number of very rare medieval manuscripts, among them the Nibelungs Saga, Schwabenspiegel and Parsifal Saga.

Freiburg: *Augustinermuseum,* Augustinerplatz, especially fine collection of medieval and baroque art from the Upper Rhine region. *Naturkundemuseum,* Gerberau 32, natural history. *Museum für Völkerkunde,* Adelhauser Strasse 32-ethnography. Kunstverein, Talstr. 12a, periodic art exhibitions.

Furtwangen: *Uhrensammlung,* clock museum of historic and other clocks.

Gutach: *Freilicht Museum,* open-air museum of old Black Forest farmhouses and other farm buildings.

Triberg: *Heimatmuseum,* local history, folk dress, carvings and Black Forest clocks.

Villingen: *Städtische Sammlungen, Altes Rathaus,* antiquities, medieval art. *Schwarzwald-Sammlung,* am Riettor, folklore, interiors of old farmhouses.

SPORTS. Baden-Baden has a **swimming** stadium with 5 pools in addition to other swimming facilities. Freiburg has several outdoor swimming places in addition to indoor pools. Badenweiler, which has an outdoor thermal swimming pool also has a monumental marble indoor pool. Wildbad has a thermal pool open in summer and closed by sliding glass doors in winter. Bad Liebenzell has a large indoor thermal pool. All resorts and larger towns have outdoor pools. Swimming also in the lakes of Titisee and Schluchsee, where **sailing** and **rowing** are practised. There is a sailing school at Schluchsee. **Tennis** courts are in all resorts and larger towns; important international tennis tournaments are scheduled every year in Baden-Baden. **Golf** courses exist at Baden-Baden, Badenweiler, Herrenalb, and Freudenstadt. Freiburg has an **ice rink.**

Horseback riding schools are at Baden-Baden, Freiburg and Freudenstadt (new riding hall); saddle horses also in Badenweiler, Villingen and many other places. World famous **horseraces** take place at the Baden-Baden race track Iffezheim, which has been in operation since 1858; the most important yearly events are the International Race Week and the Great Week of Baden-Baden, the latter always the last week of August.

Important **motor races** take place on the Schauinsland mountain course above Freiburg, aiersBbronn and Bernau have **kite flying** (hang gliding) schools.

Black Forest streams are among the best in Germany for trout **fishing.** In Titisee and Schluchsee you can also catch pike, perch and tench. **Hunting** is practised widely in this forested region; roe deer is the most frequent game while mountain cock is perhaps the most prized.

The Black Forest is one of the best regions in Germany for **hiking** through the woods and over medium-low (compared to the Alps) rolling mountains. There are hundreds of trails and in the Freudenstadt area alone, for instance, there are 95 miles of them. Three principal trails cover the Black Forest in a north–south direction: Westweg (West Trail), marked by a red diamond, from Pforzheim to Basel, total length about 170 miles; Mittelweg (Middle Trail), marked by a white stem in a red diamond, from Pforzheim to Waldshut, total length about 140 miles; Ostweg (East Trail), marked by a black and red diamond, from Pforzheim to Schaffhausen, about 133 miles. As the starting point of three trails, the tourist association of Pforzheim offer one-night accommodations for DM49, including maps, brochures, a lunch voucher and a cultural evening. The health resort of Lossburg near Freudenstadt offers special hiking weeks in May and September from DM169 per week for bed and breakfast. Alpirsbach in the upper Klinzig Valley offers a hiking week in June for DM182. A seven-day tour covering 100 km and called "Spätzlepfaden" belongs to the "Wandern ohne Gepäck" (hiking without luggage) scheme, and costs DM385 until the end of May. Luggage is transported from one destination to the next without charge. Enquire at Schwarzwald Information, Marktplatz 1, 7530 Pforzheim.

WINTER SPORTS. For economy skiing vacations, this area is tops, offering many inexpensive to reasonable accommodations. In addition, most of the places listed below have inexpensive-moderate bungalows and/or vacation apartments. Up to 2,300 feet skiing lasts from Christmas until the end of February; up to 3,300 feet, from early December until mid-March; above 3,300 feet, two or three weeks longer. Ski tours are possible everywhere up to the highest elevations of the Black Forest (over 4,900 feet). Long stretches of prepared cross-country ski-tracks *(Loipen).*

Bernau, 3,000 feet, bus from Freiburg. Six ski lifts, tobogganing, ski instructors, children's ski school. Many inexpensive inns and pensions.

Bühlertal, from 760 to 3,280 feet, bus from Baden-Baden; 16 ski lifts, ski jump, instructors. Many inexpensive inns and pensions.

Feldberg, 3,280 feet, bus from train stops Feldberg-Bärental and Todtnau. Considered the birthplace of skiing in Germany and now has a modern residential training center for skiers with private ski jump, gymnasium, sauna bath. Sports facilities in the area: chair lift, more than 40 ski lifts, ski jump, ski school, bobsled tobogganing. This is also the starting point for the scenic cross-country ski tour, *Panorama Spur.*

Freudenstadt, 2,420 feet, fast train stop, 2 ski lifts, ski jump, ski school, skating rink, horse sleighs, tobogganing, ski tours. There are a double chair lift, 10 ski lifts, 3 ski jumps, tobogganing and horse sleighs in nearby Baiersbronn.

Hinterzarten, 2,950 feet, fast train stop. Six ski lifts, 3 ski jumps, instructors, ice-skating, curling, tobogganing, horse sleighs, ski tours.

Schauinsland-Hofsgrund, 4,200 feet, bus plus cable car from Freiburg. Cable car, 9 ski lifts, ski jump, instructors, tobogganing.

Titisee, 2,820 feet, fast train stop. In the area: 3 ski lifts, ski jump, instructors, skating rink, curling, tobogganing, ski tours, horse sleighs. In nearby Saig, 3,280 feet (2½ miles by bus from Titisee or Lenzkirch), is another ski lift, ski school, ski jump, skating rink, ski tours and tobogganing.

Todtmos, 2,800 feet, bus from Freiburg or Säckingen. 5 ski lifts, instructors, curling, tobogganing, ski tours, ski jump, ski school.

Todtnau, 2,130 feet, train stop. Chair lift, 2 ski lifts, ski jump, ski school. In nearby Todtnauberg (3,350 feet), increasingly important as ski center, are 6 ski lifts and a ski school.

Triberg, 2,300 feet, fast train stop. Ski lift, ski jump, ski school, skating rink, hockey, curling, tobogganing.

Unterstmatt, 3,050 feet, bus from Baden-Baden. 4 ski lifts (lighted at night), ski school.

Wildbad, from 1,400 to 2,460 feet, train stop. Ski school, ski jump, ice skating, curling, ski tours, tobogganing. At Sommerberg, reached by cable car, there are 4 ski lifts and an artificial ski run.

 USEFUL ADDRESSES. Tourist information: Baden-Baden Kurdirektion, Augustaplatz (also room reservations) and Reisebüro Baden-Baden, Sophienstr. 1b, for sightseeing tours and guides; Freiburg, Verkehrsamt, Rotteckring 14 (also room reservations) and Schwarzwald-Reisebüro at the same address for sightseeing tours. For the whole area: Landesfremdenverkehrsverband Baden-Württemberg, D-7 Stuttgart, Charlottenplatz 17.

LAKE CONSTANCE AND THE ALLGÄU

Sailboats and Snow

Lake Constance, called in German the Bodensee, is shared by three countries: most of its shoreline is German, while Switzerland has a substantial section on the southwestern side, and Austria gets a foothold on its southeastern end. In spite of belonging to three different states, the inhabitants around the lake speak one language, German, and what is more, they actually speak the same dialect of German. This fact, increased by numerous blood relation ties, makes them a homogenous group in spite of and beyond any political borders.

Tucked away between Lake Constance on the south and the Swabian Mountains on the northwest is a small corner of Baden-Württemberg. This is the Oberschwaben, which changes in the southwest into the

Allgäu region of Bavaria, known chiefly to skiers and mountain enthusiasts.

EXPLORING LAKE CONSTANCE AND THE
ALLGÄU

Coming from the Black Forest, we enter the Lake Constance region through the Hegau, of clearly volcanic origin. We first encounter the lake at Radolfzell, on the Untersee. Lake Constance is shaped like some weird crustacean, with a thick body, the Bodensee proper, from which two claws stretch out towards us, the northeastern one known as the Überlingersee, the southwest one, from which the Rhine flows after its course through the lake, as the Untersee.

Progressing from here towards Konstanz, we pass into the space between the two claws, hugging the shore of the Untersee. To our right we see the island of Reichenau. Anthropologists say that the earliest culture on German soil of which there is any knowledge began here. In more "recent" times, in 724 A.D., a Benedictine Abbey was founded here; at the peak of its glory, it harbored as many as 1,600 monks and was the seat of one of the most famous medieval schools of painting. The abbey was secularized in 1799, but the three notable churches at Mittelzell, Oberzell, and Niederzell are standing testimonials to its resplendent past.

Now the lake narrows to a mere thread (actually it is again reduced to the Rhine, connecting the Untersee and the Bodensee proper, for the former is not quite a true arm of the main body of water, as the Überlingersee is) and we cross that narrow water course to enter another frontier anomaly, the city of Konstanz, or Constance. The oddity here is that all the rest of this side of the lake is Switzerland. Konstanz, the largest city on the lake, lies all alone on this side of it, surrounded on all sides by Swiss territory, except where it fronts on the water, across which is the land to which it belongs.

Because of the proximity of the Swiss frontier the war hardly touched Konstanz and many of its old buildings (those which have not been sacrificed for contemporary monstrosities) still stand as they have for centuries. The main sights include the 14th-century Council Hall, originally the seat of the linen weavers' fair and later named after the Council of Konstanz (1414–18), because the conclave which elected Pope Martin V was held in this building in November 1417; the imposing cathedral, whose construction was started in the 11th century with additions of all styles dating up to 1856; Insel Hotel once a Dominican Monastery and a hotel since 1875, still preserving the original magnificent cloisters—Count Ferdinand von Zeppelin, the inventor of "Zeppelins," was born here and a memorial to him stands at the boat landing stage nearby; the Renaissance City Hall; Rheintor and Schnetztor tower gates and Pulverturm, "the powder tower," since it was used in the old days as a depot for gunpowder; St. Stephan's Church at the square of Obermarkt surrounded by old patrician houses.

The lake has a moderating influence on the climate and nearby Mainau Island, at the beginning of the Überlingen section of the lake, has had a long gardening tradition. Its floral treasure includes tulips, narcissi and hyacinths in April and May; rare varieties of irises and lilies blooming through July; dahlias beginning to bloom in September; and a great variety of roses all through the summer; in addition to hothouses of orchids, palms, lemon and orange trees, and rare and old trees in its arboretum. The baroque palace on the island used to be the summer residence of the Grand Dukes of Baden, and was inherited shortly after World War II by Prince Wilhelm of Sweden from his mother, Queen Victoria of Sweden, a sister of the Grand Duke of Baden. Abundantly blessed with good hotels, Konstanz makes a delightful vacation place in the summer, with the lake providing the playground for water sports of every description, while the casino operates roulette, baccarat and blackjack tables.

At the tip of the Überlingersee branch of the lake is Ludwigshafen. You will find the local atmosphere and the spell of the lake more pervasive if you penetrate a little farther into the region. Following its northeastern shore, you come to Überlingen, with its close-set old houses hugging the lakeside. Once an imperial free town, it has preserved many of its towers, defense walls and old patrician homes, such as the Reichlin-Meldegg House, built in 1462, and now containing the local museum. The five-nave Gothic cathedral has a famous Renaissance altar and the Rathaus, also Gothic, is known for its Pfennig Tower and the woodcarved grand hall from 1492. Überlingen, which is also well known for Kneipp (cold water) cures, is referred to locally as the German Nice, in reference to its mild climate, which, of course, it shares with all the lakeside resorts. From here you can go by the postal bus to Heiligenberg, in the hills back from the lake, where there is a castle containing magnificent works of art, and in which the Renaissance Knights' Hall is particularly striking. From the heights of Heiligenberg there is also a spectacular view over the lake to the Alps.

Continuing along the lake shore, you could hardly make a mistake stopping anywhere at random: Birnau, with its rococo church on the high shore; Unteruhldingen, where there are reconstructions of the homes of the ancient lake dwellers (this is another point from which you can go to Heiligenberg); peaceful Meersburg, a marvelous old town with one of its castle towers dating from the 7th century, a wine-growing center boasting several colorful old taverns, and a particularly favored summertime lake resort. A panoramic path along the heights between Meersburg and Hagnau offers another magnificent view of the entire lake and the Austrian and Swiss Alps. From Meersburg, ferryboats cross to Konstanz day and night, thus considerably shortening the journey around the lake if you are in a hurry.

Friedrichshafen and Lindau

From Meersburg we proceed along the shore to Friedrichshafen. This is a place that has helped make aeronautic history. It was the birthplace of the Zeppelins, named after Count Zeppelin, their inventor. Their hangars and the plants which built them were here, and it was from here that they started out on their transatlantic flights in the days before disaster ended their career. It was here, too, that the Dornier flying boats were built, and their powers tested over the convenient, wide, calm, landing surface provided by the lake before they took off on their flights to America. It is rather quieter today, the chief traffic being provided by ferryboats, for this is the point from which they leave for the crossing to Romanshorn, in Switzerland.

You will find the lake more attractive if you stop at smaller places than this, the smaller the better. Beyond Friedrichshafen is the charming town of Langenargen with its Montfort Castle; the town clustered along the lake is a favored vacation spot. A little further is another small place, Nonnenhorn. You will enjoy the town square with its chapel and the lakeside walks among the fruit trees and vineyards.

The other little settlements along the lake are equally entrancing— Wasserburg, with its splendid church rising from the peninsula on which it stands, and Bad Schachen, a spa in a particularly lovely setting on the lakeside.

Lindau is in the lake rather than on it—it's built on an island. It doesn't look quite credible from the shore, floating on the water as if moored by the two narrow bridges which hold it to the land like hawsers, with its towers rising here and there from its trees and houses. It doesn't look quite credible when you get there, either, with its narrow, twisting streets lined with fine old buildings. You should be warned that a lot of people have discovered how attractive Lindau is, and the place gets packed out.

At the lakeward end of the island you can sit and gaze out through the twin pillars of its little harbor (they are not identical twins; one is a lighthouse, the other a statue of a lion) towards the mountains beyond the lake. On a clear day you will be able to see the peaks known as The

Three Sisters in a tiny nearby country, Liechtenstein, the independent principality between Switzerland and Austria.

In addition to the harbor the main sights in Lindau include the beautifully frescoed old town hall; the equally beautifully built and frescoed old patrician house Zum Cavazzen, presently housing the City Museum; the two principal city churches (one Catholic and one Evangelical) on the same square; the Diebsturm ("Thief's Tower") with a section of the old town walls; the nearby Romanesque Peter's Church, reputed to be the oldest on Bodensee, with frescos by Hans Holbein the Elder (today the church is a war memorial chapel); the many narrow streets lined with romantic old houses.

Lindau's casino is small, but extremely well-appointed, and you can play roulette there. A contrast to an evening in the casino might be a moonlight sail on one of the white steamers you will see flitting about the lake.

The Allgäu

Striking northward from the lake at Friedrichshafen, you come to Ravensburg, whose impressive gates and towers date from the time when it was the Swabian stronghold of the Guelphs. A little beyond Ravensburg is Weingarten, the site of Germany's largest baroque church. From Biberach, a medieval town with a fine museum, you may visit the monastery at Ochsenhausen.

Heading in a more easterly direction from Lake Constance stop at Wangen for a look at its centuries-old gates and other romantic remains. Southeastward from here begins the skiing country. The nearest notable winter sports resort is Isny, also an old historic place.

Nearly all the towns in the Allgäu are both winter sports centers and starting points for trips through the mountains. This is true of charming Sonthofen, in the upper Iller Valley, reached from Lindau via the scenic German Alpine Road through two more winter sports centers: Oberstaufen, known especially for its unique Schroth cures based on dieting, and Immenstadt with a 17th-century castle and a baroque parish church. But Oberstdorf, a little to the south, is the best known winter sports center and Alpine summer resort in the region, lying in a broad valley ringed by lofty peaks. A three-mile-long cable lift leading to the 7,380-foot Nebelhorn and its gigantic jump for ski soaring constitute its two greatest drawing cards. Seven smaller valleys lead up into the Alpine stillness. Especially recommended is the walk along the Heilbronnerweg, reaching the Kempter refuge at 6,000 feet.

From Oberstdorf it is also possible to explore Kleinwalsertal (Small Walser Valley—the Great Walser Valley being on the other side of the mountain barrier in Vorarlberg), a mountain fastness of incomparable beauty with the villages of Riezlern, Hirschegg, and Mittelberg. Oddly enough, this is Austrian territory, but because it is inaccessible to the mother country except by twisting footpaths, it has been integrated economically with Germany for many years. German currency is used, therefore, although letters must carry Austrian stamps. In Unterbalderschwang, 9 miles northwest of Oberstdorf, you can sit in the shade of Germany's oldest tree, a double-trunked yew, reputed to be as ancient as 4,000 years old.

To the north is Kempten, Allgäu's capital. It is an old Roman settlement whose name was originally Cambodunum. The excavations on the Burghalde give us an interesting insight to the old Roman town, with its well-preserved remains. Roman, Celtic, and Alemannic finds are exhibited in the Heimatmuseum in the Kornhaus. The latter is one of the finest old office houses and is situated at the former corn market. The Kornhausplatz, as it is called nowadays, ranks among the most remarkable sights in southern Germany. The façades of the Kornhaus and the old monastery on one side, and of the beautiful Bavarian baroque church of St. Lorenz and the Residenz on the other, give the place its special romantic character.

If you are traveling from Kempten to Ulm you can stop over in Ottobeuren for a visit to the Benedictine abbey church there, constructed in the 18th century by the great South German architect Johann Michael Fischer; this is one of the finest and largest rococo churches in Germany, with 16 altars, exquisite woodcarved choir stalls and a world-famous baroque organ by Master Karl Riepp. The present huge abbey itself, with 6 courtyards, 20 halls and 250 rooms, was built only a few decennia earlier than the church, although it was originally founded in 764.

The main road to Ulm goes through Memmingen. Memmingen, once a free imperial city, has preserved five towers and part of its walls; the Rathaus square and several narrow streets are lined with gabled, arcaded or half-timbered houses, while Martin's Church contains fine Gothic choir stalls and the Frauenkirche frescos from the same period. East of Memmingen and Ottobeuren, among forests and meadows, lies Bad Wörishofen, the principal cold water health resort in Germany, where Father Sebastian Kneipp invented and started the famous cold water treatments in the last century. The Kneipp Museum is in the Dominican Convent and a monument to him stands in the town which from a little village has become an important spa with up-to-date installations and all modern amenities, including many outstanding accommodations for health-seekers.

PRACTICAL INFORMATION FOR BODENSEE
AND ALLGÄU

HOTELS AND RESTAURANTS. Many delightful hostelries cluster about and above the shores of Lake Constance, or Bodensee. Allgäu accommodations are available in all price ranges, right down to rustic, comfortable country inns.

In the Bodensee localities, order tender *Blaufelchen* and *Trüsche,* whose large liver is fried separately and is as good as the fish itself. To go with the Bodensee fish, try *Weissherbst,* a slightly pinkish dry wine produced around Meersburg.

Balderschwang. *Alp Chalets Sporthotel* (M), modern hotel rooms plus 21 separate chalet-style apartments, good restaurant with charcoal grill dishes and terrace; indoor pool and various sports facilities. *Luisenhof,* 42 beds, is (M). Many inexpensive inns and pensions.

Fischen. Hotels: *Gastehaus Burgmuhle,* Auf der Insel 4, all rooms with bath or shower. *Haus Rosenstock* (M), all rooms with balcony. A bit outside and higher up: *Haus Tanneck* (M), next to ski lift, 80 beds, 40 baths and showers, excellent restaurant and small indoor pool and sauna.

Café-Pension Maderhalm (I), nearby at about 3,000 ft., inexpensive.

In nearby Langenwang, *Hotel Sonnenbichl* (M), most rooms with bath or shower, small indoor pool, tennis.

Friedrichshafen. Hotel: *Buchhorner Hof* (M), Friedrichstr. 33, has 100 beds, about half of rooms with bath, a good restaurant with the accent on local fish and game.

Hindelang, popular winter sports resort. Hotels: *Sonne* (M), in town proper, 60 rooms, cozy restaurant of note and dance-bar.

In Bad Oberdorf section: *Kurhotel Luitpold* (E), 160 beds, good food, bar, tennis court and swimming pool, health cures in house.

Two small (M) inns with colorful restaurants and good food are *Bären* and *Alpengasthof Hirsch.*

In five-mile-distant Oberjoch (3,700 ft.) is *Haus Ingeburg* (M), dance-bar, tennis court and small indoor pool.

Isny. In the vicinity: *Berghotel Jägerhof* (M), five miles northwest (follow the signs). Allgäu-style farmhouse but modern interiors; excellent restaurant, indoor pool, fishing, hunting and in winter skiing.

Historic *Gasthof Adler* (I) in three-mile-distant Grossholzleute has 100 beds, gemütlich Alpine-style Stuben (avoid the large, functional dining room) and private swimming.

Several inexpensive and moderate Gasthofs in the picturesque old town section of Isny.

Kempten. Hotels: All (M) are—*Neue Rose,* Mittleres Entenmoos 4, 18 beds, and *Post; Bahnhof-Hotel* at the station, and *Haslacher Hof.*

Restaurants: *Weinhaus zum Strittigen Winkel* (M), historic wine tavern at the street stairs at Fischerstr.; *Zum Stift* (M), large, near Kornhaus; *Haubenschloss* (M), especially for game.

Kleinwalsertal, actually in Austria but can only be reached by road from Oberstdorf, so integrated with Germany. Among the numerous delightful mountain-style hotels, many of which require pension terms: In Riezlern: *Sporthotel Riezlern* (M), 130 two-room apartments, all with bath or shower and some with kitchenette, indoor pool, sauna, horseback riding.

All (M) are—*Stern,* most rooms with bath, bar and dance café. *Montana,* all rooms with bath or shower, indoor pool, sauna. *Erlebach* and *Bellevue,* both with indoor pools.

In Hirschegg: *Ifen-Hotel* (E), noted restaurant, bar, indoor pool, sauna. *Walserhof* and *Der Berghof* are (M).

In Mittelberg: All (M) are—*Alte Krone,* indoor pool. *Gästehaus Reinhard Leitner,* all rooms with bath or shower, indoor pool. *Alpenrose,* heated pool, *Alpenhof Wildental* and *Alpinum,* also with indoor pool.

A bit further in Baad, *Gasthof Pühringer,* all rooms with bath or shower, ski lift, is (M). Also pensions and rooms in private houses, as well as many mountain lodges in the area.

Konstanz. Hotels: *Steigenberger Insel* (L) is a former monastery on a small island near lake shore, 120 rooms, all with bath, three restaurants and private park overlooking the lake, own swimming beach.

All (M), with some rooms priced higher: *Bayrischer Hof,* garni, Rosgartenstr. 30, only 17 beds; *Seeblick,* garni, Neuhauserstr. 14, 100 beds, swimming and tennis facilities. *Bodan,* Fürstenbergstr. 2., 50 beds; the historic *Barbarossa,* Obermarkt 8, 100 beds; and the quiet small *Haus Margarete,* Seestr. 25.

Dom-Hotel St. Johann, Brückeng. 1, built in the 10th century and looking like an old church, with noted restaurant, is (I).

On nearby Reichenau Island: the smaller *Schloss Königsegg,* a castle in private park, and the larger *Strandhotel Löchnerhaus,* facing the lake, both have restaurants, private lake swimming facilities and are (M).

Both (I) are—*Kaiserpfalz,* next to Münster, 45 beds, with wine tavern and pleasant garden. The colorful and small *Seeschau* on the lake.

Restaurants: *Casino* (E), in Casino building, with Tessiner rustic-style room, pleasant terrace overlooking the lake, outstanding cuisine, dance-bar.

Stefanskeller (M), Stefansplatz 41, historic wine tavern. *Konzil* (M) in old Council Hall building, with terraces and lake view. *Zur Linde* (M), Radolfzeller Str. 27, also café and *gasthof* with pleasant, comfortable rooms.

Graf Zeppelin (M–I), Stefansplatz 15, colorful old Gasthaus. *Domkeller* (M–I), next to cathedral. *Grünenberg* (M–I), Stefansplatz 5, serves Bavarian beer. *Engstler* (I), at lake corner of Markstätte, with large beer garden.

On Mainau Island: historic *Comturey-Keller* (M) with a huge wine barrel; and restaurant *Schwedenschenke* (M).

Langenargen. All the hotels mentioned are located on or near the lake front. Leading at the time of this writing are *Kurhotel Seeterrasse* (E), 80 beds, about half of the rooms with bath, restaurant with lakeside terrace, heated pool and own beach, and *Schiff,* Marktplatz 1.

About the same size and (M) (rooms with bath usually higher) are *Schiff, Litz* (combined with *Helvetia*), *Löwen* and *Engel* (combined with *Marta*), all with lakeside terraces.

Smaller and (I–M) are *Seemann* in town and *Schwedi* a bit outside and very quietly located.

Lindau. On the lake promenade facing the small picturesque harbor, most with pleasant terrace restaurants and cafés, all (M) are—*Bayerischer Hof,* 140 beds, most rooms with bath, closed in winter; next door and smaller is *Reutemann,* also most rooms with bath (open all year); *Seegarten,* 40 rooms; *Helvetia,* 70 rooms, most with shower; and *Lindauer Hof* (all closed in winter).

Old town hostelries (I) include *Zum Stift,* Marktplatz, *Alte Post,* in Fischergasse, *Goldenes Lamm,* Schafg. 3, all with good restaurants.

In Bad Schachen, health resort in western suburbs of Lindau: lakeside *Hotel Bad Schachen* (L), park, tennis, beach, water sports, cure facilities, acupuncture.

Also very fine, located on the lakeside beyond Bad Schachen towards Wasserburg: *Gästehaus Hof Reutenen* (E), in park, private swimming and sailboat harbor, limited number of rooms and suites, antique-style furnishings.

In Wasserburg: *Schloss Wasserburg,* built in 1386, a small castle hotel with wine cellar tavern and private beach. *Lipprandt,* with fine cuisine, small heated pool and private beach. Both (M) rooms with private bath higher.

Restaurants in Lindau (most serving among their specialties Bodensee fish and game when in season): *Spielbank* (E), in casino building in city park, also café, bar, and dancing; *Zum Lieben Augustin* (E), on Seepromenade (in Hotel Seegarten), evening wine tavern with musical entertainment and dancing.

Weinstube Frey (M), old wine tavern (since 1560), Hauptstr. 15, upper floor; *Zum Sünfzen* (M), Hauptstr. 1, used to be an old patrician drinking place and has a large coat-of-arms on the wall to attest the fact.

Schlechterbräu (I), In der Grub 28, a large beer restaurant.

Mainau. Restaurant: not surprisingly, the heart of Mainau catering has associations with Sweden and the *Schwedenschenke* (Swedish Inn) offers first-class food; for local specialties try *Torkelkeller* with its outsize wine barrel.

Meersburg. Hotels on lake front (all closed in winter). All (E–M) are—*Strandhotel Wilder Mann,* outdoor and indoor glassed-in terrace restaurant and café with music and dancing, and the new and modern *Rothmund am See,* with balconied rooms overlooking the lake. *Zum Schiff,* at the old town gate. On the hill above the lake with marvelous view are the modern *Villa Bellevue* and *Terrassen-Hotel Weisshaar.* The half-timbered *Drei Stuben* in the upper old town has a very fine restaurant.

Inexpensive, atmospheric old inns include *Löwen* and *Zum Bären.*

Restaurants (which in Meersburg means mostly wine taverns): *Zum Becher* (M) serves outstanding food; *Ratskeller* (I), the vaulted town hall cellar; *Burg-keller* (M) has garden and musical entertainment.

Winzertrinkstube (I) serves wines of the local wine growers' cooperative; *Zum lieben Augustin* (I) is also a small hotel.

Nesselwang. Hotels: *Marianne, Bären,* with good local specialties in its restaurant, and *Kurhotel Marburg* are (M). On the 4,900-ft. Edelsberg, *Sportheim Böck* offers (I) rooms and a wonderful view, can be reached only by cable car and a two-minute walk (baggage delivered separately).

Oberstaufen. Hotels: Both (E) are the *Büttner,* indoor pool, and the *Alpina,* with period-furnished public rooms. All (M) are—*Rosenalp,* all rooms with bath or shower, attractive wood-paneled rooms, nice view from comfortable restaurant, Schroth cures. *Hirsch,* garden terrace, Schroth cures; colorful chalet-style *Löwen,* very fine food and wine, with game from own preserve.

Oberstdorf. Hotels: *Kurhotel Adula* (L), in Jauchen outskirts, 130 beds, all rooms with bath and balcony, apartments, indoor pool, cure facilities, rustic bar and restaurant.

All (E–M) are—*Filser,* 150 beds, excellent restaurant, indoor pool, cure facilities; *Exquisit,* 75 beds, all rooms with bath or shower, garden terrace, indoor pool; *Wittelsbacher Hof,* 115 beds, many rooms with bath, noted restaurant, bar, heated pool (closed April and May and Oct.–mid-Dec.); *Kappeler Haus,* beautiful location, outdoor pool, garni; *Alpenhof,* 45 beds, built in Allgäu country style, indoor and heated outdoor pools.

All (M) are—*Sporthotel Eisstadion,* at the ice stadium, small, most rooms with shower, *Nebelhornbahn,* next to valley station of Nebelhorn cable car, and *Berghotel Höfatsblick* (6,330 feet), at upper station of same cable car, good food.

The old, Bavarian-style inn *Hirsch,* with music in the evening, is (I).

Pfronten. Hotels: *Schlossanger-Alp,* nice quiet location, (M–I).

Pension Zugspitzblick, terrace and indoor pool; *Bayerischer Hof* in Kreuzegg district; *Gasthof Krone* in Dorf district; all (I).

Scheidegg. Winter and summer resort in Allgäu. *Kurhotel Scheidegg* (E), all rooms and apartments with bath and balcony, indoor pool, tennis, ice skating, Kneipp watercures, restaurant, bar, beautiful location with view of Alps, pension terms only. *Der Allgäu Stern* (M), Auf der Steiger Alp, 850 beds, all amenities and cure facilities; *Gästehaus Rex* (I), garni, Jahnstr. 17.

Sonthofen. Hotels in town: *Sonne,* 45 beds (I).
Outside and above town: *Kurhotel Sonnenalp* (L), 2,800 ft., 220 beds, most rooms with bath or shower, cure facilities, gymnasium, sauna, indoor and heated outdoor pools, tennis, delightful restaurant, bar. *Allgäuer Berghof* (M), 4,200 ft., reached by private toll road, 110 beds, many rooms with bath, indoor pool, tennis, cure facilities. Both in isolated locations with fine views.

Überlingen. Hotels: All (M) are—*Bad Hotel,* Christophstr. 2, 84 beds and *Seegarten,* with lakeside terrace; *Ochsen,* excellent position for sailing, good facilities; and *Waldburg* (garni) at Gallerturm.
Restaurant: *Weinstube Hecht* (M), fish specialties, also has a few moderate rooms, all with bath or shower. The youth hostel has gym and indoor pool.

THE BODENSEE AND ALLGÄU. By Car. As far as motoring is concerned it should be Allgäu and Bodensee, because the road round the lake is just a lighthearted appendage to the more serious German Alpine Road *(Deutsche Alpenstrasse)* No 308 and, if you follow it into Austria to return to Germany close by the Zugspitze, No B314 as well. It is a marvelous road, high enough to provide breathtaking views, not so high as to be barren. There are also some smaller, higher roads to explore if you are a motor mountaineer.

In this very small region there is, with help from Austria and Switzerland, the chance to experience most types of motoring except motorway, unless you use the A7 to take you away from the Allgau towards Ulm. The German side of Bodensee is much more attractive than the Swiss, because it is the Swiss mountains that provide the happy backdrop for the lake and its neat, Germanic foreground. The road is, however, well used and not one on which you can stop when and wherever you wish. That side, and the Austrian end, tend also to be a little smart; the other—to which there are two car ferries—is almost entirely pastoral.

NIGHTLIFE. Konstanz. Gambling: *Casino,* roulette, baccarat and blackjack from 2 P.M. to 2 A.M., Saturdays until 3 A.M.; also dancing in *Casino-Bar.* Dancing also in *Candy,* Am Fischmarkt, and in a number of other night bars whose mortality, however, as everywhere, is so great that it defies both the writer and the printer.
Lindau. Gambling: *Spielbank,* roulette and baccarat after 3 P.M., blackjack after 5 P.M.; also dancing. *Zum lieben Augustin,* musical entertainment and dancing. Dancing and show: *Tanz-Café Rathaus-Bar.* Humoristic entertain-

ment and dancing: *Zum lustigen Simpl.* A number of nightspots can be found in the narrow old town street called *In der Grub.*

Oberstdorf. Bars, music, dancing: in principal hotels as well as in several locales, among them *Trettachstüble,* near Nebelhorn cable car lower station.

Kleinwalsertal. *Spielcasino* in Riezlern, roulette, baccarat and blackjack after 5 P.M. Music and dancing in about two dozen bars, cafés, taverns and hotels in Riezlern, Hirschegg and Mittelberg.

 MUSIC AND THEATER. Konstanz has its own theatrical company appearing in *Stadttheater.* Important guest groups from Munich, Stuttgart, Augsburg and elsewhere appear in the *Stadttheater* of Lindau. *Bauern-Theater* in Oberstdorf performs folk-type plays. Konstanz has a regular concert season with guest orchestras and the local *Städtisches Orchester;* open-air performances during summer months in the city park and the Rathaus courtyard; the International Music Days are scheduled in June–July.

Lindau has outdoor concerts at the port promenade from May to September and guest musical performances throughout the year. Überlingen stages concerts in the modern Kursaal during summer season. Folklore evenings are held particularly in all more important Allgäu resorts.

 MUSEUMS. Konstanz: *Rosgartenmuseum* in Rosgartenstrasse, art and culture of Bodensee region and prehistoric, collection; City Painting Gallery, in Wessenberghaus periodic exhibits.

Kempten: *Allgäu Heimat Museum* in the Old Corn House (*Kornhaus*) has an ancient coin collection and exhibits on local history.

Lindau: *Stadtmuseum* on Marktplatz local history and culture.

Überlingen: *Heimatmuseum* in the 15th-century Reichlin-Meldegg patrician house, local history; 15th-century Armory.

Unteruhldingen, not far from Meersburg: Stone and Bronze Age pile lake dwellings, Meersburg: Stone and Bronze Age pile lake dwellings.

 SPORTS. Lake swimming in all the localities on Bodensee; in Allgäu in some lakes, especially Grosser Alpsee and Forggensee, and in many indoor and outdoor pools. There are frequent pollution checks on all the lakes.

Water skiing, sailing, rowing and **motor boating** in principal localities on Bodensee and also on Grosser Alpsee and Forggensee. There is a water skiing school on Inselee in Allgäu, **windsurfing** schools in Konstanz, Meersburg, Überlingen, Immenstadt and Füssen; Oberstdorf has a school of **kayaking;** and for **kite flying** (hang-gliding) it is Oberstdorf and Nesselwang. **Sailing** schools at Lindau, Wasserburg and Nonnenhorn on Bodensee, Dietringen on Forggensee and Lechbruck on the artificial Lech Lake; international regattas in Konstanz and Lindau; sailboats for rent in Konstanz, Friedrichshafen and Überlingen. **Tennis** courts abound; international tournaments in Konstanz.

Golf courses in Lindau, Oberstdorf and Konstanz. **Horseback riding** in Konstanz (also a riding hall, instructors and races), Überlingen, Oberstdorf (also a riding school) and elsewhere. Landing sites for **gliders** are at Konstanz and Kempten. In Oberstdorf in Allgäu there is an international *balloon* contest.

Best for **fishing** are Bodensee (lake trout, char, pike, perch, tench, eel) and the rivers of Iller, Wertach and Lech in Allgäu (especially for trout, grayling, pike, carp, tench). Among the best in Allgäu, in addition to Bodensee, are: Oberstdorf (in several small lakes and streams nearby), Füssen-Bad Faulenbach, Oberstaufen, Wertach, and Bad Wörishofen.

Mountain climbing (rock scaling) is an important activity in the Alps of Allgäu. The best valley bases are Oberstdorf, Hinterstein, Hindelang, Unterjoch, Pfronten, Schwangau. An excellent mountain climbing base is Kleinwalsertal above Oberstdorf, in Austria but integrated with the German economy on account of its geographic position.

For high mountain **hiking** there is a 37-mile trail leading over the heights of the Allgäu Alps from Oberstdorf to Oberjoch with the highest point at 8,500 ft. and the lowest at 5,200 ft., disclosing magnificent Alpine scenery all along. It is well protected and secured but nevertheless not for those who have no experience in mountaineering. There is an alpine mountain climbing school in Oberstdorf.

WINTER SPORTS IN THE ALLGÄU. The skiing season in this region lasts from December until March in the localities from 2,600 feet to 3,300 feet, until April in the places higher up, and even longer on the highest terrains. Several of the high valleys are closed to motor traffic. Oberstdorf and Hindelang having started this movement some years ago. The valleys of Stillach, Trettach, Birgsau, Spielmannsau and Oytal come in this area. Here you move by horse sleigh, on skis or on foot.

Accommodations in this area are about 10–20% less than in their counterparts in the Bavarian Alps. Most of the following localities also have bungalows and vacation apartments, at prices ranging from moderate to reasonable.

Balderschwang, 3,424 feet, bus from Oberstdorf. Seven ski lifts, ski school.

Fischen, 2,400 feet, fast train stop. Chair lift, 2 ski lifts, ski jump, ski schools, curling. Ski tours up to 7,300 ft. 10 miles of marked cross-country ski tracks.

Füssen, 2,600 feet, train stop. Ski lift, instructors, 2 ski jumps, covered ice stadium, 6 curling rinks, and bobsled school. Ski tours up to 6,000 ft. 37 miles of prepared cross-country tracks.

Gunzesried, 2,950 feet, bus from Sonthofen (fast train stop). Chair lift, 4 ski lifts, ski schools.

Hindelang, 2,760–3,770 feet, bus from Sonthofen. Chair lift, 18 ski lifts, ski schools, ski jump, skating rink, curling, tobogganing. Ski tours up to 7,500 feet. Chair lift to Iseler mountain. 25 miles of cross-country ski tracks.

Immenstadt, 2,400 feet, fast train stop. Cable car, chair lift, 12 ski lifts (one for children), ski school, ski jump, skating rink, hockey, curling, tobogganing. Ski tours up to 6,000 feet. Over 30 miles of marked cross-country skiing.

Isny, 2,350 feet, train stop. 5 ski lifts, sleigh lift, instructors, 2 ski jumps, skating, curling, tobogganing. Ski tours up to 3,700 feet. 25 miles of marked cross-country ski tracks.

Kleinwalsertal. Riezlern, Hirschegg, and Mittelberg, all close together and between 3,660–3,900 feet high. Bus from Oberstdorf. This tiny valley has 2 cable cars, 3 chair lifts, 29 ski lifts, ski jumps, instructors in every village, skating rinks in Riezlern and Mittelberg, curling, tobogganing (with lift), bobsled school in Riezlern. Ski tours up to 7,200 feet. 28 mountain lodges in area.

Nesselwang, 2,950 feet, fast train stop. Cable car, 2 chair lifts, 7 ski lifts, ski jump, ski school, ice skating, ski tours. 14 miles of prepared cross-country ski tracks.

Oberstaufen-Steibis, 2,750 feet, Oberstaufen is fast train stop. Steibis (two miles away) can be reached by bus. Chair lift and 10 ski lifts in Oberstaufen; mountain rail and 17 ski lifts in Steibis; ski schools in both places, bobsled school and curling in Oberstaufen. Ski tours up to 6,100 ft. Après-ski in Oberstaufen. Almost 80 miles of prepared cross-country ski tracks.

Oberstdorf, 2,740 feet, fast train stop. Joint winter sports center with Nebelhorn (6,330 feet) and Fellhorn (6,452 feet) above it. Two cable cars, 3 chair lifts, 18 ski lifts, 3 ski jumps (one the longest in the world), ski and bobsled schools, skibobbing, year-round ice stadium for skating, hockey, curling, horse sleighs, tobogganing, ski kindergarten. Ski tours up to 7,500 feet. Considerable après-ski. 34 miles of prepared cross-country ski tracks.

Pfronten, 2,900 feet, train stop. Cable car on Breitenberg, chair lift, 13 ski lifts, 2 ski jumps, instructors, skating rink, hockey, curling, tobogganing. Ski tours up to 6,500 feet. 43 miles of cross-country skiing.

Schwangau-Hohenschwangau, 2,625–3,280 feet, train stop. Cable car to Tegelberg (5,640 feet), 2 chair lifts, 6 ski lifts, ski school, bobsled school, curling, horse sleighs, ski tours, tobogganing. 15 miles of cross-country skiing.

Sonthofen, 2,460 feet, fast train stop. Three ski lifts (one for children), ski jump, instructors, skating rink, hockey, curling, tobogganing. Ski tours up to 7,200 feet. 30 miles of prepared cross-country ski tracks.

Wertach, 3,000 feet, train stop. Four ski lifts, instructors, tobogganing. About five miles away, reached by bus, is Unterjoch (3,770 feet) with ski jumps, 4 ski lifts, ski schools. 13 miles of prepared cross-country skiing. About three miles from Wertach is Jungholz (3,770 feet), reached by bus and located across the border in Austria but economically integrated with Germany like Kleinwalsertal; also has ski school and 4 ski lifts. From these three places ski tours can be made up to 5,900 feet.

USEFUL ADDRESSES. Tourist information: Schwaben-Allgäu Fremdenverkehrsverband, 89 Augsburg, Halderstr. 12. Konstanz, Verkehrsamt, Bahnhofplatz 6. Lindau, Fremdenverkehrsamt, opposite main railroad station.

THE ROMANTIC ROAD

Picturo Book Germany

The Romantic Road from Füssen to Würzburg is a progression through a continuous pageant of history, art and architecture. On it you have no need to cudgel your brains to work out the best-value itinerary. Accept the ready-packaged journey of around 260 miles, providing the concentrated essence of picture-book Germany. If the founders of the places through which you pass had deliberately set out all the worthwhile spectacles of the region in a line, so that you could pass through them successively and see everything you wanted to see without having to deviate along the way, they couldn't have done it better.

EXPLORING THE ROMANTIC ROAD

The southern beginning of this well-known and much-followed south-north route is at Füssen, on the Austrian border, in Bavaria.

Füssen-Bad Faulenbach, spa and winter sports resort, is an old mountain town that owes its location to the fact that it constituted the fort guarding a pass through the Alps; but its site might just as easily have been chosen with the idea of giving it perfect scenic surroundings. From a majestic wall of mountains behind the town, the river Lech comes tumbling down to the green plains cradled within the encircling heights, and flows by the ancient stone buildings of the town. Lakes dot the country about Füssen—the Alpsee, the Schwansee, the Bannwaldsee, the Hopfensee, the Weissensee and the lake-river formed by the broadening of the Lech, the Forggensee. The famous view of Füssen is from a point where the Lech rolls over a long low fall. Beyond it rise the ancient walls of the castle, the churches, and the medieval buildings of the town; beyond them rise the Alps. Wander through the town, and you will find that all the streets are picturesque; but what you should particularly not fail to visit are the castle (Hohes Schloss), once the summer residence of the Prince Bishops of Augsburg; the St. Mangkirche, which has a much admired Romanesque crypt; and Hiebeler's *Totentanz* (Death Dance) in St. Anne's Chapel.

About three miles southeast of Füssen are two of the most magnificent castles in Germany, Neuschwanstein and Hohenschwangau. Neuschwanstein in particular, thrusting fantastically shaped towers and turrets and pinnacles and gables into the air and occupying a solitary perch in the midst of mountains, seems a picture from a fairy tale. In summer, occasional Wagnerian concerts are given in the magnificent setting it provides—an appropriate one, for it was built for Wagner's benefactor, King Ludwig II.

After royal architecture come three stunning examples of ecclesiastical, all close to road No. B17 which you will be following to Augsburg. At Steingaden is an old Guelph Minster, which you will not want to miss, and then you make the only detour from the main road required anywhere on the trip. It is worth it to see the building known as "The Wonder of the Wies"—the exuberantly-adorned church constituting the last and greatest masterpiece of Dominikus Zimmermann (he lies buried here), which is considered by connoisseurs to be the most beautiful rococo church in all of Germany. The third member of this great trio is the rococo monastery church at Rotternbuch.

At Schongau we again meet the Lech, which we left at Füssen. Schongau calls itself "The Town in Front of the Mountains," for this is the point—if you were coming from the opposite direction—where for the first time you would see the backdrop of the Alps looming beyond a settlement. Schongau today is a quiet rural center, but it was once a lively way station on the frequented medieval trade route between Italy and Augsburg, and as a result its small area is crammed with old city walls, towers, and historic buildings.

Beyond Schongau, the Lech runs through a series of artificial lakes. Following it, we come to Landsberg, an old medieval city richly adorned with baroque and rococo. Here you meet in profusion the works of Dominikus Zimmermann, whose finest creation we have seen at Wies. Among his works in Landsberg are the Johanniskirche, built in 1740–54, and the Ursulinenkirche. The present façade of the Rathaus was added by him in 1720 to a building which was originally put up in 1699. The Bavarian Gate of Landsberg, dating from 1425, is rated as one of the finest Gothic gates in Germany; and the visitor should not miss either the central square, with the 13th-century Schöner Turm (Beautiful Tower) and its 18th-century fountain, nor the 15th-century parish church containing the Madonna of Multscher. Every fifth year the Rüthen Festival in the middle of July (during which 1,500 children parade in historical costumes) draws hordes of visitors to this city.

Augsburg

From Landsberg, the road crosses the Lechfeld, where German Emperor Otto the Great in 955 inflicted a crushing defeat upon the Magyars, stopping forever their predatory incursions into Germany and contributing to their pacification and final settlement in what is today Hungary. The road then takes you through the Red Gate (Rotes Tor), providing a spectacular introduction to a spectacular city, the greatest city on the Romantic Road—Augsburg. This impressive complex of tower, bridge, ramparts, and moat, against whose massive background open-air opera is staged in summer, gives you a foretaste of the architectural riches of a city that also has been accumulating them for 2,000 years.

Augsburg was an important center in the 10th century, an international center of trade and the richest town in Europe in the 15th and 16th centuries. Its leading businessmen were the Fuggers and the Welsers, two of the most powerful families of medieval Europe. A Welser once *owned* Venezuela! The Fuggers were wealthier than the famous Italian Medicis. They financed wars and pulled strings that determined the elections of Emperors.

Both Holbeins were born in Augsburg. Mozart was not born here, but his father, Leopold, was and Augsburg treated the composer with more respect than did his native city of Salzburg, in Austria, while his compositions for the piano were much influenced by the improvements which Stein made to that instrument in Augsburg. Elias Holl, the architect who built the Rotes Tor, is buried here.

Augsburg is known also by an important date in German history. In 1555 the Augsburger Religionsfriede (Religious Peace of Augsburg) was ratified in the form of a treaty between the Catholic and Lutheran princes of the Holy Roman Empire, which provided that any member-state of the empire might set up either form of faith as its official religion. Those who refused to conform were guaranteed the right to dispose of their estates and emigrate. The treaty was based on the Confessio Augustana by the theologian Melanchthon (1530).

Augsburg is the seat of the oldest social settlement in the world, the Fuggerei, built in 1519 to house indigent but deserving families at a nominal rent and still doing so. The present rent is the same as at the time of its foundation, the equivalent of one Rhenish Florin of those times, or, in today's terms, one mark and 71 pfennigs *per year*. Augsburg is also important industrially, it has been the biggest textile center in southern Germany for 500 years, it is the birthplace of Rudolf Diesel, inventor of the Diesel engine, and in addition to the Diesel plant, important factories here include those of the Messerschmitt airplane makers and the National Cash Register Company.

A complete list of the sights of Augsburg, this collection of Gothic churches and Renaissance palaces, would fill an entire book. Among the most important are the cathedral, begun in 995, which boasts the oldest stained glass in the world (11th century) and altar paintings by Hans Holbein the Elder; an early 11th-century bronze door, and a series of tombs in the cloister (from the 13th to the 18th century); St. Ulrich, which not only has two towers but is two churches—for as a Protestant *and* Catholic church, it embodied in stone the spirit of the Religious Peace of Augsburg, achieved in 1555; the Maximilianstrasse, considered the finest Renaissance street in Germany; the Perlach tower and the Rathaus beside it, one of the most impressive creations of German Renaissance style, if not the most impressive, by Elias Holl; and in the Schaezler Palais, where the municipal art collections are displayed, is the Festive Hall, opened in 1770 to receive Marie Antoinette, then on her way to Paris from Vienna to become the bride of Louis XVI; a triumphal procession which was the first stage on the route to the guillotine.

For contemporary outdoor recreational needs Augsburg has constructed the Rosenaustadion, a thoroughly up-to-date athletic stadium, seating 45,000 spectators and located near the Wertach River, and the world's first canoe-slalom stadium (24,000 spectators), on the Lech River, site of this event in the 1972 Olympics. Also in the southern outskirts of the city but nearer to the Lech River in the pleasant Siebentisch woods are the botanical garden and a fine zoo of the modern cageless type.

Medieval Cities

Leaving Augsburg on Route 2, we continue north through Bavarian Swabia to Donauwörth, where we encounter the Danube (whose German name is Donau). Once again we are in a medieval town, and a well-preserved one, with the old town walls still running along the banks of its second river, the Wörnitz; the quaint Färbertörle gate, the baroque Holy Cross Church, and the regional parish church, with its medieval frescos, should be visited.

The Romantic Road follows the Wörnitz, leaving northern Swabia on Route 25 to enter Franconia (Franken), and comes to the little old town of Harburg, with its stone bridge spanning the water. Above it on a hill is Harburg Castle, a powerful 13th-century fortress. The well-preserved walls harbored collections of such richness that a new museum was opened to display the art treasures of the castle to better advantage. Among them are works by Riemenschneider, Romanesque ivory carvings, a fine collection of Gobelin tapestries and a huge library.

Nördlingen is called "the living medieval city," and that is just what it is, for not only does it retain its old walls and old buildings, but its old customs as well. At night you will hear the watchman's call echoing through the narrow streets as it has for centuries. The wider market places are made lively during the day by peasants from the Ries plains wearing the local costumes which also have not changed for centuries. The city's holidays hark back to medieval times too. The Stabenfestival, held in May at the old bastion, goes back several centuries; the Anno 1643 pageant commemorates the town's time of troubles at that date; and the Scarlet Derby (Scharlachrennen) is Germany's oldest. The open-air stage provides an appropriate setting for these performances, which accord perfectly with the solid ancient walls that encircle the old town, with the fine patrician houses of this former Imperial Free City, with the medieval shops and homes, with St. George's Church and its 300-foot tower (familiarly referred to as "Daniel"), with the Church of the Savior and its 13th-century frescos, with the Rathaus (14th century) and with the Kürschnerhaus, the oldest fair building in Germany.

Proceeding north we enter Dinkelsbühl, another old imperial free city. In July, Dinkelsbühl holds its Kinderzeche (Children's Tribute), with sword dances, guild dances, and an historical festival play in memory of the saving of the city from destruction during the Thirty Years' War. To that event we owe the fact that once again we have here a medieval city preserved intact, its walls still standing, complete with moat, bastions, gates, and towers. The atmosphere is dreamlike. Swans float lazily on the still waters of the moat. Nördlingen was a medieval town still living its medieval life (plus a good admixture of modern life); Dinkelsbühl is a medieval town that has drifted off to sleep.

The Tauber Valley

At Feuchtwangen, the monastery church, with its row of arches, serves as a background for outdoor presentations of plays on warm summer evenings. If you stop for them, don't miss the excellent Heimatmuseum collection of folk crafts.

Rothenburg-above-the-Tauber, which was also an imperial free city, is today (having survived the last war unharmed) the best preserved example of a medieval town in Germany. It was named "Model Tourist Town" of the European Architectural Year, an award it richly deserved. Here again we have a walled city, with sentry walk, with towers and gates intact, a fairy-tale city whose old fountains are alive with scarlet geraniums. It would be very difficult to recommend this town highly enough to anyone who has a taste for atmosphere.

At Whitsuntide, and again in September, it holds a festival centered about a play given in the Rathaus, *Der Meistertrunk,* which you can translate "The Master Drink," "The Mighty Draught," or anything else that conveys the idea of a formidable feat of swallowing. It is performed to commemorate the drinking feat that saved the town from destruction in 1631. The enemy commander who conquered the town first ordered it to be destroyed; he then offered to save it on condition that one of the town councillors empty with a single draught a 3-liter mug of wine (over three U.S. quarts). The old mayor, Nusch, succeeded in draining the sizeable container and the town was saved. During the summer, shepherd dances and Hans Sachs comic plays are performed. You can also see *Der Meistertrunk* clock play every day at 11, 12, 1 and 2 o'clock on a house near the Rathaus.

There is plenty to see in Rothenburg outside of festival time, too— particularly the masterly carving of the Holy Blood altar in the west choir of the St. Jakobskirche, executed by Tilman Riemenschneider of Würzburg, whose work is encountered throughout the Tauber Valley. The church itself is an impressive example of the Gothic style and it also contains the famous winged High Altar painted by Hans Herlin in 1466 and beautiful stained-glass windows.

Following the Tauber on a secondary road, we pass through the little village of Detwang, whose church also possesses carvings by Riemenschneider, and come to Creglingen, where his masterpiece, the intricate altar with the *Ascension of Mary,* is in the Herrgotts Church. The Tauber now draws us more to the west than to the north, so that we are back in Baden-Württemberg. We pass through Weikersheim, the site of the oldest residence of the Princes of Hohenlohe, set in its own baroque garden. If you want a glass of wine, you can go down into the cellars of the castle and have it served to you, with the great casks as a background.

From 1525 to 1809, Bad Mergentheim was a center of the Teutonic Knights, and their castle is still the great sight of the old city on the south bank of the Tauber, where high-roofed buildings of the Middle Ages confront you at every turn. When Napoleon dissolved the order, it appeared that Mergentheim's chief claim to distinction was at an end, that however interesting it might remain as a museum, it was doomed to fade away so far as active contemporary life was concerned. Then a shepherd, Franz Gehrig, grazing his sheep on the north bank of the river in 1826 discovered mineral springs. A new Mergentheim, baptized Bad Mergentheim, rose across the stream from the old town. The healing springs turned out to be four in number, each slightly different in its chemical composition, with the Albert Spring producing the strongest sodium sulphate and bitter salt waters in Europe. Excavations disclosed that the springs had been in use in the early Bronze and late Iron Age, and had then apparently silted up and become lost until their lucky rediscovery gave to a town apparently destined for decay a new lease of life. If you stop at Bad Mergentheim, you should not fail to visit the village church of Stuppach, a few miles to the south, to see one of the most famous canvases of one of the most famous painters of Germany—*The Virgin with the Infant Christ* by Matthias Grünewald (1519).

The Main Valley

From Bad Mergentheim we come to Tauberbischofsheim with its old, round watchtower, once part of a mighty fortress, and some half-timbered houses and baroque courtyards; in the parish church is a fine side altar, the work either of Riemenschneider or of his pupils. From here the Romantic Road moves back into Bavaria to end at the city of Würzburg on the river Main.

But we continue down the Tauber Valley to Wertheim, where the Tauber flows into the Main. Here the slender Kittstein Tower rises beside the Tauber like a gun-barrel standing on end, while on the heights beyond we see the massive castle of the Counts of Wertheim. Narrow streets in the old town are lined with venerable houses (Wertheim acquired city rights in 1306) and the market square is framed by fairy-tale half-timbered architecture.

Wertheim is still in Baden-Württemberg at its northernmost point, but our next stop, Miltenberg, down the Main River, brings us back into Bavaria. Its market square with the 16th-century fountain offers one of the most beautiful half-timbered pictures in Germany while several medieval tower-gates still watch the approaches to the city, and fishermen dry their nets along the bank of the Main. Across the river from Miltenberg are the green forested hills of Spessart. Proceeding downstream on No. 469, we come to Aschaffenburg and eventually to Frankfurt.

Only a few miles south of Miltenberg is Amorbach, founded by Benedictine monks in 734. The abbey church is today in baroque style, containing the biggest baroque organ in Europe, and the parish church is rococo. West of Amorbach is the heart of the Odenwald region in the state of Hesse.

PRACTICAL INFORMATION FOR THE ROMANTIC ROAD

HOTELS AND RESTAURANTS

Augsburg. Hotels: *Steigenberger Drei Mohren* (L), Maximilianstr. 40, 120 rooms and apartments and operating since 1723, is one of Germany's historic hotels; Russian Czars and German Emperors have been guests, as well as Mozart and Goethe. Fine restaurant, terrace café, dance-bar.

Turmhotel-Holiday Inn (L), adjoining the Kongresshalle in the Stadtpark, all rooms air-conditioned and with bath, radio and balcony in large 35-story supermodern tower; grill specialties in the top-floor *Turm-Restaurant,* bar, indoor pool.

All (M) are—*Alpenhof,* Donauwörther Str. 233, in the northwest suburbs, 220 beds, most rooms with bath or shower, indoor and outdoor pools; *Ost,* Fuggerstr. 4, 100 beds, good restaurant, bar; *Hotel Langer,* Gögginger Str. 39, near station, 25 rooms all with bath, peaceful, international restaurant.

Riegele, at main station, smaller, good restaurant; and *Post,* Fuggerstr. 7, 90 beds, most rooms with shower and terrace restaurant *Poststube. Dom-Hotel,* Frauentorstr. 8, very quiet position in the old town, near the station, 37 rooms, 20 with bath or shower.

Thalia, Obstmarkt 5, 63 beds, is (I).

Restaurants (in addition to those listed above): *Berteles Weinstuben* (E), Philippine-Welser-Str. 4, a tavern for gastronomes. *Ecke-Stuben* (M), Elias-Holl-Platz, old Augsburg atmosphere and good wines, artists' hangout.

Ratskeller (M), in the Rathaus with Elias-Holl-Stube. *Fuggerkeller* (M), Maximilianstr. 38. *Sieben-Schwaben-Stuben* (I), Bürgermeister-Fischer-Str. 12, Swabian specialties.

Goldene Gans (I), Karolinenstr., serving the oldest beer in Augsburg. *Agnes-Bernauer-Stuben,* Ludwigstr. 19, local specialties and agreeable music in evenings. Closed Sunday evenings (M).

There is a *Wienerwald* hotel on Rosenaustrasse.

A rare dining experience is offered by the *Welser-Küche* (E), in the old patrician Stiermann house. Here you can enjoy original medieval recipes in complete 16th-century style. On Fridays and Saturdays only and at 7 P.M. promptly; prior telephone arrangements are a must.

Another gastronomic delight is offered by *Gasthaus Gunzenlee* (M), about 6 miles southeast, with an unusually large selection of worldwide specialties and charcoal grill on garden terrace; also a few inexpensive rooms.

Bad Mergentheim. Hotels: *Viktoria* (E), 140 beds, most rooms with bath and glassed-in balconies, restaurant service in several atmospheric rooms, in a heated outdoor atrium and on roof terrace which also has a heated swimming pool with sliding glass partitions.

Extensively renovated *Kurhaus* (E), 160 beds, 60 baths, indoor swimming pool, cure facilities and mineral water taproom in house.

Both (M)—*Kurhotel Steinmeyer*, smaller, with nice view and cure facilities. *Garni am Markt*, also small.

There are several (I) hotels like *Petershof*, *Haus Wanfried* and *Irmgard*.

Dinkelsbühl. Hotels (all with restaurants): *Deutches Haus*, the most original half-timbered house in town, built in 1440 and with delightful local specialties in its historic restaurant, and *Goldene Rose*, renovated in 1976, with atmospheric *Ratskeller;* both (M).

Goldene Kanne, fine local food, (I–M).

Goldener Hirsch, (I), with a big golden stag above the door.

About 2 miles northeast in Gersbronn, *Haus Hildegard* (M), is a delightful, quiet hotel garni, all rooms with shower or bath.

Füssen. Hotels: *Hirsch*, Augsburger-Tor-Platz 2, 80 beds, authentic rustic furnishings; and *Sonne*, Reichenstr. 37, 64 beds, are (M).

Alpenkurhotel Filser (I), Säulingerstr. 3, quiet location and with Kneipp water cures.

In the Bad Faulenbach suburb *Kurhotel Wiedemann*, quiet and pleasant, also with Kneipp cures, is (M).

Hohenschwangau, near the two romantic castles. *Hotel Lisl und Jägerhaus*, in hunting manor style, and *Müller*, with attractive restaurant and *Kutscherstube*, are (E).

Miltenberg. Hotels: *Riesen* (M), historic (1590) half-timbered inn used by knights during the Middle Ages, 50 types of Franconian wines in wood-paneled *Riesen Restaurant* adjoining.

Rose, centuries-old guild house of river boatmen and fishermen, and *Mildenburg*, terrace café, both overlook the Main; *Brauerei Keller*, good restaurant with large wine list. All (I–M).

Nördlingen. Hotels: *Sonne*, established in 1477, next to Rathaus; *Hotel am Ring*, at station; and *Schützenhof*, fine local specialties in its restaurant, are (M).

Historic and picturesque hostelries include *Alte Post* and *Zum Golden Lamm*, both (I).

Rothenburg ob der Tauber. Hotels: *Eisenhut* (E), Herrengasse 3–5, two historic buildings in exquisite antique style, 90 rooms, excellent cuisine and wine cellar, luxurious. *Goldener Hirsch*, Untere Schmiedgasse 16, 80 rooms, very colorful old building, fine dining on the Blue Terrace with outstanding view of town.

Somewhat less expensive are *Zum Bären,* Hofbronneng. 9, an old and steep narrow street below the Rathaus, 90 beds and indoor pool; and *Burg-Hotel,* Klosterg. 1, with panoramic view over the Tauber Valley, indoor pool; and *Gotisches Haus,* in a 700-year-old house.

The colorful *Adam,* Burgg. 29, small (most rooms with bath or shower), but great on the menu; *Markusturm,* at the tower of the same name, are (M), and *Roter Hahn,* with ancient half-timbered balcony-corridors in the back, is (I).

Inexpensive: the half-timbered *Reichsküchenmeister,* with fine food and café-terrace facing St. Jakobi Church; and *Gasthof Zur Glocke,* with good food and wines.

Restaurants (in addition to those mentioned above): *Baumeisterhaus* (M), Obere Schmiedg. 3, perhaps the most attractive building in town, built in 16th century in Renaissance style; good food and wines, period furnishings.

NIGHTLIFE. Augsburg. Variety: *Apollo-Bar,* Theaterstr. 12; *Maxim,* Theaterstr. 6; *Griffin,* Fuggerstr. 14. Primarily for dancing and drinks: *Drei-Mohren-Bar* in hotel of the same name; *Rainbow Club* in Holiday Inn; *Moby Dick,* discothèque in Hotel Weisses Lamm; *Afra-Tanzbar,* Afrawald 2; and *Westside,* Kesterstr. 28. **Nördlingen:** *Dehlers Disco-Nightclub,* Hallgasse 7.

MUSIC AND THEATER. Augsburg has regular theater and concert seasons in the following establishments: *Stadttheater,* Theaterplatz, opera, operetta, drama, season October–June; *Schauspielhaus Komödie,* Vorderer Lech 8, plays and ballet, October–June; *Kongress- und Konzerthalle,* Stadtpark, symphony concerts; *Marionetten-Theater,* Spitalgasse 15; *Freilichtbühne am Roten Tor,* season July–August, open-air opera.

In **Füssen** theatrical performances by guest companies are given in the *Volksbühne* and concerts in the *Fürstensaal* of the former Benedictine monastery.

Folklore evenings of music and dance are regular features during summer and winter. **Rothenburg** stages its festival plays at Whitsun (Der Meistertrunk) and Hans Sachs Spiele June/July, also mid-Sept. festivals, *Rolf Trexler's Puppet Show* (Apr.–Oct.), as well as open-air concerts; **Bad Mergentheim** also has frequent musical events and open-air plays are performed at *Alte Bastei* in **Nördlingen.**

MUSEUMS. Augsburg. In the Schaezler Palais, Maximilianstr. 46, *Deutsche Barockgalerie,* German baroque masters as well as works by Rembrandt, Veronese, Tiepolo. In the former Dominican Church, entrance in the Schaezler Palais, the *Staatsgalerie* with old German masters including Holbein the Elder and Dürer. The *Römisches Museum,* Dominikanergasse 15, has prehistoric, Roman and old German exhibits. *Maximilianmuseum,* Philippine-

Welser-Str. 24, local history, arts and crafts. *Mozarthaus,* Frauentorstr. 30, birthplace of Mozart's father and now converted into a Mozart memorial.

Nördlingen. *Reichsstadtmuseum,* paintings, arts and crafts, local history and culture with *Vor- und Frühgeschichtliches Collection,* important pre-historical and early historical finds.

Rothenburg ob d. T. *Kloster-Museum,* local history, including the Meistertrunk mug used by Mayor Nusch during the Thirty Years War. *Craftsman Museum* in 13th-century house; Staatsgalerie; guided tours of Rathaus.

SPORTS. Swimming in the beautifully situated lake establishments near Füssen; **windsurfing** with school on the Schongauer artificial lake. **Golf** courses exist in Augsburg and Bad Mergentheim, **tennis** courts also in Füssen, Rothenburg and elsewhere.

You can engage in **horseback riding** in Nördlingen, Rothenburg, Augsburg and Bad Mergentheim. The Scharlachrennen in Nördlingen is the oldest (since 1438) **horseracing** event in Germany is held at the end of August.

You may try your **fishing** luck in the Tauber River in the Bad Mergentheim section, in the several lakes and Upper Lech in the Füssen area, or in Wertach and Schmutter streams near Augsburg; all primarily for trout, huck, grayling and pike. Lech River is good for **kayaking:** it is very scenic from Füssen to Schongau and difficult in some spots; from Schongau to Landsberg it goes through artificial lakes and dams (9 portages), from Landsberg to Augsburg it is easy.

For **winter sports** in the Füssen area consult the practical information section for Allgäu.

USEFUL ADDRESSES. Tourist information: Augsburg, Verkehrsverein, Bahnhofstr. 7 (including room reservations), and ABR (Official Bavarian Travel Office), at the main station and Philippine-Welser-Strasse 14; Bad Mergentheim, Verkehrsamt, Rathaus; Dinkelsbühl, Verkehrsamt; Füssen, Kurverwaltung, Augsburger-Tor-Platz; Miltenberg, Verkehrsbüro, Rathaus; Nördlingen, Verkehrsamt, Marktplatz 15; Rothenburg, Verkehrsverein, Marktplatz.

SOUTHEAST
GERMANY

SOUTHEAST GERMANY

The Holiday Land

Southeast Germany means Bavaria, by far the largest state in the Federal Republic. For centuries, Bavaria was a nation of importance in itself. Its historical beginnings date from the 6th century, when an independent Duchy was established by the early Bavarians. They were one of the original Germanic peoples and settled in Bavaria during the "migration of the nations" at the end of the Dark Ages. Bavaria remained a Duchy, within the Holy Roman Empire of the German Nation, until 1623 when it became an Electorate. After the dissolution of the Empire in 1806, Bavaria became a Kingdom and a member of the newly-established German Confederation, later the German Empire. Her official name, the Free State of Bavaria (Freistaat Bayern), proudly displayed on her borders, reflects her distinctive history and her somewhat idyosyncratic traditions and staunch individualism.

Bavaria is split approximately in half by the Danube, running west to east across the state. North of the river, the principal areas and cities are the Spessart mountains, the Rhön hills, Würzburg and the vineyard-laden Main valley. These are all in Lower Franconia (Unter-Franken). In Middle Franconia (Mittel-Franken) are medieval Nürnberg, the leading city of northern Bavaria and Franconia, the southern section of the Franconian hills (Franken Alb) and the lovely Altmühl valley which runs into the Danube.

Upper Franconia (Ober-Franken) is to the northeast of Lower and Middle Franconia. Its two principal cities are Bamberg, dripping with history, and Wagnerian Bayreuth. The whole region is mountainous and wooded and exudes a peculiarly Germanic sense of mystery. At the northern extremity of the area is the Franconian Forest (Franken Wald), which just touches the edge of Thuringia in the Soviet Zone of Germany. Upper Franconia continues south along the East German frontier through the mountain group of Fichtelgebirge and the spectacular scenery of Swiss Franconia (Fränkische Schweiz)—confusingly named as it is many miles from Switzerland—to the Franconian hills and the Oberpfälzer Jura. The rest of Northern Bavaria is a remote and hilly region running along the Czechoslovakian frontier. The two principal ranges are the Upper Palatinate Forest (Oberpfälzer Wald) and the Bavarian Forest (Bayerischer Wald), squeezed between the Danube to the west and Czechoslovakia to the east.

The area south of the Danube is Lower Bavaria (Niederbayern). Further south still is Upper Bavaria (Oberbayern) in the mountains. Its name refers to its altitude.

Lower Bavaria is rich, agricultural country, interspersed with fine medieval cities such as Regensburg, Passau on the Austrian border and Lanshut. It is an unspoiled, hilly, forested landscape, with little villages nestling in peaceful sunlight.

Upper Bavaria can be summed up in two names, Munich and the Alps. Munich is the capital of the state and lies approximately halfway between the Danube and the Alps. It is probably Germany's best-known city and offers something of everything, from one of the world's most important and rich collections of paintings to the best-known brewery in the world. The Bavarian Alps, immediately to the south, are Germany's top holiday resort, and have a beauty all their own, from their strangely green forests to their terrifying rock escarpments. It is this region, more than any other, that is usually considered most typically Bavarian and hence German.

MEDIEVAL FRANCONIA

The Wagner Heartland

Franconia, or Franken as it is called in German, is the northern region of the state of Bavaria. Its western edge includes most of the northern section of the Romantic Road and in the Spessart hills reaches a point only 20 miles from Frankfurt. Its northern border runs along the frontier of the Soviet Zone. In the east it extends to Oberpfalz (Upper Palatinate) and in the south it reaches Lower Bavaria on the Danube.

Franconia is the region of the courts and castles where famous Minnesingers composed the rhymes that formed the beginnings of German lyric poetry, of walled towns where Mastersingers sang songs to the beat of their artisan tools, of splendid baroque and rococo cities built by art-loving prince-bishops. It is the region, too, of quiet wooded hills through which the river Main winds its meandering course, and on whose sunnier banks the golden grapes mature into pale, dry wines.

EXPLORING FRANCONIA

The most direct route from Frankfurt to Würzburg, the chief city of Unter-Franken (Lower Franconia), passes through Aschaffenburg, only 25 miles southeast of Frankfurt and still on the Main but already within the borders of the state of Bavaria.

Aschaffenburg is a rather important cultural and trade center endowed with some outstanding buildings in really beautiful parks and surrounded by lovely countryside. The most notable is the 800-year-old monastery church of St. Peter and Alexander; its main treasures are the Romanesque cloister with superbly graceful arches and one of the finest paintings by Matthias Grünewald, showing the dead Christ. Aschaffenburg calls itself "the city of Grünewald"; though the artist was born in Würzburg he lived for several years in Aschaffenburg where he also collaborated on the construction of the imposing Renaissance Johannisburg Castle which dominates the view of the city from the Main side with its fortress-like bulk and its four turrets. A curious structure is the Pompejanum, an imitation of the Castor and Pollux house in Pompeii, built at the whim of Ludwig I of Bavaria. Aschaffenburg should not be dismissed without special mention of its beautiful parks—Schönbusch with its small neo-classic palace mirrored in the tranquil waters before it, and Schöntal, about two miles outside, whose pond reflects the ruins of an old cloister church and which is resplendent in spring with the bloom of magnolias.

Aschaffenburg is the gateway to Spessart, a region of undulating hills, mostly covered by forests, many of them old oak forests, with a few atmospheric quite small towns and villages hidden among them. Mespelbrunn is noted for its Renaissance moated castle while Rohrbrunn, approximately in the center of the region on the main route between Aschaffenburg and Würzburg, has an interesting hunting castle and many hiking paths for Spessart is a walker's paradise.

Proceeding along the main route through Spessart we meet the Main River again near Marktheidenfeld. At this spot we either cross the river, continuing straight to Würzburg, or follow the longer but much more interesting road along the right bank. This route passes through a series of picturesque small towns: Hafenlohr, where regional rustic pottery is made; Rothenfels, with its medieval castle; Gemünden, where the Sinn and Saale rivers flow into the Main; Karlstadt, with 13th-century walls and gates, the ruins of an even older castle across the river, and an exquisite 15th-century Town Hall.

Just a few miles before reaching Würzburg is the baroque Veitshöchheim Castle, with rococo adornments and a beautiful, formal park; this was the former summer residence of the prince-bishops of Würzburg.

Würzburg

The prehistoric finds in the immediate vicinity of Würzburg have shown that this area was already inhabited 120,000 years ago. A chain of fragmented pottery leads us through the dawn of history to the Celts who for several centuries lived in their hearth-heated huts at the foot of Marienberg and built a defense fort on the top of the same hill (on the site of the present castle), where they retreated in times of danger. Germanic tribes settled on the present city site at the beginning of the Christian Era, but became christianized much later when Kilian, the Irish missionary—called the Apostle of the Franks—came to this area together with his companions Kolonat and Totnan. Their efforts eventually bore fruit, but not until after all three of them had been put to death upon the request of a duchess, for Würzburg at that time was the seat of Frankish dukes and some of them at first rejected Christianity. In spite of this early opposition the city was made a bishopric as early as 742 and it was only half a century later that the Würzburg bishops acquired secular power as well; as prince-bishops, they ruled the city for 1,000 years.

Kilian, who was canonized after his martyrdom, is buried in a crypt over which the baroque Neumünster Church was later erected. The nearby monumental cathedral is also named after him; basically in Romanesque style, it has many later additions. Neumünster was once an abbey church (Stiftskirche) and in the former cloister courtyard—today the site is called Lusamgärtlein—the canons were buried, and among them, by special imperial order, Walther von der Vogelweide, the famous Minnesinger, who spent his last days in this monastery and died in 1230. Other outstanding churches in the city are the Gothic Marienkapelle (St. Mary's Chapel) on the market square and the half-Romanesque and half-Gothic St. Burkard's, named after the first bishop of Würzburg and located at the foot of the vineyards rising to Marienberg Fortress.

The fortress (Festung) is one of the main attractions of Würzburg. Not only is it a majestic sight, when seen from the pleasant promenade on the right river bank or from the 15th-century Old Main Bridge, but it also offers a splendid view over the city from its terrace garden. You can walk up from the Old Main Bridge (Alte Mainbrücke), or drive up by a roundabout way, first following route No. 27 (marking the beginning of the Romantic Road) to the heights south of the river, and then taking the narrow Oberer Burgweg, which is the street leading through several gates of the fortress to one of the main courtyards. From this courtyard a gate leads into the castle proper; here stands the former arsenal, today housing the Mainfränkisches Museum. Of outstanding artistic interest in the museum is the section devoted to the sculptor Tilman Riemenschneider, where some of his best works in wood and stone are displayed; Riemenschneider was born in the Harz region but spent most of his life in Würzburg, where he became a city councillor and mayor, and where he was imprisoned for a brief period in 1525 for having sided with the peasants in the great peasant rebellion of the same year.

In the interior castle courtyard stands the round Marienkirche, one of the oldest churches in Germany (built in 706), with the outward appearance of a large defense tower rather than a church. Nearby is the 341-foot well that provided the fortress with water, and a tower called Sonnenturm, where the treasury and the archives were kept and in whose dungeon Riemenschneider was imprisoned. The castle suffered severe damage from incendiary bombs towards the end of the last war and while the exteriors have been largely repaired and rebuilt, the precious interior furnishings were almost totally lost.

The prince-bishops lived in the fortress until the 18th century, when they moved into the splendid castle-palace (Residenz) in the city, built by the famed baroque architect Balthasar Neumann. Although the greater part of the Residenz was burned out during the same air raid which set the Marienberg fortress and the rest of the city ablaze, its façade, most beautiful halls, and unique Grand Staircase miraculously escaped serious damage. The Grand Staircase, with the huge ceiling painting by Tiepolo representing the four continents, is one of the finest examples of the baroque style in Europe, while the Kaisersaal (Emperor's Hall), where the Mozart Festival concerts are performed in summer by the light of thousands of candles, and the Hofkirche (Court Church), in the southeast corner of the palace, are considered among the best specimens of early rococo in Germany and also contain frescos and paintings by Tiepolo. Intricate wrought-iron gates, 18th-century masterpieces by Oegg, lead into the adjoining palace garden, which is full of smiling rococo statues.

Rococo is everywhere in Würzburg: in the original Julius Hospital Pharmacy; on the façade of the Haus zum Falken on the market square, once a proud patrician dwelling; on the figures of Rokokobrunnen and Vierröhrenbrunnen, two fountains near the Rathaus which, however, is much older; in the interior decorations of Käppele pilgrimage church, on a hill next to Marienberg, whose architecture, however, is one of Balthasar Neumann's baroque achievements. But the rococo of Würzburg is not the over-gilded and bejeweled style usually encountered elsewhere; the rococo of Würzburg is younger and simpler, with white rather than gold reflecting the sun. The local wine seems to share its heart-lifting exuberance, and the Bocksbeutel, the flat, unevenly round, dark green and long-necked wine bottle used only in Franken, is most probably also one of its products. And the Bocksbeutel Road we shall take now also meanders up the Main Valley in rococo style.

Bocksbeutel Road

To be exact, we have already traveled on the Bocksbeutel Road before reaching Würzburg. But its heart, assuming that the heart of a wine road has to be filled with the best of its wine, is shaped by a huge southward bend of the Main. It begins a bit northwest of Würzburg and ends, following the river, a few villages north of Escherndorf. This is a tiny village with a big reputation among wine drinkers, for it is here that the Escherndorfer Lump (The Rascal of Escherndorf) gushes from the wine presses into the barrels and bocksbeutels and matures into "The Rascal."

The medieval watchtowers of two ancient towns stand guard at the lower point of the Bocksbeutel heart: Ochsenfurt, with its Gothic Rathaus and Glockenspiel, and Marktbreit, preferred by painters for its idyllic old motifs. On the right bank of the Main, north of Marktbreit, is Kitzingen, a center of the wine trade, whose curiosity is a medieval tower with a leaning spire; it is located on the direct route from Würzburg to Nürnberg. Farther up the river is Dettelbach, a small town founded in 515, still enclosed by 15th-century walls with 36 towers.

Iphofen, an authentic medieval town, and nearby Rödelsee are important wine-growing centers. Volkach's principal sights include the 16th-century Town Hall, baroque Schelfenhaus, and the *Rosary Madonna* by Riemenschneider in the pilgrimage church on the nearby Kirchberg. All three of these towns are situated on the edge of Steigerwald, a region of low hills reaching to Bamberg.

Approximately in its center, on the direct Würzburg to Bamberg road, stands the 13th-century monastery church of Ebrach, one of the best examples of early German Gothic (with interior additions from later periods), and the adjoining baroque monastery with five courtyards and some fine interiors. Follow a side road at the western edge of Steigerwald for Schloss Weissenstein near Pommersfelden, about 12 miles south of Bamberg, built in the early 18th century by the Bamberg architect Johann Diezenhofer with the assistance of Lukas von Hildebrandt, the famous Austrian baroque master. This splendid castle, with a spectacular grand staircase, a series of richly-decorated halls, and a gallery of paintings, rivals the finest baroque castle-palaces of southeastern Germany.

Instead of crossing the Steigerwald, we can proceed northward to Schweinfurt, an industrial town whose specialties are dye-stuffs and ball bearings. Its finest buildings, the 16th-century Town Hall and the Protestant Johanniskirche were fortunately not hit by wartime bombings. A few miles to the southwest is baroque Werneck Castle, while the northbound road leads to the Franconian spa region at the foot of the Rhön hills.

Bad Kissingen is the leading spa of this area and a one-time favorite of Bismarck. It has several thermal and mineral springs, lovely parks, 16th-century Old Rathaus, baroque New Rathaus, a large Kurhaus (Regentenbau) with several halls and with arcades connecting it with the mineral water outlets in Brunnenhalle, and with Wandelhalle, a huge promenade lobby; there is also a gambling casino, a fashionable entertainment program during the season, and an airport for small private planes or air taxis. Bad Kissingen also offers some very unusual attractions: a giant 33-foot-square chess-board with 3-foot figures, installed by the spa management for the benefit of the guests who wish to exercise their brains and their muscles at the same time; and a 9-seat bright yellow stagecoach, drawn by four white horses, with blue-liveried coachmen, running daily from early May through October between Bad Kissingen and the 5-mile-distant Bad Bocklet, operated by the German Federal Post and still transporting mail in addition to passengers, the only service of this kind still existing in Germany.

On the market square in Bad Kissingen you will see a bust of Peter Heil, who in 1643 devised an ingenious defense stratagem while the town was beleaguered by hostile forces during the Thirty Years War: he advised his fellow town defenders, who had run out of ammunition, to hurl beehives from the city walls upon the attackers, and the latter fled in panic. A new fountain on Rathausplatz has been erected to honor the *Minnesänger* Count Otto von der Bodenlauben.

To the north lie Bad Neustadt, in a lovely location on the Saale River, with the nearby Salzburg fortress, one of the largest in Germany, and Bad Brückenau, surrounded by woods in the dreamy Sinn Valley with the border of Hesse just beyond it. For beautiful views of the surrounding region drive up the scenic roads to Wasserkuppe, the highest summit in Rhön (over 3,000 feet) and one of the main German gliding centers, or to Kreuzberg, which is almost as high and on whose top stand the three crosses of the Crucifixion.

Resuming our upstream journey along the Main from Schweinfurt, we pass through Hassfurt, a medieval town that has retained its old gate towers and its 15th-century Gothic Ritterkapelle (Knight's Chapel) with 240 coats of arms of Franconian noble families. North of Hassfurt are the wooded hills of Hassberge, with numerous castles, quiet, unspoiled villages, rushing streams, and hundreds of pleasant and easy hiking paths.

Bamberg

The Regnitz River, which joins the Main just a few miles below Bamberg, flows through the city in two arms. Its left arm cuts through the heart of the city and once represented the borderline between the section on its left bank, which was the Bishop's Town, and the section on its right bank, which was the Burghers' Town. This accounts for the fact that the Old Town Hall, which had to administer both halves of the city, is picturesquely located in the middle of a bridge that connects them, like a stone ship. As an industrial center of some importance (Bosch spark plugs, among other items, are made here), Bamberg was badly bombed; fortunately the Bishop's Town, its oldest and most interesting section, suffered no serious damage.

The foremost sight in Bamberg, as well as one of the main architectural and artistic attractions in Germany, is the famous cathedral, whose four spires rise above the city and whose mighty two-choir Romanesque building dominates the Bishop's Town. The construction was started by Emperor Heinrich the Holy in 1003 and the consecration took place on Heinrich's birthday in 1012. During the ensuing two centuries it was enlarged and partially rebuilt, acquiring Gothic additions. The exquisitely-figured Adam's Portal, St. Mary's Portal, and Prince's Portal lead into the interior with its numerous artistic treasures. Let us mention only the most important individual pieces: the nobel equestrian statue known throughout the world as the Bamberg Rider, chiseled in stone around 1230 by an unknown master and interpreted as the personification of medieval German knighthood; the sculptures of the Visitation group and the nearby Smiling Angel; two elegant early Gothic female figures representing "Church" and "Synagogue"; the limestone tomb of Emperor Heinrich and his wife Kunigunde (both canonized after death) carved by Riemenschneider; St. Mary's or Christmas Altar, carved in wood by Veit Stoss; the 14th-century choir stalls. In the west choir of the church is the grave of Pope Clement II, a former Bishop of Bamberg and the only pope buried in Germany, while the cathedral treasury contains some of his ecclesiastical garments as well as clothing of Emperor Heinrich and Empress Kunigunde.

Near the cathedral stands the beautiful Old Residence (Alte Hofhaltung) of the Bamberg prince-bishops, now housing a regional historical museum, built in German Renaissance style except for the half-timbered wing in the inner courtyard, which is from the 15th century and which was once part of the now defunct fortress. On the other side of the cathedral square is the baroque New Residence (Neue Residenz), built by Dienzenhofer, containing baroque and rococo halls and rooms, once apartments of the prince-bishops, and a very fine gallery of paintings. The rear of the palace encloses a lovely rose garden, which offers an excellent view of another majestic ecclesiastic edifice, topping the highest hill in the city: the former Benedictine abbey with St. Michael's Church first built in Romanesque and later converted into baroque, with rich interiors.

In the narrow, romantic streets between the cathedral hill and the left arm of the Regnitz River, many old houses recapture days gone by. Perhaps the finest among them are the two baroque patrician houses, once owned by Böttinger, an influential and wealthy citizen of Bamberg, and built upon his orders: the Böttingerhaus in Judengasse and Concordia Palace right on the river.

Crossing the left arm of the river through the Old Town Hall—for one of the two bridges that support it passes through it—the waterfront presents a unique view: a row of colorful old fishermen's houses called Klein Venedig (Little Venice). St. Martin's Church in the center of the Burghers' Town is another outstanding example of baroque architecture, and the State Library next to it has among its thousands of books, manuscripts, and incunabula works by Dürer and Cranach, a 5th-century manuscript by Roman historian Livy, the Alcuin Bible from the early 9th century, and the prayer books of Emperor Heinrich the Holy and his wife Kunigunde. On Schillerplatz, across from the city theater, stands Hoffmann-Haus, today a museum, from 1809–13 the residence of writer E. T. A. Hoffmann, who was also the composer, musical director and scene painter in the Bamberg city theater, and whom Offenbach made the main character in his *Tales of Hoffmann*.

To the Sources of the Main

At Bamberg we entered Ober-Franken (Upper Franconia). Proceeding north in the valley of the Main, we come to Staffelstein, an old town with an exquisitely half-timbered Rathaus, situated beneath the Staffelberg from whose top there is an extraordinary view of the Main Valley. Nearby are two gems of ecclesiastical architecture, both with very rich interiors. One is the pilgrimage church of Vierzehnheiligen, the finest rococo church in northern Bavaria, constructed after the plans of Balthasar Neumann; its name means "fourteen saints" and it is built on the spot where, in 1445 and 1446, a young shepherd had visions of 14 *Nothelfer* (saints who help people in times of need); they are represented in a ceiling fresco. The other one is the former Benedictine Abbey of Banz, dating from 1071 and later rebuilt several times; its baroque abbey church and the main monastery building are the works of the Bamberg master, Dienzenhofer, and another monastery wing is by Neumann. Not far away is Lichtenfels, center of German basket-making, with a basket-weaving school as well as old town gates and a castle.

Situated in the valley of the Itz, Coburg was for several centuries the seat of the family of Saxe-Coburg-Gotha, a kind of royal stud farm which provided kings, queens and prince consorts to almost every royal house of Europe; one of them was Prince Albert, the consort of Queen Victoria, herself descended from the same family. A statue of Prince Albert stands in the market square, flanked by the Renaissance Stad-thaus and the Rathaus, first erected in the 16th century and later rebuilt, but preserving the original Renaissance Great Hall. But the finest example of the Renaissance style in the city is Gymnasium Casimirianum, built in 1605 and named after its founder, Duke Johann Casimir of Coburg. Opposite is the Protestant Morizkirche, with two uneven towers and with portal stone sculptures from 1420. Schloss Ehrenburg was the ducal town palace and its 17th- to 19th-century apartments and chapel are open to the public; it also contains the State Archives and the provincial library.

High above the town you will see the massive walls of a fortress, from whose interior rise the roofs of the buildings it surrounds. This is the Veste, over 900 years old and one of the largest fortified strongholds in Germany, shut in by a triple line of ramparts. The approach to it has been beautified by the creation of a park that begins at the town below and extends all the way up the slope to the castle. If you find the climb through the Hofgarten to the Veste too arduous to accom-plish in a single stage, stop halfway up and visit the Natural History Museum (one of the largest bird collections in Europe, more than 8,000 specimens). The fortress, too, houses a museum. Its apartments contain a wealth of period furniture, porcelain, silver, and its art collections include paintings by both Cranachs, and engravings by Dürer and Rembrandt.

Among the several castles on the outskirts of Coburg is Schloss Rosenau, the summer residence of the dukes and birthplace of Prince Albert. Neustadt, a town devoted to the manufacture of dolls, has a museum with 1,000 folk-costumed dolls and a toy show portraying fairy tales. Another curiosity of Neustadt is the goat bleat announcing the noon hour from the Rathaus; this recorded "baa baa" is sounded in memory of a medieval tailor who saved the town from a siege by sewing himself into a goat skin and frolicking on the ramparts to convince the enemy that the defenders had plenty of food. In the vicinity is medieval Kronach with picturesque old streets and build-ings, the powerful fortress of Rosenberg that was never captured, and the house where Lucas Cranach the Elder was born. Kronach is a good center from which to explore the thickly-forested hills of Frankenwald, harboring at its northern end the idyllic summer resort of Ludwigsstadt, with the 1,000-year-old Lauenstein Castle nearby.

Kulmbach is famous for the production of excellent beer. Its Luitpold Museum contains, among other exhibits, a collection of 32 pieces of fine goldsmiths' work of the late 16th and early 17th centuries, which was hidden so effectively during the Thirty Years' War that it was not found again until three centuries later, in 1912. The town is dominated by the Plassenburg Fortress, with a beautiful arcaded Renaissance courtyard and a series of dioramas containing over 300,000 tin figures representing all sorts of scenes from mammoth hunters to famous battles.

Just below Kulmbach, the White Main, on whose banks the town is located, and the Red Main flow together forming the beginning of the Main proper. The Red Main comes from the northeastern edge of Fränkische Schweiz and passes through Bayreuth.

Traveling up the White Main from Kulmbach, we come to its source in the Fichtelgebirge, a range of granite mountains and plateaus covered with conifers, an unpretentious summer and winter vacation area. Coming from the west we enter them at Bad Berneck, a climatic health resort. Approximately in the center of the Fichtelgebirge are lovely Fichtel Lake and the winter sports center of Ober-Warmensteinach. In the vicinity is the old town of Wunsiedel, with the nearby Luisenburg, which is the name given to an amazing natural pile of huge rocks near the top of a hill; their position is so intricate that the marked path leading through them is a veritable labyrinth, and it takes two hours of twisting and turning to cover its mile and a half. The great rock pile provides a fine background for the Luisenburg drama festival that is held here every summer.

North of Wunsiedel are Selb, the famous porcelain manufacturing city, and Hof, a textile and brewing center. Another specialty of Fichtelgebirge is glass blowing and decorating. The town of Bischofsgrün, the highest climatic resort in these mountains, has the longest ski lift in Europe and an 800-year-old glassmaking tradition, while there are glass factories in many other places.

Wagner's City

Bayreuth is known throughout the world as the city where the yearly Wagner Festival is given in the theater designed by Richard Wagner himself for the presentation of his operas under ideal conditions. Today it is impossible to move two steps in Bayreuth without being reminded of Wagner. The shops are packed with souvenirs, the streets are named after his family and characters from his operas, it is Wagnerville all the way. You should be warned that prices of nearly everything rise by 100% during the Festival.

However, Bayreuth was an important center of arts and music even before Wagner opened his theater in 1876. The Margraves of Bayreuth had been longtime sponsors of the arts, particularly during the mid-18th century. When Wilhelmine, the favorite sister of Frederick the Great, married into the Bayreuth ruling family, she and her husband made the city a center of art and music, and during their lifetime the finest buildings of Bayreuth were built. At the command of Margravine Wilhelmine, the famous baroque Margrave's Opera House was built, where Wilhelmine often acted herself, but it was a private Margrave's Theater and performances could be attended only by invited guests. Today the Franconian Festival Week, featuring baroque music, is staged in it every year in late spring.

Wagner designed his Festspielhaus (Festival Theater) primarily to achieve perfect acoustics for his operas: for this reason the seats have no upholstering, a cloth is suspended in a horizontal position about 25 feet below the ceiling, and the orchestra pit is almost completely covered by a wooden boarding. This last innovation ensures that a balance is kept between the orchestral sound and the singers, a balance that very few other opera houses can provide. The stage is very high and very deep and has an excellent lighting system. The building cost vast amounts of money and Wagner never had sufficient financial means to give the theater a fancy finish; that is why it has a simple look, both inside and out. The present productions at Bayreuth, staged in accordance with the most modern techniques, are highly impressive, but differ greatly from the traditional productions which were staged by Wagner himself.

Richard Wagner and his wife Cosima, the daughter of the composer Franz Liszt, lived in Haus Wahnfried and are buried in the garden behind it. The house is now a museum. Liszt also spent his closing years in a nearby villa, where he died three years after Wagner; he is buried in the city cemetery.

A section of the New Castle, once the residence of the Margraves and now a museum, includes the State Gallery of Painting, City Museum, and a regional collection of natural history. The Old Castle and Old Town Hall were severely hit by wartime bombing but have been rebuilt. You should not fail to visit Eremitage, a rococo-style park with two pleasure castles and elaborate fountains, also built and formerly owned by Margraves, about three miles outside the city.

Fränkische Schweiz

Southwest of Bayreuth, inside the triangle formed by the roads connecting Bayreuth–Nürnberg–Bamberg–Bayreuth, is Fränkische Schweiz (Swiss Franconia), a group of romantic, narrow valleys and dolomite hills, with strange stone formations protruding here and there out of steep, wooded flanks. The name is a misnomer since, except for its idyllic, pastoral character, the area has little in common with Switzerland. Medieval castles stand guard on many cliffs, whose interiors harbor some 40 caves rich in stalactites and stalagmites, where many fossils and bones of prehistoric animals were found, most of which were removed to museums but some left in place. The best starting points for an exploration of Fränkische Schweiz are the towns of Hollfeld in the north, Forchheim in the west, Gräfenberg in the south and Pegnitz in the east.

The Wiesent River flows south from Hollfeld through quaint villages to Behringersmühle, where it turns west and is joined by two other streams: the Alisbach, coming from Rabenstein Castle (near the stalactite cave of Sophienhöhle), and the Püttlach passing through the town of Pottenstein, dominated by a 10th-century castle, with the famous Teufelshöhle, or Devil's Cave nearby (open to the public, as are all the other caves mentioned, and easily reached from Pegnitz on the Bayreuth–Nürnberg autobahn). In the town proper is the parish church of St. Bartholomew, with its enormous high altar and priceless woodcarvings. Across the river is the climatic health resort of Gössweinstein, with a baroque pilgrimage church by Neumann and an impressive castle atop the hill above it that is well worth the short but steep drive up, also for the view. Two or three miles east is 15th-century Gaillenreuth Castle in whose neighborhood is the Gaillenreuther Zoolithenhöhle, a cavern where prehistoric human bones were found next to those of Ice Age animals. At Streitberg, flanked by the ruins of two castles, are the underground stalactite treasures of Binghöhle.

Forchheim is a bustling textile center whose documentary history dates back to 805. Note the half-timbered Rathaus square, 17th-century Nürnberg Gate, remains of old walls, 14th-century castle (now museum), and Gothic parish church with baroque onion-shaped spire. If you wish to see the colorful regional folk dress, visit the nearby village of Effeltrich on a church holiday, and particularly at Easter.

We enter Mittel-Franken (Middle Franconia) at the university town of Erlangen, which consists of two parts: the Old Town and the New Town. The latter was built by Margrave Christian Ernst of Bayreuth in a grid street pattern around his castle-palace for Huguenot refugees from France, who found haven here towards the end of the 17th century. Among the eminent sons of Erlangen was Simon Ohm, famed German discoverer of the electrical unit named after him, the ohm. Important engineering and electrical industries are also located here.

Nürnberg

The principal city of Franconia and second only to Munich in Bavaria, Nürnberg was a great imperial city dating back at least to the year 1040. Nürnberg owed its supremacy to a number of factors: its position at the crossroads of all important trade routes of medieval Europe, the genius of its citizens, and the favor of the emperrors—Charles IV in the Golden Bull of 1356, a medieval constitution of the Holy Roman Empire of the German Nation transforming it from a centralized monarchy into an aristocratic federation, ruled that every emperor should convoke his first diet in Nürnberg.

Nürnbergers were renowned for their intellect and their skill at handicrafts. Its citizens included Minnesingers—among them Tannhäuser, who was neither an invention of German sagas nor of Richard Wagner, but who lived for a while in Nürnberg in the 13th century—and particularly Mastersingers, whose center was Nürnberg and whose most famous member was Hans Sachs, a shoemaker-poet, who was born and died in the city, and who combined intellectual power and manual skill.

In the field of the arts Nürnberg can boast that it was the birthplace of: Albrecht Dürer, probably Germany's greatest painter; Michael Wolgemut, another painter, in whose atelier Dürer learned to paint; one of the greatest woodcarvers, Veit Stoss; one of the greatest German sculptors in stone, Adam Kraft; and one of the greatest workers in brass, Peter Vischer—the last particularly fitting, since the development of brass founding was one of this prolific city's inventions. The first pocket watch, the gunlock, gun casting, mechanical toys, the clarinet, are some of the other Nürnberg inventions. The first geographical globe (now in the Germanic Museum) was also made here by Martin Behaim in 1490–92 before Columbus, using the nautical tables of the Nürnberg astronomer Regiomontanus, had demonstrated by his voyage that the world was a globe. The city is still at it: the German Inventors Exposition is held here every September. A toy fair is held every year in February.

Nürnberg does not have the elegant, aristocratic air of many German provincial cities that were the seat of princes and bishops. It has always been a democratic place, ruled by the genius of its citizens and reflecting in its streets and comfortable houses their ideas of how to live. Food figures largely here, and you will find many budget restaurants and beer halls specializing in bratwürst, Nürnberg grilled sausages. Have a nibble on the local gingerbread, too.

EXPLORING NÜRNBERG

Although wartime air raids almost totally wiped out the genuinely and extraordinarily medieval Nürnberg, the clever and faithful reconstruction of the principal centuries-old buildings has to a large extent restored to the city its former air. Nürnberg is a double city, whose two halves are separated by the Pegnitz River. During nearly 150 years of its historic existence, the parts led a separate life. Each was enclosed by its own walls, and not until the end of the first quarter of the 14th century were they united in a single strong defensive unit, still almost intact, with their double walls, their moats and their great gates and watch towers. Possibly the Number One attraction in Nürnberg is the walk around the circuit of the walls, and the floodlighting of the old buildings, which you must not miss and which occurs daily during the summer season and during the famous Christmas Market period as well as when the frequent congresses and conventions are held. A good place to begin and end this circuit is the castle-fortress (Burg).

The proud Burg sprawls along a sandstone cliff, dominating the city from above. Architecturally and historically it is subdivided into three groups: the 12th–16th-century Imperial Castle (Kaiserburg), on the western part of the rock, with the Imperial Hall, Knights' Hall, suites, the Renaissance double chapel (above and below), the courtyard, 165-foot well, and Sinnwellturm, the round watch tower that offers an excellent view of the city; in the center, the remains of the earliest Burgrave's Castle (Burggrafenburg), with the pentagonal tower and the bailiff's house; the Kaiserstallung (Imperial Stables) in the eastern part of the fortress, with several rows of dormer windows on its high roof, built as a granary in the 15th century, rebuilt after the last war and converted into a youth hostel, connected with the pentagonal tower of the middle section of the Burg.

Below the western part of the fortress is a picturesque small square with the Tiergärtner Gate and Albrecht-Dürer-Haus, a fine example of an old Nürnberg burgher's house with original interiors and a collection of originals and copies of works by Albrecht Dürer, who lived in this house from 1509 until his death in 1528. Following the Bergstrasse downhill, we come first to Dürer Square with a monument to the painter and then to St. Sebaldus Church (now Protestant) built in the 13th century, whose style represents the transition from late Roman-

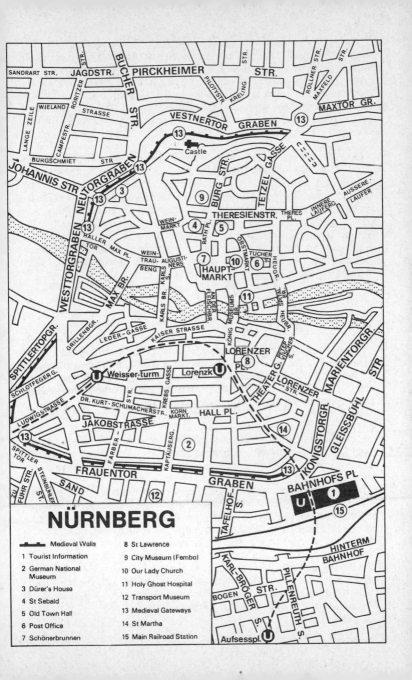

NÜRNBERG

- ━━━ Medieval Walls
- 1 Tourist Information
- 2 German National Museum
- 3 Dürer's House
- 4 St Sebald
- 5 Old Town Hall
- 6 Post Office
- 7 Schönerbrunnen
- 8 St Lawrence
- 9 City Museum (Fembo)
- 10 Our Lady Church
- 11 Holy Ghost Hospital
- 12 Transport Museum
- 13 Medieval Gateways
- 14 St Martha
- 15 Main Railroad Station

esque to Gothic. It contains the famous Sebaldusgrab, a masterpiece in brass created by Peter Vischer and his sons; resting curiously on the shells of snails this shrine supports a silver coffin with relics of St. Sebaldus and is ornamented with scores of realistic figures, including those of the Twelve Apostles and of the artist himself. Among other artistic treasures in the interior of the church are several works by Veit Stoss and on the exterior side of the east choir is a sculptured tomb by Adam Kraft.

Opposite the church on one side is the parish house, with a magnificent Gothic bay window, and on the other side is the Rathaus, with underground dungeons hewn out of rock around 1340. In the court square of the Rathaus stands the Gänsemännchenbrunnen (Gooseman's Fountain) with a figure of a 16th-century peasant taking two geese to the market, cast in bronze by Pankraz Labenwolff about 1550. Nearby in Theresienstrasse is a monument to the navigator Martin Behaim and in the Burgstrasse is the Fembohaus, a dignified patrician dwelling from the Renaissance period, presently housing the Old City Museum.

The Hauptmarkt

Between the Rathaus and the Pegnitz River is the main square (Hauptmarkt), with the 60-foot, spire-like Schöner Brunnen fountain ornamented with 40 statues, and the 14th-century redstone Frauenkirche, both in Gothic style. The Frauenkirche contains the Tucher-Altar, a fine example of 15th-century Nürnberg painting, and statuary by Kraft. Under the little tower facing the main square is the Männleinlaufen, an artistic mechanical clock of 1509, that performs every noon and represents Emperor Charles IV receiving homage from the seven Electors. The traditional Christkindlmarkt for Christmas tree decorations and toys is held on the main square in front of the church every December.

Near the Frauenkirche, bridging one arm of the river that forms an island here, is the picturesque Holy Ghost Hospital (Heilig-Geist-Spital), founded in 1331, with several wooden-galleried inner courtyards, among them the Crucifixion Court with the group by Adam Kraft. On the square in front of it is the Hans Sachs Monument. A few bridges downstream is a romantic sight that should not be missed: the Henkersteg (Hangman's Bridge) leading to the 14th-century Water Tower (also called Hangman's Tower) which is connected with the late Gothic, half-timbered Weinstadel (Wine Storehouse), originally built as a hospital and now containing a students' hostel.

St. Lorenz Church

Proceeding from the main square over the Museum Bridge, we come to the Gothic St. Lorenz Church, the most beautiful in Nürnberg. The building was started in the 13th century, finished in the 15th, severely damaged during the last war and rebuilt with the generous help of Rush Kress of New York, whose ancestors emigrated from this area to America in 1752. Its Rosette window is one of the most famous in Germany, and it possesses two other particularly prized works of art, the *Angelic Salutation* by Veit Stoss, carved in wood and suspended from the vaulting, and the Tabernacle by Adam Kraft, chiseled from stone and including the figure of the artist himself. The restoration of the church was possible only because the pillar with the Tabernacle remained standing after the air raids, supporting part of the choir superstructure, a fact which is today considered a miracle by many inhabitants of Nürnberg.

Outside the church is Tugendbrunnen (Fountain of Virtue), with the jets of water springing occasionally from the breasts of the dignified female figure representing six main virtues, and topped by a statue representing Justice. Opposite the church and the fountain is the Gothic, tower-like Nassau House, a patrician city dwelling whose cellar and lower floors originate from the 13th century. About halfway between the St. Lorenz Church and the powerful Königstor is the dormer-windowed Mauthalle (Customs Hall), first built as a granary around 1500. Near Königstor is a reconstructed medieval craftsmen's courtyard called "Alt Nürnberg," where you can watch blacksmiths, potters, bakers, silversmiths, and even coin minters at work in summer. Nearby is the 14th-century St. Martha Church where the Mastersingers had their singing school from 1578 to 1620.

Not far from the Mauthalle is the Kornmarkt, the former grain market square, where the main entrance into the Germanic National Museum is located. This museum is unique in Germany and its exhibits represent the development of the art and culture of all German lands from the earliest times until the 19th century. Its several buildings include the former 600-year-old Carthusian monastery and church.

Proceeding west from Kornmarkt we come to the reconstructed Gothic St. Jakob's Church and to Ludwigstrasse with the White Tower, also rebuilt, and beyond it the fountain with a bronze figure of Peter Henlein, the pocket-watch inventor.

At the other end of Ludwigstrasse are the Spittlertor and the Fürther Gates and beyond them the Fürther Strasse takes us to five-mile-distant Fürth, virtually an extension of Nürnberg but a city in its own right, old industrial tradition and an interesting City Hall (an imitation of Florence's Palazzo Vecchio).

In the northern outskirts of Nürnberg are Neunhof with a moated castle, opened on summer weekends as a hunting museum, and Kraftshof with a fortified 16th-century church, destroyed during the last war and restored mainly through the great financial help of the same Rush Kress who contributed to the rebuilding of St. Lorenz Church in Nürnberg; his ancestors had founded the church in Kraftshof.

Between Nürnberg and the Danube

East of Nürnberg are medieval Altdorf (once a university town) Lauf, with an interesting moated castle; and Hersbruck, with old gates, the Shepherds' Museum, and a collection of 50,000 hand-painted lead soldiers. Southwest of Nürnberg, on the Castle Road, is Heilsbronn with the Gothic Minster, once a Cistercian abbey church, furnished with many works of art, particularly the Gothic altars and stained-glass windows. Beyond Heilsbronn is Ansbach, founded over 1,200 years ago and now known as the city of Franconian rococo. The splendid Margrave's Palace, built in Italian baroque style and containing interiors furnished in luxurious rococo, is the best preserved 18th-century castle-palace in Franconia, with the single exception of the Residenz in Würzburg.

Turning off the Castle Road we first come to the medieval walled town of Wolframs-Eschenbach, birthplace of famed Minnesinger Wolfram von Eschenbach, the author of *Parzival*. Then we proceed to Gunzenhausen, with medieval towers and the remains of the Roman limes; Ellingen, with the impressive castle-palace of the German Order; Weissenburg, another medieval walled town whose Ellinger Gate is particularly admired and which also has the remains of a Roman fort; and to the nearby 16th-century fortress of Wülzburg, where deer are kept in the dry moat.

South of Weissenburg is Treuchtlingen in the narrow, green Altmühl Valley, whose most romantic scenery extends from here to Kelheim. Its most interesting town is Eichstätt, situated some 15 miles west of the Nürnberg–Munich autobahn. A bishopric for 1,200 years, its many fine buildings include the baroque Residenz, former residential palace of the prince-bishops, and the cathedral, with Romanesque towers, mostly Gothic interior, and a baroque façade. On an elevation near the city is the massive Willibaldsburg fortress. In the limestone quarries in and around nearby Solnhofen are found some of the best and most interesting bird and fish fossils in Europe, among them *archaeopteryx lithographica*, which, when first found in 1861, caused quite a stir in scientific circles since it was the first example of a transition from reptile to bird. Today it is in the British Museum in London, but five further specimens found in the Altmühl Valley—including the so-called "Eichstätt Specimen" found in Solnhofen in 1951 and perhaps the best specimen of its kind—can be seen in the recently opened Jura Museum in the Bishops' Residence on Willibaldsburg.

At the old fortress town of Ingolstadt we cross the Danube and enter southern Bavaria. Among its many fine buildings note the Gothic Liebfrauenmünster (Basilica of Our Lady), with a magnificent Renaissance-style stained-glass window; the rococo Maria Victoria Church by the Asam brothers, a marvel of intricate decoration, including a large ceiling painting; the 13th-century Herzogkasten, the only remaining building of the Old Castle; the New Castle, with late Gothic interiors, and today the Bavarian Army Museum. A good portion of the 14th- to 15th-century city walls has been preserved, together with over 40 towers and gates, among them notably the elaborate 14th-century tower-gate known as the Kreuztor. Also well worth seeing are the St. Moritz and Minoriten Churches. The Nürnberg–Munich autobahn passes through the eastern suburbs of Ingolstadt.

PRACTICAL INFORMATION FOR FRANCONIA

 HOTELS AND RESTAURANTS. During the Wagner Festival, hotels in Bayreuth are crowded and rates are considerably higher than at other seasons; reserve rooms well in advance. The summer and winter skiing resorts of Fichtelgebirge, Rhön and Frankenwald offer price-worthy vacation possibilities, including apartments and bungalows.

The best known all-Franconian pork dish is probably *Schlachtplatte* (butcher's platter) consisting of several types of fresh sausages and meat. It can be served with *Fränkische Klösse,* the Franconian version of dumplings. In addition to Nürnberg, whose culinary specialties we describe separately, Coburg also produces excellent sausages, and its ham is perhaps even better. When you are in Würzburg, don't forget to order *Meefischli,* very small fish from the Main River, fried and eaten whole. Würzburg also offers a number of other excellent river fish, but the best trout come from the Wiesent River in Fränkische Schweiz and the best carp from Weissenstadt in Fichtelgebirge.

Excellent dry white wines come from the banks of the central Main section, particularly in the Würzburg area. Try *Würzburger Stein, Würzburger Neuberg, Escherndorfer Lump, Iphöfener Julius-Echter-Berg, Randersackerer Teufelskeller,* or *Rödelseer Kuchenmeister.*

Franken also produces many good beers; those of Hof are among the best known locally, while the dark *Echtes Kulmbacher* is drunk all over the world. Another beer specialty of Kulmbach is *Bayrisches G'frornes* (Bavarian frozen beer); it is made with a frozen extract and has the highest alcoholic content of all beers. Other special types of beer are: *Rauchbier* of Bamberg, with a smoked flavor as the name implies, and *Back'nbier* (baker's beer) of Bayreuth, which is brewed by bakers as a sideline and is supposed to acquire a special bakery taste.

Among harder drinks there is *Sechsämtertropfen,* a bittersweet fruit liqueur from Wunsiedel; similar in taste are *Fichtelgebirgskräuter,* made from the mountain herbs of Fichtelgebirge, and *Streitberger Bitter,* from Streitberg in Fränkische Schweiz.

Abenberg. The peaceful castle hotel *Burg Abenberg* (M) has 24 beds, large restaurant and cellar wine tavern, swimpool, garden terrace, panoramic view.

Ansbach. Hotels: *Am Drechselgarten,* all rooms with bath or shower, terrace-café with fine view, wine tavern and nightclub, reasonable. *Christl* and *Platengarten* are (M).

Aschaffenburg. Hotels: *Post* (E), Goldbacher Str. 19, 124 beds, excellent dining in several atmospheric rooms, indoor swimming. *Aschaffenburger Hof* (M), Frohsinnstr. 11, 130 beds.

An atmospheric old hostelry is *Wilder Mann* (M), at the Main bridge, with 80 beds and delicious Main fish and Franken wine in its wood-paneled Stuben.

Restaurants: *Schlossweinstuben* (M), in Schloss Johannisburg, wine tavern with view of Main Valley. About 3 miles west is *Mainparksee* (E), also a few moderate rooms with bath.

Bad Brückenau. *Kurhotel Bad Brückenau* (E), Armand-von-Busek-Str., first class and quiet. *Staatliche Kurhäuser,* a number of quiet and comfortable jointly run spa hotels ranging from (M) to (E); tennis, outdoor pool. The country-estate-style *Pilsterhof* (I), 5 miles out, surrounded by forested hills, has 30 beds and tasty food prepared from own farm products.

Bad Kissingen. Hotels (most open only Apr–Oct.): *Steigenberger Kurhaushotel* (L), all 83 rooms with bath, cure facilities, rustic-antique *Kissinger Stüble,* bar and garden terrace.

Both (E) are—*Das Ballinghaus,* Martin-Luther-Str. 3, 70 rooms, indoor pool, thermal baths; *Kurhotel 2002,* Von-der-Tann-Str. 18, new, with cure and various sport facilities.

All (M) are—*Diana,* Bismarckstr. 40, 75 rooms, most with bath, indoor pool; *Sonnenhügel,* above town, recent, in large grounds, many sports facilities, also apartments. *Vier Jahreszeiten,* Bismarckstr. 3–7. *Fürst Bismarck,* Bismarckstr. 90. café, indoor pool.

Am Ballinghain (I), Schillerstr. 1, on the outskirts. Quiet.

Restaurants: Spielbank Restaurant, *Le Jeton* (E), at the Luitbold Park near casino. Very comfortable, excellent food with dancing from 6 P.M. Cafe open from 2 P.M.

Ratskeller (E), in the Rathaus, music and dancing in the evening. *Weinstube zum Rebstock* (M), Kurhausstr. 14.

Bratwurstglöckle (M), Grabengasse 6, Franconian sausages, 10 kinds of beer. Afternoon music and dancing in the evening at *Kurgarten-Café* in spa park.

Bamberg. Hotels: *Bamberger Hof,* Schönleinsplatz 4, 70 beds, first class superior. *National, Straub, Alte Post* (all near station), and *Altenburgblick* (garni), with fine view, Panzerleite 59, are (M). The quiet *Evengelisches Hospiz,* Promenadestr. 3, is (M); *Roter Ochse* (I), Untere Königstr. 13.

Restaurants: *Messerschmitt* (M), Lange Str. 41, good food and wines (game and fish specialties), garden terrace. *Schlenkerla* (I), Dominikanerstr. 6, old-style tavern in 15th-century house, serving Rauchbier (smoked beer). *Theaterrose* (M), Schillerplatz 7, garden. *Scheiner* (M), Katzenberg 2, wine tavern. *Steinenes Haus* (M), Lange Str. 8, local fish dishes. *Michaelsberg* (M), on hill of same name, beer restaurant, café, terrace view.

A pleasant excursion is to the brewery restaurant *Windfelder* (M), on a small lake at Stegaurach about 4 miles southwest; carp when in season (Sept.–April).

Bayreuth. Be sure to have *confirmed* ticket reservations before reserving hotel room. For room reservations, contact the Bayreuth Tourist Office, Luitpoldplatz 9.

Hotels near station: 98-bed *Bayerischer Hof,* roof-garden evening restaurant, *Reichsadler* (garni); *Goldener Hirsch,* and *Haus Weihenstephan,* all (M). In the same category are the quiet *Am Hofgarten* (garni), Lisztstr. 6, and *Goldener Anker,* Opernstr. 2–6.

Zum Edlen Hirschen (I), Richard-Wagner-Str. 77.

Restaurants: *Eule* (M), Kirchg. 8, atmospheric, calls itself an artists' tavern. *Postei* (M), Friedrichstr. 15. *Wolffenżacher* (M), Badstr. 1. *Mohrenstube* (M), Mittelstr. 2, is an evening wine tavern with local color. Metropol (M), with view over city from ninth floor of Haus Deutscher Ring, has café and grill, evening dancing.

A very fine hostelry about 4 miles from Bayreuth is *Schloss Thiergarten* (E), a period-furnished castle hotel, excellent cuisine and well-stocked wine cellar, bar, large garden terrace. To reach it leave autobahn at Bayreuth-Süd, then follow the signs.

About 16 miles south in Pegnitz is *Pflaum's Posthotel,* in the same family since 1787, fine restaurant, beer tavern *Posthalterstuben,* attractive bar, all rooms with bath and TV, (M–E).

Bischofsheim. About 3½ miles north is *Jagdschloss Holzberg* (I), a hunting castle with rustic but atmospheric accommodations: no electricity; candlelight and oil lamps only. Hunting, fishing, riding.

Coburg. Hotels: All (M) are—*Goldene Traube,* Am Viktoriabrunnen 2, *Der Festungshof,* a pleasant, manor-like house next to fortress, with fine restaurant and café-terrace; *Goldener Anker,* Roseng. 14, indoor pool and roof terrace; and the quiet *Haus Blankenburg,* Rosenauer Str. 30, café-terrace; *Stadt Coburg,* Lossaustr. 12; *Coburger Tor,* Ketschendorferstr. has a fine restaurant.

A few km northeast is *Schloss Neuhof,* a reasonable castle-hotel with restaurant in the Knights Hall.

Restaurants: *Speisehaus Schröck* (M), Hahnweg 1, game and fish specialties, closed in June. (I–M) wine taverns: *Alt-Coburg* and *Weinstuben Pieper,* both in Steinweg; Künstler-Klause, Theaterplatz 4a; *Burgschänke* (I), at the fortress with view from the ramparts; *Lorely,* Herrngasse 14, south of town at the Zeughaus.

Hammelburg in Lower Franconia. Castle hotel *Schloss Saaleck* (M), on a hill above town, colorful restaurant with own wines, very quiet.

Hofheim in Lower Franconia. About 2 miles northeast is castle hotel *Bettenburg,* owned by the Barons of Truchsess since 1343. Swimpool, horseback riding, hunting and fishing possibilities, moderate.

In **Gossmannsdorf,** 2 miles southeast on the road B2, and in the country estate hotel *Landhaus Sulzenmühle* (M), quiet, with indoor pool, sauna and horseback riding.

Ingolstadt. Hotels: *Rappensberger* (M), Harderstr. 3, 170 beds, indoor pool, particularly comfortable.

The quiet *Bavaria,* Feldkirchner Str. 67, café and indoor pool; the 96-bed *Adler* (garni), Theresienstr. 22; and the newer 50-bed *Donau-Hotel,* Münchenerstr. 10, are all (I).

Near the autobahn exit the recent *Holiday Inn* (E) offers 125 modern rooms, all with bath, radio and TV; grill restaurant and attractive tavern; pool.

Restaurants: *Theater-Restaurant* (E), Schlosslände 1, with terrace and fine cuisine. *Schumann-Stuben* (M), Schumannstr. 21, courtyard dining in summer.

Lauenstein. Castle hotel *Burg Lauenstein* (I), reached by road No. 85 from Kronach. Built in 915, one of the best preserved medieval castles. Rooms furnished in authentic period style, 40 beds, restaurant in romantic setting, inexpensive.

Nürnberg. Hotels: The best hotels in the city are concentrated in the area around the railroad station and the nearby Königstrasse. Most are new or completely renovated.

Both (L) are—*Grand-Hotel,* Bahnhofstr. 1, has 220 beds, some suites, excellent cuisine in restaurant *Fürstenhof,* bar, café, 60-car garage; *Carlton,* Eilgutstr. 13, on other side of station, 175 beds, rooms with radio and TV, excellent restaurant, dancing in night bar.

(E) and farther away in the direction of the south entrance to the autobahn, is the *Crest Hotel,* Münchenerstr. 283, 90 rooms, all with bath or shower, *Puppengrill* restaurant, bar and nearby the *Atrium Hotel,* Münchenerstr. 25, 300 beds and pool, sauna, solarium and restaurant.

Also (E) are—*Merkur,* Pillenreuther Str. 1, behind main station, 142 rooms; *Am Sterntor,* Tafelhofstr. 8, in quiet location near station and shops, 120 rooms; *Victoria* (garni), Königstr. 80, off main station square, 64 rooms. *Novotel,* Münchenerstr. 340, 170 rooms, 234 beds.

All (M) are—*Kaiserhof,* Königstr. 39, near St. Lorenz Church, 100 beds, restaurant, café, and *Pfälzer Fass,* a colorful cellar wine tavern serving Pfalz wines and presided over by a huge barrel and picture of a saint; *Deutscher Hof,* Frauentorgraben 29, also in vicinity of main station, 80 beds, cozy *Holzkistl* restaurant; *Reichshof,* Johannesg. 16–20, in quiet, narrow street near Mauthalle, 65 rooms.

Also (M) are—*Am Hauptmarkt-Kröll,* on main square, Hauptmarkt 6, small but modern; *Schöner Brunnen* at No. 17; *Am Heideloffplatz,* Heideloffplatz 9, modern facilities; *Deutscher Kaiser,* Königstr. 55; all garni.

All (I–M) are—*Blaue Traube,* Johannisg. 22, near Mauthalle; *Drei Linden,* Äussere Sulzbacher Str. 1–3, in northeastern section of city on street leading to autobahn, 31 rooms.

Both (I) are—*Lorenz* (garni), Pfannenschmiedsg. 4, near St. Lorenz Church, 27 rooms; and the quiet *Tiergarten,* near the zoo, with 62 rooms, most with bath or shower; restaurant closed in the evening.

Restaurants: Best known among the Nürnberg culinary specialties are, of course, the delicious *Nürnberger Bratwürstel,* small, fresh, grilled sausages which are eaten by the dozen or half dozen and are served with sauerkraut, mustard or horse-radish. Another genuine Nürnberg dish is the spicy *Ochsen-maulsalat,* a cold meat salad made with onions, spices, oil, and vinegar. A favored fish course is carp, either boiled or fried, eaten only in the months with an "r". Nürnberg is also well known for the production of delicately-flavored cakes and cookies, such as *Nürnberger Lebkuchen* (gingerbread), chocolate-coated almond cakes, and various macaroons, wafers and *Pfeffernüsse* (cookies flavored with ginger). A selection of eating and drinking places follows (see also under Hotels).

Very atmospheric (M–E) are—*Essigbrätlein* am Weinmarkt 3, near the Dürer Haus, with garden terrace. *Waffenschmied,* Obere Schmieg. 22, period furniture, terrace; specialties include Franconian potato soup and entrecôte steak.

Nassauer Keller, the deep 13th-century cellar of the Nassau House; try chicken, duck, or the pork cutlet with egg and tomato; good wines, music.

Goldenes Posthorn, at the St. Sebaldus Church, founded in 1498, once frequented by Albrecht Dürer and Hans Sachs, international grill specialties washed down by German and French wines.

Walliser Kanne, Königstorgraben, Swiss specialties.

Meistersingerhalle, Münchener Str. 21, in the southeast suburbs, garden terrace. *Ranbritter,* Untere Schmiedgasse 4. Another deep cellar in an ancient house. Specialties are mixed grill, salmon.

All (M) are—*Marientorzwinger* at the Marien Gate of the city wall, not far from main station, also café; *Ratsstuben,* Rathausplatz 1, comfortable; *Patrizier,* Pfannenschmiedsg. 1; *Zum Löblein,* Bayreuther Str. 36, grill-bar and Schwarz-wald-Stube, good wine list. *Helilig-Geist-Spital,* Spitalg. 12, heavy wooden furnishings and over 100 wines from all German districts; *Kronfleischküche* (also small hotel), Kaiserstr. 22, on two floors with windows on Regnitz River. The restaurant in *Hotel Tiergarten* (the Zoo) is pleasant for food and surroundings.

Nürnberg sausages and local color: *Bratwurst-Herzle,* Brunnengasse 11; *Bratwurst-Häusle* at Rathausplatz 1; *Bratwurst-Friedl,* Hauplatz; *Bratwurst-Glöcklein,* in the Alt Nürnberg Waffenhof near Königstor; *Zunftstube,* Obstmarkt 5 and the famous *Historische Bratwurstküche im Handwerkerhof.*

Beer restaurants: *Mautkeller,* Königstr. 60, music on weekends; *Herrenbräu,* at Hauptmarkt, serving Humbser beer; *Tucher-Bräustübl,* Kartausertor 1. *Schlenkerla,* Bergstr. 31, smoked beer and sausages.

Two fine restaurants in the suburb of Grossreuth are the colorful *Zur Grünen Weintraube* (M), in an old Franconian half-timbered house, pleasant garden, closed Aug., and *Gasthaus Rottner* (M).

CAFES AND PASTRIES: *Kröll,* Hauptmarkt 6, on the second floor, with large terrace with unique view of the main square area. *Porten,* Luitpoldstr. 15, music and dancing; *Corso,* Klaragasse 1, day café; *Berger,* Königstr. 70, primarily for pastries; *Konditorei Scheuermann,* Winklerstr. 29, excellent pastries, shipping Lebkuchen anywhere.

Rabenstein, in Fränkische Schweiz. Both (M) are—*Berghaus Rabenstein,* a 12th-century castle hotel, atmospheric restaurant with open fireplace, rococo garden; *Hotel Linde,* 80 beds, very quiet with fine view, indoor and outdoor pools, solarium and terrace restaurant.

Riedenburg. Castle hotel *Burg Eggersberg* (M), 2½ miles northwest, with beautiful view over Altmühl Valley. Former hunting castle of Bavarian dukes, it dates from the 9th century. Antique furnishings, colorful tavern; fishing and riding; concerts. Also (M) and very comfortable, if small, *Tachensteinerhof,* peaceful surroundings at Burgstr. 26, 30 beds, pleasant garden restaurant.

Weissenburg. "Romantik Hotel" *Rose* (E), opposite Rathaus, inn dating back to 1625; 50 beds, baroque breakfast room, elegant gourmet restaurant, and Ratskeller, serving Franken and Baden-Württemburg wines.

Wunsiedel. Hotels: best is *Kronprinz von Bayern,* with noted restaurant, moderate. *Bayerischer Hof* and *Weisses Lamm,* both small, are (I).
Berggasthof Waldlust (M), a pleasant inn with garden and glassed-in terrace, on Luisenburg hill, 2 miles south. *Jagdschloss Fahrenbühl* (I), 20 miles north, riding and rustic castle atmosphere.

Würzburg. Hotels: *Rebstock* (E), Neubaustr. 7, a neo-baroque building with modern facilities, all rooms with bath or shower, colorful wine tavern.
All (M) are—*Schoss Steinburg,* sited on the famous vineyard hill, outdoor pool, terrace and weekend dancing; *Franziskaner,* garni, on Franziskanerplatz, with fine *Klosterschänke* restaurant; the modernized *Walfisch,* Am Pleidenturm 5, front rooms with view of river and fortress; *Amberger* (garni), Ludwigstr. 17, near city theater; the simple *Schönborn* (garni), Herzogenstr. 2; *Russ,* Wolfhartsg. 1, with good restaurant, garage.
Among (I) hotels: *Luitpoldbrücke,* near Luitpold bridge at Pleechertorstr. 26; *Gasthof Stadt Mainz,* Semmelstr. 39, with good restaurant (Franconian dishes, fine wines and smoked beer).
About 5 miles southwest of city is quiet *Erbachshof* (E), a converted estate manor house, 40 beds, most rooms with bath or shower, first class superior.
In Biebelried, about 7 miles east, *Gasthaus Leicht* (M), in same family since 1469, tops in pleasant eating.
Restaurants (all with excellent local wines): *Burggaststätte* (M), Marienberg Fortress, with terrace, fine view and a candlelit tower room; *Ratskeller,* Langgasse 1, with antique furniture, terrace and extra beer tavern. *Schiffbäuerin* (M), Katzeng, 7, colorful, specializing in local fish, including Meerfischli.

Bratwursterzle (M), Theaterstr. 7, open 11 A.M. through midnight; *Schnabel* (M), Haugerpfarrg. 10, freshwater fish from glass tank and own butchery.

Himmelsleiter (M), Katharineng. 3, Franconian dishes; *Silberner Karpfen* (M), Spitalg. 5, Meefischli and other fish; *Buhl'sche Weinstuben* (M), am Dom; *Martinsklause* (M), Martinstr. 21, evening cellar restaurant; *Russ* (M), Wolfharsg. 1, for trout.

Maulaffenbäck (I), Maulharng. 9, snacks only, hangout of students and other wine drinkers.

Taverns serving wines from their own vineyards: *Bürgerspital,* Theaterstr. 19, old tavern with several levels, hidden corners and leather-aproned waiters; *Juliusspital,* Julius-promenade 19, simpler but as good on wine; *Hofkellerei Weinstuben* in a rebuilt annex of the Residenz Palace, rambling and with garden; *Stachel,* Gressengasse 1, near market square, founded in 1413.

Weinhaus Maulaffenbäck, Maulhardgasse 9, open from 8 A.M. until 10 in the evening, and guests are encouraged to bring their own picnic lunch, for which they receive plates and cutlery from this quaint tavern's small kitchen.

FRANCONIA. By Car. This is the area of wine and culture in which the car will be used from one point of special interest to another, rather than in its own right. Situated in the center of Germany, this mild, easy motoring country has what might be described as sensible roads, not too hilly, many of them designated "scenic." Although driving among vineyards quickly palls, the region is studded with castles, and small towns full of art riches.

Nürnberg. One could say that all roads lead to Nürnberg rather than Rome: they also lead on. The north-south autobahn E6 enters West Germany near Hof and goes to Nürnberg, Ingolstadt and Munich. It is the best way to get to Münich, and therefore the playgrounds of Bavaria, in spite of the fact that the lower road via Stuttgart and Augsburg seems a better bet. All the lorry drivers act on that assumption. To the northwest the E5 autobahn leads to Frankfurt and Wörzburg, while to the southeast it goes to Regensburg and the Austrian border. Nürnberg itself has an inner ring-road which is nearly all dual carriageway but not quite, so you need to remain alert. Nürnberg also has an outer one running from the southeast to the northwest, clockwise, which assists drivers to return to the autobahn from the city center. The inner road encircles the original town, which is where tourists want to be. There are 14 car parks within it, and a few more just outside. A good town map is essential because virtually all the streets are one-way. People who don't want to visit the place can ride by it on autobahns 3, 6 or 9.

MUSIC AND THEATER. Bad Kissingen. Seasonal events include performances by visiting opera and theatrical companies in *Kurtheater,* concerts by visiting orchestras in *Regentenbau,* daily concerts by Kurorchester in *Wandelhalle* and spa park.

Bamberg. The home of the famous Bamberger Symphoniker, one of the top German orchestras. Symphonic concerts are given in *Zentral-Saal* and *Kulturraum,* several chamber music ensembles perform in the Imperial Hall and the Rose Garden of the New Residence and in the Böttingerhaus.

Bayreuth. The home of Wagner's *Festspielhaus* (Festival Theater) and the site of the famous Wagner Festival from late July through August. Franconian Festival Week of baroque music is staged in late spring in the baroque Margrave's Opera House. Bookings can be made through the *Bayreuther Festspiele,* Postfach 2320, 8580 Bayreuth 2.

Coburg. Opera, operetta and plays in *Landestheater.* Outdoor performances in summer at the fortress. Also concert season and during summer organ concerts in St. Moritz Church. **Schweinfurt.** *Stadttheater* for plays and opera.

Nürnberg. *Opernhaus,* Richard-Wagner-Platz, opera and operetta. Next to it is *Schauspielhaus,* where drama and comedy are performed. *Neues Theater,* Luitpoldstrasse, experimental and avant-garde plays, *Stadttheater* of Fürth, neighbor of Nürnberg, opera, operetta and plays. Nürnberg is the home of the *Nürnberger Philharmoniker, Fränkisches Landesorchester* (Franconian Orchestra) and several other orchestral and choral groups. Concerts are given in the ultramodern *Meistersingerhalle,* a large building with two concert halls, conference rooms, a restaurant and other premises, used also for congresses, conventions, balls and similar events. There are also concerts in the hall of the School of Music, organ concerts in St. Sebaldus and St. Lorenz churches. An important International Organ Week takes place every year in June. Summer outdoor concerts are given in the Schwedenhof of the Imperial Castle and in the courtyard of the Holy Ghost Hospital. Hans Sachs Plays are performed in Schwedenhof, the city park, and in Rosenau park on Wednesdays during summer months.

Schweinfurt. *Stadttheater* for plays and opera.

Würzburg. *Stadttheater,* for opera, operetta, and plays. In a gate tower in Sommerhausen near Würzburg is the small *Torturm-Theater* with its twin *Mitternachtsbühne,* both experimental type. City Philharmonic Orchestra; concerts given in Imperial Hall of the Residenz Palace, also in Huttensäle, Virchowstr. 2, and Staatskonservatorium. There is a Mozart festival in September.

 MUSEUMS. Ansbach. *Kreis- und Stadtmuseum* contains local exhibits, especially porcelain from the Ansbach factories.

Aschaffenburg. *Museum der Stadt,* Stiftsplatz, fine collection of art and handicrafts, notable pieces including Riemenschneider's wood carving of St. Joseph and Rembrandt's *John the Baptist.*

Bad Winsheim. *Fränkische Freiland Museum* in Fischgrund near Bad Windsheim, is, as its name implies, an "open-air" museum. Still under construction, this museum with a difference is a collection of reconstructed typical farm buildings, village inns, windmills and peasants' cottages of architectural significance of the last centuries in and around Franconia. Each building is being reconstructed exactly according to plan and museum objects will be mainly those buildings of cultural-historical significance of the region threatened with demolition or not under protection of the preservation of monuments' act. The museum layout nestles on gently undulating ground just south of the old town of Bad Windsheim, bordered by the rivers Alter- and Neuer Aisch. To complete the setting a large goldfish pond and small reservoir are planned and the entire concept is designed to take the visitor back in time and give a firsthand insight into how the farmhouse and farm life of the peasants who lived there has developed down through the centuries.

Bamberg. *Diözesan-Museum,* Domkapitelhaus, on the square in front of the Cathedral: unique collection of Byzantine and Roman textiles (for example the cloaks of Emperor Heinrich II and Empress Kindigunde, a complete papal regalia from the 11th century and the burial shroud of the holy Bishop Gunther from 1065); also sculptures, stained glass, Gothic hand-woven carpets and religious art from the Byzantine to Baroque periods.

Coburg. The museum in *Coburg Fortress* has medieval wood carvings, paintings by Lucas Cranach, armor, original letters of Martin Luther and a 300,000-piece graphic collection. *Natural History and Ethnological Museum,* with large bird collection.

Erlangen. *Städtische Sammlung,* Halstatt-period finds; *Heimatstuben,* with weapons, toys and collection of 17th-century stocking looms which belonged to the Huguenot refugees who settled in this area.

Ingolstadt. *Bavarian Army Museum* (formerly in Munich), in Herzogsschloss, Bavarian Army history from medieval times to 1870.

Nürnberg (for opening times consult the current issue of the official monthly program published by Verkehrsverein and obtainable at the tourist information office in the main station). *Germanic National Museum,* Kornmarkt 1. Paintings by Wolgemut, Dürer, Altdorfer, Cranach, Holbein, Baldung Grien; sculptures by Adam Kraft, Veit Stoss, Peter Vischer, Riemenschneider; 11th-century Golden Gospel of Echternach, the Gold Cone (a sort of helmet) from about 1000 B.C., found in the village of Etzelsdorf in the Nürnberg area; the first geographical globe made by Behaim in 1490–92 before the discovery of America; the first pocket watch made in 1430 by Peter Henlein; the original score of Richard Wagner's opera *The Mastersingers of Nürnberg;* weapons from the 14th to the 17th centuries, particularly the richly-ornamented armor; ancient farmhouse interiors and folk dress; clothes and furnishings from the baroque and rococo periods; a collection of over 1,100 musical instruments of all epochs.

Imperial Castle (Kaiserburg), the interior can be visited.

Albrecht-Dürer-Haus, Albrecht-Dürer-Strasse 39, mementos and works of Dürer, who lived here from 1509 to 1528.

Stadtmuseum, in Fembohaus, Burgstr. 15, city history and Nürnberg period house furnishings from 16th to 19th century.

Alt-Nürnberg, in the Waffenhof at Königstor. A "living" museum of medieval craftsmanship. Open mid-Mar. to end Nov.

Spielzeugmuseum, Karlstr. 13, a rich collection of toys and dolls from medieval times to present, in an old Renaissance house.

Gewerbemuseum, Gewerbemuseumsplatz 2, applied arts from many countries, ceramics and glass collection.

Verkehrsmuseum, Lessingstr. 6, traffic museum with models of old post coaches and railroad cars, history of communications, large collection of stamps; the model of the first German train, which began running between Nürnberg and Fürth in 1835 (another smaller-sized model is used for transportation within the zoo area).

Dungeons, under the Rathaus (Town Hall), hewn out of rock around 1340, called *Lochgefängnisse* (Hole Prisons).

Würzburg. (Most museums closed Mondays.) *Marienberg Fortress*, guided tours of interiors, summer 9–5, winter 10–4. *Mainfränkisches Museum*, at fortress; Riemenschneider sculptures, paintings, tapestries, world's oldest known clock (1380), prehistoric and early historic collections; summer 10–5, winter 10–4. *Residenz Palace*, interiors open summer 9–5, winter 10–4; garden open until dark. *Otto-Richter-Halle*, Maxstrasse, near Residenz, exhibitions of contemporary art. *Veitschöchheim Castle*, in vicinity, guided tours of interiors, summer 9–12 and 1–6, garden open until dark, closed in winter. The *Martin-von-Wagner Museum* of the University of Würzburg, bequeathed to the University by sculptor, painter, and art collector Martin von Wagner towards the end of the 18th century, in the Residenz Palace; excellent collection of ancient vases.

PARKS. Nürnberg is surrounded by parks and forests, offering pleasant short and long walks. One of the best known is *Volkspark Dutzendteich*, in the southeastern suburbs, with several ponds and beyond them the large area of the sports fields, including Stadion, Langwasserwiese, and Zeppelin Wiese where Hitler used to stage his huge parades. Northeast of Dutzendteich is the *Tiergarten*, a large zoo set in natural surroundings with the animals roaming in apparently complete freedom. In the eastern section of the city is *Wörhder Wiese*, pleasant meadows along the Pegnitz River. Northeast is *Stadtpark* (city park) and farther on in the same direction, the *Erlenstegen Forest*. In the west is *Rosenau*.

Bamberg. Between the two arms of the Regnitz is Bamberg's biggest nature park, The Hain, richly forested with rare trees.

SPORTS. Among the principal localities with **tennis** courts are, Ansbach, Aschaffenburg, Bad Kissingen, Bamberg, Bayreuth, Coburg, Ingolstadt, Nürnberg and Würzburg. **Golf** courses exist in Bad Kissingen, Ansbach, Bayreuth, and Nürnberg.

Horseback riding in Bad Kissingen at Reithausstr. 1 and in Bamberg at the riding stadium (Reitstadion), both also indoors; in Würzburg contact the Reit- und Fahrverein and in Ansbach the riding school (Reitschule); saddle horses in Aschaffenburg, Erlangen, Ingolstadt and other places.

Bad Kissingen has a terraced **swimming** establishment with four pools. Indoor swimming pools are in Würzburg, Bamberg, Coburg and elsewhere, outdoor facilities in all resorts and larger towns. The best for **kayaking** is Main from Lichtenfels through Bamberg, Schweinfurt, Würzburg, Aschaffenburg to the confluence with Rhine below Frankfurt (slow current, 275 miles).

Many pleasant and rewarding **hiking** paths in Spessart, Rhön, Fichtelgebirge, Frankenwald, Hassberge and Steigerwald.

The Main River and its tributaries, especially Regnitz and Saale, are good **fishing** waters for pike, carp, perch, tench and eel. Fränkische Schweiz and Franken Alb have excellent trout waters.

The principal **winter sports** centers in Fichtelgebirge are Bischofsgrün, Alexanderbad, Bad Berneck, Warmensteinach and Wunsiedel; skiing also in the Rhön mountains and in Frankenwald—all are bargain ski areas.

The top place for **gliding** in all Germany is on Wasserkuppe in Rhön; other gliding fields at Saupurzel (north of Nürnberg), Greding in Altmühltal and Ebermannstadt in Fränkische Schweiz (last two with schools).

 USEFUL ADDRESSES. *Tourist Information:* Ansbach, Verkehrsamt; Aschaffenburg, Verkehrsverein, Weissenburger Str. 1; Bad Brückenau, Kurverwaltung in Rathaus; Bad Kissingen, Kurverein in Regentenbau; Bamberg, Verkehrsamt, Hauptwachstr. 16; Bayreuth, Verkehrsverein, Luitpoldplatz 7; Coburg, Fremdenverkehrsamt in Rathaus; Ingolstadt, Stadtverwaltung, Rathausplatz 4.

In Nürnberg, Verkehrsverein Nürnberg, in the central hall of the main railroad station, tel. 20–42–56, open Monday through Thursday 9 A.M. to 8 P.M., Friday and Saturday 9 A.M. to 9 P.M. (including room reservations, tickets for city tours, engagement of private guides). Guided city tours between May 1 and October 31 and during Christmas Market, starting from Hallplatz. During the rest of the year, tours can be arranged by taxi through the Verkehrsverein. Wunsiedel, Verkehrsamt, Marktplatz 6.

Würzburg, Fremdenverkehrsamt in the pavilion facing the main railroad station (also for room reservations) and in Haus zum Falken (also for guided city bus tours); boat trips on the Main from Am Alten Kranen.

Tourist Information Franken at the Spessart-Rasthaus Rohrbrunn on the Frankfurt–Nürnberg Autobahn (also room reservations). For the whole area: Fremdenverkehrsverband Nordbayern, D–85 Nürnberg 8, am Plärrer 14.

Travel agencies in Nürnberg: Amlitches Bayerisches Reisebüro (official), various travel services including transportation tickets and money exchange, with offices at main rail station, at Hauptmarkt, and Hallplatz 11. Hapag-Lloyd-Reisebüro, Hallplatz 5, also travel correspondent of American Express. Wagons-Lits in Konigstrasse.

Money change in Nürnberg: exchange office inside the main railroad station, weekdays 7:45 A.M. to 8 P.M., Sundays 9 A.M. to 12:30 P.M. and 6 P.M. to 8 P.M. *Taxi:* call 20555.

Information for motorists in Nürnberg: ADAC, Prinzregentenufer 7. *Parking garages* (day and night): Parkhaus am Sterntor, Parkhaus Adlerstrasse and Parkhaus Kussberger, Gleissbühlstr. 12. *Car hire:* Selbstfahrer Union (also Auto Europe), Augustinerstr; Hertz, Untere Grasersgasse 25.

MUNICH

A City Reborn

Munich (or München), the capital of Bavaria, is a big city and still growing. Only two German cities, Berlin and Hamburg, exceed it in size.

Munich is an old city. The earliest known document in which it was mentioned is dated 1158, so it must have been still earlier when the settlement from which it grew was founded by monks and called accordingly "zu den Mönchen"—which can be loosely translated "Monksville." Hence its name and the monk on its coat of arms.

Munich is an intellectual city and generally regarded as the most important cultural center of West Germany. It has some of the finest educational institutions in Germany, especially its university, where the chemist Justus von Liebig and the physicist Wilhelm Röntgen have been among the professors, its School of Art and its School of Engineering. Scholarship and the arts are further stimulated by the Bavarian

329

Academy of Science founded in 1759, and by the Bavarian Academy of Fine Arts. Its museums are famous. There is no finer scientific museum in Germany than Munich's Deutsches Museum, no completer display of crafts than in its Bavarian National Museum, no more splendid picture galleries than its Alte and Neue Pinakothek.

But Munich is also an industrial city. Everyone knows its most famous product—beer—but it is pre-eminent in other lines as well. In line with its cultural importance, it plays a leading role in printing and publishing, in the fashion industry and in movie making. It has optical and precision instrument factories, electrical industries as well as heavier outputs such as locomotives, trucks and machinery.

Munich was so badly bombed during the last war that it would not be much of an exaggeration to say that the pre-war city has disappeared. The old city lost three-quarters of its buildings, the city as a whole one-sixth, its inhabitants one-third of their homes. Yet today you can walk through Munich without being conscious of the damage, unless you are looking for it. Many old buildings have been restored and the new ones, particularly in the old city, and with only a few glaring exceptions, have been built in a style sufficiently discreet to blend into their surroundings. Munich has also rediscovered the pedestrian, and created the pedestrian zone with trees, flowers and peaceful spots to take a rest. The largest is in the heart of the old city between Karlstor and Marienplatz, to the east, extending westwards across the road from Karlsplatz along the Schutzenstr. to the station (*Hauptbahnhof*).

EXPLORING MUNICH

The first piece of advice that should be given to the first-time visitor to Munich is not to work too hard at the job of seeing the city—not because there's so much to see that it's easy to wear yourself out, though that's true enough, but because you can easily miss the atmosphere of the Bavarian capital if you go at your sightseeing too doggedly. The soul of Munich is to be met with in the beer halls and beer gardens. If you don't spend a fair proportion of your time in good weather sitting out of doors with a stein of sound Munich brew within easy reach, or in bad weather in a beer hall, surrounded by dark paneling, leaded glass, colorful tiles, and large doses of *Stimmung* and *Gemütlichkeit,* then you're missing Munich. In the intervals you can go sightseeing.

As you leave the large central railroad station through the front exit (the two side entrances, however, are the ones to be used for access to and from the railway trains) you find yourself on the railroad station square. From here, two busy streets and a pedestrian mall (Schützenstr.) will take you into the heart of Munich, all of them converging on the square popularly called Stachus and officially Karlsplatz. Over the next three years, the entire area between the Main Station and the Town Hall Square (Marienplatz) is to be converted into a pedestrian mall. At the corner of this square and Prielmayerstrasse, one of the three streets mentioned, stands the gray Palace of Justice, which suffered severely from air raids but after rebuilding regained its impressive appearance. On one side, Stachus square continues into the broad shopping avenue called Sonnenstrasse, which ends at Sendlingertor Platz, while on the other side it merges with Lenbach Platz, adorned with the Wittelsbach Fountain, representing the destructive and beneficial powers of water. The chief above-ground landmark of Karlsplatz is the Karlstor, one of the old city gates.

In all, the fortifications of the old city of Munich between the end of the 13th and the end of the 19th centuries had a total of seven city gates: Neuhauser Tor (present-day Karlstor), Kosttor (between Maximilian and Prinzregentenstr., demolished in 1879), Einlasstor (at the crossroads of Rosental-Blumenstr., demolished in 1824), Sendlinger Tor, Angertor (at the southern end of the city on the site where today the Marionettentheater in the Blumenstr. stands. Demolished in 1871), Isartor and Schwabinger Tor (on the square in front of the Feldherrnhalle at Odeonsplatz, demolished in 1817 to make way for the extension of the Ludwigstr). The Karlstor, or Neuhauser Tor, was first built in 1302 and in addition to its two smaller side towers boasted a large central clock-tower which, following an unfortunate gunpowder explosion, had to be demolished in 1857, thus giving the Karlstor the appearance it has today. The two additional remaining city gates, Isartor and Sendlinger Tor will be described in the following pages.

In late 1970 another important landmark was added below ground: a large shopping area reached by numerous stairways and escalators from the square and the neighboring street corners. At Karlsplatz begins a broad promenade first called Neuhauserstrasse and then Kaufingerstrasse, which is perhaps Germany's most attractive pedestrian mall, leading through the old city all the way to the heart of Munich at Marienplatz. Sidewalk beer gardens, flowers and fountains, and occasional benches for loafing and resting make this one of Munich's latest attractions. Continuing from Marienplatz, through the arcade of the old Rathaus, the street changes its name again—to Tal—and, no longer traffic-free, meanders on to another gate of the now extinct city wall circuit, the Isartor.

The Isartor is the only significant city gate of Munich remaining today in much the same form as originally built in 1337. The bridge over the city moat was flanked by two towers to the fore, and at the

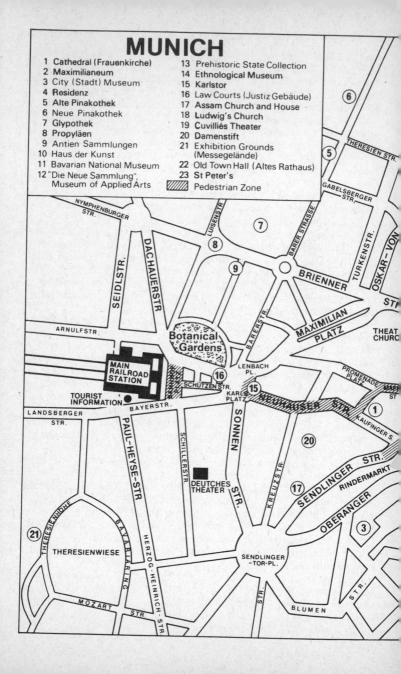

MUNICH

1 Cathedral (Frauenkirche)
2 Maximilianeum
3 City (Stadt) Museum
4 Residenz
5 Alte Pinakothek
6 Neue Pinakothek
7 Glypothek
8 Propyläen
9 Antien Sammlungen
10 Haus der Kunst
11 Bavarian National Museum
12 "Die Neue Sammlung",
   Museum of Applied Arts
13 Prehistoric State Collection
14 Ethnological Museum
15 Karlstor
16 Law Courts (Justiz Gebäude)
17 Assam Church and House
18 Ludwig's Church
19 Cuvilliés Theater
20 Damenstift
21 Exhibition Grounds
   (Messegelände)
22 Old Town Hall (Altes Rathaus)
23 St Peter's
▨ Pedestrian Zone

NYMPHENBURGER STR.

LUISENSTR.

BARER STRASSE

THERESIEN STR.

GABELSBERGER STR.

TURKENSTR.

OSKAR - VON

STR.

BRIENNER

SEIDLSTR.

DACHAUERSTR.

ARNULFSTR.

Botanical Gardens

BARERSTR.

MAXIMILIAN PLATZ

THEAT CHURC

MAIN RAILROAD STATION

TOURIST INFORMATION

SCHÜTZENSTR.

LENBACH PL.

PROMENADE PLAT

ST

BAYERSTR.

KARLS PLATZ

NEUHAUSER STR.

KAUFINGER S.

LANDSBERGER STR.

PAUL-HEYSE-STR.

SCHILLERSTR.

SONNEN STR.

KREUZSTR.

SENDLINGER STR.

RINDERMARKT

DEUTCHES THEATER

OBERANGER

THERESIENHÖHE

BAVARIARING

HERZOG-HEINRICH-STR.

THERESIENWIESE

MOZART STR.

SENDLINGER -TOR-PL.

STR.

STR.

BLUMEN

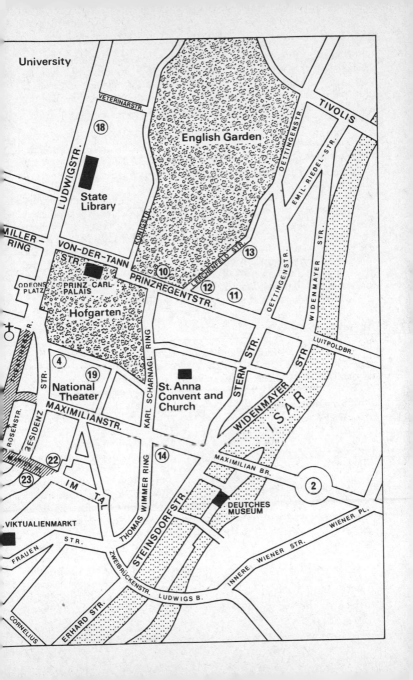

axle of the drawbridge rose the large main tower. In the left-hand tower lived the city's wheelwright and in the right-hand tower the customs collector. An urgent restoration of the Isartor took place between 1833 and 1835, during which time Bernhard Nehers completed his famous fresco depicting the triumphal entry of Kaiser Ludwig of Bayern after the Battle of Ampfing in 1322.

Architectural sights in Neuhauserstrasse of particular interest are the Renaissance St. Michael's Church (not to be confused with the beautiful baroque church of the same name in the eastern suburb of Berg am Laim) and the small Bürgersaal chapel with rococo interiors, both of them restored after the war. On a square just off Kaufinger-strasse stands the cathedral of the city, the much photographed Frauenkirche. Its twin towers, with their rounded domelet tops, have become a trademark of Munich. Built in the 15th century in Bavarian Gothic style, it was largely destroyed between 1943 and 1945, but it has been rebuilt. One of the few items that have remained untouched is the tomb of Emperor Ludwig the Bavarian, with interesting bronze figures. The 332-foot north tower of the church can be ascended by an elevator (operating only in good weather) and the top offers a magnificent view of the city, on a nice day extending to the high peaks of the Alps.

The Rathaus

The steeple soaring from the middle of the Neues Rathaus on Ma-rienplatz (278 feet high), which is also serviced by elevator, offers another fine view of the city—including perhaps the best view of the external architecture of the Frauenkirche, which cannot be had from the small square where the church stands because there is not enough space to step back for a full view. From the tower one can also see the intricate courtyard architecture of the Rathaus itself.

The Neues Rathaus, the New Town Hall, was built in the second half of the last century in neo-Gothic style. Its façade, richly ornamented with buttresses, pinnacles, crenels, arches and balconies, dominates Marienplatz and explains its past fate with the following curt description: "Built 1867–1874, Enlarged 1888–1908, Destroyed 1944–1945, Rebuilt 1952–1956." The colorful figures standing outside the open arched bay windows on the tower begin to move in the remarkable *Glockenspiel* every day at 11 A.M.: the upper level represents a tourna-ment event held on the occasion of the marriage of Duke William V and Renate of Lorraine in 1567.

During the Thirty Years' War the Swedes occupied Munich, but did not destroy it (as they did most of the other towns they occupied), and in gratitude the Elector of Bavaria in 1638 erected in the middle of Marienplatz the Mariensäule, a marble column topped by a statue of the Madonna (hence the name of the square). In the direction of the Tal, Marienplatz is halfway closed by what remains (after rebuilding) of the 15th-century Altes Rathaus (Old Town Hall), only some walls of which still stood at the end of the war. While this section has been externally restored (the rich interiors were burned out), the old Rathaustor, the tower gate connected with it, and the section across the street were completely shattered.

Just a few steps away from Marienplatz is St. Peter's Church, another landmark of Old Munich and its oldest parish church, first built in the 11th century and rebuilt several times since then, including as recently as a few years ago. Its tower, over 300 feet high and offering an excellent view (you have to walk up this one) is fondly called *Der Alte Peter* (Old Peter) by the people of Munich. Before walking up look at the north side of the platform: if you see a red disc there, the visibility over the city is good and if the disc is white the view is clear all the way to the Alps. Behind the church is Viktualienmarkt, Munich's lively outdoor food market.

Although it will require extra steps, we suggest a diversion at this point. It is worth the trouble to leave the Marienplatz on the Rosenstrasse and continue along Munich's newest pedestrian zone, the Sendlingerstrasse. Closed off almost completely to traffic at the end of 1980, Munich city planners have made great efforts to ensure that this important shopping street is even more attractive. Strolling past the 46 nostalgic lanterns lining the mall you will reach the small church of St. John Nepomuk, better known as the Asamkirche, for the Asam brothers who built it. They deserve the honor, for while architects as a rule are paid for putting up buildings, the Asam brothers built this one, next to their home, out of their own pockets, for sheer love of the job. The result must have gratified them. It is a beautiful rococo building, and though it was hit several times, it was lucky in that most of its rich interior decoration was saved, though unfortunately the great ceiling painting was almost totally lost.

At the end of Sendlingerstrasse, a little beyond Asamkirche, is Sendlinger Tor, another old city gate. The main tower of the Sendlinger Tor gate disappeared in 1808. The two outer towers and connecting wall with its opening remained until 1860 in their original form, when, in 1862, two small archways for pedestrians were broken through and the Sendlinger-Tor-Platz was built. The present-day form of the central archway was constructed by Wilhelm Bertsch in 1906. Beyond is the large Sendlingertor square, mentioned previously. A few fine old patrician houses still stand in the narrow streets behind the Asam Church, particularly in Hackenstrasse and Damenstiftstrasse. In the latter street are also the partially restored Damenstiftskirche (inside, more of the Asam brothers' work was lost) and the completely rebuilt Kreuzkirche.

Back at Marienplatz we continue on our route through the archway of the Old Town Hall to Tal and Isartor and from there to the river.

Museum Island and Maximilian's Street

The green Isar flows under many bridges that connect the center of Munich with its eastern districts. Most of its right bank offers pleasant green walks. At the point where we reach it, the river forms an island in its middle, called the Museum Island because the Deutsches Museum is located there. This colossal museum of natural science and technology, founded in 1903 by the German engineer Oskar von Miller, is very probably the best of its kind in the world. Here you can follow industrial production methods and their historic development in fascinating models and displays; you can also study in its vast library. The main stairway is adorned by a large fresco representing the great men of arts and sciences from ancient times to the Renaissance.

Strolling from the museum island down the river on its right bank, we come to a circular place in which stands the building known as the Maximilianeum, built for the Bavarian King Maximilian II less than 100 years ago and presently the seat of the Bavarian Parliament. Here we cross back to the left bank of the Isar over Maximilian's Bridge which leads us into Maximilianstrasse, presided over by the bronze statue of King Maximilian II.

Maximilianstrasse is an approximate parallel, a few blocks to the north, of the Kaufingerstrasse-Marienplatz-Tal thoroughfare we have covered. Only this time we are proceeding in the opposite direction, i.e., from the river through the city. A little more than halfway on Maximilianstrasse a narrow street called Am Kosttor takes us left to the tiny square called Platzl, on which stands the famous Hofbräuhaus, today a state brewery, founded by the Bavarian Duke Wilhelm V in 1589. The taproom is a *must* for the visitor, as much for the atmosphere as for the beer. The late Gothic Alter Hof in the nearby Burgstrasse used to be the medieval residence of the Bavarian Dukes and also of Emperor Ludwig of Bavaria.

Our walk through Maximilianstrasse ends at Max-Joseph-Platz, framed on one side by the Residenz. Continuing straight in the same direction through a few short streets, we could come to Lenbachplatz. Most of the beautiful 18th- and 19th-century palaces that used to exist in this area were destroyed during the war. Some façades have remained and the rebuilding of the rest has been carefully carried out. The rococo Palais Holnstein in Kardinal-Faulhaber-Strasse, called Erzbischöfliches Palais after the archbishops of Freising moved their seat to Munich in 1821, however, was not touched. The baroque Dreifaltigkeitskirche (Trinity Church) in Pacellistrasse, with ceiling frescos by C. D. Asam, was only slightly damaged and has been restored. An interesting architectural sight is Maxburg, a new, modern shopping and office block at Pacellistrasse-Lenbachplatz-Maxburgstrasse.

The Residenz

A large complex of buildings, the Residenz was once the residential palace of the rulers of Bavaria, dukes at first, then electors, and kings from 1806 until World War I. Before it was almost totally destroyed during the last world war, its architecture and interior furnishings and decorations made it one of the most valuable artistic monuments of Europe, a unique representative of Renaissance, baroque, rococo, and neo-classical styles, since its various wings and sections were built and period-furnished between the 16th and 19th centuries. Laborious and painstaking reconstruction restored the interiors which have been refurnished with the movable items that were saved. By the time of the 800th anniversary of the city of Munich in 1958, more than 50 rooms and sections had been reopened, including the Old Court Chapel and the glittering and chandeliered rococo theater where the first performance of Mozart's *Idomeneo* took place in 1781, directed by the composer himself.

The Residenz is in four sections:

Alte Residenz and the central sections of the palace, including the splendid rococo Cuvilliés theater, with entrance from the Residenzstrasse;

Königsbau at Max-Joseph-Platz, also restored and reopened in 1958;

Festsaalbau along the Hofgartenstrasse with the new Hercules Hall (Herkulessaal) built to replace the old one and serving today as a concert hall;

The Hofgarten or palace park, framed by arcades and noted for its flowerbeds, a mass of color in spring and summer.

Königsbau and Festsaalbau were built in the first half of the 19th century by the famous Munich architect Leo von Klenze, upon the instructions of King Ludwig I. The Residenz also houses the famous Schatzkammer of the Wittelsbachs, the rulers of Bavaria for almost 750 years prior to 1918. The richest piece in this glittering treasury, one of the finest in Europe, is a small Renaissance statue of St. George studded with 2,291 diamonds, 209 pearls and 406 rubies.

Since 1963, with the reconstruction of the Bavarian National Theater, the Max-Joseph-Platz has returned to its full neo-classic splendor. This imposing building, the home of the Bavarian State Opera, is probably the most beautiful and also functionally the best opera house in the world. The high standard of acoustics is guaranteed by such special features as the double wooden dome, the wooden-floored semi-circular orchestra pit resting on beams, and the wooden backs and arms of the seats, which for this reason have been only partially upholstered. The columned, marbled, mirrored, chandeliered, stuccoed and gilded interiors provide almost as splendid a spectacle as the masterful performances.

Across from the Alte Residenz at the beginning of Theatinerstrasse, a pedestrian shopping street leading to the Rathaus, is the basilical Theatinerkirche, built in Italian baroque style. Between them, facing Odeonsplatz and Ludwigstrasse, is Feldherrnhalle, an open loggia built towards the mid-19th century upon the initiative of King Ludwig I in imitation of the Loggia dei Lanzi in Florence; it contains the statues of some famous field marshals from Bavarian history.

King Ludwig's Street and Schwabing

From Feldherrnhalle the view opens on Ludwigstrasse, one of the great carefully-planned streets of Munich. It begins at Odeonsplatz, named for the concert hall which was destroyed in the war. The equestrian statue of King Ludwig I stands on this square, appropriately guarding the street which not only bears his name but was constructed as a magnificent and uniform whole at his orders. "I wish to make of Munich a city that will be of such honor to Germany, that no one will be able to claim to know Germany without having seen Munich," were his proud words which became reality. Upon his initiative and later following his example, monuments and palaces, important schools, museums, and scientific institutions, beautifully planned streets and squares were built and founded, attracting artists and scholars from many lands and making Munich, particularly at the turn of the century, one of the cultural centers of Europe. King Ludwig I was a great admirer of ancient Greek architecture and it was his own desire to introduce the neo-classical style to Munich. His architect Leo von Klenze was the author of the architectural designs but the king himself worked very hard on planning, construction details, financing, and similar matters. His court had to live frugally in order to save money for the great building plans and Ludwig I spent about 20 million guldens (30 million dollars) of his private funds for their realization. At his death he left all the buildings erected with his money to the Bavarian State and to the city of Munich.

King Ludwig's Street is one sight of the city that you may still appreciate as it was before the war. While many buildings were reduced to empty shells, the façades remained, the rest was rebuilt, and the general effect has not been lost. Following the street brings us to the cultural center of Munich: the Bavarian State Library, the University of Munich, and the Academy of Fine Arts which is located in a side street left of Siegestor. The continuation of Ludwigstrasse beyond Siegestor is called Leopoldstrasse, leading into the heart of Schwabing, the artists' and students' quarter. Siegestor (Arch of Victory) was also built upon the orders of Ludwig I after the pattern of the Arch of Constantine in Rome.

It is natural that the city's artists' colony should center on the university and the Academy of Fine Arts. If Schwabing's colorful bars, discos, nightclubs and jazz dives filled with students and artists provide the atmosphere common to art colonies elsewhere, its buildings do not, for Schwabing is not an old quaint district of winding streets, but a modern quarter, erected mostly in this century, and a popular residential section. It is the rendezvous of international youth the whole year round. Here young people meet to drink, dance, flirt, debate—in summer in the sidewalk cafes flanking the Leopoldstrasse. And those people who really get to know this atmosphere of easy-going optimism, tolerant conversation, the pleasure of turning night into day—in fact, of just taking life easy—will soon discover that Schwabing is not just a district, it is more a way of life. During the warm months, and some not so warm, artists and would-be artists line the Leopoldstrasse with their products ranging from artistic handicrafts to paintings and even outbursts of poetry.

Lying along the east side of Schwabing is the English Garden, a large natural park. It was the brain-child of Count Rumford, who was born Benjamin Thompson to farmer parents in Woburn, Mass., some 200 years ago. In the American Revolution Thompson sided with the British against the American colonies, received a knighthood as a reward, was a British Colonial Office official for a while, then made the acquaintance of the Elector of Bavaria, served as his minister of war and police, and was made a count. In the English Garden there is Rumford Hall as well as a Rumford Monument, and another statue of him stands on the Forum, which is the name for the large, square-like section of Maximilianstrasse near the Isar.

In the northern part of the attractively landscaped English Garden is a pleasant small lake, called Kleinhesseloher See, on which you can go boating in summer or skate in winter; in the middle of the park are the Chinese Tower, encircled by its famous beer-garden, and Monopteros, resembling a small Greek temple and from which you can get a fine veiw.

The southern section is bordered by Prinzregentenstrasse, which connects Isar with Ludwigstrasse and runs in a parallel manner to Maximilianstrasse. The Haus der Kunst (House of Art) with its collection of modern paintings and sculpture and its year-round art and antique furniture exhibitions, as well as the Bavarian National Museum and Schack Gallery, are located here.

The Alte and Neue Pinakothek

Returning from the Haus der Kunst towards Ludwigstrasse, crossing it, and continuing in the same direction (roughly northwest) for four blocks, we come to the square with the Alte Pinakothek, one of the finest and most famous art galleries in the world. Its palatial building was also constructed by Leo von Klenze on orders from Ludwig I; it, too, was destroyed during the war and rebuilt. The Alte Pinakothek (Old Painting Gallery) was given this name because it was to include only old paintings, whereas Neue Pinakothek (New Painting Gallery), was intended for contemporary paintings. In March 1981, the Neue Pinakothek was finally reopened after a closure of some 32 years. The gallery was founded originally in 1846 by Ludwig I but was badly bombed in the war and subsequently demolished. But it was not until 1975 that work began on the *new* Neue Pinakothek, which stands on the site of its predecessor in Barer Strasse. The collection features predominantly English paintings but also has works by Goya, the Romantics, the Munich School and both the French and German Impressionists.

The Alte Pinakothek grew out of a small court gallery started by Bavarian Duke Wilhelm IV in the early 16th century into today's very representative collection of European painting from the 14th to 18th centuries. Only about one-eighth of the some 7,000 canvases it possesses are presently exhibited. All important masters are represented, but the collection is particularly rich in the earlier German painters, Altdorfer, Dürer, Cranach, Flemish, and Dutch are well represented too; Roger van der Weyden, Memling, Quentin Metsys, and others, while the great names of da Vinci, Raphael, Rubens, Fra Angelico and Fra Filippo Lippi, Murillo and El Greco all help to swell the incredible wealth that covers the walls.

In Arcisstrasse, across the street from Alte Pinakothek, is the Technical University. Continuing along Arcisstrasse towards the center of the city, we come to Königsplatz, laid out for Ludwig I by Leo von Klenze, who was the architect of two of the neo-classical structures framing it: the Glyptothek, housing a fine collection of Greek and Roman sculpture, and the Propyläen, a giant gate built in imitation of the propylaea of the Acropolis in Athens. The third building houses the State Collection of Antiquities, a superb museum of classical art.

At right angles to Arcisstrasse is Briennerstrasse, which will take you to Odeonsplatz and Residenz. The continuation of Arcisstrasse is Meiserstrasse, which ends at the Old Botanical Garden, now a park.

The Theresienwiese

If you are in Munich at the time of the Oktoberfest, you will certainly visit it, and perhaps you might want to take a look at the part of town where it is held in any case. It lies south and a little west of the railroad station. If you take Goethestrasse, on the south side of the railroad station, and turn right when you reach Pettenkoferstrasse, you will come out onto the wide open space of the Theresienwiese, where the festival takes place.

On a height of the Theresienwiese is a statue of Bavaria, 98 feet high. You can go up into her head, if you don't mind climbing 130 steps, and enjoy the view through small windows; but if it is summer, don't go in the afternoon. The statue is of bronze, and by noon it has become a furnace.

The fair ground proper (Messegelände) lies off the west side of the Theresienwiese. A model of its kind, it lost many of its decorative details in the air raids but the large halls have been rebuilt and new ones added; all the important trade exhibitions and fairs are again staged here.

Nymphenburg

One attraction of Munich you mustn't miss is Nymphenburg, far out in the northwest part of the city. If you have been doing your exploring in the center on foot—the best way to get acquainted with any city, if you are hardy enough—you will have to abandon that method for this particular trip. Trams 17 and 21 go there from the center of the city.

Schloss Nymphenburg is an exceptionally lovely baroque palace which was used by the electors and the monarchs of Bavaria as a summer residence. It was started in the 17th century, and building went on for more than 100 years before the palace reached its present form, while the park in which it stands, even more beautiful than the palace, was altered, enlarged and improved over a period of nearly a century and a half.

The showpiece of the castle is the great Festsaal, in rococo style, where you can hear concerts during the summer. You will find an extraordinary collection of gilded and richly decorated coaches and sleighs in the Marstallmuseum. Also interesting are the workshops of the famous Nymphenburg Porcelain (Staatliche Porzellanmanufaktur Nymphenburg), located in one of the small buildings facing the palace; the factory, founded some 200 years ago by the ruling Wittelsbach family, is now run by the state and can be visited; in its showroom you can also place orders and have them shipped to your home.

Several small castles and pavilions are located in the park; water courses, small lakes, and a cascade add to its charm. Particularly delightful among the park buildings are the rococo Amalienburg with hunting motifs, Badenburg with a unique bath, and Pagodenburg, which serves as tea pavilion. Adjoining the palace park on the north side is the Botanical Garden with large hothouses for tropical plants and the Botanical Institute of the university. Its magnificent rhododendrons are in full bloom during May and June, but at any season it is a pleasant excursion with which to end your stay in Munich.

In the northern suburbs of Munich, to the northeast of Nymphenburg, is the Olympia Park, the site of the Olympic Games in 1972. Brilliantly designed stadiums, artificial lakes and the former Olympic Village spread out around the 961-foot Olympia-Turm (Olympic Tower), completed in 1968, which also serves as a TV tower. At the height of about 570 feet the tower has a round three-floor observation "nest," with the lower floor protected by glass and housing the proverbial rotating restaurant, and the upper two as open platforms. The "nest" is reached by very fast elevators in 30 seconds. When the weather is clear there is a magnificent view over Munich, of the Bavarian Alps and a large portion of Upper Bavaria.

Excursions from Munich

Dachau, eleven miles north of Munich, was notorious during the last war for the concentration camp set up by the Nazis in its vicinity, where a monument to its victims now stands. Dachau itself however has always been a pleasant old town (dating from at least 800), popular with landscape painters for the beauty of its scenery. It's also a light-hearted kind of place, with a mid-August festival in local costumes and races, not of horses, but of oxen.

Altomünster, 19 miles farther north, on the same road and railway line, has a convent dating from 730, with a fine 18th-century church. If you go by road, you should stop between Dachau and Altomünster at Indersdorf to visit the old monastery and the fine 13th-century church, Romanesque outside and rococo inside.

Schleissheim, 12 miles north of Munich, east of Dachau, is noted for its three castles. The late German Renaissance Altes Schloss, built by the Elector Maximilian in 1626, was almost wiped out by air raids, but you can still lunch at the Schlosswirtschaft restaurant in it. The Neues Schloss (1701–4), with its fine staircase, frescoed dome, Festival Hall and Victory Hall, where in summer you can enjoy evening concerts of Baroque music; the Jagdschloss Lustheim, late 17th century, has a valuable Meissen porcelain collection.

Winter in Berchtesgarden, with a view
of the Parish Church

Auditoria, ancient and modern; the Palace
Theater, Munich, built by Cuvillies in the 1750s,
and the Berlin Philharmonic Hall, built in 1963

**Ancient American art evocatively displayed
in the Berlin Ethnographic Museum**

One of the most popular spots in Berlin; the Zoological Gardens, with the Siberian Tigers

Freising, twenty miles in the same general direction from Munich, was once the seat of the bishopric of this region, which accounts for the official title of the prelate of the capital, who is Archbishop of Munich and Freising. Thus it has a cathedral, a Romanesque basilica, of which the earlier parts date from 1160. The Benediktuskirche is as old, and has a particularly fine stained-glass window. There are three other notable churches here, an interesting Rathaus, the former bishop's palace, a local museum, and, on the nearby heights, the Weihenstephan Benedictine monastery, now containing the School of Agriculture of Munich University with the Bavarian State Brewery, which continues the brewing activities started by the monks in 1040.

The Isar has cut a deep valley through the hills that rise as they move southward until they become the high Alps. This valley is a good region for tranquil weekends. Grosshesselohe, six and a half miles from Munich, can be reached by bus or by suburban train in 20 minutes.

On the other bank of the river is Grünwald, eight miles from Munich, which can also be reached by streetcar; it has an interesting castle which was first built in the 13th century as a hunting castle for Duke Ludwig the Strong, and later rebuilt. From Grünwald we can cross back to the left bank of the Isar over a bridge standing at one of the most scenic spots of the valley. Proceeding south we come to the Schäftlarn Benedictine Monastery, founded in the 8th century, whose 18th-century church is a beautiful example of Bavarian baroque. A few miles farther south is Wolfratshausen, an old market town with picturesque houses in a scenically beautiful location.

The Lakes

A number of natural playgrounds for the citizens of Munich are afforded by the lakes to the southwest of the city, or Fünf-Seen-Land (literally, five lakes land) as the area is known. The lakes are Starnbergersee, Ammersee, Wörthsee, Wesslingersee and Pilsensee. All are within the radius of Munich's fast suburb electric train network (S-Bahn), and can be reached directly from the center. The largest are Starnbergersee and Ammersee. The former, over 12 miles long, has a steamer service that makes for a relaxing and picturesque trip, or you can hire a motorboat or rowboat. Starnberg rises on terraces from the lake shore, though at this north end of the lake the country behind it is comparatively low. The 16th-century castle of the Princes of Bavaria, the 18th-century parish and the local museum are its chief attractions.

Easy trips from here are to the Hindenburghöhe, with a wonderful view; the Herrgottsruh chapel, where there are prehistoric tombs; Leutstetten, the site of the model stud farm of the late Crown Prince of Bavaria, Rupprecht, and Mühltal, with its fish hatcheries. Tutzing is a popular summer resort, and many wealthy Munich families have vacation homes here. There are three good bathing beaches. Seeshaupt, at the south end of the lake, has a towering wall of snowclad Alpine peaks for a backdrop. Pleasant country, numerous bathing beaches, and an opportunity to explore the Osterseen sector—a region of 21 small marshy lakes.

The Ammersee (10 miles) is not as long as the Starnbergersee but it's more interesting, partly because it is in more mountainous country, partly because it's farther from Munich, and you feel yourself to be away from the madding crowd. Herrsching, on a bay, is a much frequented summer resort. Its chief excursion is the climb to the Benedictine priory of Andechs, on the Heiliger Berg (Holy Mountain), altitude 2,333 feet, and then quench your thirst with the special dark beer brewed by the monks. Diessen, a market town as well as a summer resort, has a fine Bavarian rococo church, and if you want to take up sailing, a yachting school. Diessen is also an artists' colony; visit some of the potteries, or watch pewter models being made. Holzhausen is a rendezvous for artists. Schöndorf is a pretty place with a fine bathing beach.

Wörthsee is a typical marshland lake, where you can sooth and tone up your skin in the peat baths. In winter, ice-sailing is popular. Pilsensee and Wesslingsee are the smallest of the lakes but by no means the least attractive. In the summer they are the first to warm up and in winter they are frozen the longest. You need only stroll around the lakes to enjoy the peaceful scenery: green bullrushes, red knotweed blossom, fine-membraned milfoil and the water-hemlock's pebble-shaped fruits.

PRACTICAL INFORMATION FOR MUNICH

 WHEN TO COME. So far as climate is concerned, any time. Munich is near the Alps (in clear weather you can see them from the Rathaus and Olympic Towers), and the result is unpredictable weather, with the thermometer bobbing merrily up and down. The tourist season, is, of course, as all over the world, summer. This is the time if you want to attend the festivals of the Bavarian State Opera from mid-**July** through the first week of **August.**

The German Handicrafts Fair in **March** is interesting, as is the Christkindl Markt preceding Christmas. The Auer Dult, a grandiose flea market with country-fair atmosphere, is held three times a year on Maria-Hilf-Platz; 9 days each, beginning end of **April,** end of **July** and in **mid-October.** Other, smaller flea markets take place almost every Sunday at Münchner Freiheit and Berliner Str. (by the Ungererbad).

But the most typical fair is the Oktoberfest, which is held in **September** (all, that is, except the last few days of its fortnight's course). This is theoretically a country fair (in a big city!), but agriculture becomes somewhat swamped by that offshoot of cereal production, beer. On the Theresienwiese, where the fair grounds are located, the big breweries put up tremendous beer halls able to seat several thousand persons each. Bavarian brass bands are everywhere, the humor is fast, furious, rowdy, and unconfined.

Its top attraction is the big parade that takes place on the first Sunday of the *Fest* and includes gay beer floats and numerous folklore groups, particularly *Gebirgsschützenkompanien* (clubs of mountaineer marksmen), who come not only from Bavarian mountains but also from Tyrol, Styria, Salzburg and Carinthia, in Austria, and from South Tyrol (now in Italy). Folklore groups from other European countries, especially Switzerland, also participate in the parade.

Fasching, the carnival time preceding Lent is no longer as lively as it used to be. However, during its last few days you are apt to meet costumed refugees from masquerade balls almost anywhere; on Shrove Sunday there are outdoor gatherings, *mit Musik,* on several different squares, and the festive foolishness culminates on Shrove Tuesday, particularly at Viktualienmarkt (the market square), where the market women close shop early and dance, costumed, with one and all round the square, and in the Marienplatz pedestrian zone, where everyone dons a remnant of fancy dress—if only a large red nose—to dance to open-air music, link arms and ring out the end of *fasching.*

HOTELS. Munich is well supplied with hotels, but it is nonetheless advisable to book in advance (during the Oktoberfest and the Fashion Weeks—*Mode Woche*—in March and October it is essential). Hotels here are among the highest priced in Germany, but tourist deflation in the past years has created panic among many, particularly the new American chain-hotels, who were among the first to join the special all-inclusive, out-of-season "Munich Weekend" package, which includes city and countryside tours, museum fees, etc.

These low-price arrangements include such packages as: "Munich Weekend Key", "Munich Christkindl Key" (valid from Nov. 27 to Dec. 24), "Munich's New Year's Eve Key" (valid from Dec. 25 to Jan. 6), "Munich Fasching Key" (valid from Jan. 7 to Feb. 20), "Munich Summer Stop" (valid from June 5 to Sept. 5), and "Munich 7-Day Key" (valid from Oct. 10 to Sept. 5 of the following year with some exempted week ends). In addition to the reduced hotel prices, they include breakfast, city sightseeing tour or an afternoon excursion to one of the Bavarian lakes, free ride to the top of the Olympic tower, shopping coupons, free admission to all museums and galleries as well as to the Nymphenburg Palace and the Botanical Gardens. The German Federal Railway (Bundesbahn) offers a considerable reduction on train fares in conjunction with these packages. The special arrangements offered by the City of Munich can be booked on all railroad stations or through a travel agency. Information from the Munich Tourist Office (tel. (089) 2391–226).

Deluxe

Bayerischer Hof, Promenadeplatz 6, has 700 beds, all rooms with bath or shower, some with large floor-level bath; studio rooms and suites also available. Sauna bath and heated rooftop swimming pool. Bayerischer Hof acquired the famous Montgelas Palais next door, had it restored and reopened as a hotel annex containing elegant period-furnished apartments and banquet and private dining rooms, some fashionable shops, and the rustic-style *Palais-Keller.* Whereas the accommodations and environment are tops, the culinary efforts are less: *Grill* is so-so, and *Trader Vic's* is as pseudo-Polynesian as in the U.S. Dancing in the *Night-Club,* usually a very loud affair.

Hilton, Tucherpark between the English Garden and the Isar River, with several restaurants: *Tivoli-Grill* serves "international" food; *Bayernstube* Bavarian; *Isar-Café* mainly pastries; recent small beer-garden overlooking the little Eisbach river; and the rooftop *Marco Polo* with bar (dine and dance) advertises "a culinary Marco Polo Trip." Also swimming pool, sauna, shopping arcade, large underground parking facilities. Its 500 rooms each have private bath and balcony, TV and other amenities.

Königshof, on Karlsplatz (Stachus). All 120 rooms sound-proof, airconditioned, and most with bath. First-class food in the restaurant overlooking Stachus. 180-car underground garage (entrance from Bluntschlistrasse).

Vier Jahreszeiten, Maximilianstrasse 17. Palatial, it has served royalty and other important international figures and is still the leading hotel of Munich. Owned now by the Kempinski (of Berlin fame) chain, it has a new super-modern wing (fortunately at the back) with roof-top pool, convention facilities and other similar amenities. There are several restaurants, dine-dancing in *Vier Jahreszeiten Bar,* but the days of the old famous chef Walterspiel who used to own the place are gone, with the exception of the very fine restaurant bearing his name.

Expensive

Arabella, 400 beds on the upper floors of a supermodern 22-story apartment building in Arabella Park in the Bogenhausen suburb, restaurant and indoor pool with sauna on the top floor with magnificent view.

Ambassador, Mozartstr. 4, in a quiet spot near Theresienwiese, a 100-bed hotel with studio suites only, all with bath, radio, TV and kitchenette with ice-box (filled with drinks); was the first of its kind in Germany and the original idea of Herr Carl Gross, the owner. Also good restaurant.

Continental, at Max-Joseph-Strasse 5, near Maximiliansplatz, has 200 beds, all rooms with bath, private suites available. Fine food in the atmospheric *Conti Grill* and in the rooftop restaurant. Cocktail lounge and terrace garden. Furnishings include valuable antique and art objects.

Deutscher Kaiser, Arnulfstr. 2, a towering 16-story building at the main station, 300 beds, most rooms with bath, but those without have inconvenient bathing facilities; fine view from 15th-floor restaurant and café. Underground garage.

Excelsior, Schützenstr. 11, on quiet side street near main station, to become pedestrian mall. 180 beds. All rooms with bath and radio, top floor terrace suites with TV. Game specialties in the atmospheric *St. Hubertus.*

Holiday Inn, at Leopoldstrasse 194 on the outer edge of Schwabing, with 400 comfortable modern rooms and a series of elegant suites spaced in three buildings, which are connected by a huge hotel hall. Swimming pool, several restaurants and cocktail lounges and the unique *Yellow Submarine* nightclub. Virtuoso zither playing every night except Sun., in the Almstube.

Holiday Inn International, Schleissheimer Str. 188, out in the suburbs near the 1972 Olympic Grounds. All 151 rooms with bath. Restaurant and bar.

Penta, across the Isar on the Rosenheimer Berg at Hochstrasse 3, near downtown (walking distance). Largest (600 rooms) of the Munich hotels. It offers rooms in two different price categories: one closer to luxurious and one nearer first class reasonable. Restaurant, cocktail lounge, self-service restaurant and automats. The *Münchner-Kindl-Stuben* offers an attractive menu in traditional, rustic, old-Munich surroundings, ranging from cold and hot buffet-bar to Bavarian dishes and international cuisine, with a fine selection of grill specialties. Open until 2 A.M. Rooftop swimming pool. The hotel is part of a large permanent exhibition and shopping center called "Motorama" featuring German and foreign cars, and including also other shops.

Preysing (garni), Preysingerstr. 1 near Deutsches Museum, 92 beds, all rooms with bath, radio, TV; apartments available (also on monthly basis).

Residence, Artur-Kutscher-Platz 4 in Schwabing, the latest in architecture; 300 beds, swimming pool in the basement, restaurant *Die Kutsche.*

Senator, Martin-Greif-Str. 11 at exhibition grounds and Theresienwiese, 28 rooms, all with bath, underground garage.

Sheraton, at Effnerplatz in the Arabella Park section of the Bogenhausen suburb, overlooking the city with outstanding view from the top floors, 1,300 beds in 650 rooms, convention hall seating 1,500 persons and equipped with simultaneous translation units, all other modern amenities and several restaurants, bar, nightclub.

Moderate

Ariston, Unsöldstrasse 10, near Haus der Kunst, garni, 100 beds, all rooms with bath or shower, modern, quiet location.

Arosa, Hotterstrasse 2, in the center (not far from Marienplatz), garni, 86 rooms with bath or shower. Underground garage.

Central (garni), Schwanthalerstr. 111, on Theresienhöhe in the Hacker-Pschorr-Zentrum, 50 rooms and 18 apartments.

Domus, St.-Anna-Str. 31 near Haus der Kunst, all rooms with bath and balcony, underground garage.

Leopold, Leopold Strasse 119 in Schwabing, old-fashioned Gasthaus in front, modern wing in the garden in the back; 120 beds, many single rooms, parking lot and underground garage.

Metropol, Bayerstr. 43, opposite the south exit from main station. 200 rooms, all with radio, most with bath, large underground garage.

Nikolai, on Nikolaiplatz, a small, reasonably quiet square in Schwabing. Of recent vintage, all 64 rooms have bath, refrigerator and cooking facilities.

Nymphenburg, Nymphenburger Strasse 141, about halfway between the main rail station and Nymphenburg Palace, 80 beds, all rooms with bath or shower, restaurant.

Olympiapark. On the Olympic grounds, good subway connections to downtown. Recent, 100 rooms with bath, restaurant, and indoor pool.

Platzl, Munzstr. 8, opposite the Hofbräuhaus, 200 beds, 100 baths, own parking lot. Indoor pool. The well-known Bavarian folklore shows are presented nightly in the large beer restaurant. Ownership and management by Ayinger Brewery. Rooms on the Hofbräuhaus side are boisterously noisy.

Reinbold, Adolf-Kolping-Str. 11, near main station and Stachus. Recent, 74 rooms, small but well appointed, with ice-box stocked with drinks, air-conditioned.

Schweizerhof, Goethestr. 26, near main station, good restaurant.

Also *Moderate* are: In City—**Bosch,** Amalienstr. 25, 80 beds; **Dachs,** Amalienstr. 12, 110 beds; **Drei Mohren,** Schuberstr. 6, 60 beds, quiet; **Schwabing,** 90 beds, Fendstr. 2 in Schwabing; **Senefelder,** Senefelderstr. 4, 106 beds, most with bath or shower; **Stachus,** Bayerstr. 7, 120 beds. Most are garni.

In suburbs—**Moorbad Wetterstein,** Grünwalder Str. 16, 100 beds, all rooms with bath or shower, heated pool, mudpack and Kneipp cures. **Edelweiss Park-Hotel** (garni), Menzingestr. 103, in Obermenzing, not far from Nymphenburg Gardens, a small modern hotel in a quiet residential section; also in Nymphenburg, **Pension Krimhild,** Guntherstr. 16, 30 rooms, all with bath or shower.

Gästehaus Haustein, Wolfratshauser Str. 149 in the Solln area (south).

Hotels **Atlantik** and **Pazific** in Ottobrunn suburb (southeast), near Salzburg Autobahn.

Inexpensive

A few of Munich's many inexpensive hostelries: **Pension Beck,** Thierschstr. 36, near the Max II Monument. **Coburg,** Franz-Josef-Str. 38, near Leopoldstr. in center of Schwabing, very tastefully furnished. **Münchner Kindl,** Damenstiftstr. 16, near Sendlinger Tor. **Hungaria,** Briennerstr. 42. **Tannenbaum,** Kreuzstr. 18, is near Theresienwiese.

 RESTAURANTS. Lunch is ordinarily served in Munich restaurants from noon until about 2:30 P.M., dinner from 6 P.M. Among the best known Munich specialties are *Leberkäs,* a meat loaf made from pork and beef, and *Weisswurst,* a small, white, nonsmoked sausage made from veal and various other ingredients; both are eaten warm, with sweet Munich mustard, and as a snack rather than a main meal course and call for copious drafts of beer; tradition has it that the Weisswurst should be eaten only between midnight and noon. Delicious *Brathendl* (chicken from spit) and *Steckerlfisch* (fish grilled on sticks) are served primarily during the Oktoberfest and are intended to work up your beer appetite. Other typical Munich dishes include *Kalbshaxe* (veal shank), *Schweinshaxe* (pork shank), and various types of *Geselchtes* (smoked pork), accompanied by the Bavarian type of *Knödel* (potato or bread dumplings). *Radi* (white or red radishes) are another beloved bite to go with beer.

Although there are numerous restaurants with first-class wine cellars and taverns specializing in wine from certain regions, such as Pfalz or Franken, the "national" drink of Munich is, of course, beer. In the most typical beer halls the minimum you can order is a *Mass,* a "measure" which in this case means a 1-liter mug (a bit over a U.S. quart); elsewhere *ein grosses* (½ liter) or even *ein kleines* (¼ liter) can be had. You order *helles* (light) if you like the regular or *dunkles* (dark) if you prefer a bit heavier and sweeter type. You will meet the product of several dozen breweries, but the great names among them have remained the same for several centuries: Löwenbräu, Paulaner-Salvator-Thomasbräu, Hackerbräu, Spatenbräu, Augustinerbräu, and Pschorr Bräu. Weihenstephan beer produced in the nearby Freising since 1040 is the oldest in Germany. Among the several seasonal types of beer, all of them stronger than the "regular", are: *Wiesenbier,* brewed for Oktoberfest which takes place on the Wiesen (meadows) hence the name; various kinds of *Starkbier* (strong beer) produced during the Lent season, called with Latin names, the best known of which is *Salvator; Maibock,* brewed and drunk in May. If none of these should be available and you wish a strong beer, ask for *Bock* (light or dark). If you prefer wheat beer, order a *Weissbier;* it is served with a slice of lemon in it.

The following lists can only be a short selection of more than a thousand of Munich's eating and drinking establishments. Previously mentioned hotel restaurants are not repeated.

In all cases you should check opening times and particularly the *Ruhetage* or closing days each week.

There are two **Mövenpick** restaurants (M–I), one at Lenbachplatz 8, the other at Hopfenstr. 1, for easy eating.

Expensive

All of the restaurants mentioned in this category primarily serve wines with the meals and their wine cellars rate from very good to excellent.

Die Aubergine, Maximilian's Platz 5 (entrance in Max Joseph Str.). Munich's finest and most expensive restaurant (5-star), serving highest quality French cuisine. Small, quiet and elegant, with aubergine-colored decor. Reservations from 12 to 1:30 and 6:30 to 9:30. Closed Sundays and during the first three weeks of August. Advanced booking essential. Allow at least 4 hours for your meal.

Käferschänke, corner of Prinzregentenstr. and Schumannstr. Another delicatessen paradise with large store downstairs; restaurants upstairs, and in the cellar they serve everything from truffles to quail eggs and vintage champagne.

Tantris, Johann Fichte-Str. 7 in the north of Schwabing. In a modern building a little out of the center you can sample the widest selection of French food in town. Open from 12 to 2 and 6:30 to 10:45. Good parking facilities. Rather overpriced.

Die Kanne, Maximilianstr. 30, intimate, candlelit rooms, some decorated with theatrical mementos, fine meat, fish and game dishes, good wine list.

La Cave, Maximilianstr. 25, an elegant and exclusive evening restaurant and bar, open until 2 A.M. Mostly French-style cuisine; crawfish is one of the specialties.

Le Gourmet, Ligsalzstr. 46, next to the Fair Grounds. Particularly comfortable first-class restaurant with antique furnishings. Open from 6 to 11; Wed. and Thurs. also from 12 to 2.

Böttner, Theatinerstr. 8, a tiny restaurant in the back room of a small specialty delicatessen shop. Lobster, caviar, and goose liver pâté rate high. Delicatessen tasters will find great joy here. Reservations essential.

Maximilian Stube, Maximilianstr. 27. International specialties, but with the accent on Italian cuisine. Evening dining with zither music as accompaniment.

Haxnbauer Stuben, a twin rustic-style establishment, the larger one at Sparkassenstrasse and the smaller one, with original mountain wooden hut interiors, around the corner at Münzstrasse 5. Schweinshaxen and Kalbshaxen from open fireplace, as well as other Bavarian delicacies. Rustic in everything but prices.

Dallmayr, Dienerstr. 14. Delicious selections in the small rooms upstairs from the huge (and world-famous) ground-floor delicatessen.

König-Promenadeplatz, Promenade Platz, opened in 1980. In relaxing, elegant surroundings, with seating for 85 in four separate rooms, tastefully furnished with French and English antiques, first-class French food is served from a small but exclusive menu daily from 11.00 until 1.00 A.M. In addition to an imposing wine list, freshly drawn *Pils* or lager-beer from the proprietor's own brewery is a specialty served at the bar.

K.u.K. Monarchie, Reichenbachstr. 22. Evening restaurant with specialties from all the far reaches of what once was the Austrian Empire.

Schwarzwälder's Naturweinhaus, Hartmannstr. 8. New ownership of this once famous establishment has lowered the quality considerably, although it can still boast the largest wine-list in Munich, with a selection of high-quality vintages from all over the world. Still mentioned here only for its old interiors, a landmark of Munich. Otherwise the only thing "first class" is the cost.

Rauchfang, in Schwabing district. Excellent food in old Bavarian atmosphere.

Moderate with Local Atmosphere

Neuner, Herzogspitalstr. 8, old wine tavern with good food and wines.

Torggelstuben, on Platzl. Antique furnishings in the restaurant rooms on the upper floor, rustic and wine décor in the ground-floor restaurant and in the cellar wine tavern. Outstanding food in the restaurant rooms; mostly wine drinking only in the cellar.

Goldene Stadt, Oberanger 44 near Sendlinger Tor, perhaps not particularly atmospheric but serving fine food, particularly Bohemian specialties.

Zum Spöckmeier, the famous old Munich restaurant in a new house in the Rosenstrasse, with summer sidewalk tables on the pedestrian mall.

Drei Rosen, another famous old Munich restaurant has been rebuilt and reopened at Rindermarkt 5 near St. Peter's Church in the "House of Three Roses" (city tourist office is on upper floor).

Zum Bögner in Tal 72, halfway between Rathaus and Isar Gate, is yet another old Munich restaurant.

Nürnberger Bratwurstglöckl, Frauenplatz 9, at the Frauenkirche, specializes in Nürnberg sausages and charcoal-grilled meats in colorful old-style interiors.

Zur weiss-blauen Rose, in basement of Beck Store on Marienplatz. Excellent old-style Bavarian lunch dishes; popular and usually filled up by 12:30. Has charming courtyard in the summer.

Hannen Stube, Prannenstr. 2, behind Bayerischer Hof hotel. In addition to Bavarian dishes, specialties from all over the world are offered.

Ratskeller, in the cellar of the Rathaus, Marienplatz. A series of more or less modern rooms, some small and inviting, some uncomfortably barn-like, replaced the old, tradition-filled Ratskeller. The food, however, remains good, with emphasis on Bavarian specialties, which are served until midnight.

Inexpensive

In addition to the beer halls and restaurants listed below, mostly inexpensive, there are a number of good and penny-saving sources of protein such as **Donisl,** Weinstr. 1, with zither music (Sun. only), *Weisswurst* and Pschorr beer; they are the traditional caterers to Munich hangovers (open Fri., Sat. and Sun. until 6 A.M.); **Grüner Hof,** Bayerstr. 35, opposite the south exit of main station; and **Am Kühbogen,** a delicatessen on the corner of Theatinerstr. and Salvatorstr., cafeteria downstairs.

Gebo's, Blumenstr. near Viktualienmarkt. Café-restaurant serving snacks and gourmet meals at very reasonable prices. Open from 10 A.M. until 8 P.M. for breakfast, lunch and early dinner. English spoken.

BEER RESTAURANTS

These are usually sponsored, if not owned, by large breweries. They are intended, however, primarily for eating and serve mainly Bavarian fare and the sponsor's beer, although some wine can be had in most of them. Prices range from moderate to inexpensive. Most of them are vast establishments, often occupying several floors.

Altes Hackerhaus, Sendlinger Str. 75, among oldest. The **Peterhof** on Marienplatz offers a series of cozy corners on the ground floor and a fine view of the Rathaus from its upstairs windows. **Pschorr** is a large establishment at Neuhauserstr. 11.

Augustiner Grossgaststätten, Neuhauserstr. 16, is a historic beer restaurant. **Franziskaner und Fuchsenstuben,** Perusastr 5. All of these are located in the center, near or not far away from the Rathaus.

TRADITIONAL BEER HALLS

These establishments, mostly owned by large breweries, are enormous in size. Enormous also are the mugs of beer, the portions of food, and the waitresses serving them. The liveliest activity is concentrated in the large main hall (in summer usually in a vast garden) where a brass band plays merry folk tunes, although a series of restaurant rooms is often attached to the place. Usually dancing on weekends. Prices are inexpensive to moderate.

Among the most venerable in this category is the famous **Hofbräuhaus,** dominating the tiny Platzl square, with the rough and rowdy Schwemme ("watering" place) on the ground floor, a first-class restaurant for Bavarian specialties one flight up, a large hall with brass band and dancing further up, and a courtyard garden in summer. **Löwenbräukeller** at Stiglmaierplatz is a similar indoor and outdoor establishment.

Mathäser Bierstadt (beer city) in Bayerstrasse near Stachus Square is also owned by Löwenbrau, and true to its name is probably the largest beer hall in the world; a special cellar-restaurant features Weissbier.

Salvator-Keller, at Hochstr. 49 on Nockherberg, is particularly lively in March when the strong Salvator is on draft for a few weeks.

Augustiner-Keller, Arnulfstr. 52, has the largest beer garden in the city.

Thomasbräukeller, Kapuzinerplatz 5. is near the South Station.

Hackerkeller and **Pschorr Keller** on Theresienhöhe, near the Trade Exhibition Grounds, are housed in modern sterility and have lost the old flavor.

WINE TAVERNS

Munich has a series of genuine wine taverns where the accent is on drinking rather than on eating. In addition to the long lists of bottled wines they usually offer some two dozen types of open wine, sold by the ¼-liter glass, prices ranging according to quality. Long tables call for making acquaintances with your drinking neighbors. Prices are moderate to inexpensive.

Hahnhof sells wines from its own vineyards in Pfalz and has five establishments in Munich, the most popular of which is at Leopoldstr. 32 in Schwabing.

Pfälzer Weinprobierstube in the Residenz Palace, entrance at Residenzstr. 1, also specializes in Pfalz wines.

Weinstadl, Burgstr. 5, very atmospheric in what is probably the oldest house in Munich (last rebuilt 1551).

Weinkrüger, Maximilianstr. 21, a short walk from the National Theater and a favorite meeting place for opera and theater goers; and Feilitzchstr. 25 in Schwabing, recent, but in old tavern tradition, wines from all over Germany.

For Austrian wines and Viennese atmosphere: **Grinzing,** Marktstr. 6 in Schwabing, zither music, and **Lamm's Heuriger,** Prinzregentenstr. 60.

MAINLY OUTDOORS

Hirschgarten (M), Hirschgarten 1, in the Nymphenburg section of the city, in a large wildlife (deer and stag) park of the same name.

Chinesischer Turm (I), in English Garden at the foot of the pagoda-like "Chinese Tower," a decorative building. Beer and food are strictly Bavarian.

Zum Aumeister (M), at Sondermeierstrasse 1, off the Frankfurter Ring at Munich-Freimann; former hunting lodge of the Bavarian Kings.

FOREIGN FOOD

Munich has a vast array of foreign food restaurants and the number is still growing, due to numerous foreigners, especially foreign workers, and also to the German passion for all foreign food. The Balkan-type restaurants serve hot and spicy food, perhaps not suitable for the more delicate stomach.

In addition to the expensive French restaurants at present dominating the culinary scene in Munich, for notable French food at reasonable prices, try:

Aquitaine, Amalienstr. 39 in Schwabing, specialties from Bordeaux.

Bouillabaisse, Falkenturmstr. 10, opposite the opera, offering wide variety of fish specialties as well as fine all-round menu. Cozy surroundings on two floors with cellar wine tavern. Open until midnight and meeting place for performers from the ballet and opera.

Bistro Terrine, Amalien Passage also in the Amalienstr., typical French bistro-style restaurant, small and simply decorated but with good quality food. Reservations essential; moderate.

Le Medoc, Häberlstr 1, new and spacious; lamb, scampi and other grill specialties. Excellent wines.

For lovers of oysters and scallops, **Austern Keller Pils Bar** in the Stolbergstr., near Maximilianstr., where freshly caught fish and shellfish are flown in daily from the South of France.

One of the coziest is **Walliser Stuben** (E), Leopoldstr. 33 in Schwabing, featuring *Swiss* food and wines. Fine Swiss cuisine also in **Chesa Rüegg** (M), Wunzerstr. 18.

For *Hungarian* food, gypsy music and puszta décor visit **Csarda Piroschka** (E) in Haus der Kunst; original gypsy orchestras from Budapest.

Spanish food: **Don Quijote** (E), Biedersteiner Str. 6, quaint cellar with corner tables; menu from shrimp with garlic to Steak Torero, good Spanish wines; flamenco guitar on Saturdays. **Casa Pepe,** Klopstockstr. 4, newly-opened modern, reasonably-priced restaurant, spacious, on two floors with extensive menu and first-rate Spanish and South American music.

Food from *Caucasus, Turkestan* and *Russia:* **Datscha** (E), Kaiserstr. 3, wooden hut interiors; in summer colorful courtyard with open grill; some waiters wear fierce moustaches. **Kasak** (M), Friedrichstr. 1, folklore décor and *intime* setting.

Romanian: **Klein Bukarest,** Thalkirchnerstr. 186, near Isar. High quality Romanian and Balkan specialties in rustic surroundings.

Italian: **El Toula** (E), Sparkassenstr. 5; **La Fattoria** (M), Pündter Platz in Schwabing. **Il Tartufo,** Prinzregenten Platz 11, a newcomer on the scene.

Greek: **Sorbas Le Grec** (E), Ungererstr. 65; *Costa* (E), Barer Str. 42; **Mykonos** (M), Georgenstr. 105; **Scorpios** (M), Leopoldstr. 35; all in Schwabing.

Far Eastern: **Mifune** (E), Ismaninger Str. 136 in Bogenhausen suburb (Japanese). For the best Chinese food in town, **Tai-Tung** (E), recently moved into the beautiful old Stück Villa on the corner of Prinz Regenten and Ismaningerstr. Comfortable, relaxed surroundings and personal service by proprietor.

Cafés and Pastry Shops

Café Glockenspiel on the top floor of Marienplatz 28 offers fine pastry and an excellent view of the Rathaus; this is the place from which to watch the Glockenspiel at 11 A.M., as is **Peterhof** on the fifth floor or Marienplatz 22, For a magnificent view of the city and far beyond, if the weather is nice, go to **Hochhaus-Café** on the 16th floor of Hotel Deutscher Kaiser. **Luitpold,** Brienner Strasse 11, has a grill room and sidewalk tables.

Among the best for pastries are **Hag,** Residenzstr. 26, **Kreutzkamm,** Maffeistr. 4, **Passage-Café** in Hypo-Passage with entrance from Theatinerstr. 9, **Feldherrnhalle,** Theatinerstr. 38 and **Conditorei-Cafe Waltl** (new 1980), Stolbergstr. 22 (corner Maximilianstr.), a café/cake-shop opened by the renowned Munich pastry cook of the same name, in *art nouveau* style, with hand-painted glass ceiling, shady garden and a menu with over 30 different pastries and 12 ice-cream specialties, all home-made. **Franzmann** in Gloria-Passage at Lenbach Platz, **Maxburg Espresso** in Pacellistrasse, and **Alte Börse** in the passage at Maffeistr. are modern.

THEATER. Munich has always been a great city for drama and now has 22 theaters. Get the Munich official monthly program, containing all cultural events. Tickets for the Opera can be purchased at the Opera ticket office, Maximilianstrasse 11, open 10–1 and 4–6; Saturdays, Sundays and holidays 10–1. Other ticket agencies: *ABR-Theaterkasse,* am Stachus: *Max Hieber,* Kaufingerstr. 23; *Bauer,* Landschaftstr. 1 (in Rathaus building); *Radio-RIM,* Theatinerstr. 17 and in some other radio and bookshops. Information about the

Munich Festival can be obtained from *Festspiele der Oper zu München,* Brieffach, 8 München 1.

As befits the city that was host to the world premières of four Wagner operas, Munich has a fine opera company in the *Bavarian State Opera,* which performs in the *Bavarian National Theater* (Munich State Opera House) at the Max-Joseph-Platz, reopened in 1963 and rebuilt exactly according to the original appearance: the auditorium with Corinthian columns, stuccoed ceiling and a gigantic, 180-light chandelier suspended from the dome, and the ancient Greek-style promenade halls with large mirrors reflecting the lights of numerous crystal chandeliers. A 450-car underground garage for opera visitors beneath the Max-Joseph-Platz is connected with the theater directly by an underground passage.

Other principal theaters include *Theater am Gärtnerplatz,* at Gärtnerplatz 3, where operettas and light opera are performed, while for plays there are the *Münchner Kammerspiele,* Maximilianstr. 26, and the *Bayerisches Staatsschauspiel* in the Residenztheater, Max-Joseph-Platz 1.

The rococo *Altes Residenztheater,* better known under the name Cuvilliés-Theater, is where baroque-period operas, Richard Strauss and Molière are performed. *Theater in der Brienner Strasse,* at No. 50 in the street of the same name, and *Theater am Marstall,* Marstallplatz, are mainly for drama.

Among the several smaller theaters, giving mainly comedies, are *Intimes Theater in Künstlerhaus,* Lenbachplatz 8; *Die Kleine Freiheit,* Maximilianstr. 31; and *Kleine Komödie* with two halls, at Promenadeplatz Passage (Bayerischer Hof) and at Max II Denkmal.

Munich has two puppet show theaters: *Marionettentheater,* at Blumenstr. 29a, and *Puppentheater* at Lenbachplatz 8 (Künstlerhaus).

 NIGHTLIFE. Munich has scores of night spots. Folklore variety shows are headed by *Platzl* on the tiny square of the same name—if you want to expose yourself to a heavy dose of highly typical and far from subtle rustic humor. Yodeling and *Schuhplattler dances* are regular features of these shows.

For variety shows mixed with striptease: *Maxim,* corner of Färbergraben and Altheimer Eck. Striptease primarily or only: *Intermezzo,* Maximilianstr. 34; *Lola Montez,* Am Platzl 1; *Fernandel,* Hans Sachs Str. 2, near Sendlinger Tor.

The "better" class dance at *Nightclub* in Hotel Bayerischer Hof, in *Club P-1* in Haus der Kunst and in *Eve's Cabaret,* Oskar-von-Miller-Ring. Munich would-be-society gathers at *Saint James Club,* Brienerstr. 10. For a large selection of cocktails and mixed drinks in plush surroundings, try *Harry's New York Bar* in Falkenturmstrasse.

A unique nightclub is *Yellow Submarine* in Hotel Holiday Inn in Schwabing, Leopoldstrasse 200; it is an underwater nightclub, built into a steel tank where the guests, protected by thick glass, are surrounded by 40 swimming sharks from Florida. Other luxury hotels also have nightclubs and dancing, although less spectacular. You might try the *Marco Polo Bar* in Hilton or Sheraton's *Vibraphon.* Be prepared for stiff bills in all three places.

Munich's newest nightclub is the *Boccaccio* in the Brienner Str., open until 4 A.M.

If you wish to dance, are past school-age and not looking for pro-company: *Ball der einsamen Herzen* (Ball of Lonely Hearts), Klenzestr. 71; *Philoma,* Schleissheimer Strasse 12, specialized for merry widows and mature bachelors. For *intime* drinking: *King's Corner Club* in Hotel Königshof; *Bei Heinz,* Herzog-Wilhelm-Strasse 7.

In **Schwabing,** there are many additional night spots, some with way-out atmosphere and décor. You might try *Der brave Schwejk,* Neureutherstr. 15, or *Ba-Ba-Lu,* Ainmillerstr. 1. Among dozens of discothèques: *Drugstore,* Freilitizschstr. 12; *Scotch-Kneipe,* next door; *Gaslight Club,* Ainmillerstr. 10; *Rumpelkammer,* Trautenwolfstr. 1; *Capt'n Cook,* Occamstr. 8. *Die Fregatte,* Josephspitalstr. 14.

MUSIC. The big concert halls of Munich are the *Herkules Saal in der Residenz,* and the *Kongress Saal* of the Deutsches Museum, on its island in the middle of the Isar. Soloists and chamber music groups appear in the *Sophiensaal,* Sophienstr. 6, where there is a fine organ; the *Festsaal* of *Künstlerhaus,* Lenbachplatz 8; *Galerie im Lenbachhaus,* Luisenstr. 33; and in the *Hochschule für Musik,* Arcisstr. 12.

Munich has four symphony orchestras: the *Munich Philharmonic,* the *Bavarian State Orchestra,* the *Bavarian Radio Orchestra* and the *Symphony Orchestra Kurt Graunke.* There are several choral societies including the famous *Bach Choir,* the *Münchner Motettenchor,* and the *Musica Viva,* the latter for contemporary music.

The best church music is provided by the choirs of St. Michael's and St. Matthew's and the Cathedral Choir *(Domchor),* which sings sometimes in the Frauenkirche and sometimes in the Dreifaltigkeitskirche.

CONCERTS IN HISTORIC PALACES AND CASTLES IN AND AROUND MUNICH

The following concerts will give you a chance not only to enjoy marvelous music making, but to see some of the interesting places in and around Munich under different conditions. The concerts are held both indoors and in the expertly kept grounds of historic buildings.

Open-Air Concerts in the Brunnenhof of the Residenz in Munich. Throughout the summer months from end of June through September. In bad weather the concerts are transferred from the courtyard to the Herkulessaal of the Residenz. Advance booking from all large travel agents or from concert organization (tel. 609 11 98).

Schloss Nymphenburg in Nymphenburg, West Munich. Summer Music Festival from 22 June to 13 July in the Steinerner Saal of the palace. Tickets from all large travel agents.

Schlosskirche Blutenburg at Schloss Blutenburg on the River Würm in Obermenzing, West Munich, near autobahn Munich-Stuttgart. Indoor concerts in the castle's chapel or Barocksaal of castle. Outdoor concerts in the monastery garden at Würminsel near the Marienplatz square in Pasing about 1 mile south of the castle. In addition, concerts of Renaissance music arranged by the Schloss Blutenburg organization take place in the French Gardens of Schwaneck Castle down on the Isar at Pullach, ten miles southeast of central Munich. Advance bookings from Theatergemeinde, Goethestr. 24.

Schloss Amerang, near Wasserburg. Médieval castle about 30 miles east of Munich with summer concerts from 28 June until 23 August. Baroque music and folklore. Concerts take place in the courtyard of the castle, which in bad weather is covered. Tickets from all large travel agents.

Schloss Schleissheim in Schleissheim, 12 miles north of Munich. Concerts throughout the summer, June to September, in the Grosser Barocksaal. International Music Weeks from 1–29 June. Tickets can be booked in advance from all large travel agents or from the Concert Organisor, Schleissheim (tel. 609 11 98).

Benediktbeuern Monastery, Benediktbeuern near Bad Tölz. In this famous 1,200-year-old monastery you can enjoy indoor and outdoor concerts of baroque music, as well as performances by the world-renowned Tölzer Knabenchor. Taking place from June until end of August, indoors in the Barocksaal or the Basilika the famous double-towered church, and outdoors in the courtyard of the cloisters. Advance bookings for concerts in the *Basilika* only from the theater box office (Theaterkasse) of the *Amtliches Bayerisches Reisebüro*, at Stachus-Karlsplatz in Munich (tel. 5 98 15).

Schloss Herrenchiemsee on the island of Herrenchiemsee. Concerts of chamber music from 17 May through 27 September in the majestic ballrooms of the palace, illuminated with thousands of genuine wax candles. Concerts take place in the evenings at 7:30 and 8:30 every Saturday and ferryboats transfer visitors from Prien on Chiemsee to the island in accordance with the times of the concerts. Last ferry back from Herrenchiemsee at 9.50. Bus excursions from Munich also offered by American Express Company and Autobus Oberbayern, Lenbachplatz 1, with whom advance bookings (concert and ferry tickets) can be made.

 MUSEUMS. For opening times consult the official monthly program of Munich events obtainable at newsstands. *Alte Pinakothek*, Barer Strasse 27, European paintings from the 14th to the 18th centuries. Among the chief treasures of this museum are works by Van der Weyden, Memling *(The Seven Joys of the Virgin)*, Hieronymus Bosch, Holbein, Dürer (including one of the most famous self-portraits), Grünewald, Breughel, a rich group by Rubens, Van Dyck, Frans Hals, fine Rembrandts, Poussin, Chardin, Boucher, El Greco, Velasquez, Giotto, Botticelli, Leonardo da Vinci, Titian, Raphael, Tintoretto.

The Neue Pinakothek, Barer Str. 29, right across the lawn from the Alte Pinakothek. Munich's museum of 19th-century painting and sculpture in a brand new building. A collection strong on German Romantics and French Impressionists. Among the great names here are Goya, Turner and Manet.

Haus der Kunst, Prinzregentenstr. 1. The west wing houses works belonging to the Neue Staatsgalerie and represents a good cross-section of modern art. Important art exhibitions are scheduled round the year.

Schackgalerie, Prinzregentenstr. 9. Late 19th-century German painters (Böcklin, Feuerbach, Schwind).

Bavarian National Museum, Prinzregentenstr. 3. Contains a remarkable collection of medieval art and sculpture, miniature art, arts and crafts, folk art, applied art, etc. Also the prehistoric and early history museum is housed here. Among its more notable exhibits are the largest collection of early German sculpture in the country, the best tapestries in Germany, a fine group of wood-carvings by Tilman Riemenschneider, 16th-century armor, and the unique Krippenschau, Christmas Crib collection.

Prehistoric State Collection, next to the National Museum in Lerchenfeldstr. 2. Prehistoric and early history with special exhibitions.

"Die Neue Sammlung" (Museum of Applied Arts), Prinzregentenstr. 3, collection of articles of everyday use from end of 18th century to present day.

Deutsches Museum, Museum Island (full name, German Museum of Master-works of Natural Science and Technology). Gradually reopened, this first-rate scientific museum covers just about everything in its realm. See the mining exhibit, showing just how mines are and were worked, and the 16th-century alchemists' workshops. A planetarium capable of projecting some 4,500 stars inside its semi-circular dome (as well as the sun, moon, and planets, of course) is one of the many attractions, along with the historical railroad and astronaut sections.

BMW Museum. Reopened in 1980 after a period of closure for renovation, the soup-bowl shaped BMW Museum out on the Petuelring near the Olympic Park now offers a lot more than an exhibition of vintage cars and motorcycles from the history of the Bavarian Motor Works. The visitor is guided through the museum with the aid of the most modern audio-visual aids. Headphones provide a running commentary describing not only the technical details of each exhibit from the world of motor sport and transport, but supplementing the descriptions with historical film material, video tapes, and often portraying the exhibits in a setting of some suitable event from modern history. On the top floor of the museum is a relaxation area—again an innovation—where visitors can sit back in comfortable car seats and enjoy film-slide shows. On the ground floor a computer is at the disposal of visitors to compile and print out their own individual museum catalogue.

Staatliche Antikensammlungen, Königsplatz 1. Collection of Greek, Roman and Etruscan art.

Glyptothek, Königsplatz 3. Collection of ancient Egyptian, Greek and Roman sculpture.

Städtische Galerie im Lenbachaus, Luisenstr. 33. The works of Lenbach, and noted collection of the Blaue Reiter (Blue Rider) school (Kandinsky, Marc, Macke) and Paul Klee.

Residenzmuseum, Max-Joseph-Platz 3. Staterooms and princely suites in Renaissance, rococo, and neo-classic styles, porcelain, silverware. *Schatzkammer* (Treasury) in the same building features masterpieces in gold and precious stones from the last ten centuries. The previously mentioned rococo theater is also a part of the Residenz Palace and can be visited daily, entrance Residenzstr. 1. The State Collection of Egyptian Art is now also located here, entrance near the obelisk in Hofgartenstr.

Münchner Stadtmuseum, St.-Jakobs-Platz 1. Munich history and antiques. Includes also the *Deutsches Brauereimuseum,* historical museum of beer brewing through the centuries.

Deutsches Jagdmuseum (German Museum of Hunting) in the former Augustine church, Neuhauserstr. 53. Among exhibits are 3,000 hunting tropies, historic hunting weapons, 200 stuffed animals in dioramas representing their natural surroundings.

Schloss Nymphenburg, with rococo interiors in the main palace and the attached Marstallmuseum (Bavarian Royal coaches and sleighs) and the museum of Nymphenburg porcelain manufacture. Also beautiful gardens with several garden pleasure buildings (Amalienburg, Badenburg, Pagodenburg and Magdalenenklause).

State Graphic Collection, Meiserstr. 10/I, drawings and prints from the late Gothic period until the present.

Theatrical Museum, at Galeriestr. 4a (Hofgartenarkaden). Collection still has its 40,000-volume library, portraits of actors, designs for stage sets, etc.

Bavarian State Library, Ludwigstr. 23. This great library lost 500,000 of its 2,000,000 books (the collection has now grown to over 3,000,000) in the bombings, but saved all its 16,000 incunabula and its priceless medieval books, including the Bible of Emperor Otto III, with its Reichenau illuminations dating from about 1000, and its ivory binding inset with gems.

SHOPPING. Generally considered Germany's most varied shopping city, Munich boasts a variety of fascinating streets. Among them: the pedestrian mall from Karlsplatz (Stachus) to Marienplatz at the Rathaus; from here two shopping arteries lead to Odeonsplatz: Wein and Theatinerstrasse, and Diener and Residenzstrasse; other fine shopping streets are Briennerstrasse, Maximilianstrasse, the Maxburg block at Pacellistrasse and the small streets near the Hofbräuhaus and the new pedestrian zone in Sendlingerstrasse. Highlights of Munich shopping include, of course, Bavarian handicrafts, such as woodcarvings, pewter, handblocked prints, and elaborate wax candles; and antiques and contemporary art.

Antiques. *Antic Haus,* Neuturmstr. 1 near Hofbräuhaus; in a large house about 50 different antique dealers are spread over 3 floors; check your coat at the entrance and wander for hours upstairs and down: there is a café on top floor for resting.

Beer steins and pewter. *Ludwig Mory* in the Rathaus, particularly beautiful and varied pewter articles and large selection of beer mugs. *Wallach,* Residenzstr. 3, for original beer steins; also *Josef Pemsel,* Orlandostr. 2 near Hofbräuhaus.

Clocks. *Andreas Huber,* Weinstr. 8. *Hauser,* Marienplatz 28 and Neuhauserstr. 19.

Dirndls and folk dress. *Wallach,* Residenzstr. 3. *Dirndl Ecke* on Platzl near Hofbräuhaus. *Trachten-Alm,* Herzogspitalstr. 13. *Dirndlstube,* Karlsplatz 8. *Loden-Frey,* famous for Bavarian clothes, Maffeistr. 7–9.

Handicrafts. For wax-art candles: *Seitz,* Pacellistr. 2; *Koron,* Mazaristr. 1; *Wachszieher am Dom,* Sporerstr. 2. *Bayerischer Kunstgewerbeverein* (Bavarian association of artist-craftsmen), Pacellistr. 7, for Bavarian handicrafts with a modern touch. *Wallach,* Residenzstr. 3, a bit of everything. For Oberammergau woodcarvings *Karl Storr,* Kaufingerstr. 25.

 TRANSPORTATION. If you arrive by **train** you have to get off at the Hauptbahnhof (main station) which is located very near the center of the city. Other important railroad stations in Munich are: Starnberger Bahnhof, which is now a section of the main station, and where you take trains for Starnberger Lake and Garmisch; Holzkirchner Bahnhof, Bayerstr. 14, at the other end of the main station, where the trains for Tegernsee, Schliersee, Bayrischzell, Bad Tölz start; Ostbahnhof, Orleansplatz 1, which serves the eastern section of the city and has a direct line to Wolfratshausen south of Munich.

Airport buses leave from the north side (Arnulfstrasse) of the main railroad station every 20 minutes between 5:40 A.M. and 8:40 P.M. Fare DM 3.50.

Munich has a closely knit network of public transport to get you quickly and comfortably to anywhere you wish to go. Modern suburban **electric trains** *(S-Bahn),* **underground** *(U-Bahn),* **trams** and **buses** are at your service from early morning till late at night, and the underground network is at present being extended even more to link the eastern and western perimeters with the city center.

The **S-Bahn** operates seven different lines, numbered S1 to S7. S7 was opened in 1981 and is the latest addition to the transportation system, linking Munich's eastern main station, the *Ostbahnhof,* with the old market town of Wolfratshausen, a favorite starting point for exploring the Isar valley and the foothills of the Alps. Connections to all the other lines can be made at the Ostbahnhof.

The underground, or **U-Bahn,** also operates six lines (U1-U8), traversing the city from north to south and east to west, with many extensions under construction. Of these, the most important, the new U8 opened in October '81, and linking Munich's "new town" area of Neuperlach and the residential areas on the eastern borders of the city, with the Main Station and the western suburbs. A northern extension of this line to the suburbs of Bogenhausen and Cosima Park is at present under construction.

The S-Bahn provides quick links with some of the most beautiful recreation areas of the countryside surrounding the capital of Bavaria. For example, with the S6 you can be down at the lakeside on Starnberger See within half-an-hour from the city, or with the S5 to Herrsching on the delightful Ammersee and with the S4 in the depths of Ebersberger Forest. Another S-Bahn excursion which should not be omitted is a trip out to Aying on the S1 (direct connection) to visit the famous Gasthof-Brauerei Aying, a first-class restaurant set in picturesque surroundings with its own old-established brewery.

Tickets. The same tickets are valid for U-Bahn, S-Bahn, trams and buses. Your ticket is valid everywhere and connections can be made from one line to another. Single and strip-tickets (for several journeys) can be obtained from automatic ticket dispensers at all train, bus and tram stations, together with schematic information regarding the tariffs. A green-strip ticket with 12 strips costs DM10 (six rides in the metropolitan area). A blue-strip ticket with six strips costs DM5 (three rides). A trip within the metropolitan Munich area costs two strips, equivalent to DM1.66. Your strips entitle you to as many transfers as you like in one direction for two hours.

However, as you have to calculate yourself the number of fare-stages through which you are going to travel and cancel your ticket accordingly (in one of the blue automatic cancelling machines called *Entwerterautomaten,* marked with a large, yellow "E") before starting your journey, visitors to Munich who intend to make full use of all the public transport services offered and who wish to be spared the trouble of learning the system thoroughly, are recommended to use the 24-hour ticket. With one of these tickets you can travel for 24 hours wherever you like and as often as you like on all forms of public transport in and around Munich. There are 2 kinds of tickets: one for DM 6 (children 4 to 14 years DM 2) which is valid only in the inner area (blue) of the schematic tariff plan for travel in the city center, and one for DM 10 (children DM 4), which is valid for the whole transport area (blue and green zones). You can buy these tickets from the automatic ticket dispensers or from ticket kiosks with the sign *"Mehrfahrtenkarten"* and a white "K" on a green background, from the Official Bavarian Travel Agency (ABR) or from tourist offices. Before you begin your first journey you must sign the ticket and cancel it in one of the blue cancelling machines. The ticket is then valid for 24 hours.

A word of warning: never use the Munich Transport System without a valid ticket, or with a ticket cancelled insufficiently, otherwise you are liable to pay a DM 40 fine! Regular checks are carried out on all forms of transport and being "a foreigner" is no excuse for not having a ticket.

Two booklets which will help you get about in Munich and easily explain the ticket system are *Rendezvous mit München* and *Verbundfahren in München,* with English translations, which are published by the Munich Transport Office *(Münchener Verkehrs Verbund)* and available from the city's Information Center in the underground shopping precinct at the Karlsplatz.

PARKING. As in all large cities, parking is a problem. Several, albeit crowded, outdoor parking lots exist all over the city. Many streets in the center have meters. Large above-ground and underground parking garages are available especially in the main railroad station area and in the section near the Rathaus. Some of them (open day and night) are: *Parkgarage* in the main station (the first completely automatic type in Europe); *Parkhaus am Stachus* entrance from Bayerstr. and Sonnenstr.; *Mathäser Tiefgarage,* Bayerstr. 5; *Central-Garage,* Maxburgstr. 4; *Parkhaus am Färbergraben,* entrance from Altheimer Eck and Marienplatz; *Fina am Hofbräuhaus,* entrance from Tal and Maximilianstr.

SIGHTSEEING. The blue buses, with conducted sightseeing tours in German and English, leave from the main train station square, corner of Prielmayerstrasse, all year round. No student reductions. Trips to the Upper Bavarian lakes and mountains by buses operated by German Railroads or by German Post Administration, usually start at the main railroad station, or by guided bus tours, organized by several travel offices. City sightseeing by air can be done from the airport and is fairly inexpensive; inquire at Bayerischer Flugdienst at the airport. Helicopter flights can be taken in winter from the airport to some winter sports centers in Upper Bavaria.

Among the tours which start from the Main Station are the following:

Short tour (1 hour), daily; 1 May - 31 Oct., 10:00 A.M., 11:30 A.M., 2:30 P.M.; 1 Nov. - 30 April, 10:00 A.M., 2:30 P.M. Price: DM9.50.

Short tour with trip to Olympic Tower (2½ hours), daily; 1 Nov. - 30 April, 10:00 A.M., 2:30 P.M. Price: DM17.

Long tour with visits to Cathedral, Glockenspiel and Alte Pinakothek (2½ hours), daily except Monday; 10:00 A.M. Price: DM19. With visits to Nymphenburg Palace and Schatzkammer (2½ hours), daily except Monday; 2:30 P.M. Price: DM19. With visit to Olympic Park and Olympic Tower (2½ hours), daily; 1 May - 31 Oct; 10:00 A.M., 2:30 P.M. Price: DM19.

Munich by Night (approx. 5 hrs.) daily at 7:30 with visit to three typical Munich nightspots. Price, including dinner, DM 80.

SPORTS. All kinds of sports installations are available on the grounds at Oberwiesenfeld, constructed for the 1972 Olympic Games. **Football** (soccer): the most important matches take place there at the Olympic Stadium; others at the stadium in Grünwalderstr.

Golf courses are at Strasslach near Grünwald (18 holes) and at Thalkirchen (9 holes).

Horseback riding schools are Universitätsreitschule in Königinstrasse 34, and four schools belonging to the large sports store *Sport-Scheck* (inquire there). **Horse Racing:** flat races at Riem, trotting at Daglfing, take the S-Bahn from the center of the city for either.

Bicycle races at the Amorbahn, Baumgartnerstr. 50 beyond the Theresienwiese.

Skating at the Eissportstadion (ice stadium) on the Olympic grounds (also **hockey** matches), and at Prinzregenten Stadium. There is also outdoor skating on the lake in the English Garden and on the Nymphenburg Canal.

Bowling (American-style) at Brunswick Bowling, corner Forstenrieder Allee and Züricherstrasse in the suburb of Fürstenried, 20 automatic alleys, bowling instruction; or at Bavaria-Bowling, Lazarettstrasse 3, both with restaurants.

The largest all-weather (indoor and outdoor) **tennis** installations are at Münchner Strasse 15 in München-Unterföhring (7 indoor and 18 outdoor courts) and at the corner of Drygalski-Allee and Kistlerhofstrasse in München-Fürstenried (5 indoor and 11 outdoor courts). In addition there are about 200 outdoor courts all over Munich.

Swimming, outdoors, in the Isar at Maria-Einsiedel, if you are a hardy character; the river flows from the Alps, and the water is frigid. Warmer natural swimming is provided by the bathing beaches of the lakes within reach of Munich (Ammersee and Starnbergersee, for instance). There are many swimming pools, among the best; *Dantebad,* Dantestr. 6, outdoors but heated in cold months; *Volksbad,* Rosenheimerstr. 1; *Michaelibad,* Heinrich-Wieland-Str. 24; and the *Olympia-Schwimmhalle* on the Olympic grounds. *Florian's Mühle,* Floriansmühlerstr, in Freimann suburb.

Sailing and Wind-surfing on the nearby lakes of Ammersee (with sailing school) and Starnbergersee, but windsurfers should pay attention to restricted areas at bathing beaches. Further information from *Verband der Deutschen Windsurfing Schulen,* Weilheim, (tel. 0881 5267).

 **USEFUL ADDRESSES. Local tourist information:** Fremdenverkehrsamt in the central front section of the main railroad station (also room reservations) and in the main hall at the airport; the main office is at Rindermarkt 5 (Haus Drei Rosen); all with the central tel. 2–39–11. Fremdenverkehrsverband München-Oberbayern, Sonnenstr. 10. **Train information,** tel. 59–33–21. **Air travel information,** tel. 92–11–27. *Alpine Auskunftstelle,* for information on mountaineering and skiing tours, tel. 29–49–40.

General tourist information: ABR (Official Bavarian Travel Office) with branches in the main railroad station, at Promenadeplatz 12, Stachus (corner Sonnenstrasse), Sendlinger Strasse 80, Feilitzschplatz, Tegernseer Landstr. 11, Arabellapark, Pasing—all with the central tel. 5–90–41, and at the airport, tel. 92 21 71. American Express, Promenadeplatz 3. Cook's Lenbachplatz 3.

For motorists: ADAC (General German Automobile Club), Baumgartnerstr. 53 and Sendlinger-Tor-Platz 9. ADAC emergency service, tel. 22–22–22. Driving guides: Lotsendienst München, Valpichlerstrasse 9/0 and at the exits of all four autobahns (Salzburg, Garmisch, Stuttgart and Nürnberg) and Highway 13 from Holzkirchen. English-speaking sightseeing-guides also available.

Official representation: U.S. Consulate General, Königinstr. 5–7. British Consulate, Amalienstr. 62. Amerika Haus, Karolinenplatz 3; British Council, Giselastr. 10/I.

Business: Chamber of Commerce, Maximilianplatz 7. Lost and Found: in general, at Police stations anywhere; on city streetcars and buses, Tal 70/V; on trains, main station; in post offices, Bahnhofplatz 1.

Money change (also before and after regular banking hours): Wechselstube in the main station from 6 A.M. to 11:30 P.M. and in the arrival hall at the airport from 7 A.M. to 8:30 P.M., both daily.

International pharmacist: *Internationale Ludwig's Apotheke,* Neuhauser Str. 8, in the pedestrian mall (tel. 260 30 21).

English-language church service: Munich Baptist Church, Holzstrasse 9; Sunday at 12:45 (tel. 690 85 34).

THE BAVARIAN ALPS

Snow Trails and Rocky Faces

Along the southern border of Bavaria, the high walls of the Alps separate Germany from Austria. These are real mountains—Germany's highest peak, the Zugspitze, is here, rising to nearly 10,000 feet—and one might expect, accordingly, that it would be difficult to get about in country so abundantly provided with natural barriers. But the Bavarian Alps, on the contrary, are highly accessible.

This region of the Bavarian Alps (Upper Bavaria) is the most typical, or at least the most representative of most people's idea of Bavaria. The people here are easy-going, the village inns resound with zither music, village squares with brass band tunes, the mountains with the yodels of hunters and lumbermen, and on Sundays every true villager wears the folk dress. The houses are large and the roofs long, low and sloping; usually they are chalets, with wooden balconies running along them; their façades are often elaborately painted.

EXPLORING THE BAVARIAN ALPS

Munich lies very close to the Alps and unless you are coming from Austria, chances are it is from Munich that you will enter this region. If you first wish to visit Oberammergau and the Garmisch area, you travel through Starnberg on the Starnberger Lake and then continue through the old market town of Murnau, located at Staffel Lake with its wooded islets, to either Oberammergau or Garmisch. A scenically more rewarding route to Oberammergau (you must have a car for this one) is from Starnberg through Weilheim to Schongau on the Romantic Road; then through Rottenbuch with its rococo decorated monastery church and over Echelsbacher Brücke, a single-span bridge 250 feet above the Ammer River, to Oberammergau.

Oberammergau

Oberammergau is known the world over for its Passion Play, given every ten years in the year ending with a zero. Even if there is no play the year when you are visiting, you can see the theater in which it is given and the bearded actors who will play the roles of Christ and other important parts carrying on their everyday occupations—many of them carving wood, for Oberammergau is a great woodcarving center, with a school that teaches the craft. The play, which was first given in 1634 in fulfillment of a vow to present it every decade if the Black Plague were ended, requires over a thousand performers. As they are all natives of Oberammergau, whose population is only 5,000, it is evident that it is the focal point of life in the town.

Play year or not, Oberammergau is a rewarding place to visit, with its attractive old houses and its pleasant parish church lying peacefully among broad grassy fields, from which the great rocks of the Alps rise abruptly. From it you can take the bus trip into the Graswangtal Valley, to visit Schloss Linderhof, one of Ludwig II's most fanciful castles. In front is an artificial pond with a gilded statue of Flora and a 105-foot fountain. The castle itself was built in rococo style and has a number of ornate suites. In the park King Ludwig II also had constructed an artificial blue grotto in imitation of the one at Capri and a Moorish Kiosk with enameled bronze peacocks.

Oberammergau is also an ideal starting-off point for hiking tours in the surrounding mountains. There are a variety of marked footpaths to choose from, and every year on 24 August anyone can take part in an organized Mountain Hiking Day (Gebirgswandertag) called "In King Ludwig's Footsteps" in memory of the "Dream King" of Bavaria. The day ends with a spectacular sight when, at dusk, huge bonfires are set ablaze on the surrounding mountainsides.

Proceeding from Oberammergau or Linderhof to Garmisch the road passes through Ettal, known mainly for its beautiful Benedictine Abbey founded in 1330. Its church was built first in Gothic style and was changed in the early 18th century into a baroque structure with a large dome whose ceiling was painted by Johann Jakob Zeiller.

A good route from Munich to Garmisch-Partenkirchen moves southward from Wolfratshausen, the farthest point from Munich mentioned in the list of excursions from that city, the railroad making straight for Bichl, while the motor road makes a slight loop to the east to pass near Bad Heilbrunn. From this minor spa, or from Bichl via Bad Heilbrunn, it is a short side trip to a major one, Bad Tölz, delightfully located on the Isar against a background of high mountains. It is an old place (the Romans had a settlement here in the 5th century, named Tollusium) and it remains conscious of tradition. This is local costume country and if you happen to be on hand on November 6, you can take in the Leonhardi Ride, in honor of the patron saint of horses.

Continuing south from Bichl, road and rail alike pass through Benediktbeuern, where there is a 1,200-year-old monastery, whose double-towered church bears the familiar onion domes of this region. At Kochel there is a lovely lake, the railroad ends and train travelers must take to the bus. The road continues through Walchensee, where there is another delightful example of the beautiful lakes that characterize this region, with the mountains rising steeply straight from the water; Wallgau, a pleasant little village of 900 inhabitants, nestled in a small valley cupped by mountains, and Krün, somewhat larger but in a situation much the same, to Garmisch-Partenkirchen.

Garmisch-Partenkirchen

This town is very probably the world's Number One winter sports center; in any case, there can be no doubt that it is Germany's. It was the growing popularity of skiing that made Garmisch-Partenkirchen the world-renowned place it is. Before World War I, there was only a village here; it took ten hours to reach the peak of the Zugspitze, where, in those days, it was assumed only eccentrics would want to go. Now thousands reach its top every year in minutes by the cable car from the nearby Eibsee.

Garmisch-Partenkirchen lies on comparatively flat ground, from which mountains spring to terrifying heights on every side. The giants of the group are the Wank to the east, 5,840 feet; the Kreuzeck to the south, 5,420 feet; to the southeast the Alpspitze, 7,284 feet; and to the southwest, on the Austrian border, Germany's highest mountain, the majestic Zugspitze, 9,782 feet. These great peaks, plus Garmisch's famed sunny climate, which made it a health resort before skiing seized upon it, and the fact that snow can be depended upon here from the latter part of November until the middle of May, are the natural factors which account for the popularity of this resort. Manmade attractions have completed its assets.

The Olympic Ski Stadium and Olympic Ice Stadium were built for the winter Olympic Games held here in 1936. The Olympic Ski Stadium has two ski jumps and a slalom course. There is room for 100,000 people, although "only" 30,000 of them can be accommodated in the grandstands. The Olympic Ice Stadium provides nearly an acre of ice surface and its grandstands can take 12,000 spectators; ice skating competitions and ice hockey games can be held at night because the ice rink can be floodlit to daylight brilliance by powerful reflectors. Another rink, with stands for 6,000 persons, is next to the first one.

There are any number of breathtaking excursions from Garmisch. There is a beautiful four-mile walk to Grainau, offering superb views. There are two gorges well worth visiting, the Partnachklamm and the Höllentalklamm. The lovely little Riessersee is a lake on the outskirts of Garmisch, while further away is the Eibsee, with the tremendous rock wall of the Zugspitze rising above it. The Wank is reached from Partenkirchen by a suspended cable car; the Kreuzeck, Graseck, and Eckbauer are reached similarly while a cable car will take you to Hausberg. But for the Zugspitze, the Number One excursion from Garmisch, you have your choice between a Bavarian mountain railway and cable car and a Tyrolean cable car (from Obermoos which can be reached by train and bus from Garmisch), since the Zugspitze marks the border between Germany and Austria.

For the full variety of the marvelous scenery, the best idea is to go by one route and return by the other. On the Bayrische Zugspitzbahn you pass the dark-blue Eibsee, framed by deep-green pine forests, and reach Schneefernerhaus through a long tunnel. At this point a broad skiing area spreads out, the highest in Germany, the Zugspitzplatt; if your object is not skiing, but the view, a cable car will take you still higher, to the Summit Station, anchored by cables to the lofty pinnacle on which it stands, from which you can see all the way to the central Alps of Switzerland. You can also reach the peak of Zugspitze directly from Eibsee by cable car.

Garmisch, together with Partenkirchen, however, is not only a sports center and a point of departure for trips and excursions. It is a very attractive town in its own right, with many wooden balconies and painted façades on its Alpine-style houses, and with the baroque parish church and 15th-century Church of St. Martin. Garmisch is also a health resort with a lovely Kurpark where outdoor concerts are held in summer.

Some ten miles southeast of Garmisch, in the valley of the Isar, which is still very young here, is Mittenwald, one of the most beautiful Alpine towns, with the rugged rocky face of Karwendel rising almost vertically above it. Many colorful houses line the streets, some with magnificent façade paintings, such as the Neunerhaus at Obermarkt. The baroque church with frescoed tower was originally built in Gothic style. In front of it stands the monument to the violin-maker Mathias Klotz, who in the 17th century introduced his craft to the town, and set Mittenwald on the path to world fame in this field. In the regional museum at Obermarkt 7, you may view an exhibition of the violin-making craft. A two-stage lift (first stage chair and second stage gondola) takes you to the 4,560-foot Kranzberg with a magnificent view of the Karwendel and Wetterstein mountain ranges and a cable car takes you close to the top (to about 7,350 feet) of the grandiose Karwendel scenery.

To Tegernsee and Chiemsee

In the vicinity of Mittenwald are several small blue-green lakes such as Lautersee, Ferchensee and Barmsee. A few miles north of Mittenwald are the villages of Krün and Wallgau which we have passed earlier on one of our routes to Garmisch. Proceeding further north we can return via Walchensee and Kochel to the picturesque old town of Bad Tölz, one of the oldest spas of Bavaria, with its natural iodine rich mineral springs and thermal baths, or to Munich. Another very scenic and less frequented road follows the Isar Valley (toll road for a while) from Wallgau through Fall and the unpretentious climatic resort of Lenggries to Bad Tölz.

East of Bad Tölz in a ring of high mountains lies Tegernsee, one of the most beautiful Bavarian lakes, dotted with sails in summer and spinning ice skaters in winter; its tree-lined shores adorn it with flowers in the spring and depict in the autumn a magnificent contrast between the red and golden leaves and the already snow-capped peaks in the background. All the localities on the lake are summer and winter resorts; the most important are Gmund in the north; Tegernsee with the former Benedictine monastery (now ducal castle and parish church), which was founded in 747, on the eastern shore; Bad Wiessee with chloride, iodine, and sulfuric springs and a large spa establishment on the western shore including a modern covered promenade connected with the music pavilion; Rottach-Egern with Walberg Mountain, reached by cable car, at the southern end. Farther south is the idyllic village of Kreuth from where the road continues through Wildbad Kreuth, a tiny spa, and Glashütte to Austria.

Continuing eastward from Tegernsee we come to another lovely lake, the Schliersee, whose main community bears the same name, and less than seven miles south of it is yet another blue gem of the Bavarian Alps, the tiny Spitzingsee. About ten miles southeast of Schliersee is the village of Bayrischzell with a sharply-pointed church spire, another important skiing center and summer resort. Above Bayrischzell to the north is Wendelstein Mountain, which can be reached via a new cable car. On its north side a cogwheel railroad, the oldest in Germany, begins at Brannenburg above the Inn Valley, and takes you almost to the top.

The Inn River comes rushing from Austria and flows north under the high bridge of the Munich–Salzburg autobahn, reaching Rosenheim a few miles beyond it. Rosenheim, which has been a market town since 1328, is a busy industrial city. The Old Town has several picturesque old façades, onion-shaped steeples, and arcaded streets, and is separated from the New Town by the 14th-century Mittertor (Middle Gate). About seven miles west of the city is Bad Aibling with peat and mud baths, one of the nicest Kurparks in Bavaria with a modern concert hall, music pavilion and remodeled Kurhaus. About five miles east of the city is the quiet lake of Simsee, the summer playground for the inhabitants and visitors of Rosenheim.

Proceeding farther east, you reach Prien, and find yourself on the shores of the largest lake in Bavaria, the Chiemsee, sometimes called the Bavarian Sea, whose greatest attractions are the two islands, Frauenchiemsee, with a 1,200-year-old convent and minster church, and Herrenchiemsee, where one of the fantastic castles built by Ludwig II stands. On Saturday nights (in summer) the great ballroom is lighted with thousands of candles, while chamber music groups perform selected works of classical music.

In addition to Prien and its lake section of Stock, from where the lake boats take you to Herreninsel and Fraueninsel, a cluster of small and unspoiled towns is strung around Chiemsee. Not much more than five miles from the eastern shore of the lake is Traunstein, a market town with a long history, which is presently known primarily as a health resort offering brine and mud baths and cold water Kneipp cures. South from the Chiemsee in the Chiemgau, as this part of Bavaria is called, is the very popular Alpine resort of Reit im Winkl, close to the Austrian border. If you are coming from Prien, there is no direct railway connection, but postal buses leave five times daily for this tranquil vacation spot. As a winter sports center, it has the reputation of receiving the heaviest snowfalls in Bavaria.

From Reit im Winkl we proceed on the very scenic section of the German Alpine Road to the pleasant town of Ruhpolding, another summer and winter resort, surrounded by high mountains—there is a cable car on Rauschberg—and with its houses hugging a small hill crowned by a church.

Berchtesgaden

Continuing on the Alpine Road we come to the biggest tourist attraction of the eastern Bavarian Alps—the Berchtesgaden region called Berchtesgadener Land, with its rugged giant mountains and its Alpine lakes of exquisite beauty. We first come to the village of Ramsau, an excellent mountain-climbing base for the peak of Hochkalter which towers above it; nearby is Hintersee, a small lake locked by steep slopes. Then we pass by the tumultuous torrent that pours down through the Wimbach Gorge and originates in the snowfields separating Hochkalter from the even higher and wilder Watzmann.

Berchtesgaden is the center of this area and an old market town, so rocky and so densely wooded that only one-sixth of it could be cleared for the erection of buildings. It has been described as being as high as it is wide. As a skiing center it is probably second only to Garmisch.

The main sight in town is the castle-palace, which was once an Augustinian abbey and later belonged to the Wittelsbach family, the rulers of Bavaria. Now arranged as a museum, it is accessible to the public. A part of it is the twin-spired former abbey church, first built in the 12th century in Romanesque style and later partially rebuilt in Gothic. Berchtesgaden is also a famous woodcarving center with a woodcarving school, and in its Heimatmuseum, at Schiesstättbrücke 8–12, you can see fine local masterpieces of this art. A visit to the Salzbergwerk, or salt mine (from May 1–October 15), in existence since 1517, is highly rewarding; you will be given special protective clothes and taken through the mine on old, historic mine trams.

Numerous first-class excursion spots near Berchtesgaden include Königssee, in a deep cut between almost vertical mountain walls. In order to see its majestic beauty you take an electric boat (only electric boats and rowboats are allowed in order not to disturb the peace in this wildlife preserve area) to St. Bartolomä country castle and chapel, once the summer residence of the Prince-Bishops of Salzburg, later the hunting castle of the rulers of Bavaria, and now a historic inn; today only an innkeeper, a hunter, and a fisherman are permitted to live here permanently. No building is allowed on the shores of the lake except at the very beginning where the hotels are located; but this is only a small bay which is actually hidden, due to the curve of the lake, and if you do not take the boat you have to follow the footpath to a spot called Malerwinkel, from where the lake opens in front of you in its unspoiled natural magnificence.

Another very rewarding excursion from Berchtesgaden is the drive up the Rossfeld mountain road, Rossfeld-Höhenring-Strasse, a toll-road running in a loop around the 4,900-foot Rossfeld and offering breathtaking vistas of the Berchtesgaden region as well as of the Austrian mountains across the border. You can combine this excursion with a visit to Kehlstein, the former "eagle's nest" of Adolf Hitler, which can be reached from Obersalzburg by postal bus and elevator. On a clear day the view from Kehlstein (over 6,000 feet) is one of the most magnificent in the entire Alps. Other top excursions are the visit to the Schellenberg Ice Caves, Wimbach (mentioned earlier) and Ambach Gorges, and the trip to 6,200-foot Jenner by cable car.

Bad Reichenhall

From Berchtesgaden we turn north to the fashionable spa of Bad Reichenhall, with its Romanesque St. Zeno church (according to legend founded by Charlemagne). This is one of the places that give you the full treatment—luxurious hotels, finely equipped cure establishments, well-tended parks, Kurhaus with auditorium for concerts and plays, gambling casino, and so forth. Although Bad Reichenhall's big season is the summer, in winter it is a skiing center. Summer and winter a cable car runs up to Predigstuhl from which there is a splendid view of the rocky giants of the Berchtesgaden region.

Continuing north from Bad Reichenhall and leaving the Waginger and Tachinger Lakes off to the west, we follow the Salzach River, which here forms the German-Austrian border, through the picturesque old towns of Laufen and Tittmoning to Burghausen. This 1,000-year-old town, in a very scenic location between the Salzach River and Wöhr Lake, has retained a considerable portion of its medieval aspect: a large and powerful fortress whose defense walls are among the longest in Germany; the city walls which are connected with the fortress.

A few miles below Burghausen the Salzach flows into the Inn and continuing down the Inn River there are less than 50 miles to Passau in East Bavaria. But instead of taking this route we shall follow the Inn upstream to Neu-Ötting. Al-Ötting, its twin town about a mile from the river, is one of the most frequented pilgrimage places in Bavaria. Its Holy Chapel is one of the oldest churches in Germany and the Gothic parish church (formerly Collegiate Church) contains works of art of all periods; in its treasury is one of the finest examples of goldsmith work in Germany, made about 1400 and officially known as the

Adoration of the Infant Jesus, but more generally referred to as the Golden Horse. Further up the Inn River is Wasserburg, a charming old town with its Gothic parish church, 16th-century castle, 15th-century Rathaus, and several other fine old buildings. From Wasserburg to Munich it is less than 35 miles.

PRACTICAL INFORMATION FOR THE BAVARIAN ALPS

 WHEN TO COME. This is a summer and winter region, typified by its leading resort, Garmisch-Partenkirchen, whose summer season runs from mid-**June** to the end of **September.** Although you can count on being able to ski in Garmisch by the latter part of **November,** and the first ice hockey games are scheduled then, the real winter season gets under way about Christmas, when the first ski jumping contests are held, and ends about the end of **February,** though ice hockey and minor ski meets go on through **March** and indomitable skiers prolong the season until the middle of **May.**

The big week is the International Winter Sports Week, in **January,** when everything is going full blast—ski jumping, slalom, races, bobsled contests, and all other varieties of winter sports. In **March** the longest ski trail in Europe, at Oberammergau, is the site of the King-Ludwig-Langlauf (long distance ski run), and late spring skiing features are the international Zugspitze races at Garmisch and Dammkar races at Mittenwald.

Special events are the historic Schwertertanz and George Ride festival in Traunstein on Easter Monday and the traditional Leonhardi Ride on November 6 at Bad Tölz. Many tour operators offer exclusive package visits. Consult a German National Tourist Office.

 REGIONAL FOOD AND DRINK. Most of the basic Munich dishes are also the dishes of Upper Bavaria, to which Munich belongs. For meat dishes the emphasis remains on *Geselchtes* (smoked pork), *Kalbshaxe* (veal shank), and *Schweinhaxe* (pork shank), but the *Knödel* (dumplings) are served here as a side dish to most of the meat courses, and the portions are even more ample than those of Munich. The rich juices of the meats flavor the Knödel and color the *Sauerkraut,* which appears beside the meat as often as dumplings. The Upper Bavarian lakes and streams contain a large number of excellent fish, particularly *Forelle* (trout), *Saibling* (char), and *Renke* (salmon trout).

If you want to finish off your meal with a Bavarian hard drink, try *Enzian,* a schnaps that goes well after the hearty meals you'll get here.

 HOTELS AND RESTAURANTS. Garmisch-Partenkirchen and Berchtesgaden head the field in this region, which is bountifully supplied with accommodations in all categories and special spring, fall and, particularly, winter 7-day packages. Although prices are higher here than in other mountain areas, there are still many lesser-known resorts (Inzell, Kreuth) and inexpensive hotels and pensions everywhere, plus a number of beautifully situated mountain hotels. A few of the resort hotels may close for a short period in the fall.

Ampfing. On the 2-mile-distant Palmberg hill is *Schloss Geldern* (M–E), a castle hotel with 40 beds in comfortable rooms, all with bath; swimming pool, fishing and hunting possibilities.

Bad Reichenhall. Hotels: *Steigenberger's Axelmannstein* (L), on Salzburgerstrasse, 167 rooms, most with bath, excellent restaurant with terrace, cocktail bar, own thermal bath establishment, located in large park with swimming pool, also indoor pool and tennis courts.

Both (E) are—*Kurhotel Luisenbad,* Ludwigstr. 33, fine cuisine, bar, indoor pool, garden terrace, cure facilities, most rooms with private facilities, some apartments; *Panorama,* Baderstr. 3, indoor pool, cure facilities, bar and café.

All (M) are—*Bayerischer Hof,* Bahnhofplatz, 45 rooms and 18 apartments, pool on roof terrace, café with afternoon music, nightclub and three restaurants; *Salzburger Hof,* Mozartstr. 7, small, all rooms with bath; *Tiroler Hof,* with colorful, wood-beamed restaurant, indoor pool, some apartments; *Aparthotel am Schroffen,* 19 apartments, most with terrace or loggia, indoor pool, fitness rooms, restaurant and wine tavern, panoramic views; *Tivoli,* Tivolistr. 2, 40 beds, and the much smaller *Landhaus Prosinger,* same street.

Berghotel Predigtstuhl (M), at the top station of cable car (4,320 ft.), 40 beds.

Deutsches Haus (I), Poststr. 32, with timbered restaurant.

About a mile northwest is the *Alpenhotel Fuchs*(M), in quiet location with attractive view; and about 3 miles east is the *Schlossberghof* (I), 100 beds, with folklore shows on Saturdays.

Restaurants: *Bürgerbräu,* Rathausplatz, Gasthof and beer restaurant; *Kloster-Klause,* Poststr. 52, colorful, with musical entertainment in the evening; both moderate. *Café Reber,* old coffee house with long tradition and good pastries.

Bad Tolz. Hotels: *Kurhotel Jodquellenhof* (E), on left bank of Isar at Ludwigstr. 13–15, large, most rooms with bath, 3 swimpools, one with thermal iodine water, open March–October.

All (M) are—*Diana,* Breumayerstr. 18, garni, small, all rooms with bath or shower, indoor pool; *Hotel-Pension Hiedl,* Ludwigstr. 9, 28 beds, cozy, rustic-style hotel with particularly good cooking in its *Bürgerstuben* restaurant; *Kolberbräu,* Markstr. 29, in same family since 1600, good restaurant. Many inexpensive pensions.

Restaurants: *Schwaighofer* (M), Markstr. 17. *Mauthäusl* (I), Kapellengasteig.

Bad Wiessee. Hotels (almost all chalet-type and many closed in winter): All (E) are—*Kurhotel Lederer,* 190 beds, 90 baths, in lovely location on lake with own beach and tennis courts, comfortable restaurant and Martinsklause cellar tavern; *Kurhotel Rex,* 100 beds, 30 baths, park; and *Terrassenhof,* 86 rooms, most with bath, pool, café, wine tavern and summer dancing.

All (M) are—*Kurheim Wilhelmy,* in pleasant location, 28 rooms; and *Resi von der Post,* 30 rooms; *Kurhotel Seegarten,* terrace; *Westfalen,* small, most rooms with bath; and *Wiesseer Hof, Der Kirchenwirf.*

Numerous pensions.

Restaurants: *Taverne* (M). *Alpenhof mit Schmiede* (E), a bit outside, also has a few moderate rooms. Excursion restaurants with view: *Berggasthof Sonnenbichl* (M) (2,740 ft.), with own ski lift, and *Berggaststätte Freihaus* (I) (2,760 ft.), both with (I–M) rooms. *Bauer in der Au* (M–I) (almost 3,000 ft.), with a 200-year-old covered courtyard.

Bayrischzell. Hotels (all with restaurants): Both (M) are—*Schönbrunn,* with period-furnished tavern and fine wine list; and *Meindelei,* small indoor pool and 6 bungalows.

Alpenrose and *Alpenhof,* the latter with indoor pool and a bit outside in Osterhofen, are (I–M).

On the Alpenstrasse eastwards there are several (I) mountain inns, all with terraces and views: *Sudelfeld, Brenneralm, Feuriger Tatzelwurm,* with restaurant.

Berchtesgadener Land. Many package arrangements are offered by groups of hotels. For full details write to the *Kurdirektion, Berchtesgadener Landes, Postfach 240, 8240 Berchtesgaden.* Hotels in Markt Berchtesgaden: *Geiger* (E), in quiet location on outskirts, all rooms with bath, indoor and outdoor pools, trout specialties in restaurant, antique and rustic furnishings.

All (M) are—*Königliche Villa,* built by King Maximilian II, and *Fischer* and *Bavaria,* about 40 beds. *Krone* is small, quiet.

Gästehaus Weiherbach (I), heated pool.

In Schönau, both (M) are—*Stoll's Alpina,* some apartments, indoor and heated outdoor pools, sauna; *Hanauerlehen,* indoor pool.

On Königsee: Both (M) are—*Alpenhof,* indoor pool and sauna; *Königsee-Betriebe,* a huge establishment with heated pool, 5 restaurants, bar and Casino with dancing and Bavarian folklore shows.

Schiffmeister, 20 beds, indoor pool and terrace, is (I).

In Ramsau: *Alpenhotel Hochkalter* (M), 200 beds, pool, sauna. On Hintersee lake, *Alpenhof* and *Gamsbock,* with lakeside terrace garden, are (M).

Zum Türken (I) is a small mountain hotel in quiet location with fine view in Obersalzberg next to Hitler's air-raid shelter. In Bischofswiesen, *Gästehaus Elvira,* heated pool, is (I).

Restaurants in Berchtesgaden: *Gasthof Neuhaus* (M), Marktplatz 1; café and restaurant (M–E) in the new *Kur- und Kongresszentrum,* also nightclub; *Zum Bier-Adam* (M), Markplatz 22; *Haslinger* (M), am Luitpoldpark.

Excursion restaurants in beautiful natural setting: *St. Bartolomä Historische Gaststätte* (I) on far side of Königsee, next to chapel of same name and in the former hunting castle of the rulers of Bavaria; *Berggaststätte* (M), at upper station of Jenner cable car at Königsee, excellent view. Also *Café Lockstein,* on the Lockstein hill; *Berggasthof-Dora* on the Rossfeld-Höhenring-Str. and *Kehl-steinhaus* up at the Eagle's Nest.

Chiemsee. Numerous hotels (several open May to mid-October only) in many small localities strung along the banks of this largest Bavarian lake, among them, in **Prien:** All (M) are—*Wagner,* most rooms with bath or shower, indoor pool; *Sport-und Golf-hotel Prien,* terrace, indoor pool and sauna. *Chiemsee* and *Bayerischer Hof* are (I–M).

In **Gollenshausen:** comfortable *Haus Heimburg* (I–M), chalet style, garni, library, boathouse, fishing gear, small, with own beach.

Seebruck: *Post* (M), on the lake, own bathing beach, 100 beds, garden restaurant bar.

Ising: *Gutsgasthof Zum Goldenen Pflug* (E), 120 beds, most rooms with bath, in 5 charming old houses around a courtyard, all rooms in antique style; colorful restaurant and *Stuben;* horseback riding with instructors.

Seeon: *Pension-Restaurant Gruber-Alm,* 50 beds, no through traffic, homemade bread and wine, sauna, solarium,

On the two islands: *Schlosshotel Herrenchiemsee* (restaurant open all year), own beach on Herreninsel; and on Fraueninsel the *Linde* with pleasant garden restaurant; both (I–M). Also on Fraueninsel are the *Inselwirt* restaurant (M), with pleasant garden, which serves excellent fish from the lake, and the nearby *Kloster-Café,* where you may taste the famous Chiemseer Klosterlikör, a liqueur made by the nuns of the 1,200-year-old island convent. These last three open only in summer.

Garmisch-Partenkirchen. Hotels: *Holiday Inn* (new 1980), Mittenwalderstr., Partenkirchen. With 117 rooms, all with bath, the resort's largest hotel (L). Offers first-class comfort and every possible amenity from excellent restaurant with Gourmet Club and nightclub, indoor pool, tennis courts, sauna and solarium, to individually compiled sport-action and/or cultural programs for guests at no extra charge.

Alpina (L), Alpspitzstr. 12, with heated swimpool, also indoor pool, all rooms with bath, radio, some with TV

All (E) are—*Partenkirchner Hof,* near the station, 67 rooms, excellent dining in Reindl-Grill; *Golf-Hotel Sonnenbichl,* at the golf course, 100 rooms, cozy interiors with many pieces of antique furniture, own tennis courts, music and dancing also on the outdoor terrace, with splendid view; the recent *Königshof* at the station, roof-terrace pool, café, *Jagd* restaurant with Bavarian game specialties, nightclub; *Clausings Posthotel,* a baroque chalet on Marienplatz with richly statue-ornamented façade and outstanding Bavarian cuisine, dancing in the evening. *Bellevue,* garni, Riesserseestr. 9, rooms and apartments with kitchenette, indoor pool.

All (M), some rooms higher, are—*Obermühle,* garni, Mühlstr. 22, in rustic Bavarian style, all rooms with bath and balcony, indoor pool, in same family since 1634; *Wittelsbach,* Von-Brug-Str. 24, 100 beds, all rooms with private bath or shower, most with balcony and panoramic view, indoor pool; *Posthotel Par-*

tenkirchen, Ludwigstr. 49, original stagecoach post, 90 beds, first class service, good restaurant and wine tavern with music.

Also (M) are—*Seecafé–Riessersee,* very small, Reiss 9; also *Bavaria,* 50 beds, Partnachstr. 51; *Garmischer Hof,* Bahnhofstr. 51, 58 beds; *Buchenhof,* Brauhausstr. 3, 20 beds; *Drei Mohren,* Mohrenplatz; and *Roter Hahn* (garni), Bahnhofstr. 64, indoor pool. *Gasthof Schützenhaus,* Münchner Str. 66 and *Katharienenhof,* Zugspitzstr. 86, 18 beds (garni) are (I).

In nearby Grainau, the quiet *Badersee,* with noted restaurant, boating; *Haus Hirth,* with pool; and the particularly comfortable and peaceful *Gästehaus Barbara,* Am Krepbach 12, are (M). Cheaper than any of these are the *Zugspitz,* Klammstr. 19, with 72 beds, and the *Vier Jahreszeiten* (which means the "Four Seasons"), Bahnhofstr. 23, near the station, with 100 beds.

Garmisch is also rich in good accommodation in private houses, from about DM16 for bed and breakfast. *Grainauer Hof* and *Post* are (M).

Schneefernerhaus on Zugspitze, reached by cogwheel railway, is the highest hotel in Germany (over 8,700 feet), with large public rooms and sun terraces, 30 beds; and also reached by own cable-car is the *Forsthaus Graseck,* situated at 3,000 feet above Garmisch in idyllic surroundings with 74 beds, indoor pool, restaurant and terrace with panoramic view. Both (M–E).

Restaurants: *Chesa Reindl* (M), Schmiedstr. 1, Swiss specialties; *Bauer* (M), Griesstr. 1, music; *Isis Goldener Engel* (M) on Marktplatz, café, bar, wine tavern.

Grassau. about 10 miles north of Reit im Winkel. *Sporthotel Achental* (M–E), all rooms with shower, an attractive Bavarian-style sports hotel in beautiful location, horses with riding hall and fields, pool. *Gasthof Sperrer* (M), has a panoramic view from garden restaurant terrace.

Inzell. Hotels: Modern, large *Kurhotel,* all rooms with bath, restaurant, café, cozy wine tavern and Alpine-style *Albmar* (M). *Gasthof Schmelz* (M), smaller, with heated pool, Iceland ponies, a bit outside in pleasant location near ski lifts.

All (I) are—expensive: *Binderhäusl,* small, with Bavarian restaurant and good view; *Hotel-Restaurant Eisstadion,* at the skating rink, indoor pool; in center: *Kienberg,* with verandah restaurant; *Gasthof Zur Post,* and garden restaurant; *Alpen-Hotel Gastager,* indoor pool, inexpensive apartments.

Kreuth. Hotels. *Gasthof Batznhäusl* and *Bachmair,* 90 beds, are both (M–I).

Lenggries. *Brauneckhotel* (M), recent, 84 rooms with bath. *Seemüller* (M), small, all rooms with bath or shower. Many inexpensive inns and pensions.

Mittenwald. Both (E) are—*Wetterstein,* Dekan-Karl-Platz 1, indoor pool, cure facilities, restaurant, bar and café, and *Rieger,* same square at No. 28, 80 beds, indoor pool, terrace, café, cure facilities.

All (M) are—*Post,* Obermarkt 9, 130 beds, 3 restaurants, garden café, indoor pool and cure facilities; *Gästehaus Franziska* (garni), Innsbrucker Str. 4, comfortable, with garden and nice view; *Alpenrose,* Obermarkt 1, in 13th-century house, music evenings in *Josefkeller; Alpenhotel Erdt,* Albert-Schott-Str. 7, good food; and *Jägerhof,* Partenkirchner Str. 35. *Jagdhaus Drachenburg,* Elmauer Weg 20, with view over town, game specialties in restaurant.

Many inexpensive pensions and vacation apartments and bungalows.

About 2 miles west of Mittenwald is *Sporthotel Lautersee* (50 beds), near the lake of the same name; and about 3 miles north, *Tonihof,* in lovely, quiet location, indoor pool; both are (M–E).

Oberammergau. Hotels: Both (E) are—*Alois Lang,* St. Lucas-Str. 15, 50 rooms, most with bath and balcony, cozy restaurant and bar; *Bold,* König Ludwigstr. 10, 62 rooms, most with bath or shower, panoramic views, bar, terrace and restaurant.

All (M) are—*Wolf,* Bavarian atmosphere, outdoor pool; *Turmwirt,* most rooms with bath or shower; *Friedenshöhe,* small, all rooms with bath or shower, and *Alte Post,* with magnificent old façade, garden and pleasant Ludwig-Thoma-Stube. Special winter-season rates for six days' half-board from beginning of January to end of April through local tourist office.

Both (I) are—*Wittelsbach,* 100 beds, beer tavern, and *Ambronia,* 54 beds, garden restaurant.

Reit Im Winkl. Hotels: *Steinbacher Hof* (E), on hillside and with ski lift, quiet and luxurious with fine view, all rooms with bath, indoor pool; *Unterwirt* (E), 69 rooms, most with bath, pool, bar and restaurant.

Both (M) are—*Post* and *Pension Sonnenblick,* indoor pool.

Two very pleasant hotels, quiet locations with fine views are *Alpengasthof Winklmoosalm,* 45 beds, and *Alpengasthof Augustiner,* 25 beds, both at Winklmoosalm (3,800 ft.) about 7 m. southeast of Reit im Winkl. Both have restaurants and are (I).

Rottach-Egern. Tends to be expensive as a result of its fashionable reputation. **Hotels:** The super-deluxe *Bachmair am See,* hotel complex on lakefront with 400 beds in its eight houses, all rooms and apartments with bath; seven restaurants, with particular atmosphere in the *Barthlmä-Stuben;* evening entertainment, dancing in *Nightclub;* indoor and heated outdoor pools.

Seehotel Überfahrt (E), also on lakefront, is nearly as large, with indoor pool, lakeside terrace, nightclub.

Hotel Jaedicke (M–E), garni, set in its own beautiful park, has 45 rooms, each individually decorated and offering highest comfort. Particularly attractive is the cozy cafe, serving superb home-made pastries.

Bachmair-Weissach (M) just out at Weissach, 35 rooms, excellent Bavarian specialties in attractive restaurant.

Seerose, 70 beds, garden restaurant and *Strandhotel Prasserbad,* water sports facilities, are (M). *Wallberghotel* (I), garni, at top of Wallberg cable car.

At the lower station of the cable car and in the wildlife preserve is the excellent restaurant *Alpenwildpart* (E).

Ruhpolding. Hotels: Both (E–M) are—*Zur Post,* Hauptstr. 35, 650-year-old Gasthof, tastefully furnished in traditional style. 100 beds, most rooms with bath, indoor heated swimming pool, sauna, solarium, terrace. *Post Keller-Bar* with first-class restaurant and dancing every evening. *Steinbach,* Maiergschwendterstr. 8, Ruhpolding's largest hotel with 167 beds, all rooms with bath or shower, balcony or terrace. Many rooms furnished with hand-painted rustic furniture in traditional local style. Self-service breakfast buffet, *Pils*-Tavern and fine food in *Hobelspan* restaurant with large garden terrace.

(M) are—*Gästehaus am Westernberg,* Am Wundergraben 4, peacefully situated on hillside with panoramic view, 70 beds, indoor pool, thermal baths, sauna and fitness center. Twenty minutes from Stud Farm Brendlberg. *Haus Wittelsbach,* 87 beds, fine food, including breakfast buffet bar, *Die Klause* tavern with dancing and afternoon concerts, terrace. *Ruhpoldinger Hof,* Hauptstr. 30, 76 beds, central position, most rooms with bath or shower, indoor pool with underwater massage. First-class food, particularly from own trout farm. Dancing in the *Hubertus Keller.*

Among many (I) hostelries are *Hotel Diana,* Kurhausstr. 1 with its *Dianastuben* restaurant; the elegant, rustic *Hotel-Garni Alpina,* particularly quiet and comfortable *Haus Heidelberg* and the *Cafe-Restaurant Taubensee* at the foot of the Rauschberg cable car. Also large choice of apartments. Addresses from *Verkehrsamt.*

Schliersee. Hotels: *Schliersee Hotel im Europa Ferienpark* (M–E) at Kirchbichlweg 18. New, modern apartment-hotel located in large holiday park offering 130 luxurious hotel apartments, rooms and holiday flats for 2–7 persons. All apartments, rooms and flats have balconies or terraces. In addition, indoor pool, sauna, solarium, cure facilities, bowling, rustic-style *St. Sixtus Stube* restaurant and cozy wine and beer taverns with open fireplaces.

Hotel Reiter, Silence-Hotel (M), Risseckstr. 8. As name implies very quietly located hotel on hillside above lake with fine views of lakeside and mountains. 29 rooms, most with bath or shower, 2 apartments, sun-terrace, indoor pool, cozy bar with open fireplace.

Schlierseer Hof–am See (M), 80 beds, lakeside terrace, own lake swimming facilities.

In nearby Neuhaus is the (I) *Maria Theresia,* 35 beds, and on Spitzingsee, about 7 miles south, are the fairly recent *Spitzingsee-Hotel* (M), 68 rooms and apartments, all with bath, radio and balcony, seven restaurants and Hubertusstuben in rustic décor, bar, indoor pool. *Zur Alten Seilbahn* (M), Spitzingsattel 2, 25 beds; and the *Postgasthof-Café St. Bernhard* (I), both with terrace and lake swimming facilities.

Attractive restaurants in Schliersee are *Ratskeller* and *Reiter,* both (M).

Starnbergersee. Hotels: in Starnberg: (M) are—*Seehof,* 60 beds, attractive Tessiner Stuben restaurant, lakefront café and dance-bar; *Seehof,* 60 beds, own lake swimming facilities. *Bayerischer Hof,* in front of the station, with garden restaurant, cafe and tennis.

Both (I) are—*Zur Au,* Jos. Jäger-Huberstr., 15 beds, garni; and *Tutzinger Hof,* 65 beds.

About 1½ miles north is *Forsthaus Mühltal* (M), a pleasant garden restaurant, with trout specialties and Waldkeller dance-bar, also a few inexpensive beds. In Berg: *Strandhotel Schloss Berg* (E), in quiet location, 40 beds, 10 baths, grill specialties in fine restaurant, bar, tennis, lake swimming facilities, ferry landing-stage.

In Feldafing: *Kaiserin Elisabeth* (M), at golf course in lovely country surroundings, 125 beds, cozy outdoor dining terrace, bar, tennis, riding, and swimming facilities, Schroth cures.

In Tutzing: *Hotel Seehof* (M), 90 beds, very pleasant outdoor restaurant and café on lake, moderate. The quiet *Dehn* (garni) is (I).

Tegernsee. Hotels: Moderate and very convenient location is the *Bastenhaus am See* in the main street at Hauptstr. 71, with 36 beds, good food, particularly local fish, lakeside terrace and own bathing beach; *Haus Bayern,* beautiful surroundings, every facility and large, indoor pool, and *Alte Post,* 51 rooms, on lakefront, are (M). *Luitpold,* Hauptstr. 42, restaurant and café on lake, is (I–M). *Berggasthaus Leeberghof* (I), quiet location above Tegernsee, small, colorful tavern.

The *Eybhof* (M), garni, 27 rooms, is located on the main road about halfway between Tegernsee and Rottach, very modern, noted for food, own beach.

Among other restaurants, try *Fischerstüberl am See* (M) for excellent fish from the lake, also 34 inexpensive beds; or *Schlosskeller* (M), in the castle.

Wendelstein. Almost 6,000-foot mountain above Brannenburg in Inn Valley. A mountain railway takes you near the top where *Berghotel Wendelstein* is located (I); the oldest mountain hotel in the Bavarian Alps, built in 1883 by Max Kleiber, a pioneer climber; 60 beds, restaurant, bar. Rather crowded in summer.

MUSIC AND THEATER. There are summer concerts in many spas and health resorts, including Berchtesgaden, Garmisch-Partenkirchen, Mittenwald and Bad Reichenhall. Garmisch-Partenkirchen often has guest performances in its Kurtheater, and there are folklore theaters at Bayrischzell, Berchtesgaden, Partenkirchen, Mittenwald and several other localities. Rosenheim has a regular theater and concert season. Folklore evenings featuring music, singing and dancing by local folk dress groups are scheduled at least once weekly during the summer and winter seasons in all the resorts.

Evening concerts by candlelight are held in summer at Herrenchiemsee Palace, near Prien, every Saturday from May 17 until September 27. Motorboats leave Chiemsee-Frasdorf Recreation Area in the evening at 6:30 and 7:30, as well as regular ferry services from Prien. Concert tickets should be bought in advance and can be obtained from Benno Spremberg, Künstlerhaus, Lenbachplatz 8, Munich, or a combination of concert plus ferry booking can be made at all large travel agencies. The American Express operates a bus service from

382 THE BAVARIAN ALPS

Munich (Lenbachplatz 1) to Chiemsee, departing every Saturday at 2 P.M. Excursion coaches also run from most of the large resorts of Southern Bavaria.

 SPAS AND CASINOS. Bad Tölz, Bad Reichenhall, Bad Wiessee, Berchtesgaden, Garmisch-Partenkirchen, Kreuth, Prien am Chiemsee, Rottach-Egern, and Tegernsee are all health resorts and have cure facilities. Bad Wiessee, Garmisch-Partenkirchen and Bad Reichenhall also have casinos where you may try your luck; the first is located at Münchner Strasse 10, the second at Marienplatz; the third is open daily after 3 P.M. for roulette and baccarat.

 **SPORTS. Swimming** in all lakes; modern indoor pools in Garmisch-Partenkirchen, (its Alpspitz-Wellenbad, with waves, is one of the finest swimming pool/fitness centers in Europe; it has 6 different pools, saunas, solarium and a sports center), Berchtesgaden, Bad Reichenhall (salt water), Oberammergau (with waves), and Inzell and Trimini pool (with waves) and fitness center at Kochelsee Lakes. **Sailing** on all principal lakes; Sailing and **windsurfing** schools on Chiemsee, Tegernsee, Starnbergersee and Ammersee. **Water Skiing** and **rowing** on the lakes. Best for **kayaking** are the Isar from Bad Tolz through Munich-Landshut to the Danube near Deggendorf (easy, sometimes torrential in upper part); and the Inn from the Austrian border at Kufstein through Rosenheim, Wasserburg, Neu-Otting, and along the German-Austrian border to Passau (easy).

A more daring and extravagant sport which is rapidly gaining popularity is **hang-gliding** or *Drachenfliegen*. Schools exist in most of the large resorts in the mountains, where the terrain and air currents are suitable. Instruction for beginners and hiring of equipment from the hang-gliding school of Aichach near Munich, adress: Drachenflug Aichach, Attention Herr Förster, Postfach 1112, 889 Aichach, Oberbayern. No previous experience is necessary. This is the best place for foreigners to obtain a good basic training before going off independently to the various resorts. Of these, some of the most popular are the grassy slopes of the mountainside at Brauneck near Lenggries and around Tegernsee.

Tennis courts in all spas and resorts, some indoor and open year-round. **Golf** courses in Garmisch, Berchtesgaden, Chiemsee, Bad Wiessee and Feldafing on Starnberger Lake. **Horseback riding** schools and facilities in many areas, including Wasserburg (very large) and Berchtesgaden.

Fishing is good in almost all the streams and lakes.

 MOUNTAIN CLIMBING. The Bavarian Alps are the most important climbing region in Germany. An efficiently-run net of mountain lodges provides direct access to rock faces and mountain guides are available at all important points of departure; Garmisch-Partenkirchen has a school (Bergsteigerschule Zugspitze). The principal valley bases are: Garmisch and Grainau for the Wetterstein group, which includes Zugspitze; Mittenwald and Krün for the Karwendel group; Rottach-Egern, Wildbad Kreuth, and Bayrischzell for the German offshoots of the Mangfall group, most of which is in Austria; Berchtesgaden, Ramsau, and Bad Reichenhall for the Berchtesgaden Alps. Rock-scaling tours in the Bavarian Alps, and thousands of easy hiking paths.

 WINTER SPORTS. The Bavarian Alps constitute the principal winter sports region of southeastern Germany and of Germany as a whole. The skiing season lasts in the valley areas from December to early March, above 5,000 feet until late April, and above 6,500 feet from November until late May. For cross-country skiing *(Langlauf)* all the main centers offer long stretches of prepared ski tracks or *Loipen,* which run through some of the most beautiful winter scenery.

Special winter sports trains run in the winter season between Munich and the principal skiing centers at reduced rates. All of the following centers are express train stops unless otherwise indicated. The roads leading to various of the winter resorts have recently been improved considerably. There are even well equipped winter camping sites at Berchtesgaden, Königsee, Ruhpolding, Reit im Winkl and Mittenwald-Krün. In the absence of "natural" snow a snow-making machine provides during the winter for a 440-yard long and 140-yard wide ski slope, with an ascent of 300 feet, on the Griessberg near Oberalting (Ammersee).

Aschau, 2,000 ft., with skiing terrains up to 5,000 ft. train from Prien. Cable car, chair lift, 6 ski lifts, ski jump, ski schools, ice skating, curling. In nearby Frasdorf and Sammerberg there are an additional cable car and 6 ski lifts.

Bad Reichenhall, 1,630 feet; cable car, 3 chair lifts, 3 ski lifts, ski school, ski jump, ski tours up to 8,100 feet, cross-country tracks in and around town, 2 ice skating rinks, ice hockey, curling, tobogganing. Fashionable après-ski.

Bayrischzell, skiing terrains from 2,600 to 5,000 feet, tours up to 6,000 feet; cable car, 3 chair lifts, 21 ski lifts, 3 ski jumps, bobsled school, ski school, ice skating rink, curling, tobogganing, horse sleighs. 40 km of prepared cross-country tracks.

Berchtesgaden, 1,700 to 2,500 feet; in the area known as Berchtesgadener Land: 2 cable cars, chair lift, 34 ski lifts, 2 with floodlights, 10 ski schools with instruction in ski hiking, 3 ski jumps, ice stadium, hockey, bobsled school, curling, tobogganing. Over 200 km of cross-country ski tracks. Late spring ski race on Blaueisgletscher. Considerable après-ski. An artificial toboggan run with sprinkler system, lighting and telephone system has recently been added, as well as a ski school for children.

Bergen, 1,800 feet. The Hochfelln cable car takes you to skiing terrains up to 5,500 ft. 5 ski lifts (one for children), bobsled school, curling, ice skating, ski school.

Garmisch-Partenkirchen, 2,500 feet, One of the top winter sports centers in the world with a ski stadium and ice stadium. Other facilities in this area, including nearby Grainau and Zugspitze, include: cogwheel railway, 12 cable cars, 2 chair lifts, 26 ski lifts, 4 ski jumps, ski schools, bobsled run and school, tobogganing and curling. Ice hockey in the ice stadium, skating there (also in summer) and on other rinks. From Eibsee, the cable car rises to the Zugspitze. Over 60 winter sports events scheduled every year. Ski tours are possible up to the elevations of over 9,100 feet. In the valley, numerous cross-country ski routes on prepared tracks. Fashionable après-ski. On the Zugspitze plateau, there is skiing all year albeit rather expensive. Tourist Association offers special winter ski-training weeks from 21 Oct.-15 Dec. with special cheap rates for hotels plus ski courses.

Inzell, 2,300 feet; 9 ski lifts, ice stadium with international ice racing events, ski tours, with school.

Kreuth, in Weissach Valley near Tegernsee, 2,580 feet; chair lift, 8 ski lifts, curling, tobogganing, 2 ski jumps.

Lenggries, about 2,250 feet. Cable car, 2 chair lifts, 17 ski lifts, ski school, curling, horse sleighs, snow cat. Ski tours up to 6,000 feet. Panoramic cross-country ski routes on well-prepared tracks in nearby Jachenau, Fall and Vorder-riss.

Mittenwald, about 3,250 feet. Two cable cars, chair lift, 6 ski lifts, 2 ski jumps, ski school, ice skating rink, curling, tobogganing, horse sleighs. Ski tours up to about 8,800 feet. In nearby Krün and Klais, another ski lift, 2 ski jumps, ski teacher, skating, curling, and tobogganing facilities. Many important international skiing events. Considerable après-ski. Artificial ice stadium.

Oberammergau, 2,520 feet, train stop, changing from fast train at Murnau. Cable car, chair lift, 10 ski lifts, 2 ski jumps, ski schools, one for children in English and French, ice skating, ice hockey, curling, tobogganing. Ski tours up to 6,000 feet. 90 km of cross-country tracks. Après-ski. In nearby Unterammergau: 2 ski lifts, ski school, curling and ice skating.

Oberaudorf, 1,600 to 3,000 feet. Two chair lifts, 15 ski lifts, 2 ski jumps, bobsled school, ski schools, ice skating and curling.

Reit Im Winkl, bus from the train stop at Marquartstein (8 miles). Skiing terrains between 2,300 and 4,000 feet, ski tours up to 6,000 feet, and with 65 km of prepared and sign-posted cross-country ski tracks, covering 8 different routes, one of the best resorts for *Langlauf-ski* in the whole of Germany. 2 chair lifts, 17 ski lifts, 3 ski jumps (also in summer on special mats), ski and *Langlauf-ski* schools, ice skating, curling, tobogganing. Après-ski.

Rottach-Egern, on Tegernsee, 15 minutes by bus from express train stop at the town of Tegernsee, 2,400 feet. Cable car, 3 chair lifts, 4 ski lifts, 2 ski jumps, 52 km of first-class prepared cross-country ski tracks. In nearby Tegernsee (town) are two more ski lifts; in Bad Wiessee (on same lake, less than 3 miles from Rottach), 4 ski lifts, ski jump. Ski schools exist in all the places mentioned, as well as curling and tobogganing facilities, ice skating in places on lake. Many international skiing events. Ski tours are possible up to 6,000 feet. Après-ski.

Ruhpolding, train stop. Skiing terrains between 2,100 feet and 3,600 feet, skiing tours up to 5,600 feet. Cable car, 3 chair lifts, 15 ski lifts, 2 more for children, 2 ski jumps, ski school, ice skating, also new artificial ice skating rink, curling, and tobogganing facilities. Ski tours. Après-ski.

Schliersee, on lake of same name, with nearby Spitzingsee. Skiing terrains between 2,600 and 3,600 feet, tours up to 6,200 feet. In Schliersee and immediate vicinity are 3 cable cars, 3 chair lifts, 20 ski lifts, 2 ski jumps, ski schools at Schliersee, Neuhaus, and Spitzingsee, 4 marked cross-country ski tracks, totaling 22 km, the *Schliersee Loipe,* floodlit at night; ice skating, curling, and tobogganing facilities and ice hockey at the ice stadium in nearby Miesbach. Après-ski.

 USEFUL ADDRESSES. Local Tourist Information and room reservations: Bad Reichenhall, Verkehrsverein, Bahnhofstr. 17; Berchtesgaden, Kurdirektion, opposite railroad station at Königseer Str. 2 (inquire also in office at Königsee parking lot for hotel rooms there); Garmisch-Partenkirchen, Verkehrsamt, at railroad station; Mittenwald, Verkehrsamt, Dammkarstr. 3; Oberammergau, Verkehrsamt, Dorfstr. 9; Reit im Winkl, Verkehrsamt, in Rathaus; Rottach-Egern, Verkehrsamt, Nördliche Hauptstr. 9.

For **General Information** on Upper Bavaria: Fremdenverkehrsverband München-Oberbayern, Munich, Sonnenstr. 10.

Mountain-climbing guides: Bayerischzell, inquire at Gustl Müller sports shop; Berchtesgaden, Hellmuth Schuster, Locksteinstr. 5. Heinz Zembsch, Burgergraben 11, 8244 Strub. Garmisch-Partenkirchen, (inquire at Deutschen Alpenverein, Bahnhofstr. 13), several in Grainau; Mittenwald, consult board showing names in Bahnhofstrasse; Bad Reichenhall, inquire at Sport-Noack, Innsbrucker Strasse 5.

EAST BAVARIA

A Quiet, Forested Corner

East Bavaria has the approximate shape of a triangle whose longest side is represented by the Czech border, the second side runs north-south from Fichtelgebirge to the Danube to a point about a dozen miles below Ingolstadt, and the third side cuts in a southeasterly direction from the Danube roughly to the confluence of the Salzach and Inn. The various regions of East Bavaria are: Oberpfalz (Upper Palatinate) in the north with Oberpfälzer Wald (Upper Palatine Forest) along the Czech border and Oberpfälzer Jura touching the eastern sections of Fran-conia; Bayerischer Wald (Bavarian Forest) between the Danube and the Czech border; and Niederbayern (Lower Bavaria) south of the Danube.

Although East Bavaria to the southeast shares a short stretch of border with Austria, most of its frontier faces Czechoslovakia. For the traveler it is an impressive coincidence that the natural scenery along the Czech border is the scenery of solitude. You come closer to savagery here than in any other German landscape. Here you will find large stretches with no trace of settlements, and, when there are towns and villages, inhabitants who are following customs hallowed by centuries, uncorrupted by influences from the outside world. Thus in the Bavarian Forest, when a man dies he is laid upon an oval board, and after the funeral the board is planted upright by the roadside. You will pass those boards as you make your way through this region, and on each one you will see the name of the man whose body lay upon it and a request that you say a prayer for him.

EXPLORING EAST BAVARIA

Regensburg is the principal city of East Bavaria and the fourth largest in Bavaria. It is the best point of departure for the exploration of this region. If you are coming from Munich inspect Landshut on the way, although this route is a bit longer than the direct one.

Landshut is an interesting old city with gabled houses of the 14th and 15th centuries lining its central squarelike streets of Altstadt and Neustadt, and Dreifaltigkeit Square. It has been the seat of government of Lower Bavaria since 1839. The impressive Gothic Church of St. Martin, built in the early 15th century, has a richly carved portal, superb and very high interior vaulting, the high altar from 1424, and a 436-foot brick church tower supposed to be the highest in the world. Stadt-Residenz (City Residence Palace), once inhabited by the Dukes of Bavaria, shows Renaissance, baroque and neo-classical influences and contains a very fine painting gallery and several museum collections in addition to the period-decorated suites of the 16th and 18th centuries. Landshut is dominated by Burg Trausnitz, a powerful castle-fortress on the hill above it, with the 13th-century double chapel and Wittelsbach Tower, and with such interior details in the main building as the "Fools' Staircase," so called because it is decorated with scenes from Italian comedy.

The city has many other interesting buildings, such as the rococo church of Seligenthal Abbey, but Landshut is just as renowned for its recollection of the very good time it once had at a wedding. That event took place in 1475, when Prince George, the son of the reigning Duke, married the Polish Princess Hadwiga. The feasters consumed 333 oxen, 275 hogs, 40 calves and 12,000 geese, with, it must be assumed, a few side dishes as well, and something to wash it all down. Landshut has never forgotten that celebration, and every three years it enacts the

Princely Wedding all over again, with most of the population turning out in medieval costume.

Ancient Regensburg

Much bigger and older than Landshut, Regensburg was originally a Celtic town, taken over by the Romans about 2,000 years ago. Next to the Celtic settlement, to which the name Radasbona was given, the Romans built a military fortress town and called it Castra Regina. When the Bavarian tribes migrated to this area in the early 6th century, they occupied it, made it the seat of their dukes, and apparently on the basis of the Latin name, called it Reganesburg and hence the present name. Later the city became the capital of the Carolingian monarchs and in the Middle Ages developed into a commercial center of European importance. Later it became a free imperial city and for some 150 years was the site of the Imperial Diet. Reminders of its glorious past are everywhere in the city. It is not, however, simply a monument of the past. It is a busy modern city and the head of navigation on the Danube, with a lively port which is well worth a visit.

To get a general view of Regensburg, walk to the far end of the Steinerne Brücke, the Stone Bridge, the end which touches the trans-Danubian suburb of Stadtamhof. This early 12th-century structure was an engineering miracle for its time and is the oldest bridge in Germany. Penetrating into the city, keeping straight ahead from the bridge, you will come to the square where the magnificent St. Peter's Cathedral stands. It was built in its present form between the 13th and 15th centuries and rates among the finest examples of the German Gothic ecclesiastical architecture; the magnificence of its twin-towered façade is surpassed probably only by the cathedrals of Cologne and Strasbourg. In addition to many other works of art (the Gothic sculptures deserve special note), it has preserved some of the 14th-century stained-glass windows and its treasury contains valuable items from the late Middle Ages. In the cathedral you can hear the famous Regensburger Domspatzen (Regensburg boys' choir). The cathedral is connected by an arcaded courtyard with the early Romanesque St. Stephan's Church and the late Romanesque All Saints Chapel. At the eastern end of the cathedral square is the 13th-century St. Ulrich's Church.

At the nearby Alter Kornmarkt is the Romanesque Alte Kapelle (Old Chapel), of which the earlier parts date from about 1000 and which was the church of the ducal castle that stood here in the Middle Ages. This is also the area where the Roman fortress was located and in a narrow street between the cathedral and the Danube you can still see Porta Praetoria, constructed in 179, which was one of its gates. The continuation of the same narrow street towards the west is called

Goliath Strasse because the Goliath House is located here, which in turn received its name from the giant 16th-century fresco.

Several other centuries-old patrician houses and narrow streets give this section of the city a truly medieval appearance; particularly interesting examples are the 13th-century Baumburger Turm on Watmarkt and the 9-story Goldener Turm in Wahlen Strasse, both built in the form of towers. Goliath Strasse ends at Kohlenmarkt and Rathaus Square, with the Old Town Hall built in 1350. Its star exhibit is the Reichstagssaal (Imperial Diet Hall), where the Diet sat, but it also boasts dungeons, instruments of torture, and some fine, richly medieval rooms.

Continuing in the same westerly direction and crossing the Haidplatz, which was a tournament field in the Middle Ages, we come to the twin squares of Arnulfsplatz and Bismarckplatz, separated by the city theater. At the Jakobstrasse corner is Schottenkirche St. Jakob, a 12th-century Romanesque church built by Scottish and Irish monks, particularly known for its north portal, on which Christian and pagan sculptural motifs are curiously intermixed. Not far from it, in Beraiterweg, is Dominikanerkirche, a noted 13th-century Gothic basilica, with some murals of the 14th and 15th centuries.

One other particularly important sight in Regensburg is the palace of the Princes of Thurn and Taxis, their residence since 1748, set in a pleasant park not far from the railroad station. This was originally the Abbey of St. Emmeram, and the adjoining St. Emmeram's Church, a Romanesque basilica parts of which go back to the 8th century (St. Emmeram's tomb, over which it is built, is even earlier, since he was buried there in 652), is one of the most interesting of this group of buildings.

Excursions from Regensburg

There are two particularly notable excursions (which can be made by boat if you like) from Regensburg. One is southwest along the Danube to Kelheim, where there are two principal sights. The first is an impressive rotunda, the Befreiungshalle, which commemorates the wars of Liberation against Napoleon. The other is the Benedictine monastery of Weltenburg, which was founded shortly after the year 600, where there is a splendid baroque church built in the early 18th century by the Asam brothers and containing a lifesize figure of St. George on horseback above the altar. In good summer weather, this can be made a delightful trip by walking from the Befreiungshalle to the monastery, which will take you about an hour, by a lovely clearly-marked forest path which takes you past the pre-Roman ramparts, and returning to Kelheim by motorboat, through a spectacular piece of the

Danube Valley, known as the Donaudurchbruch, where the river narrows as it forces its way between limestone cliffs which run up to some 400 feet. Every year on the first Saturday in July at Kelheim there is a spectacular illumination of the gorge known as "Flammende Donau" (Danube in Flames).

The other classic excursion from Regensburg is along the Danube in the opposite direction, to the east, and takes you to Donaustauf, where there is a remarkable view from the ruins of the Romanesque castle of the Bishops of Regensburg, and from Walhalla, the Hall of Fame, a temple designed in imitation of the Greek classical style by the architect Leo von Klenze spurred on by King Ludwig I, and containing marble busts and memorial plaques of some 200 famous Germans.

Proceeding farther downstream along the Danube, we enter the pleasant town of Straubing, also a Celtic and a Roman settlement, whose chief landmark is the 16th-century city tower crowned by several pinnacles. Straubing lies in the middle of a particularly fertile plain stretching between the mountains of the Bayerischer Wald north of Regensburg southwards to the hilly region of lower Bavaria around Passau. As far back as historical records go, this region has been famous for its agriculture and cattle rearing and became the granary center of Bavaria. Every year in mid-August the traditional Gäuboden Folksfest takes place, when the town of Straubing celebrates with folklore processions, music and country fair its rich and plentiful "Gäuboden." The town's Gäuboden Museum is also well worth a visit with its rich prehistoric collection, including the world-famous Römischen Schatzfund (Roman Treasure Trove) excavated in 1950 and comprising golden masks, armor, harnesses and bronze figures.

Straubing is also the city of Agnes Bernauer, accused of sorcery in the year 1435 by Duke Ernst of Bavaria, who could see no other reason to explain why his son had married her, and so had her thrown into the Danube. Her tombstone is in the graveyard of the 12th-century Peterskirche, though her body, under the circumstances, is not; every four years Straubing gives summer performances in the Ducal Palace of Friedrich Hebbel's tragedy which recounts the story of Agnes Bernauer. The next performance will be in July 1984.

Still farther down the Danube is Deggendorf, another very old town, founded around 750, which has also preserved its 14th-century city tower as well as its 16th-century Rathaus. It is a gateway to the Bayerischer Wald whose hills rise immediately to the north. In the vicinity of Deggendorf are several interesting excursion spots; the Benedictine abbey at Metten and Egg Castle are both situated at the beginning of Bayerischer Wald, while another Benedictine abbey at Niederalteich and the baroque and rococo Altenmarkt monastery church with interiors by the Asam brothers are further down the Danube. Another city tower, this time in Renaissance style, can be seen in Vilshofen, also an old town on the Danube. From here to Passau, about fifteen miles away, the road on the left bank of the river is very scenic but before visiting that city we shall explore the area north of the Danube.

Oberpfalz and Bayerischer Wald

About 45 miles north of Regensburg is Amberg which refers to itself as "the Rothenburg of Oberpfalz" because, like that famed town on the Romantic Road, it has preserved its old walls, with their sentry walk and their four gates. In addition, there are many buildings of interest—the 15th-century Gothic St. Martin's Church, the unusual 14th-century Gothic St. George's Church, and the 17th—18th-century baroque Mariahilf pilgrimage church on the outskirts; the 13th—14th-century castle of the Counts Palatine, with its fine Gothic chapel and 15th-century glass, and the 17th-century Elector's Palace; the 14th—16th-century Gothic Rathaus and the 17th-century building of the Knights of Malta.

Near Amberg, at Hirschau there are huge hill-like piles of white kaolin sand where skiing can be practised in summer. This is a porcelain-making area and kaolin is used for porcelain paste. It is supposed to be the best substitute for snow as far as skiing is concerned, or so the local people claim.

Through Weiden we proceed southeast, following the Ostmark Road along the Oberpfälzer Wald and through the Bayerischer Wald, the largest stretch of unbroken mountainous forestland in Germany, with the first German National Park, covering over 300 square miles of idyllic wildlife reserve. This is strictly a trip for scenery and any road branching off our main route will open up an unspoiled hilly and forested landscape of rare beauty.

Shortly after Weiden we come to Leuchtenberg Castle ruins on a wooded hill, easily reached from the road and worth walking up for the view from its top. A little beyond it, the road connecting Nürnberg with Prague takes us to the idyllic village of Waidhaus near the Czech border. From Waidhaus a very scenic road—though in poor condition —runs through Oberpfälzer Wald near the Czech border, passing through Schönsee and Tiefenbach to the small 1,000-year-old town of Waldmünchen, which can be reached more directly from Rötz on the parallel Ostmark Road. A net of rewarding hiking paths surrounds Waldmünchen which, however, is better known for its annual Trenck-the-Pandour Pageant, named in memory of the terrible occupation time it had to suffer some time in the 18th century at the hands of Baron Trenck and his wild Croatian pandours (mounted constabulary).

Dragons and Castles

Furth im Wald, some ten miles southeast of Waldmünchen and very near the Czech border, is noted for its Dragon-Sticking Pageant (Drachenstich) which takes place every August, and in which a most realistic dragon is done to death in the streets of the town. Accompanying the Drachenstich is a procession with costumed folklore groups, horses, musicians and decorated floats. The best way to reach Furth im Wald from Ostmark Road is via Cham, idyllically located on the Regen River.

We are now in the Bayerischer Wald, which, along the Czech border, almost acquires the character of a virgin forest. It has a remarkably clean and unpolluted air and numbers among the most therapeutic areas of Germany. The Regen flows into the Danube at Regensburg. In the section of the Bayerischer Wald between the Regen and Danube are many old castles and quiet villages offering simple vacations, ideally designed for those who wish to get "away from it all." Farther along the Ostmark Road is Viechtach, an unpretentious summer and winter resort, and the town of Regen with the nearby Pfahl ridge of natural rocky towers soaring from the earth and the ruins of Weissenstein Castle where, according to an old saga, a Count Hund (Dog) had his wife immured alive because she drowned their baby in the Regen River, afraid of a bad prophecy.

The Regen River that flows through the town of Regen is actually the Black Regen and joins the White Regen—which passes through the folk-costume-conscious village of Kötzting—shortly below Höllensteinsee into the Regen River proper. The Black and the White Regen form a giant pair of pincers that include in their grip Arber, the highest mountain of the Bayerischer Wald (4,780 feet), whose top can be reached by a chair lift and you can drive up to the lower station. This is a skiing and hiking area with several pleasant winter and summer resorts dotted around the mountain, such as Bayerisch-Eisenstein, Lam, and Bodenmais, Grosse and Kleine Arbersee, the two Arber lakes, two blue gems set in deep woods in exquisitely unspoiled landscape. The largest locality near Arber is Zwiesel, an old glass-making town, only a few miles northeast of Regen.

Passau

Geography has given Passau a delightful setting. The old city lies on land which narrows to a point as the Inn and the Danube come together on either side of it (the little Ilz, dwarfed by the other two, enters modestly from one side, opposite the point) and on the two flanking banks across from the city, on both rivers, rise wooded heights. Its old buildings lining the waterfront, the varying levels of the streets rising to the hill in the center of the old city, and picturesque architectural details such as the archways joining one house with another all combine to make it a thoroughly delightful city—Humboldt called it one of the seven most beautiful cities in the world.

It is the 15th-century St. Stephan's Cathedral that dominates Passau, situated as it is on the highest point in the town. It is of rather unusual appearance, with an octagonal dome built over the point where the transept and nave roofs cross, as well as the more conventional two towers of the west façade. In it is the largest church organ in the world—17,000 pipes, 208 stops—which you may hear played at noon every day during the summer, with an additional recital at 6 P.M. in July and August. On the choir side of the cathedral is the Residenzplatz, surrounded by fine old patrician houses, a testimonial to the wealth of Passau in the past centuries. On Residenzplatz also stands the baroque 18th-century New Residence Palace of the Prince-Bishops (hence the name of the square), with beautiful staircase, hall and rococo interiors. Passau—which in Roman times was called Castra Batava and was a Roman military town—has been the seat of a bishop since 739. At that time the bishopric was set up mainly for the support of the missionary activities in the eastern territories. Later Prince-Bishops ruled Passau for many centuries.

Among other outstanding buildings in the central section of the town are: the Gothic Rathaus on Landeplatz near the Danube with two large halls containing murals that depict the scenes of Nibelungen sagas; the Old Residence of Prince-Bishops, now Law Courts, in Zengergasse; the former Niedernburg Abbey (now a girls' school) with Holy Cross Church, founded in the 8th century as a convent, rebuilt in baroque style—in the church is the grave of Abbess Gisela, the sister of Emperor Heinrich II and the widow of St. Stephen, the first Hungarian King (the cathedral is named after him). Across the Inn River, on a hill with a fine view of the city, is Mariahilf pilgrimage church.

You cross the Danube by the Luitpoldbrücke for the second most important building of Passau, the Veste Oberhaus, also on a dominating position on the heights. This is a great fortress, started in the early 13th century by the Prince-Bishops, and continually added to for the next seven and a half centuries.

Discoveries made in 1974 on the south bank of the Inn River have disclosed the long-sought Roman town Boiotro, where St. Severin was known to have lived in the 5th century, when he undertook the Christianization of the Germanic tribes. Although the archeological work is not completed, to date they have unearthed the remains of the Roman fortress, with walls four meters broad, five defense towers, and a well, which still, after 1,500 years, is full and fresh.

There are many excursions which start from Passau. One would be a visit to the 11th-century Schloss Neuberg, about 7 miles south on the River Inn. Buses make circuits through the Bayerischer Wald, or you can take a motorboat at the Rathausplatz or the Inn Promenade for a river ride.

In fact a boat trip on the Danube is a must for any visitor to Passau. Fast, comfortable cruise steamers of the Danube Steamship Company with first-class restaurants, sun decks and cabins on board leave the Rathausplatz daily for excursions to Regensburg, the Austrian Danube Valley, an afternoon's "Three Rivers Tour" (Dreiflusserrundfahrt) around Passau on the Danube, Inn and Ilz or directly to Vienna from where passenger steamers of Austrian, Hungarian, Czech or Russian shipping lines offer exciting tours of the Danube ports in five different countries on the way to the Black Sea. Whether you take a half-day or a fortnight's trip with a Danube steamer, you will not fail to experience a combination of relaxation, good food and the chance of an insight into the history and culture of a cross-section of lands and people at this waterway to the East.

PRACTICAL INFORMATION FOR EAST BAVARIA

 WHEN TO COME. Hiking is the great attraction in summer and skiing in winter. From **December** to the end of **March** is the season for the slopes, with the later dates at the higher altitudes. Two interesting events take place every year on Whit Sunday: a religious procession on horseback, dating back to 1412, in Kötzting and a pilgrimage procession to the church of Bogenberg by the inhabitants of Holzkirchen, carrying a 40-ft. pole transformed into a giant candle. Special events are Landshut's triennial Princely Wedding, taking place on three Sundays during **June** and **July,** Waldmünchen's annual Trenck the Pandour pageant in July, and the Dragon-Sticking pageant to be seen at Furth im Wald during the second week in **August.** In **September,** the harvest festival in Kösslarn in Lower Bavaria includes a folksy children's parade.

 REGIONAL FOOD AND DRINK. Although East Bavaria shares most of its dishes with Franconia and Upper Bavaria, it has a number of its own specialties that should not be missed. *Regensburger* are the short, thick, and spicy sausages of Regensburg, which have to be charcoal-grilled, similar to those of Nürnberg. A sausage of a different kind, made mostly in the area further down the Danube is *Milzwurst,* very delicately flavored and made with spleen; along with it you may try *Deggendorfer Knödel,* a special type of dumpling, if you happen to be in the Deggendorf area. Another special type of sausage is *Bauernseufzer* (Farmer's Sigh) of Amberg.

The Danube provides a number of excellent fish, particularly tasty the *Donauwaller* (Danube sheatfish) of Passau, which is served *blau* (boiled) or *gebacken* (breaded and fried). The town of Tirschenreuth in the north is the home of especially delicious *Karpfen* (carp). East Bavaria also has its own version of radishes, the *Weichser Rettiche,* to be washed down with very good locally produced beers.

 HOTELS AND RESTAURANTS. This area has been too long overlooked by tourists; there are many unpretentious, but no less charming, summer and winter resorts and accommodations are for the most part in the lower price categories, especially in the low season or April/May and Sept./Oct. The hotels remain open all year round, and most of them have restaurants. There are also a great many inexpensive bungalow villages and vacation apartments available.

Abensberg. *Klosterhotel Biburg* (M), in the old monastery; period furnishings, own brewery.

Aicha Vorm Wald. *Schloss-Pension* (I), in a castle, parts of which are over 1,000 years old, quiet, rich in atmosphere.

Amberg. Hotels: All (I–M)—*Brunner* and *Bahnhof-Hotel,* both with garden, near station; *Goldenes Lamm,* Rathausstr. 6., in pedestrian zone.

Restaurant: *Casino Altdeutsche Stube* (M) is most atmospheric and is at Schrannenplatz 8. Wine taverns: *Bacchus Klause,* Batteriegasse 1, and *Pfälzer Weinstube.*

Bayerisch-Eisenstein. Both (M) are—*Pension am Regen,* Anton-Pech-Weg 21, a quiet and comfortable small hotel with 24 rooms, indoor pool, sauna, solarium and garden terrace; *Berggasthof Brennes,* on Arber, about 3,400 feet high, a hotel with 65 beds, bar, terrace with excellent view and a small pool.

Bischofsmais, near Regen in Bayerischer Wald. **Hotel:** *Wastlsäge* (M), in a beautiful isolated location with view, outside the village, 90 beds, 44 baths, indoor pool, cozy restaurant, bar.

Bodenmais. Hotels: Both (M) are—*Steigenberger Sonnenhof,* all rooms with shower, apartments, 2 restaurants, tavern-bar, nightclub and beauty farm; *Andrea,* first class reasonable, *Andrea,* most rooms with shower; on edge of forest.

Bayerwald-Hotel-Hofbräuhaus (I–M), all with indoor pool, sauna.

Burg Falkenfels, about 12 miles north of Straubing in the Bavarian Forest. Medieval castle-fortress, first mentioned in 1100. Inexpensive hotel with heated outdoor pool, fishing. Good food.

Cham. Hotels: Modern *Randsbergerhof* (M), near Grasselturm, 65 rooms, lovely garden café, weekend dancing, good restaurant, own cinema.

Ratskeller and *Goldenes Lamm* are (I).

Grafenau. Hotels: Both (M) are—*Steigenberger Sonnenhof,* all rooms with bath or shower; *Sonnenberg,* indoor pool.

Landshut. Hotels: *Hotel-Garni Bergterrasse,* Ger.-Hauptman-Str. 1, small and quiet; *Goldene Sonne,* Neustadt. 520, garden restaurant; both (M).

Peterhof (I), Niedermayerstr. 15, 11 beds.

Restaurants: *Klausenberg* (M), on hill of same name, with fine view of city from its terrace. *Beim Vitztumb,* Landg., closed August.

Passau. Hotels. All (M–E) are—*Weisser Hase,* Ludwigstr. 23; *Stiehler,* Spitalhofstr. 73, balconied rooms; *Zur Laube,* small, with good terrace restaurant, and *Schloss Ort* (last two at point where the three rivers join).

Both (M) are—the colorful *Schwarze Ochs,* Ludwigstr. 22; *Zum König,* Rindermarkt 2, all rooms with shower.

Hotel-Pension Abrahamhof (I), Innstr. 167, just out of town, terrace garden.

Restaurants (all moderate): *Ratskeller* in Rathaus, with terrace on the square. *Heilig-Geist-Stiftschenke* in Heilig-Geist-Gasse, an historic wine tavern founded in 1358, with large garden; *Gasthof Blauer Bock,* Fritz Schaeffer Promenade with waterfront terrace and lively music.

Regensburg. Hotels: All (M–E) are—*Avia,* Frankenstr. 1, in suburbs across the river, 95 rooms, garden, good restaurant, bar; *Karmelitin,* Dachauplatz 1; and the newly renovated *Park Hotel Maximilian,* Maxstr. 28; *Bischofshof,* Krauterermarkt 3, with pleasant restaurant; *Kaiserhof am Dom,* Kramg. 10, all rooms with shower.

All (I–M) are—*Weidenhof* (garni), Maximilianstr. 23; *St. Georg,* near Thurn. u. Taxis Palace, Karl-Stieler-Str. 8, with garden terrace; *Münchner Hof,* Tändlerg. 9.

Restaurants: *Historisches Eck Zur Stritzelbäckerin* (E), Watmarkt 6, colorful wine tavern in 13th-century house.

Ratskeller (M), Rathausplatz 1, Donauwaller is specialty. *Kaiserhof* (M), outdoor terrace faces cathedral.

Historische Wurstküche (I), Weisse-Lamm-G. 3, at the Stone Bridge, 900-year-old tiny tavern serving delicious Regensburg sausages and potato soup. *Kneitinger Garten* (I), Müllerstr. 1, with nice view of city. *Kuchlbauer's Schiffskuchl,* Werftstr., seaman's specialties.

Inexpensive beer restaurants: *Brandl-Bräu-Gaststätte,* Osteng. 16, *Spitalgarten,* Katharinenplatz 1, serving beer since 1300, and *Hofbräuhaus,* Rathaus Platz.

Wine taverns: *Falks-Weinstuben,* Bismarckplatz 4; *Zum Steidlwirt,* Am Ölberg 13; *Zum Alten Patrizier,* Baumhackerg. 2.

St. Englmar. Hotels: All (M) are—*Kur- und Sporthotel St. Englmar, Aparthotel Predigstuhl,* 400 apartments with kitchen, also hotel rooms, and *Haus Berghof,* all rooms with bath. All have pools and many sports facilities.

Straubing. Hotels: *Seethaler,* Bavarian cooking; *Heimer,* and *Motel Lermer* (garni) are all (M), small, all rooms with bath or shower.

About 14 miles from Straubing in the quiet village of Schwarzach is the 25-room delightful hotel *Zum Degenberg* (I), with fine local food.

Viechtach. Hotels: *Schmaus,* 68 rooms, indoor pool, sauna; *Dischinger,* 36 rooms, fishing, ski tour school. Both (M).

Weiden. In Oberpfalz. **Hotels:** All (M) are—*Europa,* all rooms with shower; *Parkhotel,* Bohemian specialties in restaurant; and *Waldlust.*

EAST BAVARIA. By Car. This region has a way of getting left out, which is all the better for motoring in it. Unless you want to go into Czechoslovakia or Austria, there is little reason why motorists should find themselves in East Bavaria; but there are very good reasons for going into it deliberately. The fact that on the far side of the Bavarian Forest is the Eastern European frontier, means that people who motor there are going to have it to themselves. It is in any case a somewhat primitive place and forest, of course, means not only trees but mountains. It is a region for touristic one-upmanship. Down in the plain leading to the Austrian frontier there is the usual slight emptiness of such places—enhanced, as far as the motorist is concerned, by a very good road system.

CAMPING. East Bavaria offers a wide selection of campsites for tents and caravan trailers and the following are only some of the many sites with modern facilities to be found in the Bayerischer Wald and Oberpfalz:

BAYERISCHER WALD

Comfort Campingplatz, Hohenwarth, in the valley of the Regen with view mountain ranges of the Bayerischer Wald.

Knaus-Comfort-Campingplatz, Lackenhauser, vast campsite in forest park at foot of Dreisessel peak with kilometers of hiking paths, swimming, boating, riding, tennis.

Campingplatz Am Höllenstein in Viechtach, at the Höllensteinsee. Small and on unspoiled meadowland at the side of the lake.

Aral Ferienzentrum Bayerischer Wald, Zwiesel. Large camping holiday estate in the spa town of Zwiesel, primarily for caravans.

Campingplatz Tröpplkeller, 1 km outside Zwiesel in Bodenmais; small.

Komfort-Campingplatz Gaisweiher, Flossenbürg, near the castle ruins of the same name, situated in beautiful meadowland with panoramic views of surrounding countryside. Swimming in the Gaisweiher lake or in heated swimming-pool, boats for hire, tennis nearby.

OBERPFALZ

Campingplatz an der Altmühl, Beilngries. Modern campsite on the banks of the river Altmühl with bathing beach.

Campingplatz Rasthaus Talblick, Riedenburg, with view of Altmühl valley. Own tavern, boats for hire, indoor pool.

Terrassencamping Sippenmühle, terraced campsite in the wildlife reserve of the White Laaber river. Many bathing possibilities in the river or in heated outdoor pool.

MUSIC AND THEATER. Regensburg has an excellent *Stadttheater,* Bismarckplatz 7, presenting opera, operetta, and plays. Concerts are given in the *Neuhaussaal, Herzogssaal,* and in summer in the *Kreuzgarten* of the City Museum. The cathedral *Boys' Choir* is famous throughout Germany. Guest companies appear in the Municipal Theater at Amberg. Passau also has a City Theater, which offers a varied program, particularly during European Festival Weeks in June-July. Concerts and theatrical performances in Landshut, Weiden and Straubing.

  MUSEUMS. Landshut: *Trausnitz Fortress* and Stadtresidenz (City Residence Palace), with princely suites; the painting gallery and local museum are open daily 9–12, 2–6 (in winter 2–4), Sundays 9–12.

Amberg: *City Museum* in Castle of Palatine Counts.

Passau: at *Oberhaus Fortress.*

Regensburg: *City Museum,* Dachauplatz 2, with a notable collection of prehistoric and medieval arts and crafts, of which one of the most unusual exhibits is the Medallion Carpet woven in Regensburg in the 14th century; *Ostdeutsche Gallerie* (City Art Gallery), Stadtpark, showing local art and concentrating especially on the works of important East German artists and other examples of East European art and culture; *Reichstagmuseum* (Imperial Diet Museum), in Old Rathaus: Imperial Diet hall, princely suites, in the cellar a medieval courtroom with torture chamber and prisons. *Marstallmuseum* of the Prince of Thurn and Taxis, coach museum located in the Residenz riding hall.

Straubing: *Gäuboden Museum,* Frauenhoferstr. Notable prehistoric collection and world-famous Römischen Schatzfund (Roman Treasure Trove) with its rich works of gold and bronze among the finest to have been excavated in N. Europe.

 SPORTS. Hiking is a favorite pastime in this region, especially around Waldmünchen and the Arber area. Sturdy mountain walkers and those in search of real wilderness will find the mountains to the southeast of Arber along the Czech border (several mountain lodges on the German side) and their approaches from Zwiesel, Grafenau, Freyung, Finsterau, Frauenberg, and Haidmühle particularly challenging.

Swimming in the Ilz and Danube Rivers and in many indoor and outdoor pools. Water sports, including **motor boating** and **water skiing,** forbidden on many other lakes, are allowed on the dammed section of the Danube near Obernzell.

Gliding schools in Amberg, Regensburg, Landshut and Straubing.

There is a **squash** court in Pocking, south of Passau; **tennis** courts in most towns; and **golf** courses at Regensburg, Eggenfelden, Schmidmühlen and Waldkirchen in the Bavarian Forest. **Horseback riding** in Passau and Regensburg; some countryside hotels also have saddle horses.

Fishing is rewarding in the rivers of Bayerischer Wald and Oberpfalz, particularly for trout, although almost two dozen other kinds are also present. A fish specialty of the area is huck (Huch), a large and savage river salmon, caught in the Danube and its tributaries; in cold months they average 25 pounds, and specimens of 35 pounds are not unknown.

Some of the principal bases for **hunting** are Bogen, Falkenfels, Kötzting, Regen, Schwarzach, Tittling, Viechtach and Zwiesel, all in Bayerischer Wald; and Eschenbach, Moosbach, Oberviechtach, Schönsee, Waidhaus, all in Oberpfälzer Wald.

The best rivers for **kayaking:** Danube through Ingolstadt and Regensburg to Passau; and Altmühl from Treuchtlingen to Kelheim where it joins the Danube (85 miles, easy, lovely scenery). Canoe and kayaks are for hire in Kelheim.

WINTER SPORTS. The best winter sports centers are in the Bayerischer Wald where the skiing season lasts from December until early March, above 3,200 feet until the end of March. Ski tours are possible up to about 3,750 feet. There are at least two dozen quiet and unpretentious towns with good skiing terrains and inexpensive hostelries, among them:

Bayerisch-Eisenstein, about 2,330 feet, train stop. Chair lift above town on the Arber, 7 ski lifts, ski jump, ski school, curling, tobogganing.

Bodenmais, 2,300 feet, train stop. 4 ski lifts, ski school, ski jump, ice skating, curling, tobogganing, Arber chair lift only about 7 miles away by road.

Grafenau, 2,000 feet, train stop. 2 ski lifts, ski school, ski jump, curling, tobogganing.

Philippsreut - Mitterfirmiansreut, 3,200 feet, bus from Passau. In the area: 6 ski lifts, ski school; many inexpensive hostelries.

St. Englmar, almost 3,000 feet, the highest village in Bayerischer Wald, bus from Straubing, near train station at Steinburg, 13 ski lifts.

Schöfweg-Langfurth, 3,330 feet, bus from Passau. 7 ski lifts, ski school, curling, ski tours. Inexpensive inns.

Viechtach, 1,620 feet, skiing terrains mostly above the town, train stop. Ski lift, ski teachers, ice skating rink, curling, tobogganing.

USEFUL ADDRESSES. *ABR (Bavarian Tourist Office),* Nibelungenhalle, Passau. **Local Tourist Information:** Amberg, *Verkehrsamt,* Hallplatz 2; Cham, *Verkehrsamt,* Rosenstrasse; Landshut, *Verkehrsverein,* Altstadt 79; Passau, *Verkehrsverein,* Nibelungenhalle; Regensburg, *Fremdenverkehrsamt* (about city), Altes Rathaus, and *Fremdenverkehrsverband Ostbayern* (about East Bavaria), Landshuter Str. 13; Weiden, *Verkehrsamt,* Rathaus.

For information about the National Park Bayerischer Wald, contact Nationalparkverwaltung 8352 Grafenau.

Information for Danube boat-trips from Passau from: *Schiffahrtgesellschaft Wurm und Köck,* Bräugasse 8, 8390 Passau. Excursions from Regensburg from: *Personenschiffahrt Gebr. Klinger,* Jurastr. 31, 8401 Tegernheim.

NORTH
GERMANY

NORTH GERMANY

The Seagirt Land

North Germany comprises the states of Lower Saxony, which forms by far the bulk of the area, Bremen and Hamburg, the smallest states in the Federal Republic, and Schleswig-Holstein, the most northerly state. Geographically, it is in sharp contrast to the rest of the country, being almost exclusively flat. The only mountainous area, the Harz, is in the southeastern corner, south of Hannover, the capital of Lower Saxony.

North Germany is the only region with any outlet to the sea. Historically, it is this fact more than any other that distinguishes the area. This is the region that gave birth to the Hanseatic League in the 14th century, which turned Germany into not only the most powerful force in the Baltic but into one of Europe's leading commercial and seafaring nations. Today Bremen and Hamburg still proudly call themselves "Hanseatic Cities." To a very large extent, the pre-eminence they gained through the Hanseatic League enabled them to remain states of the Federal Republic in spite of their size. Both sit on the two principal rivers of the north, Hamburg on the Elbe and Bremen on the Wesser.

To the east and north of Bremen, on the North Sea coast, is East Frisia, a picturesque and quiet land where traditions have survived into the present day and where the people still unselfconsciously dress in traditional peasant clothes on holidays and during festivities. Lying a few miles off shore and running northeastward from the point on the North Sea where Holland and Germany meet are the East Frisian Islands. These islands are really a kind of fringe of the coastline, several miles out, a necklace of sandy outcroppings, each one nearly all beach. They all have good ferry services from wherever the nearest point on the mainland may be. They are all of them attractive in their own ways and are relaxed, essentially open-air places where, provided the weather is good, a healthy holiday is guaranteed.

The bulk of Lower Saxony is rich and fertile land, but not surprisingly for such a large area it is by no means entirely unvaried. Apart from the inevitable spas, there are vast forests, heaths and lakes, and, in the Harz mountains, increasingly popular winter-sports centers. In the farming regions, the wide plains are dotted with low farmhouses that seem almost unable to bear the weight of the wide-spreading thatched roofs that cover them. The geography of the area has had another important effect on its architecture. A lack of stone and wood has made this the kingdom of brick. Throughout North Germany, there are examples of intricate and beautiful brickwork.

Schleswig-Holstein lies to the north of the Elbe. Its western limit is the North Sea, its northeastern limit the Baltic, which the Germans call the East Sea (Ost See). Historically it is a newcomer to Germany. Until 1864 it had belonged to Denmark. Bismarck, however, then managed to force the Danes to cede the two separate Duchies of Schleswig and Holstein to the German Empire. Today, after 117 years of unification, they are indisputably part of the fabric of the modern state.

Schleswig-Holstein is a quiet land and, more than any other part of the country, it is Germany's flat land—a wide plain of soft green heaths, sandy dunes, rich fields and blue waters. The area abounds in architectural and artistic treasures. In the center, it is a fertile, agricultural region whose villages of thatched-roofed cottages and windmills in green fields offer an attractive contrast to the wind-blown grass clinging to the sandy dunes of the coast.

SCHLESWIG-HOLSTEIN

Sand Dunes and Thatched Roofs

Schleswig-Holstein is Germany's northernmost province, the land that lies north of the Elbe, and the one most conscious of the sea. Its western limit is the North Sea, its northeastern boundary the Baltic, which the Germans call the East Sea. This is Germany's flatland—a wide plain of soft green heaths, sandy dunes, rich fields, and blue waters. The land of several historic Hanseatic cities, Schleswig-Holstein abounds in architectural and artistic treasures. In the center, it is a rich agricultural area whose villages of thatched-roof cottages and windmills in green fields offer an attractive contrast to the wind-blown grass clinging to the sandy dunes of the coast.

EXPLORING SCHLESWIG-HOLSTEIN

North of Hamburg in an almost straight west-east line and on the road which crosses the Schleswig-Holstein peninsula from Brunsbüttel in the west to Lübeck in the east lie three important spas: Bad Bramstedt with new spa buildings located a mile or so out of town which is traversed by several small streams operating two water mills in the center; Bad Segeberg, separated from Bad Bramstedt by the Segeberger Forest, whose chief attraction is the Kalkberg, a 300-foot rock formation, the only place in Schleswig-Holstein where mountain climbing can be practised and at whose foot is a large outdoor theater where plays based on Karl May's novels are performed every summer (Karl May was the romantic German writer who wrote adventure stories about the American Indians in the last century); and Bad Schwartau which is located in the immediate vicinity of Lübeck.

Lübeck

Lübeck, "Queen of the Hansa," no doubt owed its dominating position in the Hanseatic League—which made it an important influence in the development of all of northeastern Europe—firstly to its favorable location on the Trave River, just above the point where it empties into the Baltic. The old harbor buildings and docks along the river give visible evidence today of the ancient prosperity of this port, which in the time of the Hohenstaufen Emperors became an Imperial Free City. Its wealth is obvious also from the fine old buildings in its center. Most spectacular of these is the City Hall. Lübeck is famous for its brickwork, and the Rathaus is probably the finest example of it, retaining in part the black glazed tiles characteristic of the region. It is a striking building, with its arches resting on pillars on the ground floor and curious rounded cylinders, each capped with a pointed spire like a dunce's cap, embedded in its walls.

Other buildings worth visiting in Lübeck include its famous cathedral, founded in 1173 by Henry the Lion, in which you will find the *Triumphal Cross,* carved in wood by the famous artist of the north, Bernt Notke, in 1477; the Holstein Gate, two massive towers, again with conical roofs, connected by a central section whose façade rises in a series of steps; the city walls, St. Mary's Church, also founded by Henry the Lion in 1159, at the same time the city was founded, and the Heiligen-Geist-Spital (Hospital of the Holy Ghost), built in 1280 with an early Gothic church. Both the cathedral and St. Mary's Church, like so many other fine buildings in Lübeck, were badly damaged by bombs, but both have been partially restored; some of their movable treasures have been returned, others are still in the St. Annen Museum. St. Peter's Church has also been repaired and its tower can be ascended (by elevator) for a magnificent view of the city. Also in a special class is the Buddenbrooks House, in the Mengstrasse; it provided the background for the famous novel by Thomas Mann, who was born in Lübeck.

South of Lübeck along Die Alte Salzstrasse (The Old Salt Road) are several interesting towns. The first is Ratzeburg, huddled on a tiny island in the Ratzenburger Lake in the center of a lovely lake region. The top attraction of the town itself is the outstanding 12th-century Romanesque cathedral. The next stop is medieval Mölln, also on a lake and with a Romanesque church where Till Eulenspiegel is allegedly buried; the inscription on the tombstone says that he died in Mölln in 1350. South of Mölln is Schwarzenbek at the edge of Sachsenwald, and then we reach the Elbe at Lauenberg which we visited during one of our excursions from Hamburg.

Travemünde and the Coast Resorts

Northeast of Lübeck is the beach resort of Travemünde. This is the most popular of all Baltic holiday spots, and it manages to keep up its gaiety all year around, thanks to the luxurious gaming casino overlooking the beach. If Travemünde is the point where you first touch the Baltic, you will make acquaintance there with beaches whose pattern is repeated all along this coast. Thick pine woods run down to sandy beaches, of the dune type. Where bathers concentrate, you will find the characteristic enormous wicker chairs, in which you can shut yourself up to change in your own individual bathhouse, each chair sitting in the middle of a crater scooped into the sand, to prevent it from upsetting in high winds.

Travemünde is the first of a whole string of beaches enjoying a sheltered position on the Baltic bay that cuts in behind the long peninsula running north from this point. It is a large, beautiful seaside resort with a nautical Cornwall or Massachusetts flavor, filled with restaurants, casinos, and hotels. If you arrive by sea, you will find one of the prettiest seaside locations around today, right in the town, with handsome craft from Finland and Sweden, gliding up the Trave, and lit up at night. Travemünde is a good place to visit, even if only for a day trip—it's 20 minutes from Lübeck and an hour from Hamburg. One of the colorful sights is a marvelous fish, fruit and vegetable market, held in the morning near St. Lorenz Church.

Across the bay is East Germany and an hour's drive away in the other direction is Hamburg's international airport. All the resorts along this part of the coast are lively. Next comes Niendorf, a little fishing village, which has preferred to stay that way instead of going cosmopolitan like its next-door neighbor to the north, Timmendorfer Strand, with its fine white-sand beach and extensive woods. Next come Scharbeutz, Haffkrug and Sierksdorf, all quiet vacation spots. From the old town Neustadt (with the name of "new town"), the railroad and main road run directly through Oldenberg to Grossenbrode from where you cross to the island of Fehmarn over a bridge; on the other side of Fehmarn you reach Puttgarden, the ferry port for Denmark. Along the coast, however, there are several important beach resorts, among them Grömitz, Kellenhusen, and Dahme.

Eutin, to the northwest of Neustadt, takes us away from the coast and puts us back on the road to Kiel. Eutin has several claims to fame: it is the gateway to "Holstein Switzerland," is the birthplace of the composer Carl Maria von Weber, is noted for its rose cultivation, has an old moated castle set in a beautiful park, and it is on a charming lake.

This last is not much of a distinction here. We are now in the lake district. Our next town, Malente-Gremsmühlen, a health resort, offers a popular Five Lakes Tour. Plön with a castle known as a "miniature Versailles," which succeeds it, is completely surrounded by lakes. Across the Greater Plön Lake you can go by boat to the little resorts of Dersau and Bosau, hence the rather loose comparison with Switzerland. Next comes Preetz, where there is an old convent, and we exit from Holstein Switzerland without having seen anything remotely resembling an Alp.

Kiel

This brings us to Kiel, which happens to be a university town, but unfortunately it is difficult to think of that today since its old university, founded in 1665, was completely demolished in the last war, as well as the old castle of the Duke of Holstein-Gottorf. The world over, this name automatically brings to mind the Kiel Canal—except in Germany, where this great engineering achievement, which has converted the only mainland Denmark possessed into one more island, is known as the North Sea-East Sea canal. Its entrance—or exit, depending on your point of view—remains one of the major sights of Kiel.

Once the chief naval port of Germany, Kiel remains today one of the country's greatest centers for both inshore and deepsea fishing, and its fish market is another of its spectacles. Everyone knows of Kiel Week, of course, early in summer, the international regatta during which craft of all sorts, wind, motor, or muscle-pulled, race on the waters of Kiel Fjord. This is the gathering time of the international set, for the leading yachtsmen the world over participate in its competitions.

There are a number of interesting trips to be made from Kiel. By boat there is a pleasant ride to Laboe, near the opening of the fjord at whose base Kiel itself lies. There is an impressive monument at Laboe, but its finest attraction is a flat sandy beach, protected by the lie of the land from the sharp eastern winds, which because of its gentle slope is particularly safe for children. On the same side of the fjord is Schönberg, with another fine beach, reached by a local railway line from Kiel.

Schleswig and Flensburg

From Kiel the direct road for Schleswig passes through Eckernförde, with its 500-year-old Town Hall and wine cellar hewn out of solid rock. But if you travel by train you have to pass through Rendsburg with an impressive bridge over the North Sea-Baltic Canal.

If you come into Schleswig by car, you will pass a signpost bearing in small letters the name, "Schleswig," and under them in larger characters, another and stranger title, "Haithabu." Surmounting the whole is the carved replica of a Viking ship. For Schleswig was a Viking city, and Haithabu was the name of this locality in Viking days. Today it is Haddeby, and you may visit it on Schleswig's outskirts.

The oldest city in Schleswig-Holstein, Schleswig, from the 9th to the 11th centuries, was an important center of foreign trade. It has two major attractions you must not fail to visit. One is St. Peter's Cathedral, begun in 1100. It is a fine building, and its great drawing card is not the cathedral itself, but the fact that it contains one of the most famous works of art in all Germany—the Bordesholm Altar. This is a remarkable specimen of the woodcarver's art, a richly ornamented altar piece containing no less than 392 figures, which was made by Hans Brüggemann in 1521. It originally stood in the Augustine abbey of Bordesholm, a small place in the Schleswig lake district, where very few persons saw it; so in 1666 the Duke of Schleswig had it removed to the cathedral of his capital.

The other great sight is Gottorf Castle, on an island in the Schlei, the largest castle in Schleswig-Holstein. The original building was constructed about 1150 for the Bishops of Schleswig, and became the residence in 1268 of the Dukes of Schleswig-Holstein-Gottorf, who held it for some four and a half centuries. In 1713 it fell to the Danish crown and was stripped of its treasures; in 1842 it was completely destroyed. In 1864 Schleswig-Holstein was returned to Germany and later the castle was rebuilt; the present building is a faithful restoration of the old one. It contains the great Landesmuseum of Schleswig-Holstein with a fine collection of medieval ecclesiastical art, of arts and crafts from the 16th to 19th century and of folk art, as well as the King's Hall and Castle Chapel. It also contains one of the largest and finest collections of prehistory and early history in Germany, including the only stone with a runic inscription ever found in this country, objects found in old Viking graves, and the Nydam Boat, an Anglo-Saxon craft of the 4th century, the sort of ship in which the Angles and Saxons sailed from this neighborhood for the conquest of Britain.

The area between Schleswig, Flensburg, Flensburg Fjord and Schlei deserves mention since it gave its name to the language you are at this moment reading. It is called Angeln, and from it, 1,500 years ago, came the Angles, the men who crossed the North Sea to the British Isles and settled in England.

"The Gate to the North," Flensburg, is full of picturesque old houses. One of them is the Nordertor—built in 1595 and formerly a city gate—a Gothic brick structure with a series of stepped gables, which, gate though it is, harbors a house inside. So does the Kompagnietor (1603), which also served as a guildhouse. The Old Flensburg House and St. Mary's Church (1284), with a neo-Gothic tower added in 1880, the arcaded North Market (1595), and the fishing quarter of Jürgenby, with its picturesque boats and fishing nets, are also worth visiting. A more modern attraction of Flensburg is the fact that it produces rum. One of the local brands, of which there are some 128 produced by 28 distilleries, is known descriptively as "Flensburg Fire."

When in Flensburg, make the excursion to Glücksburg Castle, once the residence of the Glücksburg line of the House of Oldenburg and the cradle of the royal houses of Denmark, Norway, and Greece. Mirrored in the lovely lake that almost completely surrounds it, Glücksburg Castle stands in majestic solitude over the still waters and the encircling green forests. The castle itself, built between 1582 and 1587, houses one of the best collections of tapestries in Germany.

North Frisian Islands

At Flensburg, we are on the Baltic, but a westward drive of less than 30 miles puts us in North Frisia, on the North Sea. Offshore lie the North Frisian Islands, the most famous of which is Sylt. On the island of Sylt you get your first taste of this healthy vigorous country—sometimes too vigorous, on the days when gales sweep in from the open sea, holding the dune grass flat against the ground and making the sand of the beaches ripple like waves. At Keitum you can see the answer of the old shipmasters to the wind, in the snug staunch thatch-roofed homes they built in order to spend their declining days looking out upon the element on which in their younger years they lived. In Keitum they picked a propitious spot, for it is usually sheltered from the gales, for these islands; indeed it has a considerable reputation as a climatic health resort. Its immunity from the full force of the gales is shown by its numerous trees; most of the territory of the North Frisian Islands has been swept bare of them. To visitors, Keitum offers several spectacles—the old Frisian House, the Regional Museum (Heimatmuseum), and the 12th-century church at St. Severin, once the most important on the island and built on the site of a shrine dedicated to the Germanic goddess of marriage, Frigga.

Westerland, Sylt's most famous resort, is a busy center, with a gambling casino, fashion shows, sporting events, and all the bustle of chic vacation spots. Some distance from the more frequented localities, however, Westerland has staked out a sector more in tune with the natural surroundings of the island—a section of the beach reserved for those who want to enjoy sunbathing in the nude.

Another attractive stop on the Isle of Sylt is at Kampen, the most expensive and elegant "village" on the island. If you like horseback riding, a canter from Wenningstedt to Kampen along the shore will long remain in your memory. A favorite excursion from Kampen or Westerland is a boat ride to the islands where seals bask and play in the sunshine.

Two other delightful North Frisian isles are Föhr and Amrum. Föhr has the mildest climate of the North Sea Islands—roses bloom well into the winter at Wyk, its loveliest and oldest resort, a noted health center, where the traditional Frisian costumes are worn.

Amrum has three resorts, which, oddly enough, are quite widely known in the United States in spite of their remoteness, for many Frisians emigrated to America from here. They are Wittdün, whose 6-mile-long beach is sheltered by sand dunes ninety feet high; Nebel, with an interesting ancient cemetery; and Norddorf, just beach and bird sanctuary—and an unusual type of hunting: for seals.

Helgoland

Probably the most interesting of the North Sea Islands, however, is Helgoland, located about halfway between the North Frisian and the East Frisian Islands. Its red sandstone cliffs rising regally out of the green water have viewed a stormy past: originally a health resort of the early Frisians, it later provided secret shelter to sea pirates. Its strategic location has made it a long-fought-over prize to many seafaring nations, including Denmark and England. Although no longer the smuggler's paradise it has been in the past, particularly when Europe was blockaded during the Napoleonic wars, it is today the shopper's paradise, for it is a duty-free oasis for the bargain-minded.

There is whisky galore on Helgoland and at the same prices that you would pay in the various duty-free airport shops. With the right set of vacationers Helgoland could easily become a "Tight Little Island." Since Helgoland is a duty-free area you have to pass customs when leaving for the mainland but the quantity you can take along customs free may change from time to time.

Sea swimming is mainly from the dune island facing the port, connected with it by motorboat service, but there is also excellent swimming in the town itself, in the large twin swimming pool, filled with seawater and whose indoor and outdoor sections are connected by a water corridor. Not far from the swimming pool, which is located in the sports and recreation area, is the very interesting aquarium containing almost all specimens of the North Sea fauna. The regular ships cannot dock in Helgoland and therefore you have to transfer to small boats which will take you in and out. Everything on Helgoland was blown up by the Allies at the end of the last war (although you will notice that some thick defense walls at the sea level below the red cliff remained almost unscarred by the dynamiting attempts) and therefore everything on Helgoland is new. Small hotels and pensions are being added, and an elevator connects the lower part of the town with the upper part. The buildings, spotless and neat, designed along the most modern lines, and painted in pastel colors, almost give the impression of neatly arranged toys. The importance of Helgoland as a tourist center and health resort has increased tremendously during the past years and if you contemplate spending some time there during the summer you should make your reservations well in advance.

On the Mainland

Back on the mainland again, we proceed south to Husum, opposite the small group of Halligen Islands, embattled against the sea, even more out of the main current than those we have just visited. South of Husum is Friedrichstadt, separated from the sea by the Eiderstedt peninsula which pushes into the North Sea at this point, into which you might want to make a side trip to the beach resort of St. Peter-Ording, with a year-round season, or the smaller one at the mouth of the Eider River, Tönning. From Friedrichstadt, our route passes through Heide, with an interesting museum (from here there is a side trip to Büsum, once a simple fishing village but now a bathing resort devoted to horseracing on the sand flats and also a spa which bathes its patients in the North Sea mud that is reputed, perhaps because of high iodine content, to have powerful health-restoring qualities); Meldorf, whose

Church of St. John the Baptist, built in 1220–30 in early Gothic style, presides over a city where handicraft still flourishes; and brings us to Brunsbüttel, at the south end of the North Sea-Baltic Canal.

Crossing the canal, we proceed to Glückstadt, famous for its *Matjes,* a special kind of marinated white herring. The best time for tasting it is from the beginning of June to August: 'Matjes Weeks''. Here, where we might pause long enough to admire the six-sided Market Square, from which no less than 15 streets branch out, before taking the ferry over the Elbe to Wischhafen, we cross out of Schleswig-Holstein and into Lower Saxony.

PRACTICAL INFORMATION FOR
SCHLESWIG-HOLSTEIN

HOW TO GET ABOUT. The most popular way to reach the North Frisian islands is by boat. **To Sylt:** In season, steamer from Hamburg via Cuxhaven and Helgoland; by road and railroad (over the Hindenburg Dike) from Flensburg (a stop on the Jutland-Hamburg and beyond express train route), as well as by direct trains from Hamburg and direct cars from Cologne and Frankfurt. **To Helgoland:** During the summer there are daily services by comfortable ships from Hamburg and Bremerhaven, as well as frequent connections from Wilhelmshaven, the East Frisian islands, Büsum, and Sylt; year-round sailings from Cuxhaven. **To Föhr:** Year-round sailings from Dagebüll via Föhr depending on the tides; during the summer from Hörnum and Bongsiel. **To Pellworm:** Year-round sailings from Husum depending on the tides. From April through October, Helgoland and Sylt have air services from Hamburg, Bremen and Bremerhaven, and from several Frisian islands during summer.

REGIONAL FOOD AND DRINK. In Schleswig-Holstein you can have your fill of seafood. A particular regional specialty is the seaman's *Labskaus,* a stew prepared from pickled meat, potatoes, and sometimes herring, depending on the temperament of the cook, and garnished with a fried egg, sour pickles and a lot of beetroot. Famous *Holstein Schnitzel,* invented here and best here, is a golden fried breaded veal cutlet topped with a fried egg and anchovy. A really unusual and wonderful mixture is the *Gefüllte Schweinerippchen,* pork chops stuffed with toast, raisins, apples, and laced with rum.

In Büsum you must try the *Krabben,* a sort of tiny and very delicious shrimp, while Lübeck is famous for its marzipan.

In Schleswig you might try their specialty, gull's eggs: in Kiel *Sprotten* (baby herrings salted and then smoked to a golden luster), and in Flensburg kippered eel. Good eating requires good drinking, and the *Holsteiner,* drunk with juniper-scented *Korn* or *Bommerlunder* brandy should see you through nobly.

HOTELS AND RESTAURANTS. In addition to the higher-category hotels in the larger centers, there are many inexpensive, modest accommodations in this area. Most establishments remain open all year round. You will find Autobahn-Hotel accommodations in this area listed in the regional practical information for Northern Germany.

Resorts in Schleswig-Holstein, in common with many other German resorts and cities, offer off-season reductions.

A seaside resort complex, named (oddly to us) *Damp 2000,* is located between Eckenförde and Kappeln. Covering 15 acres, it consists of a year-round holiday complex of apartment houses and bungalows with every sort of indoor and outdoor sport imaginable. There are 3 heated pools, children's playgrounds, kindergarten, babysitter service. There is no through traffic and cars stay at the entrance to the resort.

Flensburg. Hotels: *Am Wasserturm,* Blasberg 13, 35 beds, and *Flensburger Hof,* Süderhofenden 40, 38 rooms, are (M).

All (I) are—*Europa,* Rathausstr. 1–5, 120 beds in a central location, with smoked eel as the specialty of its restaurant; *Am Stadtpark,* a quiet location at Nordergraben 70, with a good view overlooking the Flensburg Fjord; *Flensborghus,* Norder Str. 76, 15 rooms; *Union,* garni, Nikolaistr. 8, 38 rooms.

In nearby Glücksburg: *Intermar Hotel Glücksburg* (M–E), Fördestr., all rooms with bath; indoor pool, sauna, riding, tennis, water sports, fishing. *Parkhotel Ruhetal* (I), Flensburger Strasse 2, 35 beds, on Rüder Lake, garden, restaurant.

Restaurants: *Piet Henningsen,* at Schiffbrücke 20, an unusual place at the harbor, in itself a small sailing "museum," 18 varieties of rum. *Gnomenkeller,* Holm 1–3, expensive, specialty is lobster.

In nearby Oeversee, the *Historischer Krug,* an atmospheric restaurant in a 450-year-old thatched-roof house, offers good local specialties and an excellent selection of German wines. Much of the historic interior was destroyed by a fire in 1979.

Helgoland. All hotels on Helgoland are recent, as the entire settlement is completely rebuilt. Further establishments, mostly small hotels and pensions, are being added all the time. One of the best places for bed and breakfast is the (M) *Lieselotte,* Am Südstrand 5, all rooms with bath; tennis, water sports, fishing.

All (I–M) are—*Hanseat* and *Hans Baer,* both facing the port, and *Hansa-Hof* in Schifferstrasse. On the upland, *Haus Nickels,* Kurpromenade 33 and *Fernsicht,* with very fine view.

Felsen-Eck (I), also on upland, is small, and its terrace café offers a beautiful view over the harbor.

Restaurant: *Westfalen-Schänke* in Lung Wai.

There is a bungalow town on the dune island, where the swimming is best; small, inexpensive 2- and 4-person recently-built bungalows (without cooking facilities or running water) stand among sand dunes, protected from the wind. Next to them is a large camp site. A restaurant and tiny airport are located on the island, as well as some small provision shops. Travel to and from Helgoland proper is by motorboat (daytime only), about a 10-minute ride.

Kiel. Hotels: Both (E) are—the fairly modern *Conti-Hansa-Hotel am Schloss-garten,* in a beautiful park area near Oslokai on the Kiel Fjord, 150 beds, all rooms with bath or shower, some with terrace; *Maritim,* Bismarckallee 2, 105 rooms with bath; indoor pool, sauna, tennis, riding, water sports, fishing.

All (M) are—Modern *Astor* on top floors of a 10-story building at Holstenplatz, 1–2, 59 rooms with bath or shower and radio, rooftop café-restaurant; *Flensburger Hof,* Grosser Kuhberg 9–13, 100 beds, 21 baths; *Berliner Hof,* Ringstr. 6, 110 beds; *Consul,* Walkerdamm 11, 70 beds; and *Kieler Kaufmann,* Niemannsweg 102, 51 rooms, in park.

Restaurants: Renowned for fish specialties is *Restaurant im Schloss,* Wall 80; *Ratskeller,* in Rathaus; *Siechenbrau,* Eggerstedstr., with music.

Cafés with dancing and night bars: *Florida-Tanzcafé,* Dänische Strasse 14; *Allianz Tanzcafé,* Holstenbrücke 8. *Drathenhof* (M), in nearby Flintbek, Hamburger Landstr., situated in a museum is well worth a visit.

Lübeck. Hotels: *Lysia* (E), 65 rooms, some suites, all with bath, radio, TV and beverage refrigerator, has interesting restaurant, café, bar and dance bar, garage.

All (M) are—*Parkhotel,* Holstentorplatz 7, modern, 100 beds, all rooms with bath, cozy restaurant, and *International,* at the station with 200 beds, *Jensen,* Obertrave 4, and the 85 bed *Kaiserhof,* Kronsforder Allee 13.

Restaurants: *Schabbelhaus,* Mengstr. 48–52, historic (frequented by Thomas Mann), atmospheric, expensive. *Ratskeller* in the Rathaus is picturesque.

The *Haus der Schiffergesellschaft,* Breite Strasse 2, is a historic seamen's inn (since 1535), with ship models hanging from the ceiling and other décor to please a seaman's heart. *Zum Kulmbacher,* Fleischhauerstr. 16. *Alte Kate Anno 1748,* near Travemünde in Ivendorf, an historic, extremely expensive restaurant. *Cafe Niederegger,* Breite Str. 89, opposite the Rathaus; Johann Georg Niederegger first produced marzipan here in 1806.

Schleswig. Hotels: Both (M) are—*Strandhalle,* an outstanding if small hotel (50 beds) on Strandweg, overlooking the yacht harbor. *Goldener Stern,* Gottorfstr. 7, only 24 beds, is moderate.

Both (I) are—*Skandia,* 50 beds, Lollfuss 89; *Deutsches Haus,* 32 beds, Lollfuss 114.

Outside the city: *Historisches Gasthaus Haddeby,* on the Schlei in the old Viking settlement about 1½ miles south, 30 beds, atmospheric; restaurant specialty: Haithabu-Topf; also fishing facilities. *Waldschlösschen* in Pulverholz, just outside, 47 rooms; both are (I).

Timmendorfer Strand. Both (L) are—*Maritim Golf Hotel,* An der Waldkapelle, 250 rooms, and *Maritim Seehotel,* Strandallee, 241 rooms, with heated pool, sauna. *Seeschlösschen* (E), Strandallee, 150 rooms with bath, has pool, sauna.

Both (M) are—*Holsteiner Hof,* 21 rooms, with restaurants, and *Krug's Hotel Meeresblick,* 50 rooms, has an old-style beer tavern.

In the Niendorf section are the cheaper places hereabouts and though small and simple they are excellent value: *Altdeutsches Haus, Haus Evers, Haus Annegret, Seeluft, Haus Lotti. Hotel-Café Carstens,* thatched roof restaurant with terrace on the beach.

Restaurants: *Schloss-Keller* in Schloss Gottorf; *Hollandia,* moderately priced, on Timmendorfer Platz (with 18 beds).

Travemünde. Hotels: *Maritim* (L), Strandpromenade, 240 rooms with bath, thermal baths.

Kurhaus (E–L), Aussenallee 10, 104 rooms, all with private facilities, for those who appreciate 19th-century elegance with this century's comforts. Part of the Kuraus complex is the *Casino,* which includes a restaurant, nightclub, and beautiful terrace in addition to roulette and baccarat.

Golf (E), Helldahl 12, 60 rooms with bath, quiet. *Deutscher Kaiser* (M), Vorderreihe 52, 45 rooms some with bath. *Cafe Seegarten* (I), Kaiserallee 11, 20 rooms, garni, is a very good find.

Tremsbüttel. For a peaceful vacation in this region outside of the big cities, a most exceptional hostelry is the *Schlosshotel Tremsbüttel* (E), 40 beds; lying about halfway between Hamburg and Lübeck (near Bargteheide). Built as a hunting castle for the Dukes of Holstein-Gottorf in 1644 and surrounded by a large estate, it has been converted into a hostelry offering period-furnished accommodations, from singles to suites; tennis, riding, hunting, and fishing facilities.

ON SYLT ISLAND

Kampen. Hotels: *Rungholt,* with 55 rooms, has half-pension only; *Waltershof,* 24 apartments for 2–6 persons, pool. Both (E). *Westerheide,* 23 rooms, moderate. Several (M) and (I) pensions. Most establishments open Mar.–Oct. only.

Restaurants: For a bit of local color, visit the tavern *Kupferkanne,* the "Copper Kettle," an old bunker reconverted and decorated in a style which might be termed "seafaring modern," very popular with artists and writers, whose special province is Kampen. *Sturmhaube* is a moderately priced restaurant with a fine view of sand dunes and sea. Only cold foods available. *Kamp Krog,* very typical thatched roof restaurant; good for steaks, fish and fondues.

Wenningstedt. Hotels tend to be seasonal, May–Oct. Crab and lobster are restaurant features. *Pilz,* Hochkamp 9 is small and good quality (25 beds). *Klasen,* pretty and well equipped; *Friesenhof,* similar, and *Seefrieden* are (I–M).

Restaurant: *La Bonne Auberge,* Am Dorfteich 2, also has 7 rooms. *Green Onion,* Westerlandstr. 12, good grill restaurant.

Westerland. Hotels: In the (M) category are—*Stadt Hamburg,* Strandstr. 2, 110 beds, 30 baths; *Strandhotel Miramar.* Friedrichstr. 43, 100 beds, open

May through Sept.; and *Strandhotel Monbijou,* Andreas-Dirks-Str. 6, 50 beds, open May–Oct. *Windhuk,* Brandenburgerstr. 6, 46 beds. *Wünschmann,* Andreas-Dirks-Str. 4, 50 beds.

All (M) are—*Vierjahreszeiten,* Johann Möllerstr. 40, 43 beds, simple; *Hotel-Pension Agnes,* Johan Möller Str. 2, 30 beds, good facilities, also riding.

Restaurants: *Altfriesische Weinstuben,* Elisabethstr. 5, Frisian-style tavern with lobster, oysters and sole as specialties and a huge wine list. *Hardy auf Sylt,* Norder Str. 63, restaurant richly furnished with antiques; also has six apartments. *Landhaus Stricker,* Tinnum, nearby Westerland, Boy-Nielsen-Str. 10, 250-year-old Frisian house. Specialty: milk lamb.

Om de Eck, Friedrichstr. 33, close by, is good. In the large *Kurzentrum* (Cure Center), there is a very pleasant and large terrace café-restaurant with protected booth-tables permitting enjoyment of the sea air in any weather.

SCHLESWIG-HOLSTEIN. By Car. With the completion of the E3 autobahn from Hamburg into Denmark, the land between the seas, North and Baltic, has been set free. By nature beautiful, it has been graced by generations of good farmers and architects and has a maze of little roads from which to enjoy the fruits of their labors. Besides the autobahn already mentioned, and one from Hamburg to Lübeck, there are only three other great roads: No 5 which feeds the west coast; No 404/76 going east of Hamburg to Kiel, and the old central route to Flensburg which looks on a map as though it were fighting a running battle with the upstart motorway. All this makes for excellent holiday motoring where time is no object but peace and quietness everything. The many islands in the west are mostly accessible by car with the aid of ferry boats or, as in the case of Sylt, train ferry from Niebüll. In a land so narrow, about 70 miles in its widest part, it can be bracing rather than relaxing. For a chance of more warmth, try the Baltic.

MUSIC AND THEATER. Kiel has two new and modern theaters, *Grosses Haus* for opera, operetta and ballet and *Schauspielhaus* for plays; in summer, productions are given in Krusenkoppel and Neumühlen-Dietrichsdorf open-air theaters. Opera, operetta and plays are staged in Lübeck by *Bühnen der Hansestadt* and in Flensburg by *Städtische Bühnen.* Plays are performed in the *Nordmark Landestheater* in Schleswig.

The traditional Karl May summer festival performances are staged in natural open-air theaters at Bad Segeberg and Eutin. Flensburg, Kiel and Lübeck have symphonic orchestras and concert seasons. At Westerland during the summer the Flensburg Nordmark Symphony plays on the bandstand on the promenade. Westerland has a Lieder society and a good choir in St. Nicholas Church. The promenade is also the scene of outdoor performances from June to September. Concerts are scheduled during the summer in Travemünde and Helgoland.

MUSEUMS. For opening times inquire at the local tourist information offices. **Flensburg:** the *Municipal Museum,* Lutherplatz 1, contains ecclesiastical art, arts and crafts of Schleswig from prehistoric times to 19th century; *Natural Science Museum,* Nordergraben, fine collection of butterflies, local birds and pressed plants.

Kiel: *Kunsthalle,* Düsternbrookerweg 1, paintings of the 19th and 20th centuries; *Theater Museum,* Olshausenstr. 40, costumes, models for stage sets, etc., from 17th cent. to present; *Zoological and Ethnological Museum,* Hegewischstr. 3, Stone Age cultures of America and South Pacific, ancient Chinese coins. At Rammsee, near Kiel, open-air working museum village of farms, artisans' workshops and windmills of the region. Crafts and baking by traditional methods are demonstrated.

Lübeck: *St. Annen,* St. Annenstr. 13, North German art, especially medieval. Some fine woodcarving by Bernt Notke; *Behnhaus,* Königstr. 11, interiors of an 18th-century patrician house and modern art; *Holstentor,* in the historic gate of the same name, city history.

Schleswig: *Provincial Museum,* in Gottorf Castle, collection from Viking period, medieval and folk art.

WATER SPORTS. Yachting under ideal conditions is possible in the waters of the extensive Flensburg Fjord, which for some distance separates Denmark and Germany, and sailboat regattas are held frequently at Flensburg during the summer. There's also excellent sailing in the Kiel Fjord and along the coast, but once out of the shelter of the fjord, experience is required. You have about 190 miles of coastline along which to sail on either side of Kiel, between Lübeck and Flensburg. Prevailing winds are westerly. The two-mast yacht *Germania V,* built in 1955 and carrying almost 2,000 sq. ft. of sail, is now at the disposition of the Hanseatic Yachting School in Glücksburg. Long distance yacht races are scheduled every year in several places but the most famous sailing regattas take place during the traditional (since 1882) Kiel Week, usually in late June, when more than 600 international boats compete for the already legendary cups and prizes.

Boating and canoeing are very good on the Trave River. From Lübeck you can do the 14-mile trip to Travemünde, on the Baltic, or up the river making for Bad Oldesloe (22 miles), or Bad Segeberg, 14 miles farther upstream.

Swimming, motorboating, and other water sports are practised at these resorts. Indoor seawater swimming pools with artificial waves, nicely warmed, at Westerland, Büsum, St. Peter-Ording, Wyk, Grömitz, Haffkrug, Borkum and Eckernförde. Many have glass façades with a view of the sea. Helgoland has a unique twin seawater swimming pool divided by a water corridor into an outdoor and an indoor section; you can swim here in winter. Travemünde's modern indoor glassed-in seawater pool is connected directly with the Kurhaus, has a sauna and sun terraces.

OTHER SPORTS. Golf courses at Kiel, Travemünde, Wyk and Lohersand. **Tennis** in Kiel, Westerland, Kampen, Helgoland, Travemünde, all larger towns. **Horseback riding** schools and instructors in Flensburg, Lübeck, Kampen and elsewhere. Riding across tidal sands is popular along the North Sea coast. **Shark fishing** high sea excursions are organized from Helgoland.

DUTY FREE PORT OF HELGOLAND. You are allowed to take back to the German mainland the following items free of duty: 1 liter (about a quart) of liquor with more than 22 percent alcohol content (or instead of liquor: 2 liters of either champagne or spirits with less than 22 percent alcohol content) *and* 2 liters of regular wine; either 200 cigarettes or 50 cigars or 250 grams of tobacco; 50 grams of perfume, ¼ liter toilet water, 500 grams coffee, 100 grams tea and other articles not in excess of 300 German Marks. **Note:** subject to change!

USEFUL ADDRESSES. Tourist information: Flensburg, Verkehrsverein, Süderhofenden 1; Helgoland, Kurverwaltung, near the port on the main street; Kiel, Fremdenverkehrsamt, Auguste-Viktoria-Strasse 16; Lübeck, Verkehrsverein, Rathaushof 14; Schleswig, Verkehrsbüro, Friedrichstr. 7; Travemünde, at the beach rail station: Westerland, at the rail station.

HAMBURG

Germany's Greatest Port

The Elbe is one of Europe's greatest rivers and Hamburg, standing at its mouth, was for centuries the busiest port in Europe. The ships of Hamburg, and those of her partner cities in the Hanseatic League—Bremen and Lübeck—brought fabulous wealth to their owners, and through them to thousands of their fellow citizens. From the splendid red-brick warehouses that still stand along the river's northern shore to the copper-domed churches and public office buildings, and beyond these to the palatial suburban houses of the wealthy burghers, the city is still an impressive sight. Every year some 15,000 ships sail up the lower Elbe from the sea, loaded with cargos which range from oriental gems and carpets to raw minerals and timber. Many tourists also arrive by sea.

And yet the wealth and grandeur of Hamburg is not what it was. The elegant hotels still glitter with chandeliers, the best shops are still

421

exquisite, but elsewhere the city is less grand. The war took its toll, of course, and the many new buildings are more functional and less ornate than the old. The way of life is more functional too: the traditional, rather rigid politeness of the people has given way to a more straight-forward, friendlier approach. Pompous pride lingers on in the older establishments, an interesting phenomenon in the 1980s, but for the most part Hamburg is thoroughly cosmopolitan.

Water dominates Hamburg, not only because of the harbor but also by virtue of the tiny river, the Alster, that flows south, through the old city, into the Elbe. Once little more than an insignificant waterway, the Alster is central to the Hamburg scene, for during the 18th century it was dammed—just north of the old city—to form a lake. Divided into two at its southern end, this lake is known as the Binnenalster (Inner Alster) and the Aussenalster (Outer Alster), the two parts are separated by a pair of bridges. Surrounded by gardens, grand hotels and private mansions, the lake is a fine sight. In spring, the gardens burst with rhododendrons, in summer there are open-air cafés where you can take a meal and watch the boats. Sailing and wind-surfing are popular, though the winds are unreliable. You can also ride the ferry boats, which stop at landing piers along the shore before plying north along the suburban canals, which are lined with the gardens of elegant 19th-which are lined with the gardens of elegant 19th-century houses.

Water also plays a part in sustaining another Hamburg specialty—the lively nightlife. Ports must always cater to the frustrated demands of seamen newly ashore after a long voyage, and the St. Pauli area, by the waterside just west of the old city, specializes in the business of sex. Here you will find club after club, some ringing to dance bands, others offering pools and sauna and massage—some reputable, others not. The atmosphere throbs with its own unique vitality. Passers-by are encouraged to part with their money, so don't take more than you intend to spend. But don't worry. The club owners, restaurateurs, waitresses, pimps and whores who work here are no less businesslike or dishonest than elsewhere. To preclude any opening for disagreement, order your own drinks, rather than letting a hostess do it for you, and pay as soon as they are served.

A trip to St. Pauli is part of any good look at Hamburg. You might start your evening in another part of town with a good meal, a concert or a few hours in one of the city's celebrated cabaret spots, where drinks are served and a satirical show performed, then go to the Reeperbahn, look around, and explore one of the clubs listed later in this chapter.

EXPLORING THE CITY

The true city of Hamburg, the Alt-Stadt, can be seen on foot in a day, if you have stamina and a good pair of walking shoes. Only a small fraction of the city's 1.7 million people live here, but much of their historical tradition is found within the old city walls. The actual walls no longer exist, but where they stood the streets are called "wall," (or *Wallanlagen*), so you will easily be able to trace the old boundaries.

Let us begin at the main railway station (Hauptbahnhof), which is the terminus for every kind of train, from the local underground (U-bahn), the wider ranging suburban trains (S-bahn), the simple wooden-seated regional trains that stop at every station (D-zug), to the express trains south and west (Inter-City) and the luxurious first-class trans-European expresses (T.E.E.) Simply to stand beneath the vast vaulted glass canopy of the station roof and watch Europe's most efficient railway system in action is an experience. Later we shall return for trips out of town, but now we head out towards the Alster. Glockengiesser-wall is a rather monstrous street, heavy with traffic—follow the example of the good citizen and stop when the pedestrian light is red. As with so many of the regulations that are observed in Germany, these lights will make your walk more relaxing.

On your right is the monolithic domed Art Hall (Kunsthalle), which is certainly worth visiting. It is a powerhouse of genius, and especially of the 20th-century German artists who—despite two wars, or perhaps because of them—have produced some extraordinary work.

When you emerge, cross the Alster by the Lombard Bridge (Lombardsbrücke), pause to sample the curious blend of salt-sea air and city smoke, then press on along the Esplanade, passing the ultra-modern Opera House on your left. The first opera house in Germany was built here in 1677 on the site of the old Gänsemarkt (Goose Market) and Hamburg has been closely linked with opera ever since. Straight ahead of you is the Botanical Garden, first laid out in 1821 on the site of the original Hamburg fortress. The Palmenhaus (Palm House) and the Victoriahaus with its water lilies from the Amazon are particularly interesting. Beyond the Botanical Garden and bordering Jungius Str, is the most famous park in Hamburg, the Planten un Blomen (Plants and Flower), laid out in 1936 and relaid in 1973 for the National Garden Show. The masses of tulips in spring are followed through the year by displays of flowers in season. After dark in summer, there is a water ballet played out by special fountains accompanied by colored lights and music.

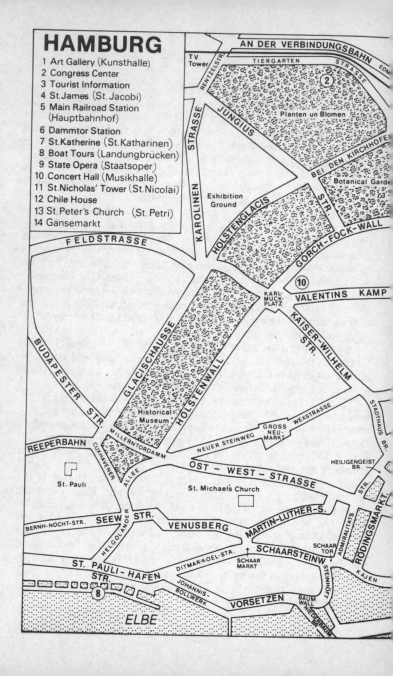

HAMBURG

1 Art Gallery (Kunsthalle)
2 Congress Center
3 Tourist Information
4 St. James (St. Jacobi)
5 Main Railroad Station
 (Hauptbahnhof)
6 Dammtor Station
7 St. Katherine (St. Katharinen)
8 Boat Tours (Landungsbrücken)
9 State Opera (Staatsoper)
10 Concert Hall (Musikhalle)
11 St. Nicholas' Tower (St. Nicolai)
12 Chile House
13 St. Peter's Church (St. Petri)
14 Gänsemarkt

AN DER VERBINDUNGSBAHN
TV Tower
TIERGARTEN STRASSE
EDM
RENTZELSTR.
(2)
Planten un Blomen
JUNGIUS
STRASSE
BEI DEN KIRCHHÖFEN
KAROLINEN
STRASSE
Botanical Garden
STR.
Exhibition Ground
HOLSTENGLACIS
GORCH-FOCK-WALL
FELDSTRASSE
(10)
KARL-MUCK-PLATZ
VALENTINS KAMP
KAISER-WILHELM STR.
BUDAPESTER STR.
GLACISCHAUSSE
HOLSTENWALL
STADTHAUS BR.
Historical Museum
WEXSTRASSE
GROSS NEU-MARKT
REEPERBAHN
MILLERNTORDAMM
CUXHAVENER ALLEE
NEUER STEINWEG
HEILIGENGEIST- BR.
St. Pauli
OST - WEST - STRASSE
STR.
St. Michaels Church
RÖDINGSMARKT
BERNH-NOCHT-STR.
SEEW
HELGOLÄNDER STR.
VENUSBERG
MARTIN-LUTHER-S.
SCHAARSTEINW
SCHAAR TOR
ADMIRALITÄTS
ST. PAULI - HAFEN
STR.
DITMAR-KOEL-STR.
SCHAAR MARKT
STEINHÖFT
KAJEN
(8)
JOHANNIS-BOLLWERK
VORSETZEN
BAUM WALL
WANDEBAHN

ELBE

We are now just outside the Gorch-Fock-Wall. Beyond the park stands the Fairground (Messe) with congress halls and exhibition grounds, where there is a year-round program of trade fairs. To the north of the railway—the line that runs from the Hauptbahnhof to Dammtor and beyond—is the University (an interesting area if you care to return there another day, with book-shops, student cafés and the Harverstehude area with some notable architecture).

But our tour follows the wall, and next we come to Karl-Much Platz, with Hamburg's premier concert hall (Musikhalle), where the great composer Brahms heard his works performed before returning to his simple room north of the city. Continuing along the Holstenwall, with parkland on the right, your next important stop is at the Hamburg Historical Museum (Museum for Hamburgische Geschichte) with a splendid collection of marine models which demonstrate the development of the port and ships that have used it. In the Kaufmannsdiele, there are concerts once or twice a month.

St. Pauli and the Port

Swinging southwest towards the river, we now enter the St. Pauli district. At night it is a buzz of neon lights, music and street life, but by day it is rather quiet, ideal for a first visit to aquaint yourself with the layout of the streets. Follow the Reeperbahn which runs parallel to the river. When you come to the crossing with Davidstrasse, where Hamburg's most famous police station stands, turn left and walk through towards the river. On your right is the walled-off Herbertstrasse, painted a lurid red and marked with a warning, "No ladies admitted"; though this is not strictly true.

Now the ground slopes down towards the Elbe, across what was once the most fascinating part of St. Pauli, the old huddle of riverside buildings which stood along the narrow streets is gone, and a new complex of offices, shops and flats is under construction. Walk past it down to the waterfront. On the left are the St. Pauli Piers (Landungsbrücken St. Pauli), where local passenger ships and excursion boats tie up. Check the times of the tours around the port, a trip which takes in miles of quayside, hundreds of freighters, ocean liners, floating docks, and a good view of the animated men at work there.

To your right, the road leads to Altona, with its fascinating Sunday morning fish market and, above, the graceful town hall and State Museum, which contains an interesting marine display. It is worth returning here another day and walking west along the river shore to Övelgönne, a narrow, riverside way with extremely beautiful old houses.

Near the St. Pauli piers, you can see the dome above the old Elbe tunnel, built in 1911. A new one, which is further west, was opened in

1975: 2 miles long—the longest in Europe—it diverts much of the through traffic from the city center.

To get back to the Alt-Stadt, turn away from the river and go up Helgoländer Allee towards the Bismarck memorial. As so often happens with former heroes, Bismarck's Prussian warmongering during the last century has largely been romanticized. His statue stands, with its fierce moustache, huge jack-boots, spiked helmet and sword, as a reminder of the destructive forces that have swept across Europe—more than once.

The Inner City

As we approach the inner city, the fruits of war are all too apparent. The heart of Hamburg was ripped to shreds during the last war, and though construction speeds on there are still vast, gaping holes. One building that survived the holocaust was St. Michael's Church, which now comes into view on your right, surrounded by a cluster of small red-brick houses, the Krameramtsstuben, tiny, 17th-century houses that today are art galleries, inns and cafés. From the green-topped spire of St. Micheal's Church, the watchman blows his trumpet every day at 10 A.M., to east and west, and again at 9 P.M. to all four directions. You can climb to his windy music stand, just below the clock, and gaze across the entire city and the port—a splendid panorama.

The Ost-West-Strasse now takes us into town, but first there is that maze of old warehouses, bridges, water-worn stairways and abandoned quays around Rödings Markt, and the canals, called Fleete, which connect the Elbe with the Alster. There is something here of Venice and Amsterdam. When you have seen enough, follow your nose towards the high spires of the Town Hall (Rathaus), which will guide you to the Alt-Stadt center, her most elegant shops and restaurants, and the chance to rest your feet.

One of the most exquisite shopping arcades in Europe is in the Alster Arcade, alongside the canal that borders the Rathausplatz. Here you will find furs, diamonds, ancient apothecary boxes and modern manicure kits, Bavarian lederhosen and Chinese porcelain—in short, the best consumer goods from all over the world. If you have the money to spend, this is a good place to spend it.

The cheaper, larger department stores lie to the east of the Rathaus, but before you head in that direction, check the times when the Rathaus itself is open. This daring Renaissance structure has a fine festival hall, noble vaulted ceilings, elaborate doorways and offers a rare view of German official architecture at its proudest.

The Alster Lakes

If the weather is fine, now is the time to head for the Alster, a short walk which takes you out onto the elegant Jungfernstieg. Here there is a café on the lakeside, and the chance to check the boats that leave every few minutes to cross the Alster waters. On a gustier day, you might prefer to cross the Rathausplatz and explore Mönkebergstrasse. Largely rebuilt after the war, there are nevertheless a couple of architectural gems here—the Petrikirche and, next door to it, a 300-year-old house which gives a startling impression of how this street might once have been before the invention of steel and plate glass. Across the road, in Gerhard Hauptmannplatz, is the Hamburg TIP, an information center where you can find out about everything from current concerts and excursion trips to Schleswig-Holstein, to who needs a drummer for his band and who is offering a ride to Berlin on Wednesday. Outside there is always a gathering of young people, relaxing on the pleasant wooden benches designed by Hamburg architect Jost Vieth. Here, too, you find the Thalia Theater, even more popular than the German theater.

A little further along Mönkebergstrasse is the best Hamburger place in town, entirely American in conception, for the universally useful meal-in-a-bun which takes its name from this city has truly nothing to do with Germany. For authentic local sausages, and fine local breads and cakes, continue a little further to the café/conditorei *Otto Vernimb*. Here, from a first-floor window, you can watch the city come and go, enjoying succulent desserts at acceptable prices. The pedestrian precinct below is full of shoppers and the atmosphere is always relaxed.

South towards the river from here, there are some interesting pieces of architecture, notably the Chilehaus, the Spinkenhof and the Ballinhaus—built during the last century and happily survivors of the war. They deserve an afternoon on their own, as does the immense television tower, 890 feet high and visible throughout the city. From its summit, you will have a stupendous view of Hamburg, particularly at night.

At the end of Mönkebergstrasse is the main station again, and beyond it the Arts and Crafts Museum (Museum für Kunst and Gewerbe), in Steintorplatz, and the German Theatre (Deutsches Schauspielhaus) off the KirchenAllee. The former, like all Hamburg's museums, is closed on Mondays. The latter, with productions from Goethe to the modern Peter Handke, has a notable reputation.

Excursions from Hamburg

Downstream from the city along the Elbe shore is the quaint riverside village of Blankenese, where narrow streets and winding step-ways (Treppe) connect the main road above with the waterside and beach below. There are several pleasant restaurants here, where you can sit and gaze at the ships as they rumble up and down the river, You can catch an S-bahn train from the main station, which carries you quickly and comfortably, but the most interesting ride is certainly by car along the the the Elbchaussee, with its elegant parks and attractive old mansions.

On the other, southern, side of the river, beyond the refineries which have made the Elbe unsafe for swimming with their effluence, lies the agricultural Alte Land, the Old Land. This can be reached by local ferry from St. Pauli Piers via Wedel (at Welcome Pier) to Lühe. A drive through this very traditional region, with its vast timbered farmhouses in which people, animals and crops are all housed under one roof, is a dip into history. Canals, simple taverns, fresh air and men hard at work are the characteristics of this flat Saxon land. One goal of this trip might be Stade, an old Hanseatic city, with many of its medieval buildings still intact. The best time to visit is April/May, when the fruit trees are in blossom, or in June for the cherry harvest.

For a look at the mouth of the mighty Elbe, which is fed by waters from Czechoslovakia over 700 miles away, take a boat from Hamburg to Cuxhaven and, beyond it, to the island of Helgoland. In fine weather, this is a delightful ride, and you can still get back to the city before nightfall. If you have the time, spend the night on Helgoland, which will refresh you for another bout of tourist life back in the city.

East of Hamburg, riding up the Elbe, lies the glorious wild Saxon Forest (Sachsenwald). You can get there by S-bahn through a series of rather dismal industrial dormitory towns like Bergedorf and Reinbek, stopping off, if you have a mind to, at the Bismarck Museum in Aumühle, where the Iron Chancellor died, in the bosom of land presented to him by Kaiser Wilhelm in 1871, for services rendered. It is, however, much more pleasant to drive through these woods, in which case you might turn north, follow the little Bille through its valley, and make your goal the picturesque old watermill at Grander-Mühle or, a little further along, the bathing beaches at Grossensee and Lütjensee.

East of Hamburg, again, but further to the north, is Lauenberg, a pleasant little town at the point where the Elbe-Lübeck Canal leaves the river. It is reached by boat from the St. Pauli Piers or by suburban train, but the point is the boat ride through lovely country. On the way, you pass The Four Lands—Vierlande—large stretches of land, growing fruits and vegetables for the Hamburg market, separated by various branches of the Elbe, canals, and other rivers, that under the very eye of Hamburg have maintained their old customs and costumes (the latter particularly colorful, involving, for the women, a curious head-dress that looks like an inverted bowl). Shortly before the goal is reached are Geesthacht, an old town creeping onto the hill above it, and several bathing beaches along the Elbe. Until less than a hundred years ago Lauenburg was the seat of an autonomous duchy of the same name and the half-timbered architecture of the lower town is witness to its historic past while the terrace of the former castle in the upper town provides a good view of the Elbe, bridged here for one of the main connections between north and south, at the point where it is joined by the Lübeck-Elbe canal.

If you have a spare afternoon, and the weather is good, take the U-Bahn northwest to Hagenbeck, where the zoo is situated. The ani-mals roam in open enclosures, with moats rather than cages to contain them. The great-grandson of the founder still runs the zoo, which was built up as a private business. Wild animals are still trained here for circuses.

PRACTICAL INFORMATION FOR HAMBURG

 WHEN TO COME. Hamburg boasts a year-round program of cultural, sporting and trade events which are listed in the periodic City Guide, available from German tourist offices throughout the world. Some of the most important are the Boat Exhibition in January; the two-week Spring Festival (Frühlingsfest) in February and March; the Spring Show (Frühlingsschau) in April and May, with flower parades, firework shows and many sports and musical events; the Equestrian Tournament in June and Derby week in July; the German tennis and golf championships late in July; and the great folk festival (Hamburger Dom) in November and December, with its fairground, beer tents and general merriment.

  HOTELS. Hamburg has many hotels but advance booking is necessary in summer and whenever large conventions or congresses are taking place—and this is quite often. Central booking offices (Hotelnachweise) can arrange this for you: there is one in the main station, on the KirchenAllee side (tel. 32–69–17), and another at the airport arrival hall (tel. 50–84–57).

Deluxe

Atlantic Hotel (Kempinski), An der Alster 73, on the lakeside, with 400 beds, most rooms with bath, 20 suites; elegant furnishings, glittering public rooms, roof-top swimming pool, nightclub and fine restaurant.

Hamburg Plaza, Am Dammtor, 1,134 beds, most rooms with bath, color TV and radio. Swimming pool and sauna, two good restaurants and rooftop cocktail lounge with a fine view.

Inter-Continental, Fontenay 10, on the lakeside. 600 beds, all rooms with private bathroom, several restaurants and bars, indoor pool, sauna, conference rooms, shops, large carpark.

Vier Jahreszeiten, Neuer Jungfernstieg 9, also on the lakeside, with 300 beds, most rooms with bath, antique-style suites and excellent food. Impeccable service.

Expensive

Alsterhof, Esplanade 12, near Lombard Bridge. 130 beds, most rooms with bath, suites with a view over the lake; restaurant and bar.

Ambassador, Heidenkampsweg in Berliner Tor district. 200 beds, most rooms with shower/bath; bars and swimming pool; grill restaurant.

Berlin, Borgfelderstrasse 1, near the autobahn exit. Modern. 120 rooms with bath and outside view; suites with TV; excellent food.

Bellevue, An der Alster 14, on the northern lakeside. 103 beds, all in the new wing with bath/shower; good restaurant and bar.

EuroCrest, Mexicoring, near Hamburg City Park. 270 beds, all with bath/shower; two restaurants and a bar. Convenient for airport and shopping.

Europäischer Hof, Kirchenallee 45, opposite main station; 450 rooms, most with bath/shower; good restaurant; garage.

Moderate

Bellevue, An der Alster 14, on the lakeside. 103 beds, conference room, restaurant.

Dänischer Hof, Holzdamm 4, near the southern lake. 70 beds, meals for hotel guests.

Eden, Ellmenreichstrasse 20. Pleasant and modern; 170 beds, meals for hotel guests.

Elbbrücken, Billhorner-Mühlenweg 28. 60 beds, parking.

Kronprinz, Kirchenallee 46. 107 rooms, some with bath. Bar.

Metro, Bremerreihe 14, near main station; 104 beds, meals for guests, large garage.

Motel Hamburg International, Hammer Landstrasse 200. 78 beds, evening meal for house guests.

Pacific, Neuer Pferdemarkt 30, near Heiligengeistfeld; 100 beds.

Parkhochhaus, Drehbahn 15, near the Opera. 100 rooms, all with bath/shower; restaurant.

Prem, An der Alster 9, on the lakeside. 75 beds, most rooms with bath/shower.

St. Raphael, Adenauerallee 41, near main station; 160 beds.

Wedina, Gurlittsrasse 23. Pleasant; 40 beds.

Aachener Hof, St.-Georg-Strasse 10; **Immke,** Neuer Kamp 21, in St. Pauli; **Am Bahnhof,** Präsident-Krahn-Str. 13, in Altona; **Stadt Altona,** Louise-Schröder-Str. 29, in Altona.

 RESTAURANTS. Perhaps Hamburg's most famous dish at home is *Aalsuppe* (eel soup), worthy of comparison with the *bouillabaisse* of Marseille. In fact, most of the Hamburg soups are worth a trip north—especially the *Arfensuppe mit Snuten un Poten,* a thick pea soup made with pig's feet, and the *Hamburger Frische Suppe,* made of beef, veal meat balls, and the vegetables in season. Other Hamburg specialties are the *Stubenküken* (chicken), *Vierländer Mastente* (duck), *Birnen, Bohnen und Speck* (pears, beans and bacon), and the sailor's favorite *Labskaus.*

Expensive

Atlantic Grill, in the Atlantic Hotel, with many local specialties.

L'Auberge Francaise, Rutschbahn 34, with excellent French cooking, and including delicious seafood recipes.

Daitokai, Mittelweg/Milchstrasse 1, Japanese cuisine at its best.

Haerlin Restaurant, in the Vier Jehreszeiten Hotel, shares the hotel's high standards, with view of the Dinnen Alster and marvelous cooking.

Schümanns Austernkeller, Jungfernstieg 34, also specializes in seafood; solemn wooden décor with pretty booths. Closed Sun.

Nikolaikeller, an old Hamburg tavern serving local specialties including several kinds of *Matjes.*

OLD HAMBURG

Moderate

Ratsweinkeller, the beautifully vaulted cellar restaurant of the Rathaus (City Hall); entrance from Grosse Johannisstrasse (corner of City Hall Square).

Zum Alten Rathaus, Börsenbrücke 10, vaulted, atmospheric and noted for food; local type of entertainment in its cellar tavern *Zum Fleetenkieker.*

Also good are—**Achter der Kark**, Zeughausmarkt/Gerstackerstrasse; **Brahms Stuben**, Ludolfstr. 43; **Petershof**, Rodig Allee 293,

FISH RESTAURANTS

Three restaurants specializing in seafood are—**Fischerhaus**, St. Pauli-Fischmarkt 14; **Fisch-Fiete**, Grindelhof 77; **Übersee-Brücke**, St. Pauli Piers.

FOOD WITH A VIEW

Restaurants that can be recommended and with a view over the port area are **Bavaria-Blick**, on the top floor of Bernhard-Nocht-Strasse 99 in St. Pauli, **Landungsbrücken** at St. Pauli piers and the glassed-in *Überseebrücke* at the overseas passengers' pier, also on the St. Pauli side.

Fernsehturm, a revolving restaurant (one turn an hour) 420 feet high up on the 890-ft. TV tower with outstanding view. Two sections: the upper section is a fine and higher priced restaurant; the lower section is self-service.

Restaurant im Finnlandhaus, Esplanade 41, near the opera house, has a panoramic view and the food is deliciously fresh. Expensive.

Inexpensive

Among the many comfortable restaurants with good, reasonable food are— **Friesenhof**, Hamburgerstr./Winterhude Weg; **Kanzelmeyer**, ABC-Strasse 8; **Shalou**, Steindamm 53, for Indian dishes.

Vegetarische Gaststätte over the Alsterarkaden is the oldest and the largest vegetarian restaurant in Germany.

The two chains, **Wienerwald** and **Block House** (steak houses), provide easy and fairly reasonable eating. They both have branches all over the city.

OUT-OF-TOWN

Overlooking the Elbe, and all (M) are—**Op'n Bulln,** Blankensee landing stage; **Zum Elbwirt,** Oevelgonner Hohlweg 12; and **Süllberg,** a vast indoor and outdoor restaurant and café in a castle-like structure on a hill above Blankensee.

Cafés (all with fine food)

Alsterpavillon, where everybody meets, on Jungfernstieg overlooking the Inner Alster, music in the afternoon and evening, especially pleasant outdoors; **Otto Vernimb,** Spitaler Str. 9 and Mönckebergstr. 10 is worth visiting; the elegant **Gustav Adolf,** Grosse Bleichen 32, has fine pastries and a lunch bar. These three also have full restaurant service. Primarily for pastries: **Schröder,** Alsterarkaden 9.

TRANSPORTATION. By Train: The city and suburban U-bahn and S-bahn are excellent. Tickets are purchased from automatic vending machines in each station, which accept 2DM, 1DM, 50 and 10 pfennig pieces, but also dispense change. A map of all stations is available at tourist offices.

By bus: Hamburg is well served by street public transport, though it is helpful if you can speak a little German. The advantage of the bus over trains is that you can view the city as you travel. A bus map is available from tourist offices.

By boat: Regular Alster taxis leave the Jungfernstieg pier for points along the lake and the canals. A 50-minutes Alster cruise, and a 2-hour canal cruise depart regularly, returning to the same pier. Inquiries can be made by phone (34–11–41). For harbor trips from St. Pauli Piers, with commentary in English, check the timetable of HADAG ships (31–96–280) or Harbor Launches (31–96 –227).

Car-hire: *Autorent,* Gertrudenstrasse 3. (33–59–98); *Auto-Sixt,* Ellmenreichstr. 26. (24–14–66); *Avis,* Drehbahn 15 (34–16–51 or 50–83–14); *Hertz,* Kirchen Allee 34 (280–21–21); *InterRent,* Tangstedter-Landstr. 81 (52–01–81).

Parking: Open-air and inside facilities are available throughout Hamburg. A map is available from tourist offices. Several parking lots offer 50% reductions to visitors parking between 8 P.M. and 8 A.M.

SIGHTSEEING. The buses for city sightseeing start from Hachmannplatz at the main railroad station. Guided boat tours of the port leave from St. Pauli Landungsbrücken (Piers). Guided motorboat tours of the Alster lakes leave from Jungfernstieg about every half hour, and Saturday moonlight cruises with dancing on board. Round air flights over Hamburg in summer and in winter in clear weather from the airport. Beautiful view of the city from the tower (elevator) of St. Michael's Church, landmark of the Hamburg port area.

MUSEUMS. Most Hamburg museums are closed on Mondays. Many also have days when entry is free. However, as with opening times, these tend to vary, so it's best to check with the local tourist office or with the official monthly program.

Ethnology Museum, in Rothenbaumchaussee 64. Particularly good collections of African and South American culture, as well as many other exhibits from all over the world. Open 10 to 5.

Hagenbeck Zoo, in the northwest suburb of Stellingen and easily reached by U-Bahn or bus. Originally founded in 1907, this was one of the first zoos to adopt the system that houses animals in open-air pens and not in cages. It has also been responsible for capturing, training and selling wild animals to other zoos and circuses throughout the world.

Hamburg Historical Museum (Museum fur Hamburgische Geschichte), Holstenwall 24. Apart from the displays concerning Hamburg's history, the most interesting items are nautical and are particularly concerned with the development of the port. Open 10 to 5.

The Kunsthalle, Glockengiesserwall 1. Hamburg's principal art gallery and contains some of the best works of art in Germany. The collections include paintings from the late Middle Ages to modern times. European and American (from the '60s onwards) schools are particularly well represented, but perhaps the finest piece is the Grabow Altarpiece, executed by the Master Bertram in the late 14th century. Open 10 to 5; Wed. till 7.

Museum of Decorative Arts and Crafts (Museum fur Kunst and Gewerbe), Steintorplatz 1. The collections cover centuries of development in the applied arts. Among them are some remarkable medieval gold and silver work, but there is also much Renaissance furniture, 18th-century porcelain and some marvelous art nouveau.

North German Regional Museum, Museumstrasse (in the suburb of Altona). This fine museum contains a wealth of interesting exhibits on the culture and life of North Germany. Open 10 to 5.

 MUSIC. From opera at the State Opera House (tickets are not always easy to get as many seats are held on subscription) to symphony concerts given by Hamburg's own three orchestras, from mainstream jazz at the Altona Fabrik to rock and roll at the Logo, in the University area, Hamburg boasts one of the most comprehensive music scenes in Germany.

A complete list of concerts is available at tourist offices, at many hotels and at the Hamburger TIP in Gerhart Hauptmann Platz, near the Rathaus. Look out for open-air concerts in summer, and notices of the many church concerts.

THEATER. Traditional theater is well represented, with drama and comedy at the *Deutsches Schauspielhaus*, which has a good reputation, the *Kammerspiele* and the Thalia. More experimental plays are sometimes produced at the tiny *Theater im Zimmer*, while the *Hansa* is one of the last old-style variety houses left in Germany, with drinks and light meals served at tables in the auditorium. As with music *(above)*, a complete list of current productions is available in the city.

Ticket Agencies: *Theaterkasse Altona*, Neue Grosse Bergstrasse (38–62–64); *Hamburg TIP*, Gerhart-Hauptmann-Platz (32–54–12); *Theater- und Konzert Kasse Collien*, Eppendorfer Baum 25 (48–33–90); *Konzertkasse Gerdes*, Rothenbaumchaussee 77 (45–33–26); *Theaterkasse Schumacher*, Colonnaden 37 (34–30 –44).

 NIGHTLIFE. For elegant restaurants with dancing, try *die Insel*, Alsterufer 34 (tel. 44–66–51), with its splendid view over the Alster or *Boccaccio*, Kirchenallee 50 (tel. 24–94–44) near the main station: others in this vein are *Marieville*, Hoheluftbrücke/Isebekkanal (tel. 49–71–48) and the *Life Club*, Rothenbaumchaussee 185 (tel. 45–57–80).

If you want a floor show, try *Homa*, Bei den Muhren 91 (tel. 36–67–16), with belly-dancing on Saturday nights; or *el Flamenco*, Hoheluftchaussee 132 (tel. 460–13–38), which features Spanish dancing. Both are highly respectable. Other nightclubs: *Chesa*, Beim Schlump 15; *186*, Dorotheenstr. 186; *Member's*, Milchstr. 25, in Harvestehude; all expensive. Famous for Hamburg cabaret is *Das Schiff*, a converted ship moored at Holzbrücke near Ost-West-Str./ Deichstr.

There are more informal dance locales in the Reeperbahn, such as the *Bayrisch Zell* (tel. 31–42–81) and the *Café Keese* (tel. 31–08–05), where there are hostesses but the atmosphere is still respectable. For a more liberal venue, with freer ladies, try *Colibri, Safari* or the notorious *Gross Freiheit* (Great Freedom). None of these gets going till 10 P.M. and they will happily accommodate you until the early hours. St. Pauli at night is a much safer place than it was ten years ago, but visitors should still take note of our recommendations at the beginning of this chapter: order your own drinks, rather than letting the hostess do it for you, and pay as soon as you are served; go with a friend or in a group. If in doubt, you can always take the tourist-office tour, which provides a variety of bars and a sex show, while getting you to the main station soon after midnight. Sex shows of a pretty up market type at *Salambo*, Grosse Freiheit, and *Pulverfass*, Pulverhof near Steindamm, which puts on a superior drag show.

If you want to dance with abandon, Hamburg offers a large number of good discos: *Grünspan, Trinity Star Club, Shave* and many others are open to all, though frequented mostly by the young. If you prefer live music, there are fifty or so clubs in and around the city, playing everything from rock and jazz to the blues. Near the University, try *Logo* or *Remter;* in Altona, the *Fabrik* is excellent, with facilities for children as well as adults; in Eppendorf.

SPORTS. Tennis: public outdoor courts are situated in all the main parks; heated indoor courts are open in winter in the Planten un Blomen Park, and all the year round in the Tennishalle at the Horn race track. **Swimming:** there are 22 heated indoor pools; admission is usually cheaper on Tuesdays. The largest and most popular is the Alsterschwimmhalle near Uhlandstrasse U-bahn (tel. 22–30–12). There are also saunas and turkish baths: consult the telephone directory under Badeanstalten u. Bäder or ask at the tourist office.

Sailing and rowing are popular summer events on the Alster and the Elbe: boats are for hire and there are several regattas. **Horseback-riding** is popular among the Hamburgers: there are over 40 riding schools. For information telephone the Association (36–66–06). There are regular trotting events in Bahrenfeld (S-bahn to Altona, then bus 188 or S-bahn to Holstenstrasse, then bus 288: it's easier to drive). Flat-racing takes place at the Horn race track and jumping tournaments at Gross-Flottbek, where there is also polo.

Ice-skating: a vast new ice palace was opened in 1978 at Berner Heerweg in Farmsen (tel. 643–32–00), and there are regular hockey matches here. An older rink is in the Planten un Boomen Park, where there are also roller-skating facilities. **Skittles and bowling:** there are several skittle alleys in Hamburg, notably those in Adolph-Schonfelderstr. and in Meinendorfer Mühlenweg. Bowling alleys are in Am Millerntor in St. Pauli, in Wagnerstrasse near Hamburgerstrasse, at the Elbe shopping Centre in Osdorferlandstrasse, and elsewhere. Consult your hotel or the tourist office.

USEFUL ADDRESSES. Tourist information: near Main Station: Bieberhaus, Hachmannplatz (24–87–00); at the airport: Arrival Hall (50–84–57); near Rathaus: Hamburg Tip, Gerhart-Hauptmann Platz (32–57–60); St. Pauli Piers: Hafen Tip (31–39–77); Motorway ADAC: Stillhorn Services (754–46–03).

Hotel Reservations: at Main Station: Hotelnachsweis, Kirchenallee (32–69–17); at the Airport: Arrival Hall (50–84–57); Tourist Office (24–87–00).

Transport telephone numbers:
Airport. 50–87–53
Auto traffic: 28–999
Train times: 33–99–11
Boat trips: 34–11–41 (Alster); 31–96–281 (port).

Consulates: American: Alsterufer 28 (44–10–61); Canadian: Esplanade 41 (35–18–05); British: Harvesterhude Weg 8 (44–60–71).

LOWER SAXONY

The Land of Contrasts

Lower Saxony is bounded by the Elbe on the north, by East Germany on the east, Holland on the west, and by Westphalia and Hesse in the south. It includes also the East Frisian Islands in the North Sea. This is a land of wide variety, containing within its borders sea-bound islands and coastal harbors, great river ports and vast heaths, medieval Hanseatic cities and university towns, forests, lakes and spas, and even, as a climax to the extremes, mountains high enough for winter sports.

EXPLORING LOWER SAXONY

Moving westward on the southern bank of the Elbe, the first place of importance we come to is Cuxhaven, which some of the big ships use as a port for Hamburg instead of sailing up the river all the way to that city. It is also an important fishing town and, together with adjacent Duhnen, a beach resort. It calls its seaside bulwark, for some reason mysterious to outsiders, "Old Love," and is inordinately proud of its Kugelbake—a stilt-mounted monster of a ball buoy which stands on the end of a jetty. This marks the beginning of Lighthouse Lane, as the heavily traveled sea route northward from this point is called. The best fun from Cuxhaven is a sail by smack to the island of Neuwerk.

Passing down the coast from Cuxhaven we come to Bremerhaven, which performs for Bremen the service Cuxhaven does for Hamburg—many ships dock here instead of sailing up the Weser to the bigger city. Bremerhaven is no mere suburb of Bremen. It is an important city in its own right. With the largest fisherman's harbor in the world (its auction hall is well worth visiting) it possesses quite naturally a Fisheries Museum, a North Sea Aquarium, and an institute of seamanship. The well-equipped building on the dock at which big transoceanic liners tie up is the modernized and enlarged overseas passengers' terminal, 850 feet long and containing passenger waiting rooms, ship reservation and travel offices, shops, post-office counters, money exchange offices, several restaurants and lunch counters. It is interesting to note that the very first ship to use the newly-founded harbor of Bremerhaven was the U.S.S. *Draper* in 1830. Like most world ports, Bremerhaven enjoys a lively nightlife.

The Great Port of Bremen

Forty miles up the Weser is Bremen, Germany's oldest and today her second port (Hamburg is the first), a great center of world trade since the days when, with Hamburg and Lübeck, it was one of the Big Three of the Hanseatic League. Since World War II the port of Bremen has surpassed its highest prewar traffic volume. Here is the landing stage from where you can take a boat tour of the port. The sightseeing boats first pass by the great three-mast sail ship *Deutschland,* an outstanding beauty, employed today by the naval school and usually at anchor near the Stephan's Brücke. Then you proceed to several sections of the great port where ship stands next to ship under rows of cranes.

Immediately upstream from the St. Martin's landing stage is the Great Weser Bridge and not far from it, a little further in from the right bank and tucked away from traffic, is the idyllic Schnoor quarter, with very narrow streets and dozens of toy-like houses from about 1600, populated by artists and containing small galleries and artistic craftsmen's shops.

Outside of the moated Old Bremen and beyond the main railroad station is the green expanse of the Bürgerpark at whose edge are the exhibition grounds with the ultramodern Stadthalle with several halls intended for congresses, conventions, musical events, great social occasions and similar. In addition to many other modern buildings in the inner city, Bremen possesses fine examples of modern architecture in such residential apartment settlements as Vahr and Neue Vahr in the eastern suburbs.

Oldenburg and the Stone Age

From Bremen, the picturesque land of East Frisia, with a fringe of fascinating islands off its coast, can be reached in a circular swing which takes in a number of other interesting points. First stop is the garden city of Oldenburg, where those glazed Klinker bricks you see in North German buildings are produced. Oldenburg is also known particularly for its Renaissance Palace, the 13th-century Lamberti Church and the 15th-century St. Gertrud Chapel. The city is in the middle of Stone Age country—the region where Stone Age man painfully gathered together the great boulders scattered over the countryside by the glaciers of the Ice Age and heaped them up into funeral monuments called here Hünengräber or Hünenbetten, giants' graves or giants' beds. They are particularly numerous on the Ahlhorn Heath south of Oldenburg, where the largest one stands—the Visbecker Bridegroom, made of 150 granite blocks forming a structure 360 feet long—Germany's Stonehenge.

To the northwest of Oldenburg is a lake called Zwischenahner Meer whose blue waters are dotted by sails, swans and seagulls and whose southern shore is presided over by the noted spa of Bad Zwischenahn. Further in the same direction is the town of Westerstede with the 12th-century St. Peter's Church, an important horseracing field and surrounded by meadows and oak woods. To the north of Oldenburg, fast rooted in the land, we make a swift transition to Wilhelmshaven, standing on the sea, at Jade Bay, where the Ems-Jade Canal cuts across the peninsula of East Frisia and makes it an island. Beside fine sunny beaches, Wilhelmshaven's specialty is relaxing therapeutic mud baths. It is a starting point for tours along the East Frisian coast and to the islands off it, or across the East Frisian peninsula, with its many moated castles.

From East Frisian Islands to Osnabrück

From Wilhelmshaven we go to Jever, the center of a district studded with castles, whose own is famous for the carved oak timbers of the ceiling in its great hall. The castle, surrounded by a beautiful park, houses one of the best local museums in North Germany; the town church contains a rich Renaissance sarcophagus, the Rathaus dates from 1609 and Jever traces its history back for over 1,000 years. Next we reach Carolinensiel on the coast, which we can then follow through country which looks like Holland—windmills, dikes and fat cattle grazing in the fields—or cut across to one or the other of the East Frisian Islands to swim from their sandy beaches, which the mainland, at this point, lacks.

The East Frisian Islands, reading from the Dutch border eastwards, are Borkum, Juist, Norderney, Baltrum, Langeoog, Spiekeroog, Wangerooge. They have been taken up in quite a big way as "back-to-nature" resorts, excellent for family vacationing.

These islands are really a kind of fringe of the coastline, several miles out, a necklace of sandy outcroppings, each one nearly all beach. They all have good ferry services, from whatever the nearest point on the mainland is, Norddeich for Juist, Norderney and Baltrum, Bensersiel for Langeoog, and so on. They are all of them attractive in their own ways.

Borkum is the largest of the chain, and very popular; here you will see holidaymakers riding horses along the vast expanses of beach at low tide, or walking for miles. In fact horse-riding is a favorite relaxation on several of the islands. Borkum is very well supplied with all sorts of accommodation, spa facilities and lots for families to do by night and day. Juist is very popular too, with even more of a family atmosphere. The special sport here is sailing land yachts on rubber-tired wheels across the long beaches.

Norderney is the oldest North Sea resort (since 1797), and has a slightly more international flavor. There is an indoor pool with artificial waves, for use when the sea is too cold, and a naturist beach here, too.

Baltrum, the smallest of the islands, has an attractive fishing village. On Langeoog the emphasis is on sport. Spiekeroog, reached from Neuharlingersiel or Carolinensiel, has an old church with mementos and objects from the 16th-century ships of the Spanish Armada. Wangerooge has unusually wide, sandy beaches, an all-the-year-round season, air which relieves hay fever and the delight of stepping straight out of your hotel on to the beach (which also goes for some of the other islands).

Tea drinking is an unexpected feature of East Frisian life, but don't expect it to resemble the European concoction. It's even more an acquired taste—a very dark brown though being so strong and taken with thick cream and a lump of sugar, rather like coffee. Seagull eggs are another novelty and no less strong, though travelers who have eaten them in the western countries of England will find them familiar.

These are not, by and large, sophisticated places for a holiday, but neither are they Coney Island or Blackpool. They are relaxed, essentially open-air places, where a lot will depend on the weather, but, if it is good, you could have a healthy holiday to remember.

On the mainland again, we might swing through Norden, notable for its Town Hall (1500) and Gothic Church of St. Ludger; Emden, home port of the herring fleet and a busy shipbuilding and shipping town (it is the trans-shipment point for the Ruhr, and at the mouth of the Ems-Jade Canal), with a fine museum containing a notable collection of medieval art, stained-glass windows, and old arms and armor; Aurich, from which you can visit Upstalsboom, where the medieval Frisian Diets met; Bagband, jumping-off point to see large-scale moorland cultivation at Wiesmoor; Leer, a picturesque old river port which is the largest cattle market in northwestern Germany; Papenburg, a typical moorland settlement; Meppen and Lingen, with their interesting town halls.

From here we go southeast to Osnabrück, a lively city for centuries. Its cathedral is more than a thousand years old and in its Gothic Town Hall, in 1648, France, Sweden and the Germanic Empire signed the Treaty of Westphalia, which ended the Thirty Years War. George I of England was born in Osnabrück in 1660 as the son of the Elector of Hannover, though he was not to be called until 1714 to found England's present ruling house, which changed its name to House of Windsor in 1917. Among the more recent achievements of this city are the production of highly-regarded pumpernickel and a potent variety of schnaps known as *Korn.*

Returning from Bremen we proceed north from Osnabrück through Damme, a pleasant old town and climatic resort in an area of wooded hills, half-timbered farmhouses, ponds and stone graves; a few miles east is the Dümmer Lake, known for the many species of birds and alive with sailboats during the warm season. North of Damme is Dinklage with a romantic moated castle and located in a fertile farm region rich in old customs. Cloppenburg, further north, is noted for its Museums-dorf, an open-air museum consisting of typical old farmhouses. Wilde-shausen, on the Hunte River and the main road to Bremen, has preserved some of its walls, gabled houses and the Romanesque Alexander Church. Nearby is Ahlhorn Heath with the previously mentioned giant grave stones.

Launching out from Bremen once more, this time in a southeasterly direction, our first stop is Verden on the Aller River, noted for two things—its cathedral and its horseback riding and racing traditions, including a horse museum. It is also an excellent place to start canoe or kayak trips. We come next to Nienburg, with its charming gabled houses, its fine town hall, its picturesque marketplace and the pleasant nearby lake, the Steinhuder Meer.

Industrious Hannover

Hannover (the English variant has one "n") is most animated in the spring, when the great international industrial fair, the most important of its kind in the world, is held here. But as a big industrial city with great cultural traditions, it always has many other fairs, exhibitions, conventions and continuous theatrical and musical programs.

The war destruction left almost nothing of the old town but the little that remained has been restored and reconstructed. The tower of the Gothic Marktkirche is again the landmark of the city; the church itself contains a notable wood-carved altar, a 15th-century baptismal font and bronze doors by the famous contemporary German sculptor Gerhard Marcks. Nearby is the beautifully restored Altes Rathaus (Old City Hall), which together with Marktkirche now represents an island amid the modern, functional buildings of the surrounding shopping streets. Not far away is another remaining piece of the Old Town, the 17th-century Ballhof, a several-winged, half-timbered building where the first opera in Hannover was performed in 1672, and a row of other half-timbered houses. The neo-classic Leineschloss, standing on the bank of Leine, has acquired an ultramodern annex and now houses the Lower Saxon Parliament, for Hannover is the capital of Lower Saxony. Also on the bank of the Leine you can observe the round Beginenturm, the only fully preserved (and once the strongest) tower of the city walls. Across the river is the Neustädter Church with the grave of Philosopher Leibniz.

The massive and vast Rathaus (the present City Hall), built during the first decade of the current century, is reflected in the small Maschpark lake, while the north shore of the large Maschsee lies only a few hundred yards away. Maschsee, which was made artificially during the years 1934–36 with the assistance of the parallel-running Leine river, is the playground for sailing and rowing enthusiasts and there is a large swimming establishment on its south shore; passenger boats ply the lake during the summer months. Hannover is known for its parks, among which Eilenriede, like Maschsee, is within easy walking distance of the city center. Eilenriede, lying beyond the main railroad station and railroad tracks, is the city forest and includes, among other features, the zoo which harbors some very fine and rare animals.

The most elegant street of Hannover is the section of Georgstrasse between Aegidientor Platz, where some of the most modern office buildings have sprung up, and Kröpcke square, the nerve center of Hannover's downtown traffic. The Opera Haus near Kröpcke on

Georgstrasse was originally built in the mid-19th century by Georg Ludwig Laves, the favored Hannover architect of that period, and it has been reconstructed since the last war. Georgstrasse continues from Kröpcke to Steintor square. Nearby in Goseriede street stands the Anzeiger Building, belonging to a publishing firm; from its top floor, reached by elevator, there is a fine view over the city.

The baroque Herrenhausen Gardens in the northwestern suburbs are among the most beautiful artificially laid out parks in Europe. They contain fountains, cascades, sculptures, several garden pavilions, orangerie and a baroque theater. In the southeastern outskirts on the other edge of the city are the fair grounds, three fair buildings, 22 exhibition halls, vast open-air exhibition area, and parking space for 40,000 cars.

Only about 12 miles southeast of the Hannover fair grounds is the 1,100-year-old town of Hildesheim, a real treasury of old architecture; although most of it was destroyed by the air raids of the last war, much of it has since been reconstructed. The most interesting churches include: the cathedral begun in 852 with bronze doors from 1015, a 13th-century baptismal font, numerous other works of art and an outstanding treasury; the 11th-century St. Michael and the 12th-century St. Godehard, both in pure Romanesque style. Among the most beautiful half-timbered houses are Wernerhaus and Waffenschmiedehaus, both from the 16th century. The Pelizaeus-Museum contains an outstanding collection of old Egyptian art.

From Weser Hills to Harz Mountains

We now swing west to Hameln (Hamelin is the anglicized version) which would be worth visiting anyway, as the town with the finest examples of the Weser Renaissance houses, but which has a particular attraction as the city of the Pied Piper. You will see his house in Hameln, along with many other palatial private homes, whose timbered façades are likely to bear inscriptions addressed to you, with words of advice, criticism or irony, all in Old German. The Pied Piper's story is re-enacted every summer, usually on Sundays, when the Piper in his medieval clothes walks through the streets of the town followed by an army of delighted kids dressed as rats and performing the Rat Dance.

Hameln is situated on the Weser in the region called Weserbergland after the river. The Weser Hill Country, as its name could be translated into English, is formed by some 15 ranges of hills, located on both sides of the Weser and extending from Hannoversch Münden, where the Fulda and Werra join the way to Porta Westfalica where the Weser breaks violently through the last range in order to enter the North

German Plain at Minden, flowing across it to Bremen and to the North Sea. Weserbergland is a region of beautiful scenery and fairy tales, of old monastaries, castles, and deep forests; the banks of the river are lined with attractive little towns and the interior is dotted with healing spas. Only a few miles south of Hameln is Bad Pyrmont, the most important one, a fashionable and well-known watering place. It has one of the most beautiful spa parks in Germany, once a favorite with Goethe. Its waters are beneficial for a number of disorders, ranging from skin diseases to blood circulation troubles. A number of other spas are to be found in the area west of Bad Pyrmont, and we have already visited some of them during our tour of western Germany, since the Weser Hill Country forms a dividing area between northern and western Germany.

Proceeding up the Weser River from Hameln we come to Bodenwerder, the town where Baron Münchhausen, the teller of the world's tallest tales, used to live; to Höxter, an old Hansa town with outstanding half-timbered houses and the nearby famous Benedictine Abbey of Corvey, founded in 822; to Karlshafen with its fine baroque buildings; to Hannoversch Münden, the "birthplace" of the Weser, with painted half-timbered buildings, a very fine Town Hall, and the remains of city walls. Not far from here is the fairy-tale Sababurg Castle of the Sleeping Beauty, in Hesse.

To the northeast is the ancient university town of Göttingen, whose 14th-century Town Hall, medieval half-timbered houses, and particularly its old students' taverns should not be overlooked. Farther northeast we reach the Harz Mountains at Osterode, an enchanting walled town with fine 15th- and 17th-century buildings, and the birthplace of the famous woodcarver, Tilman Riemenschneider. Not far from here along the southern edge of Harz are Herzberg with the 13th-century castle-fortress and Bad Lauterberg, specializing in Kneipp cold water cures. At the northern edge of the Harz, and very near the border of East Germany, is the beautifully situated spa of Bad Harzburg with chloride and ferrous waters. The Grosse Burgberg hill above it can be ascended by chair lift. In winter Bad Harzburg becomes a skiing center, and there is now a year-round casino. Just south of Bad Harzburg is the Brocken summit, the highest in Harz (3,750 feet), where the witches hold their Sabbaths, now in East Germany.

The evergreen forests of the Harz Mountains appeal both to those in search of holidays and of health. Many of the places at the highest altitudes are climatic health resorts which in winter become skiing centers, for Harz is the only important skiing region of North Germany. The principal winter sports centers and summer resorts include, in addition to Bad Harzburg, particularly Braunlage, Hahnenklee-Bockswiese, Clausthal-Zellerfeld, Schulenberg, and St. Andreasberg.

Goslar, Braunschweig and Lüneburg

If you think you have already seen everything possible in the way of medieval towns, you are likely to revise your ideas when you come to Goslar. Nestled in the beautiful country of the Harz, Goslar is an encyclopedia of the domestic architecture of past ages, as well as of ecclesiastical and public architecture, which is less rare. From its own buildings, street after street of them, it can produce a multitude of examples for each of the clearly marked periods it represents—Gothic houses built between 1450 and 1550, transitional buildings combining Gothic and Renaissance features in the last quarter century of that period, Renaissance homes from 1550 to 1650, baroque from 1650 to 1880. The 15th–16th-century guildhouses are magnificent. It has in addition some of the thickest towers of any defense works anywhere, several 12th-century churches, and the ancient (11th–12th century) Romanesque palace of the German Emperors. The latter is worth visiting if only for the grandiose, 19th-century murals depicting early German history and for its interesting chapel. The museum has a scale model reconstruction of how the town looked several centuries ago, together with many choice items of furniture, torture instruments, and other quaint items from the past.

The ancient Rathaus in the market square contains the Huldingungs-saal, a fabulous room entirely covered (walls and ceiling) with tempera paintings done by an unknown artist in 1500, and still retaining all their brilliant color. This old meeting room of the city elders also has a secret chapel.

But Goslar is more than architecture and history. To stroll along the stream that still rushes headlong through the streets, to climb the tower of the Market Church just before its bells announce the hour of day, to linger in the marketplace, is to step back into another way of life. It is not enough to study Goslar; indeed, too conscientious a visit would be a mistake. Rather it is a corner of Germany to be savored and enjoyed. Plan to allow at least a day, and save some of that time for rambles on foot.

We now come to another old city, a famous one, Braunschweig (the English version is Brunswick), which is north of the Harz. The old capital of Lower Saxony, Braunschweig is symbolized by the bronze lion dating from 1166, which stands in its Burgplatz—itself symboliz-ing Henry the Lion, who built the city's historic Romanesque cathe-dral. One of Germany's finest examples of sepulchral art is the tomb of Henry and his wife in the cathedral. Don't miss the Gothic Old City market, with its half-timbered houses representing Gothic and Renais-sance styles, and the 13th-century Old Town Hall. Still in the center of town are the early Gothic Ägidienkirche and St. Martin's Church (about 1200). The Herzog Anton Ulrich Museum, an important gallery of paintings, is in a park near the theater.

Celle is a colorful old town, with the oldest court theater in Germany. Its ducal castle is an imposing pile, its outstanding event of the year the Stallions' Parade in October—a riding and driving tournament as well as a horse show. From this point, we may take one of two routes—through Ülzen, where notable sights are the Rathaus, the Guild House, and St. Mary's Church with the "Golden Ship"—or through Soltau, near the natural park preserve of Wilsede and the painters' colonies in Fallingbostel and Bispingen. Either way brings us to Lüneburg.

Lüneburg is thought of particularly as a sort of museum of brick architecture, and it is true that there are whole streets of 15th- and 16th-century structures of that material; but there are also plenty of half-timbered buildings, with carved and brightly colored oak beams combined with the brick—mostly 14th century. The 14th-century Church of St. John and that of St. Nicholas are both fine examples of brick architecture, but the 13th–15th-century Rathaus is perhaps the finest structure in the city, with its elaborate carvings, the beautifully decorated beams and the wall painting in its banqueting hall, and the noble proportions of the Gothic Chamber of Justice. The old crane on the Ilmenau River harbor is the most picturesque sight in town.

Lüneburg gives its name to one of the most ancient lands of Germany —the Lüneburger Heide (Lüneburg Heath), covering about 45 square miles and extending roughly between the Elbe in the north and the Aller River in the south, the border of East Germany in the east and the autobahn Bremen-Hamburg in the west. Here prehistoric man lived, and left the mark of his passage by the great stones he heaped into cairns or built into passage tombs or set up into chambered forms, like the Seven Stone Houses near Fallingbostel, the burial chamber of the later Stone Age in the Klecker Forests near Bendestorf, or the tomb in Schieringer Wald near Bleckede. This is a vast area of varying scenery. of flatlands and undulating hills; of tracts of heath proper with old juniper shrubs of bizarre shape, wild flowers and flocks of sheep alternating with large forests rife with game and rich farmlands where the horse is the main animal; of elevations offering panoramic views over sections of the Heide and of tiny, shallow valleys where all you can see is the edge of the next wood, or perhaps a rock thrown from nowhere, or a swampy pond; half-timbered thatched-roof farmsteads alternate with small and colorful old towns dotted with the monuments of the past, simple village churches topped by wooden steeples with medieval cathedrals and monasteries. Here you take an inexpensive vacation in a dozen or so climatic resorts, such as Bendestorf, Hanstedt, Jeteburg, Schneverdingen or Walsrode; or, in case you need a cure in such spas as Lüneburg (for Lüneburg is also a spa) or Fallersleben, or in the Kneipp-cure (cold-water cure) resort of Fallingbostel.

As well as its old towns, pretty villages, spas, lakes and forests, the Heath also contains a landmark of a more sober nature. This is the memorial to the victims of the Bergen-Belsen Concentration Camp. It stands in solitude in a clearing on the Lüneburg Heath, about four miles southwest of the nearest town of Bergen. (The name Belsen is not found on most maps; the town is more usually referred to as *Bergen-Belsen.* It is roughly 30 miles north of Hannover and is northeast of Celle in the southwest of the Heath.) After passing the mounds that mark the sites of the common graves, you will find the obelisk honouring the victims of the Holocaust. Further on, in a clearing thickly covered with heather, is the actual site once occupied by the camps themselves.

PRACTICAL INFORMATION FOR LOWER SAXONY

 HOW TO GET ABOUT. From Bremen, during the summer there are daily trips on the lower Weser, varying from a one-hour ride to Vegesack, to a sail all the way to Bremerhaven (2 round trips daily) and a full-day excursion to the Baderen Hills. The art colony of Worpswede, in the fens north of Bremen, and nearby Fischerhude, a little gem of a village, can be reached by bus. Excursions through the Lüneberger Heide can be made via horse-drawn carriages. Inquire locally about other trips into nearby wooded or lake regions. There are also sightseeing flights over Bremen daily.

In summer there are pleasure-boat trips on the Upper Weser from Hameln to Hannoversch Münden (85 miles, very scenic), with a stopover in Corvey to visit the monastery; as well as twice-weekly boat trips to Porta Westfalica. The latter can be combined with train and bus connections.

There are twice-daily crossings from Wilhelmshaven to the East Frisian island of Wangerooge. This island can also be reached from Bremerhaven.

 REGIONAL FOOD AND DRINK. Braunschweig is noted for its sausage and a favored drink, *Mumme,* a dark, bittersweet liquid—actually beer without hops. In Hannover, *Bouillonwurst mit Meerrettich und Senf* (bouillon sausage with horseradish and mustard) and the *Grünkohl mit Brägenwurst* (kale with sausage) or *Pinkelwurst* make absolutely essential a glass of *Einbecker Bier,* which comes from this area and has been brewed here for 600 years. Or if you're in Hannover try it with *Lüttje Lage,* beer and schnaps.

In Bremen, near the sea, you'll eat as well as you can eat anywhere in Europe. Because Bremen is a port, its dishes come from all over the world—one you mustn't miss is a curry of chicken and rice, onion, coconut, eggs, and shrimp with a red hot curry sauce and small fish crumbled over all. In Bremen, a summer *must* is the *Aalsuppe grün,* an eel soup with dozens of herbs; in the fall, *Bunte oder Gepflückte Finten,* a wonderful dish of green and white beans, carrots and apples; and for any time of the year, the *Bremer Küken-Ragout,* a really fantastic dish made of sweetbreads, spring chicken, tiny veal meat balls, asparagus, clams and fresh peas, all cooked in a white sauce.

Along the East Frisian Islands, popular resort places, every kind of fish is a delight—boiled, fried, baked or smoked. There's fresh crab, and shrimp, called *Granat* or *Garnelen,* and even seagull eggs, which are considered a great delicacy.

HOTELS AND RESTAURANTS. The majority of hotels in Lower Saxony are medium- to lower-priced. They remain open all year, with the exception of the summer resort establishments, where the season runs from about May through September, occasionally starting a month earlier and ending a month later.

Bad Harzburg, spa and winter sports center in Harz. **Hotels:** *Harzburger Hof,* Kurhausstr. 23, 200 beds, 60 baths, is (L). *Bodes* (E), Am Stadtpark 48, 90 rooms, quiet location, Kneipp cures, cosmetic studio.

All (M–I) are—*Seela,* Nordhäuserstr. 5, 120 rooms, indoor pool, sauna. *Victoria,* Herzog-Wilhelm-Str. 74, 80 beds, *Landhaus am Rodenberg,* garni, Am Rodenberg 20, 15 rooms, and *Hotel Jagdhof,* Hindenburgring 12a, 106 beds.

In the vicinity: *Harzhotel Molkenhaus* (E), about 2 miles away; 40 beds, is a very fine hostelry in the middle of Harz Mountains, surrounded by forests. Game dishes are a specialty in the excellent restaurant; park, tennis, swimming, fishing, boating, skiing in winter. A unique winter experience is watching the feeding of wild animals a few yards from the hotel.

Bad Pyrmont, spa in Weser Hills. **Hotels:** *Kurhotel,* in Kurpark, 200 beds, 60 baths and showers, thermal baths in house, casino, very quiet, and *Bergkurpark,* Ockelstr. 11, with sauna, solarium and garden terrace, are both (L).

All (E–M) are—*Waldecker Hof,* Brunnenstr. 34, only 20 beds, *Bad Pyrmonter Hof* same street No. 32, 70 beds; *Güldener Pfennig,* Kirchstr. 22, 30 beds.

Borkum, summer resort in the East Frisian Islands. **Hotels:** *Hotel Atlantik* (E), with its annex *Nordmeer;* which has small flats, 225 beds altogether, 70 showers and baths.

All (E–M) are—*Nordseehotel,* 300 beds, *Ostfriesenhof,* 70 beds, and *Rheinland,* 60 beds; *Graf Waldersee,* Bahnhofstr. 6, 65 beds, and *Bruns,* Reedestr. 2.

Restaurants: There are several good restaurants, including *Der Insulaner, Heimliche Liebe* and *Stadtschänke,* some with rooms.

Braunlage, climatic resort and winter sports center in Harz. **Hotels:** *Maritim-Kongress-und-Sporthotel* (L), Am Pfaffenstieg, 275 rooms, 2 pools, sauna sports facilities, quiet location.

Kurhotel Weidmannsheil (E), Obere Bergstr., 89 rooms, garden, pool, sauna, excellent cuisine.—*Hohenzollern* (M), Dr-Barner-Str. 10, 46 rooms, half with bath or shower, pool.

Both (M–I) are 27-room *Berghotel,* Gartenstr. 1, quiet, and 53-room *Brauner Hirsch,* Am Brunnen 1.

Restaurant: *Zur Tanne,* Herzog-Wilhelm-Str. 8, local specialties, is good, fairly expensive. Also has 29 rooms (M); *Landhaus bei Wolfgang,* Hindenburgstr. 6, in Hohegeiss suburb, is a rustic, country manor with good value food (M).

LOWER SAXONY 451

Braunschweig (Brunswick), former Hanseatic League city. **Hotels:** *Atrium* (L), Berliner Platz 3, all rooms with bath. *Deutsches Haus* (E), Ruhfautchenpl. 1, 115 beds, 20 baths and showers, an old castle-like mansion, quiet location.

All (M) are *Frühlings-Hotel,* Bankplatz 7, 100 beds, 22 baths and showers; 43-room *Lorenz,* Friedrich-Wilhelm-Str. 2, most rooms with bath or shower; *Zur Oper,* garni, 65 beds, Jasperallee 22. *Braunschweigerhof,* Ziegenmarkt 7, a small, 20-bed, cozy hotel near the main railroad station, in an old house originating from 1550.

Thüringer Hof (I), Sophienstr. 1, 40 beds.

Restaurants: *Gewandhaus* (E), on Altstadtmarkt in the former guildhouse of the influential sailmakers, built in 12th century with Renaissance façade from 1590. Parts of the cellar are more than 1,000 years old. Elegant wine restaurant, attractive cellar decorated with old paintings. Seafood specialties, selection of wines, also local and Bavarian beer.

Among the (M) and (I) are: *Haus Zur Hanse,* Güldenstr. 7, in a 17th-century half-timbered house; *Das Alte Haus,* Alte Knochenhauerstr. 11; *Zum Bitburger,* Stobenstr. 15, both of these pleasant and atmospheric; *Rauchfang,* Steinweg 34, for grills; *Löwenbräu,* near railroad station, also beer restaurant; and *Zum Grünen Jäger,* Ebert-Allee 50 (Streetcar No. 8): *Wolters am Wall,* Fallersleberstr. 35.

Cafés with music: *Stadtpark,* in city park, also restaurant; *Keil,* in Schlosspassage and Wiesenstr. 11, for pastries.

Bremen. **Hotels:** *Park-Hotel* (L), Im Bürgerpark, magnificent park setting, 220 beds, all rooms with bath and radio, suites, elegant restaurant, café, bar, terrace overlooking small lake.

Columbus (E), across from the railroad station, 200 beds, most rooms with bath, suites, modern, excellent value restaurant, bar and cellar tavern.

Euro-Crest Hotel (M–E), August-Bebel-Allee 4, in the suburb of Neue Vahr, 230 beds, all rooms with bath; restaurant.

All (M–E) are—*Zur Post,* on the main station square, 250 beds, over 100 baths and showers, several restaurants, underground garage; *Schaper-Siedenburg,* Bahnhofstr. 8, 100 beds, near the station, good restaurant; *Bremer Hospiz,* Löningstr. 17–20, not far from station, 120 beds, half of rooms with bath or shower, particularly comfortable.

Both (M) are—*Überseehotel,* Wachtstr. 27–9, near Rathaus, 250 beds, most rooms with bath or shower, reception lobby on the third floor (elevators); also *Konsul-Hackfeld-Haus,* garni, Birkenstr. 34, 75 rooms, in a quiet location facing the park with the old windmill.

In Vegesack, about 10 miles downstream from the center, is *Strandlust,* Rohrstr. 11, on the bank of the Weser, a refined garden establishment with a renowned restaurant serving authentic local specialties. 12 miles upstream at Achim is the *Novotel* (M–E), Zum Klümoor.

In Horn, on the outskirts of Bremen, is the 33-room *Landhaus Luisenthal* (M), Leher Heerstr. 105, a country manor with a large park, cozy, quiet.

452 **LOWER SAXONY**

Restaurants: *Ratskeller,* in the City Hall, in existence since 1408 and supposed to be the oldest German Ratskeller; the cellar is lined with wine casks, including an enormous one that has been holding wine ever since the 18th century; it serves excellent seafood in addition to other top dishes, but is even more outstanding for its unsurpassable selection of over 600 German wines. The city fathers decided in the 15th century that only German wines would be served in their cellars and so it remains today.

Bremer Aalsuppe, fresh Weser salmon, and *Bremer Kükenragout,* with specially cured fresh herring added, figure high on the varied menu of *Flett* and its twin *Robinson* in the historic Böttcherstrasse. The original Bremen eel soup is also the specialty of *Die Glocke,* Am Dom, next to the cathedral, with summer outdoor dining in the romantic cloister courtyard.

Deutsches Haus, an old patrician house opposite the Rathaus, has many atmospheric rooms, good food and a view of the market square from the upstairs *Ratsstuben,* and a rustic *Seefahrtsstuben* on the ground floor.

In the Schnoor artists' quarter is *Schnoor 2,* at that address, old gabled house, *Alte Gilde* is in the deep, vaulted cellar of the 17th-century Gewerbehaus in Ansgaritorstrasse; all (M).

Unusual is the *Alt Bremer Brauhaus,* with 24 rooms behind half-timbered courtyard façades, each reflecting Bremen trade branches of yore (fishing, brewing, cotton, etc.).

Cafés: *Konditorei Knigge,* Sögestr. 42–4, excellent pastries and small snacks; *Konditorei Jacobs,* luscious cakes, candy and cookies in two comfortable and large locales at the corner of Sögestrasse and Knochenhauerstrasse (3 floors).

Bremerhaven. Hotels: *Nordsee-Hotel Naber,* Theodor-Heuss-Pl., near railroad station, modern, 120 rooms, 80 baths and showers, radio in all rooms, two restaurants, American-type bar, garage and parking lot (E), suites are higher.

Haverkamp, Schleswiger Strasse 27, 140 beds, is (M) and *Bremerhaven,* Deichstr. 52, 60 beds (I).

Restaurants: *Senator* (I), corner Mühlen and Prager Strasse, Balkan food. *Columbusbahnhof,* Columbuskaje at the port, overlooking the harbor; *Strandhalle,* Weserdeich, at North Sea Aquarium, view of the sea through glass wall, both (M). *Löwenbräu,* Lloydstrasse in Hochhaus (skyscraper). For fish specialties, the *Fischereihafen-Restaurant Natusch* (M) at the fish market railway station is particularly good value.

Small taverns specializing in fried fish: *Höpker* in Bismarckstr. 34; *Zum Fischbäcker,* across from the main station; *Brauns and Co.,* Keilstr. 16; *Nordsee,* Obere Bürgermeister-Smidt-Str. 44; and at Martin-Donandt-Platz 32.

Cafés: *Columbusbahnhof* (station), view of the river; *National,* Bürgermeister-Smidt-Strasse 101; *Café Bode,* beautiful cakes, at Hafenstr. 91 and *Hoops,* Rickmersstr. 43.

Cuxhaven. Hotels: Both (M–E), *Seepavillon,* at the Alte Liebe lighthouse, in beautiful location facing the mouth of the Elbe with ships passing by constantly, is modern, 100 beds; not far away, modern *Donners* (125 beds, 50 baths), also fine view particularly from the top-floor restaurant; pleasant bar downstairs.

In the Duhnen section (where you go for swimming and cures) is the (E–M) *Strand-Hotel Duhnen und Seehotel Kamp,* with a fine beer restaurant and daily (during season) dancing in Kursaal and in the bar. On the Döse beach nearby is the modern restaurant *Strandhaus Döse,* resembling the command bridge of a ship; in season it offers afternoon musical entertainment and dancing nightly.

Goslar. Hotels: *Der Achtermann* (E), 92 rooms with bath or shower. Built around one of the original (1501) towers of the old city wall. Excellent restaurant, good selection of wines; *Kaiserworth* (E), Am Markt 3, a former merchant tailor's guildhall built in 1494, with 120 beds, almost all rooms with bath or shower, terrace and economical restaurant.

All (M) are—*Niedersächsischer Hof,* 110 beds; *Schwarzer Adler,* with noted evening restaurant *Bachus.*

A bit outside, *Berghotel Zum Auerhahn* is (I).

Restaurants: *Ratsweinkeller,* in the Rathaus, atmospheric. *Zwinger,* Thomasstr. 2, with historic torture chamber. *Maltermeisterturm,* Rammelsbergerstr. 99, with a good view.

Gottingen, old university town. **Hotels:** *Gebhards Hotel* (M–E), Goethe-Allee 22–3, 90 beds, 19 baths and showers, terrace and garden.

Both (M) are—*Zur Sonne,* Paulinerstr. 10–12, 120 beds, 50 baths and showers, and *Kronprinz,* Groner-Tor-Strasse 2–3, 100 beds.

Both (I) are—*Junkernhaus,* Barfüsserstr. 5, in a building dating from 1503, is an atmospheric hostelry, with the Junkernschänke, historical wine restaurant with old wood carvings; *Stadt Hannover,* Goethe Allee 21.

Restaurants: *Alte Krone,* Weender Strasse 13–15, a traditional students' cellar whose "University Room" is decorated with drawings, cuts, and pages from old books. *Schwarzer Bär,* Kurze Strasse 12, a favorite of students. Built on the site of a medieval jousting field and later a toll house.

Other restaurants include the colorful *Alte Fink,* Nikolaistr. 1, and the *Ratskeller,* in the Rathaus, with terrace, in existence since early 1400's.

Hahnenklee-Bockswiese, climatic resort and winter sports center near Goslar. **Hotels:** *Kurhotel Hahnenklee* (I), Triftstr. 25, 125 rooms, 2 pools.

Both (M) are—*Hahnenkleer Hof,* Parkstr. 24a, 32 rooms, pool, and *Parkhotel Weissleder,* Am Bosckberg 1, 47 rooms.

Hameln (Hamelin). Hotels: All (M) are—The recent *Weserbergland,* 102 rooms with bath; the last two are in the low (M) category. *Sintermann,* at the railroad station, 50 beds, good food, bar and beer tavern, moderate; *Börse,* with fine, atmospheric restaurant and *Zur Krone,* Osterstr. 30.

Restaurants: *Im Rattenkrug-Ratsstuben,* Bäckerstr. 16, a picturesque eating place in a building dating from 1569. *Rattenfänger-Haus* in Osterstrasse is another with local color.

Hannover (Hanover). Hotels: The 8-floor *Hannover Inter-continental* (L), opposite the City Hall, with 300 rooms, has all modern amenities, underground garage and a partially covered plaza with fountains, shops and landscaped grounds, cocktail lounge, café, grill restaurant, one of this company's best.

Both (E–L) are—*Kastens,* Luisenstr. 2, 225 rooms with bath or shower, smart restaurant, bar, music, and dancing; *Am Stadtpark,* Clausewitzstr. 6, 252 rooms with bath, pool, is garni, but see restaurants.

All (E) are—*Mussmann,* opposite the main railroad station, 185 beds, 50 baths and showers, music in café and bar, modern; *Georgenhof,* Herrenhäuser Kirchweg 20, near Herrenhausen Gardens, small country-style house; quiet location; outstanding food; *Central,* on the main station square with 120 beds, 25 baths and restaurant.

All (M), some rooms higher, are—*Europäischer Hof,* Luisenstr. 4, 82 beds, 25 baths, near station; *Am Thielenplatz,* on square of the same name, modern, most rooms with bath or shower and balcony; *Körner,* Körnerstr. 24, in a quiet side street, back rooms have balconies and overlook a park; *Loccumer Hospiz,* Kurt-Schumacher-Strasse 16, 100 beds, very modern, restaurant and café; *Bundesbahnhotel,* 58 beds, at main station. *Am Rathaus,* Friedrichswall 21, facing the City Hall, recent, with small inexpensive restaurant; *Thüringer Hof,* Osterstr. 37, with an old-style cellar restaurant.

In the suburbs are the *Euro-Crest Hotel,* at the zoo, 108 rooms with bath, and *Holiday Inn,* near airport; with indoor pool, lounge, bar, discothèque, sauna, solarium, soundproof suites, color TV in all 146 rooms, both (E).

The *Park-Motel Kronsberg* (M–E), 165 beds, all rooms with bath or shower, restaurant, space for 400 cars, 2 gas stations, is in the trade fair complex, close to the motorway, air terminal and railway station.

In Garbsen (about 7 miles out on B6) is the *Landhaus Köhne am See* (M), small, only 19 rooms, but a real find, with good restaurant (closed Sunday).

Restaurants: (E) are *Alte Mühle,* Hermann-Löns-Park 3; *Ratskeller,* in Old Rathaus, with several sections, the best being the Gothic vaulted wine restaurant downstairs; *Die Insel,* also a café, Rudolf-von-Bennigsen-Ufer 81, on the south bank of the Maschsee, one of the pleasantest locations; *Stadthalle-Park-restaurant,* Theodor-Heuss-Platz, which belongs to the hotel Am Stadtpark; *Leineschloss,* in the super-modern annex of the Leineschloss Palace, with outdoor terrace. The *Georgenhof,* Herrenhäuser Kirchweg 20, in an attractive park, has excellent food, a large wine list, and a few rooms as well, but out of the center.

Beer restaurants, all (M) are—*Löwenbräu,* Georgstr. 36, Bavarian décor and Austrian music, vast; *Rotisserie Helvetia,* Georgsplatz 11, pleasantly rustic Swiss atmosphere; *Wienerwald,* Thielenplatz, excellent value, but busy like all this chain; *Härke Klause,* Ständehausstrasse off Kröpcke, local color tavern.

Wine taverns: *Fey's Weinstuben,* Sophienstr. 6, with zither music; *Wein-Wolf,* Rathenaustr. 2, in the cellar; *Weinstube Künstlerhaus,* in Sophienstrasse.

Cafés: *Konditorei and Café Kreipe,* Bahnhofstr. 12, good pastries; *Die Insel* (see Restaurants); café in main station; and in *Euro-Crest* and *Inter-continental* hotels.

Hildesheim. The *Hotel Rose* (M), 90 beds, all rooms with bath or shower, is noted for its *Arnold Restaurant.*

Norderney, one of the East Frisian Islands. **Hotels:** All (E) are—*Hanseatic,* Gartenstr. 47, 72 beds and *Kurhotel Norderney,* Weststandstr., 51 beds; *Hotel Friese,* Friedrichstr. 34, central position, 72 beds, good facilities.

All (M) are—*Kaiserhof,* 260 beds, 10 baths, directly on the sea, bar, grill, *Hotel-Pension Haus am Meer,* 106 beds, open April through Oct. Moderate: *Europäischer Hof,* 100 beds, garni, terrace directly on the sea, open May through September; *Pique,* 27 rooms, good view; *Strand-hotel Rixtine,* 100 beds, open April through Sept.

Oldenburg. Hotels: All (M) are—the *Graf von Oldenburg,* Heiligengeiststr. 10, 30 rooms, and *Sprenz,* at No. 15, 47 rooms, most with bath or shower, atmospheric Balkan Grill.

The *Kreyenbrücker Hof* (M–I), Cloppenburgerstr. 418, most rooms with bath or shower.

Restaurants: *Ratskeller,* Markt; restaurant in *Parkhotel,* Lange Strasse 16, colorful; *Alte Wache,* Cloppenburger Strasse 296.

Osnabrück. Hotels: *Parkhotel* (E), Am Heger Holz in the outskirts, swimming pool.

Hohenzollern (E), Heinrich-Heine-Str. 17, near station, 100 rooms, most with bath, pool, good food in restaurant and cozy *Löwenbräukeller.*

All (M) are—*Kulmbacher Hof,* Schlosswall 67; *Central,* Möserstr. 42, and *Klute,* Lotter Str. 30.

Hotel-Restaurant Westerkamp, Bremer Str. 120, 42 beds, is (I).

Restaurants: *Walhalla,* Bierstr. 24; *Am Röthebach,* Oelweg 55; *Aldermann,* Johannisstr. 93; *Ratskeller* in the town hall; *Ellerbracke,* Neuer Graben 8.

Cafés: *Romanisches Café,* Johannisstr. 46; *Cafe Brüggemann,* Bierstr. 13; *Cafe Läer,* Krahnstr. 4.

Rinteln/Steinbergen. *Schloss-hotel Arensburg* (M), a castle hotel located 4 miles northeast of Rinteln on the Hannover-Bielefeld autobahn. Former castle of Dukes of Schaumburg-Lippe, 30 beds, terraces, park. Closest railroad station is Steinbergen.

Wangerooge, the most eastern of the East Frisian Islands. **Hotels** (all open in summer season only): *Strandhotel Gerken* (M), Strandpromenade 21, 100 beds, open May through Sept. *Strandhotel Kaiserhof* (I–M), 90 beds. *Strandhotel Monopol* and *Fresena* are (I).

Wilhelmshaven. Hotels: All (M), some rooms (I) are—*Nordsee,* Am Ölhafen, view of port and sea; *Delphin,* at Südstrand (south beach), view of North Sea; *Flacke,* Virchowstr. 30, good food.

Restaurants: *Strandhalle* on south beach with view of sea; *Kochlöffel,* Marktstr. 51; *Jadehaus,* Rheinstr. 65.

LOWER SAXONY. By Car. One cannot really pretend that this is the best possible area for motoring in Germany. It is very large, and its stars in the north are all great ports, not the most comfortable of places for cars. Four long, fantastically busy autobahen cross it and between them a good number of trunk roads, which are useful rather than beautiful. The northern coast has no bathing beaches, nor indeed many opportunities for getting down to the sea at all. There are, however, restricted car ferry services to the west and east Frisian Islands where there are splendid beaches.

The mainland north of the Bremen to Hamburg autobahn is low, mostly flat and sparsely inhabited. To the south of the same road lies Luneburg Heath which is, perhaps, an acquired taste. For the real fun of motoring in Lower Saxony you need to go to the extreme southeast where the Harz mountains provide the scenery and steep, serpentine roads that entrance keen drivers.

 MUSIC AND THEATER. The music-lover has a choice of daily concerts at Borkum and Norderney, or those presented by Bremen's Philharmonic Orchestra and notable church choir, the Göttingen symphony, or Hannover's symphony orchestras and choral societies.

Borkum has a theater offering light plays; **Braunschweig** has a Provincial Theater and Studiobühne, in the City Park.

Bremen's Theater am Goetheplatz presents opera, operetta, and some drama, while the Kammerspiele is a small theater for plays only; its Niederdeutsche Bühne is a local dialect theater. Opera, operetta, and plays are put on by **Bremerhaven's** Municipal Theater and **Osnabrück's** Am Domhoh.

Hannover has a rich stage life and the principal theatrical companies include Landestheater, performing opera, operetta, ballet and plays in the Opera House and Ballhof; Thalia for operetta, Landesbühne for plays, both having their home in Theater am Agei and a remarkable children's theater at the Künstlerhaus, Sophienstr. 2. Hannover is also known for its rich summer theatrical and concert season in the Herrenhausen Gardens, beginning in early June and ending in early September: operas, plays, ballets and concerts take place on various indoor and outdoor stages in the beautiful park.

 NIGHTLIFE. Braunschweig: *Melodia,* Neue Str. 10, music in cafe, dancing and floorshow at *Teene,* Ebert-Allee 50 and *Königin-Bar;* disco-dancing at *Schwabing,* Gieseler 3; *Darkness-Club,* Breite Str. 6.

Bremen: Floorshows and dancing at *Katja's,* Bahnhofstr. 5, open till 5 A.M.; *Red Horse,* opposite the main rail station; in Philosophenweg (14, 15 and 23) are *Happy Night, Playgirl* and *Grüner Kakadu* respectively; *Ex,* Eduard-Grunow-Str., 29, open till 4 A.M. For dancing: *Halai Bar* in Park Hotel, elegant; *Filou,* Europahaus Birkenstr. 20; *Strandlust-Bar Kajüte,* in Strandlust hotel, Vegesack, till 4 A.M.; *Schabbalabba,* Burgerstr. 7, a touch of times past when dancing had steps; *Ball paré,* Knochenhauerstr., where women can ask men to dance.

Bremerhaven: Shows: *Roxy*, Fahrstrasse 21; otherwise go almost anywhere around Fahrstrasse, Georg-Seebeck-Strasse, Bürgermeister-Smidt-Strasse, Rickmersstrasse or Hafenstrasse and you will find shows or dancing or both. There are scores of nightclubs—but just remember that this is a port. The *Roxy* (above) is the only long-established place.

Hannover: Shows, mostly striptease: *Uhu-Bar*, opposite the Opera House; *Amourette*, Asternstr. 11; Hotel *am Stadtpark*. Dancing: *Grenadier Lounge* in Hotel Inter-continental; *Take Off*, in Holiday Inn; in the bar of the *Luisenhof* hotel; *Top of the Town*, opposite main station, the big band place; *Der Fröhliche Weinberg*, Joachimstr. 1. **Osnabrück:** Cabarets are *Bar Barella Nachtbar*, Bohmterstr. 52; *Domhof Bar*, Domhof 4c; *Namen Village*, Herrenteichstr. 1.

MUSEUMS. Braunschweig. *Herzog Anton Ulrich Museum*, Museumstr. 1, paintings by Rembrandt, Rubens, Van Dyck, Holbein, Cranach, Jordaens, and others. *Municipal Museum*, Steintorwall 14, local folk art. *Natural History*, Pockelstr. 10a.

Bremen. *Kunsthalle*, Am Wall 207, arts, crafts, 15th- to 20th-century paintings, including Holbein, Cranach, Rembrandt, Rubens, Manet and Van Gogh. *Ludwig Rosellus Collection*, Böttcherstr, 4, old German and Baroque art, woodcarving by Tilman Riemenschneider, paintings by Cranach and Rubens. *Übersee-museum*, at the main station square, with outstanding ethnographic collections. *Bremer Landesmuseum für Kunst und Kulturgeschichte* (Focke Museum), Schwachhauser Heerstr. 240, history of art and culture of Bremen and North Germany.

Bremerhaven. *Fishing Museum*, Am Handelshaven 12. *Morgenstern Museum* at Kaistr. 6, prehistoric discoveries and folk art; and an open-air museum at Parkstr. 9, of old peasant houses and furnishings from the 17th cent. At the old harbor, *Maritime Museum*, with many old vessels, including a 1380 Hanseatic trading ship. Also here, the radar tower, with observation platform.

Hannover. *Landesmuseum*, Am Maschpark 5, excellent painting gallery with works from medieval masters to 20th century. *Kestner Museum*, Trammplatz 3, arts and crafts of all times and countries, especially good Egyptian collection. *Lower Saxony Regional Museum*, Prinzenstr. 9. *Wilhelm-Busch-Museum*, Georgengarten 1. *Herrenhausen Museum*, Fürstenhaus, Alte Herrenhäuser-Strasse, furniture, paintings and etchings from the history of Herrenhausen.

Borkum and **Osnabrück** have local museums and **Norderney** the *Fischerhaus Museum* of East Frisian culture.

At **Göttingen** there is a museum for folk arts and crafts, as well as the *Municipal Museum* of prehistory, geology, etc.

PARKS AND ZOOS. Since **Bremen** has no natural woods, the citizens have for centuries devoted unusual efforts to the cultivation of green areas. The result is many beautiful parks, among them the park on Herdentorswall with a windmill; the English garden-style Bürgerpark with a small zoo; the Botanical Garden; and the Rhododendron Park (the city is famous for its rhododendrons and azaleas). There is also an aquarium and a new zoo in Oberneuland section.

Bremerhaven has a fine "grotto zoo" and aquarium, both at Am Deich, next to the Strandhalle (open 9–6). **Braunschweig's** Botanical Garden is near the Theaterpark.

Hannover has the lake of Maschsee, mostly framed by parks; the magnificently landscaped Herrenhausen Gardens, more than 300-year-old baroque landscape gardens with a magnificent open-air theater; a zoo and Tiergarten (animal park); the latter is a large forested area outside the city, where deer and wild horses roam freely. **Osnabrück** has a zoo and Botanical Garden, and **Borkum** a wildlife preserve. Wangerooge is a natural sanctuary.

WATER SPORTS. There are many opportunities for **canoeing** and **boating** from Bremen. Up the Hamme to Worpswede (the German Canoe Association has a delightful hostel near here, at Waakhausen) or a trip on the Wümme, 111 miles long through beautiful heathland, are both on currentless waters offering no difficulties even for novices. A real labyrinth of small streams and canals starting from Bremen, threading lonely peat moors studded with typical thatched farmhouses of the region and majestic old oaks, is perfect for canoeing, **kayaking,** or small boat **sailing.** The Weser above Bremen has little current, but there is a lot of traffic and many locks; below Bremen, you have ideal tidal water, but it is also busy and some skill is required. But the most delightful trip for the experienced kayaker is on the Upper Weser between Hannoversch Münden and Porta Westfalica.

A number of international **yachting** regattas are staged at Bremen. Sailing is practised off the East Frisian Islands, especially Norderney and Borkum; on the Weser between Bremen and Bremerhaven; on the Aller River; in the estuary of the Ems river; on Dümmer Lake north of Osnabrück, on Zwischenahner Meer near Oldenburg, on Steinhuder Lake northwest of Hannover and on the lake of Maschsee in Hannover. Canoeing and **rowing** regattas are a regular feature on Maschsee and sail and rowboats can be rented here. **Wind-surfing** facilities available on lakes.

Water skiing can be engaged in on the inland lakes mentioned as well as at some of the East Frisian Islands. **Swimming,** in addition to the East Frisian Islands, inland lakes, some river beaches, is done in numerous pools in all resorts and larger localities. There are a considerable number of indoor swimming pools at Braunschweig, Bremen, Bremerhaven, Hannover, and all other larger cities as well as in Braunlage, Clausthal-Zellerfeld (open winter only), and a glass-front-variety with artificial waves and seawater at Norderney.

WINTER SPORTS. The forested Harz Mountains are an important winter sports region in Germany. Their slopes are much more gentle than those of the Alps, the highest peak, the Brocken, being only 1,142 meters. The terrain lends itself particularly to cross-country skiing and is mostly easy to medium/pleasant for ski-hiking through the woods. Another specialty of the area is ski-jumping. The snow is abundant and deep and normally lasts until the middle of March. There are 11 main mountain resorts and a total of 45 ski lifts. The best pistes are at Schulenberg, the Lower Saxony Ski Alpinum, which has a 1,200-meter Olympic run, an excellent slalom course and a variety of other pistes well served by lifts. Ski lessons are available at nine different locations with special classes for children. The principal centers are listed below. They are located at elevations of between 1,600 and 2,600 ft. with skiing up to about 3,200 ft.

Altenau, bus from fast train stop Goslar, 1 ski lift, 2 ski jumps, tobogganing, ski instructors.

Bad Sachsa, train stop (fast train stop at Northeim). 1 ski lift, 2 ski jumps, skiing instructors, ice rink, ice hockey, tobogganing.

Braunlage, bus from fast train stop Bad Harzburg. Cable car to Wurmberg, 1 ski lift, 3 ski jumps, 2 ski schools, ice skating rink, ice hockey, curling. 33 ski teachers. Also ski-kindergarten. Hexenritt ski run is one of the steepest and most difficult in Harz.

Clausthal-Zellerfeld, train stop (fast train stop at Goslar). 2 ski jumps, tobogganing, curling, ice rink, ice hockey, skiing instructors.

Hahnenklee-Bockswiese, bus from fast train stop at Goslar. Skiing instructors, ice rink, ice hockey, curling, tobogganing, bobsleighing.

Hohegeiss, bus from the train stop Walkenried. 1 ski lift, 2 ski jumps, tobogganing, ski instructors, ice rink.

St. Andreasberg, bus from fast train stops Goslar and Nordheim. Chair-lift, 5 ski lifts, 2 ski jumps, ski school, ski hiking, skijoring, tobogganing, horsesleighs.

 USEFUL ADDRESSES. Local tourist information: Bad Harzburg, Kurverwaltung; Bad Pyrmont, Verkehrsverein, Arkaden 14; Borkum, Verkehrsbüro, Am Bahnhof (main station); Braunschweig, Verkehrsverein, at the main railroad station and in Bohlweg 16; Bremen, Verkehrsverein, in pavilion facing the main railroad station (also room reservations); Bremerhaven, Verkehrsamt, Friedrich-Ebert-Strasse 58; Cuxhaven, Verkehrsverein, Lichtenbergplatz; Goslar, Fremdenverkehrsamt, Rathaus; Göttingen, Fremdenverkehrsamt, Rathaus; Hameln, Verkehrsverein, Deisterallee; Hannover, Verkehrsbüro, Ernst-August-Platz 8; Norderney, Verkehrsamt; Oldenburg, Verkehrsverein, Lange Strasse; 3 Osnabrück, Verkehrsamt, Markt 8; Wilhelmshaven, Verkehrsbüro, Bahnhofplatz.

Consulates etc.: Bremen: U.S. Consulate General, Präsident-Kennedy-Platz, tel. 32–00–01; Amerika-Haus, Präsident-Kennedy-Platz. Hannover: British Consulate General, Uhlemeyerstr. 9 and 11; Amerika-Haus, Prinzenstr. 9; Bremerhaven: British Consulate, Eisewerkestr., tel. 7–10–84.

WEST
BERLIN

Ludwig van Beethoven
1770-1827

WEST BERLIN

A Different City

For a visitor to Berlin it might be useful to imagine that he is coming to a mini-state rather than a city. For Berlin is vast in area (East and West Berlin together are a third the size of Luxemburg and almost three times as big as Munich). It has large forests, lakes, agricultural land and independent villages, besides huge industrial compounds. For too many visitors Berlin has meant the partly rather seedy area around Kurfürstendamm, with its conspicuous nightclubs and bars. If one equates Soho with London one gets a somewhat distorted view of London. The visitor who is aware of this will enjoy his visit to Berlin much more and leave with a truer picture of the city in his mind.

At the end of World War II, Berlin was sliced into four pieces under the control of a four-power Kommandatura. Each piece was called a sector, and each sector reflected the policies and viewpoint of the nation that administered it. Then, in June 1948, the Soviet general walked out

of the Kommandatura, and the Berlin blockade was in effect. West
Berlin lay isolated deep inside Russian-occupied Germany, 110 miles
from the nearest West German territory. All movement of traffic by
road, rail, and canal was stopped.

But there was still the air. First ten planes a day, then a hundred,
finally a thousand shuttled back and forth between Western Germany
and the Allied sectors of the stricken city. Close by Tempelhof Airport
is the monument that commemorates this airlift and the airmen who
gave their lives to maintain it. (Flights now mostly use Tegel Airport.)

Having survived so severe a test, West Berlin has been a different city
ever since. Its main problem has been to maintain a balanced population structure, or simply to prevent any decrease in population. Career
opportunities are limited, and so an increasing number of younger
people have moved away. In spite of all sorts of tax incentives for
business many firms have transferred their headquarters to Western
Germany. The exodus of people in their late twenties to early forties
is reflected in the population image: the prevalence of older people in
the streets is striking. The many universities and institutes ensure that
there are vast numbers of young people as well, but the absence of
people in their thirties and forties, who are actually earning money and
producing, is conspicuous. The city has tried to counteract this development by giving generous incentives to people who decide to work in
Berlin. Also, there has been a development of the service industries
which attract more people to the city. With its new congress center
I.C.C. Berlin is now one of the foremost congress cities in Europe.
Rather interestingly, a lot of successful artists who could afford to live
elsewhere choose to live in Berlin. There is still something about the
social atmosphere of the city that makes it to some people preferable
to Western Germany.

In Berlin you can live anonymously. There are many sub-cultures,
and material pressures as well as pressures to conform generally are felt
much less than in the rest of Germany. Since the seventeenth century,
when the "Grosse Kurfürst" Friedrich Wilhelm gave asylum to the
French Huguenots and the first Jewish community was established
("In my kingdom every man must find his own way to heaven"), there
has always been a certain cosmopolitan tolerance in Berlin. Something
of this still exists, although even Berliners themselves complain about
an increasing provincialism, and they used to be notorious for their
boastful arrogance. "If we had your mountains they would be bigger,"
a Berliner is supposed to have told a Bavarian.

EXPLORING WEST BERLIN

For the visitor to postwar Berlin, the heart of the city is the Kurfür-stendamm, the center of activity both by day and by night. For the American, it will be Broadway and Fifth Avenue in one; for the British-er, Oxford Street and Piccadilly.

The Kurfürstendamm is itself a great shopping street, and others lined with big postwar stores are clustered about it—the Kantstrasse, which meets it at an acute angle at the Kaiser Wilhelm Memorial Church, the Tauentzienstrasse, which meets it at an obtuse angle at the same spot, the Joachimstalerstrasse, which cuts across it. The stores and office buildings that line these streets are mostly built on sites from which the ruins of war-destroyed buildings have been cleared away. You will find the best vantage point to watch the interesting and animated spectacle of the street in one or other of the sidewalk cafés, whose glassed-in terraces line the Kurfürstendamm.

At night, the quarter is just as lively, for this is a theater district as well. The Komödie is on the Kurfürstendamm, the new Schiller is nearby, the opera a block away, and there are a score or more of film palaces, not to mention nightclubs and bars.

The Kurfürstendamm starts at the Kaiser Wilhelm Memorial Church (the Gedächtniskirche), which was built anew in 1961 in a very modernistic form, with only the badly damaged tower, "Berlin's finest ruin," remaining from the prewar church. From behind and left of the church you can enter the great Tiergarten park through the precincts of one of its chief tenants, the Berlin Zoo. Even if you are not an admirer of zoos, don't disdain this one. Germans are fond of zoos and provide other distractions than the animals for their amusement while they're there. You can eat or drink well within the zoo, listen to open-air concerts, and take in various forms of amusement.

Emerging into the Tiergarten proper, you are in the great 630-acre park that was central Berlin's prewar pride—its Central Park, Hyde Park, or Bois de Boulogne. The damage done to the Tiergarten during the war was not all the result of external attack, though some of it was. A good deal of the Battle for Berlin was fought here, and shells and entrenching tools alike mutilated the ground. But it was for fuel that the Berliners cut down the lovely old trees during the bitterly cold winter of 1945–46.

Trees that took a century to grow can hardly be replaced overnight, but Berlin did what it could to restore the Tiergarten. Trees and bushes were planted, new paths laid out, and little by little the district regained much of its former charm. One of the problems was that of disposing of rubble. The solution adopted was to heap the shattered bricks and stones into artificial hills, cover them with soil and sow grass. Several of these rubble "mountains" have become part of the Berlin skyline, most notably the Insulaner at the southern tip of the Steglitz district, which is 260 feet high.

Siegessäule, Victory Column

Bisecting the Tiergarten from east to west is the Strasse des 17. Juni, named in memory of the Germans shot down by Russian tanks in 1953 when East Berlin construction workers laid down their tools in protest over greatly increased work "norms." Focal point of this broad avenue is a vast circle called the Grosse Stern or Great Star. From its center rises a 210-foot column of dark red granite, sandstone, and bronze surmounted by a gilded figure of Victory. The Siegessäule, as it is called, was raised in 1873 to commemorate the Franco-Prussian War, and originally stood in front of the Reichstag.

If your legs are strong, climb the Siegessäule for a magnificent view of Berlin's heart. As you face east and look along the Strasse des 17. Juni towards the Brandenburger Tor, the English Garden will be practically at your feet, to the left. Because it was dedicated by Anthony Eden, the then Foreign Secretary of Great Britain, Berliners often refer to it jokingly as the Garden of Eden. East of this atmospheric park-within-a-park you'll be able to pick out Schloss Bellevue, which has been restored and is the official residence of the President of West Germany; in summer months its interiors are open to the public. To the south-east you can see the concert hall of the Berlin Philharmonic Orchestra, the New National Gallery, and Berlin's latest acquisition, the Staatsbibliothek. With its 2.9 million volumes it is the largest library of its kind in the world. Its outstanding collection of manuscripts comprises many rarities, particularly in the field of music. Its beautifully light and functionally designed reading-room can accommodate 600 readers.

Before returning to street level, look west along the Strasse des 17. Juni. Immediately on your right hand rise the gaily painted and fancifully balconied apartment houses of the Hansa Viertel, a district that has been revived by the best work of architects from a dozen nations of the world. It is the site of the Interbau exposition and on your left is the Technical University plus the Hochschule für Musik and the Academy of Fine Arts.

But let's proceed east along the Strasse des 17. Juni towards the Brandenburger Tor. Somewhat more than halfway along on the left is the Soviet Victory Monument, a semicircular colonnade surmounted by a massive statue of a Russian soldier and flanked by World War II artillery pieces and tanks. Technically, this is a Russian enclave in the Western sector of Berlin.

As you continue up the Strasse des 17. Juni you will see slightly to the left the Reichstag which has now been reconstructed. As everyone knows, it was burned down on the night of February 28, 1933, providing the Nazis with a convenient pretext for outlawing the opposition. All that remained was the shell of the florid Italian Renaissance structure that was built in 1884–94 to house the Prussian parliament, and later performed a similar function for the ill-fated Weimar Republic. The building was further damaged during the last war but has now been almost completely restored.

The Eastern sector of Berlin begins a few yards in front of the Brandenburger Tor, once the Arch of Triumph of the German capital. Victorious Prussian troops used to parade through it on their return from a successful campaign. The last troops to march beneath it, however, were not on parade. They were Red Army infantrymen who stormed through it in May 1945. By then, the famous quadriga—the two-wheeled chariot drawn by four stallions—was shattered beyond repair. For a dozen years the sole adornment of the shell-pocked gate was a red flag. Then, in 1957, East German workmen began the task of repairing the Brandenburger Tor, a job that was completed late the following year. Meanwhile, the West Berliners discovered the moulds in which the original quadriga was cast. A new one was poured, gilded and hoisted to the top of the refurbished gate in a rare, remarkable instance of cooperation between East and West.

Despite this symbolic act, the Brandenburger Tor at this writing is no longer an entry point between East and West Berlin. Everywhere on the East-West boundary, there stand the hated concrete and barbed wire walls separating the two sectors, with rows of houses bulldozed down inside the Eastern sector to create a no-man's land of some hundred yards' width.

Potsdamer Platz

If you turn right at the Brandenburger Tor and follow the extreme eastern edge of the Tiergarten you shortly reach the Potsdamer Platz, where the British, American, and Russian sectors meet. Nearby is "Checkpoint Charlie" (Friedrichstrasse corner of Zimmerstrasse), the only entry for foreigners and West Germans into East Berlin. Entry for West Berliners is still restricted. The railing along the edge of the near sidewalk marks the end of West Berlin. The street and the traffic circle in its middle are all part of East Germany. Nowhere does East Berlin

BERLIN

1 Charlottenburg
2 Tourist Information
3 Opera
4 Europa Center
5 Philharmonic Hall
6 To Dahlem Museums
   and Botanical
   Gardens
7 Potsdamer Platz
8 Post Office
9 Checkpoint Charlie
10 Berlin Museum
11 National Gallery
12 Brandenburg Gate
13 Museum Island
   (Pergamon, Bode etc)

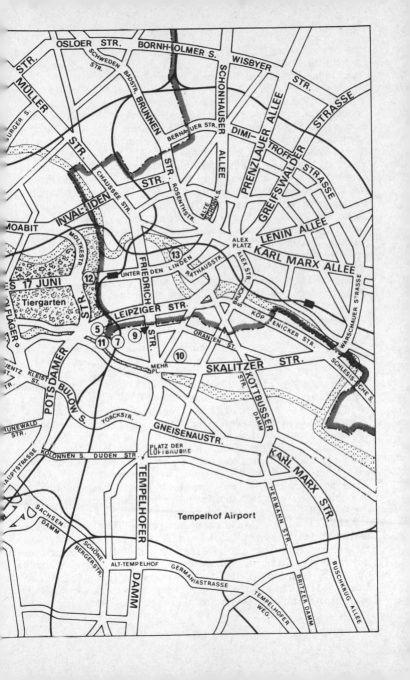

look more desolate than here with ruins on every side. A few hundred yards to the northeast are the covered remains of Hitler's reinforced concrete bunker, where his final days were passed in a frenzy of self-pity.

If West Berlin has risen like a Phoenix from its pyre, cleared away its rubble, put up new buildings, so has East Berlin, though this looks even less like its prewar state than West Berlin. Except for the once splendid Unter den Linden, the storied avenue of stately trees, great stores, embassies and famous hotels that used to lead to the Royal Palace (blown up by the Russians and paved over to form the Marx-Engels Platz), this was originally the working quarter of Berlin with row on row of solid, clean apartment houses. Though never a slum, it was congested and thus particularly vulnerable to bombing. Today you notice the Stalinist style of East Berlin's principal buildings and the newer high-rise apartment blocks, which are a faceless feature of town planning throughout the world.

Close by the western approaches to the Potsdamer Platz you'll likely note a thicket of small shops selling foodstuffs, candy, shoes, cheap clothing, and the like. Here, too, have taken place many of the most dramatic escapes in the stormy history of the cold war.

Berlin's Liberty Bell

From here we turn south and head towards the district called Schöneberg whose Rathaus or City Hall now houses the Senate and the House of Deputies, West Berlin's governing bodies, and the Burgermeister or mayor. The open square in front of the building is used for a market two mornings a week, one of those small-town activities that often give Berlin a peculiarly provincial air.

Each day at noon, however, the deep tones of the Freiheitsglocke ring out to remind Berlin and the world that "all men derive the right to freedom equally from God." If you can spare the time, climb the belfry and take a closer look at this replica of America's Liberty Bell. In a room at the base of the tower are samples of the 17,000,000 American signatures that are stored behind a door carved with a text describing the events that motivated this expression of solidarity with the West Berliners.

Another symbol of Allied intervention is the Platz der Luftbrücke in front of nearby Tempelhof Airport. A soaring, three-pronged concrete monument salutes the 31 American and 39 British airmen who lost their lives flying in food, medicine, and other necessities of life during the grim year of the blockade. Between June 24, 1948, and October 6, 1949, over 2,325,000 tons of supplies were flown into Berlin in an airlift that ultimately reached the tempo of a thousand planes per day. West Berliners wryly refer to the structure as the Hunger Rake, perhaps justifiably, as memorials of this kind are usually ugly.

At the foot of the Mehring Damm, a few minutes' walk from the southwest corner of the Eastern sector, is the American Memorial Library. A magazine room with more than a thousand periodicals and a music department equipped with booths for listening to records and tapes complete its facilities.

We continue south, however, beyond the Insulaner rubble mountain already mentioned on whose lower slopes an ultra-modern outdoor swimming pool has been installed. Soon we are in Steglitz with its outstanding botanical gardens and botanical museum. The display of plants, flowers, shrubs, trees, and bushes, large and small, rare and common, is beautifully set among smooth green lawns, statuary, and little pools, in a triumph of the landscape architect's skill. Besides the museum there are hothouses for the cultivation of tropical vegetation.

Dahlem's Museums and the Free University

Practically next door, but in the Dahlem district, is a cluster of museums, institutes and archives headed by the Gemälde Galerie, with an outstanding collection of paintings, especially Rembrandt. Berlin is less rich in art than before the war. The state museums were in what is now the Eastern sector, along with the castles of Eastern Berlin and Potsdam. Many of their treasures were removed to the West and distributed all over Germany.

The collection in the Gemälde Galerie is really splendid, for examples of work of most of the European masters are on view—Dürer, Holbein, Brueghel, Giotto, Raphael, Titian, Caravaggio, Guardi, as well as many French, Flemish and Dutch masterpieces, with, of course, the ubiquitous Rembrandt well represented, especially by his famous *Man in a Gold Helmet*. Also in this complex of museums is the Ethnographic Museum, with art from far regions of the world, brilliantly displayed; the Museums of Indian, Islamic and East Asian Art; and also a Sculpture Gallery, especially strong in medieval and Baroque sculpture. Nearby is the Free University, founded in 1948 with more than 25,000 students, almost entirely German. It is a vital center of German intellectual life.

Eastwards lies the Grunewald, Berlin's largest park and summer playground. Lake Havel and the Teufelsberg wintersports center are both popular parts of the park, while the Grunewald Hunting Lodge, built in 1542, contains not only hunting trophies, but also a representative collection of Dutch and German painters, with emphasis on the Dutch 17th century. In summer candlelight concerts are held in the courtyard.

The south end of Clayallee intersects Berliner Strasse at one of the many points where this broad thoroughfare changes names, in this instance to Potsdamer Strasse and, presently, to Potsdamer Chaussee and König Strasse.

Just before you reach the bridge that marks the end of the American sector of Berlin and the beginning of the Eastern zone of Germany, a right-hand turn will bring you to the delightful Nikolskoe Blockhaus, a log house built by Frederick William III for Crown Prince Nicholas of Russia in 1819, today a restaurant with one of the better views of the Havel River. A few hundred yards more bring you to the Pfaueninsel or Peacock Island (you can hear the screams of the peacocks from which the island takes its name) reached by ferry. Here Frederick William II built a château to resemble a partly-ruined Italian castle. Two centuries earlier, the Great Elector provided an alchemist with a laboratory here and commissioned him to find a method for turning base metals into gold.

Retracing our steps to the bridge that divides the Kleiner Wannsee from the Grosser Wannsee, we take the left-hand fork and turn north along the shores of the Wannsee and the Havel, a run that can take more than an hour on Sunday afternoons when the lake is full of sailboats and the shore a mass of bathers. The Wannsee Strandbad is an attractive place to swim, with those lovely old-fashioned beach chairs that give you comfort and protect you from the wind. There is real sand imported from the North Sea beaches, but in summer it tends to get very crowded.

Charlottenburg

Alternatively, we could take the autobahn itself, which penetrates Berlin as far as the Charlottenburg quarter. This stretch of the divided highway is called the Avus. The end of the Avus marks the beginning of the Messegelände or Fair Grounds, a whole city of exhibition buildings grouped around the 490-foot-high Funkturm or Radio Tower. An elevator carries you to its top for an extensive view of the surroundings, including the Olympic Stadium to the west with the British compound and the open-air Waldbühne theater—and, of course, the international congress center I.C.C., which makes Berlin one of the foremost congress cities in Europe. It has room for 5,000 people at a time, and there is a corresponding number of smaller rooms to enable large gatherings to split into reasonably sized working-parties. The I.C.C. is extremely well-sited, next to the exhibition grounds of the Funkturm complex and with direct access to the motorway.

One edge of the Messegelände impinges on Theodor-Heuss-Platz, in whose center burns an eternal flame on top of an altar-like monument to Justice, Liberty, and Peace.

If we leave Theodor-Heuss-Platz behind us and turn east along Kaiser Damm and Bismarck Strasse, the Victory Monument glitters distantly in the sun. Before completing our circuit of West Berlin, however, we branch off to the left on Schloss Strasse and immediately see the restrained proportions of Charlottenburg Palace, not only a lovely building in itself, but the home of yet another collection of museums. Berlin is a city of museums! A guided tour will take you through the state apartments with their memories of the great kings and queens of Prussia. The rooms are sumptuous, crowded with fine decoration and works of art. There is a porcelain collection, in the China Cabinet, which will startle you with the amount of plates and vases all over the walls and as if the variety wasn't enough, reflected in large mirrors. The rococo Golden Gallery is a most impressive hall, with delicate plasterwork in gilt. Frederick the Great's rooms are close by. After such a display of decoration it is quite natural to find the Museum of Arts and Crafts in one wing of the palace. In the balancing wing there is the Museum of Ancient History and space for exhibitions.

Opposite the front of the palace is the Museum of Egypt, with a rich collection of ancient Egyptian treasures, including what is probably the most famous portrait bust in the world, that of Nefertiti. Beside this museum is the Museum of Antiques, with a hoard of gold and silver pieces that is a must for anyone interested in jewelry from the classical world.

The park surrounding Charlottenburg is also worth visiting. It is designed in the English landscape tradition, which was so popular with the late 18th-century German monarchs (remember the great English Garden in Munich). Tucked away in these extensive grounds are the mausoleum where some of the Prussian royal family is buried, and the Belvedere, a pretty retreat, built with a view of the lake.

As a parting thought for West Berlin it may please you to know that within a stone's throw of the Wall at Klingsorstr. 59 there is a revival of a former Berlin delight, in the shape of Berlin's wine school for viniculturalists. Berlin has two vineyards, one in Neukölln and the other in Kreuzberg and the result is delicious. They don't export it any more—it was going to eastern Europe in the 19th century when a liter cost 12 pfennigs—because of fiercer competition from cheaper southern wines and Bavarian beer. But you can get Spreewein (the river Spree is Berlin's river) locally and the vineyards are probably Berlin's most soothing sight.

PRACTICAL INFORMATION FOR WEST BERLIN

 WHEN TO GO. Berlin's liveliest period is between **September** and **April.** This is when theaters, concert halls, and nightlife are going full blast. The big fairs and festivals also occur during this period: Berlin Festival Weeks and German Industry Exhibition from **September** to **October;** International Book Exhibition, Ballet Weeks and Berlin Jazz days in **November;** the mammoth Christmas Fair in **December** which fills nine exhibition halls; Press Ball, Film Ball, Fashion Ball and the International Green Week in **January;** Opera Ball in **February;** and the International Boat and Water Sports Exhibition in **March.** The last week in February and the early days of March are also enlivened by the Berlin Film Festival with its gala premières, lavish ball and a rich selection of some of the world's best contemporary films.

Apart from September, this is not, however, the ideal time of year from the standpoint of weather. There is a good deal of rain, some snow, and occasionally freezing cold weather. Spring which usually comes in late in March, is mild and pleasant. Berlin's many fruit trees burst into blossom in **April.**

Summer, of course, is best. Other events (the opera season doesn't close until mid-July and then begins again the end of August) plus the good weather favor a visit at this time. Excessively hot days are rare even in mid-summer, and Berlin is full of delightful parks, not to mention the broad waters of the Wannsee.

 HOW TO GO. West Berlin's location creates special problems in reaching the city from the West. The best solution is to fly in from Hamburg, Hannover, Frankfurt, Munich, Düsseldorf, Cologne, Stuttgart, or Nürnberg on *Pan Am,* or *British Airways* planes. There are about 80 flights daily to and from West Berlin; the trip takes as little as an hour, and there are special reduced excursion fares. These airlines now use Tegal Airport, the main civilian airport in the Western sectors. Regular express bus services connect Zoo Station and Tegel. Other airlines, however, have occasional services to Schönefeld Airport in East Berlin, but to minimize formalities it is simpler to fly into West Berlin.

Tourists may use the regular train services to Berlin or drive their own cars. However, they must obtain a transit visa at a border checkpoint.

Transit visas are issued at the following border crossing points: Helmstedt-Marienborn (rail/road); Rudolphstein-Hirschberg (road); Ludwigstadt-Probstzella (rail); Büchen-Schwanheide (rail); Herleshausen-Wartha (road); Hof-Gutenfürst (rail); Warnemünde and Sassnitz ferry landings. These, incidentally, are the only routes permitted to American and British tourists. See that your exit point is indicated correctly—if you don't say anything, your return transit visas will be issued for the same border checkpoint as your entry. Speed limits for cars in East Germany are 100 k.p.h. on the autobahns, 80 on main roads and 50 in built up areas.

HOTELS. Berlin lost all of its great old luxurious hotels during World War II but during the last decade it has acquired a number of ultramodern, top-class hotels with international reputation and more are being built every year. The city is also rich in small hotels and pensions. Because of the great business activity, frequent fairs, conventions and other periodic events, as well as the large number of tourists visiting the city throughout the year, it is recommended to wire or write for reservations in advance, especially for rooms in the hotels listed below. At Tegel Airport there is a hotel indication board showing where rooms are vacant.

If you do not write direct to the hotel, or reserve your accommodation through your travel agent, then you might wish to contact the hotel reservation service of the Berlin Tourist Office (Verkehrsamt) at the Zoo railway station, tel. (030) 31–70–94.

Deluxe

Ambassador, Bayreuther Strasse 42, 120 rooms, all with bath, radio, TV; French restaurant and roof pool.

Am Zoo, Kurfürstemdamm 25, 145 rooms, garni, very central.

Bristol Hotel Kempinski, corner of Kurfürstendamm and Fasanenstrasse. The annex (all rooms airconditioned) now gives it 350 rooms, all completely renovated, three outstanding restaurants, two bars, indoor pool with Spanish-style patio and recreation area. On Sunday mornings there is brunch and jazz in the popular *Caroussel-Veranda.*

Hilton, Budapester Strasse. Its 350 rooms (600 beds) all have private bath, and there is a choice of three restaurants, three bars, a café, and a roof garden. The Starlight Room, on the top floor of this skyscraper building, gives you two contrasting views—one onto the brilliantly-lit Kurfürstendamm and the other over East Berlin.

Intercontinental, Budapester Strasse 2, a very good link in this chain's hotels, 314 rooms and top comforts.

Palace, Europa Center, Budapester Strasse, among the newest. 175 rooms with bath; two elegant restaurants and a well-stocked bar.

Schweizerhof, Budapester Strasse 25, with annex, 450 rooms including apartments and studio rooms, all rooms with bath or shower. Swiss-style grill restaurant, swimming pool, shops.

Expensive

Arosa, Lietzenburgerstr. 79, 107 rooms, some apartments, good facilities, including open-air pool. Garni, but has *Walliser Stuben* restaurant.

Bremen, Bleibtreustr. 25, garni, 48 rooms, welcoming venue.

Schlosshotel Gehrus, Brahmsstrasse 4–10, Grunewald. For those who like an exclusive, quiet location, we can recommend enthusiastically this former private palace-style residence converted to a small hotel. In the park district of Grunewald, it has 30 rooms plus apartments.

President, An der Urania 16, is also one of the newer but smaller, 60 rooms with bath or shower and refrigerator; roof garden and sauna.

Savoy, Fasanenstr. 9. Near the Kurfürstendamm. Modern and efficient with the best service in town. Garni. All 115 rooms with bath.

Seehof, Lietzensee Ufer 11, overlooking the Lietzensee, 77 rooms, suites; restaurant and lakeside café terrace. Verges on deluxe.

Steigenberger-Berlin, Wielandstr. New 1981, a member of the chain of deluxe hotels of the same name.

Sylter Hof, Kurfürstenstr. 114–16, 130 rooms with bath, restaurant in Empire style, bar in baroque style.

Tourotel, Albrechtstr. 2 (in Steglitz), modern, very comfortable with 440 beds, sauna, solarium and restaurant.

Parkhotel Zellermayer, Meinekestr. 15, just a three-minute walk from Kurfürstendamm. All 140 rooms have bath.

Moderate

Ariane, Keithstrasse 45, medium-sized hotel, some rooms with bath.

Askanischer Hof, Kurfürstendamm 171–172, for bed and breakfast only.

Astoria, garni, Fasanenstrasse 2, quiet, good value for the rather classy neighborhood. Between the Zoo and the Technical University, so close to center.

Aviv, Lietzenburgerstrasse 82, attractive, modern, excellent value, and central with it. Some rooms have kitchenettes. Highly recommended.

Börse, Kurfürstendamm 34. Restaurant/hotel, bang in the center and busy.

Hospiz Friedenau, garni, Fregestrasse 68. Just south of Schöenberg and not far from the Insulaner sports center. Small, pleasant, well-run place.

Frühling am Zoo, Kurfürstendamm 17. Excellent, central value. (Don't confuse with the **am Zoo,** see above.)

Hotel-Pension Helvetia, Mommsenstrasse 55, 23 beds, rooms with shower or bath.

Kardell, Gervinusstrasse 24, pleasant situation not too far from the Charlottenburg rail station. Some rooms with showers.

Pichlers Viktoriagarten, Leonorenstrasse 18. Small, high value hotel, with restaurant; just south of the Insulaner complex and virtually on the Teltowkanal. Quite handy for Dahlem.

Rastätte-Motel Grunewald, Spanische Allee 177. Furthest out of all the selection, just beyond the Dahlem museums and near Lake Havel. Worth it to be in an attractive area with a view. Reasonably priced for facilities and with fair restaurant.

Savigny, garni, Brandenburgischestrasse 21. On wide avenue, midway along the Kurfürstendamm. 60 rooms.

Hotel am Studio, Kaiserdamm 80–81, near Funkturm (radio tower and exhibition halls), 93 beds, all rooms with baths.

Inexpensive

The best bet for reasonable accommodation is to find a pension, but be sure to check in advance on the price, for some pensions can be every bit as expensive as a fully fledged hotel. The following is a selection from the dozens available, all centrally located, most of them in the Kurfürstendamm/Zoo area. All are bed and breakfast.

Ansbach, Ansbacherstrasse 11; **Atlas,** Uhlandstrasse 172; **Elton,** Pariserstrasse 9; **Fischer,** Nürnbergerstrasse 24A; **Flora,** Uhlandstrasse 184; **Masovia,** Clausewitzstrasse 7; **Nürnberger Eck,** Nürnbergerstrasse 24A (the same address as the Fischer); **Riga,** Rankestrasse 23; **Savignyplatz,** Grolmannstrasse 52. In the suburbs: **Pension Havelhaus,** Imchenallee 35, on the banks of the River Havel with own bathing beach and boats for hire. Quiet and good value; restaurant next door.

Also possible is the **Dom,** Hohenzollerndamm 33, which is simple and adequate, good for the young tourist.

 RESTAURANTS. The three favorite food specialties of Berlin are *Bockwurst* (a chubby frankfurter); yellow pea soup with *Bockwurst* and/or a slice of bacon; and *Eisbein* (pig hock) and sauerkraut. You will find these three specialties almost everywhere you drop in to eat. *Bockwurst* stands are as common as the proverbial hot-dog stand in America. *Berliner Kindl* restaurants are a sure bet for *Eisbein:* these are a chain of restaurants located all over West Berlin. Another popular priced chain is *Aschinger.*

Berliners also like *Schlesisches Himmelreich:* roast goose or pork with potato dumplings, cooked with fried fruit in a rich gravy. *Königsberger Klops* are meatballs, herring, and capers—a wonderful combination of meat and fish. Fresh carrots, peas, asparagus, and mushrooms make a dish called *Leipziger Allerlei,* and there's wonderful smoked goose breast. *Kasseler Rippenspeer,* concocted long ago by a Berlin butcher named Cassel, is salted pork, fried golden in butter, then cooked slowly until well done. A traditional summer dish is *Aal grün mit Gurkensalat,* tiny pieces of eel from the nearby river, cooked in rich sauce, and served with boiled potatoes and cucumber salad.

Expensive

Berlin is full of expensive restaurants, most of them excellent. Here are one or two that might fill the bill for a special evening out without breaking the bank.

Alexander, Kurfürstendamm 46, fine food in an interesting restaurant, well frequented by artists, attracted, perhaps, by the open fire. Corner of Ku-damm and Bleibtreustrasse.

Conti Fischstuben, Sybelstr. 14, is good for local fish dishes and excellent. Cheaper dishes at lunchtime.

The **Grill** at the **Ambassador Hotel,** Bayreutherstrasse 2, is open to 2 A.M., comfortable and thoroughly reliable. This is also true of the **Grill** at the **Berlin Hotel.** Considering the quality and surroundings, surprisingly reasonably priced for this category.

Maitre, Meinekestrasse 10. This really is a gourmet spot, with superb food (French, of course); bouillabaisse on Tues. and Fri. is a must.

Moderate

Alt-Berliner-Bier Salon, Kurfürstendamm 225, decorated with objets d'art and nostalgic bric a brac from the days of the Empire; central and popular. Large portions of north German specialties especially *Eisbein* (boiled knuckle of pork) and *Schalachtplatte* (mixed offal and sausage). Dancing after 8 P.M.

Alter Krug, Königin-Luise-Strasse 52. Not far from the Dahlem Museums, certainly near enough for lunch when seeing the exhibits or the Botanic Garden. Attractive restaurant with outdoor dining.

Le Bou-Bou, Kurfürstendamm 103, bistro-type restaurant, art-deco interior, not too expensive and usually full of life.

Drei Bären, Kurfürstendamm 22. You can't get more central than this very popular spot, it actually spills over onto the sidewalk, right where all the world passes. Excellent for local food, especially dumplings filled with eels, and Eisbein.

Heckers Deele, Grolmannstrasse 35. Westphalian-style restaurant with Westphalian specialties and many kinds of beer. Also has 25 rooms.

Mampes Gute Stube, Kurfürstendamm 14. Old Berlin again, and excellent cooking, too.

Ratskeller Schmargendorf, Barkaerplatz 1. A very typical Berlin eating house, popular with locals from the neighborhood. No frills, but excellent fare.

For a wide selection of gastronomical varieties at moderate prices, try the **Silberterrasse** in the huge department store *Ka-De-We* in Tauentzienstr. 21 (not far from Europa Center).

Zlata Praha, Meinekestrasse 4. Here's a restaurant that is something out of the usual Berlin run, for it specializes in food from Eastern Europe, Hungary, Bulgaria, Czechoslovakia and so on. The menu is really a budget snip for value, and the range of beer quite something, for, amongst others, it sells Pilsner Urquell, which is a fairly strong brew.

Inexpensive

Two excellent spots for lunch are the restaurants at the **Berlin Museum** and the **Dahlem Museums** (for location see the Museum lists following). Naturally they are only lunchtime venues, but both have really excellent, reasonable menus. The Berlin Museum's **Weissbierstube** serves typical local food (as a kind of gastronomic extension of the museum's exhibits!) and it also has Berlin's popular beer, caller Berlinerweisse, which is flavored with raspberry juice. The Dahlem Museum has a wide variety of dishes, again, at super prices.

Hardtke, Meinekestrasse 27, just off Kurfürstendamm, near center, perhaps the most typical of all Berlin restaurants, with bare wood steins and gargantuan portions of hefty fare. This is the one we heartily recommend for atmosphere and value.

Provinz, Galvaniastrasse 12, this charming restaurant, somewhat hidden in a quiet location (five taxi-minutes from Kurfürstendamm) has a very pleasant atmosphere. Popular with students and artists.

Ratskeller Schöneberg, at Schöneberg Rathaus. When visiting the Liberty Bell, have lunch here. Atmospheric and with excellent, filling set meals.

Schultheiss Bräuhaus, Kurfürstendamm 220, full of life and high spirits. They hold suckling pig feasts here sometimes on a Saturday, with hurdy-gurdies and all the trimmings. Otherwise it's a solid, beer cellar setting with food to match.

Tai Shan, Meinekestrasse 7, good Chinese food at reasonable prices.

If you are looking for a snack, or a coffee break, try one of the city's **Konditoreien** for delicious cakes and pastries. Three on Kurfürstendamm will tempt you, **Cafehaus** at 234, **Kranzler** at 19, or **Carrousel** at 27.

IN THE SUBURBS

Blockhaus Nikolskoe (M), Wannsee. Russian-style blockhouse dating back to 1819 in a charming spot at the southern end of the Wannsee (on the Havel) and a long, long taxi ride from downtown. If you are going by car, turn off Königstrasse on Nikolskoer Weg. Closed Thurs.

Wannsee Terrassen (M), Wannseebadweg. Terraces that overlook the Wannsee and closer to town than the Blockhaus though still quite a way. But worth it in good weather. Also near the Strandbad Wannsee where you can swim before having a meal. Dancing, but not every night. Closed Mon.

Historischer Weinkeller, Alt Pichelsdorf 32, Spandau, vast choice of German wines in centuries-old wine cellar. From October until April every Wednesday, Thursday and Sunday, **Feuerzangenbowle** (a pair of coal tongs is placed over a large punchbowl. On it a sugar cone soaked in rum is lit) and zither music. Closed on Mondays.

In Grunewald: **Chalet Suisse** (M), on Königin-Luise-Str. Has terraces and attractive dining areas. Not far from Dahlem; also, **Weinstuben Habel** (M), Hohenzollerndamm 93, pleasant restaurant with garden and quite close to the Schloss Gehrhus (see Hotels).

In Tegel, there is the more expensive **Alte Waldschänke,** Karolinenstr. 10, with particularly praiseworthy cuisine in very comfortable rustic surroundings.

HOW TO GET ABOUT. Because of its vast, yet compacted, area, Berlin is not the kind of city that can be comfortably covered on foot. In fact you would find yourself easily exhausted if you tried to do so. But, luckily, Berlin has a really magnificent network of public transport, which is especially a blessing for the budget tourist, who is not likely to be hiring a car or wanting to invest in taxis.

BVG (the Berlin Tourist Corporation) has 83 city bus routes and 8 subway (underground) lines. You can get a special map with the entire system of bus and underground routes and the timetable booklet containing all lines, fares, the first and last buses and underground trains, from ticket offices at underground stations.

The **U-Bahn** (underground) and the **S-Bahn** (surface trains) provide high-speed services all over the city. There are three U-Bahn lines that go through to East Berlin and one S-Bahn. There are special reduced tickets available, the Touristenkarte (Tourist Pass), for use on the U-Bahn and the buses (not on the S-Bahn). These currently cost DM20 and are valid for 4 days, or DM11 for 2 days and are available from the Berliner Verkehrsbetrieb (BVG) main ticket office at the U-Bahn station Kleistpark or the Zoo station.

SIGHTSEEING TOURS. One good form of tour is the one you work out yourself and then implement by getting a Tourist Pass. But if you want to get yourself orientated in the city before striking out on your own, the *Berliner Baeren Stadtrundfahrt* has several daily departures from the Memorial Church; *Berolina Stadtrundfahrten* leaves several times daily from the corner of Meinekestrasse and Kurfürstendamm; *Severin/Kühn* leaves from Kurfürstendamm 215–216. If the tour is going to be taking in East Berlin, remember to have your passport with you. Be prepared to pay an extra DM7 for an official East German guide. Naturally the prices of these tours vary with the company and the length of the trip, but a 2–4 hour tour will average out at DM30, with longer ones going up to DM65.

In the summer, special excursion buses operate from the Zoo underground station almost non-stop to Wannsee and the neighboring lakeside resorts.

VISITING EAST BERLIN Tourists with non-German passports use the international transit point at the corner of Friedrichstrasse and Zimmerstrasse; this is the famous Checkpoint Charlie, featured in endless newscasts and spy stories for the last thirty years. It is open round the clock. A special permit is obtainable at the checkpoint, costing DM5. You have to present a valid passport.

You can also go through on the underground (U-Bahn) or the normal rail (S-Bahn) both to Friedrichstrasse, from 7 A.M. to 8 P.M.. Private cars must carry a registration certificate, international insurance (green) card and car sticker of country of origin. The charge for road fee is DM10 for the car.

Visitors are obliged to exchange DM6.50 on entry into East Berlin. The transit pass for non-Germans is valid until midnight and the visitor must leave through the same checkpoint as the one he entered by.

Sightseeing tours of East Berlin are made by three authorized West Berlin companies (see Tours above). Unlimited sums of DM and other western currencies may be taken in but it is strictly forbidden to take out currency of the GDR or other Eastern European countries.

Please be sure to check these points before taking a trip into East Berlin, as they are liable to change.

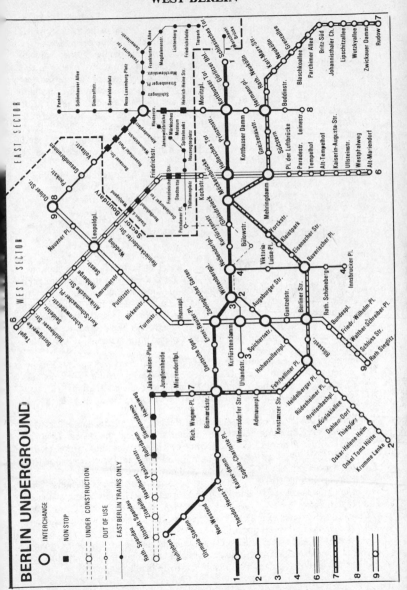

BERLIN UNDERGROUND

○ INTERCHANGE

■ NON STOP

○—○ UNDER CONSTRUCTION

○--○ OUT OF USE

●—● EAST BERLIN TRAINS ONLY

MUSIC. Berlin is a music center. The *Berlin Philhar-monic,* under Herbert von Karajan is the focus of musi-cal activity. There is also the *Radio Symphony Orchestra* (the radio orchestra). Internationally famous soloists and ensembles appear in Berlin. Among the pleasantest musical events in the former capital are the summer concerts given in the *Eichengalerie* of the *Charlot-tenburger Schloss* or outdoors in the courtyard of the Jagdschloss Grunewald. The principal concert halls in West Berlin are the *Philharmonic Concert Hall* at Kemperplatz in the Tiergarten quarter and the *Konzertsaal der Hochschule für Musik* on Hardenbergstrasse, in the Charlottenburg quarter. The Philhar-monic Concert Hall, home of the Berlin Philharmonic Orchestra, rebuilt and reopened in 1963, 20 years after its destruction during the war, is one of the most modern buildings of its kind in Europe.

The *Deutsche Oper Berlin* is in Bismarckstrasse, Charlottenburg, and stands on the site of the prewar Opera House. There are daily performances of the standard operatic repertoire. Light opera can be heard at the *Berliner Operetten-theater,* Schlossstr. 5 in Steglitz quarter, and musicals at the *Theater des Westens,* Kantstr. 12. Twice-weekly concerts are given in the glass-sheathed Memorial Church and Bell Tower next to the old Kaiser Wilhelm Memorial.

 THEATER. The Theater in Berlin is quite outstanding but of course except for operetta and the (non-literary) cabarets it is mostly for those who understand German well. The city has 18 theaters in all, including the two state-subsidized theaters, the *Schiller-Theater,* Bismarckstr. 110 (which has an excellent workshop: *Werkstatt*) and the *Schlosspark-Theater,* Schloss Str. 48, have a repertory of modern and classical plays, with acting of a very high standard.

The most renowned among the private theaters is the *Renaissance-Theater,* Hardenbergstr. 6, but in recent years the *Schaubühne am Halleschen Ufer* has proved artistically most interesting and it can claim some international success. At present the *Mendelsohnbau* at Lehniner Platz is being rebuilt as a new home for the company.

Mainly for Boulevard plays there is the *Komödie,* Kurfürstendamm 206, the *Theater am Kurfürstendamm,* Kurfürstendamm 207, and the *Hebbel-Theater,* Stresemannstr. 29. The outdoor Waldbühne *Theater,* behind the Olympic stadi-um, seats 24,000. Among the experimental and small intimate theaters is the *Tribüne,* Otto-Suhr-Allee 18–20, a youthful enterprise.

Berlin has a long tradition of literary and political cabaret-theaters. The Berlin idiom is savage and debunking, and therefore admirably suited to social and political satire. Today there are the *Stachelschweine* in Europa Center, *Die Wühlmäuse,* Lietzenburger Ecke Nürnberger Strasse, and the very aggressive *Reichskabarett,* Ludwigkirchstr. 6.

At tourist bureau offices and hotels you can get the *Berlin Programm,* giving events in the theaters, concert halls, nightclubs, museums, fairs, etc., published in German, as well as many useful folders in English.

Cinema. There are over 200 cinemas in West Berlin. Most cinemas show one film for several weeks. Among art cinemas showing two or three different films a day, almost without exception in the original, there are: *Arsenal,* Weisestr. 25, *Filmbühne am Steinplatz,* Hardenberstr. 12, *Die Lupe I und II,* Kurfürstendamm 202.

A newsreel theater at Hardenbergstrasse 27 shows the latest *Aktualitäten* or news, plus short subjects, from 9 A.M. to midnight.

 NIGHTCLUBS. Berlin's nightlife has always been famous, not to say notorious. There are a number of small places of no particular distinction, almost indistinguishable from one another—small smoke-filled rooms, minute bars, barmaids with plunging necklines, three-piece bands—but the specialty of Berlin is entertainment with shows of varying elaborateness. *Severin* and *Kühn* and *Berliner-Bären,* Berlin tour operators, have two nightclub tours, starting at 8 P.M. and 9 P.M. respectively, one with dinner, four stops and four drinks, the other with three stops and three drinks. Price between DM75 and DM85.

The one thing to warn you against is taking the advice of a taxi driver and heading for Potsdamerstrasse or Stuttgarter Platz. Here are two or three established possibilities that will give you a good night out without breaking the bank.

Coupé 77, Kurfürstendamm 177; very chic discotheque decorated to represent a carriage of the Orient-Express railway. Lots of atmosphere.

The *New Eden,* Kurfürstendamm 71, dancing to two bands, strip shows and reasonably priced drinks. Stick to beer if you can, which is true wherever you go.

Chez Nous, Marburgerstr. 14, near Europa Center. Empire style plush and Cabaret-Revue with world-famous drag show. Open from 9 to 3 with two shows a night.

Revue Theater *La Vie en Rose,* Waitzstr. 22, at Adenauer Platz. Spectacular cabaret show with light effects and international stars. If you like easy-going entertainment and original humor bordering on the outrageous, this is the place. Book ahead. Open from 9.

Big Eden, Kurfürstendamm 202. For the younger tourist, a strobe heaven, but if you can stand the decibels you'll love the price.

Riverboat, Hohenzollerndamm 174. Mississippi riverboat décor and Berlin liberation make it a great spot whether you are alone or in a group. (Closed Mondays.)

Rheinische Winzerstuben, Hardenbergstr. 29, has been on the go, on and off, since 1899. Twice nightly, at 10 P.M. and midnight, there is a terrific Rhine panorama, thunder and lightning, rain included.

 **SHOPPING.** Kurfürstendamm is a curious mixture of inspired prosperity and tawdriness. Streets branching off what is always known as Ku-damm offer good shopping, and at its end, where the Memorial Church stands, is Breitscheid Square with the Europa Center, a large intertwined group of buildings with dozens of shops on street level, below and above ground. Don't miss *Ka-De-We,* either; this is West Berlin's mammoth department store, located on Wittenberg Platz in the vicinity. Excellent shopping streets are also *Schloss Strasse* (Steglitz) with the department store *Forum,* Wilmersdorfer Strasse which is partially roofed over and a pedestrian precinct. Some 100 central shops stay open until 11 P.M.

 MUSEUMS AND GALLERIES. One extremely welcome point to start with—the entrance to the State Museums in Berlin is *free.*

The Museums at the Charlottenburg Palace Open 9–5, closed Fridays. *Museum of the Prehistoric and Early Stages of Man,* in the West Wing of the palace, originally the Orangery. This consists of the pre-historic remains of this part of Germany, i.e. Brandenburg. *Museum of Applied Arts,* in the East Wing (the Knobelsdorff Wing). A wonderful amassing of loot from the Middle Ages to the late 19th century. The highlight is the Guelph Treasure, but there is much else besides in gold, silver, porcelain and lesser materials. *The Egyptian Museum,* in front of the palace. The main thing to see here is the most famous portrait bust in the world, that of Nefertiti, queen to Aken-Aton the heretic. German archeologists excavated his city of Amarna, and much of their findings is on display here, along with lovely things from many centuries of Egyptian civilization. Next door is the *Museum of Antiques and Treasure Department,* and never was museum better named! Upstairs are relics of ancient Mediterranean peoples, while downstairs is the Schatzkammer, the treasure house, glittering silver and gold from three thousand years. The Hildesheim Hoard of Roman silver vessels, Scythian gold, and endless delicate ancient jewels.

The Dahlem Museums Open 9–5, closed Mondays. *Gemälde Galerie* (Gallery of Paintings). Entrance on Arnim Allee. One of the great collections of paintings. Great in more than one sense, it's vast. There's some fine early German works (especially by Dürer *(Jerome Holzschuher),* Cranach *(Fountain of Youth),* Holbein *(Flight from Egypt);* many lovely Flemish and Dutch pieces; French— Fouquet's *Etienne Chevalier* represents the work of a master rarely seen, while Chardin and Poussin give another, later, side; the great Italians, Raphael, Titian, Botticelli and Giotto are all well represented, as are the Dutch and Flemish masters. Lastly, you should not miss the Rembrandts. *Ethnographic Museum.* Entrance Landstrasse 8. A marvellous collection of ethnic works from all over the world, as notable for the art itself (Mayan carving, masks from the South Seas, Benin bronzes) as for the superb, modern display techniques that bring them all to life. (Literally in the case of the shadow puppets from Java and Thailand.) If you have any time left, see the *Museums of Islamic Art, of East Asian Art, of Indian Art;* they all have fine collections in their own fields. The

Sculpture Gallery has examples of plastic art from ancient times to the 18th century. Outstanding are German medieval pieces and those from the Italian Renaissance.

Not far away is the *Botanical Museum,* Königin-Luise-Strasse 6. Open 10–5, closed Mondays.

New National Gallery, Potsdamerstrasse 50, Open 9–5, closed Fridays. 19th and 20th century art, following the development of European and especially German, artistic movements. The building itself is a modern gem, designed by Mies van der Rohe.

Bauhaus Archives and Museum, Klingelhöferstr. 13. Open 11–6, Wed. 2–9, closed Tuesdays. Admission 1.50DM. Home of the currently 'in' '20s school of architecture, founded by Walter Gropius.

Berlin Museum, Lindenstrasse 14. Open 11–6, closed Mondays. Admission 1.50DM. Three hundred years of Berlin is seen through its art and culture. The museum is in the beautiful building of the former Altes Kammergericht (Court Chambers). Also has a moderately priced restaurant with local fare.

Brücke Museum, Bussardsteig 9. Open 11–5, closed Tuesdays. Admission 1.50DM. Collection of the work of an Expressionist group (The Bridge), which flourished in the first two decades of this century.

Museum of Musical Instruments, Bundesallee 1–12. Open 9–5, closed Mondays. Fascinating for anyone with a taste for musical history (it includes Frederick the Great's flute among other instruments of the famous).

State Museum's Art Library, Jebenstrasse 2. Closed Sundays. Architectural drawings, poster collection, library of costumes, etchings, etc.

Zoological Garden. Open summer 8–7, winter 9–7. Admission 4 DM. Very popular with Berliners and a delightful place to wander in, look at the animals, excellently housed and imaginatively displayed, and eat at the handy restaurant.

 SPORTS. Berlin is a big sports center. The Olympic Stadium on the Heerstrasse, completed for the 1936 Olympic Games, seats 95,000, and can provide standing room for 25,000 more. International football (soccer) matches are held here as well as gymnastic competitions, a sport of which Germans are fond. There is also a swimming pool, where championship meets take place, and athletic fields.

Motorcycle and automobile races take place on the speedy Avus racetrack, which runs from the Funkturm (Radio Tower) through the Grunewald to the Wannsee. As many as 350,000 spectators have turned out at a time here for the big international motorcycle races in May and the principal automobile races in July. Nearby is the Deutschlandhalle, Messedam 26, Germany's largest, with seats for 16,000. The Sporthalle is also near the Funkturm. It is here that wrestling tournaments are held. Horseracing, trotting and flat, takes place at the Mariendorf track.

The favorite place for **swimming** in Berlin is the Wannsee Strandbad. The Wannsee is also an excellent place for rowing, canoeing or sailing. Practitioners of these sports can penetrate into the very heart of Berlin, on the Spree, one of

Berlin's two rivers. The other is the Havel, also suitable for boating, as are the Tegeler and Heiligen lakes. If you try **boating** in Berlin, be careful to keep in the Western sector—there are parts of the Wannsee (more correctly, the Havel) that belong to East Germany. The efficient East German water police, using speedy motorboats, delight in pouncing—and keeping—any West Berlin craft that venture into their area. There is a thermal bathing establishment in the Europa Center, with underwater massage, sauna, various thermal baths, as well as swimming pools.

In addition to some 65 tennis installations having about 350 **tennis courts,** an "aeroform" covered tennis court at the Blau-Weiss Tennis Club gives the players the conditions of an open-air court while they are protected from cold in winter by a plastic shell.

Also in winter Berliners, adults and children, get great fun out of **ice-skating** in the open air. There are several skating-rinks among them *Eisstadion Wilmersdorf, Eisstadion Neukölln,* and the skating rink in *Europa-Centre.* At all of them boots and skates may be hired.

USEFUL ADDRESSES. Tourist Information: The *Berlin. Tourist Office,* Europa-Center, D-1000 Berlin 30 (tel. 240111). This is the place to go with any problems that you may have while in Berlin. There are two *Information Pavilions,* one, an Arrival Pavilion, near the Zoo Station, Hardenbergstrasse 20, (next to Amerika Haus); (tel. 317094/95). Open daily 8 A.M. to 10.30 P.M. The other Information Pavilion is at Tegel Airport. Tel. 41013145; open daily 8 A.M. to 10.30 P.M.. *Taxi,* Berlin Radio Taxi (tel. 6902).

American Express, Kurfürstendamm 11. *Thomas Cook,* Kürfurstendamm 42. **Consulates:** *American,* Clayallee 170 (tel. 832 40 87). *British* Uhlandstrasse 7/8; (tel. 309 52 92/3/4). *French,* Kürfurstendamm 211 (tel. 881 80 28).

Amerika Haus, Hardenbergstrasse 21–24. British Center, Hardenbergstrasse 20. Maison de France, Kurfüstendamm 211.

Aussenkommission der Freien Universität, Ihnestr. 24, D-1000, Berlin 33 (tel. 308381), arranges programs for student groups, as does *ASTA* (Allgemeiner Studentenausschuss), Sekretariat, Hardenbergstr. 34, 1 Berlin 12 (tel. 3112202); both usually open 8–12 noon.

Motorists: Information: *ADAC* (German Automobile Club), Bundesallee 29 (tel. 86865); *AvD* (Automobile Club of Germany), Schöneberger Ufer 83–91, (tel. 2616084). **Car hire;** *Selbstfahrer Union* at Tegel Airport and Kurfüstendamm 179; *Hertz,* Meinekestrasse 19 and airport; *Avis,* Budapesterstrasse 43, at Eden-Haus and at the airport.

Emergencies: Medical emergencies, tel. 2585. *Post Office* open 24 hours a day at the Zoo Railway Station.

Lost Property: Polizei Präsidium, Tempelhofer Damm 1 (nr the airport).

EAST
GERMANY

Johann Wolfgang von Goethe
1749-1832

EAST GERMANY

The German Democratic Republic

If Communism (known in Eastern Europe as socialism) had to come to Germany—and the spoils of World War II made that inevitable—it was not unreasonable that it was the most easterly provinces that fell under the hammer. And unlikely though it is that the electorate of those provinces would have freely returned a government that paid allegiance to its old enemy, the U.S.S.R., it was in these provinces that the concentration of left-wing sympathy was to be found.

In reconstructing the separate development of the two Germanys—after nearly a century of unity—you meet a latter-day Thirty Years War, albeit for the most part a cold one, between the U.S.A. and her political allies, and the U.S.S.R. and hers. Divided Germany is the linchpin. The American influence in West Germany is clear, materialistic and ideological, in that order. The Russian influence in East Germany is equally clear, but totally, thoroughly ideological, unaccompanied by the financial aid that the U.S.A. was able to put into West Germany. Propaganda, blatantly pedestrian in the East, more sophisticated in the West, can have the effect of dulling the sensitivity and consciousness, or heightening it. But the seasoned observer of Germany sees today, in both East and West, a hybrid.

But while it might be fair to observe that the Western hybrid has reached maturity, it is harder to see this in the East, because the process has been slower. It is also largely due to hitherto-strained official connections between East Germany and those who did not recognize its sovereignty, which threw a smokescreen over the already heavy pall of official attitudes toward life there. Accustomed as they were to the upheavals of European history, four million East Germans, battered physically and emotionally by two world wars, did not feel able to remain in their own territories to see the emergence of yet another society there. So only 17 million remain and these have weathered the colossal strains on resources of all kinds imposed by emergent regimes.

Since 1961, movement to the West has been virtually confined to persons whose permanent absence could only be a blessing to the economy. The erection of the Berlin Wall, said, very understandably, to have been necessary because of the hitherto continuous undermining of the East German economy, also ensured that passage between the two Germanys could be strictly controlled.

Certainly open-minded thinkers will allow for, if not excuse, the restriction of movement in terms of the diminished labor force, and even justify it in terms of the economic miracle that has made East Germany the fifth strongest industrial power in Europe. Clearly, too, the younger East German, with easy access to West German television, has enough material security and a measure of incentive to want to stay put and to establish independent development. Officially, the East German publicists still whirl about words like "fascism" and "imperialism" as idly and over-readily as the West uses the words "communism" and "socialism." Often misnomers, these terms are of very little importance these days.

But people and events are. And with some moves toward European unity, U.N. recognition of East Germany, and current overtures—especially in matters of trade—coexistence looks at least a hopeful possibility for the two Germanys, for East and West Europe, and for the everyday lives of people in East Germany.

The country is unlikely to draw back her lost citizens, since émigrés and refugees are not noted (at least in Europe and America) for retracing their steps. Yet it will earn its own respect, thanks to its recovery.

East Germany has been deeply preoccupied, at least in theory, and, as far as the old order of society goes, in practice, in eradicating elements which it considered slowed down material (and in a sense spiritual) progress, and which brought about the two world wars. Her methods and achievements, like most people's, are open to strong criticism. Where resources are minimal and planners and administrators are new to their tasks, progress is slow and it is precisely these factors and their consequences that give East Germany rather a dour exterior. As a tourist, one misses terribly the family-run business or inn, for example, and feels slightly disconcerted by the fact that people are easily thrown by direct and perhaps unexpected requests, and that the wheels of life seem to lack oil. This is where one observes how sparse the labor force is and how great an effect the loss of a country's experts and skilled workers can have, together with the disappearance of the little touches that are indigenous to life in older-established ways of society, but which have no place here.

East German Voices

One sign of security, self-possession and maturity is being able to admit one's faults. Another is letting one's citizens' individuality speak for itself, thus indicating collectively the measure of the society. Probing for evidence in these spheres is a pastime that few tourists visiting East Germany may feel inclined to indulge. But it is far more valuable to be able to read, hear or see the works of, for example, contemporary writers and artists, and more valuable for that country to extol them, than to have too much of the official voice telling you in terms of political propaganda and half-truth about the achievement of a country, and in half-truth terms. East Germany has few such contemporary cultural envoys whose works are known abroad, nor publications.

East German films are now finding their way into European film festivals. But having said this much it is still more appropriate to dwell on the rich sources of art and music in previous centuries in East Germany. Considering the amount of work of this kind, as well as that of great philosophers and literary figures, East Germany is today a Sleeping Beauty, waiting for a prince to bring her wonders to life.

Treasures of the East

Berlin's treasures are more obvious, albeit—like the city itself—somewhat divided. Frederick the Great's superb Watteau collection, for instance, though intended for display at East Germany's Sans Souci Palace, is now in West Berlin's Charlottenburg Palace, and the Dahlem Museum has finished up with most of the great Prussian art treasures. But the Pergamon and Bode Museums in East Berlin still have the largest classical architectural structures in the world to be housed inside buildings; and, in the Bode Museum, highly important Egyptian works; the German State Library is also here.

Your visit may coincide (almost haphazardly, for advance information is scarce) with important special exhibitions. For example, the National Gallery in East Berlin had a rare showing of Art Nouveau (or Jugendstil as it is known in Germany), with Kipling and original Beardsleys included.

Aside from Dresden, Weimar is the other great cultural treasure house that tourists will probably be shown only fleetingly. (Though they may be directed to the ugly and less significant Halle, Karl-Marx-Stadt or, worse infamous Buchenwald.) Bach, Goethe, Schiller, Luther, Herder, Liszt and Wagner are just a few of the great men who spent many years in historic Weimar. There is good documentation on the private as well as the public side of their lives and works to be found in hotels and museums.

Dresden has 16 other important museums besides the Zwinger, while Leipzig, synonymous with Bach, has a magnificent Bach archive, while the University (Schillerstrasse) has the largest Egyptian collection of its kind in Europe. And anyone devoted to the medieval poets and the romantic revival of the 19th century will find a haven in the Wartburg Castle, primarily, of course, associated with Luther.

Money for maintenance is one of the serious drawbacks facing East Germany, but much restoration has been done, and quite as beautifully and as lovingly as any in West Germany. There is considerable public appreciation of music, opera, drama and art, and the official attitude is positive, with the result that East Germany has 86 theaters and opera houses functioning. Berlin and Dresden are the best testimony to the reconstruction of churches, cathedrals and art galleries, so much so that one tends to forget that they *have* been restored, at great cost in time, money and effort, and to notice instead the no-man's-land around the frontier with West Berlin and the rather "anonymous international" style of contemporary hotels and public buildings. But to English visitors particularly, a visit to Dresden is more than a homage to the Sistine Madonna and all the other great treasures of the Zwinger; for this great city of art, set so graciously on the Elbe, was destroyed by British and American bombers partly in retaliation for German attacks on Britain.

East Germany is much smaller than her westerly neighbor. After World War II, East Prussia ceased to exist and the people living there were expelled—bearing out once again the moral often to be observed elsewhere in this world that it is best not to live on the borders of another state, or even another province. So, with territory east of the Oder and Neisse rivers in Polish hands, East Germany is now made up of the provinces of Mecklenburg, Brandenburg, Saxe-Anhalt, Thuringia and Saxony—about 67,000 square miles. The prettiest parts form a ring, all bordering on East Germany's neighbors: Saxon Switzerland, as it is known (bordering West Germany and Czechoslovakia), the Erzgebirge (mountains forming a natural barrier with Czechoslovakia), the Thuringian Forest, the Harz Mountains and the Baltic Sea resorts (all adjoining West Germany). In between the territory is pretty flat: it is an extension of the immense Baltic Plain, whose sandy soil has been partly won back from the marshlands. Cold in winter, hot in summer, this sparsely wooded land is a forerunner of the Russian steppes.

Unless you happen to be in Karl-Marx-Stadt or Magdeburg, it is unlikely that East Germany's very considerable industrial activity will be apparent. More noticeable in the new order of life there are university buildings and technical colleges, which are to be found in almost every important town and city. Homes, too, have changed in appearance in recent years, a feature that many visitors will understand and brood over with mixed feelings, for back-to-back dwellings have given way to tower blocks, offering people streamlined kitchens and flush WC's but taking them away from the land and contact with neighbors on the same street.

Food and Drink in East Germany

Dishes on East German menus in cities are heavily influenced by Eastern European cuisine. Explanations are usually given in several languages, including English, and generally speaking regional specialties manage to make themselves known. In Berlin, for instance, you will find the famous *Eisbein mit Sauerkraut* (knuckle of pork with pickled cabbage), *Rouladen* (rolled stuffed beef), *Spanferkel* (suckling pig), *Berliner Schüsselsülze* (potted meat in aspic), *Schlachteplatte* (mixed grill), *Bürgermeister-Suppe* (thick soup), *Hackepeter* (minced meat), and *Kartoffelpuffer* (potato pancake).

Just outside Berlin, in the haven and tranquility of Spreewald (the Spree woods) and their "streets" of waterways (much of this district has no roads, so boats are the only means of transport) freshwater fish dishes are served, as well as the familiar sausages peculiar to every spot of Germany, East or West. Good ones to try are *Spreewälder Wurstplatte mit Meerrettich* and *Quark mit Leinöl* (various types of sausage with horseradish and cream cheese), *Fisch in Spreewaldsosse* (fish in season with a local sauce) or *Aal mit Gurkensalat* (eel and cucumber salad).

Thuringia specializes in venison, poultry and fish. *Röstbrätl* (pot-roast), *Thüringer Sauerbraten mit Klössen* (pickled roast meat and dumplings), *Bärenschinken* (ham) are typical, and *Thüringer Kessel-*

fleisch, Würzfleisch, Schlachteplatte, Thüringer Wurstplatte are all local sausage dishes.

In the Harz Mountains, you may come across *Halberstädter Käsesuppe* (cheese soup), *Harzer Köhlerteller mit Röstkartoffeln* (meat cooked over a charcoal grill and served with roast potatoes).

In the north, popular dishes are *Mecklenburgischer Schinkenbraten* and *Katenschinken* (similar dishes of baked ham), *Fleischfondue* (meat fondue), mushrooms cooked in various ways, and, of course, on the coast and nearby, fish, sometimes flavored with paprika. There are seafood restaurants throughout East Germany, many of them called *Gastmahl des Meeres.*

Wines and spirits tend to come from eastern rather than western climes, and Bulgarian wines and Polish and Russian vodkas are worth sampling. A local throat-scorcher, found particularly around the Harz Mountains, is *Schierker Feuerstein.*

EXPLORING EAST BERLIN AND POTSDAM

If you have arrived via West Berlin (have your passport with you) you will enter by "Checkpoint Charlie" and turn along Friedrichstrasse to Unter den Linden, Berlin's beloved pre-1939 and still elegant avenue. If you arrive directly in East Germany, city tours follow a similar circuit. Besides the Soviet Embassy and the restored opera house, the contemporary version of the street is lined with many ministerial buildings. Humboldt University founded in 1810 by Wilhelm von Humboldt, is at its lower end. The German State Library with over 4 million volumes is here, also the Museum of German History in whose courtyard concerts are held in summer, the German State Opera, the Opera Cafe (once the Princesses' Palace), the former Royal Library, used today by the University, St. Hedwig's Cathedral, and the National Gallery.

In a moment you arrive at a great open expanse, and if you knew Berlin before the 1939–45 war, you will gaze at it in bewilderment. This was the heart of the city in those days, where stood the great museums, the cathedrals, and the massive buildings of the old Imperial Palace. Begun in 1538, the palace, thanks to the genius of Andreas Schlüter, has been one of Berlin's most prized architectural monuments for four centuries. It was severely damaged during the war, but not to such an extent that it could not have been restored. In 1951 it was razed and every trace of its existence obliterated, to make way for the bare desola-

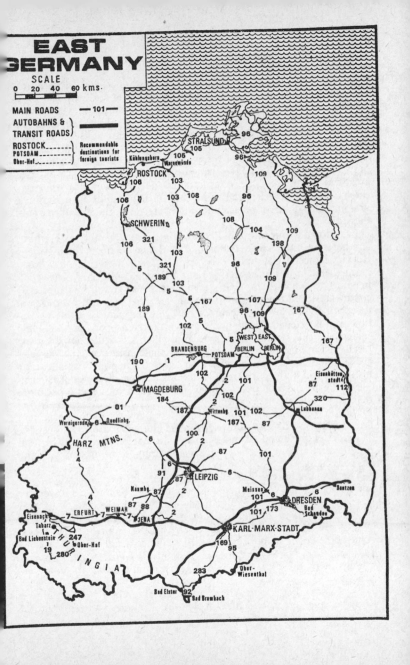

tion of the Marx-Engels-Platz, the Red Square of Berlin and somewhat calling to mind Munich's Königsplatz.

Passing East Berlin's town hall, usually festooned with slogans emblazoned in white letters against a red background and near the 14th-century Marienkirche, you come next to Alexanderplatz, with several HO stores. A few blocks more and you are at the beginning of the monolithic Lenin Allee, a double row of apartment houses and stores built in what is sometimes called Moscow gingerbread style. It was here that the protest meetings of the men who were building Stalin Allee (now Karl-Marx-Allee) developed into the riots of June 17, 1953. This area, which contains hotels, restaurants, the TV tower and other eye-catching monuments, is the showpiece of newly built East Berlin; a uranium clock, surrounded by fountains, tells the time in all parts of the world.

Last stop on your tour will likely be the Soviet cemetery at Treptow, another monolithic construction built with marble taken from Hitler's Reich Chancellery, among other places. On either side of a broad avenue leading to a massive figure of a Russian soldier are bas-reliefs in white stone portraying episodes of World War II and interpreted by commentaries in Russian and German. Guides the world over are not noted for their historical accuracy and you may find local interpretations of this place unconventional. However, the propaganda is cooling somewhat; and remember, it's because all this is still comparatively recent history that one reacts to it. Abominable insults and inaccuracies are bandied about concerning older wars (cold and hot) and only historians will notice, or care. This monument is as depressing as most.

East Berlin has well over a million inhabitants, but never looks more than half full; of these, a goodly proportion look foreign, and are. Berlin, deep in the lowlands of East Germany, with big lakes and forests (Spreewald) extending right to the municipal area, is industrial, as well as cultural and administrative. One quarter of each of the total production in the fields of electrical engineering, printing, and clothing happens here.

The Brandenburger Tor, landmark of the former German capital and later the East-West crossing point, has been restored to its former state, complete with gilded Quadriga—the two-wheeled chariot drawn by four stallions. It dominates Unter den Linden which leads down to Marx-Engels-Platz and Karl-Marx-Allee, with its many new buildings, some borrowed in inspiration from Russian neo-academism. This 300-foot-wide and 2-mile-long avenue certainly is *kolossal,* even though dominated by the TV tower, 1,187 feet high and offering the best view over the city.

The famous Pergamon Altar and the Market Gate of Milet are on display at the Pergamon Museum, whose collection of ancient cultural monuments of the Near East is surpassed only by those of the Louvre and the British Museum.

Berlin is a theater town *par excellence,* with 13 theaters, including the famous State Opera. Famous too are the productions by Dr. Felsenstein at the Comic Opera, which opened its magnificent new building in 1966. There is operetta at the Metropol Theater. Near the Brecht theater on Schiffbauerdamm is Schumannstrasse is the German Theater with the Kammerspielen where Max Reinhardt once worked. Among the theater companies is the Berliner Ensemble, where the late Helene Weigel carried on the traditions which were begun by her husband, Berthold Brecht.

Trips from Berlin include traveling by boat on the canals in the Spreewald. This is enchanting, and local costume is often worn by the Sorb minority (Slavs) living here. Regional dishes are to be found at Zum Fröhlichen Hecht (The Happy Pike) at Lehde and at Zum Grünen Strand der Spree at Lüddenau. The Spree forest is about an hour south of Berlin by car or train and all transport here is by waterway. In Lehde is a museum of typical regional homes and farm buildings with exact replicas of original interiors. At Lübbenau is another dealing with history and folk art of the region.

In addition to trips organized by the Reisebüro DDR, which is responsible for tourism in East Germany, there is a one-day trip to Potsdam twice a week for visitors living in West Berlin. A smallish settlement, Potsdam became a flourishing town in 1660 when the Prince Elector Friedrich Wilhelm decided to build his castle there. A few years later he admitted a large number of Huguenot refugees from France, who introduced many arts and crafts and thus contributed to the town's prosperity. His successors, the Kings of Prussia, of whom Frederick the Great is the best known, embellished Potsdam in the Versailles manner, and left many a gem of baroque architecture. Of the many palaces in Potsdam the finest is *Sans-Souci,* built by Knobelsdorff in 1745. Its Concert Room is the best, but you may also want to see the room where Voltaire lived. Next door is the Picture Gallery, with works by Rubens, Van Dyck and Caravaggio. A side-trip to the Cecilienhof, the 20th-century palace where the Potsdam Agreement was signed by Truman, Stalin, and Churchill in 1945, is worthwhile, although the propaganda about the meaning of the Agreement is inevitably one-sided and fails to make clear that Germany was a pawn, whether she liked it or not, in the power game between the U.S.A. and the U.S.S.R. Lip-service to the U.S.S.R. is endemic throughout East Germany though not from the man-in-the-street.

Potsdam, an hour from Berlin by car or train, has over a million inhabitants, a considerable industry, predominantly metallurgy, vehicle production and electronics. The surroundings are densely forested and the river Havel flows through a number of its beautiful, unspoiled lakes.

Dresden and Saxon Switzerland

Splendidly situated on the banks of the Elbe, Dresden can be visited briefly on a day trip leaving once a week. Though the city was the capital of Saxony as early as the 15th century, its architectural masterpieces, heavily damaged during the war and now restored, date from the 18th century. The most outstanding baroque buildings are the Zwinger Palace, the Opera House, the Cathedral, with a fine Silbermann organ, and the National Gallery, which once again houses a unique collection of paintings. The Picture Gallery in the Semper Building of the Zwinger Palace complex is one of the most highly concentrated exhibits of magnificence in the world. In addition to its most famous masterpiece, Raphael's *Sistine Madonna,* there are 12 Rembrandts, 16 Rubens and 5 Tintorettos, to mention only a few of the masters. In short, for Italian and Dutch paintings of the 16th and 17th centuries, few museums can match the Zwinger collection. There are over 20 museums. Combine your visit with the cable-car trip to Weisser Hirsch, a hill overlooking the city, where you can dine at the famed Luisenhof restaurant. From the TV tower, where there is a café, there is a splendid view to the Albrechtsburg Castle in Meissen. including the Karl May Foundation's Red Indian Museum, illustrating the history of the North American Indians.

The Zwinger apart, you have to look fairly hard for reminders of Dresden's former architectural glory, but indicative of this and the modern concept of town planning is a walk through Weisse Gasse where the statue of the Goose Thief (Gänsedieb) stands, Webergasse, now a shopping center and Gewandhausstrasse with its Children's Frieze (Kinderfries). Prager Strasse connects new with old Dresden and leads to the arcades of the Altmarkt, through baroque Schlossstrasse with its expertly restored Georgentor and over the Dimitroff Bridge to the right bank of the Elbe.

A short trip down-river brings us to the city of Meissen, famed for its porcelain. Its castle and late-Gothic cathedral (an excellent Cranach in the latter) are vivid reminders of the town's ancient history. Halfway, a few miles inland, the baroque Moritzburg Castle, former hunting lodge of the Saxon kings, houses a fine museum. Turning upstream by river boat, you can enjoy the scenery of flat-topped sandstone mountains rising steeply from both banks of the meandering Elbe, sometimes to a height of 1,300 feet. The most impressive of all hills is the Lilienstein, opposite the fortress-town of Königstein. Bad Schandau, near the Czechoslovak border, is the most important tourist center of the region.

Leipzig, Trade Center

As a center of the printing and book trade, as well as of the European fur trade, Leipzig acquired world renown soon after the Napoleonic Wars. One of the greatest battles, which led to the Emperor's fall, was fought here in 1813, commemorated by the ponderous Völker-Schlachts-Denkmal. Richard Wagner was born here in 1813 and was molded by a long-established musical tradition which boasts such names as the Gewandhaus Orchestra, founded in 1781, and the St. Thomas Church Boys' Choir, closely associated with Johann Sebastian Bach. Astride great trade routes, Leipzig became an important market town in the early Middle Ages. Thus the scene was set for the twice yearly Trade Fair (March and September) which has brought together exhibitors and buyers from all over the world for more than half a century. Today the Fair is the most important single meeting place of East and West for commerce and industry. Little is left of old Leipzig, but among the places to see are—the 12th-century market place, with Renaissance Town Hall and now housing Town Museum, which possesses valuable documents about Leipzig, including a diorama of the Battle of Nations (1813). You can go through a gateway in the Town Hall to the Nasch Market, Leipzig's most famous square, formed by the façade of the 17th-century Old Trade Exchange.

There are many associations with Goethe in Leipzig—he was a student here—and also with Johann Sebastian Bach, notably the Thomas Church, originally the center of a 13th-century monastery and rebuilt in the 15th century. This church, with its tall Gothic roof over the nave, is Bach's burial place. Today it is still the center of Bach tradition in Germany and the home of the Thomaner Choir. More Gothic ecclesiastical architecture in the early 16th-century Paulinen Church. You can walk through it—it's the sole remnant of a 13th-century Dominican cloister.

Of recent vintage are the New Opera House in Karl-Marx-Platz, and the enormous sports stadium. Train-lovers will like to know that here is Europe's largest station—26 platforms. But train-spotters beware, your motives may be misunderstood, especially when taking photographs.

Today Leipzig has the biggest German-language library, hosts the International Book Art Exhibition, and trains personnel in book production. Book production goes with music and art production too. Also printed here, and exported, are seven million packs of playing cards per year.

Fur processing, from East German mink and fox, and fur auctions are still important features. Most enterprising, though, is the successful breeding and export of wild animals, including lions (particularly), then bears, hyenas and Siberian tigers.

In Gohlis, a Leipzig suburb, stands a small farmhouse, now a museum, which tells you that Schiller wrote his "Ode to Freedom" here in 1785. Gohlis Castle, set behind a magnificent wrought-iron gate in a fine park, was a meeting place for Leipzig's intellectual and artistic world under Goethe's teacher, Böhme. Today it houses the Bach Archives. Close-by is the Zoo, where they breed animals for export. Southwest, and following the Martin-Luther-Ring, stands the Georgi Dimitroff Museum, the Supreme Court of the Reich from 1895 to 1945. In the Great Hall in 1933 the Dimitroff (Reichstag Fire) trial took place. Dimitroff was the leader of the Bulgarian Communist Party. Behind this museum is the music center of Leipzig, focused on the Gewandhaus. Southwest of Leipzig, German and Russian troops defeated Napoleon in the 1813 Battle of Nations, and the inevitable monument is there.

Other excursions that can be made from Leipzig are to Lutherstadt Wittenberg, Halle, Eisleben, Namburg and Altenburg.

Lutherstadt Wittenberg, is the center of the German Reformation, whose history is exhibited in the early 16th-century monastery of the Augustines and former residence of Luther. Humanist Philipp Melanchthon was born in a Renaissance house here and in the Town Church, Wittenberg's oldest building (14th and 15th centuries), are paintings by Cranach (the Elder), and Vischer, better known as a contemporary of Dürer's in Nürnberg. Luther and Melanchthon are buried in the 15th-century Schlosskirche (Castle Church), totally destroyed in the Seven Years War and rebuilt only in the 19th century. From the tower you have a fine view of the old town and its narrow streets. Statues to the two men stand in front of the 16th-century Town Hall.

Halle is the birthplace of Händel (statue in the market place). His house is an important musical instrument museum, spanning five centuries.

At Eisleben there is a wry piece of history. On August Bebel Square is Lenin's statue, said to have been stolen from Leningrad by the Fascists in 1944. Why, one wonders? Anyway, the anti-Fascists, whoever they were, saved it from destruction and as a thank you and to show how much they valued it, the Soviets off-loaded it on to Eisleben. You might think this dramatic gesture ended the matter. But no, the East Germans came up with a reprisal by sending the Soviets a monument of the East German Communist leader Ernst Thälmann. Seriously, this town is the birth and death place of Martin Luther.

Further trips can be made to the medieval towns of Naumburg and Altenburg—where they make playing cards and where the Castle Museum has a collection of playing cards.

Harz Mountains

The Harz is the best known of mountain districts in central Germany. Delightful surroundings help to enhance the medieval character of Wernigerode, dominated by a feudal castle. The thousand-year-old Quedlinburg is now a dreamy little town, with its half-timbered houses, winding lanes and its outsize cathedral. Accommodations are very limited and it may be advisable to stay at the Magdeburg Interhotel and make excursions from there. Magdeburg has Germany's first Gothic cathedral, some fine baroque buildings, and several theaters, including a puppet theater.

From here one can also visit the timber-framed houses of Halberstadt. Thale is best reached via Quedlinburg and the Devils' Wall. Thale's surroundings include the beautiful Bode valley, the witches' dancing place (Hexentanzplatz) and the Harz mountain theater, also accessible by cable railway. So on to Rübeland with stalactite caves, and Stolberg in the southern Harz with fine renaissance houses, baroque castle and museum.

Thuringia

This region, 100 km long and between 10 and 35 km wide, lies at the most southwesterly point in East Germany, vying with the Harz (to the north) and Erzgebirge (east) in sheer unspoiled, undeveloped wooded mountain slopes, forests, clear streams, rare plants, and traditional craftsmanship, notably glass and wooden toys. Walkers will enjoy particularly the Schwarztal, Inselberg and Rennsteig regions; the air is the most remarkably heady in all Germany. At the two extremities of the Thüringer Wald lie two historic cities: Eisenach and Saalfeld, the latter with the most beautiful stalactite caves in East Germany—really fairytale grottos. Eisenach is dominated by the 900-year-old Wartburg Castle, mentioned in many a German legend. Here minstrels like Tannhäuser, Walter von der Vogelweide and Wolfram von Eschenbach sang of noble lords and lovely ladies. During the stormy days of the Reformation it served as a refuge for Martin Luther, who translated the New Testament into German here in 1521.

Bach was born in Eisenach in 1685; and incidentally the Wartburg car is manufactured here. Further east, Erfurt, seemingly untouched by history, remains one of the finest of German cities, with its cathedral and the church of St. Severin, its matchless Gothic and German

Renaissance houses, and its 600-year-old bridge, with 33 houses built
on it. Erfurt has long been associated with flowers and there is a
summer horticultural show (of plants from Communist countries) in
the grounds of Cyriak Castle.

Only a few miles away, Weimar retains the atmosphere of the old
residential town of German princes. Lucas Cranach lived and worked
here. Its greatest period came at the turn of the 18th century when
Goethe, Schiller, Wieland and Herder, giants of the era of German
humanism, made this town famous in the realms of literature and
philosophy. Later on, Böcklin and Lenbach founded the Weimar
school of painters here. For historical significance, true peace and
graciousness, Weimar is unsurpassed in East Germany.

Among the interesting places to visit are—Goethe's residence in
Frauenplanstrasse, and his summer house in the beautiful park on the
Ilm; the Dower Palace of the Duchess Anna-Amalia; Schiller's house
opposite the Gänsemännchen (Little Goose Boy) well; his and Goethe's
vault; the Liszt Museum; the Herder Church with Cranach Altar. This
is a town where history can be observed and felt, unimpeded, for the
most part, by contemporary comment.

That is more than can be said for Buchenwald, the Nazis' terrible
concentration camp a little to the north, on the Ettersberg. This is not
a place for the over-sensitive and the horror endured by the 56,000
people murdered here is made no easier on the eye and mind by the
whitewashing messages purporting that the blame for these vile camps
must really be laid at the West German door alone. The wretched
victims are loosely described as anti-Fascist, which they most probably
were. But mostly they were Jews, and that is why they were there.
Today the almost total absence of Jews in East Germany makes it
currently easier for authorities to observe racial tolerance within its
boundaries.

Near Weimar are Apolda, with Germany's oldest bell foundry and
bell museum, the 13th-century cathedral town of Naumburg, and Jena,
with its 16th-century university. Schiller was a professor and Karl
Marx wrote his doctor's thesis on philosophy here. Also here is the
Zeiss planetarium which should be visited even if you find this subject
difficult. Gera is a very beautiful patrician and Renaissance town where
one can still see the 16th-century town hall, a 17th-century chemist's
shop, patrician houses spanning four centuries (1500–1900) and fine
botanical gardens and orangery. Several castles are nearby: the 600-
year-old Osterburg at Weida and the 1000-year-old Ranis Castle.

Oberhof, a year-round resort, is the tourist center of Thuringia and
in winter the scene of bobsled and toboggan runs, skating and skiing.
Suhl is the capital of the Thuringian Forest, known for gun manufac-

ture for four centuries. Suhl country comes second only to that of the Baltic coast for popularity as an East German holiday region.

Christmas decoration fanatics should visit the glass-blowing town of Lauscha, home of such delights—three centuries of the glass industry are celebrated in the museum.

The Erzgebirge

This most powerfully dramatic, wooded mountain landscape forms a natural barrier with Czechoslovakia and is idyllic for walkers and motorists, both rejoicing to find even less traffic than elsewhere in East Germany.

Karl-Marx Stadt is the principal city. Badly damaged in World War II it is long since re-established as a center for heavy industry, turning out modern automatic weaving machines and everything to do with the knitting, spinning and calico printing industries, plus bicycle manufacture. If you have to be here—and most people prefer the countryside—there is a 250-million-year-old petrified tree trunk in front of the Textile Museum on Theaterplatz.

The Schlosskirche and Schlossberg museum are nice to look at, likewise the Siegert House with its carefully restored baroque facade. Of the former 25 medieval military towers only the Rote Turm still stands today. There are also some fine patrician houses but the jewel is the late Gothic cathedral with wooden sculptures and its Silbermann organ from 1714, the oldest of the still existing 31 organs he made. The Golden Door of the Marienkirche, dating from the 13th century is built into the south side of the cathedral.

Freiberg is attractive and still has the remains of its ancient fortifications as well as tiny miner's houses in narrow streets—"Erzgebirge" means "ore mountains." The highest located East German town is hereabouts, Oberwiesenthal, which lies at the foot of the Fichtelberg. Spas, as we have said elsewhere, figure highly in East as in West German recreation and round here they have Bad Brambach and Bad Elster, the latter in a charming parklike setting. Diabetics find this place most helpful.

From Karl-Marx Stadt, mentioned above, you can take a trip to the 800-year-old Burg Rabenstein and the Rabenstein group of rocks, a network of caves hollowed out by mining, with also the remains of a 17th-century castle. Ten km away is Pelzmühle with pleasure steamers and recreation.

At Küchwald is an open-air theater if what is on is understandable to you. The Augustusburg is a formidable Renaissance building, built in 1572 as a hunting center and now houses a museum of the creatures caught in these mountains. In the castle church is an altar painting by

Lucas Cranach the Younger and many people get pleasure from a well here which is 170 meters deep. Water sportsmen head for the Kriebstein Dam 25 km distant, a relaxing area, or to Sachsenring, the international motorcycle race course.

Seiffen, deep in the mountains, is not to be missed: famous, like mountain villages the world over for woodcarving, its toy museum is a joy, as are the workshops of the turners and carvers.

Close to Annaberg in the Sehma valley is the Frohnauer Hammer, an iron processing installation from the 15th century and framework house of the former owner of the forge, today a local art museum with bobbin-lace room. Musicians may know the names Klingenthal and Markneukirchen, for centuries centers for musical instrument manufacture. A large collection of musical instruments is at the museum in Markneukirchen. Annaberg is a bobbin-lace center but was formerly famous for silver mines, long since closed, but there are some houses which indicate local prosperity. The church dates from 1520.

The Baltic (Ostsee)

Crossing the northern lakeland district we soon reach that part of the coast known as Ostsee (German name for the Baltic). Old Hanseatic cities alternate with well-known beach resorts. Largest of East German ports, Rostock lies almost in the geographical center of the coastline. Its architectural unity has been broken by war damage, but there are still several items of interest to see. The Town Hall has seven towers, spanning 13th to 18th centuries. Medieval Rostock can still be seen in the Stone Gate and parts of the old town wall. The Kröpelin Gate is now a museum for local history and important examples of ecclesiastical architecture are Kreuz Church, St. Mary's Church and the 13th-century Nikolai Church. The busy modern harbor is also of interest. The train and car ferry for Denmark (about the cheapest in Europe and thoroughly comfortable) leaves the coast at Warnemünde, one of the best-known seaside resorts.

To the west, Wismar, for nearly two centuries a Swedish possession (1648–1803), gives evidence of old Hanseatic traditions, but architecturally the most enchanting place is Stralsund, with its quaint streets and venerable, red-brick public buildings and churches, fine examples of northern Gothic. Further inland, Schwerin was the seat of the Dukes of Mecklenburg and is typical of the old German provincial capitals, with its stately castle (with lovely silk tapestries in the hall and superb gardens) and opera house. In fact throughout the north of East Germany, right down to Frankfurt/Oder and Potsdam, you meet the red-brick Gothic architecture now so much admired but favored in the Middle Ages solely because of the lack of natural building stone.

Excursions that can be made from Rostock include a trip round the port and boat trips to Hiddensee Island and to the beach at Warnemünde; to Bad Doberan with 14th-century Gothic cathedral and numerous art treasures; narrow gauge railway to seaside resorts of Heiligendamm (the first German bathing resort, established in 1793) and Kühlungsborn. Also to Wismar, second largest seaport with nice 14th-century market square and Alte Schwede burgher house.

Neubrandenburg is another old town with many fine churches, the east gable of one (St. Mary's) being in Gothic brick and in imitation of Strasbourg Cathedral. From here you can make a side trip to Lake Müritz with East Germany's biggest nature reserve on the east bank, excellent for hiking on marked paths.

The woodlands of the Darss Peninsula represent perhaps the last example of primeval forest formations in Europe and were declared a national park some 30 years ago. To the east, the narrow island of Hiddensee was always a favorite summer haunt of artists and bohemians. Gerhart Hauptmann, the playwright, came here every year from the turn of the century and was buried on the island in 1946. The highlight of the coast is Rügen, Germany's largest and most beautiful island. It is dented by hundreds of bays and creeks. The vast Bay of Lietzow, protected from all sides, is ideal for sailing. Chalk cliffs of Stubnitz, 400 feet high, and dropping almost vertically into the sea, are the landmark of Rügen. Of the many fishing villages and beach resorts, Binz is the best known and has some good hotels. The Munich-Berlin-Stockholm train reaches the ferry-boat at Sassnitz. Southwest of Rügen is the island of Usedom, with a string of seaside resorts, some famous, like Heringsdorf and Zinnowitz, some infamous, like Peenemünde, cradle of the World War II V1 and V2 missiles.

PRACTICAL INFORMATION FOR EAST GERMANY

WHAT IT WILL COST. Hotel rates vary according to class, from about $19 to $63 a day per person, covering bed and breakfast. The additional daily charge for full board is $11 or $6 for half board. Food and drink vouchers are obtainable from travel agents, value 5, 10 and 20 marks and are accepted at all Interhotels and official government hotels and are exchangeable at any hour in bars, nightclubs and restaurants. Youth hostels (Western style) cost MDN8 a day for bed, breakfast and one main meal, but official travel agencies abroad have stopped promoting them. [See *Youth Hostels.*] Children aged 2–6 get a 50 percent reduction at all East German hotels if they share the parents' room and take half-size meals. Camp site vouchers cost $14 plus $4 service fee and VAT and part of the money—MDN25—is returned to you for use on food, camping fees, parking charges and other expenses.

SEASONAL EVENTS. The Leipzig Trade Fair (see page 515) is usually held in the first week of March and September; Weimar holds a Shakespeare Festival in April; in July the Hanseatic cities of Rostock and Stralsund stage a week of festivities, known as the Ostseewoche; September/October see the Berlin Music and Drama Festival. Dates may vary slightly, so check when booking.

MONEY. The monetary unit is the mark (Mark der Deutschen Notenbank, or MDN), which is divided into 1,000 pfennigs. There are bills worth 5, 10, 20, 5, and 100 marks; coins are issued in the denominations of 20, 10, 5, 2 and 1 mark; 50, 20, 10, 5 and 1 pfennig. Present exchange rate is *approx.* MDN 2.30 to the dollar, about MDN 4.72 to the pound sterling, but subject to change.

Foreign currency may be imported unlimited into the German Democratic Republic on declaration subject to the foreign exchange regulations of the countries concerned. The import of banknotes and coins of the GDR is not permitted. For private visitors from non-communist foreign countries the obligation exists to change currency in the equivalent of—MDN13—per person and day of stay. This mimimal amount is not re-changeable, i.e. this money must be spent. Diners Club and American Express credit cards are now accepted by many restaurants, shops, car-rental firms and hotels.

HOW TO GO. Be prepared for minute attention to detail and formality from the East German authorities. Having planned your itinerary, go see your travel agent. He will need to know your passport number, surname, forename, age, profession, address, and nationality. He will then send these, together with a request for hotel reservations, to the Reisebüro DDR, the official East German travel organization. As soon as he receives confirmation of the hotel reservations, he will issue you with a hotel voucher. With your voucher and a valid passport, you can enter East Germany. Visas are issued at entry point on arrival. Prepaid booking and reservation is still the practice and visas are issued only for the number of days you pay for. Two agencies in the U.S. with much experience in dealing with travel to East Germany are *Koch* and *Maupintour* (addresses below). It usually takes from 6–8 weeks to get a GDR visa, and the fee is $25.00. For "express handling" (about 5 weeks) the fee is $30.00. All bookings must be completed and in the hands of the Reisebüro at least 21 days before your arrival in the GDR.

Transit visas for a stay of up to 72 hours are issued at certain entry points, but accommodation must be booked and paid for at the same time. Direct transit visas for road travel (without an overnight stop) can be obtained at stated frontier points against payment of visa fee, road tolls.

Hotel booking can be effected in Berlin at the Reisebüro DDR, Alexander-platz 5; at Berlin-Schönefeld Airport, or through authorized travel organizations abroad, such as: *Koch,* 206 East 86 St., New York, N.Y. 10028; *Maupintour,* 900 Massachusetts St., Lawrence, Kansas 66044 and other cities. *Travelworld,* 6922 Hollywood Blvd., Los Angeles, CA., runs East German along with other East European trips. *Berolina Travel Ltd.,* 20 Conduit Street, London W.1., the representative in Britain for the Reisebüro DDR, will make reservations. Lists of British agents dealing with East Germany can be obtained there. For a £2 fee Berolina will handle the whole operation. Or, travelers may take their hotel vouchers and passport to the Consular Section of the East German Embassy, 34 Belgrave Sq., London S.W.1. to obtain a visa, which costs £4.10. In the U.S., the East German Embassy is at 1717 Massachusetts Ave., N.W., Washington, D.C. 20036; however, the Embassy refers visa applications to such authorized travel agents as *Koch.*

Note: Business people traveling to East Germany frequently and at short notice sometimes experience delay in obtaining hotel vouchers before receiving visas. Note that visas are granted at any of the Eastern sector entry points at Berlin to travelers holding written confirmation for hotels Metropol or Palast in Berlin. No vouchers are required, clients settle accounts direct with hotel. Reservations can be made through Supernational Reservations in London or Interhotel in East Berlin, tel. (2) 220–4281.

Apart from *Berolina* in London there are in Western Europe three other offices of the *Travel Representation of the German Democratic Republic.* They are: in Sweden at: 10122 Stockholm 1, Kungsgatan 30 III/Box 197; in Denmark at: 1620 Copenhagen V, Vesterbrogade 84; and in Austria at: 1011 Vienna 1, Brandstätte 1.

GETTING TO EAST GERMANY

BY AIR. From New York there is direct service to East Berlin's Schönefeld Airport by *Aeroflot Soviet Airlines, Czechoslovak Airlines* and *LOT Polish Airlines. LOT* also flies there directly from London, Paris, Brussels, and Amsterdam. The airport is about 15 miles from central Berlin, a 40-min. bus ride, cost 30pf., also for metro; by taxi, MDN25. For transit travelers an hourly coach service leaves Schönefeld airport for the Helios travel agency and the Radio Tower Bus Station in West Berlin, and vice versa. Fare: DM (West) 5.00. *Interflug,* the East German national airline offers direct connections from Amsterdam, Copenhagen, Helsinki and Vienna in Western Europe; from thirteen cities of Eastern Europe; from Nicosia, Beirut, Cairo, in the Near East; as well as from Havana, Hanoi, Bagdad and other less-frequented centers. *Pan American, British Airways* and *Air France* are the only airlines authorized to fly into West Berlin's main airport, from which you can cross into East Berlin.

BY TRAIN. There are through coaches to East Berlin from Paris, Ostend, Hook of Holland, Basel, and, of course, from all the large West German cities. Trains are frequent, fast and comfortable. Western rail frontiers: Herrnburg, Schwanheide, Oebisfelde, Marienborn, Gerstungen, Probstzella and Gutenfürst, at all of which entry and transit visas can be obtained.

Some of the best-known international trains to come through East Germany are the Vindobona (Berlin-Prague-Vienna), the Spree Alpen Express (Berlin-Innsbruch-Villach), Sassnitz Express (Stockholm-Berlin-Munich) and Moscow Express (Berlin-Warsaw-Moscow).

Alternatively, you may be given a pass and instructed to collect your visa at your first destination point. The Reisebüro will fix this for you.

BY CAR. There are twenty-two road-crossing points into East Germany, including Hirschberg (Munich-Hof-Berlin Autobahn); at Marienborn (Hannover-Berlin); at Wartha (Frankfurt/Main-Eisenach); and at Horst bei Boizenburg (Hamburg-Berlin, no. 5 highway); Selsmdorf (from Lübeck to Schwerin). You may also enter or transit coming from Denmark (Gedser-Warnemünde car ferry) or Sweden (Trelleborg-Sassnitz ferry). Another auto-route is open for Scandinavia-bound transit motorists from Lübeck to these two ports. There is a road toll.

VISITING EAST BERLIN FROM WEST BERLIN. Foreign nationals may enter East Berlin from Checkpoint Charlie at the corner of Friedrichstrasse and Zimmerstrasse. The checkpoint is open to all those in possession of a valid passport. (Permit for sojourn DM 5,-.) Do not take East marks or West newspapers with you. It is an East Sector requirement that all currency be declared upon entry, and all expenditures made in East Berlin be accounted for on departure. All foreign nationals, except those taking one of the official sightseeing tours, are required to exchange a minimum of DM 6.50 at a rate 1 to 1. East marks beyond this amount may be changed back into other currencies when you leave East Berlin. You are not allowed to take surplus East marks with you.

East Berlin may also be entered by taking the subway from Zoo (Schlesisches Tor line) changing at Hallesches Tor (Tegel line) to Friedrich Strasse. Foreigners must have left Berlin by midnight, and must also return through the same Checkpoint. (See *West Berlin* for tour information.)

CUSTOMS. Customs officials are courteous. Generally you can take in any article for personal use but articles of value such as cameras or musical instruments must be declared at the frontier. You can also take in 250 grams (8 ounces of tobacco, 1 liter of spirits, 2 liters of wine, and personal gifts up to MDN500 (prices computed by GDR standards). On leaving the country gifts and articles purchased up to the value of MDN100 can be taken out duty free.

Currency Regulations: There is no limit to the amount of foreign currency tourists may bring into East Germany but they must declare it on a special form to be shown when leaving the country. Do not try nor be persuaded to change foreign money on the black market, as penalties are severe. No East German marks may be taken in or out.

East Germany, like other East European countries, has two basic rates of exchange—trade and tourist. The latter is kept artificially high vis à vis western visitors as a source of much needed hard currency. Most favorable tourist rates of exchange are to be found outside East Europe. Switzerland and Hong Kong tend to offer best rates, but banks in western Europe and non-Communist Asia offer East European currencies at a discount on the official tourist rate. Look for a rate about one-third of the officially quoted tourist rate inside East Germany. Black market exchange rates are often good but there is a risk of the dealer being a police informer. Be wary of touts if heading by car for Poland. They flag you down and try to sell Polish currency, which is weak against the East German mark and the differential between the black and official rate is 300%! They trade Polish money against East German marks at 1/20 though the official rate is 1/4.

TRAVELING IN EAST GERMANY

BY CAR. There are nearly 1,000 miles of motorway and nearly 7,000 miles of trunk roads. Generally they are in a good state of repair. Gasoline (petrol) and oil may be obtained at reduced prices against coupons value MDN5, 10 and 20, which you can purchase at official agencies abroad, frontier crossing points, and some Reisebüro (travel agency) city branches.

A liter of gasoline (petrol) up to 96 octane costs MDN0.88 with petrol coupons; without, it costs MDN1.50–1.65. Always carry an international driving license. Speed limit: autobahns, 100 kilometers per hour (63 m.p.h.); other roads 90 kilometers per hour (55 m.p.h.); built-up areas 50 kilometers per hour (31 m.p.h.). Foreign cars pay a Road Users' Tax *(Strassenbenützungsgebühr),* about MDN5.00, 15.00, 20.00 or 25.00 for up to 200km, 300km, 400km, or 500km respectively. Tolls are payable in foreign currency.

Minol denotes motorway filling stations, and *Mitropa* service stations, which are also sometimes motels. Drink-and-drive is strictly forbidden.

Car hire. Cars may be booked through the official tourist agencies or your local travel agent, or the Rent-a-Car service at any Interhotel. They can be collected at one place and left at another, and can be used for excursions into Czechoslovakia and Poland. The Lada 2101 costs $15.12 daily, $88.56 weekly, the Lada 2103 $19.44 daily, $108 weekly; the Fiat 1315 costs $25.92 daily, $136.08 weekly; the Renault 18TL costs $28.08 daily, $149.04 weekly and the Fiat 132 costs $32.40 daily, $168.48 weekly. For the first two add 21¢ per km, for the last three 31¢.

AUTOBAHN MOTELS: There are well-equipped motels at Sassnitz (the *Rügen*) with 275 beds, at Hermsdorfer Kreuz in the south, to the west of Karl-Marx Stadt, 46 beds; at Berlin-Schönefeld airport, 110 beds; Meissen, 35 beds; Magdeburg-Börde, 40 beds; and Usadel, near Neubrandenburg, 100 beds.

DRINK/DRIVE: On the spot fines are imposed just for entering a car after leaving a bar at closing time. Leave earlier but if you are ever challenged and cannot easily persuade police that you are not in an unfit state to drive pay up: MDN 400–500.

BY TRAIN, UNDERGROUND, BUS AND BOAT. The U-Bahn (underground) is operated by the West Berlin authorities and the S-Bahn (district and local railway) by the East Berlin authorities, although both run in each sector. Fares are inexpensive. Local trains in East Germany are also moderately priced, as are the buses. Supplementary fares are required on certain express services. Taxis in East Germany are also moderately priced although not always easy to obtain.

The *Weisse Flotte* (White Fleet) boats ply on rivers and lakes in summer.

BY AIR. Berlin (Schönefeld) is connected with Dresden, Leipzig, Erfurt, and the two Baltic resorts of Barth and Heringsdorf by the national airline, Interflug.

TOURS. The Reisebüro DDR organizes several group tours, as well as making inclusive arrangements for individuals; special-interest tours cover railway tours, health spas, farming, riding, and so on, and last 3 to 12 days. For instance, Dresden, Spree Forest, Berlin, Potsdam, Rostock and Warnemünde on the Baltic coast, Leipzig, Naumburg, Erfurt, Weimar, Halle, Wernigerode, Karl-Marx Stadt and Meissen lasts 12 days and costs around $430. This includes flight from London and half board accommodations (breakfast and lunch). These tours are in July and August. Do try to take the minimum of luggage as porters in some places are evidently an extinct breed.

Shorter trips cover Berlin, Potsdam, Cottbus (Spreewald and center of Sorb culture, a Slav minority) in 3 days or Berlin, Dresden, Meissen, Leipzig in 4 days, costing from $105 and $120, half board accommodation and coach only).

In 7 days one can have Berlin, Dresden, Meissen, Leipzig, Weimar, Erfurt, Eisenach, Potsdam.

Special interest tours center on famous galleries (4 days $140), Bach and Handel (6 days, $155), Gottfried Silbermann, the organ maker (6 days costs $170), also classical German literature. These are on full-board accomodation basis and there are others.

Four days around Rostock, Warnemunde, Stralsund and Rügen island costs $95, 4 days in Spreewald, Cottbus and Dresden costs the same; 6 in Thuringia (Berlin, Weimar, Eisenach, Arnstadt, Rudolfstadt and Saalfeld) cost $165; 5 days in Berlin, Dresden and Meissen costs from $160. You need at least this amount of time to appreciate these places.

A week in Oberhof in the Thuringian Forest at the Ernst Thälmann Hotel costs $145. Oberhof is particularly a winter sports resort and Thälmann was the East German Communist party leader murdered in Buchenwald concentration camp which will almost certainly be part of a visit if you are anywhere near Weimar.

Ask for details and fix bookings for these trips through your travel agency: Koch or Maupintour in the U.S., or through Berolina Travel, 20 Conduit Street London, W1. Services of an English/German speaking guide are of course included and they use the best hotels *i.e.* most modern facilities.

From West Berlin: Foreigners touring West Berlin may now visit Potsdam, East Berlin, Dresden, and Karl-Marx-Stadt and so long as there is a minimum of 15 persons, autobus excursions are offered on a per person basis: afternoon and full day trips go to Potsdam· full-day excursions to Karl-Marx-Stadt and to Dresden. Groups of 25 or more can go any time by mutual agreement. Bookings are accepted by the *Deutsches Reisebüro,* Berlin W 30, Kurfürstendamm 17, up to 6 P.M. two days before excursion date, and by the principal hotels. There are several inclusive weekends available at Hotel Metropol in East Berlin, including pick-up from Tegel (West Berlin) airport, from $157.

Visitors from West to East Berlin get passes at the road crossing point (Friedrichstrasse-Zimmerstrasse) or the Friedrichstr. station if coming by underground or suburban railway. You must change DM6.50 (about $3) into East German marks.

STAYING IN EAST GERMANY

 HOTELS AND RESTAURANTS. Berlin (East) Hotels: The most luxurious of all East Berlin hotels is the
Palast, the most expensive hotel in East Germany and
situated close to the Palace of the Republic, the shop-
ping area of Alexanderplatz, the island museums. It accommodates 1,000 guests
in 600 air-conditioned rooms or suites. Restaurants include one French and one
Asian, Berlin coffee-house, grill room and even a traditional Berlin pub. Indoor
pool, sauna, gymnasium, bowling alley. *Avis* and *Hertz* car rentals are here too.

Stadt Berlin Interhotel, Alexanderplatz, 40 stories high, 2,000 beds with
private facilities, TV, and radio, several restaurants, underground parking with
servicing and repairs, travel agency bank, shop, sauna, hairdresser.

Metropol, Friedrichstrasse, 700 beds, indoor pool, solarium, sauna, every
possible facility and service including arranging sightseeing tours throughout
East Germany.

Berolina Interhotel, Karl-Marx-Allee 31, 677 beds, all with private facilities,
radio and, in the doubles, TV; restaurants, roof garden with service in summer,
currency exchange shop, attended parking.

Unter den Linden Interhotel, 400 beds, all with private facilities, radio and
TV, restaurant, theater and nightclub reservations, shop, parking.

Newa, much cheaper and has no rooms with bath.

Restaurants: *Ganymed,* Friedrichstr., international cuisine, book in advance.
Moskau, Haus Budapest, and *Café Warschau,* with bar and dancing, are on
Karl-Marx-Allee; *Telecafé* restaurant, 600 feet up in TV tower; *Operncafé,* once
the Princesses Palace and with elegant décor, with music and dancing.

Also the *Linden-Corso, Ratskeller,* historic setting in basement of Town Hall;
Raabe Diele, authentic Berlin dishes in cellar of 18th-century Ermeler House
Märkisches Ufer (old town).

Nightlife: *Opern Café, Moskau,* 37th floor of *Hotel Stadt Berlin, Sofia, Takay-
er Keller, Linden-Corso.*

DRESDEN. Hotels: Top grade: *Newa Interhotel,* Leningrader Str. 34, at the
main station, 640 beds all with private facilities, bar, restaurants *Leningrad* and
Baltic, international cuisine, dancing, shop, parking, and garages. Tantalizingly,
they offer, too, their Repin and Pushkin salons which have "variable formation
possibilities," so they say. Any reader putting this offer to the test should let us
know the results!

Interhotel Astoria, Ernst Thälmann Platz 1, 114 beds and similar facilities,
plus extensive car services. Located between trunk roads nos. 170 and 172.

Motel Dresden, on outskirts, 274 beds, restaurant, Interhotel shop, filling
station.

Good quality: *Prager Strasse Interhotel* with the Bastei, Königstein, and Lilienstein houses, 1,500 beds, similar facilities. *Gewandhaus* (hotel garni), some rooms with private facilities.

Adequate: *Waldpark*, no rooms with private facilities.

Restaurants: *Luisenhof*, reached by cable car, above the city and with views over the Elbe. *Szeged*, good Hungarian cuisine. *Radeberger Bierkeller; Café Prag*, at the TV tower.

In **Meissen** the *Vincenz Richter* restaurant is agreeable and in the vicinity of Moritzburg the historic *Waldschänke* and *Räuberhütte* are worth a visit.

EISENACH. Hotels: Good quality: *Stadt Eisenach*, some rooms with private facilities; *Parkhotel;* and adequate *Thüringer Hof*, but no private facilities.

ERFURT. Hotels: Top grade: *Erfurter Hof Interhotel*, Am Bahnhofsvorplatz, 350 beds, all rooms with private facilities, radio and TV; good restaurants, bars, nightclub, wine cellar, cafés with dancing. *Kosmos* Interhotel, huge hotel with disco, 3 restaurants, bars and panoramic view.

Good quality: *Tourist*, all rooms with private facilities.

GERA. Hotel: *International Stadt Gera*, with Thuringian specialties in the restaurant.

JENA. Hotel: *International*, moderate.

KARL-MARX STADT. Hotels: *Kongress*, some 30 stories high, massive, slab-like, all international facilities, all right for businessmen; *Moskau*, less daunting and cheaper; *Chemnitzer Hof*, old style and moderate.

Restaurants in the region: *Oberwiesenthal* has plenty of eating choice on the summit of the Fichtelberg. *Annaberg* has the *Wilder Mann* with local specialties and the *Frohnauer Hammer*, formerly a forge-owner's house.

KÜHLUNGSBORN. Hotel: *Robert Koch*. A week's holiday here, on the tideless Baltic coast, nice sandy beaches, costs £73 ($160.60), full-board accommodation.

LEIPZIG. Hotels: Top-grade, *Astoria Interhotel*, Platz der Republik, 556 beds, private facilities, TV and ice-box if required, restaurants, good service and cuisine, dancing, shop, hairdressing, parking. Very comfortable and furnished in good taste. Similarly the brand new *Merkur*.

Am Ring (formerly Deutschland Interhotel), Karl-Marx-Platz, 512 beds, similar facilities, plus garden with fountain. *Stadt Leipzig Interhotel*, Richard Wagner Str. 1–5, 570 beds, similar facilities. *International Interhotel*, Troendlinring 8, 155 beds, similar facilities.

Good quality: *Interhotel Zum Löwen*, Breitscheidstr., 174 beds, cheerful, pleasant and with similar facilities, if slightly less opulent; more practical.

Adequate: *Parkhotel.*

At **Halle,** 22 miles away, is the *Interhotel Stadt Halle,* 410 beds, all rooms with bath, excellent, and at **Lutherstadt Wittenberg** there is a simple hotel (no private facilities), the *Goldener Adler.* Try the restaurant in the castle.

Restaurants: Famous *Auerbach's Keller,* 16th-century locale of a scene in Goethe's *Faust; Zum Kaffeebaum,* also historic; *Falstaff.*

Panorama, above university in Karl-Marx Platz; *Stadt Dresden, Ringcafe, Cafe an Brühl,* all close by but reserve if possible.

Stadt Kiev is inexpensive (MDN 20–30 for two including wine and schnapps); *Plovdiv* is Bulgarian and moderate; *Moderna* is Cuban (MDN 40–50 for 2); *Gastmahl des Meeres,* seafood and found in other cities, costs more:MDN 180 for two.

Game is a specialty at the *Altes Kloster* in the center. If it's busy, tip about DM5.

Nightlife: There are some six nightclubs: *Intermezzo, Tivoli* and *Orion* have a band and good Cuban floorshow. Cost: about MDN200 for 4 with food and Russian champagne. It may be necessary to arrive at 8 P.M. to reserve a table. Do this through the head waiter *never* the manager who is to be avoided. Tip headwaiter DM5 on arrival. Appreciate and seek his advice and tip around $6 when leaving.

NEUBRANDENBURG. Hotel: *Zu den Vier Toren,* looking to town walls, moderate, with restaurant.

OBERHOF. Hotel: Top grade: *Panorama Interhotel,* Theo-Neubauerstr., whose twin buildings are designed to look like a ski jump; 900 beds, all rooms with private facilities, TV, ice-box; several bars and restaurants, nightclub, children's playroom (with teacher), gymnasium, sauna, swimming, bowling, volley ball, table tennis; and unusual feature of rambles first thing in the morning. Winter sleigh rides are popular, lighted by torch at night.

POTSDAM. Hotels: Top grade, *Interhotel Potsdam,* 17-story hotel beside the water, 400 beds, all rooms with private facilities, radio, and TV; shop, restaurants, grill-bar and self-service. Water sports facilities.

Good quality, the *Cecilienhof,* some rooms with private facilities. One week's full board accommodation costs £79 ($173.80).

ROSTOCK. Hotels and Restaurants: Top grade: *Warnow Interhotel,* Lange Str., 558 beds, all rooms with private facilities, TV sets in apartments, or on request, restaurants, nightclub, bars, shop, parking, and garages with servicing. Clay pigeon shooting and horse-riding arranged. Try local Mecklenburg dishes in the restaurant; and visit the old *Teepott* restaurant in the old lighthouse.

Adequate, but with no private facilities, *Hotel Am Bahnhof* (at station).

SASSNITZ. Hotel: Top grade: *Rugen Hotel,* 277 beds, all rooms with private facilities; restaurants and cafes, sauna, roof garden, pool.

SCHWERIN. Hotels: Top grade: *Stadt Schwerin,* all rooms with bath. Adequate: *Hotel Polonia,* some rooms with private facilities.

STRALSUND. Hotels: Adequate: *Bahnhofshotel* and *Baltic,* few rooms with private facilities.

SUHL. Hotel: Top grade: *Thüringen Tourist Interhotel,* Ernst-Thälmann-Platz, 184 beds, all doubles with shower, all apartments with TV, balcony and bath; restaurants, cafés, nightclub, hairdresser, parking, garage and servicing.

WARNEMÜNDE. Hotels: Top grade: *Neptun,* 715 beds, all rooms with private facilities and overlooking the ocean, with balcony, restaurants, bars, two pools, one with real waves, numerous sporting facilities, massage, library, hairdresser, shop, parking with servicing—the most comprehensive and modern hotel in East Germany, and open year-round.
First class: *Warnow.*

WEIMAR. Hotels: Top grade: *Elephant Interhotel,* Am Markt 19, where Goethe, Schiller, Herder, Wagner, Liszt—and Hitler—stayed. Vastly modernized (hardly surprising, since it was founded in 1696); 170 beds, all rooms with private facilities, several restaurants, bars, garden with terrace, nightclub, shop.
Restaurant: *Zum Weissen Schwan,* historic inn.

ZINNOWITZ. Hotel: *Philip Müller.* Acceptable moderate like *Koch* (see Kühlungsborn). Same price for full-board accommodation. Good beaches, swimming, tennis.

CAMPING. (See also *What It Will Cost.*) There are over 30 camp sites with electricity, water, and sanitation and many other useful facilities. They are in Berlin, Zierow (Baltic coast), the Mecklenburg lake district, Dresden, Erfurt, Leipzig and the Hartz mountains. Full details from Berolina, Koch or Maupintours. The official camping season in the GDR is May 1 to Sept. 30.

Youth Hostels. (See also *What It Will Cost.*) There are youth hostels in Berlin, Dresden, Potsdam, Weimar, Erfurt, Halle, Leipzig, Kuhlungsborn, Binz, Straslund, Saalfeld, and Bad Schandau; however, western tourists are no longer legally allowed to use them. In fact, campers are sometimes let in if space is available, and the charge is then about MDN8 per night. For a list of hostels, apply direct to Jugendtourist, 1026 Berlin, Alexanderplatz 5, DDR. Age limit is 30 years.

LEIPZIG FAIR. Official fair cards are required and visas are issued without further payment to holders at all frontier posts or in their own country before they leave. Fair cards may be obtained from *Globe Travel Service,*

127 N. Dearborn Street, Chicago; *Koch Overseas Co.,* 206 East 86 St., New York, N.Y. 10028; and *Leipzig Fair Agency,* 20 Conduit Street, London W.1. Fair cards are also obtainable at the *Leipziger Messeamt,* DDR–701 Leipzig, Postfach 720, and from frontier posts on the East German border. In Britain, bookings are also being handled by Morland and Co., 308 Regent St., London W1R 5Al, and by Barry Martin Travel Ltd., Suite 309, Albany House, 324 Regent St., London W1R 5AA.

All visitors and exhibitors to the Fair are required to exchange the equivalent of MDN 13 minimum per person per day in the currency of their country. It will be useful for tourists to effect the compulsory money exchange through a travel agency in their home country, and accommodation may be booked in advance.

Taxi services are likely to be a cause for concern and better is to have your own car or fly to West Berlin and hire one there. Hiring in Leipzig is expensive for a dubious quality machine. Use a visitor's sticker from the U.K. or U.S.A. One's own car allows for more freedom over accommodation, too. It is still a feasible alternative not to pre-book but head for the Leipzig Accommodation Bureau Zimmernachweis, Auslander Treffpunkt (Foreign Visitors' Center) on Universitätsstr. Ask for good-quality rooms in a private household in a suburb like Borlitz-Ehrenberg, Knautkleeberg or Markleeberg. Show your appreciation with a small bottle of perfume or the like, discreetly handed over. Room cost will be about MDN 7 and householders are often nice. But find accommodation within 24 hours of arriving as penalties for being without could be imposed. Should the accommodation not suit, just go and change it. Suburban accommodation in Leipzig is much pleasanter than hotels which lack friendly atmospheres and whose personnel epitomize officialdom.

At the Fair, the Information Center and restaurants tend to be overcrowded, so eat in town. East German trade officials tread a delicate course between being astute professionals surviving against quite different odds from yours. They will expect you to know that they are enmeshed in a régime which mistrusts the West and its business tactics. Try no suavity, play it straight, don't discuss politics, appreciate as much as you can, emphasize what you really do like; and be seen to change a little money at the official rate. Safe subjects to discuss are sport and music. Maintain a diffident attitude toward your home politics. Don't entertain too lavishly.

 HOLIDAYS AND BUSINESS HOURS. Holidays are January 1; Good Friday; Whit Monday; May 1 (Labor Day); October 7 (Republic Day); December 25 and 26. Closing hours are variable. Stores mostly open from 9–6 outside Berlin and from 10–7 (8 on Thurs.) in Berlin. Only departmental and larger stores open Sat. morning.

Banks are open from 8 A.M. to midday, Mon–Fri., and from 2:30 P.M. to 5:30 P.M., Tues. and Thurs., closed Sat.

MUSIC AND THEATER. Berlin (East): East Berlin has long been famous in the world of theater for the brilliance of its modern production techniques, not only in drama, but also in opera. Although both Berthold Brecht and his wife Helene Wiegel are now dead, the impetus that they gave to drama in East Germany lives on. Their company, the Berliner Ensemble, is well worth a visit, as is the Deutsches Ensemble. For opera, in all its forms, the German State Opera and the Komische Oper both repay a visit, especially for those who prefer not to sit through plays in a language they do not fully understand.

Dresden: The Dresden State Opera House saw Wagner, Carl Maria von Weber, Richard Strauss and others perform their work here. Reconstruction after war-time devastation is after Gottfried Semper, architect of Semper Gallery in the city. Two orchestras play regularly, the Philharmonic and the State. Zwinger Serenades, with the Kreuz Choir, in inner court of Zwinger. Modern and classical drama in the Great House. Open-air theater in the Great Garden, seating 5,000.

Leipzig: Opera House and five theaters and concert halls, notably housing the Gewandhaus Orchestra, of which Mendelssohn-Bartholdy was director.

Rostock: The Volkstheater. Arena open-air theater in the Barnsdorfer Wood.

Weimar: As the home of Schiller and Goethe, this city has a long and honorable history of theater production. Today it is upheld by the National Theater.

SHOPPING. Apart from the normal run of duty-free drinks, cigarettes, perfume, cameras, radios (and so on) to be bought at *Intershops,* found in all Interhotels, in exchange for convertible foreign currency, the specialist is going to have a better time hunting for items of interest than the layman.

Berlin, particularly the Frankfurter Allee and Unter den Linden, will be the best place to search. Cameras (Zeiss), and antiquities are best bought in the capital. Antiquarian books are to be found on Unter den Linden and the shop for the sale and export of antiquities is on Frankfurter Allee, at no. 80. This deals mainly in items of furniture, china plates and so on. Gramophone records are very cheap in East Germany and, certainly in the classical category, of exceedingly good quality. They cost about 10 marks.

East Germany produces and exports all types of musical instruments in large quantities. Leipzig is the place for pianos—*Blüthner, Zimmerman* and *Römisch*—and other principal orchestral instruments are made at Klingenthal and at Markneukirchen in the Erzgebirge. These mountains are also known historically, like many other mountainous regions in other lands, for woodcarving, this being formerly a form of supplementary income for farmers in the winter. Now the art enjoys a status in its own right and at the pretty little village of Seiffen, in the Erzgebirge, you can buy exquisite and beautifully made wooden toys—animals, Christmas decorations, nutcrackers and so on—which makes all these places well worth a morning's drive from Dresden or Karl-Marx-Stadt.

Dresden china is actually made at the nearby and very lovely town of Meissen, and examples can be bought by visitors there. The workshops can be viewed as well, as can the exhibition hall, which has examples of old and new Meissen porcelain on display.

ELECTRICITY. 220 volts AC.

MEDICAL SERVICES. Some medical services are free for visitors to East Germany, but medical insurance is strongly advised.

TELEPHONES. For direct dialing to U.S.A. from East Germany, dial 012–1 then the town and subscriber's number. For Britain, dial 012–44 then the town code, omitting the first 0, then the subscriber's number.

TOILETS. Most easily located and best maintained in hotels and their restaurants, and in public buildings. Grafitti are remarkable only by their absence and it is inadvisable to break with this tradition.

TIPPING. Officially abolished, but generally accepted in hotels and restaurants.

USEFUL ADDRESSES. British Embassy, Unter den Linden 32–34, (tel. 220 2431); **American Embassy,** Schadowstrasse 4, 108 Berlin (tel. 220 2741).

ENGLISH-GERMAN
VOCABULARY
Useful Phrases and Words

The most important phrase to know (one that may make it unnecessary to know any others) is: "Do you speak English?"—*Sprechen Sie englisch?* If the answer is "Nein," then you may have recourse to the list below:

Border Crossing	Zollgrenze
I have nothing to declare	Ich habe nichts zu verzollen
No tobacco	Kein Tabak
No spirits	Keine Getränke
For personal use	Für personlichen Gebrauch
Worn articles	Gebrauchte Sachen
How much is the Customs duty?	Wie hoch ist der Zoll?
Passport	Pass
Identity papers	Personal-Ausweis
Driving license	Führerschein

Days of the week	Tage der Woche
Monday	Montag
Tuesday	Dienstag
Wednesday	Mittwoch
Thursday	Donnerstag
Friday	Freitag
Saturday	Samstag, Sonnabend
Sunday	Sonntag
Holiday	Fejertag

Everyday Conversation	Tägliche Unterhaltung
Good morning, afternoon, evening	Guten Morgen, Tag, Abend
Good night	Gute Nacht
How do you do? / How are you?	Wie geht es Ihnen?
How do you say in German?	Wie sagt man auf deutsch?
All right	Gut
Permit me to introduce Mr. X	Ich erlaube mir, Herrn X vorzustellen
I am pleased to meet you	Ich freue mich, Sie kennenzulernen
Yes	Ja (yah)
No	Nein (nine)
Many thanks	Vielen Dank
Don't mention it	Bitte sehr

I beg your pardon	Verzeihen Sie, entschuldigen Sie
Please	Bitte
I am ready	Ich bin fertig
Welcome	Willkommen
I am very sorry	Es tut mir sehr leid
What time is it?	Wieviel Uhr ist es
It is 2 o'clock, a quarter past two, half past two, a quarter to three	Es ist zwei Uhr, viertel nach zwei, halb drei, viertel vor drei
I understand	Ieh verstehe
Right	Rechts
Left	Links
Straight ahead	Geradeaus
Is this seat free?	Ist dieser Platz frei?
This seat is taken	Dieser Platz ist besetzt
Where is . . .	Wo ist . . .
—the airport?	—der Flughafen?
—a bank?	—eine Bank?
—the bar?	—das Buffet?
—the barbershop (or hairdresser)?	—ein Friseur?
—the bathroom?	—das Badezimmer?
—the ticket (booking) office?	—der Schalter?
—a chemist's shop (drugstore)?	—eine Apotheke?
—the cloakroom?	—die Garderobe?
—the American (British) Consulate?	—das amerikanische (britische) Konsulat?
—the customs office?	—das Zollamt?
—the lavatory?	—die Toilette?
—the luggage?	—das Gepäck?
—the police station?	—die Polizei?
—the post office?	—das Postamt?
Have you . . .	Haben Sie . . .
—any American (English) cigarettes?	—amerikanische (englische) Zigaretten?
—a time-table?	—einen Fahrplan?
—a dictionary	—ein Wörterbuch?
—a room to let?	—ein Zimmer zu vermieten?
—anything ready (food)?	—etwas fertig?
I need a doctor, a dentist	Ich brauche einen Arzt, einen Zahnarz
I should like something to eat, drink	Ich möchte etwas essen, trinken

IN THE RESTAURANT

Breakfast	Frühstück	**Meat (Fleisch)**
Lunch	Mittagessen	
Dinner	Abendessen	
Bill of fare	Speisekarte	
Bill (check)	Rechnuug	
Waiter!	Herr Ober!	

Bacon	Speck
Beef	Rindfleisch
Ham	Schinken
Lamb	Lammfleisch

Mutton	Hammelfleisch	Grapes	Trauben
Pork	Schweinefleisch	Ice Cream	Eis
Sausage	Wurst	Orange	Apfelsine, Orange
Veal	Kalbfleisch	Peach	Pfirsich
Venison	Rehfleisch	Pear	Birne
		Plum	Pflaume
		Stewed fruit	Kompott

Poultry (Geflügel)

Chicken	Huhn
Duck	Ente
Partridge	Rebhuhn
Turkey	Truthahn

Drinks (Getränke)

Applejuice	Apfelsaft
Beer	Bier
light	helles
dark	dunkles
Champagne	Sekt
Cocoa	Kakoa
Coffee	Kaffee
Grapejuice	Traubensaft
Milk	Milch
Orange juice	Orangensaft
Raspberry juice	Himbeersaft
Red wine	Rotwein
Tea	Tee
Water	Wasser
White wine	Weisswein

Fish (Fisch)

Clams	Muscheln
Crabs	Krabben
Lobster	Hummer
Oysters	Austern
Salmon	Lachs
Trout	Forelle

Vegetables (Gemüse)

Asparagus	Spargel
Beans	Bohnen
Carrots	Karotten, Möhren
Cauliflower	Blumenkohl
Celery	Sellerie
Cucumber	Gurke
Lettuce	Grüner Salat
Mushrooms	Pilze
Onions	Zwiebel
Peas	Erbsen
Potatoes	Kartoffeln
Radish	Rettich
Spinach	Spinat
String beans	Grüne Bohnen

Miscellaneous

Boiled	Gekocht
Boiled egg	Gekochtes Ei
Cake	Kuchen
Cream	Sahne
Fried	Gebraten
Fried egg	Spiegelei
Honey	Honig
Jam, marmalade	Marmelade
Mustard	Senf
Pepper	Pfeffer
Roast	Gebraten, geröstet
Salt	Salz
Scrambled eggs	Rühreier
Sugar	Zucker
Whipped cream	Schlagsahne

Desserts (Nachtische)

Cheese	Käse
Fruit	Obst

SHOPPING

I need . . . I should like	Ich brauche . . . ich möchte
I want to buy	Ich möchte kaufen

I want something in silk, cotton, wool, linen.	Ich wünsche etwas aus Seide, Baumwolle, Wolle, Leinen
How much is that?	Was Kostet das?
I like it	Es gefällt mir
I do not like it	Es gefällt mir nicht

Colors (Farben)

Black	Schwarz
Blue	Blau
Brown	Braun
Green	Grün
Grey	Grau
Orange	Orange
Red	Rot
Violet	Violett
White	Weiss
Yellow	Gelb
Gold	Gold
Silver	Siberfarbig

Clothing (Kleidung)

Clothing	Kleidung
Belt	Gürtel
Blouse	Bluse
Dress	Kleid
Gloves	Handschuhe
Handkerchief	Taschentuch
Hat	Hut
Overcoat	Mantel
Shoes	Schuhe
Skirt	Rock
Socks	Socken
Stockings	Strümpfe
Underwear	Unterwäsche

INFORMATION SIGNS

Entrance	Eingang	Ladies	Damen
Exit	Ausgang	Gentlemen	Herren
Open	Offen	Occupied	Besetzt
Closed	Geschlossen	Free	Frei
Push	Drücken	Hot	Warm
Pull	Ziehen	Cold	Kalt
Smoking	Rauchen	Diversion (traffic)	Umleitung
Forbidden	Verboten		

MOTORING TERMS

Accelerator	Anlasser	Frame	Rahmen
Axle	Wagenachse	Front axle	Vorderachse
Ball bearing	Kugellager	Fuel	Brennstoff
Body	Karosserie	Garage	Garage
Brake	Bremse	Gasoline	Benzin
Bumper	Stossfänger	Gearshift	Schaltung
Carburetor	Vergaser	Headlight	Scheinwerfer
Chassis	Chassis	Ignition	Zündung
Clutch	Kupplung	Lubricant	Schmierstoff
Crank	Kurbel	Motor car	Wagen
Crankshaft	Kurbelwelle		Kraftwagen
Engine	Motor	Oil	Öl

Radiator	Kühler	Windscreen	windschutz- scheibe
Screw	Schraube		
Spare parts	Ersatzteile	Windscreen wiper	Scheibenwischer
Spark plug	Zündkerze	To clean, wash	Waschen
Speedometer	Geschwindig- keitsmesser	To decarbonize	Entrussen
		To hire a car	Einen Wagen mieten
Spring	Feder		
Steering wheel	Steuerrad	To inflate	Aufpumpen
Tail light	Schlusslicht	To lubricate	Abschmieren
Tank	Tank	To polish	Polieren
Tire	Reifen	To repair	Reparieren
Tube	Schlauch	To shift	Schalten
Valve	Ventil	To start	Starten, abfahren
Wheel (front-, rear-)	Rad (Vorder-, Hinter-)	To stop	Halten

NUMBERS

The answer to many of the questions you ask will be numbers. Therefore you need to know what they sound like. We suggest you learn the numbers below, with their pronunciations (in parentheses).

1 eins (ighnss)	19 neunzehn
2 zwei (tzvy)	20 zwanzig (tzvansig)
3 drei (dry)	21 einundzwanzig (ighnoontzvantzig)
4 vier (fear)	
5 fünf (funf)	22 zweiundzwanzig
6 sechs (zex)	30 dreissig
7 sieben (zeeben)	40 vierzig
8 acht (ahkt)	50 fünfzig
9 neun (noyn)	60 sechzig
10 zehn (tzayn)	70 siebzig
11 elf (elf)	80 achtzig
12 zwölf (zvuhlf)	90 neunzig
13 dreizehn (drytzayn)	100 hundert (hoondert)
14 vierzehn (feartzayn)	110 hundertzehn
15 fünfzehn	200 zweihundert
16 sechzehn	1000 tausend (towzent)
17 siebzehn (zeeptzayn)	1500 fünfzehnhundert
18 achtzehn	

Index

The letters H and R indicate hotel and restaurant listings
(See also **Practical Information sections at the end of each chapter for additional details.)**

West Germany

East Germany

GERMANY

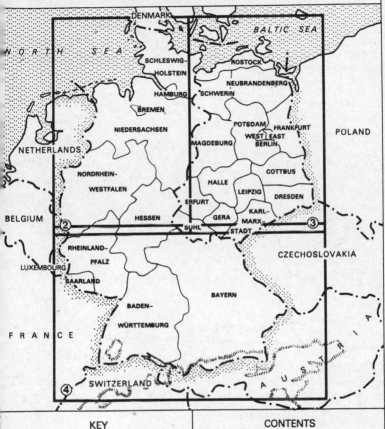

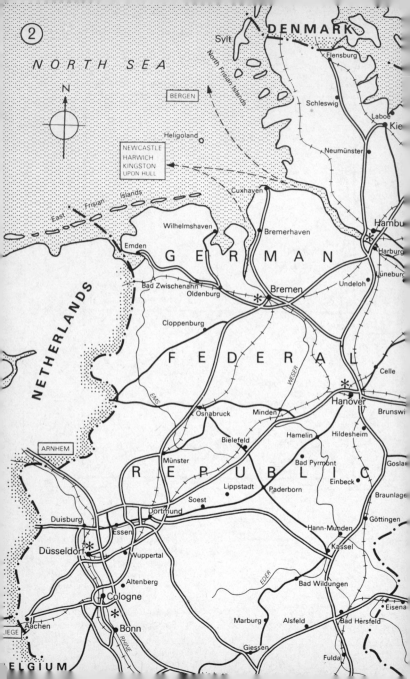

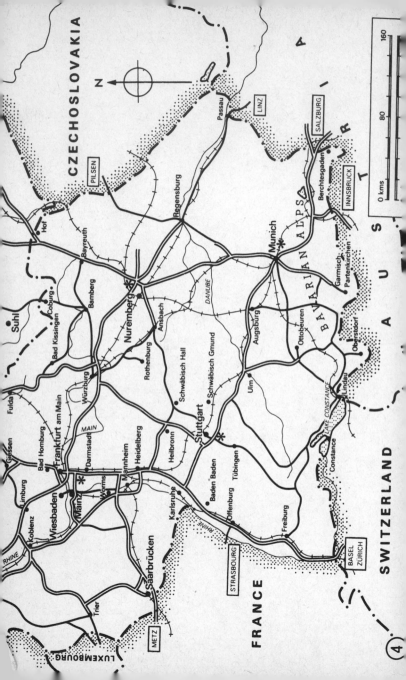